SIXTH EDITION
ENVIRONMENTAL LAW

Nancy K. Kubasek, J.D.

Department of Legal Studies
Bowling Green State University

Gary S. Silverman, D.Env.

Environmental Health Program
Bowling Green State University

Chapters 6 and 8

PEARSON
Prentice
Hall

Upper Saddle River, New Jersey 07458

Library of Congress Cataloging-in-Publication Data

Kubasek, Nancy.
  Environmental law / Nancy K. Kubasek, Gary S. Silverman.—6th ed.
    p. cm.
  Includes bibliographical references and index.
  ISBN 0-13-614216-8 (alk. paper)
  1. Environmental law—United States. 2. Environmental protection—
United States. I. Silverman, Gary. II. Title

KF3775.K83 2008
344.7304'6—dc22

                                                    2007019325

AVP/Executive Editor: Steve Sartori
Product Development Manager:
  Ashley Santora
Project Manager: Kerri Tomasso
Editorial Assistant: Marybeth Ward
Associate Director, Production
  Editorial: Judy Leale
Managing Editor: Cynthia Zonneveld
Production Editor: Melissa Feimer
Permissions Coordinator: Charles Morris
Associate Director, Manufacturing:
  Vinnie Scelta

Manufacturing Buyer: Michelle Klein
Design/Composition Manager:
  Christy Mahon
Cover Design: Bruce Kenselaar
Cover Illustration/Photo: Getty Images
Manager, Cover Visual Research &
  Permissions: Karen Sanatar
Composition: Integra
Full-Service Project Management:
  Kavitha Kuttikan, Integra
Printer/Binder: R.R. Donnelley
Typeface: 10/12 Times

Credits and acknowledgments borrowed from other sources and reproduced, with permission, in this textbook appear on appropriate page within.

Pearson Education LTD.
Pearson Education Singapore, Pte. Ltd
Pearson Education, Canada, Ltd
Pearson Education–Japan

Pearson Education Australia PTY, Limited
Pearson Education North Asia Ltd
Pearson Educación de Mexico, S.A. de C.V.
Pearson Education Malaysia, Pte. Ltd.

10 9 8 7 6 5 4 3 2 1
ISBN-13: 978-0-13-614216-4
ISBN-10:   0-13-614216-8

CONTENTS

❦

Preface   xi

PART I: AN INTRODUCTION TO THE LAW   1

CHAPTER 1   The American Legal System: The Source of Environmental Law   3

Sources of Law   3
The Legislative Branch as a Source of Statutory Law   3
The Judicial Branch as a Source of Case Law   9
The Executive Branch as a Source of Law   11
Administrative Agencies as a Source of Law   14

Classifications of Law   14
Case and Statutory Law   14
Public and Private Law   14
Criminal Law and Civil Law   15

Constitutional Principles Underlying the American Legal System   29
Federalism   29
Federal Preemption   30
The Commerce Clause   31
The Fourth Amendment   35
The Fifth and Fourteenth Amendments   36
A Constitutional Right to Environmental Protection?   43

Questions for Review and Discussion   47

For Further Reading   47

On the Internet   48

Notes   49

Resolving Controversial Environmental Issues   51
The Contradictory Behavior of the EPA   51

CHAPTER 2   The Litigation Process and Other Tools for Resolving Environmental Disputes   52

The Adversary System   52
An Introduction to the Adversary System   52
Criticisms of the Adversary System   52
The Federal Court System   55
The State Court System   55
Choice of Courts   57

Primary Actors in the Legal System 60
  The Attorney 60
  The Judge 60
  The Jury 62

Steps in Civil Litigation 63
  The Threshold Issues 63
  Pretrial 70
  The Trial 74
  Appellate Procedure 77

Alternatives to Civil Litigation 79
  Arbitration 80
  Mediation 82

Concluding Remarks 84

Questions for Review and Discussion 85

For Further Reading 85

On the Internet 86

Notes 86

Resolving Controversial Environmental Issues 87
  Does a Turtle Have More Rights than a Human? 87

**CHAPTER 3   Administrative Law and Its Impact
             on the Environment   89**

Creation of Administrative Agencies 90

Functions of Administrative Agencies 90
  Rule Making 90
  Adjudication 96
  Administrative Activities 100

Limitations on Agency Powers 101
  Statutory Limitations 101
  Institutional Limitations 102

Important Agencies Affecting the Environment 106
  Executive Versus Independent Agencies 106
  Hybrid Agencies 107
  The Environmental Protection Agency 107
  Interagency Cooperation 116
  The Department of the Interior and Its Agencies 118
  The Department of Agriculture and Its Agencies 121
  The Department of Labor and Its Agencies 121

Concluding Remarks 122

Questions for Review and Discussion 122

For Further Reading 122

On the Internet 123

Notes 123

Resolving Controversial Environmental Issues   125
    In Some Cases, We Do Not Want Power
      by the People   125

PART II: THE ENVIRONMENTAL LAWS   127

CHAPTER 4   An Introduction to Environmental Law and Policy   129

The Need for Regulation   129
    Tragedy of the Commons   129
    Free-Rider Problem   130
    Pollution as an Externality   131
    Environmental Ethic   131

Alternative Ways to Control Pollution   132
    Tort Law   132

Subsidies, Emissions Charges, and Marketable Emissions Permits   134
    Green Taxes   136
    Direct Regulation   137

Evolution of Our Environmental Policy   138
    The Origins of Our Environmental Policy   138
    The 1970s: The Environmental Decade   139
    The 1980s   139
    The Early 1990s   140
    The Middle to Late 1990s   141
    Increasing Use of "Market Forces"   144
    ISO 14000   145
    The Beginning of the 21st Century   146

National Environmental Policy Act   149
    Council on Environmental Quality   150
    Environmental Impact Statement   152
    Alternatives to the EIS   158
    Effectiveness of NEPA   160

Pollution Prevention Act of 1990   160

Concluding Remarks   162

Questions for Review and Discussion   164

For Further Reading   164

On the Internet   164

Notes   165

Resolving Controversial Environmental Issues   167
    The Right to Pollute   167

CHAPTER 5   Air-Quality Control   168

The Major Air Pollutants   168
    Sulfur Dioxide   169

Nitrogen Oxides   *170*
Carbon Monoxide   *171*
Ozone   *173*
Particulates   *173*
Lead   *174*
Airborne Toxins   *175*

Some Significant Air-Quality Problems   175
Acid Deposition   *175*
Depletion of the Ozone Layer   *177*
Human-Induced Global Climate Change   *179*
Indoor Pollution   *186*

The Initial Approach to Air-Quality Control   187
Air-Pollution Control Act of 1955   *188*
Motor Vehicle Control Act of 1960   *188*
Clean Air Act of 1963   *188*
Motor Vehicle Air-Pollution Control Act of 1965   *189*
1967 Air-Quality Act   *189*

Current Approaches to Air-Quality Control   190
National Ambient Air-Quality Standards   *191*
No Significant Deterioration   *197*
New Source Review   *198*
Mobile Source Performance Standards   *200*

The 1990 Clean Air Act Amendments   203
1990 Air Toxics Program   *203*
Acid Rain-Control Program   *207*
Enforcement of the 1990 Act   *208*

The Clear Skies Initiative   210

Solutions Beyond the Clean Air Act   210

Concluding Remarks   211

Questions for Review and Discussion   211

For Further Reading   212

On the Internet   212

Notes   213

Resolving Controversial Environmental Issues   216
Equal Rights Among Autos   *216*

CHAPTER 6   Water-Quality Control   217

The Major Water Pollutants   217
Pathogens   *218*
Conventional Organics   *220*
Toxic Trace Organics   *221*
Nutrients   *222*
Heavy Metals   *223*
Ionizing Radiation   *223*
Other Measures   *224*

Some Significant Water-Quality Problems   225
   Trace Levels of Toxic Organics   225
   Lead and Copper   227
   Radon and Other Radionuclides   228
   Coastal Contamination   229
   Concentrated Animal Feedlots   230

Protecting Water Through Government Actions   230
   Water Rights   231
   Protecting Surface Water Quality   236
   Protecting Groundwater Quality   246
   Protecting Drinking Water Quality   248

Concluding Remarks   254

Questions for Review and Discussion   255

For Further Reading   255

On the Internet   256

Notes   256

Resolving Controversial Environmental Issues   259
   What Lurks Behind that Faucet   259

CHAPTER 7   Controlling Toxic Substances   261

Identification of Potentially Toxic Substances   261
   Scientific Uncertainty   262
   Risk Assessment   263
   TSCA   268
   FIFRA   271
   FFDCA   278
   FQPA   278
   Pesticide Environmental Stewardship Program   280
   Progress Under the Acts   280

International Regulation of Toxic Substances   281
   Rotterdam Convention   282
   Registration, Evaluation, and Authorization of Chemicals   283

Toxic Torts   283
   Theories of Recovery   283
   Problems in Establishing Causation   285
   Enterprise Liability   287
   Punitive Damages   288

Concluding Remarks   290

Questions for Review and Discussion   290

For Further Reading   290

On the Internet   291

Notes   291

Resolving Controversial Environmental Issues   294
   EPA Too Cautious with Pesticides   294

CHAPTER 8   Waste Management and Hazardous Releases   295

Waste Control Techniques   295
Municipal Solid Waste   301
Hazardous Waste   304
Enforcement of RCRA   312

CERCLA: An Overview   314

Emergency Response Plans and Right to Know   314

Federal Response to Contaminated Sites   317
Removal Action   318
Remedial Response   319
Brownfields   325

Underground Storage Tank Program   327

Concluding Remarks   331

Questions for Review and Discussion   332

For Further Reading   332

On the Internet   333

Notes   334

Resolving Controversial Environmental Issues   336
As Superfund Turned the Corner?   336
Superfund Summary of Significant Accomplishments   336

CHAPTER 9   Energy   339

Energy Policy: A Historical Overview   340
The Crisis Begins   340
A Return to Complacency   342
A Bright Spot: The Energy Policy Act   343
A "Voluntary" Energy Policy   345
Transportation   346
National Energy Policy Plans   347

Energy Consumption and Production   350

Coal: The Oldest Energy Source   353
Problems with Coal   355
Regulation of the Mining Industry   357

Petroleum and Natural Gas   360
Onshore Development Problems   360
Offshore Development Problems   361
Oil Spills   364

Nuclear Energy   366
History of Nuclear Energy Development   367
Problems with Nuclear Energy   368
Regulation of the Nuclear Industry   370

Renewable Fuels   372
Hydropower   373

Solar Energy   374
Wind Energy   375
Biomass Energy   376
Geothermal Energy   377
Hydrogen Fuel   377

Concluding Remarks   377

Questions for Review and Discussion   378

For Further Reading   378

On the Internet   379

Notes   379

Resolving Controversial Environmental Issues   384
Oil is the Best Form of Energy   384
Funds for Alternative Energy Needed   385

CHAPTER 10   Natural Resources   386

Protecting Public Lands   386

Forests   387

Rangelands   388

Regulation of Public Lands   389

Wetlands, Estuaries, and Coastal Areas   395

Benefits of Wetlands   397

Destruction of Wetlands   397

Regulations to Preserve Coastal Areas, Estuaries,
      and Wetlands   399
Commerce Clause Restrictions on Wetlands Preservation   399
Marine Protection, Research, and Sanctuaries Act   401
Coastal Zone Management Act   402
*Coastal Wetlands Planning, Protection, and Restoration Act
      of 1990   403*
*The Convention on Wetlands of International Importance Especially
      as Waterfowl Habitat   403*
"Swampbuster" Provisions of the 1985 Food Security Act   403
National Estuary Program   404
"No-Net-Loss" Policy   404
Estuary Restoration Act of 2000   407

Protection of the Great Lakes   408

Wild and Scenic Rivers System   409

Endangered Species   409

The Global Extinction Crisis   416

Concluding Remarks   418

Questions for Review and Discussion   418

For Further Reading   418

On the Internet   419

Notes   420

Resolving Controversial Environmental Issues   422
Ban on Snowmobiles Best Policy for Yellowstone   422
Ban on Snowmobiles Unnecessary   422

CHAPTER 11   International Environmental Law   424

The Need for International Environmental Law   424
Overpopulation   424
Loss of Biological Diversity   427
The Global Commons   428
Environmental Disasters and Transboundary Pollution   430

The Nature of International Law   430

Sources of International Environmental Law   431
Conventional Law   431
Customary Law   432

Institutions that Effectuate and Influence International
     Environmental Law   434
United Nations   434
World Bank   437
Global Environment Facility   438
European Union   439

Addressing Specific International Environmental Problems   441
Transboundary Pollution   441
§ 902 Interstate Claims and Remedies   442
Choice of Forums   446
The global Commons   448
Preservation of Biological Diversity   456
Madrid Protocol   459

The Future of International Environmental Law   460
Rio Summit   460
Environmentalism and Trade   462

Concluding Remarks   466

Questions for Review and Discussion   467

For Further Reading   467

On the Internet   467

Notes   468

Resolving Controversial Environmental Issues   471
Amend the WTO   471
Process and Production Methods Cannot Be Regulated   472

APPENDIX   Abbreviations and Acronyms   473

Index   478

PREFACE

When I began teaching environmental law to undergraduates in 1982, there were very few such courses offered outside of law schools. There were even fewer resources available for teaching courses to anyone other than law students. My first semester, I taught the course using one of the two available law school texts.

The next year, I began putting together my own materials, materials that over the next few years evolved into an environmental law "text" designed especially for nonlaw students that I made available to my students through a copy service. To improve the quality of the materials before attempting to publish them, I asked my colleague Dr. Gary Silverman, the director of our university's Environmental Health Program, to write the chapters on water-quality control and management of waste and hazardous releases, areas in which he has special expertise.

The result was the first edition of *Environmental Law,* a book designed to introduce those without any legal or special scientific training to the system through which our nation attempts to preserve the environment. Although this book was written for college students at either the undergraduate or master's level, I had hoped that it would also be useful to anyone interested in learning about our system of environmental law and that it would be a helpful reference for anyone in business who is attempting to negotiate the morass of environmental regulations that affect businesses today. From the comments that I have received from users of the book, it is clear that, in some sense, the book is meeting these goals. Readers of the book range from graduate and undergraduate students to businesspersons and ordinary citizens interested in environmental law.

Reflecting the fact that background knowledge is often important for understanding specific areas, this book provides two key types of background necessary for understanding environmental law. First, the initial chapters explain how our legal system functions in general. Second, the initial portions of the latter chapters provide the basic scientific knowledge necessary for understanding environmental law. Thus, the reader may gain a fundamental understanding of not only what the laws are but also why they are needed.

Several people helped to make the first edition of this book, and consequently this fifth edition, a reality, and I thank them for their contributions. Thorough and insightful reviews were provided by the following professors:

James Carp, Syracuse University
William Clements, Norwich University
Frank Cross, University of Texas

David Hoch, University of Southwestern Louisiana
May Kieffer, Ohio University
Richard Kunkle, The College of St. Thomas
Patricia Tulin, University of Hartford

Their reviews led to vast improvements of the final version of the first edition of this book. In fact, it is only because of a suggestion of one of these reviewers that a very important chapter of this book was written, the chapter on energy policy and natural resource protection.

When changes in environmental law necessitated the first revision of *Environmental Law,* helpful reviews were provided by Paula C. Murray, of the University of Texas, and Eric Oates, of the Wharton School. Numerous changes were made in response to their comments.

Reviewers were once again helpful when it came to the third edition of this text. I once again thank the following professors for their helpful insights:

Donald A. Fuller, University of Central Florida
Mary Keifer, Ohio University
Michael Magasin, Pepperdine University
Michael A. Tessitore, University of Florida

Perhaps the most significant contributor to the third edition was Carrie Williamson, a former environmental law student and my research assistant at the time of the third revision. Having used the book in class, she was able to point out places where it was unclear and make suggestions for its improvement. She also spent numerous hours doing research to ensure that the edition contained the most up-to-date figures possible at the time of publication. Finally, she contributed to the improvement of the book by drafting essays featured in the new "Thinking Critically About Issues in Environmental Law" section. Her assistance on this revision was invaluable.

With the fourth edition of this text, the former Chapter 9, Natural Resources and Energy Policy, was divided into two separate chapters to allow expansion of both of these areas. Many users were saying that they would like to devote more time to natural resource issues and the energy crisis of 2001 certainly stimulated growing interest in energy issues. Many questions, such as whether we should build more nuclear power plants, were considered nonissues in the 1990s but were being hotly debated as the fourth edition went into press and continued to be on the front burner as the fifth edition was being written.

Special credit for the improvements in the fourth edition goes to my former assistant, Anne Hardenbergh. A former student in my environmental law class, she used her experience with the book as a student to suggest areas of improvement. She also helped to upgrade the quality and number of Web sites at the end of each chapter. Many users of the book sent in suggestions that helped improve the fourth edition, but three stand out for their unusually valuable contributions: Thomas Ostrom, Mike Eckhoff, and Lester Lindley.

As with previous editions, many of the improvements in this fifth edition came from suggestions of users and readers of the text, and their contributions are invaluable. Reviewers who made helpful suggestions for this edition included:

Craig Collins, University of California at Davis
Timothy Dixon, Nova Southeastern University
Debora Halbert, Otterbein College
Laurel Phoenix, the University of Wisconsin at Green Bay
Alex Sauders, Central Carolina Technical College
Jefferey M. Sellers, University of Southern California
Dennis Nettiksimmons, University of Montana

My research assistant, and future lawyer, Alex Frondorf, did extensive research for the fifth edition, as well as all of the individuals at Pearson Prentice Hall who helped to pull this edition together: Alana Bradley, my editor; Jane Avery, her assistant; Denise Culhane, production editor; and Colleen Franciscus, project manager. And finally, the students and professors who used the first four editions of this book and offered helpful criticisms cannot be omitted. Although they are too numerous to list by name, their contributions were invaluable.

In revising this book for the Sixth Edition, I was extremely fortunate that my former research assistant, Alex Fronforf, who did such good research for me on the Fifth Edition, was willing to work with me again on this newest edition. His contributions were invaluable. I was also assisted in this revision by two other research assistants, Daniel Tagliarina and Amanda Valentine. Again, several reviewers made useful suggestions. They include:

Christopher Robinson, Clarkson University
Michael Campenni, McLennan Community College
John Sutherlin, University of Louisiana, Monroe
Mark Imperial, University of North Carolina Wilmington
Britt Bailey, College of Marin
Leonard Champney, University of Scranton
Jude Benavides, University of Texas at Brownsville
David Steffy, Jacksonville State University
J. David Aiken, University of Nebraska-Lincoln
David Jensen, Texas A&M—Corpus Christi
John Marshall, Pulaski Technical College
James Reed, Christopher Newport University
Joe Arruda, Pittsburg State University
Victor Okereke, Morrisville State College
Charles Kliche, South Dakota School of Mines and Technology
Murel Jones, Virginia State University
Kate Joyce, Plattsburgh State University
Paul Pavlich, Southern Oregon University
Nicholas Lees, Columbia Southern University
Susan McCabe, Kellogg Community College
Bonnie Alexander, Valley City State University

Peter Julovich, Ivytech Community College of Indiana
Romy Knittel, St Bonaventure University
Brent Sipes, University of Hawaii at Manoa
Lori Poloni-Staudinger, Northern Arizona University
Gordon Bennett, University of Texas, Austin
Brian Swenty, University of Evansville
Jean Watts, Bluegrass Community & Technical College
Robert J. Shostak, Ohio University
LeGene Quesenberry, Clarion University
Haydn Fox, Texas A&M University—Commerce
Rodney Clinkenbeard, Oklahoma University Health Sciences Center
J. Joseph Wilder, Hilbert College
Leverett Nelson, Loyola University: Chicago
Tim Eastly, Kent-Trumbull Campus
Wendy Scattergood, St. Norbert College
David Downie, Earth Institute at Columbia University
John McGill, York Technical College

Finally, I acknowledge the contributions of those at Prentice Hall, without whom this book could not have been revised. They include: Executive Editor Steve Sartori, Project Manager Kerri Tomasso, Editorial Assistant Marybeth Ward, Production Editor Melissa Feimer.

This is the second revision of the book made during the tenure of President George W. Bush. Unfortunately, the second President Bush has turned out to be a much greater foe of the environment than most had predicted. His administration was given an "F" on the League of Conservation Voter's 2003 Report Card for performance on environmental issues. During his first term, in conflicts between protecting the environment or protecting the timber, mining, and oil industries, the Bush Administration clearly favors the latter over the former. During his second term, as changes in the text will illustrate, his administration has continued to downplay the importance of environmental interests, although there have been a few positive changes. Just before publication of this edition, the election lost the president the control of Congress. Many see this result as meaning that, at minimum, we will not see as much reduction in environmental protection as we have seen in the recent past.

In finishing the sixth edition of this book, I realize that despite the conscientious review of all stages of the book's production by many people, it is almost inevitable that mistakes have crept in, for which I accept responsibility. I would therefore appreciate readers' corrections and comments as to how future editions may better achieve the goals this book is designed to attain. Please send your comments, criticisms, corrections, or suggestions to me at the Department of Legal Studies, Bowling Green State University, Bowling Green, Ohio 43403, or e-mail me at nkubase@cba.bgsu.edu.

Nancy K. Kubasek

PART I

AN INTRODUCTION TO THE LAW

A useful prelude to a functional understanding of environmental law is an appreciation of the U.S. legal system itself. The materials contained in Chapters 1 through 3 will help you gain that appreciation.

CHAPTER 1
THE AMERICAN LEGAL SYSTEM: THE SOURCE OF ENVIRONMENTAL LAW

SOURCES OF LAW

Particular contexts dictate reactions to environmental threats. Therefore, as a preface to outlining the possible reactions to environmental harm, you must understand our legal system. The first step in this review is understanding the origins of our laws. Three articles of the U.S. Constitution create a federal government composed of three major branches: The legislative branch (under Article I) primarily creates laws; the executive branch (under Article II) primarily enforces laws; and the judicial branch (under Article III) primarily interprets laws. While performing their major functions as described in the relevant articles, the executive and judicial branches also create laws. Administrative agencies are a fourth source of laws. The following sections describe how each of these branches serves as a source of laws. Table 1-1 summarizes where you can find the laws created by these branches of the federal government, as well as laws created by state and local governments. In looking for environmental laws, you will find that they may be created by all these branches and, therefore, may be found in all these sources.

THE LEGISLATIVE BRANCH AS A SOURCE OF STATUTORY LAW

Article I, Section 1, of the U.S. Constitution states, "All legislative Powers herein granted shall be vested in a Congress of the United States which shall consist of a House and Senate." It is important for you to understand the process by which Congress makes a law (called a statute) because Congress creates most environmental laws. If you wish to change environmental laws, you must understand how to work through the legislative process. Groups that may be affected by a proposed law will seek to influence the proposal through lobbying at every stage of the legislative process. Some of these groups are highly organized forces that attempt to influence any proposed environmental legislation in Congress. Other groups are loosely knit, ad hoc organizations that emerge to influence only a particular proposal. Although most congressional lobbyists, especially those working on behalf of business interests, are paid professionals, a large number of lobbyists for environmental legislation are extremely committed volunteers.

TABLE 1-1 Where to Find Environmental Law

Level of Government	Legislative Laws	Executive Orders	Common Law/ Judicial Interpretations	Administrative Regulations
Federal	United States Code (USC) United States Code Annotated (USCA) United States Statutes at Large	Title 3 of the Code of Federal Regulations Codification of Presidential Proclamations and Executive Orders	United States Reports (U.S.) United States Supreme Court Reporter (S.Ct.) Federal Reporter (F., F.2d) Federal Supplement (F.Supp.) Environmental Law Reporter (ELR) Federal agency reports (titled by agency; e.g., FCC reports)	Code of Federal Regulations (CFR) Federal Register
State	State code or state statutes (e.g., Baldwin's Ohio Revised Code)		Regional reporters State reporters	State administrative code or state administrative regulations
Local	Municipal ordinances		Varies; often difficult to find. Many municipalities do not publish case decisions, but keep them on microfilm. Interested parties usually must contact the clerk's office at the local courthouse.	Municipality administrative regulations

The lobbying process for environmental issues is somewhat complicated. The situation is not always one of business lobbyists working against
environmental lobbyists. Divergent opinions about proposed legislation are
frequently seen within the environmentalist community. Established groups,
such as the Defenders of Wildlife and the Environmental Defense Fund,
tend to take more moderate positions and are more open to ideas for
cutting the costs of environmental regulation. The moderate stances of such
groups have prompted some former members to join organizations that
take more extreme positions, such as Earth First! which has essentially given
up on the governmental process and takes its case directly to the media by
staging protest actions.

Those in the moderate group see themselves as practical and effective.
They believe that, especially in recessionary climates, you will be ignored if
you do not take economic arguments into account. Those in the more
extreme group perceive the moderates as having sold out. Some of them
also believe that the best way to get on television, and thus generate public
support for one's position, is to take an extreme stance. Even when they
hold divergent positions, some members of both camps view the prolifera-
tion of environmental lobbying groups, even when they hold diverse positions, as being positive because it means more voices sending the message to
Congress that the public wants the environment protected.

During the 2000 election cycle, environmental groups contributed just
over $2 million to candidates.[1] In 1999, spending on lobbying by environ-
mental groups totaled more than $4.5 million.[2] This amount appears huge,
but it is small in comparison with the amounts expended by various business
sectors. For instance, in 1999, the oil and gas industry spent more than
$60 million on its lobbying efforts.[3] Nevertheless, the amount spent by envi-
ronmental lobbyists alone indicates that the lobbying effort is a significant
aspect of the political process.

How much influence do environmental groups have on the federal
government? Every other year, *Fortune Magazine* used to rate the most
influential lobbyists and publish its "Power 25." The magazine surveyed
members of Congress, their staff, and White House officials to determine
which groups were most powerful. For 2001, the last year the list was published, the Sierra Club was the only environmental group to make the list, at
number 52.[4] In previous years, groups such as the League of Conservation
Voters, Natural Resources Defense Council, Environmental Defense Fund,
and the National Wildlife Federation made the list.[5]

With the increased use of the Internet, some environmental groups are
trying to get ordinary citizens involved in what could be described as "grass
roots email lobbying." Groups such as Environmental Defense have set up
Web sites that will send messages to Congressional representatives and the
president on behalf of citizens who make such a request. To see how this
process works, you can go to http://www.environmentaldefense.org/action
center.cfm. Once there, you can choose to e-mail your representatives about

How does a group decide which candidates to endorse? Let us look at the Sierra Club's endorsement process as an example.

1. Send questionnaires to all candidates to determine their position on issues they are likely to face. (However, sometimes the Sierra Club looks only at the past record of the candidates. If one candidate has a strong record in supporting the environment whereas the other has demonstrated a bias against the environment, the club will endorse based solely on past records.)
2. Examine the questionnaires and schedule interviews with the candidates.
3. Complete interviews and make recommendations to the respective political committee (chapter political committee for state and U.S. Congress races; group political committee for local or county races).
4. Vote. Two-thirds of the body must vote to endorse.

Adapted from the Sierra Club San Diego Chapter Web site, *http://sandiego.sierraclub.org/bylaws/index.asp?content=political.*

any of various environmental issues. Once you send one message from the site, you will regularly receive e-mail notices, telling you about new issues as they arise and inviting you to come back to the site to express your opinion on those new issues.

The focus for environmental lobbyists has traditionally been in Washington. But during the 1990s, as action at the state level became more important, we saw a shift toward more lobbying below the federal level. Many national organizations, for example, have local affiliates that lobby state legislatures when their interests are affected. Groups such as the Sierra Club and the National Audubon Society have local chapters that work to address issues at the state level. That shift of resources became even more dramatic during the 2006 mid-term elections, as more environmental lobbying groups started donating more money to state candidates and ballot issues, reflecting the increasing role in environmental regulation as the federal role is shrinking.

Steps in the Legislative Process

The federal legislative process is similar in many respects to the process followed by state legislatures, but each state constitution may require slightly different procedures. We focus on the federal process because it is the model on which state processes are based and because most environmental legislation is either federal or modeled on federal law. The reason our environmental laws are primarily federal is that environmental problems do not recognize state borders and, therefore, necessitate a uniform, nationwide approach.

All laws originate from legislative proposals called bills. A bill is introduced into the House or Senate by a single member or by several members. The bill itself may well have been drafted by a lobbyist. As explained above, most environmental groups have lobbyists who attempt to persuade

TABLE 1-2 Organizations Engaging in Environmental Lobbying

Business Interests	*Environmental Interests*
Business Roundtable	Environmental Defense Fund
Chemical Manufacturing Association	National Audubon Society
National Chamber of Commerce	National Resources Defense
National Environmental Development Council	Council Sierra Club
(a coalition of industries)	Wilderness Society
Utility Air Regulation Group (a coalition of utilities	
and trade associations)	

environmentally conscious legislators to introduce and support their bills. Various business interests also hire their own lobbyists. Table 1-2 lists some of the more active lobbying organizations that influence environmental legislation.

Once introduced, a bill is generally referred to the committee of the House or Senate that has jurisdiction over the subject matter of the bill. For example, a bill seeking to provide subsidies to firms willing to get half their energy from solar power will be referred to the House Committee on Energy and Commerce, which will in turn refer it to an appropriate subcommittee. Table 1-3 lists some of the committees and subcommittees to which environmental legislation may be referred. In most cases, a bill is simultaneously introduced into both the Senate and the House and referred to the appropriate committee and subcommittee in each. Once the bill is referred, the subcommittee holds hearings on the bill, listening to testimony from all concerned parties and establishing a hearing record. Lobbyists will be active during this time, sometimes by testifying at congressional hearings.

Following these hearings, the bill is marked up (drafted in precise form) and referred to the subcommittee for a vote. When the vote is affirmative, the subcommittee forwards the bill to the full House or Senate committee, which may accept the subcommittee's recommendation, put a hold on the bill, or reject it. If the House or Senate committee votes to accept the bill, the committee brings it to the full House or Senate membership for a vote. Throughout this process, the bill may be amended several times in attempts to secure its passage. Sometimes, opponents of a bill will also amend it, in an attempt to water down the bill or to cause it to be defeated. As a bill is going through this process, interested parties may follow its progress in the *Congressional Quarterly Weekly,* a publication that keeps track of what is happening to proposed legislation. (Most university libraries subscribe to this publication.)

By the time the bill is passed by both the House and the Senate, different versions of the proposed law will usually have been adopted by the two chambers. Therefore, the bill will need to go to a Senate–House Conference Committee, which, after compromise and reconciliation of the two bills, will

TABLE 1-3 Congressional Committees and Subcommittees Influencing Environmental Legislation

Senate	House

Agriculture, Nutrition, and Forestry Committee
    Subcommittee on Forestry, Conservation, and Rural Revitalization
Appropriations Committee
    Subcommittee on Agriculture, Rural Development, and Related Agencies
    Subcommittee on Energy and Water Development
    Subcommittee on Interior Commerce, Science, and Transportation
    Subcommittee on Oceans and Fisheries
Energy and Natural Resources Committee
    Subcommittee on Energy Research, Development, Production, and Regulation
    Subcommittee on Forests and Public Land Management
    Subcommittee on Water and Power
Environment and Public Works
    Subcommittee on Clean Air, Wetlands, Private Property, and Nuclear Safety
    Subcommittee on Fisheries, Wildlife, and Water
    Subcommittee on Superfund, Waste Control, and Risk Assessment
Finance Committee
    Subcommittee on International Trade
Foreign Relations Committee
    Subcommittee on International Economic Policy, Export and Trade Promotion
Health, Education, Labor, and Pensions Committee
    Subcommittee on Public Health
Indian Affairs Committee
Judiciary Committee
    Subcommittee on Constitution, Federalism, and Property Rights
	Agriculture Committee
	    Subcommittee on Department Operations
	Oversight, Nutrition, and Forestry Committee
	    Subcommittee on Conservation, Credit, Rural Development, and Research
	Appropriations Committee
	    Subcommittee on Agriculture, Rural Development, Food and Drug Administration, and Related Agencies
	    Subcommittee on Energy and Water Development
	    Subcommittee on Interior
	Energy and Commerce Committee
	    Subcommittee on Energy and Air Quality
	    Subcommittee on Environment and Hazardous Materials
	    Subcommittee on Health
	Government Reform Committee
	    Subcommittee on Energy Policy, Natural Resources, and Regulatory Affairs
	International Relations Committee Resources (formerly known as Interior)
	    Subcommittee on Energy and Mineral Resources
	    Subcommittee on Fisheries Conservation, Wildlife, and Oceans
	    Subcommittee on Forests and Forest Health
	    Subcommittee on Health
	    Subcommittee on National Parks, Recreation, and Public Lands
	    Subcommittee on Water and Power
	Science Committee
	    Subcommittee on Research
	    Subcommittee on Energy
	    Subcommittee on Environment
	Transportation and Infrastructure Committee
	    Subcommittee on Water Resources and Environment Science
	Small Business
	    Subcommittee on Rural Enterprise, Agriculture, and Technology
	Ways and Means
	    Subcommittee on Trade
	    Subcommittee on Health

produce a single bill to be reported to the full House and Senate for voting. Very often, you will hear discussions in the media about differences between House and Senate versions of environmental laws that are making their way through this process. Often, one chamber's version will be supported by business interests and the other by environmental groups. The president will often throw his support publicly to one version or the other.

A final affirmative vote by both houses of Congress is required for a bill to become law. If passed, the bill is then forwarded to the president, who may either sign or veto the bill. When the president signs the bill into law, it becomes a statute. It is then written down and codified in the *United States Code* and the *United States Code Annotated.* If the president vetoes the bill, it may still become law if two-thirds of the Senate and House membership vote to override the veto. If the president takes no action within 10 days of receiving the bill from Congress, the bill becomes law without his signature; the exception to this procedure is that if Congress adjourns before the 10-day period has elapsed, the bill does not become law. The bill will have been pocket vetoed by the president; that is, the president will have "stuck the bill in a pocket"—vetoed it by doing nothing. Supporters will then have to reintroduce the bill during the next session of Congress.

Because Congress is responsible for passing environmental laws, citizens who wish to ensure that our environment is protected should keep themselves informed about their congressional representatives' voting records on environmental issues. The League of Conservation Voters has made it easy for concerned citizens to view their representatives' voting record on environmental issues by placing those records in an easily reachable database that can be found at http:www.lcv.org/scorecard/scorecardmain.ctm. This Web site also contains contact information of members of Congress.

THE JUDICIAL BRANCH AS A SOURCE OF CASE LAW

The federal courts and most state courts (discussed in Chapter 2) constitute the judicial branch of the government and are charged by their respective constitutions with interpreting the U.S. Constitution and statutes on a case-by-case basis. Most cases interpreting these laws are reported in large volumes called reporters, which are compilations of federal or state case laws. When two parties disagree about the meaning of a statute, they bring their case to the courts for interpretation. For example, if a bill to provide solar energy subsidies was signed by the president and became law, two parties might still disagree about its meaning and ask the federal courts to interpret it.

One disagreement that might arise with regard to such a bill is the time limit within which a firm must obtain half its energy from solar power. Although you would think that something as important as a time limit for conversion would be clearly stated in the statute, such an omission is not unusual. Congress, especially in the environmental area, often makes very broad laws and leaves it to the courts to fill in the gaps. As one senator said when Congress was about to pass the Superfund legislation, "All we know is the American people want these hazardous waste sites cleaned up . . . [L]et the courts worry about the details."

Congress may have also made the law intentionally vague because a more specific bill could not garner sufficient support for passage. The sponsors may have specifics in mind, but knowing there will be strong opposition to those details, they water down the language in the bill and hope that the courts will interpret the law to impose the specifics the drafters had in mind. This strategy can be risky because Congress never knows exactly how the courts will interpret a law. However, in the event that the judiciary interprets the law in a manner not intended by Congress, the legislative body can always amend the law, in effect overruling the judicial interpretation.

When interpreting a law, the judicial branch sees itself as trying to ascertain congressional intent. The court first looks at the "plain language" of the statute; that is, words are given their ordinary meaning. The court then looks at the legislative history to determine the intent of the legislature. This history is found in the hearings held by the subcommittees and committees, as well as any debates on the Senate and House floors. Hearings are published in the *U.S. Congressional News and Administrative Reports* and may be ordered from the Government Printing Office or found in the government document section of most university libraries. Debates about a bill are published in the daily *Congressional Record,* which also may be found in most libraries. When arguing before the court on behalf of their interpretation of the law, lawyers will draw from the *Congressional Record.* Thus, when trying to get a watered-down bill passed, its drafters will often try to insert language into the *Congressional Record* that would be supportive of their preferred interpretation of the law.

Not all judicially created laws are based on statutory or constitutional interpretation. Such laws for which there is no such basis are referred to as common law. Common law emerges from actual court cases. It develops when a problem arises for which there is no applicable statute or constitutional provision. We then have what is known as a case of first impression. Cases of first impression obviously provide judges with the greatest latitude to make law. The judge must create a law to resolve the problem. The rule laid down to resolve this case is called a precedent. If a similar case arises in the future, the courts have a tendency to follow the precedent. Very few environmental laws, however, are created in this manner; most environmental laws are based on statutes.

The rule that the court lays down when interpreting a statute or ascertaining its constitutionality is also known as a precedent. Such precedent will be relied on in the future when other judges are ruling on interpretations of statutes and the Constitution. This process of reliance on precedent is called *stare decisis,* which literally means "let the decision stand."

Not all precedents are equally important. Precedents are binding only on courts on a lower level and in the same system. For example, precedents from the Ohio Supreme Court bind the Ohio appellate and the Ohio trial courts; they do not bind the Michigan courts. However, an Ohio precedent may be used in a Michigan case as a persuasive device. In other words, lawyers in a Michigan case may point out how Ohio Supreme Court resolved the law and argue that the Ohio court's reasoning was logical and, therefore, should be adopted. Likewise, in the federal system, a Fifth Circuit Court of Appeals decision would not have any precedential effect on another circuit court appeal. However, the precedent would be binding on the district courts within the Fifth Circuit.

Although the process of *stare decisis* seems straightforward, its application actually provides the judge with an opportunity to impose his or her values on the law. Judges have discretion, in part, because no two cases are ever exactly the same. Judges, therefore, will usually be able to distinguish (a legal term) the case at bar from the case that others are arguing should provide the precedent. When distinguishing a case, judges find a difference between the case before them and the precedent-setting case significant enough to allow them to rule differently in the second case. In many cases, one lawyer will be arguing that the case before the court is similar to the potential precedent, and the opposing lawyer will be trying to point out significant differences between the two.

Another factor that makes reliance on precedent less predictable than you might assume is that there are frequently conflicting precedents, especially at the trial and initial appellate levels. Finally, a judge may always simply overrule the clearly applicable precedent. The judge will generally cite some reason for overruling the precedent, such as changes in technology or community values since the precedent was established, but he or she does not need to do so. He or she may simply say that the prior ruling was erroneous and that overturning the precedent is simply a matter of "correcting" the law.

The U.S. Supreme Court and most state supreme courts have what is generally known as the power of judicial review (i.e., the power to determine whether a statute is constitutional). Although not expressly provided for in the Constitution, the Supreme Court established this right in the landmark case of *Marbury v. Madison,* making the Supreme Court the final arbiter of the constitutionality of every law. Judicial review gives the Court ultimate power to restrict the activities of the legislative and executive branches.

Because most environmental law is federal statutory law, and because the U.S. Supreme Court is the final arbiter of the constitutionality of laws, most decisions you will read about in this book will be from the Supreme Court. As you will see, through its case-by-case interpretation of the Constitution and statutes, the Supreme Court has established a line of authoritative cases on various environmental matters.

THE EXECUTIVE BRANCH AS A SOURCE OF LAW

The executive branch includes the president, the president's staff, and the cabinet. The heads of all executive departments (e.g., the secretary of state, the secretary of labor, the secretary of defense, and the secretary of the treasury) make up the cabinet. The executive office is composed of various bodies, such as the Office of Management and Budget (OMB) and the Office of Personnel Management (OPM). The executive branch is influential in the rule-making processes of both the legislature and the administrative agencies. The president influences Congress by proposing legislation, by publicly supporting or opposing proposed laws, and by using the veto. The OMB's role in influencing administrative regulations through cost–benefit analysis is detailed in Chapter 3. The executive branch exercises direct rule making through its power to make treaties and issue executive orders.

Treaty Making

The president has the power, subject to the advice and consent of the Senate, to make treaties. These treaties become the law of the land based on the supremacy clause of the Constitution (Article XI); they supersede any state law. For instance, when President Reagan entered into the Montreal Protocol, a treaty mandating reductions in the production of chlorofluorocarbons (CFCs) and halons, that treaty became the law of the land, and its provisions superseded any existing federal or state laws inconsistent with the treaty. Thus, the Kentucky legislature could not subsequently pass a law that would allow the unlimited production of those chemicals within the state borders.

Treaty making is one of the few ways that the United States can influence the environmental policies of other nations. Even though treaty making is primarily the job of the executive branch, we cannot overlook the Senate's role. For example, in December 1997, the executive branch negotiated the Kyoto Treaty, aimed at reducing the production of gases believed to cause global warming. As of May 1998, the Kyoto Treaty had been signed by 34 countries. However, in December 2000, the treaty had not even been presented to the Senate for approval, to a large extent, because the executive branch was not confident that it would be able to secure enough votes for ratification. In 2001, a new president took office and declared that the United States no longer intended to be a party to that treaty, and even though there would be no formal "unsigning," the document would not be submitted to Congress during his term as president.

The United States has displayed increased antagonism toward environmental treaties in recent years. The Bush administration's unilateral stance on international issues was loudly demonstrated in 2002 when President Bush announced that he would not attend the Johannesburg World Summit on Sustainable Development. The United States is currently in default of a pledge made at the 1992 Rio Summit to reduce greenhouse gas emission to 1990 levels. Despite this nation's current reluctance to participate in international agreements, environmental problems are increasingly going beyond the scope of national boundaries. Consequently, treaties are becoming more essential in creating effective environmental policy solutions, but the United States is no longer taking a leadership role in this area. Chapter 11 further discusses the use of treaties in the creation of international environmental law and identifies a number of additional international environmental treaties that the United States has yet to sign and ratify as of 2006.

Executive Orders

Throughout history, the president has made laws by issuing executive orders. For example, President Reagan, by virtue of an executive order, ruled that all executive federal agencies must do a cost–benefit analysis before setting forth a proposed regulation for comment by interested parties. In 1999, President Clinton issued executive order 13123, "Greening the Government through Efficient Energy Management," which promoted energy conservation in federal facilities by mandating a 30 percent reduction in energy use by 2005. The executive order also promotes the use of renewable energy technologies and set the goal of installing 20,000 solar energy systems at federal facilities by 2010. Executive orders made by one president can be superseded by a contrary executive order made by the next president. For example, during his last year in office, President Clinton issued an executive order that made federal contracts difficult to get for companies that violated federal law, including environmental law. However, upon taking office, President George W. Bush reviewed, and rescinded, many of Clinton's executive orders, once again making it easier for federal contracts to be granted to those who are found to repeatedly violate environmental laws. Thus, although an executive order may be a quick way to achieve a goal, the victory may be short lived because the next president may undo the order. (Interested citizens can now easily find executive orders by searching the *Federal Register* Web site http://www.archives.gov/federal_register/executive_orders/executive_orders.html.)

The executive order as a source of law is also used by governors to respond to emergencies and budgeting problems. Often, a governor will call out the National Guard by executive order. In some states, the governor may use these orders to implement particular aspects of the budget process. For example, he or she may order a freeze on hiring in the state university system or order an across-the-board cut in budgets in all state departments when quarterly tax revenues are lower than anticipated.

Signing Statements

During his first 6 years in office, President George W. Bush issued 800 signing statements, which are a way of diluting or changing laws passed by Congress rather than vetoing them. According to his administration, the president has the authority through these statements to "revise, interpret, or disregard legislative measures on national security or constitutional grounds." Although other presidents have used this power on occasion, President Bush has used it more than all other presidents combined. The president's use of this power has been condemned by the American Bar Association, and there has been discussion by some Congresspersons about the need to limit the president's use of this tool, but thus far no legislation has been passed to limit its use.

ADMINISTRATIVE AGENCIES AS A SOURCE OF LAW

Less well known to the general public as a source of law are the federal regulatory agencies, among them the Environmental Protection Agency (EPA) and the Occupational Safety and Health Administration (OSHA). Congress has delegated to these agencies the authority to make rules governing the conduct of business and labor in certain areas. This authority was delegated because it was thought to be in accord with the public interest, convenience, and necessity. There was some concern, however, about the delegation of so much power to bodies with no elected representatives, so their rule-making processes (described in Chapter 3) are especially open to public participation. Proposed rules, as well as the rules finally implemented by an agency, must be published in the *Federal Register,* and the public must be given the opportunity to comment on these proposals.

Because of their substantial impact on the laws of this nation, administrative agencies sometimes represent what many observers have called a fourth branch of government. Because most of the federal environmental laws mandate the creation of many administrative regulations, we describe this fourth branch of government in greater detail in Chapter 3.

CLASSIFICATIONS OF LAW

CASE AND STATUTORY LAW

As noted earlier, laws are classified as either case laws or statutory laws, depending on how they are made. Judges make case laws; legislators make statutory laws. We generally find case law in case reports and statutory laws in codes. Even though this distinction is frequently made, it is important to remember that the two types of law are entwined through the process of statutory interpretation. We really do not know what a statute means until it is interpreted by the courts, whose judges attempt to construe congressional intent. Sometimes, the court's interpretation is not as was intended by Congress. Congress may then respond by amending the statute to make its meaning clear.

PUBLIC AND PRIVATE LAW

Aside from the distinction between statutory laws and case laws, another classification may be helpful in your study of environmental law—the distinction between public law and private law. Public laws are those set up to provide for the public welfare; they are generally applied by administrative agencies. These laws usually regulate classes of people or organizations. Environmental laws are considered public law. Other branches of public law include securities laws, labor laws, and antitrust laws.

On the contrary, private laws generally regulate the conduct between two individual parties. Private laws may sometimes be used in environmental matters. For example, if a company does not properly test a chemical and, consequently, sells a product that injures a consumer, that consumer may be able to bring a private action for compensation against that company. Such a private action is called a tort or personal injury case. Other private law actions include breach of contract and fraud.

CRIMINAL LAW AND CIVIL LAW

Perhaps an even more important distinction is that between civil and criminal law. This distinction is important because the rules governing each are different, as are the outcomes sought in each case.

Criminal law is made up of federal and state statutes that prohibit wrongs against the state or society in general—conduct such as arson, rape, murder, forgery, robbery, and illegal dumping of hazardous waste. The primary purposes of criminal laws are to punish offenders and to deter them and others from committing similar acts, usually through imprisonment or fines. The prosecutor, the party who initiates a criminal case, is the government, usually represented by a federal district attorney or a state prosecutor. The prosecutor is said to be representing society and the victim against the defendant, who is most likely to be an individual but may also be a corporation.

For purposes of both criminal and civil litigation, a corporation can sue and be sued, just as a person can. Corporations, in the context of litigation, are sometimes referred to as artificial or juristic persons. Of course, a corporation cannot be jailed; if a corporation is found to be guilty, a fine is imposed in lieu of a jail term.

Crimes are generally divided into felonies and misdemeanors, based on the severity of the harm the actions may cause. In most states, the more harmful felonies (e.g., rape, arson, and criminal fraud) are commonly punishable by incarceration in a state penitentiary and/or by fines. The less harmful misdemeanors (e.g., shoplifting) are crimes usually punishable by shorter periods of imprisonment in a county or city jail, as well as by smaller fines. However, what may be a misdemeanor in one state could be a felony in another.

Civil law is usually defined as the body of laws regulating relations between individuals or between individuals and corporations. In a civil matter, the party analogous to the prosecutor is the plaintiff. The plaintiff is usually seeking either compensation or equitable relief (an order for specific performance or an injunction). There is no division in civil law comparable to that between felonies and misdemeanors in the criminal system. In the civil system, laws are divided by subject matter, with the most common civil matters being tort cases and contract cases. Other substantive areas of civil law include domestic relations (family law), bankruptcy, agency law, property, business organizations, sales, secured transactions, and commercial paper.

Most people consider being convicted of a crime much more serious than being found guilty of violating a civil law. There is much greater "societal scorn" heaped on the criminal. Also, only criminal law threatens the defendant with the loss of liberty. For those reasons, the defendant in a criminal case is given much greater procedural protection. First, although almost anyone can file a civil action against another person, before a criminal defendant can be tried for a serious federal crime, an indictment must be handed down against him or her. Most states also require an indictment by a grand jury when a defendant is charged with a felony. To get an indictment, the prosecutor must convince the grand jury—generally composed of 15–23 citizens—that the prosecution has enough evidence to justify bringing the potential criminal defendant to trial.

When a defendant is charged with a misdemeanor, a local judge or magistrate will fulfill a role comparable to that of a grand jury. This initial step provides a safeguard against political prosecution. It is necessary because even when one is ultimately found not guilty, the act of being tried for a crime still tarnishes the defendant's reputation, so it is desirable to make the trial of an innocent party as rare as possible.

Another difference between criminal law and civil law lies in the burden of proof placed on the party bringing the action. In both cases, the party filing the action must prove his or her case. However, a person filing a civil case must prove that the defendant violated the law by a preponderance of evidence—proving that it is more likely than not that the defendant committed the act. If the defendant is charged with a crime, however, the prosecution must prove the defendant's guilt beyond a reasonable doubt, a much more stringent standard. Some people think of the difference as being the need to prove a civil case by 51 percent and a criminal case by 99.9 percent.

Environmental Criminal Prosecutions

Our primary concern with criminal law lies in the fact that violations of many environmental statutes constitute criminal offenses. As we examine specific environmental statutes, note that the same act often gives rise to both criminal and civil penalties. Criminal penalties are often imposed when an act is considered as willful or knowing violation. The most publicized trend in criminal actions today is the increasing use of imprisonment of corporate violators, including those who violate criminal provisions of environmental laws. Since new federal sentencing guidelines took effect in 1987, incarceration has increased, and plea bargains involving probation and community service have been less frequent. The EPA makes incarceration an important part of the criminal enforcement program. The stigma associated with incarceration serves as a greater deterrent than a fine that can be passed along as the cost of doing business. The prison sentence must be served by the violator. Also, when a company criminally violates an environmental law, an additional punishment may be the suspension of all of its government contracts.

The first major increase in the use of criminal sanctions to enforce environmental laws occurred in 1982, when the Department of Justice (DOJ) created a separate Environmental Crimes Unit in its Land and Natural

Resources Division, and the EPA established an office for Criminal Investigations. Since 1982, there has been a steady increase in the use of criminal sanctions. In 1990, the EPA referred a record 56 cases to the Justice Department for criminal prosecution, surpassing the previous year's high of 50. A record 100 defendants were charged with crimes in 1990, and 55 were convicted and sentenced to 75.3 years.

In 1994, the EPA took another major step toward increasing its ability to compel observance of the law by reorganizing its enforcement and compliance programs and creating the Office of Enforcement and Compliance Assurance, with an emphasis on targeting serious violations.

According to a report issued by the EPA in 2001, in 1997 a record 278 cases were referred to the Justice Department, with 322 defendants charged with environmental crimes. A total of 195.9 years of prison were imposed on the convicted defendants, and criminal fines of $169.3 million were imposed.[6] (See Figure 1-1 for a 13-year statistical comparison of criminal prosecutions.) The large increases in the criminal program are at least partly due to the Pollution Prosecution Act of 1990, which increased the number of criminal investigators to 200. Referrals have not continued to increase under the current Bush Administration, however. According to a 2003 EPA report, in 2001, there were 256 cases referred to the Justice Department (less than those in 1997), although there were 477 defendants charged (over 150 more than those in 1997) for 256 years of prison and $95 million in fines.

However, in the FY 2005 Annual Report, the Office of Compliance and Enforcement made changes to previously reported data, and also slightly modified the information they provided in their annual report, making it difficult to really make comparisons between enforcement before and after the year 2000. According to the most recent report prepared by the Office of Enforcement and Compliance Assurance, 320 defendants were charged environmental crimes and sentenced to 186 years. Fines and restitution totaled $100,000.[7]

In one of the toughest criminal sentences handed down in an environmental case, a Pennsylvania waste-pit owner, William Fiore, was sentenced to serve 6–12 years in a state prison for deliberately piping 1.2 million gallons of toxic leachate into the Youghiogheny River near Pittsburgh. The largest criminal penalty ever assessed an individual for violating an environmental law was given in 1990 to a trader on Wall Street. He was fined $2 million for filling wetlands without a permit.[8] The biggest criminal fine ever imposed on a corporation was the $22 million Exxon Valdez fine.[9] Similarly, in 1996 when Iroquois Pipeline pled guilty to degrading wetlands and streams while constructing a natural gas pipeline, it was assessed $22 million in fines and penalties.[10] Table 1-4 reveals some of the significant prison sentences, as well as fines, given in recent environmental cases.

Thus, since the early 1990s, the EPA has demonstrated a belief that criminal penalties have an important role in environmental enforcement. This view seems consistent with the public view but not with that of corporate

FIGURE 1-1   Office of Criminal Enforcement 13-Year Statistical Comparison

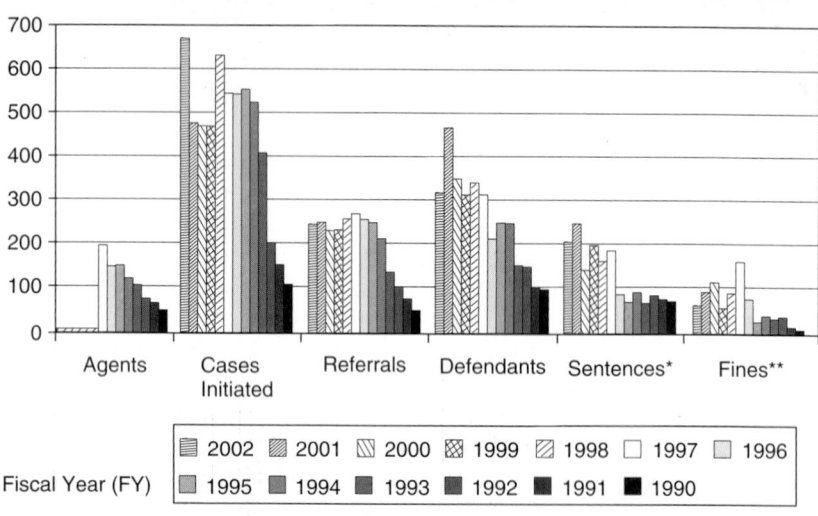

	Agents	Cases Initiated	Referrals	Defendants	Sentences*	Fines**
FY 1990	51	112	56	100	75.3	5.5
FY 1991	62	150	81	104	80.3	14.1
FY 1992	72	203	107	150	94.6	37.9
FY 1993	110	410	140	161	74.3	29.7
FY 1994	123	525	220	250	99.0	36.8
FY 1995	153	562	256	245	74.0	23.2
FY 1996	151	548	262	221	93.0	76.7
FY 1997	199	551	278	322	195.9	169.3
FY 1998	N/A	636	266	350	173.0	92.8
FY 1999	N/A	475	241	322	208.3	61.6
FY 2000	N/A	477	236	360	146.0	122.0
FY 2001	N/A	482	256	477	256	95
FY 2002	N/A	674***	250	325	215	62

*   Years of incarceration
**   Millions of dollars
***   FY 2002 Includes 190 counter-terrorism investigation initiatives.

Source: http://www.epa.gov/compliance/resources/reports/accomplishments/oeca/fy02accomplishment.pdf
(September 8, 2003) "EPA Criminal Enforcement: Major Outputs: FY 1998 to FY 2002."

executives. A poll reported in the *Wall Street Journal* on March 11, 1992, revealed that 75 percent of the general public believed that executives should be held personally liable for their environmental crimes, but only 49 percent of 500 executives of large corporations agreed.[11] A majority of the public rated environmental crime as worse than price-fixing and insider trading, whereas 80 percent of corporate executives thought that the latter two were more serious crimes.

TABLE 1-4   Significant Individual Fines, Prison Sentences, and Corporation Fines Handed Down in Environmental Cases

Fines Handed Down to Individuals in Environmental Cases

Name	*Violation*	*Date*	*Fine*
Robert Renes, vice president of Marman USA, Inc.	Forged EPA seals on false certificates of registration for pesticides his company sold abroad	1996	$150,000
Leslie Wallin, president of Eklof Marine Corporation	Charged for an oil spill off Rhode Island coast because tugs and barge were not properly equipped to safely navigate storm waters	1997	$100,000
Guy Hoy III, owner of Hoy's Marine	Discharged sandblasting residue and paint into waterways after repeated warnings to cease the harmful practice	2002	$70,000 in restitution & $27,000 in state fines
Ben Shafsky, assistant operations manager for Doyon Drilling Corporation	Violated the Oil Pollution Act (OPA) by injecting paint thinner, paint, oil, and solvents down the out rim of oil-producing wells on Endicott Island and concealing the illegal disposal of hazardous waste	1998	$25,000
Allan Sinclair, former drilling rig supervisor	Violated the OPA by mistakenly concealing the illegal disposal of hazardous waste and failing to notify federal officials about the crime	1998	$25,000
Gary Seymour	Violated FIFRA by placing pesticide on a deer carcass for the purpose of killing coyotes	2002	$23,100
Benjamin Grafton, employee of Arizona Chemical Company, Inc.	Violated the Clean Water Act (CWA) by tampering with a water-monitoring method	1997	$20,000
Benny Joe Surratt, employee of Arizona Chemical Company, Inc.	Violated CWA by tampering with a water-monitoring method	1997	$20,000

(continued)

TABLE 1-4   *(cont.)*

Fines Handed Down to Individuals in Environmental Cases

Name	Violation	Date	Fine
Ray McCune, president and owner of Reclaim Barrel Supply Company and Allstate Container Company	Illegally stored hazardous waste in two facilities	1996	$20,000
Dana Dulohery, former plant manager at a Louisiana-Pacific Corporation manufacturing company	Violated the Clean Air Act by tampering with air emission control equipment and conspired to falsify emission report data	1998	$15,000

Prison Sentences Handed Down in Environmental Cases

Name	Violation	Date	Prison Sentence
Carl Eugene Hines, owner of H&J Auto and Salvage	Illegally disposed hazardous wastes and charged with other drug, firearms, and witness intimidation crimes	1998	480 months
Daniel Martin, worked at H&J Auto and Salvage	Transported hazardous waste without a manifest, illegally stored hazardous waste, and committed drug crimes	1998	240 months
Allan Elias, owner of Evergreen Resources	Knowingly exposing his employees to cyanide gas without proper safety precautions and lying to the government	2000	204 months
Gary Benkovitz, owner of Bay Drum and Steel	Intentionally dumped toxic waste into Tampa's sewer system and waterways	1999	156 months
Donald R. Budd, owner of Texas Environmental Services	Conspired to commit and committed mail fraud on behalf of Texas Environmental Services, a laboratory he owned, by providing false wastewater and drinking water reports	1997	72 months
Johnnie James Williams, owner and operator of W&R Drum, a drum recycling facility	Illegally stored and disposed of hazardous waste in violation of RCRA in a neighborhood that has environmental justice issues	1997	41 months

TABLE 1-4   *(cont.)*

Prison Sentences Handed Down in Environmental Cases

Name	Violation	Date	Prison Sentence
Raymond Feldman, owner of Ray's Automotive	Unlawfully disposed containers of ignitable, lead-bearing hazardous paint wastes in violation of RCRA and conspired to unlawfully transport and dispose of these drums of waste	1997	37 months
Mark D. Henry, director and treasurer of Bee de Waste Oil	Convicted on two counts of wire fraud, two counts of mail fraud, one count of conspiracy to violate RCRA. Schemed to defraud approximately 75 companies trying to comply with environmental regulations. Accepted 28,000 tons of soil contaminated with hazardous waste, claiming it would be recycled	1996	37 months
Jeffery Jackson, plant manager, and Micheal Peters, environmental manager, at Hunstman Chemical Plant	Both were found guilty of violating regulations under the Clean Air Act for the discharge of dangerous levels of benzene	2002	36 months & a $50,000 fine each
Billy Joe Jones, former operator of wastewater treatment facility	Violated the CWA by knowingly allowing 65,000 gallons of raw sewage into the Ohio River	1997	27 months
Billy Jack Orange, worker at H&J Auto and Salvage	Conspired to illegally transport and store hazardous wastes	1998	27 months
Lee Poole, uncertified pesticide applicator	Illegally applied the restricted use pesticide, methyl parathion, to homes	1998	24 months
James Goldman, vice president of Tin Products	Discharged toxic waste water in violation of the Clean Water Act causing serious harm to aquatic life and the shut down of a water treatment plant	2003	18 months

(continued)

TABLE 1-4   *(cont.)*

Prison Sentences Handed Down in Environmental Cases

Name	Violation	Date	Prison Sentence
Roberto Ramilo	Tampered with samples and falsified information to conceal the fact that his water treatment equipment failed to meet safe drinking water standards	2003	15 months

Recent Criminal Fines Handed Down to Corporations in Environmental Cases

Name	Violation	Date	Fine
Refrigeration USA Corporation	129 felony counts	1997	over $37 million
Summitville Consolidated Mining Company Incorporated	Convicted of 40 counts of violating the CWA by making false statements, failing to report, and making unauthorized discharges into water	1996	$20 million
Royal Caribbean Cruise Lines	Admitted to routinely dumping waste oil and other pollutants, such as hazardous chemicals from photo processing equipment, dry cleaning shops, and printing presses, from its cruise ships; kept dummy logs, lied to coast guard about it, and tried to cover up the incidents	1999	$18 million in two cases
ASARCO Inc.	Violated CWA by illegally discharging industrial wastewater without a permit and violated RCRA by illegally storing, treating, and disposing of certain hazardous wastes	1998	$6.38 million
Hess Oil Virgin Islands Corporation	Illegally transported hazardous waste. Falsely declared that over 1,000 drums containing hazardous waste contained nonhazardous waste	1996	$5.3 million
Eklof Marine Corporation	Charged for a spill off the coast of Rhode Island. Tugs and barges were not properly equipped to safely navigate stormy waters. Spilled 826,000 gallons of home heating oil	1998	$3.5 million federal fine $3.5 million from Rhode Island Superior Court

TABLE 1-4 *(cont.)*

Recent Criminal Fines Handed Down to Corporations in Environmental Cases

Name	Violation	Date	Fine
Tanknology-NDE, International, Inc.	Fined for 10 felony counts of presenting false claims to federal agencies about underground storage tank testing services performed	2002	$1 million criminal fine & $1.29 million in restitution
Masami Cattle Ranch	Charged for violating the Clean water Act after admitting to dumping cattle waste and dead cattle carcasses into local waterways	2002	$1.7 million
Sunoco	Charged for violating the Clean Water Act and damaging natural resources	2005	Settled for $3.6 million

A single act may lead to both criminal penalties and civil liability. For example, if a businessperson willfully violates the Resource Conservation and Recovery Act (RCRA), both the person and the corporation may be subject to criminal penalties in the form of fines. In addition to criminal penalties, civil penalties may be assessed, and parties who were personally injured by the violations may also bring private civil damage suits. Many people, however, believe that the imposition of criminal penalties is more effective in deterring noncompliance.

Enforcement since 1997 has oscillated, with fewer cases initiated and referred in 1999 and 2000, but with large sentences being handed down. The largest prison sentence for an environmental crime was handed down in 1999 and upheld on appeal in 2001. In that case, Allen Elias was sentenced to 17 years in prison for knowingly exposing a worker to hazardous waste. Criminal fines were low in 1999, but they nearly doubled in 2000, although fines in both years remained at the levels set in 1997. Environmental enforcement, however, often varies with the number of people assigned to conduct inspections and enforce environmental laws. Consequently, the year 2003 saw a decrease in environment enforcement as the Bush Administration cut the number of EPA enforcement personnel by more than 12 percent, from 528 to 464, since the President took office in 2001.[12] The year 1999 was a record year for the EPA in terms of civil enforcement, with the imposition of $141 million in civil judicial penalties. The next closest year was 2001 at $101 million in civil penalties and $25 million in administrative penalties. In 2002, only $55.5 million in civil penalties were issued.

In 2001, the EPA ordered General Electric (GE) Company to pay $500 million to remove 150,000 of the 1.3 million pounds of toxic polychlorinated biphenyls (PCBs) it had dumped into the Hudson River over a 30-year period, which ended with a Congressional ban in 1977. In 1984, PCBs were discovered in the riverbed, placing a 197-mile stretch of the river on the federal Superfund list. After years of debate, GE agreed to dredge 40 miles of the river, removing 2.65 million cubic yards of contaminated sediment, making the dredging operation one of the largest in the nation's history. The dredging is scheduled to begin in 2006 after a 3-year planning period. In addition, GE will pay $28 million in partial reimbursement of the EPA's past and future cost involved in the cleanup.[13]

The improved enforcement record of the early 1990s may be attributed to two factors. First, the administrator of the EPA, William Reilly, was determined to improve enforcement. Second, the EPA's enforcement budget was greatly increased in the early 1990s. It is important to remember, however, that no matter what the enforcement level, we are not necessarily anywhere close to prosecuting most violators of environmental regulations. In January 1996, President Clinton accepted a short-term budget bill that funded the EPA as a whole at 22 percent below the agency's 1995 funding. However, EPA funding started to increase again in 1997. That year the EPA received approximately $6.7 billion compared to the 1996 allocation of $5.7 billion. Funding increased again in 1998, when the budget was $7.36 billion. However, the EPA's budget since 1998 has been relatively stable, at around $7 billion. The proposed budget for the EPA for 2007 was $7.32 billion, a slight decrease from the previous year. Table 1-5 lists the EPA's vacillating overall budget.

TABLE 1-5   Overall EPA Budget

Fiscal Year	Budget (in billions of dollars)
1990	5.5
1991	6.1
1992	6.6
1993	6.9
1994	6.6
1995	7.2
1996	5.7
1997	6.7
1998	7.4
1999	7.6
2000	7.8
2001	7.8
2002	8.1
2003	7.6
2004	8.4
2005	8.0
2006	7.6
2007 (requested)	7.3

One problem with looking at these figures, however, is that it is difficult to really know how much of the EPA's budget is actually being focused on what we have traditionally defined as environmental matters, because some of the agency's budget is now being funneled into antiterrorism activities.

An important criminal law case that has helped to make criminal sanctions more of a deterrent than they otherwise might have been is the 1975 U.S. Supreme Court case of *United States v. Park*.[14] That case laid down the rule that a corporate officer can be held criminally liable for failure to correct a regulatory violation, even when that officer directed a lower-level employee to take corrective action. The test for liability in that case was that criminal liability would be imposed when a person, by virtue of his or her position in a corporation, had the responsibility and authority either to prevent the violation or to promptly correct it and failed to do so. The defendant in such a case cannot avoid liability by claiming ignorance. If the person delegates responsibility, he or she is legally accountable for the actions or inaction of delegates.

Even when a statute requires knowledge to constitute a criminal violation, the concept of knowledge may be interpreted very broadly, with presumed knowledge considered adequate under some statutes. For example, the RCRA impose criminal liability on any person who knowingly transmits hazardous waste to a facility not permitted for that purpose. In the 1986 case of *United States v. Hayes International Corporation*,[15] a defendant had arranged to have a private hauler dispose of waste the company had generated and was led to believe that the waste was being recycled. Under RCRA, if waste is being recycled, the hauler does not need a permit. In this case, the hauler was not recycling the waste and did not have the appropriate permit. Despite the company's lack of actual knowledge that the hauler did not have a permit, both the company and its contracting officer were found guilty of violating the act. The Eleventh Circuit Court of Appeals upheld the convictions. The court created a presumption of knowledge on the part of those handling hazardous waste and said that such presumed knowledge could be used to prove circumstantially a knowing violation of the act.

Responding to Increased Enforcement

Firms are increasingly recognizing the potential for criminal liabilities being imposed on them. Because it is now clear that ignorance of neither the facts nor the law is an excuse, corporations are encouraging employees to take steps to protect themselves and their companies from liability. These steps should have been taken anyway, but often only the threat of prosecution motivates people.

First, employees in responsible positions are being encouraged to know the law. Second, when an official delegates a task mandated by an environmental regulation, he or she is advised to accompany that delegation with strict supervision to be sure that compliance occurs. In prudent corporations, all environmental policies of the company are put in writing, as are all communications with regulatory agencies, especially when an agency is waiving a regulatory requirement. Individuals who disagree with directives with respect to environmental policies are encouraged to make their objections known in writing to top corporate officials, who are encouraged to investigate such claims quickly. Prudent companies are also more carefully investigating firms that they hire to do tasks that must be done in compliance with federal environmental regulations.

Finally, firms are increasingly making use of environmental auditing, which is defined by the EPA as "a systematic, documented, periodic and objective review by regulated entities of facility operations and practices related to meeting environmental requirements."[16] The environmental audit is seen by its advocates as a means to verify environmental compliance, in addition to being an invaluable tool for assisting management in cutting costs, assessing risk, planning for growth, increasing environmental awareness in the firm, enhancing the firm's image with the public, and reducing fines and enforcement actions. Table 1-6 sets forth the elements the agency believes are necessary for a successful auditing program.

One of the stronger advocates of environmental audits is the EPA. To encourage the use of such audits and "self-policing" on the part of corporations, the administrator of the EPA issued the agency's "Incentives for Self-Policing: Discovery, Disclosure, Correction and Prevention of Violations," commonly called the Audit Policy.[17] Under this policy, issued in 1995 and revised in 2000, if a firm can demonstrate that it discovered a violation and moved to correct it, the firm will not be subject to the gravity portion of any civil penalty. Under the EPA's Policy on Civil Penalties, the gravity portion is an amount of money added to the fine that ensures that the violator derives no economic benefit from the violation; it "ensure[s] that the violator is economically worse off than if it had obeyed the law."[18] To qualify for this penalty reduction, the violator must meet nine conditions.

First, the corporation must have discovered the violation either through a voluntary environmental audit or as a result of due diligence in the corporation's compliance monitoring systems, which the EPA defines as

---

TABLE 1-6   Elements of a Successful Environmental Auditing Program

- Explicit senior management support for environmental auditing and the willingness to follow up on the findings
- An environmental auditing function independent of audited activities
- Adequate auditor training and staffing
- Explicit audit program, objectives, scope, resources, and frequency
- A process that collects, analyzes, interprets, and documents information sufficient to achieve audit objectives
- A process that includes specific procedures to promptly prepare candid, clear, and appropriate written reports on audit findings, corrective actions, and schedules for implementation
- A process that includes quality assurance procedures to verify the accuracy and thoroughness of such audits

systematic efforts to prevent, detect, and correct violations. Voluntary audits and due diligence do not include monitoring, sampling, or auditing that are required by a law, regulation, permit, judicial or administrative order, or consent agreement. Second, the corporation must voluntarily report the violation, fully and in writing, to federal, state, and local officials within 10 days of its discovery, unless it is an unusually complex violation. Third, the corporation must promptly disclose the violation. Prompt disclosure is defined as notification to the EPA within 21 days after a violation is discovered. For multiple facilities, the length of time for disclosure may be increased. Fourth, the corporation must discover the violation independently, before monitoring by the EPA, or another government agency would have found the violation. Fifth, the corporation must remedy the violation within 60 days of its discovery. Sixth, the corporation must work to prevent recurring violations. Seventh, the corporation cannot have had the same or a similar violation within the past 3 years. Eighth, the violation must not have resulted in serious harm to the environment or imminent and substantial danger to public health or the environment. Finally, the corporation must cooperate with the EPA and not hide or destroy any evidence.

If a firm meets all of the above conditions, the EPA will waive the gravity portion of the firm's civil penalty. If the firm meets all the conditions except the first, systematic discovery of violations, the firm will be eligible for a 75 percent reduction of the gravity portion. As well, the EPA may recommend against criminal prosecution for a firm that meets the nine criteria. A firm that receives a reduction based on this policy may be required to describe its due diligence practices publicly. Also, if a company must enter into a written agreement, administrative consent order, or judicial consent order resulting from the violation, those documents must be made public.

A firm that is serious about conducting an environmental audit can receive help from the EPA through its Web site. Protocols for audits to discover violations of the major environmental laws can be found at http://cfpub.epa.gov/compliance/resources/policies/incentives/auditing/, the EPA page for Compliance Incentives and Auditing.

At least 185 companies have disclosed violations at more than 457 facilities under the agency's audit policy on civil penalties. The EPA plans to study the effects of the policy and make public its review. Initial response from the environmental community to the final policy was generally favorable; response from corporate counsel was more mixed. A lawyer for the Corporate Environment Enforcement Council commended the EPA for changes it had made from an interim policy that he thought would "offer responsible companies a reliable break in penalties without letting scofflaws off the hook,"[19] but he still had some major reservations. His main criticism, shared by many industry representatives, was that the policy did not provide an absolute privilege for environmental audits, a privilege that would have kept any agency or private party from being able to obtain the audit and use it against the corporation in a legal action.

In fact, a major issue debated during the 1990s was whether these audits should be considered privileged information. Those in favor of an audit privilege argue that it is in everyone's best interest for firms to do environmental audits. After all, if firms do not know that they are in violation, how are they going to correct the violation? Yet if the management of a company knows that a violation uncovered during an audit may be used against the firm, the firm would be discouraged from doing the audit in the first place.

Initially, corporations turned to the courts to create an environmental audit privilege. Such efforts, however, have met with very little success, so corporations are now turning to both the state and the federal legislatures. By January 1998, legislation establishing an environmental audit privilege had been passed in 24 states. The bills vary somewhat, but Virginia's is an example of the type of audit privilege legislation that is supported by corporate representatives.

The Virginia statute provides that information collected, generated, and developed during the course of an environmental audit is privileged from disclosure under ordinary circumstances.[20] The information is protected regardless of whether the audit is prepared by corporate employees or an independent contractor hired by the owner/operator of the firm, and no one who helps in the preparation of the audit document can be compelled to testify about its contents or preparation.[21]

There are four exceptional circumstances under which the privilege will not be upheld:

1. When information is uncovered that demonstrates a clear, imminent, and substantial danger to public health or the environment
2. When information contained in the audit is already required to be disclosed by law
3. When information contained in the audit was prepared independently of the voluntary environmental audit
4. When the audit documents, or portions thereof, were compiled in bad faith[22]

If none of the foregoing circumstances exist, all the firm must do to assert the privilege is to prove that the audit (1) was conducted by or at the behest of the facility owner or operator, (2) was voluntary, and (3) was designed to identify areas of environmental noncompliance with the law or identify opportunities for improved efficiency or pollution prevention.[23]

Of course, state audit privileges do not apply to federal enforcement action brought in federal court or citizens' suits under federal statutes. They apply only to state actions brought in state courts. Industry representatives are, therefore, also lobbying to gain passage of a federal environmental audit privilege. A typical audit protection law introduced into, but not passed by, Congress was a 1995 House bill that would have protected companies from any administrative, civil, or criminal penalties for a violation that was discovered during an audit if the violation had been voluntarily disclosed to the EPA or another regulatory body.[24] This privilege could have been used only by firms that had not committed serious environmental violations during the 3 years before the audit.[25] In 2000, the EPA repeated its firm opposition to audit privileges in its revised Audit Policy.

CONSTITUTIONAL PRINCIPLES UNDERLYING THE AMERICAN LEGAL SYSTEM

No discussion of the American legal system would be complete without a discussion of the constitutional principles on which this system is based. The Constitution, as originally drafted, was a conservative document. Most of those who attended the Constitutional Convention were wealthy men, who understandably desired to protect their own interests. Because most of the drafters owned property, protection of private property was a major objective. Protection of private property interests, in turn, means the protection of business owners' interests.

The framers of the Constitution were also strongly influenced by philosopher John Locke, who saw government as a social compact by which people, living in a state of nature, agreed to form a government that would make rules by which all would abide. To prevent this government from being oppressive, individuals, according to Locke, had to retain certain rights. These inalienable rights included the right to the pursuit of life, liberty, and property. The U.S. Constitution was perceived as the embodiment of our social compact.

Although it is generally true that business and private property interests have consequently been well served by many of the provisions of the Constitution, there have been exceptions. As the political makeup of justices on the U.S. Supreme Court changes, interpretation of the Constitution also changes. The concepts and constitutional provisions discussed briefly in the following sections focus on those that have had the greatest impact on the scope of congressional authority to regulate private property interests and on laws designed to protect the environment.

FEDERALISM

Underlying the system of government established by the Constitution is the principle of federalism, which means that the authority to govern is divided between two sovereigns, or supreme lawmakers. In the United States, these two sovereigns are the state and federal governments. One characteristic of federalism is its allocation of the power to control local matters to the local governments. This characteristic is embodied in the Constitution. Under the Constitution, all powers not given exclusively to the federal government or taken from the states are reserved to the states. The federal government has only those powers granted to it in the Constitution. Therefore, whenever federal legislation affecting the environment is passed, the question of the source of authority for that regulation always arises. As will be revealed shortly, the commerce clause is the predominant source of authority for the federal regulation of business and, thus, the source of authority for most environmental legislation.

In some areas, the state and federal governments have concurrent authority; that is, both governments have the power to regulate the matter in question. This situation arises when authority to regulate in an area has been expressly, but not exclusively, given to the federal government by the Constitution. In such cases, the states may regulate in the area as long as the state regulation does not conflict with any federal regulation of the same subject matter. A conflict arises when a regulated party cannot comply with both the state and the federal laws at the same time. When the state law is more restrictive, and so compliance with the state law automatically constitutes compliance with the federal law, the state law may still be valid. For example, as discussed in subsequent chapters, in many areas of environmental regulation, states may impose much more stringent pollution-control standards than those imposed by federal law. However, states cannot pass less restrictive laws.

The outcome of direct conflicts between state and federal laws is dictated by the supremacy clause, found in Article VI of the Constitution. This clause provides that the Constitution, laws, and treaties of the United States constitute the supreme law of the land, "any Thing in the Constitution or Laws of any State to the Contrary notwithstanding." This principle is known as the principle of federal supremacy: Any state or local law that directly conflicts with the federal Constitution, laws, or treaties is void. Especially important for environmental law is the inclusion of rules established by federal administrative agencies as federal law.

FEDERAL PREEMPTION

The supremacy clause is also the basis for the doctrine of federal preemption. This doctrine is used to strike down a state law that does not directly conflict with a federal law but attempts to regulate an area in which federal legislation is so pervasive that it is evident that Congress wanted only federal regulation in that general area. It is often said in these cases that federal law "preempts the field."

Cases of federal preemption are especially likely to arise in matters pertaining to interstate commerce, in which a local regulation imposes a substantial burden on the flow of interstate commerce through a particular state. This situation is discussed in greater detail in the next section. The law of federal preemption is one in which there are no broad principles to be applied; the court simply looks at each individual case to determine whether Congress intended to preempt the subject matter in question from state regulation.

THE COMMERCE CLAUSE

The primary powers of Congress are listed in Article I of the Constitution. Before proceeding, it is important to recognize that Congress has only limited legislative power. Congress possesses only that legislative power granted to it by the Constitution. Thus, all acts of Congress not specifically authorized by the Constitution or necessary to accomplish an authorized end are invalid.

Commerce refers to trade or the exchange of goods or services. The commerce clause provides the authority for Congress to pass most of the federal environmental regulations. This clause empowers the legislature to "regulate Commerce with foreign Nations, and among the several States, and with the Indian Tribes." Depending on the ideological makeup of the Supreme Court, of course, interpretations of the specific boundaries of this clause vary.

Throughout history, interpretation of the commerce clause has varied greatly. Today the commerce clause is broadly interpreted. Any activity, even if purely intrastate, can be regulated by the federal government if it substantially affects interstate commerce. The effect may be direct or indirect. Thus, the federal government can regulate the price of milk that is both processed and sold in the same state. Intrastate milk competes with interstate milk; thus, the price of intrastate milk has an impact on the price of the interstate milk, thereby affecting interstate commerce.

Although many would argue that this broad interpretation of the federal government's ability to regulate Congress is so well established as to be unassailable, others still challenge some federal regulations on the grounds that such regulation is an attempt to affect private matters rather than interstate commerce. An example of such a challenge in the environmental arena is provided by the case of *Hodel v. Virginia Surface Mining and Reclamation Association, Inc.*[26] The *Hodel* case arose after Congress passed a statute establishing a number of requirements for strip mining, the most controversial being a provision that any land used for strip mining be returned to approximately its original state. The mining association argued that the principal purpose of the act was to regulate the use of private land, a matter that falls within the state's police power; thus, the act was not regulating interstate commerce.

In setting forth its rule, the Supreme Court reiterated its broad interpretation of the commerce clause with respect to environmental matters, saying,

> The court must defer to a congressional finding that a regulated activity affects interstate commerce if there is any rational basis for such a finding . . . even activity that is purely intrastate in character may be regulated by Congress where the activity, combined with like conduct by others in similar situations, affects commerce among the States or within foreign nations.

In the *Hodel* case, the Court applied this test to the facts and found that Congress had a rational basis for determining that strip mining affects interstate commerce because Congress had relied heavily on the impact of mining on water pollution. The Court pointed out the need for national standards in light of the difficulties states had encountered when attempting to regulate the problem. The Court also stated that characterization of a regulated activity as local was irrelevant if the purpose is to protect interstate commerce from adverse effects.

Until recently, most environmental regulation by the federal government, like the foregoing, has been presumed to be constitutional. In determining whether Congress has the authority to enact legislation under the commerce clause, the Supreme Court asks whether there is any rational basis for Congress to find that the activity to be regulated affects interstate commerce. If so, the Court asks whether there is any reasonable connection between the ends asserted and the regulatory scheme selected to achieve those ends. If both questions can be answered affirmatively, the legislation stands.

The 1995 case of *United States v. Lopez*,[27] however, marked the beginning of significant change in the Supreme Court's interpretation of the Commerce Clause, a change that some fear may lead to the high court's ultimately striking down some longstanding federal statutes that protect the environment. These fears have increased since the most recent appointment to the Supreme Court of Chief Justice Roberts, who has a reputation for favoring a more narrow interpretation of Congressional power under the Commerce Clause.

In the *Lopez* case, the Court ruled that Congress had exceeded its Commerce Clause authority when it passed the Gun-Free School Zone Act, a law banning the possession of guns within 1,000 feet of any school. In its ruling, the Court said that Congress could not regulate in an area that had "nothing to do with commerce, or any sort of economic enterprise."[28] The court also noted that the regulation in question must have a *significant* impact on interstate commerce.

In the 2000 case of *Brzonkala v. Morrison*,[29] the court continued its movement toward restricting Congressional authority under the Commerce Clause by striking down the Federal Violence Against Women Act, although Congress had compiled a significant amount of data illustrating the harmful effects of violence against women on the economy. As the dissent in this case noted, "it is clear that some congressional conclusions about obviously substantial, cumulative effects on commerce are being assigned lesser values than the once-stable doctrine would assign them. These devaluations are accomplished not by any express repudiation of the substantial effects test or its application through the aggregation of individual conduct, but by supplanting rational basis scrutiny with a new criterion of review."[30]

The new, more limited view of federal authority under the Commerce first affected environmental protection in the so-called *Migratory Bird Rule* case,[31] in which the high court restricted the ability of the Army Corps of Engineers (COE) to regulate wetlands that had no connection to interstate waterways but were used as resting grounds for migratory birds. Before this case, these wetlands were seen as falling under the Clean Water Act (CWA) because of the impact on tourism of the migrating birds stopping at these wetlands. Although this activity had been significant enough to justify regulating these wetlands for decades, the justices sitting on the high court in 2000 chose to overturn years of protection for those wetlands. This case is discussed in greater detail in Chapter 10.

Since the *Migratory Birds* decision, two new justices were named to the U.S. Supreme Court, both of whom seem to have a more restrictive view of Congressional authority. In the 2006 case of *Rapanos v. United States*,[32] discussed in Chapter 10, the high court further restricted the federal government's ability to regulate wetlands. What is perhaps more troubling to some environmentalists is not just this case but the fact that one of the new justices, Chief Justice Roberts, when he was a court of appeals justice, voted to hear a case questioned the constitutionality of the Endangered Species Act.[33] Thus, some environmentalists fear that the high court may no longer be willing to uphold as constitutional a number of environmental laws that have been in existence for decades.

The Restrictive Effect of the Commerce Clause

In addition to being seen as a source of power for the federal government, the commerce clause is also interpreted as an implicit restriction on the states' authority to regulate matters affecting interstate commerce. After all, under the doctrine of federal preemption, if the federal government is supposed to regulate matters affecting interstate commerce, then the states should not regulate these matters. Thus, it follows that states may not regulate interstate commerce.

This restriction has a history of changing interpretations so complex as to be beyond the scope of this book. Instead, we will focus on how the clause is being interpreted today. In brief, it is a violation of the commerce clause for a state to pass a law that on its face discriminates against interstate commerce. If, however, the legislation involves the state's engaging in a proprietary action (an action whereby the state is not functioning as a government but is acting more in the role of a business), the legislation will be upheld. If a statute does not appear on its face to be discriminatory but has discriminatory effects on interstate commerce, a test is applied, balancing the impact of the state's regulation on interstate commerce with the state's justification.

The issue of whether a state regulation is a violation of the commerce clause arises frequently in disputes surrounding the regulation of waste. States are searching for ways to restrict the importation of out-of-state waste without violating the commerce clause and are generally not succeeding. The earliest such case that went to the U.S. Supreme Court was *City of Philadelphia v. New Jersey*.[34] In that 1978 case, a New Jersey statute had prohibited the importation of solid or liquid waste generated outside the state to be buried in a landfill in the state. The Court said that the state was attempting to slow or stop the flow of commerce for protectionist reasons, an action that is clearly in violation of the commerce clause; therefore, the state law was unconstitutional and must be struck down.

Other states attempted to learn from New Jersey's experience. Ohio's legislature recognized that a statute discriminatory on its face could still be upheld if (1) the law has a legitimate purpose, (2) the statute serves that purpose, and (3) there is no nondiscriminatory alternative that would serve the same purpose. The legislature tried to pass a law that would meet that exception. The Ohio statute imposed higher taxes on out-of-state waste. Ohio had three justifications: (1) the sheer volume of waste flowing into the state, (2) the higher costs of out-of-state waste inspection, and (3) the increased threat of hazardous material entering Ohio and the consequent difficulty of policing its transportation. In striking down the law, the lower court said that protecting the environment was no justification unless something other than the source was the reason for the different treatment. The Court found the latter two justifications to be unsupported. The case was appealed in 1991, and the decision was upheld in 1992.

Michigan also tried to circumvent the restrictive impact of the commerce clause. Its law, however, fared much better than Ohio's in the lower court. Michigan's Solid Waste Management Act gave each Michigan county the right to accept or reject waste from any outside source. Because the waste was classified by county and, thus, inter- and intrastate waste were treated the same way, the lower court found no problem with the law. However, the U.S. Supreme Court did not agree.

Michigan's law, along with an Alabama law that imposed a $72-per-ton tax on out-of-state toxic waste shipped to Emelle, Alabama, commercial site, was struck down by the Supreme Court in the summer of 1992. The Court set forth in the Michigan case that states could not adopt "protectionist" measures to stop waste being generated in other states from being shipped to their dump sites. Even legitimate goals such as protecting health and the environment could not be accomplished by economic protectionism.

In the 8–1 ruling in *Chemical Waste Management, Inc. v. Hunt,* the High Court stated that Alabama could impose a special fee on the disposal of all hazardous material, not just out-of-state material, if indeed its goal was to reduce the volume of waste entering the Emelle facility. For the law to stand, the Court said that Alabama would have needed to show some distinction between hazardous waste generated inside and that generated outside the state. In the 7–2 Michigan decision, the Court likewise said that its ruling would have been different if the imported waste raised health or other concerns not presented by in-state waste. Chief Justice Rehnquist filed dissenting opinions in both cases and was joined by Justice Blackmun in his Michigan dissent. In the Alabama case, Rehnquist wrote that a state ought to be able to "take actions legitimately directed at the preservation of the state's natural resources, even if those actions incidentally work to disadvantage some out-of-state waste generators."[35]

Although most states are struggling to find a way to draft a constitutional law allowing them to keep hazardous waste out of their state, Rhode Island is trying do just the opposite: it is trying to keep commercial trash inside the state. Rhode Island's Central Landfill cannot, by law, charge the state's municipalities more than $14 a ton to receive residential trash. Because that amount does not cover disposal costs, the landfill charges up to $59 per ton for commercial trash.

The high prices made Central Landfill noncompetitive with dumps in neighboring states, which was a boon to local trucking firms, because they were now hauling tons of wastes to landfills in neighboring states. Consequently, the state's Solid Waste Management Corporation decreed that all the state's commercial trash had to go to a state-licensed disposal site—Central Landfill. A trucking firm, claiming the regulation was ruining its business, sued the state on the ground that the regulation violated the commerce clause. The district court judge agreed and issued an injunction in the summer of 1991.

Because trash disposal is such a major problem, and cases seeming to support a position that state restrictions on out-of-state waste disposal violate the commerce clause, Congress is coming under increasing pressure to pass some form of legislation that would override at least part of the Supreme Court's recent ruling and allow states to restrict the importation of waste. Indeed, Justice O'Connor specifically recognized that if Congress enacted legislation allowing for flow-control ordinances, the Court would be bound by the legislation.[36] Measures that would allow states to restrict interstate transport of nonhazardous waste have been introduced in both the House and the Senate but, thus far, have not been passed.

Like many cases before it, in the case of *Huish Detergents, Inc. v. Warren County, KY,*[37] the county ordinance requiring all waste processing to take place in a county facility was found to be discriminatory against interstate flow of waste and, thus, a violation of the commerce clause. Because the county was mandating that all trash collection be done by one private firm and that the garbage be deposited in state, Huish was unable to contract a firm to take their waste out of state. This action, the Court ruled, is a violation of the Commerce Clause.

However, in *Houlton Citizen's Coalition v. Town of Houlton,*[38] the Court upheld a plan limiting waste disposal to within the town borders because of a flow-control ordinance and bidding, thus avoiding a per se violation of the Commerce Clause. The bidding process was deemed completive, and the burden imposed on interstate commerce was not excessive in relation to the local benefits. It is the flow-control ordinance, however, that did the most to escape violation of the Commerce Clause.

THE FOURTH AMENDMENT

The Fourth Amendment protects the right of individuals to be secure in their persons, their homes, and their personal property. It prohibits the government from conducting unreasonable searches of individuals and seizing their property to use as evidence against them. If such an unreasonable search and seizure occurs, the evidence obtained cannot be used in a trial.

An unreasonable search and seizure is one conducted without government officials having first obtained a warrant from the court. The warrant must specify the items sought as well as the persons and places to be searched. Government officials are able to obtain such a warrant only when they can show probable cause to believe that the search will turn up the specified evidence of criminal activity. Supreme Court decisions, however, have recently narrowed the protections of the Fourth Amendment by providing for circumstances in which no search warrant is needed. Improvements in technology have also caused problems in the application of the Fourth Amendment because it is now simpler to eavesdrop on people and to engage in other covert activities.

The Fourth Amendment applies to corporations as well as to individuals. Fourth Amendment issues often arise when legislation authorizes warrantless searches by administrative agencies. For example, the EPA would prefer pollution-control regulations that allow them to conduct a surprise search when a firm is suspected of violating pollution limits. To the agency's dismay, the courts generally will not allow such warrantless searches. However, the standards for securing an administrative search warrant in such cases are much less stringent than those in a criminal action. In general, an administrative warrant requires that the searcher has a neutral enforcement plan that assures the court that selective enforcement will not occur.

THE FIFTH AND FOURTEENTH AMENDMENTS

The Due Process Clause

The Fifth and Fourteenth Amendments are often spoken together because both contain what is known as the due process clause—the provision that no person shall be deprived of his or her right to life, liberty, or property without due process of law. The Fifth Amendment is a prohibition on the federal government; the Fourteenth Amendment restricts states. There are two types of due process: procedural and substantive. Originally, due process was interpreted only procedurally. It required that a person whose life, liberty, or property would be taken by a criminal conviction be given a fair trial; that is, he or she was entitled to notice the alleged crime and the opportunity to confront his or her accusers before an impartial tribunal. The application of procedural due process soon spread beyond criminal matters, especially after passage of the Fourteenth Amendment.

Today, the due process clause has been applied to such diverse situations as the termination of welfare benefits, the discharge of a public employee from his or her job, and the suspension of a student from school. It should be noted, however, that the range of situations to which the due process clause applies is not being continually increased. In fact, after a broad expansion of the circumstances to which this clause applied, the courts began restricting the application of this clause during the 1970s, and they are continuing to do so. The courts restrict the clause's application by narrowing the interpretation of property and liberty. This narrowed interpretation is especially common in interpreting the due process clause as it applies to state governments under the Fourteenth Amendment.

The question of what safeguards are required by procedural due process is not easily answered. The procedures that the government must follow when there may be a taking of an individual's life, liberty, or property vary according to the nature of the taking. In general, as the magnitude of the potential deprivation increases, the extent of the procedures required also increases. For example, a student being suspended from public school for 3 days would be entitled to fewer procedural guarantees than one being expelled for a year.

The concept of substantive due process refers to the basic fairness of laws that may deprive an individual of his or her liberty or property. In other words, when a law that will restrict individuals' liberty or use of their property is passed, the government must have a proper purpose for the restriction; otherwise, it violates substantive due process. What constitutes a proper governmental purpose is, of course, subject to interpretation by the courts. Originally, proper purpose was limited to items within the traditional scope of police power (i.e., regulations that benefit the public health, safety, and welfare). The term welfare has been broadly interpreted; in some cases, it even includes such things as esthetics.

In applying the concept of substantive due process, we usually say that the government cannot act arbitrarily and capriciously. When substantive due process is analyzed, one asks whether the deprivation by the government involves the deprivation of a fundamental right. If so, the government cannot act unless it has a compelling reason to do so, and there is no less restrictive means for satisfying this compelling interest. A violation has occurred if there is an alternative way to achieve the same end that causes less deprivation. If the deprivation is for other than a fundamental right, the government action must be rationally related to a legitimate state end. In other words, the state end was an exercise of police power, and the means will logically lead to the state's specified end.

The Takings Clause

The Fifth Amendment further provides that if the government takes private property for public use, it must pay the owner just compensation. The language of the Fifth Amendment states, "nor shall private property be taken for public use without just compensation." Although the Fourteenth Amendment does not contain such a clause, the Supreme Court has interpreted the Fourteenth as incorporating this clause through its due process clause. Unlike the privilege against self-incrimination, which does not apply to corporations, both the due process clause and the provision for just compensation are applicable to corporations. The latter provision is of great importance in numerous environmental cases, where representatives of the corporation frequently argue that the environmental regulations are so onerous as to constitute a taking of their land, for which compensation should be awarded.

In cases in which a party argues that regulations are so restrictive of private use as to constitute a taking of his or her private property for public use, the government will argue that the regulations are simply an exercise of its "police power," its power to protect the welfare of the citizens. In general, the courts look at the diminution of the value of the property caused by the regulation and require compensation only when there has been a drastic reduction in the economic value of the property. In 1987, a 5–4 majority of the U.S. Supreme Court ruled that a state could impose restrictions on land use without having to compensate the owner for the land's reduced commercial value when the state "intends to prevent serious public harm."[39]

This issue of when a regulation constitutes a taking has been increasingly debated during the 1990s as both the state and the federal governments passed more regulations protecting wetlands that were often held as private property. The most significant case on this issue was argued before the U.S. Supreme Court on March 2, 1992. *Lucas v. South Carolina Coastal Council*[40] involved a dispute between a beachfront property owner and the state of South Carolina over a law prohibiting permanent construction on any eroding beach. Lucas had bought two beachfront lots for $975,000 in 1986, before the passage of the law in question. Lucas, who had not yet begun construction on his property when the law was passed, lost the right to use his property for condominiums, so he challenged the law as constituting a taking without just compensation. The state court agreed with Lucas that the regulation denied him full value of his property and thus constituted a taking, so it awarded him $1.2 million in damages. The South Carolina Supreme Court, citing the U.S. Supreme Court precedents, disagreed and overturned the lower court's decision.

Lucas appealed the decision to the U.S. Supreme Court, which handed down its opinion on June 29, 1992. This opinion reversed the state supreme court ruling in a 6–3 decision. The Court held that a state regulation that deprives a private property owner of all economically beneficial uses of property, except those uses that would not have been permitted under background principles of state property and nuisance law, constitutes a taking of private property for which the Fifth Amendment's takings clause requires payment. The Court stated that the South Carolina court erred in applying the principle that the takings clause does not require compensation when the regulation at issue is designed to prevent "harmful or noxious uses" of property.

Obviously, this decision was met with concern on the part of environmentalists, who fear that this ruling may lead to significant restraint on the part of state governments, which may fear that passing laws to protect state coastlines may now cost them millions of dollars. Even before a decision was handed down, however, the debate triggered legislative activity. A law that would require agencies to "assess" and "minimize" the potential for taking private property whenever a regulation is issued was proposed almost immediately. Another legislative proposal would have required federal agencies to compensate owners of wetlands when use of their property was restricted. Many environmentalists are understandably concerned about such proposals whenever they arise.

From the perspective of the "Property Firsters," or private property rights advocates, *Lucas* was a watershed case. *Lucas,* along with *Whitney v. United States*[41] (in which a federal court found that the federal Surface Mining and Reclamation Act constituted a taking with respect to one mining company whose land had become completely useless as a result of the act), restored to prominence the takings clause that had been relatively dormant for the previous 50 years. Strengthened by these victories, the property rights movement has been gaining momentum. A large number of property rights organizations are springing up all across the country, and many of the groups are forming informal alliances. Combining the old wings of the 1970s Sagebrush Rebellion in the West, miners, loggers, ranchers, and energy companies, with farmers and private property owners in the East and South, these groups are joining forces to attack what they see as government overreaching: wetland preservation, endangered species protection, public park and greenway expansions, scenic river corridors, land-use planning, and zoning laws and growth management plans.[42]

Table 1-7 lists some of these groups. One of the most influential organizations in the property rights movement is the Pacific Legal Foundation, the

TABLE 1-7 Property Rights Advocacy Groups

Alliance for America	A loose confederation of more than 600 property rights organizations that communicate through a fax network and host an annual "Flying for Freedom" lobbying excursion to Washington, D.C.
Environmental Conservation Organization	A coalition of organizations and individuals in America and 14 foreign countries that publishes a magazine, hosts conferences, and maintains a computer network for its membership
Virginia for Property Rights	A clearinghouse for Virginians seeking information on property rights issues
Oregonians in Action	An education center focusing on land use regulation and property rights that expanded to include a legal center
Pacific Legal Foundation	A nonprofit public interest firm that works to protect private property rights and limit government
Foundation for Research on Economics and the Environment (FREE)	A group that wants to advance and develop environmental policies featuring private property rights

first nonprofit, public interest law firm devoted to litigating in defense of "individual and economic freedoms" on a national level. Since its founding in 1973, this firm has participated in over 100 cases. Perhaps its most significant victory was *Dolan v. Tigard*,[43] a victory for the property rights movement handed down in 1994.

The city of Tigard, Oregon, had approved Dolan's application to expand her store and pave her parking lot subject to the condition that she dedicate a portion of her property for (1) a public greenway to minimize the flooding that would otherwise be likely to result from her construction and (2) a pedestrian/bicycle pathway to decrease congestion in the business district where her store was expanding. Although the Land Board of Appeals, the State Court of Appeals, and the State Supreme Court all affirmed the decision of the city, which had found that the land dedication requirements were reasonably related to her proposed construction and, therefore, not a taking, the U.S. Supreme Court disagreed. The court said that for a requirement like the one at issue to be valid, the requirement must have some reasonable relationship or nexus to the property's use, which was the standard used by the lower courts. However, in this case, what constituted sufficient evidence of that relationship for the lower courts was not sufficient for the Supreme Court.

Subsequently, property rights advocates celebrated the Supreme Court's ruling in *Palazzolo v. Rhode Island*.[44] Most of Palazzolo's property constitutes a flood-prone salt marsh protected by the State's Coastal Resources Management Program as a "coastal wetland." The State's protective regulations, which greatly limit development, existed before Palazzolo's acquisition of the property. Yet, despite having knowledge of restrictive regulations before acquiring the property, Palazzolo claimed that the State's wetland regulations constituted a taking of his property without compensation, in violation of the takings clause. The Rhode Island Supreme Court ruled that Palazzolo takings claim was not ripe and had no right to challenge regulations that predated his ownership of the property. However, the Supreme Court overturned the state court because it had erred "in ruling that acquisition of title after the effective date of the regulations barred the takings claim." The Supreme Court's ruling is significant in that it may greatly increase the number of regulatory takings claims, reducing the effectiveness of environmental regulations.

Clearly, this case was a significant victory for property rights advocates because it sends a message that the courts are now going to be looking much more closely at zoning and land use decisions than they traditionally have. Equally clear is the intent of the property rights advocates to continue to try to make gains in the courts as well as in the state and federal legislatures. They are increasingly finding friends in the legislature, as evidenced by the large number of property rights bills proposed during recent congressional terms.

A 2006 takings case that was a judicial defeat for the property rights movement may actually end up furthering their aims because the ruling has stimulated a spate of legislative proposals that may ultimately end up lessening states' willingness to impose restrictions on land use. The case was *Kelo v. New London*,[45] a case in which the high court upheld the state's taking of several private homes for a private development on grounds that the development would serve the "public purpose," that is, "public use," of creating jobs and generating tax revenue. While upholding a broad definition of public use might seem positive for environmental protection, the overall impact of the decision was to make the general public view regulation of private property as onerous and unfair. And it led to proposals in 2006 in at least six states of property rights laws that could hinder state regulation of private property for environmental protection purposes, even though the public would hardly be aware that they would be affecting environmental regulation by passing the bills.

For example, some laws provide that the government must compensate property owners for any lost property value or any potentially lost income resulting from any restrictions placed on the land. Others provide that payment for property taken under eminent domain must be determined by the highest possible use of the land. Such laws would dramatically increase the cost to states and municipalities of passing environmental regulations. It remains to be seen whether these bills will pass, and if they do, whether they will be upheld by the courts, and whether other states will follow them.

The Fourteenth Amendment contains another clause that has been gaining importance in the environmental arena since 1979: the equal protection clause. This clause provides that no state "shall deny to any person within its jurisdiction the equal protection of its laws." These words create the constitutional basis for concerns about environmental racism that are increasingly being raised by civil rights activists.

Although many claim that the movement against environmental racism began to coalesce approximately 10 years ago in South Carolina, when church-led black residents organized to protest the siting of a toxic landfill in their neighborhood, the movement started to achieve significant prominence in 1992.[46] During February of that year, the public became aware of an increasing array of statistics that appear to show that minorities receive less protection from environmental laws than whites do.

A study of EPA records by the *National Law Journal* revealed that there was a 506 percent disparity in fines assessed under the RCRA (the law regulating hazardous dumps) in predominantly black versus predominantly white neighborhoods. The average fine in white neighborhoods was $335,556, whereas the average fine in black neighborhoods was $55,318. A former EPA attorney said he believed that statistic was the most telling with respect to environmental racism.[47]

There were also much lower fines for cases alleging multiple environmental law violations in black neighborhoods. Average fines for such violations were 306 percent higher in white neighborhoods during the previous 7 years.[48] Moreover, penalties for violations of the CWA were 28 percent lower in minority communities, whereas fines for violating the Safe

Drinking Water Act and the Clean Air Act (CAA) were lower by 15 percent and 8 percent, respectively.[49]

Final evidence came from the Superfund program, which cleans up hazardous waste sites. It took an average of 20 percent more time for a dump site in a minority neighborhood to be placed on the list for cleanup than one in a white neighborhood. Actual cleanup efforts also took longer to complete in minority neighborhoods. Finally, the cleanup of sites in minority neighborhoods was more often what many perceived as a less effective "containment" action, which consisted of walling off the site. In white neighborhoods, the site was more likely to receive "permanent" treatment, such as removing the hazardous waste or treating it to eliminate the toxins.[50] Of course, some argue that the accusations of environmental racism are unfair. For example, one of the factors that the law says must be considered in assessing the size of a penalty is the financial condition of the violating facility. Often the facilities in minority neighborhoods are also in economically depressed areas, so their penalties would be lower.[51] Others claim there is no evidence for this rationale.

Close to the time of the *National Law Journal*'s story, EPA Administrator William K. Reilly created the EPA Environmental Equity Workgroup to assess evidence, indicating that minority and poor communities were at greater risk of exposure to environmental contamination than was the population at large. The workgroup was also charged with auditing the EPA's programs for any disparate impact on persons of certain races or income levels. The workgroup's report, Environmental Equity: Reducing Risk for All Communities,[52] found that although minority and low-income populations had above average exposure to some forms of environmental pollution, poverty in some instances was more determinative of the level of risk than was race. On the basis of these recommendations, in July 1992, Administrator Reilly established the EPA's Office of Environmental Equity to handle environmental justice matters and to provide oversight to the EPA in general.

On February 11, 1994, President Clinton signed into law Executive Order 12898, titled "Federal Actions to Address Environmental Justice and Minority Populations in Low-Income Populations." The order required all federal agencies to develop individual strategies to prevent environmental hazards from having disproportionately negative effects on minority and low-income populations by making environmental justice a part of decision making in every aspect of agency operations. After this order was issued, environmental justice policies were established in each federal agency. Agencies were to put pressure on recipients of federal money to evaluate the impact of their project on minority and low-income populations. According to subsequent EPA regulations, recipients of EPA financial assistance are required to agree annually in writing to comply with Title VI, which prohibits discrimination based on race, sex, national origin, color, and religion, thereby making considerations of environmental justice an accepted part of the planning and development process.

Shortly after Carol Browner took office as the EPA Administrator, she made environmental equity an agency priority. In November 1993, the EPA announced the establishment of the 25-member National Environmental Justice Advisory Counsel (NEJAC) to advise the EPA administrator on environmental justice matters and to promote communication concerning environmental justice issues. Community organizations, government, industry, academic institutions, and other groups would be represented on NEJAC. In 1993, the EPA established a small grants program to provide up to $10,000 to affected neighborhood groups or Native American tribes for environmental justice programs.

A report prepared by NEJAC and issued by the EPA at the end of 2000 attempted to assess the progress of the federal government in integrating environmental justice into its policies, programs, and activities consistent with existing laws and Executive Order 12898. The assessment was based on a survey of heads of federal agencies and environmental justice stakeholders.[53] The outcome was mixed.

All agreed that the strength of the order was that it focused attention on environmental justice and validated the concerns of the affected communities.[54] A major weakness was the lack of funds to implement environmental justice programs.[55] The biggest complaint, however, was that the order lacked any "teeth"; therefore, agencies were inconsistent in their interpretation and application of the order. Implementation of it was piecemeal and haphazard; there was no pressure to implement the order. Another related complaint was that there was no mechanism for tracking the implementation of the order.[56]

Unfortunately, things have only gotten worse since that report was issued. According to a report by the EPA's inspector general, made public in September 2006, senior EPA officials have not required regional offices and department heads to conduct environmental justice reviews despite a requirement for such reviews under Executive Order 12898. According to a survey by the IG's office, around 60 percent of the respondents—regional offices and program departments—had not conducted the reviews and 87 percent said they had not been asked to do.

The EPA's most recent statement about environmental justice, along with all official guidance's and policies about this topic, may be found at http://www.epa.gov/compliance/resources/policies/ej/index.html.

A CONSTITUTIONAL RIGHT TO ENVIRONMENTAL PROTECTION?

Because as a nation we have a tendency to look to the Constitution to protect those rights most fundamental to us, it is only natural that when concern for protecting the environment began to take the form of a national movement, people looked to the Constitution for a guarantee of a clean environment. Some have argued that the Constitution should be amended to include a constitutional right to a clean environment. Some legislators, in arguing for passage of the first major environmental statute, the National Environmental Policy Act (NEPA), argued that a constitutional right to environmental quality in fact existed;[57] their claim, however, was not widely accepted. Some environmentalists had hoped to use the Ninth Amendment, broadly interpreted, to expand the right to privacy to include a right to a clean, unspoiled environment.

Tanner et al. v. Armco Steel et al.,[58] a 1972 case in which such a claim was made, was unsuccessful. Still others have tried to argue that every time a governmental entity grants a permit to a polluting firm, that action constitutes state action, thereby making it possible for the action to be subject to claims of a violation of due process or an unconstitutional taking. The Supreme Court's reluctance to recognize such a right probably can be explained by two factors. First, there is nothing explicit in the Constitution or in its early interpretations to indicate that the drafters had any intention of protecting the environment. Second, from a practical perspective, it would be extraordinarily difficult for the courts to define the boundaries of such a right. Protecting the environment appears to be an area better left to legislators and administrative agencies.

In light of the failed attempts to obtain judicial recognition of a constitutional right to a clean environment, at least one environmental group, the National Wildlife Federation, is attempting to generate support for a constitutional amendment that would guarantee a clean environment for future generations. Although its proposed amendment is not yet in final form, the basic rights of each individual to be protected would include the right to clean air, pure water, productive soil, and the conservation of natural, scenic, historical, recreational, esthetic, and economic values of America's natural resources. The amendment would prohibit any public or private entity from impairing these rights and place the responsibility for preserving and enforcing these rights on the federal and state governments.

The Public Trust Doctrine

The idea of the government as a trustee for environmental quality is not an idea that environmentalists pulled from nowhere. The public trust doctrine is deeply imbedded in American law; it was forgotten for years but reborn in the 1970s. The concept traces its roots back to early Roman law, in which the doctrine of public trust developed around the idea that certain common properties, such as the air, seashores, and rivers, were held in trust by the government for the free and unimpeded use of the public.[59] This doctrine was subsequently applied in England to give ownership of public lands to the king but required that his subjects be given access to waterways for such purposes as fishing and trade.

On a limited scale, this doctrine has been followed in the United States, primarily for rivers, shore lands, and natural areas, although its adoption has been on a somewhat piecemeal basis. The Northwest Ordinance of 1787, for example, stated that "the navigable waters leading into the Mississippi . . . shall be common highways and forever free . . . to the citizens of the United States." The leading case establishing this doctrine is the 1892 U.S. Supreme Court opinion in *Illinois Central Railroad Co. v. Illinois.*[60] In 1869, the Illinois legislature passed a statute granting more than 1,000 acres of valuable land, including submerged lands under Lake Michigan and the shoreline along the city of Chicago's central city business district, to the Illinois Central Railroad Company. Four years later, the state passed another statute repealing this grant. It then filed an action to establish title to that property in the state's name.

The U.S. Supreme Court affirmed the state's title to the land, and in so doing explained the concept of holding title under the public trust doctrine:

> It is a title that is held in trust for the people of the state that they may enjoy the navigation of the waters, carry on commerce over them, and have the liberty of fishing therein, freed from the obstruction or interference of private parties. . . . The control of the state for purposes of the trust can never be lost, except as to such parcels as are used in promoting the interests of the public therein, or can be disposed of without any substantial impairment of the public interest in the lands and waters remaining.[61]

This precedent-setting case demonstrates the clearest application of the public trust doctrine: a situation in which title to public lands is about to be transferred to a private entity. More difficult cases arise when control of the land is being diverted to a different governmental entity that intends to put the land that is held in public trust to a more questionable public use, or, perhaps in partnership with a private entity, to develop and exploit the land for its economic value.

One example arose in Illinois in 1970 when the Chicago Park District proposed, among other endeavors, the transfer of 3.839 acres of city parkland to the Chicago Public Building Commission for the construction of a new school. Area property owners sued, arguing that the public trust doctrine required the state to retain the land in its use as parkland. The Illinois Supreme Court, in *Paepke v. Building Commission,* disagreed, stating: "The mere dedication by the sovereign of lands to public park use does not give private property owners . . . the right to have the use continue unchanged. . . ."[62]

The Illinois court noted the conflict between those who wanted to preserve the parks in their pristine state and those administrators who, "under the pressures of the changing needs of an increasingly complex society, find it necessary, in good faith, and for the public good, to encroach to some extent upon lands heretofore inviolate to change," and held that the resolution of such conflicts is a matter properly given to the legislature and not the courts. In this case, the court found that the legislative authorization in question was sufficiently broad and comprehensive to allow the transfer.

In coming to its conclusion, the Illinois court cited with approval the approach developed by the Supreme Court of Wisconsin, in cases applying the doctrine to navigable waterways and submerged lands. The criterion was developed in two Wisconsin Supreme Court decisions.[63] Both cases applied to navigable waters and submerged lands. The state approved proposed diversions in the use of public trust lands under conditions that demonstrated that

1. Public bodies would control the use of the area in question
2. The area would be devoted to public purposes and open to the public
3. The diminution of the area of original use would be small compared with the entire area
4. None of the public uses of the original area would be destroyed or greatly impaired
5. The disappointment of those wanting to use the area designated for a new use for former purposes was negligible when compared with the greater convenience afforded those members of the public using the new facility

While noting that these standards were not controlling, the Wisconsin court found them to be a useful guide for situations similar to the immediate case.

A third type of case in which the public trust doctrine may come into play is one in which lands held in trust are threatened by proposed actions of the government. These cases often involve water pollution problems created by the government or developers. Most recently, the doctrine has been applied in cases involving oil spills.

As you might infer from the foregoing discussion, the public trust doctrine is an important one in terms of public rights and responsibilities with respect to natural resources, even though it does not rise to the level of a constitutional protection. Questions as to its scope, balancing the interests of the competing segments of the public, and the extent to which the qualities of the trusted property are to be preserved against short-term use, however, still remain. We shall discuss this important doctrine later in the book.

After reviewing how our legal system is structured, you begin to realize how complex a task it is to establish a comprehensive system of laws to regulate the environment. Because the United States is organized in accordance with the basic principles of federalism, we have, in essence, two parallel systems of government: a state system and a federal system. The two systems are organized similarly, with legislative, judicial, and executive branches that are primarily responsible for, respectively, creating, interpreting, and enforcing the laws that govern our nation. A so-called fourth branch of government, administrative agencies, combines all those governmental functions and is now fully functioning at both the state and the local levels. Administrative agencies are especially important in making and enforcing environmental regulations.

The laws these governments make are both civil and criminal. Both are important in preserving the environment. These two parallel governmental systems often have overlapping responsibilities as dictated by the U.S. Constitution. But because the Constitution is a broadly worded document, subject to interpretation by the U.S. Supreme Court, it is not always clear where the lines of authority between the state and the federal governments are drawn. The commerce clause gives the U.S. Congress the authority to pass environmental regulations, whereas the states rely on the police power that they retain under the Constitution to pass such laws. Where there is potential for conflict, the courts must intervene and draw boundaries, relying on interpretations of the supremacy clause and applying the doctrine of federal preemption.

The Constitution also protects individual rights. Often, in environmental matters, individuals will argue that the government's attempts to regulate or protect the environment have gone too far and have infringed on constitutional freedoms. Cases in which such claims have arisen in the environmental area include those questioning the need for search warrants and those questioning whether a regulation is so onerous as to constitute a taking.

Although this chapter has focused on the structure and lawmaking function of the government, the judicial function of our system merits special consideration. Thus, Chapter 2 takes an in-depth look at exactly how our legal system handles conflicts.

Questions for Review and Discussion

1. Explain how statutory laws are created.
2. What does stare decisis mean?
3. Differentiate civil law from criminal law.
4. Explain the significance of the decisions in *United States v. Parks* and *United States v. Hayes International Corporation.*
5. What can corporate officials do to decrease their chances of being held criminally liable for violating environmental laws?
6. What is the relationship between the commerce clause and environmental law?
7. How does the Fourth Amendment affect enforcement of environmental regulations?
8. When does a regulation constitute an unconstitutional taking?

For Further Reading

Baker, Debra, and Bill Cason. 1997. "Getting Busy: Corporate Issues in the Early Stages of Criminal Environmental Investigation." *Journal of Corporate Law* 22: 411.

Broderick, Gregory T. 2005. " From Migratory Birds to Migratory Molecules: The Continuing Battle Over the Scope of Federal Jurisdiction Under the Clean Water Act." *Columbia Journal of Environmental Law 30*: 473.

Byrne, Peter. 1995. "Ten Arguments for the Abolition of the Regulatory Takings Doctrine." *Ecology Law Quarterly 22*: 89.

Coyle, Sean. 2004. *Philosophical Foundations of Environmental Law: Property, Rights, and Nature.* Oxford, UK: Hart Publishing.

Dorsey, Michael. 1998. "Race, Poverty, and Environment." *Legal Studies Forum 22*: 501.

Ely, James W., Jr. 2005. "Poor Relation" Once More: The Supreme Court and the Vanishing Rights of Property Owners," 2004–2005 Cato Sup. Ct. Rev. 39.

Green, Thomas. 2003. "Environmental Crimes Update: Enforcement Under the Bush Administration." *Champion 27* (August): 16.

Houck, Oliver A. 2005. *Environmental Law Stories.* New York: Foundation Press.

Lazarus, Richard. 2004. *The Making of Environmental Law.* Chicago: University of Chicago Press.

Liles, Brett D. 2006. "Reconsidering Poletown: In the Wake of Kelo, States Should Move to Restore Private Property Rights," *Arizona Law Review 48*: 369.

Martinez, Peter, Damon L. Worden, Luke M. Jones, and Jason S. Juceam. 2006. "Environmental Crimes," *American Criminal Law Review 43* (Spring): 381.

Murray, Paula C. 1995. "Dolan v. City of Tigard: Another Wrinkle on the Takings Doctrine," *Real Estate Law Journal 23* (Winter): 275.

Murray, Paula C. 1995. "The Environmental Self-Audit Privilege: Growing Movement in the States Nixed by EPA," *Real Estate Law Journal 24*: 169.

Murray, Paula C., and David B. Spence. 2003. "Fair Weather Federalism and America's Waste Disposal Crisis," *Harvard Environmental Law Review 27*: 71.

Oswald, Lynda J. 1995. "Cornering the Quark, Investment-Backed Expectations and Economically Viable Uses in Takings Analysis," *Washington Law Review 70*: 91.

Sabath, Mark. 2004. "The Perils of the Property Rights Initiative: Taking Stock of Nevada County's Measure D," *Harvard Environmental Law Review 28*: 249.

2005. Symposium: The Role of State Attorneys General in National Environmental Policy: Global Warming Panel, Part II, *Columbia Journal of Environmental Law 30*: 351.

Yeager, Peter. 1991. *The Limits of Law: Public Regulation of Private Pollution.* New York: Cambridge University Press.

On the Internet

http://thomas.loc.gov

A source for pending legislation, bill status, and directory information about members of the House and Senate

http://www.webdirectory.com/Pollution

Web directory of environmental organizations

http://www.fs.fed.us/land/envjust.html

A place to find the executive order on environmental justice

http://www.epa.gov/compliance/

Office of Compliance and Enforcement Assurance

http://sedac.ciesin.columbia.edu:9080/entri/index.jsp

Search and locate environmental treaties

http://www.lcv.org

Home page for the League of Conservation Voters, where you can access the league's "report card" on the President's and Congress' treatment of the environment.

http://projects.washingtonpost.com/congress/?referrer=email&referrer=email&referrer=email

The US Congress Votes database, showing every vote by Congress, searchable by Congress or individual member.

http://www.senate.gov/

Web site of the Senate

http://clerk.house.gov/

Web site of the clerk of the House of Representatives

http://www.motherjones.com/news/featurex/2003/09/we_531_04.html

The Ungreening of America, a report on how the Bush Administration's policies have reduced environmental protections

Notes

1. Center for Responsive Politics. "Environment: Long-Term Contribution Trends." *http://www.opensecrets.org/industries/indus.asp* (July 17, 2001).

2. Center for Responsive Politics. "Lobbyist Spending: Environment." *http://www.opensecrets.org/lobbyists/indusclient.asp?code=Q11&year=1999* (July 17, 2001).

3. Center for Responsive Politics. "Lobbyist Spending: Energy/Nat Resource." *http://www.opensecrets.org/lobbyists/indus.asp?Ind=E&year=1999* (July 17, 2001).

4. Jeffrey H. Birnbaum. 2001. "Fat and Happy in D.C." *Fortune* 143 (May 28): 94–100.

5. Jeffrey H. Birnbaum. 1999. "Washington's Power 25." *Fortune* 136 (December 8): 144–152.

6. EPA Office of Enforcement and Compliance Assurance, *Enforcement and Compliance Assurance Accomplishment Report FY 1997.* *http://es.epa.gov/oeca/97accomp.pdf* (July 17, 2001): 2–4.

7. US EPA, *Compliance and Enforcement Annual Results: FY2005 Numbers at a Glance.* *http://www.epa.gov/compliance/resources/reports/endofyear/eoy2005/2005numbers.html* (October 1, 2006).

8. Paul W. Valentine. 1990. "Trading Whiz Fined for Wetland Damage; $2 Million Md. Judgment May Be Record." *Washington Post* (May 26): A1.

9. EPA Office of Enforcement and Compliance Assurance, *Enforcement and Compliance Assurance Accomplishment Report FY 1996.* *http://es.epa.gov/oeca/96accomp.pdf* (July 17, 2001): 2–3.

10. Ibid.

11. David Stipp. 1992. "Execs Get Little Sympathy for Crimes Against Nature." *Wall Street Journal* (March 11): B1.

12. Amanda Griscom. 2003. "The Rollback Machine." *Grist Magazine* (September 4).

13. Eric Pianin and Michael Powell. 2001. "General Electric Ordered to Pay for Cleanup of Hudson; EPA Mandates $500 Million Dredging" *Washington Post* (December 5): A02.

14. 421 U.S. 658 (1975).

15. 786 F2d 1499 (1986).

16. EPA. "Incentives for Self-Policing: Discovery, Disclosure, Correction and Prevention of Violations," May 11, 2000. *http://es.epa.gov/oeca/finalpolstate.pdf* (July 16, 2001).

17. Ibid.

18. EPA. 1984. "Policy on Civil Penalties." *Environmental Law Reporter* 17 (February 16): 35083.

19. "Enforcement: Final Policy on Penalty Reductions Expanded to Include Due Diligence Systems." *Chemical Law Reporter* 19 (December 22, 1995): 1176.
20. Va. Code Annotated S. 1001–1198(B).
21. Ibid.
22. Ibid.
23. Ibid.
24. "More States Adopt Audit Privilege Laws; EPA Calls Federal Legislation Ill-Advised." *Environmental Law Reporter* (March 10, 1995): 2186.
25. Ibid.
26. 452 U.S. 264 (1981).
27. 514 U.S. 549 (1995).
28. Ibid.
29. *Bronzkala v. Morrison,* 529 U.S. 598 (2000).
30. Ibid.
31. *Solid Waste Agency of Northern Cook County v. United States Army Corps of Engineers,* 120 S.Ct. 2711, 2000.
32. *Rappanos v. United States,* 2006 U.S. LEXIS 4887 (2006).
33. *RanchoViejo LLC v. Norton,* 334 F.3d 1138, 1160 (D.C. Cir. 2003, Justice Roberts, dissenting).
34. 437 U.S. 617 (1978).
35. 12 S.Ct. 2009 at 2017 (1992).
36. 511 U.S. 383, 410 (1994).
37. 214 F.3d 707 (6th Cir. 2000).
38. 175 F.3d 178 (1st Cir. 1999).
39. *Keystone Bituminous Coal Association et. al. v. DeBenedictus,* 480 U.S. 572 (1987).
40. 112 U.S. 286 (1992).
41. 926 F.2d 1169 (1991).
42. Nancie G. Marzulla. 1995. "The Property Rights Movement: How It Began and Where It's Headed." *Land Rights,* ed. Bruce Yandle, 1–19. Lanham, MD: Rowman and Littlefield.
43. 114 S.Ct. 2309 (1994).
44. *Palazzolo v. Rhode Island* 121 S.Ct. 2448 (2001).
45. 126 S.Ct. 326 (2005).
46. Marianne Lavelle and Marcia Coyle. 1992. "Unequal Protection: The Racial Divide in Environmental Law." *National Law Journal* (September): 52.
47. Ibid.
48. Ibid.
49. Ibid.
50. Ibid.
51. William K. Reilly. 1993. "EPA's Reilly Replies to 'Unequal Treatment.'" *National Law Journal* (January 25): 16.
52. EPA Environmental Equity Workgroup. 1992. *Environmental Equity: Reducing Risk for all Communities.* Washington, D.C.: USEPA Policy, Planning and Evaluation.
53. Grover Hankins. 2000. "Pre-Meeting Report: What Progress Has the Federal Government Made in Integrating Environmental Justice into its Policies, Programs, and Activities Consistent with Existing Laws and Executive Order 12898?" *http://es.epa.gov/oeca/main/ej/nejac/pdf/11_30_premeeting.pdf* (July 16, 2001).
54. Ibid.
55. Ibid.
56. Ibid.
57. *Congressional Record* (December 20, 1969): 40, 417.
58. 340 F.Supp. 532 (1972).
59. Joseph Sax. 1970. *Defending the Environment: A Strategy for Public Action,* 163. New York: Alfred A. Knopf.
60. 146 U.S. 387 (1892).
61. Ibid at 452.
62. 263 N.E. 2d 11 (1970).
63. *City of Madison v. State,* 83 N.W. 2d 674 (1957) and *State v. Public Service Commission,* 81 N.W. 2d 71 (1957).

RESOLVING CONTROVERSIAL ENVIRONMENTAL ISSUES

- When you read an article or essay in which someone is trying to convince you to take a particular position on an environmental issue, you should identify the argument presented in the passage. An argument consists of a conclusion and reasons to support that conclusion. The conclusion is the action that the author is trying to convince you to take. The reasons offer support for the conclusion; they explain why we should agree with the author's conclusion. What is the argument (the conclusion and the reasons) presented in the following editorial?

- When people write or speak, they are often unclear or ambiguous. Furthermore, they sometimes make mistakes in their reasoning. Your job, as a reader or listener, is to actively search for instances in which the writer or speaker uses ambiguous language or makes mistakes in reasoning. You must read and listen very carefully. The author in the following EPA article confused two very different terms and is using them interchangeably. Identify these terms and explain why they are not synonyms and how their misuse affects the reasoning.

THE CONTRADICTORY BEHAVIOR OF THE EPA

The EPA claims that it does not have enough agents to adequately enforce regulations. Consequently, one would think that the EPA would support any law that would make their job easier. Yet, the EPA is adamantly opposed to one idea that would surely alleviate their responsibilities — environmental self-audit privileges. Environmental self-audits reduce the amount of work that the EPA must do. Thus, the self-audits are one way for the EPA to save both time and money. The EPA seems to be figuratively cutting off its own foot by preventing companies from conducting environmental self-audits.

Companies that report violations are often unfairly penalized. For example, the Brewer Company recently conducted a voluntary investigation of air emissions at its largest factory. When the company realized that its emissions were higher than EPA guidelines, they decided to report the emission violations and tried to correct the problem by getting permits for their factory. Their admission resulted in a fine of more than $2 million.

The reaction from the business community has been predictable. In a survey of over 500 companies, approximately 50 percent have been reluctant to conduct voluntary audits because they are afraid they will be penalized for the violations. However, in states with the self-audit privilege, companies are not as afraid and thus are much more willing to work with regulatory authorities to prevent and correct environmental problems.

If the EPA truly wants to encourage businesses to pay attention to the environment, they must allow these businesses to conduct environmental self-audits. Write to your congressman to encourage him or her to support the bill that allows businesses to conduct self-audits. If the EPA is not doing its job of protecting the environment, perhaps the legislature will pick up the EPA's slack.

CHAPTER 2

THE LITIGATION PROCESS AND OTHER TOOLS FOR RESOLVING ENVIRONMENTAL DISPUTES

Environmental problems are not resolved simply by passing environmental regulations. Once regulations are passed, disputes often arise over how the laws should be applied and whether a particular behavior constitutes compliance with the law. Thus, it is important to understand the way laws are interpreted and enforced. In our society, such interpretation and enforcement occur primarily through the use of the adversarial system referred to as litigation. The first sections of this chapter explain how this system works and also point out some of the system's flaws. Increasingly, however, litigation is being viewed as a last resort, and alternative methods of dispute resolution are favored. Thus, latter portions of this chapter discuss how various other dispute resolution processes work.

THE ADVERSARY SYSTEM

AN INTRODUCTION TO THE ADVERSARY SYSTEM

Our system of litigation is often referred to as an adversary system. In an adversarial system, a neutral fact finder hears evidence and arguments presented by both sides and then makes an objective decision based on the facts and on the law as presented by the proponents of each side. Strict rules generally govern the types of evidence that the fact finder may consider.

Theoretically, the adversary system is the best way to bring out the truth because each side will aggressively seek all the evidence that supports its position. Each side will attempt to make the strongest possible arguments for its position and point out weaknesses in the arguments of its opponents. No shred of evidence will be overlooked, and no plausible argument will be left unspoken. With all the best evidence and arguments presented, the truth, theoretically, will be easily discernible.

CRITICISMS OF THE ADVERSARY SYSTEM

Many people criticize the adversary system. They argue that because each side is searching only for evidence that specifically supports its position, a proponent who discovers evidence helpful to the other side will not bring such evidence to the attention of the court. This tendency to ignore contrary evidence prevents a fair decision, which would be one based on all the available evidence. The critics also argue that the adversary process is extremely time-consuming and costly as two groups of investigators are seeking the same evidence. Thus, there is a duplication of effort that lengthens the process and increases costs unnecessarily.

Still others argue that the adversary system, as it functions in the United States, is unfair. Each party in the adversarial process is represented by an attorney. Therefore, having the most skillful attorney is a tremendous advantage. Because the wealthier party can afford the more skillful attorney, the system unjustifiably favors the wealthy. In the environmental arena, the impact of this disparity can be seen when you consider a group of local citizens banding together to sue a corporation. The corporation may have its own staff of attorneys; and even if the firm has to hire outside counsel, it has the money to do so. The citizens' group, however, must get its money from donations. Often, if a company can tie up a group with a lot of pretrial motions, the attorneys' fees may be so high that the group may have to drop the lawsuit because it simply does not have the money to continue the action.

When used to resolve environmental disputes, the adversarial system is subject to these criticisms, as well as to others. However, perhaps the biggest criticism from environmentalists, as well as from some businesspersons, is that the adversarial process promotes strife between the parties as each seeks to be the "winner." What is really needed in many environmental cases is not a legal winner but, rather, a creative compromise. Such compromises are generally not discovered in a trial. Litigation is ideally suited for a yes or a no decision; either the plaintiff or the defendant wins. In many cases, the parties have some other objective in mind. The defendant may want to create an industrial park in an area that the plaintiff believes should be preserved. Unfortunately, those kinds of cases are not so easily resolved through our adversarial process.

A closely related criticism is that the adversarial nature of the litigation process leads to bad feelings between two parties that really need to get along with each other. When there is a conflict between a developer and conservationists, for example, many of their problems may result from an inability to discuss how a parcel of land could best be used. After a court fight, they are going to be even less able to talk with each other. Or what about an agency and a business it regulates? Litigation makes them view each other as enemies, not as parties that will need to cooperate in the future.

Our adversary system is implemented through the court systems. As makes sense under federalism, we have a dual court system. The system is depicted in Figure 2-1.

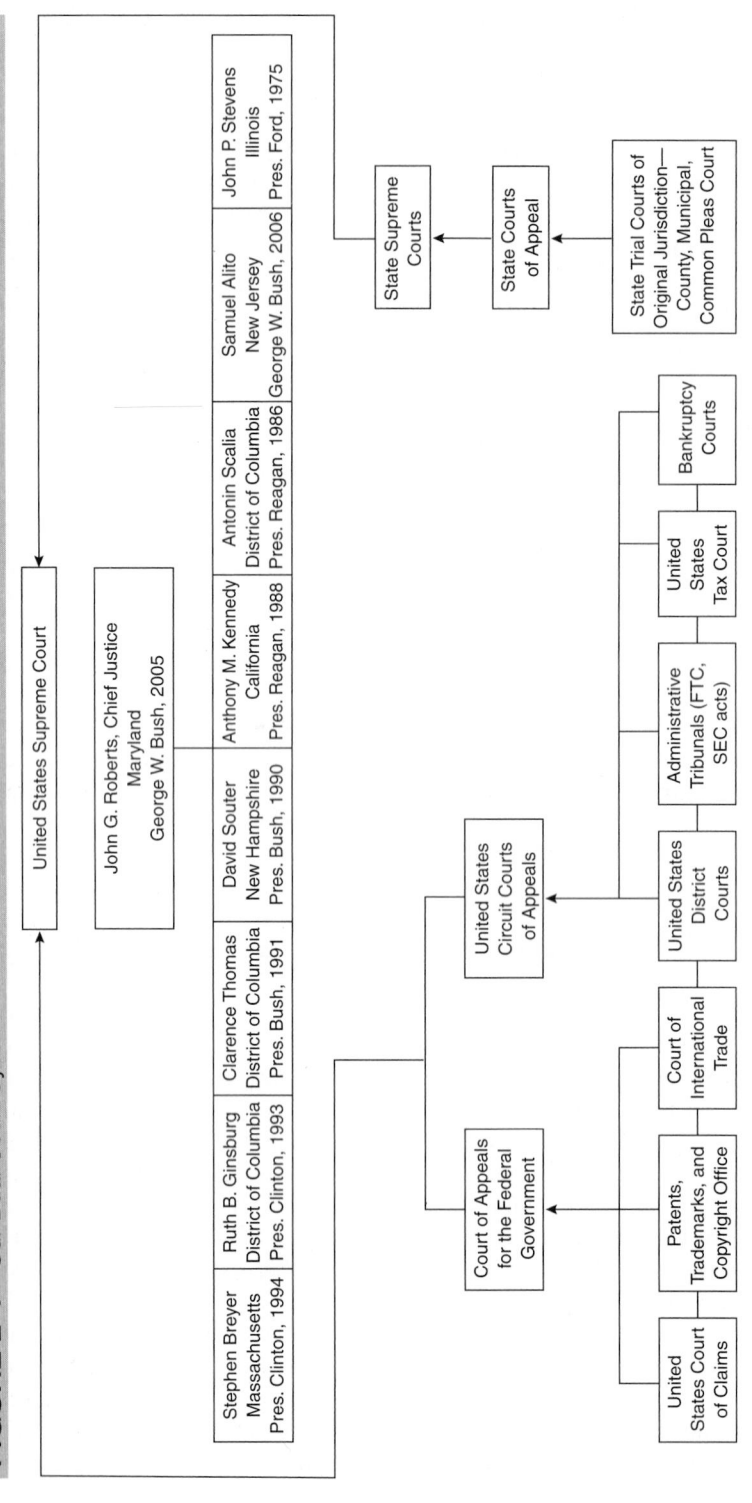

FIGURE 2-1 Our Dual Court System

Source: Nancy Kubasek, Bartley Brennan, and M. Neil Browne. 1996. *The Legal Environment of Business: A Critical Thinking Approach,* 38. Upper Saddle River, NJ: Prentice Hall. 3e 2002 111. Reprinted by permission of Pearson Education, Inc., Upper Saddle River, NJ.

THE FEDERAL COURT SYSTEM

Federal Trial Courts

Jurisdiction is the power of a court to hear a case and to render a decision. There are many different types of jurisdiction. The trial court is the court of original jurisdiction, meaning that it is the court that has the power to initially hear and decide the case. In the federal court system, the trial courts are the U.S. district courts. The United States is divided into 96 districts, and each district has at least one trial court. Almost all cases arising under the federal environmental laws will generally be heard in the federal district courts. Figure 2-2 illustrates this federal system.

Intermediate Courts of Appeals

The second level of courts in the federal system is made up of the U.S. circuit courts of appeals. The United States is divided into 12 geographic areas, including the District of Columbia, each of which has a circuit court of appeals. There are also federal circuit courts of appeals. Each circuit court of appeals hears appeals from all the district courts located within its area. Appeals from administrative agencies are heard by the federal circuit court of appeals.

Court of Last Resort

The U.S. Supreme Court is the final appellate court in the federal system. In some instances, the Supreme Court also hears cases from the court of last resort in a state system. The Supreme Court may also function as a trial court in an extremely limited number of cases, such as suits against ambassadors of foreign nations.

THE STATE COURT SYSTEM

There is no uniform state court structure because each state has devised its own court system. However, all states follow a general structure similar to that of the federal court system.

State Trial Courts

In state court systems, trial courts, or courts of original jurisdiction, are distributed throughout the state, usually by county. The names of these courts vary from state to state, including such titles as courts of common pleas or county courts. New York State is unique in using the term supreme court for its trial courts of general jurisdiction. Cases involving state environmental laws will generally be brought in these state trial courts of general jurisdiction. Also, private tort claims involving environmental matters are usually brought to these courts.

Intermediate courts of appeals, similar to the federal circuit courts of appeals, exist in approximately half the states. These courts usually have broad jurisdiction, hearing appeals from courts of general and limited jurisdiction as well as from state administrative agencies. The names of these courts often vary by state; they may be called courts of appeals or superior courts.

FIGURE 2-2 Our Federal System

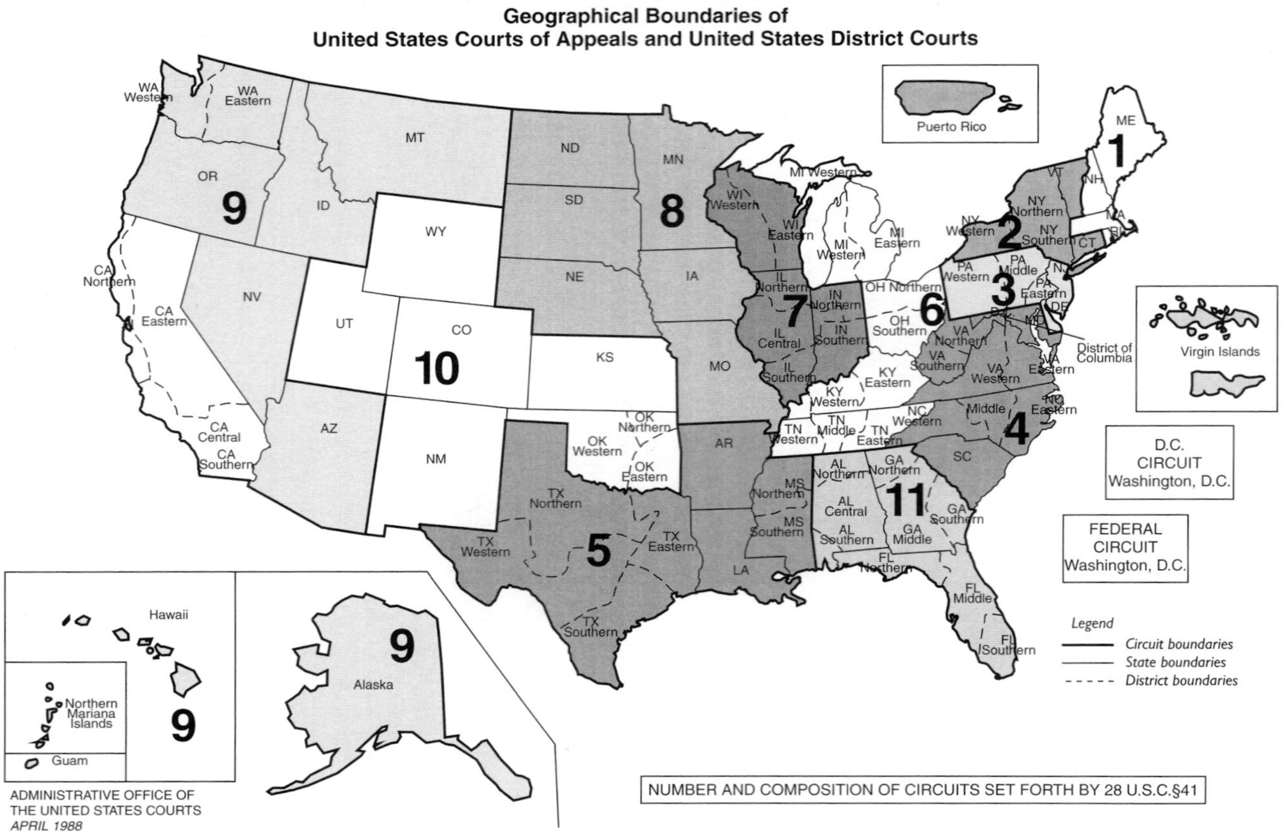

Geographical Boundaries of
United States Courts of Appeals and United States District Courts

NUMBER AND COMPOSITION OF CIRCUITS SET FORTH BY 28 U.S.C. §41

Legend
—— Circuit boundaries
—— State boundaries
- - - District boundaries

Source: Administrative Office of the United States Courts, April 1988.

Courts of Last Resort

In almost all cases filed in the state court system, the last appeal is to the state court of last resort. This court is frequently called the state supreme court. In some states, it is known as the court of appeals. In approximately half the states, this is the second court to which an appeal can be made; in the other half, it is the only appellate court.

CHOICE OF COURTS

Knowing that a case must be filed in a trial court does not tell the plaintiff which trial court will hear the case. The plaintiff must know which system is appropriate. The choice of which court system to enter is not purely a matter of deciding which forum would be the most desirable. Only in a limited number of cases does a party have the ability to choose between the federal and the state systems. Even if a party does have that choice and chooses the state system, the other party may have the right to have the case removed to the federal system. The determination of which system may hear the case depends on subject matter jurisdiction. Subject matter jurisdiction is the power of a court to hear and render a decision in a particular type of case. Such jurisdiction is extremely important because when a judge renders a decision in a case over which the court does not have subject matter jurisdiction, the decision is void, or meaningless. The parties cannot grant the judge such jurisdiction. It is determined by law as described in the following paragraphs. Figure 2-3 lists the types of jurisdiction.

FIGURE 2-3   Subject Matter Jurisdiction

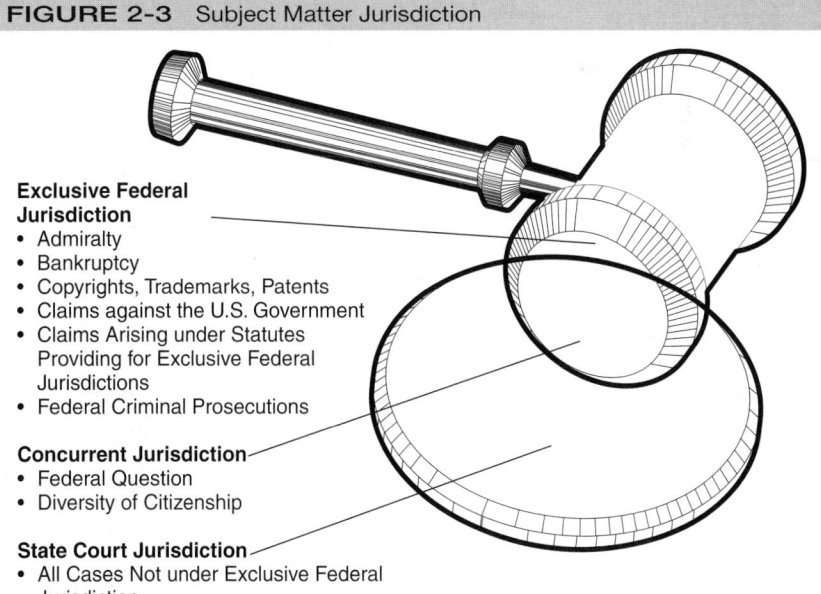

Exclusive Federal Jurisdiction
- Admiralty
- Bankruptcy
- Copyrights, Trademarks, Patents
- Claims against the U.S. Government
- Claims Arising under Statutes Providing for Exclusive Federal Jurisdictions
- Federal Criminal Prosecutions

Concurrent Jurisdiction
- Federal Question
- Diversity of Citizenship

State Court Jurisdiction
- All Cases Not under Exclusive Federal Jurisdiction

Source: Nancy Kubasek, Bartley Brennan, and M. Neil Browne. 1999. *The Legal Environment of Business: A Critical Thinking Approach,* 112. Upper Saddle River, NJ: Prentice Hall. Reprinted by permission of Pearson Education, Inc., Upper Saddle River, NJ.

Subject Matter Jurisdiction of State Courts

The state court system has jurisdiction over all cases not within the exclusive jurisdiction of the federal court system. Cases falling within the exclusive jurisdiction of the federal courts are listed in the next paragraph. Because the federal courts have exclusive jurisdiction over very few issues, it is no surprise that most litigation occurs in the state system.

Exclusive Federal Jurisdiction

A few types of cases may be heard only in the federal courts. Such cases are within the exclusive jurisdiction of the federal court system. If these cases were tried in a state court, any decision rendered by the judge would be void. Cases that fall within the exclusive jurisdiction of the federal courts include such matters as admiralty, bankruptcy, federal criminal prosecutions, claims against the United States, and claims arising under those federal statutes that include a provision for exclusive federal jurisdiction. Cases brought under such statutes must be filed in the federal district court or the appropriate federal court of limited jurisdiction. Thus, whenever an action based on a federal statute is anticipated, the statute should be read carefully to discern whether cases under the statute fall within the exclusive jurisdiction of the federal system. Many federal environmental statutes grant exclusive jurisdiction to the federal courts.

Concurrent Federal Jurisdiction

Many cases may be heard in either the federal or the state court. These cases are said to fall within the federal court's concurrent jurisdiction, meaning that both court systems have jurisdiction, so the plaintiff may file in the trial court of either system. There are two types of such cases. The first are federal question cases. If a case requires an interpretation of the U.S. Constitution, a federal statute, or a federal treaty, it is said to involve a federal question and may be heard in either state or federal court, because most federal statutes do not grant exclusive jurisdiction to the federal courts. Many federal environmental statutes give exclusive jurisdiction to the federal courts, but challenges to those that do not may be brought in state or federal court.

The second means by which a case may fall within the federal court's concurrent jurisdiction is through diversity of citizenship. When the opponents in a case are from different states, diversity of citizenship occurs. The diversity must be complete; if any two parties on the opposing sides reside in the same state, diversity is lost. For example, if the plaintiff is an Ohio resident and one of the defendants lives in Michigan and the other in Indiana, diversity exists. However, if an Ohio plaintiff is bringing an action against a Michigan defendant and an Ohio defendant, there is not complete diversity and, therefore, no concurrent federal jurisdiction. Also, when the basis for federal jurisdiction is diversity of citizenship, the controversy must involve at least $50,000.

When a case falls within the federal court's concurrent jurisdiction because of either a federal question or a diversity of citizenship, the suit may be filed in either state or federal court. If the case is filed in state court, the defendant has a right of removal, which means that he or she may have the case transferred to federal court. If the plaintiff files in federal court, the case must be heard in that court.

Why should both parties have the right to have such a case heard in federal court? In certain cases, a party may fear local prejudice in a state court. Juries for a state court are generally drawn from the county in which the court is located. The juries for federal district courts are drawn from the entire district, which encompasses many counties. Juries in state courts are, therefore, usually more homogeneous than those in district courts. One problem that this homogeneity may present to the out-of-state corporate defendant occurs when the county in which the court is located is predominantly rural. If the case involves an injury to a member of this rural community, the defendant may feel that the jurors would be more sympathetic to the local injured party, whereas jurors drawn from a broader area, including cities, may be more likely to view the victim less sympathetically. City residents are more likely to work for a corporation and, thus, may not regard corporations as unfavorably as rural residents might.

Some people believe that because federal judges have more experience in resolving questions that require an interpretation of federal statutes, they are better qualified to hear such cases. Finally, if a party anticipates that it may be necessary to appeal the case to the U.S. Supreme Court, bringing the case in a federal district court first may save one step in the appeals process.

Venue

Subject matter jurisdiction should not be confused with venue. Once it is determined which court system has the power to hear the case, venue determines which of the many trial courts in that system is appropriate. Venue, clearly prescribed by statute in each state, is a matter of geographic location. It is usually based on the residence of the defendant, the location of the property in dispute, or the location in which the incident out of which the dispute arose occurred. When there are multiple defendants who reside in various locations, the party filing the lawsuit may usually choose from among the various locales. If a corporation is being sued or filing an action, its residence is the location of the corporate headquarters, as well as where the firm has plants or offices. Thus, if a plaintiff residing in Wood County sued a defendant residing in Lucas County over an accident that occurred in Huron County, venue would be appropriate in any of those three counties, and the plaintiff may file the case in any of them.

If the location of the court in which the case is filed presents a hardship or inconvenience to one of the parties, that person may request that the case be moved under the doctrine of forum *non conveniens,* which simply means that the location of the trial court is inconvenient. This motion may be granted at the judge's discretion.

PRIMARY ACTORS IN THE LEGAL SYSTEM

An understanding of the structure of the legal system would be incomplete without an awareness of the primary actors within it.

THE ATTORNEY

The party with whom environmental groups and business representatives usually have the most frequent contact is the attorney. Although the exact qualifications for being an attorney vary from state to state, most states require that attorneys have a law degree, have passed the state's bar examination, and are of high moral character. Attorneys are the legal representatives of the parties before the court. Some corporations have full-time attorneys, referred to as in-house counsel; other corporations send all their legal work to an outside law firm. Many large businesses have in-house counsel and also use outside counsel when a problem arises that requires a specialist. Firms with large in-house staffs generally have at least one attorney who does only environmental law.

Attorneys are probably best known for representing clients in litigation, but they also provide other services. Attorneys represent their clients not only in courtroom litigation but also before administrative boards. Attorneys may serve as negotiators. For example, if a developer wants to undertake a project that the area's residents think will not be environmentally sound, the residents may hire an attorney to negotiate with the developer to try to find an alternative plan. Attorneys also serve as advisers or counselors. Finally, the attorney may serve as a draftsperson, drawing up contracts and other legal documents.

Attorney–Client Privilege

Attorneys can provide effective representation only when they know all the pertinent facts. Clients who withhold information from their attorneys may cause irreparable harm if the hidden facts are revealed in court by the opposing side. To encourage a client's honesty, the attorney–client privilege was established. This privilege provides that attorneys may not reveal information provided in confidence to them in conjunction with a legal matter without permission from the client.

This protection also extends to the attorney's work product under what is known as the work-product doctrine. The work product includes the formal and informal documents prepared by the attorney in conjunction with the client's case. Thus, if a client fears that his or her company is violating an environmental law and hires an attorney to determine whether the corporate behavior is unlawful, the lawyer may not be called to testify about the work performed in analyzing the company's behavior.

THE JUDGE

Although few people actually come into contact with a judge, the role of the judge is especially important in our legal system. The judge's function changes depending on whether he or she is a trial or an appellate court judge. A trial court judge presides over the trial, rules on all motions made in the case, and decides all questions of law, such as what evidence is admissible, what items may be obtained through discovery, and what law applies to the case. The judge explains the applicable law through the jury instructions. This judge makes sure that the case is heard with reasonable speed. If the parties waive their rights to a jury trial, or if, under the particular circumstances, they are not entitled to a jury, the judge also decides the facts in the case and renders a decision accordingly. A single judge presides over each case at the trial court level.

Although Thomas Jefferson said, "Ours is a government of laws, not of men," in reality, the "men" (and women) are as important as the laws. In an actual trial, the judge has a great deal of discretion when ruling on matters such as whether to admit a certain piece of evidence over the objection of opposing counsel. Thus, the careful litigant will always try to know something about the judge's ideology before bringing a case to trial. Certain courts earn reputations as being more pro- or antienvironment, and these reputations influence the types of cases brought to them. For example, the federal district court in Washington, D.C., is known for being proenvironment, so environmental activists file cases there whenever possible. Louisiana district courts have the opposite reputation, so business interests file in these courts whenever possible. As new appointments are made, the ideological makeup of courts may change, so attorneys must keep track of changes in the appointees.

Appellate judges serve on panels. They review cases from lower courts to determine whether errors of law were committed. Their review consists primarily of reading the transcript of the trial, reading written arguments by counsel for both parties, and sometimes hearing oral arguments from both parties' attorneys.

Aside from ideological differences, not all judges have equivalent knowledge about environmental issues. In an attempt to remedy the problem of a lack of understanding of scientific issues related to the environment, the Flaschner Judicial Institute in Boston and the Environmental Law Institute in Washington, D.C., hold a 2-day cram course in environmental law that they offer to judges all over the country. In May 1991, the first such course was taken by 48 state court judges in New England. The course was taught by both technical and legal specialists. Other training programs, such as the weekend seminars offered by the Foundation for Research on Economics and the Environment (FREE), are available for educating judges about environmental issues. However, some programs seem to display certain biases in their presentation of information. For example, FREE, a conservative property rights group, states that its program objectives are to:

- explain the linkages among science, risk analysis, and economics;
- show how secure property rights and economic freedom can foster the efficient and sensitive use of natural resources and ecosystem preservation;

- show how the application of economics to law provides insights into the public interest;
- explore and foster positive, constructive roles of government officials and federal agencies;
- describe ways in which incentives and voluntary cooperation can be used to protect and enhance environmental values while fostering economic prosperity.[1]

FREE's program seems to emphasize the importance of property rights when educating judges about the environment. In fact, funding for the all-expenses-paid, 5-day seminars comes from foundations with a significant interest in property rights and environmental law.[2] If this program is the only training a judge receives regarding environmental law, his or her rulings in environmental cases could be quite biased by the perspective offered in the seminar. FREE offered its seminars beginning in 1992 and in the following 6 years 137 judges made 194 visits to the seminars.[3]

State court judges are usually elected, although some are appointed, whereas federal court judges are appointed by the president with the advice and consent of the Senate. Federal court judges serve for life; state court judges generally serve finite terms, the length of which varies from state to state. Because of the lifetime tenure of federal judges, many people argue that the most powerful act of a president is the appointment of judges.

THE JURY

The jury is the means by which citizens participate in our judicial system. It has its roots in ancient Greek civilization, and it is often considered the hallmark of democracy. A jury is a group of individuals, selected randomly from the geographic area in which the court is located, who will determine questions of fact. The two types of juries are petit and grand.

Petit Juries

Petit juries serve as the finders of fact for trial courts. Originally composed of 12 members, in many jurisdictions juries in civil cases are allowed to have fewer members. Traditionally, jury decisions had to be unanimous. Today, however, more than half the jurisdictions no longer require unanimity in civil cases—a change made primarily to speed up trial procedures.

An important decision to be made by any party filing an action is whether to have a jury. In any civil action in which the plaintiff is seeking a remedy at law (money damages), a jury may hear the case. If both parties to the case agree, however, the jury may be waived, and a judge will decide the facts of the case. There is no rule about when a jury should be chosen, but a few factors should be considered. One is the technical nature of the case. If a case is highly technical, it may be one that can be more fairly decided by a judge, especially one with expertise in the area in dispute. Another factor is the emotional appeal of the case. If the case is one for which the opponent's arguments may have strong emotional appeal, a judge may render a fairer decision. In most environmental law cases, the remedy being sought is an equitable one, such as the granting of an injunction; whenever a court order such as an injunction is being sought, no jury is allowed.

Grand Juries

Grand juries are used only in criminal matters. The Fifth Amendment requires that all federal prosecutions for infamous crimes (including all federal offenses that carry a term of imprisonment in excess of 1 year) be commenced with an indictment (a formal accusation of the commission of a crime, which must be made before a defendant can be tried for the crime) by a grand jury. This jury hears evidence presented by the prosecutor and determines whether there is enough evidence to justify charging a defendant.

Now that you understand how the court system is structured and who the primary actors in the system are, it is time to examine how the court system works.

STEPS IN CIVIL LITIGATION

This section focuses on dispute resolution in the United States under the adversary system, in particular, examining the procedures used in a civil case. The rules that govern such proceedings are called the rules of civil procedure. There are federal rules of civil procedure that apply in all federal courts and state rules that apply in the state courts. Most of the state rules are based on the federal rules. The procedures in a criminal case are very similar to those in a civil case except for the criminal issues of pretrial release of the defendant and sentencing. Figure 2-4 shows the steps of the litigation process.

THE THRESHOLD ISSUES

Before instigating litigation, a party must be sure that his or her case meets certain threshold requirements. These requirements are to ensure that only cases really requiring adjudication come before the courts and that both sides of the case are properly represented. These objectives are met by the threshold requirements of standing, case or controversy, and ripeness. It is the requirement of standing that is of greatest importance in environmental cases, so we discuss this requirement first and also in the greatest detail.

Standing

Standing is the legal right to bring a lawsuit. One who has standing is said to be a proper party to pursue the action. In most cases, one has standing when one is personally affected by the outcome of a case. The personal involvement is believed necessary to stimulate the party to put forth the best possible case.

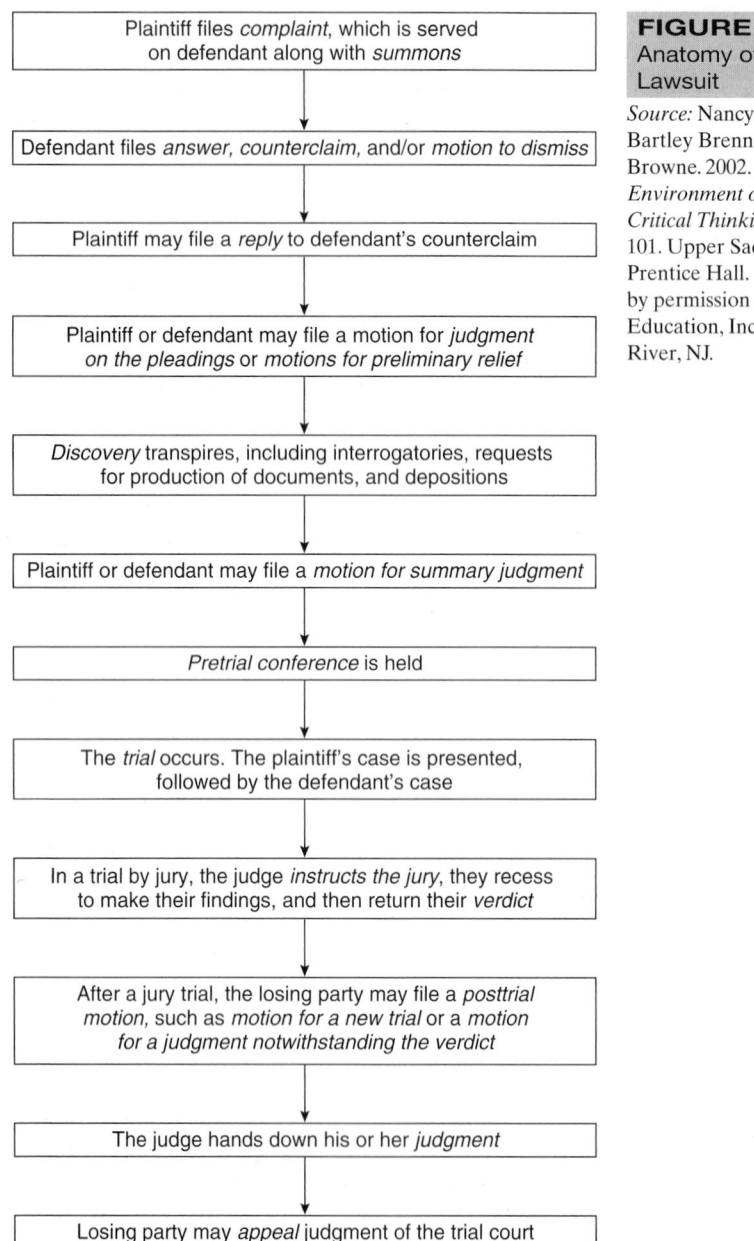

FIGURE 2-4
Anatomy of a Civil Lawsuit

Source: Nancy Kubasek, Bartley Brennan, and M. Neil Browne. 2002. *The Legal Environment of Business: A Critical Thinking Approach,* 101. Upper Saddle River, NJ: Prentice Hall. 118. Reprinted by permission of Pearson Education, Inc., Upper Saddle River, NJ.

Once thought settled, an important issue that is again in controversy is whether citizens' groups (as opposed to individual citizens) incur sufficient personal injury to have standing to bring an environmental case. The role of citizens' groups in bringing about enforcement of environmental legislation is undeniable. Almost all environmental lawsuits (except for those brought by the EPA) are filed by citizens' groups. During the "environmental decade," 1970 to 1980, when the initial environmental laws were being first interpreted, the most common lawsuit was a public interest group suing the government for allegedly abusing its discretion in administering environmental laws by not applying them with appropriate zeal.[4] These cases were heard only because a long line of cases have granted citizens' groups the right to bring lawsuits to enforce environmental statutes. However, with the more conservative, less activist courts ushered in by Reagan and Bush appointees, the broad standing granted to citizens' groups began to come under fire.

For years, political conservatives have argued unsuccessfully that environmental groups should not be able to sue for harms that affect all citizens equally. Standing requires a particularized injury, and because everyone enjoys clean air and clean water, interest groups should not be allowed to sue to enforce these laws. This argument is now being heard anew.

The case that many had feared would begin the shrinking of the role of environmental interest groups in bringing environmental cases is *Lujan v. Defenders of Wildlife,*[5] argued before the U.S. Supreme Court on December 3, 1991. In that case, the Defenders argued that the Endangered Species Act of 1973 should apply to activities that the United States funds in foreign countries. The projects at issue involved the partial use of U.S. funds for an irrigation project in Sri Lanka and funds to rebuild the Aswan Dam on the Nile River, projects that threatened the endangered elephant in Sri Lanka, the crocodile in Egypt, and other species. In addition to arguing on the merits, Lujan raised the standing issue, arguing that, at minimum, a group must show an injury-in-fact caused by the regulation that it is challenging. The Defenders argued that they have standing because they represent members of their organization who had personally visited the sites under regulation to study the endangered species that are to be regulated under the act, a basis for standing that would be sufficient under the traditional definition of standing recognized since the Supreme Court case of *Sierra Club v. Morton.*[6]

In *Sierra Club v. Morton,* the Sierra Club challenged a decision of the Forest Service and Department of the Interior to consider a proposal of Walt Disney Enterprises, Inc., to turn the Mineral King Valley, a national game refuge and quasiwilderness area, into a resort. The Sierra Club alleged it had standing to seek the injunctions against granting the permits because its membership corporation had "a special interest in the conservation and the sound maintenance of the national parks, game refuges, and forests of the country." The High Court denied standing to the Sierra Club in that case, but the Court's reason for the denial set the basis for the broad interpretation of the standing requirement. The Court denied standing because the Sierra Club failed to allege that it or any of its members would be affected in any of their activities or pastimes by the Disney development. Nowhere in the pleadings or affidavits did the Club state that its members used Mineral

King for any purpose, much less that they use it in any way that would be significantly affected by the proposed actions of the respondents.

Thus, the holding in *Sierra Club v. Morton* made it clear that an organization whose members would be adversely affected by failure to comply with an environmental statute would have standing and that the requirement of a "particularized injury" was not going to mean that the petitioners had to be the only ones affected by the action. This holding was subsequently reinforced in *United States v. Students Challenging Regulatory Agency Procedures (SCRAP 1).*[7] In SCRAP 1, an unincorporated student group sought an injunction prohibiting the Interstate Commerce Commission (ICC) from allowing the railroads to collect a 2.5 percent surcharge on goods being transported for purposes of recycling without first filing an Environmental Impact Statement (EIS). The commission challenged the standing of the organization to bring the action.

The Supreme Court found a sufficient basis for standing in the student group's allegations that each of its members "suffered economic, recreational, and aesthetic harm directly as a result of the adverse environmental effect of the railroad freight structure." The specific harms allegedly suffered were that members had to "pay more for finished products," that each member used "the forest, rivers, streams, and other natural resources surrounding the Washington Metropolitan area and at his legal residence, for camping, hiking, fishing, sightseeing, and other recreational and aesthetic purposes," and that these uses were adversely affected by the increased freight rate. The group also alleged that members breathed air that was more polluted because of the rate increase and that each member had to pay increased taxes because money had to be spent to dispose of otherwise reusable waste materials. The Court found that the allegations of those specific harms were sufficient to deny a motion to dismiss for lack of standing.

Looking at these two primary precedent-setting cases on the issue of standing in environmental cases, many thought that the defenders' position in Lujan should prevail. However, the Supreme Court today is very different from the Court of the 1970s; the Lujan court chose to restrict the right of citizens to challenge the enforcement of environmental statutes by restricting the definition of standing. Applying a rigorous standing test advocated by the Bush administration, the opinion of the 7–2 majority, written by Justice Antonin Scalia, said that the environmental group did not show that it would suffer an "injury-in-fact" or demonstrate "redressability." The High Court said that the group needed to demonstrate "not only that the listed species were in fact threatened by funded activities abroad, but also that one or more of [their] members would thereby be 'directly' affected from their 'special interest' in the subject." The Court held that the environmental group had failed to demonstrate the latter.

Reaction to the decision from environmentalists matched the feelings expressed by the dissent. Justice Blackmun, joined by Justice O'Connor, wrote that the decision was "a slash and burn expedition through the law of environmental standing." He expressed fear that the decision would impose "fresh limitations" on Congress's authority to allow citizens' suits in federal courts for injuries that were "procedural" in nature.[8] The losing counsel for the Defenders was quoted as saying, "I've been in the environmental litigation business for 18 years, and this is an attempt by the Supreme Court to put us all out of business."[9] Three years after his "dire prediction," most commentators agreed that the case had not significantly cut back on environmental litigation by citizens' groups.

However, standing continues to be a controversial issue in environmental law. In 1997, the Supreme Court ruled in *Bennett v. Spear*[10] that people can sue the government for overzealous regulations. In Bennett, a group of ranchers and irrigation districts brought a suit against the Fish and Wildlife Service (FWS), which proposed limiting the release of water from an irrigation project to protect two endangered species of fish. The ranchers argued that the restriction injured them economically. The district court dismissed the suit, and the appeals court affirmed the dismissal, finding that the ranchers lacked standing to sue. However, the Supreme Court overturned the decision, stating that the right to challenge the regulations under the Endangered Species Act did not "apply to environmentalists alone." Justice Scalia stated that the provision in the Endangered Species Act that authorizes "any person" to bring a suit challenging the way the government carries out the law does not apply only to "underenforcement" but also to "overenforcement." Although this decision might seem to deal a blow to environmentalists, environmental groups often argue that the Court needs to take an expansive view of who has the right to sue. Consequently, environmental groups did not want to urge the court to limit the view of legal standing.[11]

Not only can people who protest overenforcement gain standing to sue, but animals can also be named as parties. Specifically, the Endangered Species Act allows endangered or threatened animals to file suit. For example, three turtles—a loggerhead turtle, a green turtle, and a leatherback turtle—along with Shirley Reynolds and Rita Alexander, who stood for the turtles, recently won an appeal in the 11th U.S. Circuit Court of Appeals.[12] When sea turtle hatchlings eventually break out of their shells at night, they instinctively crawl toward the brightest light on the horizon. On an undeveloped beach, the brightest light is the moon's reflection off the surf. However, on a developed beach, the brightest light can be an inland artificial source. The turtles instituted the lawsuit in 1995 when the county council refused to ban beach driving during the nesting season for sea turtles or to ban beachfront artificial light sources that have an adverse impact on sea turtles by disorienting and misorienting hatchling turtles. Although they lost in district court, the court of appeals concluded that the turtles did indeed have standing. In addition, the court ruled that the county could be liable if turtles die on the beach because of the artificial lighting.

In 1998, standing remained a controversial issue with the Supreme Court's ruling in *Steel Co. v. Citizens for a Better Environment*.[13] Citizens for a Better Environment (CBE) brought suit against Steel Company because the company failed (for 8 years) to file reports with federal, state, and local agencies about the hazardous chemicals it was using. The Court ruled that CBE had no standing to sue Steel Company because any injury caused by the missed deadlines was not "redressable," a criterion needed to establish standing. Justice Scalia stated that the relief sought by CBE would not "serve to reimburse . . . for losses caused by the late reporting, or to eliminate any effects of that late reporting upon respondent."

Environmental supporters were worried about the effect of *Steel Co.* on environmental litigation, but a surprising 2000 ruling in *Friends of the Earth (FOE) v. Laidlaw Environmental Services*[14] seemed to allay their fears. In this case, Friends of the Earth (FOE) brought a lawsuit against Laidlaw under the CWA, alleging that the company had violated its discharge permit by discharging excess amounts of mercury and other pollutants. The District Court assessed a civil penalty of $405,800, payable to the U.S. Treasury. The case was overturned on appeal on the grounds that it was moot, because the company had already come into compliance with the law by the time of the case.

The U.S. Supreme Court reversed the ruling of the Court of Appeals. Addressing the standing issue, Justice Ginsburg reiterated the need for proving that

1. the plaintiff had an injury-in-fact that is concrete and actual or imminent;
2. the injury is fairly traceable to the challenged action of the defendant;
3. it is likely that the injury will be redressed by a favorable decision.

Ginsburg found that the members' testimony concerning how they were afraid to fish and swim in the river they used to enjoy satisfied the first two requirements. She found the redressability issue to be satisfied by the fact that civil penalties will serve as a deterrent to prevent the company (and others) from engaging in polluting behaviors in the future. The fact that the benefit to the claimants came only indirectly was not fatal to FOE's case. Thus, after this case, environmentalists once again thought that they would be able to bring actions for which the primary remedy did not flow directly to the citizens' group, but to government coffers.

Despite this ruling from the High Court, defendants continue to raise the issue of standing whenever an environmental group files a lawsuit. The case of *Nat'l Parks Conservation Ass'n v. Manson,*[15] decided in 2006, is typical of such challenges. The Bull Mountain Power Company sought permission from a state agency to construct a coal-fired, electric generating plant in the vicinity of Yellowstone National Park and a federal wilderness area. The state agency issued a permit after receiving a letter from an official of the Department of the Interior stating that the power plant would not adversely affect visibility in Yellowstone Park or the wilderness area. Originally, two Federal Land Managers had sent a letter and a report formally notifying the Montana Department of Environmental Quality (DEQ) that the proposed

Roundup Plant would "cause perceptible visibility impairment at" Yellowstone and UL Bend, but this letter had been revoked and the letter of support sent in its place after the Power Company complained to the Interior Department.

The National Parks Conservation Association and other environmental conservation organizations sued in district court, claiming that the Interior Department violated the CAA. Acting on a motion from the defendants, the district court dismissed the plaintiff's case on the grounds that the association did not have standing because they failed to demonstrate the existence of an injury-in-fact caused by the defendant that was capable of being redressed by a court order. The Ninth Circuit Court of Appeals reversed the lower court's decision, stating that "regardless whether the alleged injury is procedural or direct, it satisfies the first aspect of the standing test. As an organization dedicated to the conservation of, and whose members make use of, public lands, National Parks suffers a cognizable injury from environmental damage to those lands."[16] The court went on to say the injury was capable of being redressed by the court because the outcome they were seeking would require the secretary of the interior to consider the withdrawn letter discussing adverse effects of the permit on air quality in the park, which would be done if plaintiffs were successful in their case. The defendants petitioned the circuit court for a rehearing on the standing issue, which was denied.[17] At the time the book went to press, the case was back in the courts to be tried on its merits.

Case or Controversy

The requirement that the courts render a decision only when there is a case or controversy before them may seem like a relatively simple matter. But in actuality, the term *case,* or *controversy,* is very imprecise and, thus, has been subject to changing interpretations. Today, the requirement appears to demand that the case have three essential characteristics. First, the affected parties must be in an adverse relationship to each other. Second, actual or threatened events must give rise to a live legal dispute. Third, the courts must have the ability to render a final and meaningful judgment. Thus, the courts may give only judgments that solve an existing problem. They cannot provide advisory opinions or provide rulings with respect to hypothetical situations.

Ripeness

Ripeness simply means that there exists a present controversy for which a decision is needed. In other words, the decision must have the capacity to affect the parties immediately. This issue most often comes into play when one party argues that the issue is moot, or no longer ripe. Remember that in the previously discussed case of *Friends of the Earth (FOE) v. Laidlaw Environmental Services,* the Court of Appeals had dismissed the case on the grounds of mootness. In the part of the opinion that addressed the mootness issue, Justice Ginsburg wrote, "A defendant's voluntary cessation of allegedly unlawful conduct ordinarily does not suffice to moot a case."[18] Furthermore, "Congress has found that civil penalties in the Clean Water Act cases do more than promote immediate compliance . . . they also deter future violations."[19] The Court ruled that a case is not moot merely because of compliance with the law after the lawsuit begins. The fact that civil penalties can be seen not only as redress to the plaintiff but also as deterrence is important because that allows for a meaningful judgment to take place regardless of compliance.

PRETRIAL

Informal Negotiations

For anyone involved in a dispute, the first step is to discuss the dispute with an attorney. It is important that the attorney be given all relevant information, even if it does not make the client look good. The more relevant facts the attorney has, the better the attorney's advice will be. Together, the attorney and the client may be able to resolve the dispute informally with the other party.

Initiation of a Legal Action

Once a party decides that an informal resolution is not possible, the parties enter what is often called the pleading stage of a lawsuit. Pleadings are papers filed by a party in court and then served on the opponent. The basic pleadings (described in detail later) are the complaint, the answer, the counterclaim, and the motion to dismiss. The attorney of the person who feels he or she has been wronged initiates a lawsuit by filing a complaint in the appropriate court. A complaint is a document that states the names of the parties to the action, the basis for the court's subject matter jurisdiction, the facts on which the party's claim is based, and the relief that the party is seeking. The party on whose behalf the complaint is filed is the plaintiff. The defendant is the party against whom the action is being brought. In most environmental cases, the plaintiff is a government agency. The second most common plaintiff is a citizens' group. The most common defendants are also government agencies; the second most common defendants are corporations.

In determining the appropriate court in which to file the complaint, the attorney must determine which court has subject matter jurisdiction over the case. Once that determination has been made, the attorney must ascertain the proper venue for the case. The means used by the attorney to determine subject matter jurisdiction and venue were discussed earlier in this chapter.

The Court's Acquisition of Jurisdiction over the Person

Once the complaint is filed, the court serves a copy of the complaint and a summons on the defendant. Service is the procedure used by the court to ensure that the defendant actually receives a copy of the summons and the complaint. The summons is an order of the court notifying the defendant of the pending case and telling him or her how and when to respond to the complaint.

Personal service, whereby a sheriff or other person appointed by the court hands the summons and complaint to the defendant, has been the traditional method of service. Today, other types of service are more common. Residential service may be used, whereby the summons and complaint are left by the representative of the court with a responsible adult at the home of the defendant. Certified mail or, in some cases, ordinary mail is also used to serve defendants. When one thinks about how the rules of service would apply to a suit against a corporation, the question arises: How do you serve a corporation? The legal system has solved that question. Most states require that corporations appoint an agent for service when they are incorporated. This agent is a person who has been given the legal authority to receive service for the corporation. Once the agent has been served, the corporation is served. In most states, service on the president of the corporation also constitutes service on the corporation.

The purpose of service of the summons and the complaint is to give the defendant notice of the pending action. It also gives the court jurisdiction over the person of the defendant. This jurisdiction means that the court has the power to render a decision that is binding on the defendant. Traditionally, a defendant had to be served within the state in which the court was located for the court to acquire jurisdiction over the person of the defendant. This restriction imposed severe hardships when a defendant who lived in one state entered another state and injured the plaintiff. If the defendant never again entered the plaintiff's state, the plaintiff could bring an action against the defendant only in the state in which the defendant lived. Obviously, this restriction would prevent many legitimate actions from being filed.

To alleviate this problem, most states enacted long-arm statutes. These statutes enable the court to serve the defendant outside the state as long as the defendant has engaged in certain acts within the state. These acts vary from state to state, but most statutes include such acts as committing a tort within the state or doing business within the state. Initially, such statutes were challenged as a denial of due process to the out-of-state defendant. Such challenges were usually unsuccessful.

Defendant's Response

Once the defendant has been properly served, he or she files an answer and possibly a counterclaim. An answer is a response to the allegations in the plaintiff's complaint. The answer must admit, deny, or state that the defendant has no knowledge about the truth of each of the plaintiff's allegations. The answer may also contain affirmative defenses, which consist of facts that were not stated in the complaint that would provide justification for the defendant's actions and a legally sound reason to deny relief to the plaintiff. These defenses must be stated in the answer. If they are not raised in the answer, the court may not allow the defenses to be raised later. The defendant is required to plead his or her affirmative defenses in the answer to give the plaintiff notice of all the issues that will be raised at the trial.

When a defendant, on receiving the complaint, believes that even if all of the plaintiff's factual allegations were true, the plaintiff would not be entitled to a favorable judgment, the defendant may file a motion to dismiss. There are no factual issues being debated, so the judge accepts the facts as stated by the plaintiff and makes a ruling on the legal questions in the case. Judges generally are not receptive to such motions, granting them only when "it appears beyond doubt that the plaintiff can prove no set of facts in support of his claim, which would entitle him to relief."

If the defendant believes that he or she has a cause of action against the plaintiff, this will be included as a counterclaim. The form of a counterclaim is the same as that of a complaint: The defendant states the facts supporting his or her claim and asks for the relief to which he or she feels entitled. If the defendant files a counterclaim, the plaintiff generally files a reply, which is simply an answer to a counterclaim. In the reply, the plaintiff admits, denies, or states that he or she has no knowledge of the truth of the facts asserted by the defendant in the counterclaim. Any affirmative defenses that are appropriate must be raised in the reply.

After the pleadings have been filed, either party can file a motion for judgment on the pleadings. When such a motion is filed, the party is saying that even if all the facts are as alleged by the opposite side's pleadings, the filer should still win the case. Such motions are rarely granted.

Pretrial Motions

The early pleadings just described serve to establish the legal and factual issues of the case. Once these issues have been established, either the plaintiff or the defendant may file a motion designed to bring the case to an early conclusion or to gain some advantage for the party filing the motion. A motion is simply a request by a party for the court to do something. A party may request, or move, that the court do almost anything pertaining to the case, such as a motion for some form of temporary relief until a decision has been rendered, sometimes referred to as a motion for preliminary relief. For example, if a suit is brought over the right to a piece of property, the court may grant a motion prohibiting the current possessor of that property from selling it.

Discovery

Once the initial pleadings and motions have been filed, the parties gather information from each other through the process of discovery. At this stage, a party is frequently asked by his or her attorney to respond to the opponent's requests for information about the case. There are a number of tools of discovery through which these requests are made. One of the most common is interrogatories—a series of written questions sent to the opposing party, who must truthfully answer them under oath. Interrogatories are frequently accompanied by a request to admit certain facts. The attorney and the client work together to answer these interrogatories and requests for admission of facts.

A request to produce documents or other items is another tool of discovery. Unless the information requested is privileged or is irrelevant to the case, it must be produced. Photographs, contracts, written estimates, and forms that must be filed with governmental agencies are among the items that may be requested. One party may also request that the other party submit to a mental or a physical examination. This motion will be approved only when the party's mental or physical health is at issue in the case.

Finally, testimony before trial may be obtained by the taking of a deposition. At a deposition, a witness is examined under oath by the attorneys. A court reporter (stenographer) records every word spoken by the attorneys and witnesses. The testimony is usually transcribed so that both parties have a written copy. When a person is to be deposed in a case, it is very important that he or she and the attorney talk extensively about what kinds of questions may come up at the deposition and how such questions are to be answered. The party who requested the deposition not only is seeking information but also is laying the groundwork for identifying any inconsistencies that may arise between a person's testimony at the deposition and in court. If such inconsistencies exist, they will be brought to the attention of the fact finder, and this may result in a loss of credibility for the courtroom testimony.

Depositions may also be used when a potential witness is old or ill and may die before the trial. They are also useful if witnesses may be moving or for some other reason may not be available at the time of the trial.

As a result of discovery, each party should have knowledge of most of the facts surrounding the case. This process is supposed to prevent surprises from occurring in the courtroom. Parties must comply with requests for discovery, or the court may order that the facts sought to be discovered be deemed admitted as if they had been proved. Thus, it is important that anyone involved in litigation produce for the attorney all the requested discovery material. An attorney who thinks that certain material should not be discovered makes arguments about its lack of relevance to the case, but if the court disagrees, the information must be supplied.

Motions for Summary Judgment

At any time during this stage, either party may file a motion for summary judgment. This motion asks the judge to assume that everything the nonmoving party says is true and then to decide the case in the moving party's favor. In other words, by filing a motion for summary judgment, the defendant is in effect saying, "Even if you believe that every claim the plaintiff makes in his or her complaint is true, and disregarding my defenses, you have to decide in my favor because the plaintiff(s) has not proven I have done anything wrong."

Pretrial Conference

If the judge finds that questions of fact do exist, he or she usually holds a pretrial conference—an informal meeting of the judge with the lawyers representing the parties. At this meeting, they try to narrow the legal and factual issues and to work out a settlement if possible. When the lawsuit begins, there are many conflicting assertions as to what events actually led to the lawsuit. Questions about what actually happened are referred to as questions of fact. Many times, as a result of discovery, parties come to agree on most of the facts. Remaining factual disputes may often be resolved at the conference. Then the only questions left are how to apply the law to the facts and what damages, if any, to award. By the time of the pretrial conference, each party should have determined the limits of any settlement to which he or she is willing to agree and should have communicated those limits to his or her attorney, who may be able to reach a settlement at the conference. Judges frequently try very hard to help the parties reach agreement before trial. If no settlement can be reached, the attorneys and the judge discuss the administrative details of the trial, its length, the witnesses, and any pretrial stipulations of fact or law to which the parties can agree.

THE TRIAL

Once the pretrial stage has concluded, the next step is the trial. As noted earlier, if the plaintiff is seeking a legal remedy (monetary damages), he or she is usually entitled to a jury trial. The judge is the fact finder when an equitable remedy (an injunction or other court order) is being sought or the parties have waived their right to a jury. For example, when a plaintiff in a negligence action against a manufacturer that produced a toxic substance requests a judgment for $10,000 in medical expenses, he or she is seeking a legal remedy and is entitled to a jury trial. But a plaintiff seeking an injunction to prohibit the construction of a dam that would destroy the habitat of an endangered species is requesting an equitable remedy and is not entitled to a jury. It is important for a person filing an action to determine at the outset whether a jury is desirable, because a jury must be demanded in the complaint.

The stages of a trial are jury selection, opening statements, plaintiff's case, defendant's case, conference on jury instructions, closing arguments, and posttrial motions.

Jury Selection

An important part of a jury trial is the selection of the jury. A panel of potential jurors is selected randomly from a list of citizens. In the federal court system, voter lists are used. In a process known as *voir dire,* the attorneys and/or the judge question potential jurors to determine whether they could render an unbiased opinion in the case. In most states, each attorney is allowed to reject a minimal number of potential jurors without giving a reason. These rejections are called *peremptory challenges.* Attorneys are given an unlimited number of challenges for cause. For cause dismissals are used when questioning reveals a fact that would make it difficult for the potential juror to be impartial. For example, the potential juror may have brought a similar lawsuit against one of the defendant corporations 5 years ago.

Jury selection is deemed so crucial to the litigation process that some law firms hire psychologists or jury-selection professionals to assist them in the *voir dire* process. In fact, there is a great deal of debate about whether jury selection is indeed a science and what impact jury selection has on the outcome of a case. If jury selection is indeed a science, and the use of jury-selection consultants can influence the outcome of a case, there are important implications for environmental litigation. The party with the greater financial resources would enjoy a distinct advantage in the courtroom. In most cases, the advantaged party would be a corporate defendant.

In any event, enough people believe that jury selection is a science that jury-selection consulting firms are springing up across the country. Their services are varied and even go beyond jury selection to helping lawyers anticipate jury behavior once jurors are selected. Their fees are not cheap, often ranging from $40,000 to several million dollars per case.[20] Some of the more commonly sought services of jury-selection-consulting firms are community surveys, jury-selection assistance, mock juries, and shadow juries.[21] A community survey is a survey of potential juries, the results of which are used to develop a profile of the ideal juror. Jury-selection assistance includes the consultant's providing questions for *voir dire* and even, if allowed in the state, sitting in on the questioning. A mock jury is a jury selected to match the profile of the actual jury. The lawyers then "rehearse" their case before the mock jury and get feedback from the mock jury as to which arguments, evidence, and witnesses were persuasive and which were harmful to the case. On the basis of that feedback, the lawyers may alter their trial performance.

A shadow jury is also selected to match the profile of the actual jurors. But the shadow jurors sit in on the actual trial. At the end of each day, they meet to discuss what transpired during the trial and how the day's events affected their evolving opinion. Lawyers may alter their next day's presentation to try to remove doubts or change undesirable perceptions created that day. After trial, the shadow jury deliberates briefly to try to give the lawyers a preview of what the actual verdict will be. On the basis of input from the shadow jury, the lawyers may go to opponents with a last-minute settlement offer, or they may reject any settlement proposals they receive.

Opening Statements

Once a jury has been impaneled, or selected, the case begins with the opening statements. Each party's attorney explains to the judge and the jury what facts he or she intends to prove, the legal conclusions to which these facts will lead, and how the case should be decided.

Plaintiff's Case

The plaintiff then presents his or her case, which consists of examining witnesses and presenting evidence. The procedure for each witness is the same. First, the plaintiff's attorney questions the witness in what is called direct examination. Then the opposing counsel may cross-examine the witness; in cross-examination, only questions pertaining to the witness's direct examination may be asked. The plaintiff's attorney then has the opportunity for redirect examination, to repair any damage done by the cross-examination. The opposing counsel then has a last opportunity to cross-examine the witness to address facts brought out in redirect examination. This procedure is followed for each of the plaintiff's witnesses.

Immediately following the plaintiff's case, the defendant may make a motion for a directed verdict. In making such a motion, the defendant is stating to the court that even if all the plaintiff's factual allegations are true, the plaintiff has not proved his or her case. For example, as will be discussed in Chapter 4, to prove a case of nuisance, the plaintiff must prove that the defendant used his or her own property in a manner that interfered with the plaintiff's use or enjoyment of his or her property. If the plaintiff offers no evidence of how his or her use or enjoyment of his or her land has been diminished, then there can be no judgment for the plaintiff. In such a case, a motion for a directed verdict would be granted and the case dismissed. Such motions are rarely granted because the plaintiff will usually introduce some evidence of every element necessary to establish the existence of his or her case.

A motion for a directed verdict also may be made by either party after the presentation of the defendant's case. The party filing the motion (the moving party) is saying that even if the judge looks at all the evidence in the light most favorable to the other party, it is overwhelmingly clear that the only decision the jury could come to is that the moving party is entitled to judgment in his or her favor.

Defendant's Case

If the defendant's motion for a directed verdict is denied, the trial proceeds with the defendant's case. The defendant's witnesses are questioned in the same manner as were the plaintiff's, except that the defendant's attorney does the direct and redirect examination and the plaintiff's attorney is entitled to cross-examine the witnesses.

Conference on Jury Instructions

If the case is being heard by a jury, the attorneys and the judge then retire for a conference on jury instructions. Jury instructions are the court's explanation to the jury of what legal decision they must make if they find certain facts to be true. Each attorney presents to the judge the set of jury instructions he or she thinks will enable the jury to accurately apply the law to the facts. Obviously, each attorney tries to state the law in the manner most favorable to his or her client. The judge confers with the attorneys regarding their proposed instructions and then draws up the instructions for the jury. Attorneys listen very carefully to the instructions the judge gives because one basis for appeal of a decision is that the judge improperly instructed the jury.

Closing Arguments

The attorneys' last contact with the jury, their closing arguments, follows the conference on jury instructions. The party who has the burden of proof, the plaintiff, presents the first closing argument; the defendant's closing argument follows. Finally, the plaintiff is entitled to a rebuttal. The judge then reads the instructions to the jury, and the jurors retire to the jury room to deliberate. When they reach a decision, the jurors return to the courtroom, where their verdict is read.

Posttrial Motions

The party who loses has a number of options. A motion for a judgment notwithstanding the verdict (judgment n.o.v.) may be made. This is a request for the judge to enter a judgment contrary to that handed down by the jury on the ground that as a matter of law the decision could only have been different from that reached by the jury. For example, if a plaintiff requests damages of $500 but introduces evidence of only $100 worth of damages, the jury cannot award the plaintiff $400 in damages. If it does so, the defendant would file a motion for a motion notwithstanding the verdict. Alternatively, the dissatisfied party may file a motion for a new trial on the ground that the verdict is clearly against the weight of the evidence. If neither of these motions is granted and the judge enters a judgment in accordance with the verdict, the losing party may appeal the decision.

APPELLATE PROCEDURE

As discussed previously, the court to which the case is appealed depends on the court in which the case was originally heard. A case heard in a federal district court is appealed to the U.S. Circuit Court of Appeals for the geographic region in which the district court is located. If heard in a state trial court, the case is appealed to that state's intermediate appellate court or, if none exists, to the state's final appellate court.

To appeal a case, the losing party must allege that a prejudicial error of law occurred during the trial. A prejudicial error is one that is so substantial that it could have affected the outcome of the case. For example, the judge may have ruled as admissible in court certain evidence that had a major impact on the decision, when that evidence was legally inadmissible. Or the party may argue that the instructions the judge read to the jury were inaccurate and resulted in a misapplication of the law to the facts.

When a case is appealed, there is not a new trial. The attorney for the appealing party (the appellant) and the attorney for the party who won in the lower court (the appellee) file briefs, or written arguments, with the court of appeals. They also generally present oral arguments before the appeals court. The court considers these arguments, reviews the record of the case, and renders a decision. The decision of the appellate court can take a number of forms. The court may accept the decision of the lower court and affirm that decision. Alternatively, the appellate court may conclude that the lower court was correct in its decision, except for granting an inappropriate remedy, and so it will modify the remedy. The appellate court could also decide that the lower court was incorrect in its decision and reverse the decision. Finally, the appeals court may feel that an error was committed, but it does not know how that error would have affected the outcome of the case, so it will remand the case to the lower court for a new trial.

Although the appeals procedure may sound relatively simple compared with the initial trial procedure, appeals require a great deal of work on the part of the attorneys. They are consequently expensive. Thus, when deciding whether to appeal, a party must consider how much money he or she wishes to spend. In some cases, it may be less expensive to pay the judgment than to appeal.

However, a more important factor to consider when deciding whether to appeal may be the precedential value of the case. The case may involve an important new issue of law that a party hopes may be decided in her or his favor by an appeals court. If he or she anticipates similar suits, it may be important to get a favorable ruling. If the case appears to be strong, an appeal may be desirable. If the case is weak, the wiser move may be to accept the lower court's decision and wait for another opportunity to get an appellate ruling. Remember, an appellate precedent carries more weight than a trial court decision.

Appellate courts, unlike trial courts, are usually composed of at least three judges. There are no juries. The decision of the court is determined by the majority of the judges. One of the judges who votes with the majority records the court's decision and reasoning in what is called the majority opinion. These have precedential value and are used by judges to make future decisions and by attorneys in advising their clients as to the appropriate behavior in similar situations. If any of the judges in a case agrees with the ultimate decision of the majority but for different reasons, he or she may write a concurring opinion, stating how this conclusion was reached. Finally, the judge or judges disagreeing with the majority may write their dissenting opinion, giving their reasons for reaching a contrary conclusion. Dissenting opinions may be cited in briefs by attorneys arguing that the law should be changed. Dissents may also be cited by an appellate judge who decides to change the law.

In many important U.S. Supreme Court cases, there is one majority opinion accompanied by several concurring and dissenting opinions. A case that has only one majority opinion signed by all the judges is considered much stronger—and potentially longer lasting—than a majority opinion accompanied by numerous concurring and dissenting opinions. For most cases, only one appeal is possible. In some states where there are both an intermediate and a superior court of appeals, a losing party may appeal from the intermediate appellate court to the state supreme court. In a limited number of cases, a losing party may be able to appeal from a state supreme court or a circuit court of appeals to the U.S. Supreme Court.

Appeal to the U.S. Supreme Court

There are two types of appeals to the U.S. Supreme Court: appeal by writ of certiorari and appeal as of right. The former is the more common type of appeal. To appeal by writ of certiorari, the losing party files a petition with the Supreme Court in which he or she argues that the issue on which the appeal is based either presents a substantial federal question or involves a matter that has produced conflicting decisions from the various circuit courts of appeal and is in need of resolution. The Supreme Court reviews the petition and may decide to review the case if at least four justices are convinced that it is a matter in need of resolution.

It is often difficult to predict whether the Court will hear a case. A federal question is simply an issue arising under the federal Constitution, treaties, or statutes. Substantiality is more difficult to define. If the decision would affect a large number of people or is likely to arise again if not decided, it may be considered substantial. If the Supreme Court refuses to hear a case, such refusal has no precedential effect.

In a limited number of cases, the losing party is entitled to nondiscretionary appeal as of right. When parties are entitled to an appeal as of right, they file a notice of appeal, and the Supreme Court must review the case on its merits. For example, if a state supreme court holds that a federal statute is unconstitutional, this ruling can be appealed as of right. In both appeals by writ and as of right, the appeal may be limited to the Court's simply reviewing the transcript of the lower court case. It is up to the Court to determine whether it wants to hear oral arguments and read written briefs.

ALTERNATIVES TO CIVIL LITIGATION

The litigation process seems extremely time-consuming and expensive to many people, so unwieldy that they have turned to other means to resolve their disputes. In the environmental arena, the two main alternatives are mediation and arbitration. These two methods share certain advantages over litigation. Generally, they are less expensive and less time-consuming, and the formal hearing times and places can be set at the parties' mutual convenience. The persons presiding over the resolution process can be chosen by the parties and, in many cases, are more familiar with the area of law over which the dispute arose than a randomly assigned judge would be. These alternatives may also prevent adverse publicity, which could be ruinous to a business. They may also result in the preservation of confidentiality, which may be extremely important when a company's trade secrets are involved.

The following detailed examination of these alternative dispute-resolution methods should help you understand the types of situations in which each of these alternatives may be preferable to litigation. One problem that sometimes arises in the decision to use an alternative form of dispute resolution is that in many cases an alternative may benefit one party, whereas litigation may be more beneficial to the other.

ARBITRATION

Arbitration—the resolution of a dispute by a neutral third party outside the judicial setting—is one of the most well-known alternatives to litigation, although it is not the form most commonly used to resolve environmental matters. The arbitration hearing is somewhat similar to a trial, but there is no prehearing discovery process. The stringent rules of evidence applicable in a trial are generally relaxed in arbitration. Each side presents witnesses and evidence, and the parties are given the opportunity to cross-examine their opponent's witnesses. The arbitrator frequently takes a much more active role in questioning the witness than a judge would. An arbitrator who needs to know more information will generally ask for that information from witnesses.

Unlike at a trial, there is usually no official record of the hearing. However, the parties and the arbitrator may agree to have a stenographer record the proceedings at the expense of the parties. The arbitrator and each of the parties usually take their own notes of what transpires. Although attorneys may represent parties in arbitration, notes are not required. Often, to save money, a party may consult an attorney to help plan the arbitration strategy, but the party appears at the arbitration without the lawyer. Individuals may represent themselves or may have someone else represent them. In some cases, the arbitrator may request written arguments from the parties. These documents are called arbitration briefs.

The arbitrator usually provides a decision for the parties within 30 days of the hearing. He or she may provide the reasons for the decision but is not required to do so. The decision rendered by the arbitrator is much more likely to be a compromise than is the decision handed down by a court, for a number of reasons. First, the arbitrator is not as constrained by precedent as are judges. The arbitrator is interested in resolving a factual dispute, not in establishing or strictly applying a rule of law, although of course he or she cannot render a decision that is clearly contrary to the law. Second, the arbitrator may be more interested than a judge in preserving an ongoing relationship with the parties. A compromise is much more likely to achieve this result than is a clear win or lose decision. Obviously, if the evidence overwhelmingly favors one party, the arbitrator will rule in that party's favor, but most cases are not so clear, and arbitrators will generally try to give each party something. Finally, because an arbitrator frequently decides cases in a particular area, he or she wants to maintain a reputation of being fair to both sides so as to be selected to decide future cases.

The decision rendered by the arbitrator is legally binding. The decision may be appealed through the court system, but judges rarely overturn an arbitrator's decision. Usually, the only basis for overturning the decision is that the arbitrator exceeded the bounds of his or her authority. Such a high standard for review seems to give an arbitrator more power than the trial court!

Methods of Securing Arbitration

If arbitration of the dispute in question is not mandated by state law, there are two methods by which parties can secure arbitration. One means is to include a binding arbitration clause in a contract. Such a clause provides that all or certain disputes arising under the contract are to be settled by arbitration. The clause should also include the means by which the arbitrator is to be selected. Over 95 percent of the collective bargaining agreements in force today have some provision for arbitration.

If no arbitration clause is included in a contract and a dispute arises over its terms, the parties may secure arbitration by entering into a submission agreement, which is a written contract stating that the parties wish to settle their dispute by arbitration. It usually also states the means by which the arbitrator will be selected and the limits of the arbitrator's authority. For example, in a tort case, the arbitrator may be limited to awarding the plaintiff up to a certain amount of money.

If the parties have entered into a submission agreement or have included an arbitration clause in their contract, they will be required to resolve their disputes through arbitration. Both federal and state courts must defer to arbitration if the contract in dispute contains a binding arbitration clause.

Selection of an Arbitrator

Once the decision to arbitrate has been made, an arbitrator must be selected. Arbitrators are generally lawyers, professors, or other professionals. They are frequently selected on the basis of their special expertise in some area. If the parties have not agreed on an arbitrator before a dispute, they generally use one of two sources for selecting an arbitrator: the Federal Mediation and Conciliation Service (FMCS), a governmental agency, or the American Arbitration Association (AAA), a private, nonprofit organization.

When the disputants contact one of these agencies, they receive a list of arbitrators along with a biographical sketch of each. Once the arbitrator has been selected, the parties and the arbitrator agree on the time, the date, and the location of the arbitration. They also agree on the substantive and procedural rules to be followed in the arbitration.

Disadvantages of Arbitration

The most significant reason for not using arbitration would probably be that the decision does not create a legally binding precedent, which may be important in many cases. Less importantly, a party may want the publicity generated by a lawsuit, which arbitration does not usually provide.

Another problem with arbitration is that the lengthy court procedures that arbitration omits serve to protect parties from surprise and unfair admission of questionable evidence. The protection of thorough review on appeal is also lost.

MEDIATION

Since the mid-1970s, mediation has increasingly been used to resolve environmental disputes, especially those involving complex issues and multiple parties with different interests. Between 1974 and 1984, mediation was used to solve approximately 160 environmental disputes involving matters that ranged from air quality to land use to toxic waste. Mediation differs from arbitration and litigation in that the mediator makes no final decision. The mediator is simply a facilitator of communication between disputing parties. Mediation is an informal process in which the two disputants select a party, usually one with expertise in the disputed area, to help them reconcile their differences. Although there is no guarantee that a decision will be reached through mediation, if a decision is reached, the parties generally enter into a contract that embodies the terms of their settlement. If one party does not live up to the terms of the settlement, that party can then be sued for breach of contract. In October 1998, in an attempt to encourage mediation as an alternative to trial, Congress created the Institute for Environmental Conflict Resolution, the first federally funded organization dedicated to environmental mediation.[22] The institute was created mainly because an average of 1,000 environmental cases a year were being filed with district courts, and these cases generally take over 2 years to work their way through the courts.[23]

Having been in operation for over 5 years, the institute is playing a valuable role in the resolution of environmental conflicts. Since its inception, it has been involved in over 300 cases and projects, including mediation cases, process facilitation, conflict assessments and process designs, dispute system designs, training design and delivery, case consultation, and case referrals. The institute's work has extended into 23 different states, including virtually all the Western states along with Alaska, Connecticut, Florida, Hawaii, Maryland, Massachusetts, New Jersey, New York, Oklahoma, Tennessee, Texas, as well as Washington, D.C., and Puerto Rico.

Several projects are national or multistate in scope. The issues involved in these cases and projects include wildlife and wilderness management, recreational use of, and access to, public lands, endangered species, marine protected areas, watershed management, ecosystem restoration, wetlands protection, and urban infrastructure planning. The majority of the inquiries have come from federal agencies (headquarters and regional offices), but they also have come from federal district courts, state government agencies, tribes, and environmental groups. The institute has developed institutional arrangements with more than 10 federal agencies; cosponsored a major national conference on Alternative Dispute Resolution (ADR) and Natural Resources; hosted the Federal Environmental Conflict Resolution (ECR) Roundtable for ADR specialists at federal agencies; and launched a Federal ECR Partnership Program to support innovative and effective applications of ECR. The institute continues to become more active every year and is clearly playing an increasing role in environmental dispute resolution.[24]

Advantages of Mediation

Among environmentalists, agency employees, and businesspersons, mediation has both its supporters and its detractors. Although not all environmental issues are suitable for mediation, clearly not all environmental issues are appropriate for litigation either. The primary advantage of mediation is that because of its nonadversarial nature, it tends to preserve the relationship between the parties to a greater extent than a trial or an arbitration would. Thus, mediation is used more and more frequently in cases in which the parties will have an ongoing relationship once the immediate dispute is settled. Many times in community disputes, the parties will find themselves in conflict. Conceivably, mediation could help each understand the other better, so future disagreements might be resolved more easily.

A second advantage is that mediation can be quicker. With the ever-increasing federal court caseload, delays are inevitable. Mediation can be almost instantaneous once a mediator is agreed upon. Because many environmental issues demand a quick response, mediation may be desirable. Mediation may be less expensive than litigation. At a minimum, mediation eliminates the cost of hiring expensive expert witnesses to testify at the trial. An extremely complex mediation may cost thousands of dollars, but an expensive lawsuit may run into the millions.

Another reason why mediation may be desirable for environmental problems is that in many cases the environmental issue does not fit neatly into the two-party, right or wrong mode of litigation. Many times, the environmental matter may involve numerous groups with varying interests. What is needed is a creative solution that takes into account multiple interests. Mediation provides a forum in which an unlimited number of interests can be heard and a solution can be attained other than a "winner take all" judgment for the plaintiff or a no liability judgment for the defendant. Even if a solution cannot be reached, mediation will have at least served to educate the parties about the other's position. In the future, if the parties have to deal with each other, they may be more understanding and be able to work out problems together.

Disadvantages of Mediation

Sometimes mediation is clearly not appropriate. If you want to establish a precedent-setting interpretation of a case, you have no choice but to go to court. A related problem is that mediation may produce more inconsistent outcomes. In many places, this disparity of outcomes resulting from a matter's being mediated would be argued to be unfair.

Also, if part of a party's objectives includes getting publicity, which it hopes will turn public opinion against a project strongly enough to block it, then mediation is not appropriate. In many environmental disputes, the greatest benefit of litigation for a citizens' group may be in creating public awareness that it hopes will lead to public pressure to prohibit some action.

Finally, no one can be forced to mediate. If one person whose interests are affected chooses not to mediate, even if 20 other affected interests agree to a mediated solution, the party who did not participate may still raise the issue through litigation. Sometimes, those involved in the mediation may not be aware of an affected party who, consequently, is not included in the mediation. That party may later litigate. Even worse, a party who wants to tie up a project may agree to mediation and go through the process, fully intending not to reach any agreement. The party is simply tying the case up in mediation. Once the other party realizes what is going on, the case may then be litigated, but by that time there has been a costly delay.

Critics of mediation often argue that the informal nature of the process represses and denies certain irreconcilable structural conflicts, such as the inherent strife between developers and environmentalists. They also argue that this informal process tends to create the impression of equality between the disputants when no such equality exists. The resultant compromise between non-equals is an unequal compromise, but it is clothed in the appearance of equal influence. Despite these criticisms, mediation does have its place in the resolution of environmental disputes. It will probably always be a supplement to, but not a replacement for, litigation.

Concluding Remarks

You now understand how the U.S. dual court system is structured and functions. Dispute resolution through our courts is an adversarial process, so disputes are managed by two conflicting parties, represented by lawyers, each of whom tries to bring out the strongest evidence and make the best argument for his or her side. A neutral third party, either a judge or jury, will decide who is the winner.

This adversarial process, however, is not well suited for many disputes, especially environmental ones. It is time-consuming, generates publicity, does not lead to compromise resolutions, and often worsens the relationship between two parties who must work with each other in the future. Because of these problems, alternatives to litigation increasingly are being used to resolve environmental disputes. Some of the more common alternatives include arbitration and mediation. Mediation is probably the most common because it preserves the parties' relationship and also allows the easiest inclusion of a multiplicity of interests.

Once you appreciate how the dispute-resolution systems function, there is only one more area of the American legal system that you need to understand before you are ready to explore environmental law: administrative law. Chapter 3 introduces this important system of law.

Questions for Review and Discussion

1. Explain what is meant by an adversary system and justify the use of such a system.
2. Explain the problems associated with reliance on the adversarial process to resolve environmental disputes.
3. Distinguish subject matter jurisdiction from jurisdiction over the person.
4. Explain the various roles a lawyer may play.
5. Distinguish a grand jury from a petit jury.
6. Explain the significance of the standing cases such as *Lujan v. Defenders of Wildlife* and *Sierra Club v. Morton*.
7. Trace the steps of a civil lawsuit.
8. Explain and critique the primary alternatives to litigation.

For Further Reading

Cassuto, David. 2004. "The Law of Words: Standing, Environment and Other Contested Terms." *Harvard Environmental Law Journal 28:* 79.

Cosins, Barbara. 2003. "Water Dispute Resolution in the West: Process Elements for the Modern Era in Basin-Wide Problem Solving." *Environmental Law 33:* 949.

Hamilton, Saran. 2004. "Thinking Globally and Acting Locally to Protect Arctic Ecosystems and People." *Colorado Journal of International Environmental Law and Policy 15:* 29.

Harwood, Richard. 2005 "Planning and Compulsory Purchase Act 2004 — How the Government Takes Control of Planning Policy." *Environmental Law Review 7:* 124.

Kanner, Alan, and Tibor Nagy. 2005. "Measuring Loss of Use Damages in Natural Resource Damage Actions." *Columbia Journal of Environmental Law 30:* 417.

McDonald, Jan. 1995. "Public Interest Environmental Litigation — Chipping Away at Procedural Obstacles." *Environmental and Planning Law Journal 12:* 140.

Mendelson, Joseph III. 1997. "Should Animals Have Standing? A Review of Standing Under the Animal Welfare Act."

Boston College Journal of Environmental Affairs Law Review 24: 795.

Sax, Joseph L. 1970. "The Public Trust Doctrine in Natural Resource Law: Effective Judicial Intervention." *Michigan Law Review 68:* 471.

Sidaway, Richard. 2006. *Resolving Environmental Disputes: From Conflict to Consensus.* London, UK: Earthscan Publishing Co.

Smith, Adrienne. 2005. Note: "Standing and the National Environmental Policy Act: Where Substance, Procedure, and Information Collide." *Boston University Law Review 85:* 633.

Stone, Christopher. 1974. *Should Trees Have Standing? Toward Legal Rights for Natural Objects.* Los Altos, CA: William Kaufmann.

Wenz, Peter. 1988. *Environmental Justice.* Albany, NY: State University of New York Press.

Werner, Matthew M. 1995. "Mootness and Citizen Suit Civil Penalty Claims under the Clean Water Act: A Post Lujan Reassessment." *Environmental Law 25:* 801.

Wiygul, Robert. 1995. "Eight Years Later: Proving Jurisdiction and Article III Standing in Clean Water Act Citizen Suits." *Tulane Environmental Law Journal 8:* 435.

On the Internet

http://www.gama.com/director.htm
A directory of alternative dispute resolution providers and organizations
http://www.dnai.com/tvlf/vlf_arbitration.html
Information about alternative dispute resolution
http://www.adr.org
Home page of the American Arbitration Association
http://www.law.cornell.edu
Home page of the Legal Information Institute
http://www.ecr.gov/
Home page of the United States Institute for Environmental Conflict Resolution

Notes

1. Foundation for Research on Economics and the Environment. "Our Program Objectives." *http://www.free-eco.org/index.html* (July 17, 2001).
2. Ruth Marcus. "Issues Groups Fund Seminars for Judges; Classes at Resorts Cover Property Rights." *Washington Post* (April 9, 1998): A1.
3. Community Rights Counsel. *Nothing for Free: How Private Judicial Seminars are Undermining Environmental Protections and Breaking the Public's Trust,* July 2000. *http://www.tripsforjudges.org/crc.pdf* (July 17, 2001): 13.
4. Lettie Wenner. 1982. *The Environmental Decade in Court.* Bloomington, IN: Indiana University Press.
5. 405 U.S. 727 (1972).
6. Ibid.
7. 412 U.S. 669 (1973).
8. M. Coyle and M. Havelle. 1992. "Eco-Groups' Standing Curtailed." *National Law Journal* (June 22): 3.
9. Ibid.
10. 520 U.S. 154 (1997).
11. Linda Greenhouse. 1997. "Court Opens Species Act to Wider List of Challenges." *New York Times* (March 20): B10.
12. *Loggerhead Turtle, Green Turtle et al., v. The County Council of Volusia County, Florida,* 148 F.3d 1231 (11th Cir. 1998); see also Emily Heller. 1998. "Hardshelled and Persistent, Turtles Win Standing," *Fulton County Daily Report* (August 12).
13. 118 S.Ct. 1003 (1998).
14. 120 S.Ct. 963 (2000).
15. 414 F.3d 1 (367 U.S. App. D.C. 110, 2005).
16. Ibid.
17. 2005 U.S. App. LEXIS 21280.
18. Ibid.
19. Ibid.
20. 367 U.S. App. D.C. 110 (2005).
21. Emily Couric. 1986. "Jury Sleuths: In Search of the Perfect Panel." *National Law Journal* (July 21): 1.
22. Ibid.
23. "Institute to Mediate Disputes on Environment." *New York Times* (June 15, 1998): A16.
24. Ibid.
25. *http://www.ecr.gov/*

RESOLVING CONTROVERSIAL
ENVIRONMENTAL ISSUES

- As you learned in the first chapter, you need to identify the issue, conclusion, and reasons when reading an article. Identifying the argument in the following essay will help you better understand and evaluate it. What are the conclusion and reasons offered by this author?

- Ethical norms are ideas that guide our behavior. Everyone generally agrees that ethical norms are positive ways of behaving. Some examples of ethical norms are honesty, cooperation, and individual responsibility. If I ask you, "Do you value honesty?" you will probably say "Yes." If I ask you, "Do you value loyalty?" you will also probably say "Yes." But how do you behave when those ethical norms conflict? For example, you discover that your best friend, who is also your coworker, is stealing money from your boss. If you are loyal to your friend, you cannot also be honest to your boss. Which ethical norm guides your behavior?

Ethical norms often conflict in the law. Four ethical norms that often arise in legal controversies are freedom, justice, security, and efficiency. Try to think of more ethical norms that might guide your thinking. When you read an article, you should try to identify the ethical norms that are guiding the author's thinking. This task is difficult because the author typically will not tell you his or her ethical norm preferences. Consequently, you must infer the preferences through the reasons. Can you identify which ethical norms seem to be present in the reasons and conclusion provided in the following editorial? What ethical norm is in conflict with the author's preferred ethical norm?

DOES A TURTLE HAVE MORE RIGHTS THAN A HUMAN?

Who should be allowed to bring a case in a court of law? One might respond with the following simple answer: Anyone who has been wronged. Environmentalists claim that when environmental wrongs occur, it is often difficult for those who have been wronged to bring a case because of a perceived lack of legal standing—the legal right to bring a lawsuit.

However, environmentalists actually have had an advantage in lawsuits. Environmental groups have been permitted to file lawsuits alleging underenforcement of the Endangered Species Act; in contrast, property owners could not file suit against overzealous regulation. Environmental groups had standing whereas property owners did not. Imagine a scenario in which an individual's property use is restricted because of an endangered species living on the property. Who seems most directly injured—the property owner or the environmental group? The property owner, of course. Yet, the property owner has been unable to bring a suit against the overzealous regulation.

Luckily, the Supreme Court has rectified this unfair situation. A recent ruling gives legal standing to people with an economic stake in land and water restrictions that allegedly protect endangered species. It is about time we give legal protection to those who are truly harmed.

After all, courts have now offered legal standing to animals protected by the Endangered Species Act. For example, turtles have been successful plaintiffs in cases. Furthermore, some environmentalists claim that legal rights should be extended to forests, oceans, and rivers. We should not even consider extending rights to inanimate objects until all people have rights. Why should a river have more rights than a property owner? A person's rights must come before the perceived concern of a river or a lake.

I argue that the Supreme Court made the right decision by allowing property owners to bring cases against overregulation. Most environmental laws are like the Endangered Species Act in the sense that they allow citizens to bring suits. The Supreme Court ruling should allow property owners to bring suits under these other environmental laws. Environmental protection has gone too far when a turtle has more rights than a person. Let us not lower the protections for people while raising the protections for animals and inanimate objects.

CHAPTER 3
ADMINISTRATIVE LAW
AND ITS IMPACT ON THE
ENVIRONMENT

Environmental law is classified as a branch of administrative law. This classification means that these laws are overseen by a body known as an administrative agency and that many of the specific regulations in this area are also established by this agency. Because environmental law falls within this classification, some basic understanding of administrative law is necessary.

The first part of this chapter explains how administrative agencies are created. A description of their primary functions of rule making, adjudication, and administrative activities constitutes the second part. The third section focuses on the ways in which the primary branches of the U.S. government control these agencies. The chapter concludes with a description of some of the major agencies affecting the environment.

The first federal administrative agencies were created by Congress near the end of the 19th century and the beginning of the 20th century. They were the ICC and the Federal Trade Commission (FTC). Congress felt that separate regulatory bodies with defined statutory mandates could best control the anticompetitive conduct of railroads and other corporations. Following the crash of the stock market and the Great Depression of the 1930s, Congress saw a need for additional agencies that could assist in guiding market decisions in the public interest. Since then, numerous agencies have been created whenever Congress believed there was an area that required more intense regulation than Congress could provide.

An administrative agency is generally defined as any body created by a legislative branch (e.g., Congress, a state legislature, or a city council) to carry out specific duties. Most agencies, however, are not situated entirely in the legislative, executive, or judicial branch of government. They generally have legislative power to make rules for an entire industry, judicial power to adjudicate (decide) individual cases, and executive power to investigate corporate misconduct. Numerous agencies play a role in creating and enforcing environmental regulations; especially important is the EPA.

CREATION OF ADMINISTRATIVE AGENCIES

Congress creates most administrative agencies through statutes called enabling legislation, although the president sometimes creates administrative agencies through an executive reorganization plan. In general, the enabling statutes contain broad delegations of congressional legislative power to agencies for the purpose of serving the "public interest, convenience, and necessity." This power to create rules is sometimes referred to as quasilegislative because the scope of the agency's rule-making authority is limited to that granted by Congress. Using this mandate, a particular administrative agency issues rules that control the behavior of individuals and businesses. In many instances, such rules carry civil, as well as criminal, penalties.

When passing an enabling statute, Congress also delegates executive power to agencies to investigate potential violations of rules or statutes. Through enabling statutes, Congress also delegates judicial power to settle or adjudicate individual disputes that an agency may have with businesses or individuals. For example, the EPA administrator, using the congressional mandate under the CAA, sets forth rules governing the amount of certain hazardous air pollutants that may be emitted into the atmosphere. Using these standards, another branch of the EPA sends investigators to inspect plants suspected of violating the act. If the inspector finds a violation and the EPA imposes a penalty, the plant operator will most likely contest the imposition of the fine, and a hearing will be held before an administrative law judge (ALJ) employed in another division of the EPA.

Because the Constitution placed legislative, executive, and judicial powers in separate branches of government, the role of administrative agencies has led some to state that an unofficial "fourth branch of government" really exists. Although there is a semblance of truth to that characterization, administrative agencies are not in fact another branch, primarily because all their authority is simply delegated to them and they remain under the control of the three traditional branches of government. They are not as independent as the term *fourth branch of government* might imply.

FUNCTIONS OF ADMINISTRATIVE AGENCIES

Administrative agencies perform the following functions: rule making, adjudication of individual cases brought before ALJs by the staff of an agency, and administrative activities.

RULE MAKING

Americans are probably most familiar with administrative agencies because of their rule-making powers. Administrative agencies are granted the authority to perform the legislative function of making rules or regulations by the enabling statutes that bring them into existence. For example, the enabling statute creating the OSHA gave the secretary of labor the authority to set "mandatory safety and health standards applicable to businesses affecting interstate commerce." The secretary was given the power to "prescribe such rules and regulations that he may deem necessary to carry out the responsibilities under this act." In some cases, the procedures for implementing the rule-making function are spelled out in the enabling act. When this is not done, one of three alternative models for rule making may be used: informal, formal, or hybrid.

One reason for the creation of administrative agencies has been the idea that they could be staffed with people who had special expertise in the area being regulated by the agency and, therefore, would be capable of knowing what types of regulations in that area were necessary to protect citizens. Also, because they were not elected, agency employees, in their rule-making capacity, would not be subject to political pressure. Agencies would also be able to act more swiftly than Congress in enacting laws. Today, administrative agencies actually create more rules than Congress and the courts combined.

As you read about the administrative rule-making procedures, compare them with the legislative process. You will notice that it is much easier for the public to participate in agency rule making. One reason for the relatively great opportunity for public participation is concern on the part of Congress that people would be upset about laws being made by individuals who were not elected.

Informal Rule Making

The primary type of rule making used by administrative agencies is informal or notice-and-comment rule making. As provided by Section 553 of the Administrative Procedure Act (APA), informal rule making applies in all situations in which the agency's enabling legislation or other congressional directives do not require another form. An agency initiates informal rule making by publishing the proposed rule in the *Federal Register,* along with an explanation of the legal authority for issuing the rule and a description of how one can participate in the rule-making process. Following this publication, opportunity is provided for all interested parties to submit written comments. These comments may contain data, arguments, or other information a person believes might influence the agency's decision. Although the agency is not required to hold hearings, it has the discretion to receive oral testimony if it wishes to do so. After considering the comments, the agency publishes the final rule, with a statement of its basis and purpose, in the *Federal Register.* This publication also includes the date on which the rule becomes effective, which must be at least 30 days after publication. Figure 3-1 depicts this process.

Informal rule making is most often used because it is more efficient for the agency in terms of time and cost. No formal public hearing is

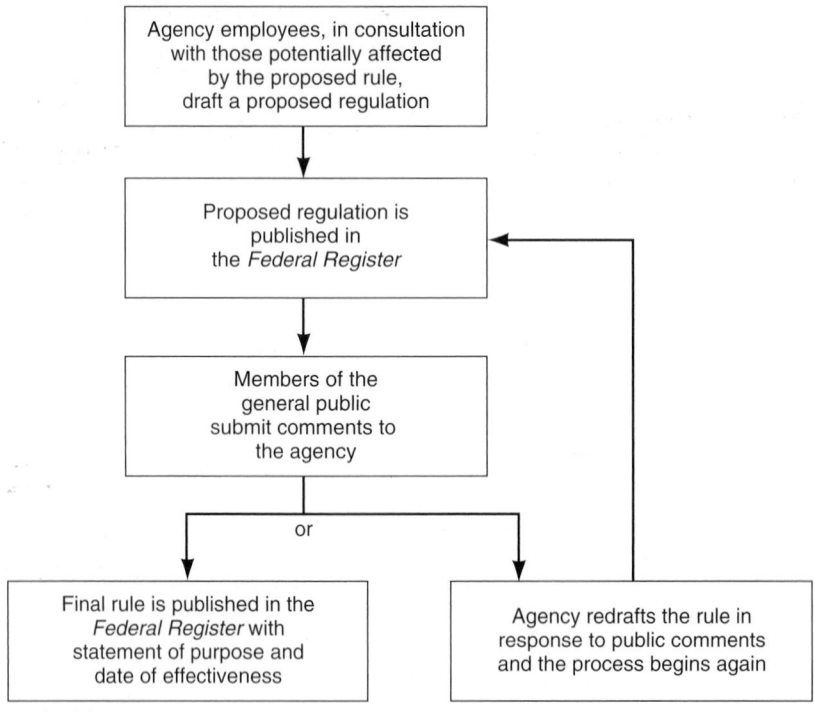

FIGURE 3-1   Stages of Informal Rule Making

required, and no formal record needs to be established, as would be true in formal rule making. Some people, however, believe that informal rule making is unfair because parties who are interested in the proposed rule have no idea what types of evidence the agency has received from other sources with respect to that rule. Thus, if the agency is relying on what one party might perceive as flawed or biased data, that party has no way to challenge those data. A second type of rule making, formal rule making, avoids that problem.

Formal Rule Making

Section 553(c) of the APA calls for formal rule making when an enabling statute or other legislation requires that all regulations or rules be enacted by an agency as part of a formal hearing process that includes a complete transcript. This procedure is initiated in the same manner as informal rule making, with publication of a notice of the proposed rule in the *Federal Register*. The second step in formal rule making is a public hearing at which witnesses give testimony on the pros and cons of the proposed rule; these witnesses are subject to cross-examination. An official transcript of the hearing is kept. On the basis of information received at the hearing, the agency makes and publishes formal findings. On the basis of these findings, an agency may or may not promulgate a regulation. If a regulation is adopted, the final rule is published in the *Federal Register* (The *Federal Register* for Environmental Documents can be found online at http://www.epa.gov/fedrgstr/). Because of the expense and time involved in obtaining a formal transcript and record, most enabling statutes do not require a formal rule-making procedure when promulgating regulations. If a statute is drafted in a manner that is at all ambiguous with respect to the type of rule making required, the court will not interpret the law as requiring formal rule making.

Hybrid Rule Making

After agencies began regularly making rules in accordance with the appropriate procedures, the flaws of each type of rule making became increasingly apparent. In response to these problems, a form of hybrid rule making became acceptable to the courts and legislature. Hybrid rule making is an attempt to combine the best features of informal and formal rule making. The starting point, publication in the *Federal Register,* is the same. This publication is followed by the opportunity for submission of written comments and then an informal public hearing with a more restricted opportunity for cross-examination than in formal rule making. The publication of the final rule is the same as for the other forms of rule making.

Exempted Rule Making

Section 553 of the APA contains an exemption from rule making that allows an agency to decide whether public participation will be allowed. The APA exempts public rule-making proceedings with regard to "military or foreign affairs" and "agency management or personnel." Exemptions are also granted for rule-making proceedings related to "public property, loans, grants, benefits or contracts" of an agency. Military and foreign affairs often need speed and secrecy, which are incompatible with public notice and hearings. Other exemptions are becoming more difficult to justify in the eyes of the courts unless they meet one of the exemptions to the Freedom of Information Act discussed later.

Also exempted from the rule-making procedures are interpretive rules and general policy statements. An interpretive rule is one that does not create any new rights or duties but is merely a detailed statement of the agency's interpretation of an existing law. These interpretive rules are generally very detailed, step-by-step statements of what actions a party would take to be considered in compliance with an existing law. Policy statements are general statements about directions in which any agency intends to proceed with respect to its rule-making or enforcement activities. Again, these statements have no binding impact on anyone; they do not directly affect anyone's legal rights or responsibilities.

A final exemption is when public notice and comment procedures are "impracticable, unnecessary, or contrary to the public interest." This exemption is used most commonly either when the issue is so trivial that there would probably be very little, if any, public input, or when the nature of the rule necessitates immediate action. Whenever an agency chooses to use this exception, it must make a "good cause" finding and include in its publication of the final rule a statement explaining why there was no public participation in the process.

Judicial Review of Rule Making

Following the promulgation of a regulation by an administrative agency and its publication in the *Federal Register,* the regulation becomes law. Often, however, businesses and other parties being regulated may not be happy with a law that an agency promulgates. These disgruntled parties have two options. First, they may immediately bring an action in the federal district court to have the law invalidated. An alternative approach is just to ignore the law. When the agency tries to fine the party for violating the law, the party's defense would be that the rule was not valid. If the ALJ upholds the rule, the party may appeal the case to the federal district court and on through the appeals process.

In general, appellate courts have accepted an agency-promulgated regulation as law unless a business, other groups, or individuals affected can prove it is invalid for one of four reasons. One reason is that the congressional delegation of legislative authority in the enabling act was unconstitutional because it was too vague and did not properly limit the agency's actions in any way. A second claim is that an agency action violated a constitutional standard, such as the right to be free from unreasonable searches and seizures under the Fourth Amendment. For example, if an agency, such as OSHA, promulgated a rule that allowed its inspectors to search a business property at any time without permission from the owners and without an administrative search warrant, this law would be struck down as a violation of the Fourth Amendment.

A third alternative is to show that the act of an agency was beyond the scope of power granted to it by Congress in its enabling legislation. In other words, the agency passed a rule that it had no authority to mandate. Finally, a party could demonstrate that the agency did not follow the proper procedures in promulgating the rule. For example, the agency was required by its enabling statute to engage in formal rule making but instead followed informal rule-making procedures.

You are correct if you believe that these four circumstances seem highly unlikely. It is very unusual for a court to strike down an administrative rule. Despite the low success rate of such challenges, firms continue to challenge agency rules. For example, approximately 80 percent of the rules made by the EPA from 1987 through 1991 have been challenged in court. Even if such a challenge is not successful, it still buys time for the firm. The firm may be able to get a temporary injunction prohibiting enforcement of the law until there is a final decision in the case. Many times, the appeals process will last for years; the resulting delay can save a firm a substantial amount of money, especially when the cost of compliance is high.

Regulated Negotiation

The exceedingly large number of challenges to regulations, as well as a growing belief that structured bargaining among competing interest groups might be the most efficient way to develop rules, has stimulated a number of agencies to adopt a relatively new form of rule making, often referred to as reg-neg. Each concerned interest group and the agency itself sends a representative to bargaining sessions led by a mediator. After the parties achieve a consensus, that agreement is forwarded to the agency. The agency is then expected to publish the compromise as a proposed rule in the *Federal Register* and follow through with the requisite rule-making procedures. The agency, however, is not bound to do so. If it does not agree with the proposal the group negotiated, the agency is free to try to promulgate a completely different rule or a modification of the one obtained through the negotiation.

The reasoning behind reg-neg is similar to that supporting the increased use of mediation. If the parties can sit down to try to work out a compromise, that solution is much more likely to be accepted than one handed down by some authority. The parties who hammered out the agreement now have a stake in making it work because they helped to create it.

Admittedly, reg-neg is not possible in all situations. If, for example, there were an unmanageably large group of interests that would have to be represented, or if any possible compromise would come as a result of one group backing away from a fundamental principle, or if two groups feel so antagonistic toward each other that they are unable to sit down and talk rationally, reg-neg would probably not even be worth trying.

Problems Associated with Rule Making

Although there is an expediency associated with this process of rule making, critics are quick to point out that there are some problems with it. Agency employees are not subject to the same political pressures as legislators, but they are not necessarily unbiased "scientists." Many of the people with the necessary expertise to regulate specific areas come from the industry they are now going to be regulating. Many believe that it will be difficult for regulators to ignore their past and potential ties to industry and pass the regulations that are in the public interest, especially when the regulations would increase costs to the industry or are opposed by the industry for other reasons. When people are discussing an agency in which they believe this problem exists, they will often refer to the agency as being a "captured" agency. The counterargument is that those who have been deeply involved in an industry know it best.

Rule making in the environmental area is especially difficult, because there is so much uncertainty surrounding the causes and consequences of pollution. There is often a significant time lag between exposure and the resultant detrimental health effects or ecological changes, making it difficult to ascertain the impact of a given pollutant. There is very little agreement as to how much certainty is needed before a regulation should be imposed.

Even when we have a little knowledge about a single pollutant's effects, we know less about synergistic effects (i.e., the effects brought about by the interactions of various pollutants).

Another problem associated with environmental rule making is that although many of the costs of regulation are borne immediately, the benefits flow primarily to future generations. Thus, many people question how much the present generation can be asked to sacrifice for future generations. This question becomes complicated by the fact that sometimes those costs are borne by those with the least economic and political power.

Regulators in the environmental arena are confronted with a difficult task. They must balance the risk to society with the cost of expenditures for pollution-control equipment with respect to almost every standard they set. They know that almost every one of those standards is going to be challenged in court by the regulated industries, which will see the standards as too stringent, and the environmental groups, which will see them as too weak.

An issue that has been increasingly arising in debates over environmental policies is the impact that the costs of compliance will have on the competitiveness of U.S. firms in a global economy. Yet, the effects of pollution-control compliance on global competitiveness are unknown. We can gather data on the costs of pollution-control equipment in the United States, but we do not know how much other nations' industries spend. Nor do we know how much increased efficiency the pollution-control equipment generates.

As you will read in Chapter 11, differences in environmental regulation have become an issue in trade agreements. We know that some firms have left the United States to go to less developed countries, where there are less stringent pollution-control regulations. But not all firms that move do so just to avoid environmental regulations. Some may also be seeking cheaper labor or materials.

Finally, regulators must be sensitive to the role the economy plays in the public's willingness to accept or support environmental regulations. When the economy is flourishing and unemployment is low, there is much greater acceptance of regulations. When unemployment is high, people are much more reluctant to accept regulations that they believe might cause workers to lose their jobs and/or cause the prices of products to rise.

ADJUDICATION

In addition to rule making by state and federal administrative agencies, adjudication of individual cases is another important agency activity. The number of cases heard by ALJs is extremely high: in 1983, one-third more cases were referred to ALJs than were filed in the federal district courts. From the beginning of 2001 to the end of 2002, the EPA's Office of ALJs made more than 160 decisions and orders.[1] The APA again sets forth the steps for adjudication, which can be modified by an agency's enabling statute. APA Sections 554, 556, and 557 set out the minimum standards for adjudication whenever an agency's adjudication is "required by statute to be determined on the record after opportunity for an agency hearing."

Agency adjudication is generally preceded by an investigation and the filing of a complaint with an ALJ by the agency staff. The party against which the agency is taking the action is entitled to notice the time and place of the hearing, the authority the agency is relying on, and the "matters of fact and law asserted." A hearing is then conducted by the ALJ, after which an initial decision is issued. An appeal to the full commission or the head of an agency may then be filed. That decision may then be appealed to the circuit court of appeals. Figure 3-2 illustrates the steps of this administrative adjudication process.

The EPA (and approximately eight other federal agencies) has so many appeals that a special board has been set up within the agency to handle certain types of appeals. On March 1, 1992, the Environmental Appeals Board (EAB), a special three-person board, began operation to handle appeals of penalty decisions made by EPA ALJs and appeals of permit decisions and civil penalty decisions in the EPA's ten regions. This board was created in anticipation of a crush of environmental disputes. With over 100 appeals per year during the early 1990s, the administrator of the EPA already had been forced to delegate authority to senior attorneys in the agency to help decide appeals. In 2002, 50 published and unpublished orders were issued by the EAB.[2] RCRA, Toxic Substances Control Act (TSCA), and Federal Insecticide, Fungicide, and Rodenticide Act (FIFRA) issues constituted the majority of matters that were subject to a formal written opinion issued in 2000 by the EAB.[3] Today, the EAB's caseload consists primarily of appeals from permit decisions and civil penalty decisions. A substantial additional portion of the EAB's caseload consists of petitions for reimbursement of costs incurred in complying with cleanup orders issued under the Comprehensive Environmental Response, Compensation, and Liability Act (CERCLA) of 1980.[4]

The administrative adjudication process is extremely important because most agencies rely primarily on administrative actions to enforce their regulations. This enforcement strategy is especially true in the environmental arena. Administrative actions are often preferred to taking a violator to trial because administrative actions are generally quicker, less expensive, and less resource-intensive than a trial. An administrative proceeding may be handled by an agency employee, whereas to prosecute a violator in court, a federal agency must turn the case over to the Justice Department and a state agency must refer the case to the state attorney general.

As a result of an administrative action, an agency can issue a compliance order, which may require immediate action by a violator, or a timetable that must be followed in moving toward compliance. The order may contain daily penalties for noncompliance or include provisions for suspension or revocation of a violator's operating permit under appropriate circumstances.

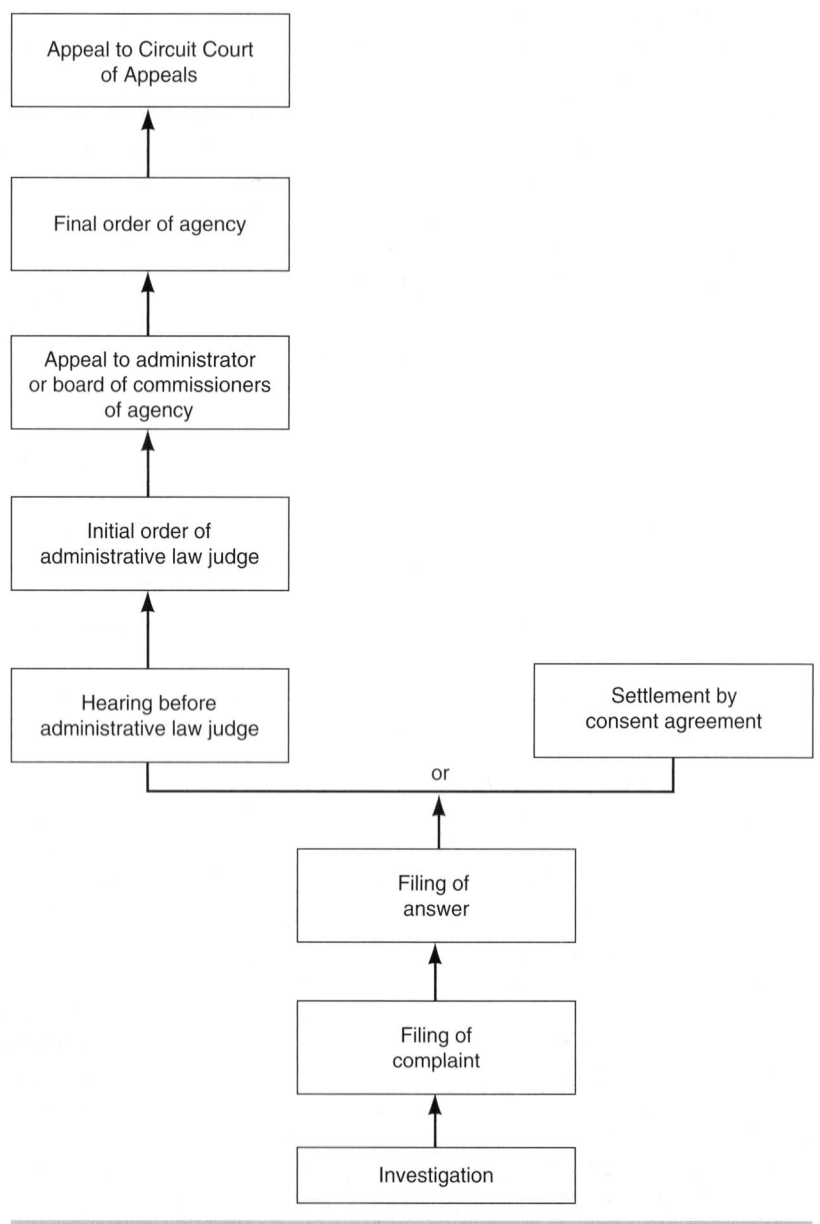

FIGURE 3-2   Steps in Administrative Adjudication

Administrative agencies may also issue corrective orders. These orders are comparable to court orders for specific performance. For example, a corrective order may require a violator that has released wastewater into a river to install equipment that would filter out the waste before the water is released.

Penalties for Noncompliance

Each of the environmental laws that you will be reading about contains provisions for administrative, civil, and criminal actions. In general, administrative penalties are less than civil and criminal penalties. By providing lesser penalties for administrative actions, violators are encouraged to settle early. In one EPA case, a violator was encouraged to settle for a $200 agency fine. The violator refused, and the case was turned over to the Justice Department. The federal district court awarded the statutory penalty of $10,000.[5] In April 1998, an EPA judge ordered DuPont to pay $1.89 million, the largest administrative penalty in history, for ignoring EPA orders to halt shipping pesticide with labels that do not warn the user to wear protective eyewear to prevent injury.[6]

In light of the substantial difference between administrative penalties and civil and criminal awards, it is not surprising that violators are often willing to settle for small administrative penalties. Table 3-1 summarizes the difference between judicial and administrative penalties assessed for fiscal years 1978 through 2002.

As Table 3-1 illustrates, even though the amount collected through administrative penalties is not as high as the amount from judicial awards, it is still significant. In fiscal year 2005, the agency issued 2,273 final administrative penalty orders and collected 27,000,000 in administrative penalties.[7]

Citizen Rewards

As you read more about specific environmental laws, you will discover that often violations are discovered not by the agencies but by the citizens.

TABLE 3-1   Penalty Assessments in Civil Cases Relating to Environmental Law, Fiscal Years 1978–2002

Fiscal Year	Civil Judicial	Administrative	Fiscal Year Total
1978	1,313,873	25,000	1,338,873
1979	4,028,469	56,800	4,085,269
1980	10,570,040	159,110	10,729,150
1994	65,635,930	48,021,941	113,657,871
1995	34,925,472	36,054,174	70,979,646
1996	66,254,451	29,996,478	96,250,929
1997	45,966,607	49,178,494	95,145,101
1998	63,531,731	28,263,762	91,795,493
1999	141,211,699	25,509,879	166,721,578
2000	54,851,765	25,509,879	80,361,644
2001	101,683,157	23,782,264	125,465,421
2002	55,571,404	25,766,401	81,337,805

Source: EPA. 1990. *Office of Enforcement and Compliance Monitoring Information Sheet* (Washington, D.C.: Government Printing Office); EPA, *Office of Enforcement and Compliance Assurance Accomplishments Report* (Various Fiscal Year Reports); *Enforcement and Compliance Program, Numbers at a Glance. http://www.epa.gov/compliance/resources/reports/endofyear/ eoy2002/5year.pdf* (October 9, 2003)

To motivate citizens, most federal and state agencies involved in environmental enforcement have reward programs to encourage citizens to bring forth evidence in cases of violations. The EPA, for example, administers the Superfund Citizen Award Provision, which pays up to $10,000 for information leading to a successful criminal prosecution.

Some citizens have started to take advantage of their ability to report violations to the EPA, and the EPA paid the first monetary awards under the CAA in February 1997.[8] The EPA awarded the maximum award of $10,000 to a citizen who learned that children were playing with bags of asbestos in an abandoned building. The citizen warned the children, contacted the local air pollution control agency, and provided other information about the large amount of asbestos improperly stored in the building. In addition, the EPA awarded three citizens $1,200 each for their assistance in a case involving a home air-conditioning service contractor who was illegally venting ozone-depleting CFCs.

ADMINISTRATIVE ACTIVITIES

Executive and independent agencies perform various less well-known but equally important tasks, including advising, conducting research, issuing permits, managing property, and providing information to regulated entities, as well as to the general public.

One of the most common ways individuals come into contact with agencies is when agencies advise businesses and individuals as to whether the agency considers an activity legal or illegal. Agencies also conduct studies of industry and markets. For example, OSHA and the Food and Drug Administration (FDA) conduct studies to determine safety in the workplace and whether drugs are harmful to the public. Agencies also devote much of their time to issuing licenses or permits. The EPA, for example, helps protect the environment by requiring certain environmentally sound activities before granting permits. Finally, agencies often are responsible for managing property.

Agencies also provide information to the general public on various matters through hot lines (Table 3-2), publications, and seminars. One of the more innovative ways the EPA provides information to regulated entities is through its Web-based compliance Assistance Centers. These centers were established in conjunction with industry, academic institutions, environmental groups, and other agencies. Each Web-based Center provides businesses, local governments, and federal facilities with information and guidance on environmental requirements and ways to save money through pollution prevention techniques. Information is provided on a sector-by-sector basis. To make use of these centers, a person would go to http://www.assistancecenters.net/, the home for Compliance Assistance Centers, and click on the sector about which they need information. They will be taken to a Web site that explains all the environmental regulations

TABLE 3-2 Environmental Hot Lines for Federal Government Agencies	
Consumer Product Safety Commission	(800) 638-2772
For information or to report a product with an actual or potential hazard	
National Institute for Occupational Safety and Health (NIOSH)	(800) 35-NIOSH
For questions concerning workplace health hazard evaluations	
National Response Center Hotline	(800) 424-8802
To report a release or spill of oil or hazardous waste materials anywhere nationwide	
Occupational Safety and Health Administration (OSHA)	(800) 321-OSHA
To report a fatality or imminent life-threatening situation; for general labor complaints contact the regional office	
U.S. Environmental Protection Agency (EPA) Safe Drinking Water Hotline	(800) 426-4791
For questions about drinking water standards and contaminants	
RCRA—Superfund Hotline	(800) 424-9346
For general information on Superfund sites and hazardous waste laws	
Emergency Planning and Community Right-to-Know	(800) 535-0202
For questions about the national right-to-know law and state and local emergency planning efforts	
U.S. Federal Bureau of Investigation	(800) 582-1766
To report potential criminal violations of environmental laws	

applicable to them in plain language, as well as links to other valuable Web sites and various Web-based tools such as compliance checklists.

LIMITATIONS ON AGENCY POWERS

STATUTORY LIMITATIONS

Certain federal statutes restrict the power of administrative agencies. One of these limiting statutes, the APA, has been discussed previously. Its rule-making procedures, for example, mandate public involvement. Two other acts are especially helpful in keeping agency action open to the public, preventing secret, arbitrary, or capricious activity: the Freedom of Information Act of 1966, as amended in 1974 and 1976, and the Government in Sunshine Act.

The Freedom of Information Act requires federal agencies to publish in the *Federal Register* places where the public can get information from agencies. The act requires similar publication of proposed rules and policy statements. Finally, it requires agencies to make such items as staff manuals and interpretations of policies available for copying to the public, upon request. The Government in Sunshine Act requires agency business meetings to be open to the public if the agency is headed by a collegiate body. A collegiate body consists of two or more persons, the majority of whom are appointed by the president with the advice and consent of the Senate. This open-meeting requirement applies only when a quorum is present. The law also requires agencies to keep records of closed meetings.

In addition, the Federal Tort Claim Act of 1946 allows private citizens to sue the government for damages caused by improper acts of employees of federal administrative agencies. The act forces an agency to waive sovereign immunity for its tortious actions and those of its employees. Tortious actions under this act include assault, battery, abuse of prosecution, and false arrest. For example, if an inspector from the EPA illegally enters a business property and pushes the owner who is trying to block the door, and if the owner is injured as a result of the assault, the EPA inspector, as well as the agency, may be held liable.

INSTITUTIONAL LIMITATIONS

Executive Branch

The executive branch limits the power of administrative agencies through (1) the power of the president to appoint the heads of the agencies, (2) the power of the OMB to recommend a fiscal year budget for each agency, and (3) the power of the president to issue executive orders. As already discussed, the president appoints the head of each agency, as well as some lower-level heads of departments and divisions that do not fall under the federal civil service system. Presidential appointees usually have the same philosophical bent as the chief executive and are often of the same party. Each president thus gains some influence over both independent and executive agencies.

As you will see in greater detail later in this chapter, the chief executive's ability to appoint an agency's head and to make recommendations can have a powerful, long-lasting effect on an agency. It is the agency's head that sets the tenor of the agency. For example, the head of the agency decides whether the agency is going to pursue violations of regulations aggressively. The importance of the heads of agencies is reflected by the vigor with which interested parties lobby the president when he is making such appointments.

The executive branch also restricts agencies through the OMB. This office reviews agencies' budgets and makes recommendations with respect to their needs for funding. Two of the most powerful agencies with respect to enforcing environmental policies—the EPA and the Council on Environmental Quality (CEQ)—were forced to curtail their actions severely as a result of President Ronald Reagan's budget and personnel decisions for 1980 through 1988.

The issuance of executive orders can also have a major impact on agencies' activities. One of the most significant of such orders is Executive Order 12291, issued by President Reagan on February 17, 1981. This order mandates that a cost–benefit analysis be performed by executive agencies for every regulation they enact.

Soon after taking office in 1989, President George W. Bush found an additional way for the executive branch to influence administrative agencies. He created the White House Council on Competitiveness. Headed by Vice President Dan Quayle and consisting of several high-ranking cabinet officials, the council ostensibly was designed to enable the administration to "speak with one voice on issues involving international competitiveness."[9] During the summer of 1990, President Bush gave the council a mandate to push for deregulation. The council was to review new regulations; any that would generate higher costs for businesses than benefits for the rest of society were to be blocked or revised.

Although some Democrats labeled the Council on Competitiveness "sinister," and others claimed its actions were "Orwellian" and "nothing short of treason and perhaps illegal," defenders of the council claimed the body has clear authority to review regulations under Executive Order 12291. Regardless of one's attitude toward the legitimacy of the council, no one would attempt to deny its impact. Some claim it became a forum for appeals on any rules that were the subject of disputes between the EPA and other agencies. The council, either alone or in concert with other agencies, helped to kill a proposal to require recycling at municipal incinerators, softened a plan to improve visibility at the Grand Canyon by reducing sulfur dioxides from a nearby power plant, and postponed an EPA plan to discourage the incineration of lead batteries, a source of toxic pollution.[10]

Legislative Branch

Congress limits the authority of administrative agencies through its (1) oversight power, (2) investigative power, (3) power to terminate an agency or amend its enabling statute, (4) power to approve or disapprove budgets, (5) power to advise and consent on the president's nominations for heads of administrative agencies, and (6) rarely used power under the 1996 Congressional Review Act (CRA) to overturn an administrative regulation within 60 days of its promulgation.

When Congress creates an agency, it delegates its legislative power over a narrow area of commerce or human rights. Through one of its oversight committees, each year Congress uses its oversight power to determine whether the agency has been carrying out its mandated function. If, for example, the House Energy and Commerce Committee, through the investigations of its subcommittee on Consumer, Finance, and Telecommunications, finds that the Securities and Exchange Commission (SEC) is not enforcing laws against insider trading and fraud, the committee orders the SEC to do so. As we shall discuss, during the 1980s, there were numerous committee hearings at which the head of the EPA was called to testify as to why the agency did not appear to be fulfilling the tasks assigned to it.

In 1996, Congress passed a statute that has the potential to significantly restrain the activities of regulatory agencies: the CRA. This law, in effect, gives Congress a "veto power" over every single regulation agencies pass.

Under this statute, a regulation cannot take effect until at least 60 working days have passed since the regulation was promulgated. If, during that 60-day period, a majority of the members of Congress pass a resolution of disapproval of the rule, and either the president signs it or Congress overrules his veto of it, the regulation is nullified.

Although the CRA appears to have the potential to affect agency regulations substantially, only six rules have ever been brought up for discussion under this law, two of which are related to the environment: OSHA's rule on occupational exposure to methylene chloride and the FWS's rule on the importation of sport-hunted polar bear trophies from Canada. Only one regulation has actually been struck down under the act: a regulation adopted by OSHA in 2001 that required most U.S. employers to set up programs to address work-related injuries once workers are determined to have such injuries and to redesign workplaces and compensate workers for repetitive motion injuries.

Since 2001, both political parties have been using the CRA with increased frequency, especially with regard to environmental issues. For example, Democratic Senator Lieberman considered using CRA to challenge some of the Bush administration's environmental decisions related to arsenic standards in water, mining regulations, and forest road construction rules. Republican Senator Inhofe similarly considered using CRA to weaken a new EPA regulation that limits emissions from heavy-duty diesel engines and lowers the sulfur content of diesel fuel. Neither senator gained the support needed to invoke CRA, but CRA remains a powerful parliamentary tool for friends and foes of the environment alike.

The greatest limitation on agency power by Congress lies in its right to approve or disapprove any agency's budget. If Congress disagrees with the agency's action or the OMB's proposed budget, it can slash the budget, raise the budget, or refuse to budget the agency. The latter action shuts the agency down.

Judicial Branch

As explained earlier in this chapter, the courts can curb excesses of the administrative agencies' rule-making and adjudication functions by reversing or modifying such actions. The U.S. Supreme Court case of *Citizens of Overton Park v. Volpe*[11] clearly stated that all agency action is subject to judicial review unless there is a statutory prohibition or "agency action is committed to agency discretion by law." This agency discretion exception has been interpreted very narrowly. The scope of review set forth in this case is that agency action must be set aside if it is arbitrary or capricious, unconstitutional, outside the scope of the agency's authority, or in violation of procedural requirements.

The power of the judiciary to control the rule-making actions of administrative agencies was demonstrated by a recent U.S. court of appeals ruling in *AFL-CIO v. OSHA*.[12] In that case, OSHA had undertaken its most extensive rule-making effort ever, promulgating permissible exposure limits (PELs) for 428 toxic substances. OSHA had promulgated only 24 substance-specific health regulations by 1989. In an effort to speed up its rule making, OSHA attempted to engage in "generic rule making."

Section 3(8) of the Occupational Safety and Health Act (OSH Act) defines an "occupational health and safety standard" as "a standard which requires conditions or the adoption or use of one or more practices, means, methods, operations, or processes, reasonably necessary or appropriate to provide safe or healthful employment and places of employment." The Supreme Court interpreted that provision to require that, before the promulgation of any new permanent health standard, OSHA make a threshold finding that a significant risk of material health impairment exists at the current levels of exposure to the toxic substance in question, and therefore, a new, lower threshold is reasonably necessary or appropriate to provide safe or healthful employment. Any subsequent standard the EPA promulgates must also comply with Section 6(b) 5 of the act, which requires that a standard adopted must prevent material impairment of health "to the extent feasible."

Industry petitioners argued that OSHA's use of generic findings, its lumping together of so many substances in one rule, and the short time for public comment created a record that was inadequate to support the rule making. The union argued that the procedure resulted in standards that were inadequate to protect employee health.

The Court, in looking at OSHA's record, agreed with the industry's position. The Court said that OSHA had a responsibility to quantify, or explain to a reasonable degree, the risk posed by each toxic substance. OSHA's discussions of individual substances contained summaries of various studies of that substance and the health effects found at various levels of exposure, but they made no estimate of the risk of experiencing those health effects; instead, OSHA provided a conclusory statement that the new limit would reduce the "significant" risk of material health effects, without any explanation of how the agency determined what was significant. There were no reasons given for why the particular standards were set. For most standards, a few studies were cited, with no explanation of why the study mandated the standard. For some, no studies were cited. The Court also faulted OSHA for failing to establish the economic and technical feasibility for each standard.

Thus, although the courts do not tend to scrutinize carefully the evidence agencies rely on, agencies must act in accordance with their statutory mandates. As the Supreme Court said in *AFL-CIO v. OSHA*, an agency cannot shortcut the proper rule-making procedures by attempting to combine multiple substances in a single rule. In addition to demonstrating the courts' power over agencies, this case also points out one of the dilemmas agencies sometimes face. They are often given a tremendous number of standards to set, and to save valuable time, they may wish to act with less than the maximum possible attainable evidence. Yet, in their haste to regulate, they may find that they have overstepped their authority.

IMPORTANT AGENCIES AFFECTING THE ENVIRONMENT

Currently, more than 100 federal agencies are in operation, as well as countless state agencies. Often, when there is a federal agency, there will also be comparable state agencies to which the federal agency will delegate much of its work. For example, the most important federal agency affecting environmental matters is the EPA. Every state has a state environmental agency to which the federal EPA delegates primary authority for enforcing environmental protection laws. However, if at any time the state agency fails to enforce these laws, the federal EPA will step in to enforce them.

This oversight authority of the federal EPA was reinforced in a 5 to 4 decision by the U.S. Supreme Court in early 2004. In a dispute between the federal EPA and Alaska's Department of Environmental Conservation over the conditions necessary for the world's biggest zinc mine to expand its operations, the high court upheld the EPA's decision to overrule the state's acceptance of the mine's proposed technology. Under the CAA, the mine was required to control its new emissions with the "best available control technology." The state agency was willing to accept the mine's proposal to install a form of technology that was less expensive but not as efficient. The federal EPA overruled the state agency's decision on grounds that the more expensive technology was more efficient and has the "best available control technology." In upholding the EPA's decision, Justice Ginsburg stated that Congress had "expressly endorsed an expansive surveillance role for the EPA," which it properly carried out by holding that Alaska's approval of the less effective technology was unreasonable.[13]

Because the EPA is the primary agency responsible for enforcement of environmental laws, we devote the greatest attention to that agency. Other agencies that affect the environment are briefly introduced, either in text or in Table 3-6, which appears later in this chapter.

EXECUTIVE VERSUS INDEPENDENT AGENCIES

Agencies are classified as either executive or independent. Executive agencies are sometimes seen as less stable in terms of their regulatory policies because the administrators of these agencies, who are appointed by the president with the advice and consent of the Senate, may be discharged by the president at any time, for any reason. In general, whenever a new president is elected, he or she will place his or her appointees in charge of executive agencies. These agencies are usually located within the executive branch, in one of the cabinet-level departments. Hence, executive agencies are often referred to as cabinet-level agencies. An example of a traditional executive agency is the Federal Aviation Agency, located within the Department of Transportation.

Although an administrator usually leads executive agencies, a board of commissioners, one of whom is the chair, is generally in charge of an independent agency. The president also appoints the commissioners of independent agencies with the advice and consent of the Senate, but these commissioners serve fixed terms and cannot be removed except for cause. No more than a simple majority can be members of one political party. Serving fixed terms is said to make these agencies less accountable to the will of the executive. These agencies are generally not located within any department. Examples of independent agencies are the FTC and the ICC.

One other difference between these two types of agencies is the scope of their regulatory authority. Executive agencies tend to have responsibility for making rules covering a broad spectrum of industries and activities. Independent agencies, often called commissions, tend to have more narrow authority over many facets of a particular industry, focusing on such activities as rate making and licensing. Executive agencies have a tendency to focus more on "social" regulation, whereas independent agencies are more often focused on "economic" regulation.

HYBRID AGENCIES

Some agencies do not fall clearly into one classification or the other. Created as one type of agency, the body may share characteristics of the other. The EPA, for example, was created as an independent agency, not located within any department of the executive branch. Yet, a single administrator who serves at the whim of the president heads it. During the early 1990s, in fact, there were discussions of the need to transform the EPA into a cabinet-level executive agency. (These initiatives did not get beyond the discussion stage.) Another example is the "independent" Federal Energy Regulation Commission, which has the typical structure of an independent agency, yet is located within the Department of Energy.

THE ENVIRONMENTAL PROTECTION AGENCY

History

By a presidential reorganization order, the EPA was created in 1970 as an independent agency. This new agency was to take over functions that were formerly carried out by the Federal Water Quality Administration in the Department of the Interior; the National Air Pollution Control Administration and the FDA in the Department of Health, Education, and Welfare (HEW); and the Atomic Energy Commission, among others. Its mission was to control and abate pollution in the areas of air, water, solid waste, pesticides, radiation, and toxic substances. Its mandate was to mount an integrated, coordinated attack on environmental pollution in cooperation with state and local governments. In 1973, the EPA had 8,200 employees. By 1982, it had grown to be one of the largest federal agencies, with 12,623 employees, and by 1999, it had nearly 19,000 employees. It has also been one of the most controversial agencies, having most of its actions criticized by either business groups or environmentalists. The EPA has often been in conflict with the executive branch and with Congress.

The EPA's first head was William Ruckelshaus, under whose 3-year tenure, the agency served as a vigorous enforcer of air-quality and water-quality standards. As Congress passed more and more environmental regulations, the agency expanded and was given increasing amounts of responsibility. In September 1973, Ruckelshaus was succeeded by Russell Train, who ran the agency during 3 more years of growth. Next, under the leadership of Carter appointee Douglas Costle, the EPA continued to grow as the new administrator attempted to streamline its regulatory process and make the agency more cost-effective.

President Reagan's tenure demonstrated how effectively an agency could be gutted by an executive hostile to the agency's mission. During his first 3 years in office, Reagan cut the EPA's research budget by 50 percent, cuts from which the agency has not yet recovered. He also appointed Anne Burford (then Anne Gorsuch) to head the agency. Burford requested budget cuts and reduced the number of enforcement actions. Fewer new regulations were issued under her leadership, and many longtime employees of the agency resigned. Conflicts arose between Congress and the agency, as Congress tried to push the agency back onto its former course; between October 1981 and July 1982, officials of the agency were called to testify before congressional oversight committees more than 70 times. Alleged mismanagement at the EPA continued until finally, in February 1983, several top EPA officials were fired.[14]

In March 1983, Anne Burford was replaced by former administrator William Ruckelshaus, followed in 1984 by Lee Thomas, who began once again to increase the number of agency enforcement orders and environmental regulations. Thomas was followed by William Reilly, the former head of the Conservation Foundation and World Wildlife Federation. The EPA's budget improved somewhat under the Bush administration, although the agency's 1990 budget, in constant dollars, actually increased by less than 20 percent over 1972 levels. This increase, however, is very modest indeed in light of all of the new environmental regulations for which the EPA has been given responsibility since 1972. If we exclude the staff employed under the Superfund, the EPA's staff was actually smaller at the end of the 1980s than it was at its inception. In September 1990, the Science Advisory Board made a report to the director of the EPA to help the agency become more effective. The SAB made ten recommendations in this report, which are listed in Table 3-3. You can read these recommendations and decide for yourself whether the agency has actually been guided by them.

In January 1993, President Clinton nominated Carol M. Browner to head the EPA in what was hoped to be an era of greater cooperation among

TABLE 3-3   Recommendations of the Science Advisory Board

1. EPA should target its environmental protection effort on the basis of opportunities for the greatest risk reduction. Because this country already has taken the most obvious actions to address the most obvious environmental problems, the EPA needs to set priorities for future actions, so the agency takes advantage of the best opportunities for reducing the most serious remaining risks.

2. EPA should attach as much importance to reducing ecological risk as it does to reducing human health risk. Because productive natural ecosystems are essential to human health and to sustainable, long-term economic growth and because they are intrinsically valuable in their own right, the EPA should be as concerned about protecting ecosystems as it is about protecting human health.

3. EPA should improve the data and analytical methods that support the assessment, comparison, and reduction of different environmental risks. Although setting priorities for national environmental protection efforts will always involve subjective judgments and uncertainty, EPA should work continually to improve the scientific data and analytical methodologies that underpin those judgments and help reduce their uncertainty.

4. EPA should reflect risk-based priorities in its strategic planning processes. The agency's long-range plans should be driven not so much by past risk-reduction efforts or by existing programmatic structures but by ongoing assessments of remaining environmental risks, the explicit comparison of those risks, and the analysis of opportunities available for reducing risks.

5. EPA should reflect risk-based priorities in its budget process. Although the EPA's budget priorities are determined to a large extent by the different environmental laws that the agency implements, it should use whatever discretion it has to focus budget resources at those environmental problems that pose the most serious risks.

6. EPA—and the nation as a whole—should make greater use of all the tools to reduce risk. Although the nation has had substantial success in reducing environmental risks through the use of government-mandated end-of-the-pipe controls, the extent and complexity of future risks will necessitate the use of a much broader array of tools, including market incentives and information.

7. EPA should emphasize pollution prevention as the preferred option for reducing risk. By encouraging actions that prevent pollution from being generated in the first place, EPA will help reduce the costs, intermediate transfers of pollution, and residual risks so often associated with end-of-pipe controls.

8. EPA should increase its efforts to integrate environmental considerations into broader aspects of public policy in as fundamental a manner as are economic concerns. Other federal agencies often affect the quality of the environment (e.g., through the implementation of tax, energy, agricultural, and international policy), and the EPA should work to ensure that environmental considerations are integrated, where appropriate, into the policy deliberations of such agencies.

9. EPA should work to improve public understanding of environmental risks and train a professional workforce to help reduce them. The improved environmental literacy of the general public, together with an expanded and better-trained technical workforce, will be essential to the nation's success at reducing environmental risks in the future.

10. EPA should develop improved analytical methods to value natural resources and to account for long-term environmental effects in its economic analyses. Because traditional methods of economic analysis tend to undervalue ecological resources and fail to adequately treat questions of intergenerational equity, EPA should develop and implement innovative approaches to economic analysis that will address these shortcomings.

Source: EPA Relative Risk Reduction Strategies Committee. 1992. *Reducing Risk: Setting Priorities and Strategies for Environmental Protection* (Washington, D.C.: Science Advisory Board).

Congress, the executive branch, and the agency. Browner was the former head of the Florida EPA, as well as the legislative director for Vice President Gore when he was a senator. At Browner's confirmation hearing, Max Baucus, chair of the Senate Environment and Public Works Committee, stated, "For the past several years, Congress and the Administration have been paralyzed by grid-lock, particularly when it comes to environmental policy. . . . Now the American people expect all that to change."[15] The only promise that the new administrator seemed to give was to provide a regulatory climate not hostile to business. Depicted as practicing a pragmatic, cost-conscious brand of environ-mentalism, she may have been chosen for her appearance of "balance." By not being clearly aligned with either environmental or business extremists, she may have been perceived as being able to balance the interests of the two groups and thereby turn the agency into a more effective regulator. She claimed that her experience with the Florida EPA had taught her that we can "ease the regulatory burden on business without compromising the environment."

Evidence of Browner's intent to do just that came from her Common Sense Initiative (CSI), launched in July 1994 and ended in December 1998. The initiative was her attempt to improve environmental regulations and stream-line permitting, while developing antipollution alternatives, such as prevention and new environmental technologies through a consensus of representatives of affected interests. Under the initiative, the EPA brought together represen-tatives from six industrial sectors and attempted to forge consensus over inno-vations in environmental management and policy. Representatives from these sectors reflected the range of affected interests including industry, labor, and environmentalists. During the 4 years of the program existence, however, only about five of the approximately 30 recommendations that came out of the var-ious CSI subcommittees resulted in any revisions of EPA regulations.

In March 1994, the EPA adopted a "place-based" or "community-based" strategy. This strategy is an effort to see how the EPA could initiate or support cross-media activities designed for specific places. The idea is to bring together many stakeholders to design smarter, more effective, multimedia approaches to complex problems that defied satisfactory management through traditional statute-driven regulations. The role of the EPA in these situations would be as a leader, partner, and enabler, primarily acting as an enabler, focusing on capacity building and indirect support to the states through flexible grants, environmental information and monitoring systems, science, and technical assistance.

In April 1995, a report by the National Academy of Public Administration, entitled *Setting Priorities, Getting Results: A New Direction for EPA,*[16] was released, recommending that the agency "hand more responsibility and decision-making authority over to the states and localities" and that a "new partnership needs to be formed, one based on 'accountable devolution' of national programs and on a reduction in EPA oversight when it is not needed." The report also recommended that the agency begin work on a reorganization plan that would "break down the internal walls between the Agency's major media program offices for air, water, wastes, and toxic substances."

The EPA offices had, in fact, already been instructed to examine whether they needed to reorganize to better meet the needs of their constituencies, and the offices submitted their reorganization plans by January 1996. By mid-1996, the EPA was still a much more flexible agency than it had been 2 years earlier, and it appears that the agency will continue evolving in the same direction. The Office of Reinvention, created to "promote innovation to achieve greater and more cost-effective public health and environmental protection," encourages the EPA to remain continually flexible.[17] The EPA is currently focusing its reinvention efforts on five key areas: building stronger partnerships, offering more flexibility to obtain greater environmental results, providing greater public access to environmental information, expanding compliance assistance, and cutting red tape and paperwork. For example, the National Environmental Performance Partnership System (NEPPS) was created because the EPA recognized that environmental progress is best achieved when the state and federal programs work together. The states and the EPA develop performance partnership agreements based on comprehensive assessments of state environmental problems. By 2000, 35 states had signed performance partnership agreements with the EPA and 45 have "opted to consolidate EPA grants."[18] Table 3-4 summarizes the various changes implemented through the reinvention program.

The Office of Policy, Economics, and Innovation (OPEI) replaced the Office of Reinvention in July 1999. OPEI was given six specific roles within the EPA:

1. To encourage integrated environmental strategies
2. To serve as a catalyst and champion new ideas
3. To identify emerging issues
4. To improve economic analysis and tools
5. To address the special needs of small businesses, local governments, and nonprofit organizations
6. To provide leadership for regulatory management evaluation[19]

In April 2000, OPEI released a report documenting the history of innovation at the EPA. The report noted several successes in innovation, including the development of clean air markets, reform of Superfund cleanups, Brownfield revitalization, the development of 20 projects under Project XL, with 30 more on the way, partnerships with states, communities, and industry, and the expansion of the Toxics Release Inventory (TRI).[20] In its proposed 2000 to 2005 Strategic Plan, the EPA set 10 goals for itself to start the 21st century:

1. Clean air
2. Clean water
3. Safe food
4. Preventing pollution and reducing risk in communities, homes, workplaces, and ecosystems
5. Better waste management, restoration of contaminated waste sites, and emergency response

6. Reduction of global and cross-border environmental risks
7. Quality environmental information
8. Sound science, improved understanding of environmental risk, and greater innovation to address environmental problems
9. A credible deterrent to pollution and greater compliance with the law
10. Effective management[21]

TABLE 3-4   Changes Underway: A Snapshot of Reinvention

Attribute	Reform Effort	Results
Flexibility with accountability	Common sense initiatives	Over 40 projects testing industry-by-industry approaches to environmental regulation
	Project XL	Three projects using alternative regulatory approaches
	Brownfields	Over 70 communities cleaning up abandoned or idled industrial and commercial sites
	Permit improvements	Streamlined administrative processes, flexible permit approaches, and increased public participation
Better access to public information	One-stop reporting	11 states developing and testing integrated environmental reporting systems
Strong partnerships	National Environmental Performance Partnership System (NEPPS)	Performance Partnership Agreements with nearly half the states
	Voluntary programs	Over 7,000 companies voluntarily improving environmental performance
Easier compliance with environmental laws	Compliance Assistance Centers	Four centers operating to help small businesses better access and understand environmental requirements
	Environmental Leadership Program	New mechanism to encourage and recognize strong compliance
Less red tape	Line-by-line review of regulations	Total regulatory burden cut by nearly 16 million hours

Source: EPA. 1997. *EPA Strategic Plan http://www.epa.gov/ocfopage/plan/epastrat.pdf*, 10.

OPEI continues to play an important role in encouraging innovation. Beginning in 2002 and continuing today, the OPEI has sponsored an annual grant project to support innovation by state environmental regulatory agencies. As of October 2006, the agency had given out approximately $5 million in grant money to states. Projects funded included 14 for development of Environmental Results Programs, eight related to Environmental Management Systems (EMSs) and permitting, five created or enhanced Performance-Based Environmental Leadership programs, two were for Watershed-based permitting, and one was for permit process streamlining through innovative information technology applications.[22]

In January 2001, President George W. Bush nominated Christine Todd Whitman, former New Jersey governor, to be the administrator of the EPA. In her Senate confirmation hearing, Whitman mentioned five principles she sees as key to the EPA's future. First, cooperation among all stakeholders is a main goal, as it was under Browner's tenure. Second, flexibility in solutions to environmental problems will be stressed, and state and local authority will be respected. Third, the EPA will place a greater emphasis on market-based incentives. Fourth, continued reliance on strong science, rather than politics, will be key to the future of the EPA. Finally, incentives for compliance will be implemented, while maintaining penalties for noncompliance.

Although brief, Whitman's tenure as head of the EPA was fraught with challenges. Whitman appeared to be as surprised as the general public to learn that President Bush had withdrawn his support of the Kyoto Protocol and regulating carbon dioxide emissions from electrical power-generating plants. Whitman's surprise foreshadowed the EPA's decreased role in the decision-making process on many important environmental issues. The Army COE, for example, issued "no net loss" rules for wetlands without consulting the EPA. Similarly, the corporate average fuel economy (CAFE) standards were sent to the National Highway Traffic Safety Administration (NHTSA) for review, without EPA input.

Environmentalists tend to be most critical of the New Source Review standards (see Chapter 5). The new standards are counter to Whitman's fifth key principle to the EPA's future, namely, maintaining penalties for noncompliance. At the urging of Vice President Dick Cheney, the EPA de-emphasized government lawsuits as an enforcement tool of the New Source Review in favor of voluntary compliance. Protesting the EPA's declining ability to enforce environmental regulations, Eric Schaeffer, the former EPA director of civil enforcement, resigned his position.

Whitman's leadership was not without its successes. She received high praise from environmentalists for her implementation of regulations, issued in the last days of the Clinton administration, to reduce sulfur emissions from diesel fuel, despite harsh criticisms from senators who threatened to invoke the CRA. In an even larger victory, the EPA ordered GE to pay $500 million for the dredging of PCB's in the Hudson River, which GE actively polluted for years.

In June 2003, Whitman resigned as EPA Administrator, citing the desire to be near her husband in New Jersey, and was replaced by Mike Leavitt, the three-term Governor of Utah who had been praised for his smart growth plans to combat urban sprawl, but strongly criticized for his ties to the oil, gas, timber, and mining industries. During his tenure as governor, Leavitt secretly struck a deal with the Bush administration, reversing a Clinton era policy that had protected six million acres of wilderness by opening the land to mining, clear-cutting, oil and gas drilling, and road building. Leavitt was also a major proponent of building a highway through wetlands and fragile shore areas along the Great Salt Lake, and it took the 10th Circuit Court of Appeals to stop the project. The highway project would have been in violation of the CWA, the very same act that, as EPA Administrator, Leavitt is responsible for enforcing. Leavitt did not make any friends among environmentalists when he announced that Bush's reelection in 2004 was a "mandate" for Bush's environmental agenda.

After 1 year on the job, Leavitt did not impress many observers of the EPA. The Property and Environmental Research Center (PERC), a group that encourages environmental policy based on free-market incentives and creative solutions rather than regulatory mandates, gave the Bush administration's approach to air quality, for which Leavitt was responsible, a grade of F and a C for overall environmental policies.[23]

A study by two very different groups, Center for American Progress and OMB Watch, likewise rated Leavitt and the agency poorly, finding that industry special interests have been given *carte blanche* to rewrite air pollution regulations to the detriment of public health. Another study by OMB Watch found that under Leavitt's watch, the EPA "shows a pattern of placing corporate interests over the public interest" and that the EPA had failed to achieve 73 percent of its "benchmarks" for cleaning up the environment that the agency announced in December 2003, just after Leavitt took office.[24] Leavitt served a mere 13 months, before being appointed Secretary of Health and Human Services.

Stephen Johnson, former Deputy Administrator of the EPA, was appointed acting administrator, pending his confirmation. His nomination was seen as *relatively* uncontroversial, as he had a 24-year record as a civil servant within the EPA. However, some members of the Senate Environment Committee attempted to use the nomination process as an attempt to get the nominee to provide them with information related to several to EPA's decisions on several controversial matters. Such documents would have been highly relevant to the nomination because the nominee was involved in these decisions, which some believed involved a weakening of environmental protections. Rather than encouraging the nominee to be forthcoming with the information, however, the president made a recess appointment of Johnson to the post, thereby circumventing the Senate confirmation process.

It is too soon to make a real assessment of Johnson's tenure, but one recurrent criticism of the EPA under all three of the most recent administrators is increased secrecy with which the EPA is acting, and the secrecy refers both to keeping secrets from Congress, a body which is supposed to have oversight authority over the agency, and secrecy from the general public. In 2005, the agency in 2005 proposed two different cutbacks in information available to the public from its landmark TRI. Since then, the changes have been opposed by the Society of Environmental Journalists, the Republican-controlled House of Representatives, and 23 of the 50 states, among others. In July 2006, the EPA's own Science Advisory Board went public with its criticism of the changes, saying that the TRI "was widely used as a scientific tool to identify pollution problems and evaluate the effectiveness of pollution control efforts"[25] and that it was "concerned about the potential negative impacts of these changes on scientific research."[26] But the EPA administrator held fast to his decision. Thus, it seems clear that Johnson does not intend to oversee a more open agency. Johnson has also been criticized by the Science Advisory Board for his failure to follow their advice regarding particulate standards. He received further criticism in 2006 for being the featured guest at an intimate Denver Republican fund-raiser attended by representatives of industries regulated by his agency.[27] Johnson was criticized by environmentalists in 2007 for dragging his feet in implementing an April 2, 2007 Supreme Court decision that found the EPA can set standards for vehicle exhaust under the Clean Air Act—if he found the emissions endanger public health.

Structure of the EPA

When the EPA was created, the agency was structured to bring regulatory authority over all forms of pollution control within one federal body—research, standard setting, monitoring, enforcement, and policy setting. This integrated management ideal, however, did not materialize, partly because of the agency's structure and partly because of its tremendous size. Basically, the EPA is headed by an administrator who is responsible for overall policy setting. The agency has a deputy administrator who helps the administrator. Figure 3-3 diagrams the structure of the agency.

As with other agencies, the EPA also has an office of ALJs. These ALJs, like others in their profession, are fiercely independent and do not always side with the EPA's enforcement officers. The EPA is frequently represented before these justices by attorneys from the DOJ's Land and Natural Resources Division.

Finally, the EPA has 10 regional offices throughout the country. The regions are illustrated in Figure 3-4, and the offices are listed in Table 3-5. Many of these offices are staffed with competent employees concerned about the environment and skeptical of industry. Unlike many other government agencies, the EPA does not have a substantial number of employees who come from industry.

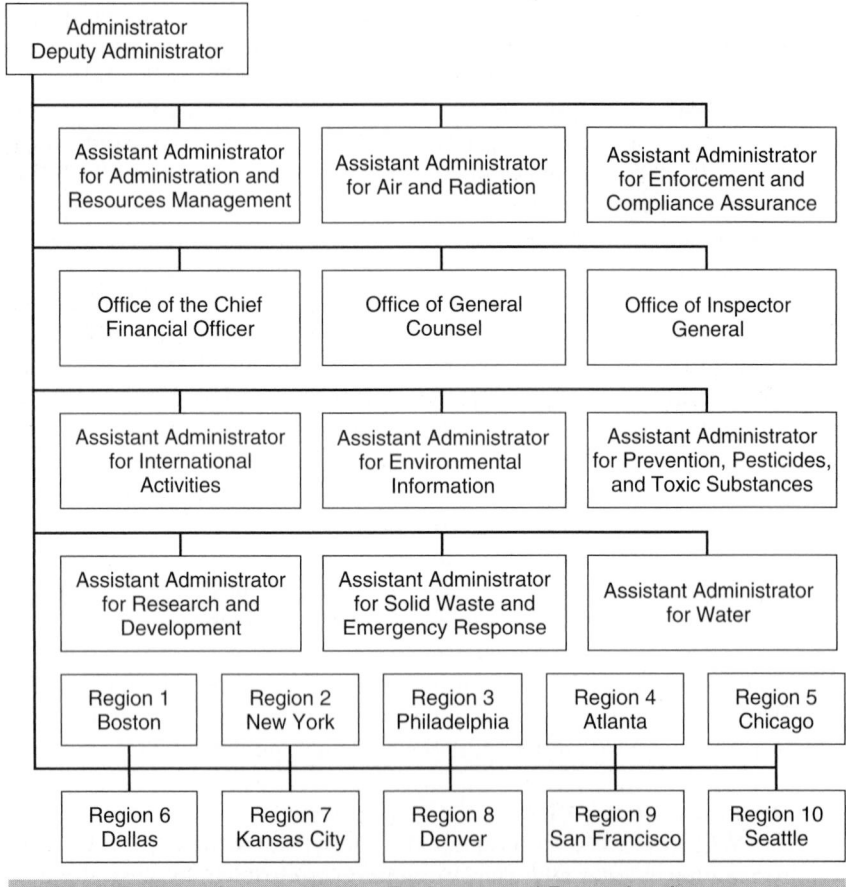

FIGURE 3-3   Structure of the Environmental Protection Agency

INTERAGENCY COOPERATION

One of the ways the EPA can be more effective is to coordinate its enforcement efforts better, not just within the agency itself but with other agencies as well. The EPA's 1997 Strategic Plan states that the EPA must work closely with approximately 20 other federal agencies to ensure that the agency's resources are directed in a way that complements federal initiatives and supports the achievement of common goals.[28] A joint venture with OSHA proved to be fairly effective. During the spring of 1991, agents from the two agencies jointly conducted surprise inspections at 29 of the nation's 140 hazardous waste incinerators run by some of the biggest corporations. Because of the sweep, corporations were charged with 395 violations of federal standards. The EPA referred 52 violations to state authorities for enforcement actions, and OSHA assessed fines totaling $92,220 on incinerator operators. Perhaps fear of these new, coordinated sweeps may make plant operators a little more concerned about following federal health, safety, and environmental laws.

FIGURE 3-4   EPA Regions

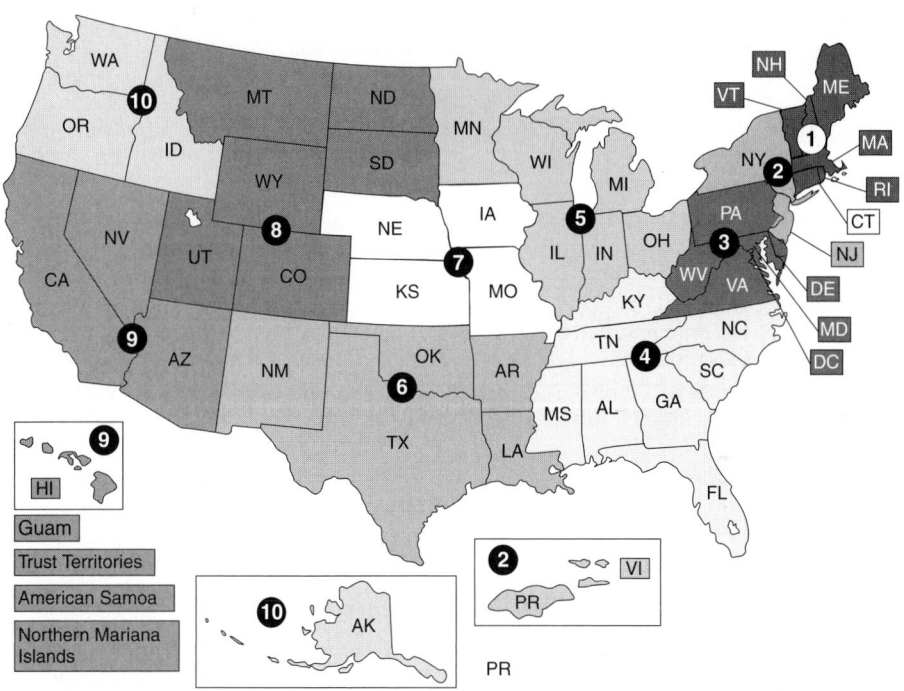

Source: EPA, http://www.epa.gov/epahome/locate2.htm

Such cooperative ventures are also being successfully undertaken with state agencies. For example, in December 1995, the cooperative efforts of the EPA's Criminal Task Force Investigation Division, the Texas Environmental Task Force, the Texas Parks and Wildlife Department, and the Texas Natural Resource Conservation Commission led to the 51-month incarceration of a violator of hazardous waste regulations. The violator Reginald Gist had been repeatedly notified by Dallas County Waste Control authorities that his business was illegally dumping electroplating waste into the sewer system. He eventually abandoned the plant, leaving behind more than 70,000 gallons of hazardous waste, cleaned up by the EPA at a cost of over $30,000. He opened a new facility in another Texas city, again illegally disposing of the waste in the sewage system and also illegally dumping on other property he owned. When these violations were ultimately discovered, he pled guilty to two counts of violating the hazardous waste laws, leading to his jail sentence and his being required to pay $75,000 in restitution and being banned from ever operating another plating business.

Many other federal agencies also aid in protecting the environment, although not always so directly. Many of these agencies are housed within departments that also play significant roles in regulating the environment. For example, the Department of the Interior and the Department of Energy

TABLE 3-5   Environmental Protection Agency Regional Offices

Region	Address	States Included
Region I	Boston, Massachusetts 1 Congress Street, 02114 (888) 372-7341	Connecticut, Maine, Massachusetts, New Hampshire, Rhode Island, Vermont
Region II	New York, New York 290 Broadway, 10007 (212) 637-3000	New Jersey, New York, Puerto Rico, Virgin Islands
Region III	Philadelphia, Pennsylvania 1650 Arch Street, 19103 (215) 814-5000	Delaware, Maryland, Pennsylvania, Virginia, West Virginia, District of Columbia
Region IV	Atlanta, Georgia 61 Forsyth Street, S.W., 30303 (404) 562-9900	Alabama, Florida, Georgia, Kentucky, Mississippi, North Carolina, South Carolina, Tennessee
Region V	Chicago, Illinois 77 W. Jackson Boulevard, 60604 (312) 353-2000	Illinois, Indiana, Michigan, Minnesota, Ohio, Wisconsin
Region VI	Dallas, Texas 1445 Ross Avenue, 75202 (214) 655-2200	Arkansas, Louisiana, New Mexico, Oklahoma, Texas
Region VII	Kansas City, Kansas 901 North 5th Street, 66101 (913) 551-7003	Iowa, Kansas, Missouri, Nebraska
Region VIII	Denver, Colorado 999 18th Street, 80202 (303) 312-6312	Colorado, Montana, North Dakota, South Dakota, Utah, Wyoming
Region IX	San Francisco, California 75 Hawthorne Street, 94105 (415) 774-1305	Arizona, California, Hawaii, Nevada, American Samoa, Guam, Northern Mariana Island
Region X	Seattle, Washington 1200 6th Avenue, 98101 (206) 553-1200	Alaska, Idaho, Oregon, Washington

play significant roles, as does the National Oceanic and Atmospheric Administration. The remainder of this chapter introduces some of these important agencies. Additional agencies that affect the environment are listed in Table 3-6. As you begin to concentrate on learning about various environmental laws, the roles of many of these agencies will be discussed.

THE DEPARTMENT OF THE INTERIOR AND ITS AGENCIES

Created as a cabinet-level department in 1845, the Department of the Interior is to natural resources what the EPA is to the regulation of pollution. It is responsible for seeking an optimal balance between the economic

TABLE 3-6   Federal Agencies and Offices that Play a Role in Environmental Regulation

Agency/Office	Primary Environmental Responsibility
Army Corps of Engineers	Regulates construction projects on navigable waterways; regulates transportation and dumping of dredged materials into navigable waterways; and undertakes projects to prevent flooding, supply water for industrial and municipal use, create recreational areas, and protect wildlife and shorelines of oceans and lakes
Consumer Products Safety Commission	Responsible for safety of consumer products, ensuring they do not contain carcinogens or toxic chemicals
Federal Energy Regulatory Commission	Issues licenses for hydroelectric power; is responsible for the safe operation of dams
Federal Maritime Commission	Certifies the financial responsibility of vessels that carry oil or other hazardous materials to cover costs of cleaning up their spills in navigable waters
Food and Drug Administration	Ensures that foods and drugs are not adulterated and do not contain toxic substances
Office of Pipeline Safety (within the Department of Transportation)	Ensures safe, reliable, and environmentally sound operation of pipelines
Office of Hazardous Materials Safety (within the Department of Transportation)	Responsible for coordinating a national safety program for the transportation of hazardous materials by air, rail, highway, and water
National Institute for Occupational Safety and Health (within the Department of Health and Human Services' Centers for Disease Control and Prevention)	Researches and develops occupational safety and health standards
National Oceanic and Atmospheric Administration (within the Department of Commerce)	Describes, monitors, and predicts conditions in the atmosphere, ocean, sun, and space environment; disseminates environmental data; and manages and conserves living marine resources and their habitats
Nuclear Regulatory Commission	Licenses the construction and operation of nuclear facilities and the possession, use, transportation, handling, and disposal of nuclear materials

(continued)

TABLE 3-6   *(cont.)*

Agency/Office	Primary Environmental Responsibility
Office of Energy Efficiency and Renewable Energy (within the Department of Energy)	Develops efficient and clean energy technologies
Office of Surface Mining, Reclamation, and Enforcement (within the Department of the Interior)	Protests against adverse effects of coal mining; establishes standards for surface effects of coal mining; and promotes reclamation of previously mined lands
Office of Wastewater Management (within the EPA's Office of Water)	Promotes compliance with the Clean Water Act
National Resources Conservation Service (within the Department of Agriculture)	Administers programs to develop and conserve soil and water resources
U.S. Geological Survey (within the Department of the Interior)	Maintains data center that conducts and sponsors research to apply data findings in mapping, geography, mineral and land resources, water resources, rangeland, and environmental monitoring
Power Resources Office (within the Department of the Interior's Bureau of Reclamation)	Develops and coordinates policy, provides advice, and assists in the power programming in the western states

growth and the preservation of natural resources. As you might imagine, the Department of the Interior is frequently a battleground between environmentalists and conservationists who want to preserve natural resources and those who want greater access to natural resources, such as those in the timber and cattle industries, mining operations, and sportsmen. State governments, especially in the West, also want to gain greater control of the public lands and natural resources within the department's control. Through its various agencies, the department is responsible for the management of more than 549 million acres of public land, administration of Indian lands and federal Indian programs, conservation and management of wetlands and estuaries, and protection and preservation of wildlife, including endangered species.

Bureau of Land Management

Created in 1946, the Bureau of Land Management is the largest landholding entity in the United States—responsible for the management of about 270 million acres of public land. About half of the land managed by this agency is in Alaska, and most of the remaining lands are in the 12 most western states. Much of the land is designated for recreational use; some has been designated for conservation as wilderness. Natural resources include timber, minerals, oil and gas, geothermal energy, wildlife habitats, endangered plants and animals, vegetation, and wild and scenic rivers.

U.S. Fish and Wildlife Service

Probably most well known for its role in the "spotted owl controversy," in which the FWS listed the owl as endangered, this agency is responsible for safeguarding and improving wildlife and wildlife habitats in the National Wildlife Refuge System. Since 1983, this system has grown to 472 national wildlife refuges, waterfowl production areas in 155 counties, and 51 coordination areas. The agency is responsible for protecting migratory and game birds, fish, and endangered and threatened species. The agency is also responsible for enforcing regulations for hunters, as well as for preserving wetlands as natural habitats.

National Park Service

This agency administers programs that conserve scenery, natural and historic objects, and wildlife in the national parks. It also is responsible for the management of 80 million acres of land.

THE DEPARTMENT OF AGRICULTURE AND ITS AGENCIES

U.S. Forest Service

This agency manages the nation's forests and grasslands. It is responsible for 33.6 million acres of wilderness. Like the Department of the Interior, this agency has to confront competing interests of those who want to conserve and those who want to exploit our natural resources, but it focuses its energies on the resource uses that occur in the forest, such as lumbering, mining, farming, and grazing. The agency is currently embroiled in controversy for such actions as clear-cutting, selling public timber below cost, and constructing roads for lumber companies in national forests.

THE DEPARTMENT OF LABOR AND ITS AGENCIES

Occupational Safety and Health Administration

OSHA is primarily responsible for promulgating and enforcing rules that affect health and safety in the workplace. A sister agency, the National Institute for Occupational Safety and Health (NIOSH), is responsible for doing research related to occupational health and safety that may be used by OSHA and the EPA in setting health and safety standards.

Mine Safety and Health Administration

This agency develops and promulgates health and safety standards for mines. It enforces standards, proposes penalties for violators, and investigates accidents. It works with states to help develop mine health and safety programs.

Concluding Remarks

Administrative agencies have enormous impact, given their authority to establish and enforce regulations. Remember, however, that their power is constrained by all of the traditional branches of government. In addition, much of our environmental law is, in fact, administrative law, developed and enforced by agencies, especially the EPA.

One of the most significant aspects of administration law is the way in which administrative regulations are created. The three processes by which these regulations can be created all invite public participation, all begin by publication of the proposed rule in the *Federal Register,* and all conclude with publication of the final rule in the *Federal Register.* If these legally binding regulations are not created following the proper steps, the courts will strike them down.

Now that you understand how the administrative law system functions, you are ready to begin study of that specialized area of law on which this book focuses: environmental law.

Questions for Review and Discussion

1. Distinguish formal from informal rule making.
2. Explain when rule making is exempt from public participation.
3. Explain the use of reg-neg.
4. Describe the grounds for which a rule made by an administrative agency can be overturned.
5. Trace the steps of adjudication that must be followed by an administrative agency.
6. Why should anyone in a heavily regulated industry be familiar with the *Federal Register*?
7. How do legislative, executive, and judicial branches each restrict the activities of administrative agencies?
8. Describe the structure of the EPA.

For Further Reading

Collin, Robert W. 2005. *The Environmental Protection Agency: Cleaning Up Our Government's Act.* Sacramento, CA: Hornet Foundation Inc.

Croley, Steven. 2003. "White House Review of Agency Lawmaking: An Empirical Investigation." *University of Chicago Law Review 70*: 821.

Farber, Daniel. 1998. "Saving Overton Park: A Comment on Environmental Values." *University of Pennsylvania Law Review 146*: 1671.

Gellhorn, Ernest, and Richard B. Stewart. 1990. *Administrative Law and Process in a Nutshell.* St. Paul, MN: West Publishing.

Gray, C. Borden. 1997. "Obstacles to Regulatory Reform." *University of Chicago Legal Forum 1*: 1.

Sanford, B. J. 2003. "Midnight Regulations, Judicial Review, and the Formal Limits of Presidential Rulemaking." *New York University Law Review 78*: 782.

Scheberle, Denise. 2004. *Federalism and Environmental Policy: Trust and the Politics of Implementation.* 2nd edn. Washington, D.C.: Georgetown University Press.

Silbergeld, Ellen K. 1995. "The Risks of Comparing Risks." *New York*

University Environmental Law Journal 3: 405.

Solow, Steven P. 1997. "The Big Chill: How Federal Agencies are Working Together to Stop CFC Smuggling." *National Environmental Enforcement Journal* (June): 14.

On the Internet

http://www.fplc.edu/risk/rskindx.htm
> Home page of RISK—Risk: Health, Safety, and the Environment

http://www.nationalacademies.org/environment
> The National Academy of Sciences/National Academy of Engineering Institution

http://www.epa.gov/opei/
> The EPA Office of Policy, Economics and Innovation

http://www.epa.gov/oalj/
> The EPA Office of Administrative Law Judges

http://www.law.indiana.edu/v-lib/vlib.asp
> The World Wide Web Virtual Library: Administrative Law

http://resource.lawlinks.com/content/legal_research/executive_orders/executive_orders.htm
> Review select Executive Orders by year or view the compiled list

http://www.archives.gov/federal_register/index.html
> The Federal Register

Notes

1. EPA Office of Administrative Law Judges. "Decisions and Orders." *http://www.epa.gov/oalj/orders2.htm* (October 10, 2003).

2. EPA Environmental Appeals Board. "EAB Unpublished Final Orders." *http://www.epa.gov/eab/unpub96.htm* and *http://www.epa.gov/eab/2002.htm* (October 10, 2003).

3. EPA Environmental Appeals Board. "Formal Opinions: Reverse Chronological Index 2000." *http://www.epa.gov/eab/2000.htm* (July 17, 2001).

4. Environmental Appeals Board, Frequently Asked Questions, *http://yosemite.epa.gov/oa/eab_web_docket.nsf/general+information/*

frequently+asked+questions? opendocument (October 15, 2006).

5. Council on Environmental Quality. 1990. *Twentieth Annual Report, 204.* Washington, D.C.: Government Printing Office.

6. "DuPont Ordered to Pay Largest Administrative Penalty in EPA History." *EPA Press Release* (May 8, 1998).

7. EPA. *Compliance and Enforcement Annual Results: FY2005 Numbers at a Glance, http://www.epa.gov/compliance/resources/reports/endofyear/eoy2005/2005numbers.html*

8. "First Monetary Awards Approved for Citizens Assistance in Enforcement." *EPA Press Release* (February 18, 1997).

9. Jeffrey H. Birnbaum. 1991. "White House Competitiveness Council Provokes Sharp Anger among Democrats in Congress." *Wall Street Journal* (July 8): B1.

10. Ibid.

11. 401 U.S. 402 (1971).

12. 61 LW 2042 (1992).

13. Alaska Department of Environmental Conservation. 2004. Environmental Protection Agency, 124 S.Ct. 983.

14. Donald J. Rebovich. 1992. *Dangerous Ground: The World of Hazardous Waste Crime.* New Brunswick, NJ: Transaction Publishers.

15. Phillip Davis. 1993. "Browner Short on Specifics in Confirmation Hearing." *Congressional Quarterly Weekly* (January 16): 127.

16. National Academy of Public Administration. 1995. *Setting Priorities, Getting Results: A New Direction for EPA.* Washington, D.C.: The Academy.

17. J. Charles Fox. Associate Administrator for Reinvention, U.S. Environmental Protection Agency, Testimony Before House Commerce Committee, Hearing on Reinvention at EPA (November 4, 1997).

18. EPA. "Executive Summary." April 2000. *Innovation at the Environmental Protection Agency: A Decade of Progress, 1–3. http://www.epa.gov/opei/decade/decade.pdf* (March 7, 2001).

19. Office of Policy, Economics, and Innovation. "New Ideas, Creative Partnerships, Sound Analysis." September 2000. *http://www.epa.gov/opei/opeibrochure.pdf* (March 7, 2001).

20. EPA. "Executive Summary," 1–3.

21. EPA. 2000. "Chapter 2: Achieving our Goals." *Draft 2000 Strategic Plan, 8–57. http://www.epa.gov/ocfopage/plan/2000sp.pdf* (July 17, 2001).

22. EPA. *Environmental Innovation, http://www.epa.gov/innovation/stategrants/sig2006.htm* (October 10, 2006).

23. Jerry Spangler. 2004. "Reports thrash EPA under Leavitt." *Desert Morning News* (October 22), *http://www.deseretnews.com.*

24. Ibid.

25. Society for Environmental Journalists. *Tip Sheet, Epa's Science Advisory Board Aghast at Tri Cutbacks, http://www.sej.org/search/index.htm* (October 30, 2006).

26. Ibid.

27. Karen E. Crummy. 2006. "Flak Hits Boss of EPA for Local Do," *Denver Post* (November 6).

28. EPA. 1997. *EPA Strategic Plan* (September 1997) *http://www.epa.gov/ocfopage/plan/epastrat.pdf* (July 17, 2001).

RESOLVING CONTROVERSIAL ENVIRONMENTAL ISSUES

- Remember that the first step of evaluating an argument is to identify the issue, reasons, and conclusion. Try to identify the argument presented in the following editorial.
- After identifying the argument in the editorial, go back and underline the reasons and the conclusion. While reading, ask yourself if the reasons logically lead to the conclusion? Are these good reasons for accepting the author's conclusion? How do you know what a good reason is?

One way to evaluate a reason is to identify assumptions inherent in the reasoning. An assumption is an unstated link between a reason and the conclusion. The author makes certain assumptions in her argument. However, are those certain assumptions necessarily good ones? Let us look at a practice example:

> Conclusion: I am going to get an A in this class.
> Reason: I've attended class every day.

To jump from the reason to the conclusion, the author needs a stepping-stone. In this example, the stepping-stone might be the following idea:

There is a link between attendance and good grades. Perfect attendance causes students to earn good grades.

How do you evaluate the worth of an assumption? After you have identified the assumption, put yourself on the opposite side of the author's position. Why might her assumption be incorrect? Look at the example again. Why might perfect attendance not lead to getting an A? Maybe you sleep in class. Perhaps you do not study at all outside of class. Your attendance has very little to do with what you are learning. Thus, the assumption is questionable.

Try to identify the assumptions and point out any problems with those assumptions in the following editorial.

In Some Cases, We do not Want Power by the People

Numerous environmental laws have given individuals the power to sue. Those who bring suits, however, are not bringing the suit simply to enforce the law. Instead, they are striving to change the law. Therefore, those environmental groups are trying to bypass the Constitution to create law through lawsuits. This practice simply must stop. It is the legislative branch's responsibility to create law.

Moreover, citizen suits are costly for the American taxpayer. Courts are already crowded, yet environmental groups insist on bringing these unnecessary suits in an attempt to win a large award. Some environmental groups have already received millions of dollars through citizen suits. Although they allegedly use this money to further environmental interests, it is not the judiciary's responsibility to redistribute money to environmental groups.

Environmentalists claim citizen suits are necessary because some regulators are willing to go easy on violators. However, environmentalists have forgotten the role of Congress, who can question and punish those regulators who are not enforcing the laws.

The citizen suit provision is unnecessary; more importantly, it is detrimental to the U.S. system of law. These cases may take over the role of Congress in their attempt to change the law. Furthermore, people who bring important lawsuits are delayed because the citizen suits clog the dockets. When we discover a wasteful element in our legal system, we should eliminate that element. The citizen suit provision is a perfect example of waste and should be eliminated.

PART II

THE ENVIRONMENTAL LAWS

The second part of this book provides an introduction to the most influential environmental laws and the dilemmas arising from implementing these laws. With the exception of Chapter 4, which discusses the basics of environmental policy, each chapter first introduces the primary environmental problems the law must resolve, providing the scientific knowledge necessary for you to understand the problem. The later sections of each chapter describe the laws themselves.

CHAPTER 4
AN INTRODUCTION TO ENVIRONMENTAL LAW AND POLICY

The area of law you are now beginning to study is one of extremely recent development. Forty years ago, there would not have been any law school or undergraduate or MBA courses in environmental law, because there was no such cohesive body of law. Environmental regulation has evolved over that brief period of time from reliance on tort law to an emphasis on end-of-pipe controls through direct regulation and finally to an emphasis on pollution prevention.

Before the existence of a cohesive set of environmental laws, how, you may wonder, did we keep the ravages of pollution from degrading the quality of our water, air, and land? The answer is that we did not. Without protective legislation, lakes and rivers became unfit for fishing and swimming, the air in many areas became severely degraded, forests were destroyed, and valuable land was eroded. Today, we are still paying the costs of cleaning up our mistakes from this era of minimal regulation.

In the first section of this chapter, we examine the justifications that led to the adoption of the regulations designed to repair the ravaged environment and prevent its future degradation. We then examine alternative ways to provide that protection. The third section traces the evolution of environmental policy. Finally, the remaining two sections discuss the two major environmental policy statutes.

THE NEED FOR REGULATION

Some believe that we did not need to enact environmental protection laws because tort law (discussed below) would protect the environment to the extent that it needed protection. In fact, for a while, tort law was the way we feebly controlled pollution, and it was in a tort class where protection of the environment was discussed, if at all, in law school. But the dying streams and polluted skies made it evident that tort law was not working; thus, the adoption of environmental regulation was seen as necessary.

TRAGEDY OF THE COMMONS

Many times when people seek to justify environmental regulation, they do so by using a story told by Garrett Hardin entitled "The Tragedy of the

Commons."[1] The tragedy develops this way: Picture a huge, lush pasture open to everyone. Many people survive by raising cattle; they take their cattle to the common pasture to graze. Each herdsman keeps as many cattle as possible. For a while, disease, famine, and tribal wars keep the number of cattle down to a reasonable level. Eventually, however, the day of reckoning comes. There is just enough land to support all the cattle.

The rational herdsman, however, asks himself, "What is the utility of adding one more animal to my herd?" Because the herdsman receives all the proceeds from the sale of the animal, he has powerful incentive to add to his herd. The negative effect of adding one more animal is the harm that results to the other herdsmen from the resultant overgrazing. Because all herdsmen share in this negative effect, the negative consequences to the individual herdsman are minimal. Consequently, herdsmen tend to keep adding to their herds. As the same conclusion is reached by each herdsman, each continues to increase his herd without limit. But the space for the herd is limited. Herein lies the tragedy. They are locked into a system that guarantees the destruction of the commons and thus their own ruin. Thus, Hardin concludes, "Ruin is the destination to which all men rush, each pursuing his own interest in a society that believes in the freedom of the commons. Freedom in a commons brings ruin to all."[2]

How, you may ask, is the tragedy of the commons related to environmental protection? Without environmental laws, the rational manufacturer finds that because the cost of a polluted river is borne by everyone, he pays only a fraction of the cost of dumping waste products into a stream. On the contrary, if he chooses not to pollute by properly treating his waste, he bears the whole cost of proper disposal. Therefore, he will pollute. Because the calculations are the same for everyone, we are trapped in a system of destroying our environment as long as we behave only as independent, rational, free enterprisers.

Just as with the tragedy of the commons, as long as there were few polluters relative to the size of the water and air, the absorptive capacities of these resources were not taxed and there were no problems. As population and industry increased, environmental tragedy emerged. Rivers became polluted, as did the air and the land. Nature's absorptive capacities were exceeded in many areas.

FREE-RIDER PROBLEM

Rather than using analogies such as *The Tragedy of the Commons,* some people justify the need for environmental laws by pointing out that clean air and clean water are public goods. Public goods are goods that are nonrival and nonexcludable—that is, once they are produced, others' consumption of the good does not affect another's consumption of the good and others cannot be excluded from using the good. Thus, when someone pays to produce the public good, not only the payer but also everyone else gets to use it. Those who do not pay become free riders. They get benefits paid for by others. No one, therefore, is going to pay for clean air and water, because every rational person would prefer to be a free rider. Each person will pollute and let everyone else pay to clean up the environment. The problem is that as everyone seeks to become a free rider, no one but a few "irrational" saints will be willing to pay for clean air and water. Because nonrival and nonexcludable goods inhibit private markets, either the good will not be produced or the government must act to provide the good. Absent government intervention, our environment will become degraded.

POLLUTION AS AN EXTERNALITY

One common justification for any government intervention in the market is to eliminate negative externalities. In the market, buyers and sellers interact to determine prices for goods and services. Buyers, through demand, communicate that certain resources should be allocated to the production of certain goods. Price is supposed to reflect the interest in allocation of resources to the production of those goods. However, sometimes third parties have an interest in a good or service, but the market listens only to buyers and sellers. Third parties have no impact on market prices; either government gives their interests a voice in production decisions or they have no voice. Thus, some argue that the government needs to step in to impose the costs of pollution on the polluting firm, so that it will have to increase the price of the product to reflect the true costs of producing the product. If the producer must pay to properly dispose of the hazardous waste created by producing the product, citizens who would have otherwise been adversely affected by the improper waste disposal will not have to pay by incurring losses to their health. The important point here is that the marketplace by itself has no mechanism for providing public goods, such as clean water, and accounting for the cost of externalities, such as the cost to third parties associated with improper waste disposal.

ENVIRONMENTAL ETHIC

Proponents of an environmentalist perspective believe that too often important decisions affecting the environment are made while taking into account only short-term impacts and economic factors, with little concern for the ongoing maintenance and enhancement of the viability of ecosystems.

Environmentalists are heavily influenced by ecology, the study of the relationships of living organisms to their environments. In ecology, land is viewed as a biotic pyramid:

> Plants absorb energy from the sun. That energy flows through a circuit called the biota, which may be represented by a pyramid of layers. The bottom layer is the soil. A plant layer rests on the soil, an insect layer on the plants, a bird and rodent layer on the insects, and so on up through the various animal groups to the apex layer, which consists of larger carnivores. . . . Land, then, is not merely soil; it is a

fountain of energy flowing through soil, plants, and animals. Food chains are the living channels that conduct energy upward; death and decay return the energy to the soil. The circuit is not closed. . . . [I]t is a sustained circuit, like a slowly revolving fund of life.[3]

When a change occurs in one part of the circuit, all other parts of the circuit must respond. Most changes that occur through evolution happen slowly, thus giving the circuit time to adapt. The more gradual and less violent the change, the more likely the successful readjustment in the pyramid.[4] The fear of ecologists is that humankind now has the capacity to make rapid changes in the circuit, and we do not know how the pyramid will respond. A substance we use to kill one harmful rodent may be absorbed into the food chain, causing death or mutation up the chain. When returned to the soil, that chemical may poison the soil, thus making plant growth impossible and resulting in a lack of food for insects, rodents, birds, and their predators in that area. Thus, the ecologists warn that we must be careful before we take steps that may interrupt ecological systems. The consequences of our actions may be graver than we anticipate. The unregulated marketplace again has little incentive to heed these fears.

Some environmentalists point out that as the dominant species in the ecosystem, with all our knowledge and power, we have a duty or responsibility to care for that ecosystem and to preserve it for future generations. We have an ethical obligation to past and future generations to be careful stewards of the legacy we have inherited. Some also make a sort of environmental noblesse oblige argument. Because our species has gone beyond the mere acquisition of food, clothing, and shelter, and we can understand the way ecosystems work, we have the special duty to preserve those systems. Because we have superior understanding, we have special responsibilities to consider the long-term impacts of our behavior. Finally, it is argued by many environmentalists, we must recognize that we are not the measure of all things. We are but a small part of the universe and have no right to destroy a significant portion of it to satisfy our own selfish desires.

As you read environmental cases, note that although the courts attempt to focus purely on the law, there are times when they go beyond a strict interpretation of the law. There are occasions when you will see the influence of the ecological perspective on a judge's decision making.

ALTERNATIVE WAYS TO CONTROL POLLUTION

TORT LAW

As mentioned earlier, tort law was the first way the United States attempted to control pollution, and it still provides a limited means of control. However, a number of limitations make tort law unavailable in many cases and unsatisfactory as an overall means of pollution control.

Under tort law, the typical action brought to control pollution is a nuisance case. An action for nuisance can be brought whenever there is an unreasonable interference with the use and enjoyment of another's land. When someone interferes with a person's use of his or her land, the one interfering can be sued for nuisance. The person suing can receive an injunction requiring that the nuisance be stopped. Because pollution of the air and water is clearly an interference with others' use and enjoyment of their land, nuisance would seem an ideal solution. The person who has been harmed by pollution could bring an action seeking an injunction, a court order prohibiting the polluting behavior and/or providing money damages for the harm caused.

The case of *Boomer v. Atlantic Cement Company*[5] reflects some of the problems of using tort law. In *Boomer,* the defendants operated a large cement plant near Albany, New York. They were sued by neighboring landowners who alleged injury to property from dirt, smoke, and vibrations emanating from the plant. The plaintiffs sought permanent injunctions and damages. After trial, a nuisance was found, and temporary damages were granted, but the request for an injunction was denied. The appellate court granted the injunction unless the defendants paid permanent damages of $185,000 to compensate for the plaintiff's economic loss. Given the relatively small amount of the monetary damages award, the injunction was essentially denied.

The ground for the denial of injunction, notwithstanding the findings that, first, there was a nuisance and, second, plaintiffs had been damaged substantially, was "the large disparity in economic consequences of the nuisance and of the injunction." In denying the injunction on this ground, the court admitted that it was "overruling a doctrine which has been consistently reaffirmed in several leading cases in this court and which has never been disavowed here, namely that where a nuisance has been found and where there has been any substantial damage shown by the party complaining, an injunction will be granted." The rule in New York had previously been that such a nuisance would be enjoined even if a marked disparity had been shown in economic consequences between the effect of the injunction and the effect of the nuisance.

The court noted that the defendant's investment in the plant was in excess of $45 million and that it employed 300 people. The court was convinced that the technology did not exist to enable the plant to operate without creating a nuisance, nor was the technology likely to be developed within the foreseeable future. The court made it clear that it was now going to balance the harm created by the nuisance with the costs of ceasing the nuisance. If the economic costs were great, no injunction would be granted. Thus, because pollution control is expensive, after *Boomer,* nuisance became an ineffective way to stop pollution. At best, tort law could be used to get damages to clean up some of the pollution's harm.

Problems with Using Tort Law

The major problem reflected in *Boomer* is the court's reluctance to grant injunctions, the only remedy that really controls pollution because what is sought is an end to the pollution. However, courts will now balance the economic harm caused by the nuisance against the costs that would result from the injunction. If the harm from the injunction would be greater, then the courts will simply award permanent damages. The problem with this approach is that it allows the pollution to go on unabated. It leaves the injured party without a remedy for unforeseen future harms. If the landowner sells the property to someone else, the courts could rule that the subsequent landowner can bring no action because permanent damages had already been awarded. Once the damages have been assessed, there is no motivation for the polluter to stop polluting.

Another problem is that of standing. Recall from Chapter 2 that standing is the legal right to bring an action. Standing in a nuisance action is somewhat different from standing in most other cases. For the purposes of standing, nuisance is classified as being either private or public. A private nuisance affects a single or a limited number of persons or affects one person in a unique way. When a nuisance is private, the affected individuals have standing to sue. If the nuisance affects a large number of persons, it is deemed a public nuisance. Only a public official can bring suit for a public nuisance. Herein lies the main problem with using nuisance law to control pollution. Most pollution is a public nuisance. Public officials, who are generally elected, may be reluctant to bring a nuisance action against a major corporation for several reasons. For one, the polluting company supplies jobs, and public officials do not want to be accused of driving jobs out of town. Also, they do not want to anger a powerful constituent who may be responsible for sizable campaign contributions.

A third problem with using tort law is the difficulty of proving one's case. Remember that in a civil action, the burden of proof is on the plaintiff. If there are multiple polluters, it is difficult to prove which one caused the damage. If seven factories are located along the stream that flows across your land, how do you demonstrate that it was the toxic chemical from the tire plant that killed the fish?

Another problem is a comparative lack of resources. In the rare instance where a nuisance is private, the plaintiff needs money to bring the action, and many people do not have the money to bring such an action. Remember, many firms would have an in-house lawyer who could spend lots of time filing interrogatories and motions that would drive up the cost of the lawsuit.

Finally, tort law is problematic because it is reactive. The problem must exist before the law comes into effect. Ideally, the law should prevent the problem.

SUBSIDIES, EMISSIONS CHARGES, AND MARKETABLE EMISSIONS PERMITS

Three alternative means of protecting the environment are subsidies, emissions charges, and marketable emissions permits. As we shift toward pollution prevention, we shall see the increasing use of these tools. Subsidies exist when the government pays, either directly by grants or indirectly by tax credit, to encourage pollution control. For example, the government might pay one-third of the cost of installing a newly developed pollution-control device. Subsidies are most likely to be effective when the polluter knows that eventually it is going to be forced to clean up the problem. So, if the company takes care of it now, the government will help pick up the tab. If the company waits until the government imposes a tighter standard, no subsidy will be available. One interesting outcome of the use of subsidies is that sometimes a firm that is able to control its emissions better because of technology installed with a subsidy may start to pressure the government to impose even stricter emissions limitations on that industry, so that their competition is held to the same standard.

Traditionally, subsidies have not fully covered the costs of reducing pollution, so businesses were likely not to use the subsidies because they did not wish to pay for pollution control when their competitors did not. In some respects, this type of thinking is encouraged by a business climate in which managers are evaluated on the basis of the bottom line at the end of the quarter or the year. Our country's managers simply do not focus on the long-term calculations of benefit and cost.

Another alternative is to require emissions charges. In essence, we are saying that the air and water belong to the community, so if you want to use them, you must pay the owners, that is, the community. The larger the per-unit fee, the more effective the charges are in reducing levels of emissions. The charges theoretically encourage development of pollution-control technology, because if a competitor could discharge less, it would lower costs and increase profits.

Emissions charges, however, are not without their problems. First, it is very difficult to monitor emissions. Second, it is also difficult to know how to set the fee. If the fees are too low, firms will simply pay the fee and continue to pollute. If there are few firms in the industry, they may even tacitly agree simply to pass on the fees to consumers. If the fees are too high, and alternative technology to reduce emissions is extremely expensive or not available, only a few firms may be able to survive, thereby creating a monopoly. In such an event, emissions charges can be a stimulus to concentrated economic power.

Renewed interests in emissions charges occurred with the release of "Strategies for a Clean Energy Future," a report by scientists from five federal research centers focusing on greenhouse gas emissions. These scientists recommended that industries and electric utilities pay $50 for each ton of carbon they emit to reduce the expected increase in carbon dioxide emissions from 1990 to 2010 by 70 percent.[6] The implementation of such a charge is unlikely, especially because the charges would add 12.5 cents to a gallon of gasoline.[7]

Despite the unlikelihood of a carbon emissions charge being implemented universally, Royal Dutch/Shell (the oil company) has decided to include the cost of emitting greenhouse gases in its decisions about new projects. The company uses estimates from the World Bank to price its carbon emissions, but in the future, the company will base carbon emissions costs on the market for carbon emissions permits, discussed below.[8] Including these estimates in financial assessments has mainly allowed Shell to decide "whether to invest in emissions-reductions equipment at the outset, or to retrofit equipment at a later stage."[9]

A related alternative is for the government not only to sell permits but also to let the polluters trade those permits among themselves, sometimes referred to as emissions trading, or marketable emissions permits. Governments would set overall emissions targets and then issue permits to meet those targets, thereby controlling the overall amount of pollution. Firms then possess incentives to reduce their emissions using low-cost methods, so they can sell their permits. The total amount of pollution can be reduced by gradually reducing the number of permits issued. The major emissions trading program in the country today is the sulfur dioxide trading program described in Chapter 5 and created by the 1990 CAA. Some have suggested using some form of marketable permits to solve global pollution problems, for example, awarding marketable permits to countries that take steps to preserve forests. Again, there are problems with this method. The government may find monitoring difficult. In addition, new entrants into an industry may be restricted by the difficulty of obtaining a permit.

GREEN TAXES

One way to help control pollution that has not been attempted to any great extent in the United States is the use of green taxes, sometimes called environmental taxes. A green tax is a tax on polluting behaviors, the revenues from which may be funneled into environmental programs. Supporters of green taxes argue that these taxes correct the market's failure to value environmental services. They also seem to be somewhat effective in discouraging polluting behavior if they are set at a high enough level. In the United Kingdom, for example, a higher tax on leaded gasoline increased the market share of unleaded gas from 4 percent in April 1989 to 30 percent in March 1990.

The member states of the European Union (EU) have been somewhat successful in implementing green taxes. Eight member states have waste disposal taxes, and an equal number of states use carbon taxes. In 2003, environmental or green taxes accounted for 6.5 percent of total tax revenue. The Council of Ministers presented a plan to the European Parliament in 2003 to increase the use of environmental and green taxes, while decreasing taxes on labor. This proposal seeks to avoid an overall increase in taxes by redistributing the tax burden to reduce environmental damage while increasing employment through reduced labor costs. Three-fourths of the EU's green taxes are levied on energy sources, which serve to promote greater energy efficiency.[10]

In the 1990s, Sweden, Finland, and Norway imposed carbon taxes to reduce the emissions of green house gasses. In 2005, New Zealand passed a similar carbon tax; however, it after receiving harsh opposition, the tax was repealed before it could take effect. That no other countries have been able to create a carbon tax indicates the difficulty of passing the true costs of carbon emissions on to either the producer or the consumer.

The United States is attempting to discourage the use of ozone-depleting CFCs with a green tax it imposed in late 1989 of $3.02 per kilogram, which increased to $6.83 per kilogram in 1995 and to $10.80 per kilogram in 1999. A comprehensive set of green taxes could reduce our nation's current level of energy consumption. In 2002, the state of New York approved the Green Building Tax Credit program, the nation's first tax credit program encouraging the design and construction of environmentally friendly buildings. The program offers strong incentives for the conservation of energy and the reduction of a building's environmental impact by allowing percentages of expenses associated with the construction of green buildings to be deducted from state taxes. For example, a 100 percent tax credit is offered for the expense of installing integrated solar panels on a building. For those owners who install a new EPA-approved air conditioner, a tax credit equal to 10 percent of the cost is offered as an incentive to reduce harmful refrigerant chemicals. A total of $25 million in tax credits may be issued over a 4-year period.[11]

In November 2006, the city of Boulder, Colorado, passed the first "carbon tax" in the United States, which is designed to reduce carbon levels in the city to 7 percent less than 1990 levels by the year 2012, which would be a 24 percent reduction. The tax, which took effect on April 1, 2007, will be based on the number of kilowatt-hours used. Officials say it will add $16 a year to an average homeowner's electricity bill and $46 for businesses.

DIRECT REGULATION

The primary means of protecting the environment is direct regulation or command-and-control regulation. By direct regulation, we mean the setting of standards and mandating compliance through threat of fines for violations. Standards may be set in terms of levels of technology that must be used or total emissions allowed. The focus of the remaining chapters is primarily on direct regulation.

These regulations are often referred to as end-of-pipe regulations because they tend to concentrate on controlling pollutants toward the end of the manufacturing process. These direct regulations have been the focus of most environmental legislation. As the final section in this chapter reveals, however, we are beginning to shift away from the end-of-pipe regulations, traditionally identified with direct regulation, and toward ways of making it economically beneficial for firms to evaluate their entire production process in search of avenues whereby fewer pollutants would be created in the first place.

EVOLUTION OF OUR ENVIRONMENTAL POLICY

THE ORIGINS OF OUR ENVIRONMENTAL POLICY

Our federal system of government allocates power and responsibility among many levels of government. Consequently, we do not have national policies on many issues; our policy, if you can call it a policy, with respect to most issues has been *laissez-faire* or "government hands off." Minimal government intervention, especially in business affairs, traditionally has been seen as desirable by those in power in this country. We are, for example, the only industrialized nation that does not have a coherent industrial policy. However, if there is any area in which our country has seemed to have adopted a national policy, it is with respect to the environment. In 1970, President Nixon signed the NEPA, which began the federalization of environmental policy.

As noted earlier, before 1970, the United States did not have any sort of environmental policy. To a large extent, this absence of environmental regulation, as well as subsequent increases in regulation, reflected the state of scientific knowledge. We were not even aware of many environmental problems. Furthermore, we did not have the ability to detect and measure low levels of chemical contaminants. For example, the ability to measure levels of many contaminants has gone from parts per thousand to parts per million.

We also did not have the computer technology available to do the types of modeling that today allow us to project the long-term impacts of certain levels of contaminants on the human environment. Even, in some cases, when we determined that a given level of pollution was harmful, we did not have the technology to reduce emissions levels immediately. Once the technology was developed, it was sometimes more costly than expected. Frequently, the cleaner the environment became, the more costly the technology for smaller and smaller reductions of emissions.

As mentioned in Chapter 2, our system of government also helped to slow the evolution of environmental policy. Strong constituencies were needed to get the legislative and executive branches moving together toward protecting the environment. Once the laws were passed, they were still subject to the courts' interpretation. As we saw in Chapter 2, the ideology of the majority of justices can change, and thus, environmental policy as enforced by the courts may change.

Finally, our environmental policy is influenced by our values—the long-ingrained values of our culture, as well as more temporary values that seem to change over time in response to economic conditions. Our independence has always encouraged a hands-off policy toward business, which would explain our lack of an earlier environmental policy. However, as our economy became stronger, other values, especially those reflecting a desire for an improved quality of life, became more dominant and encouraged the adoption of policies more favorable to the environment.

THE 1970s: THE ENVIRONMENTAL DECADE

The environmental movement of the early 1970s was inspired to a great extent by three books. Perhaps the most influential of these was Rachel Carson's *Silent Spring*,[12] which made people aware of the effects of pesticides on birds and other wildlife. The other two were Paul Ehrlich's *The Population Bomb*,[13] which alerted us to the potentially adverse impact that our rapidly increasing population could have on our natural resources, and Barry Commoner's *The Closing Circle*,[14] which explained ecological principles in terms that laypeople could understand.

Also influential in generating public interest in preservation of the environment were a few cataclysmic events, such as the 1969 oil spill in Santa Barbara, California. On April 22, 1970, the first Earth Day was celebrated, and there were "teach-ins" about environmental problems across the nation. These events created the public pressure that caused policy makers in all branches of government to perceive environmental issues as politically emergent. Seeing almost unprecedented public support for a strong environmental policy, lawmakers set about adopting tough environmental regulations, often without fully considering the costs and technological feasibility of implementing such regulations.

In terms of institutionalizing an environmental policy that would have a long-term impact, two actions were probably the most significant. One was the creation of the EPA, to bring the coordination of environmental policy under the control of one agency. The other was passage of the NEPA (described later in this chapter), which requires every federal agency to consider the environmental impacts of every major activity it undertakes.

The years from 1969 through 1979 saw the passage of 27 laws designed to protect the environment, as well as hundreds of administrative regulations. The decade of the 1970s, under this new environmental policy, witnessed vast improvements in the quality of the air, water, and land, even though many of the goals established by these laws had not been completely attained.

THE 1980s

By 1980, concern was growing over the costs of regulation in general. The economy was not in good shape, and President Reagan was elected under a banner of deregulation. As part of his general policy of "getting government off the back of business," Reagan appointed conservatives to head the EPA and the Department of the Interior, as well as to serve in key positions in these and other agencies that played significant roles in setting out and enforcing environmental policy. Many of these newly appointed officials in fact came from businesses, legal foundations, or firms that had fought the regulations they were now supposed to enforce. Subsequently, many, with their deregulatory ideas, drove a number of senior executives and professionals out of the environmental agencies.[15]

Reagan also reduced the staffs of many agencies, in particular cutting EPA personnel by 20 percent.[16] Additional reductions in enforcement were ensured by cutting the EPA's budget by more than one-third, when adjusted for inflation, between 1981 and 1983.[17] Funding for conservation programs in the Department of the Interior, as well as for renewable energy programs, was also reduced. Reacting to less money and staff for enforcement, business soon recognized that there had been a shift in environmental policy and felt less constrained by environmental regulations.

At first, Congress went along with the administration's relaxation of environmental policies. After 2 years, the public, at the instigation of numerous environmental groups, began to make its dissatisfaction known. In March 1982, ten environmental and conservation groups issued an "indictment" of Reagan, alleging that he had "broken faith with the American people on environmental protection" by taking or proposing "scores of actions that veered radically away from the broad bipartisan consensus in support of environmental policy that has existed for many years" and citing 227 ways that the administration had subverted environmental policy.[18]

Congress, perhaps in response to a perception that the public disapproved of the administration's lax attitude toward the environment, began to oppose the administration's policies toward the environment by holding several oversight hearings on the EPA's handling of specific environmental matters. Congress also voted to strengthen a number of environmental laws that came up for renewal during the 1980s. In many instances, the laws may have been stronger than they would have been with a more pro-environment president because of congressional belief that it needed to draft strong laws that could not be watered down by a weakened EPA.

Thus, the 1980s saw a reduction in funding for environmental programs and a relaxation in their enforcement, along with cutbacks in the budgets and staffs of agencies established to protect the environment. Much of the administrative burden associated with environmental policy was shifted to the states. However, by the end of the decade, there seemed to be a renewal of environmental vigor on the part of Congress.

THE EARLY 1990s

As the 1990s approached, there seemed to be renewed interest in having a strong policy to protect the environment. "Green" products began cropping up all over. Major firms, such as McDonald's, started advertising that they were changing their products to become more environmentally friendly. Public opinion polls began to show more interest than ever in environmental protection. Furthermore, enforcement at the EPA was given renewed attention. The years 1990 through 1994 produced record numbers of prosecutions and fines for environmental violations. Congress also seemed to be continuing its environmental support by passing a strong CAA.

Thus, there were many early indicators that the 1990s would see a strengthening of an environmental policy that had been weakening during the 1980s. Not all indicators were pointing in that direction, however. President Bush's appointee to head the EPA, William Reilly, although a disappointment to many environmentalists, was proving to be a bit more pro-environment and not quite pro-business enough for the president, so there were numerous conflicts within the executive branch: between the president, his Competitiveness Council, and the OMB on the one side and the EPA on the other.

In addition, by the 1990s, many federal courts were dominated by conservative appointees. Early cases indicated that these new appointees were not necessarily going to be as willing as previous courts to take pro-environment positions. Even the newly constituted U.S. Supreme Court indicated that it was going to give much less weight to preserving environmental values, even going so far as to overturn past precedents that it saw as having given too much protection to environmental concerns (EC).

As the economy continued to slump during the early 1990s, people again became more concerned about the costs of environmental regulations. They also started to recognize that once the initial gains had been made in the 1970s and 1980s, future incremental gains were going to be much more costly. Each incremental gain would also provide fewer visible benefits. These factors helped to create a shift in environmental policy away from the end-of-pipe regulation toward more pollution prevention and the use of more cost-effective ways to reduce pollution. As mentioned earlier, one of the factors that helped stimulate a concern for the environment during the late 1960s and early 1970s was the fact that the economy was doing well; there was money available to be spent. At the beginning of the 1990s, the economy was not in good shape.

THE MIDDLE TO LATE 1990s

In 1992, democratic presidential and vice presidential candidates, who were characterized by their opponents as "environmental extremists," were elected. Vice President Gore had, in fact, written a book suggesting ways to improve environmental quality. When asked by an interviewer from the *Wall Street Journal* what recent event helped shape his vision of American society, Gore replied, "The UN Conference on Environment and Development conducted in Rio de Janeiro."[19]

Articles appearing soon after the election indicated that corporate environmental lawyers were taking the election of the new presidential team as a signal, at minimum, of renewed environmental enforcement. For example, in the *National Law Journal,* in an article entitled "Girding for a Change," the author opened by warning readers, "For the general counsels at the nation's corporations, the transition period between the last weeks of President Bush's tenure and the first months of a Clinton administration calls for a thorough re-examination of their companies' overall compliance program."[20]

According to more than two-dozen regulatory and compliance experts from private law firms, corporations, public interest groups, and law schools who were interviewed for the story, the new administration would bring new rules and an overall boost in enforcement. Although enforcement in all regulatory areas was predicted to increase, the greatest increases were expected to come in the environmental area.[21]

Although the use of criminal sanctions to punish and deter environmental violations did continue to increase during the initial years of the Clinton administration, the congressional elections of 1994, which gave control of the House of Representatives to the Republicans, brought in a new group of elected officials who were committed to regulatory reform. A major component of this regulatory reform was rolling back years of environmental regulation, which these new representatives believed had been hampering business and infringing on the rights of private property owners. In fact, some of those new representatives had campaigned explicitly on a platform of protecting property rights and limiting government.

The newly elected Congress moved rapidly to attempt to fulfill its "Contract with America," a legislative plan that, if enacted, would significantly alter environmental regulation in the United States. Proposed and debated legislation would have dramatically cut the EPA's budget, exempted oil and gas production from toxic air pollution standards and citizens' suits, weakened the CWA, ended federal jurisdiction over at least half of the wetlands currently protected, eliminated the National Biological Survey, placed a 5-year moratorium on land acquisition by the Forest Service and Bureau of Land Management, allowed the leasing of the Arctic National Wildlife Refuge's coastal plain for the drilling of oil, reduced the protection given to endangered species, lifted the 14-year ban on drilling for oil along the outer continental shelf (OCS), and reduced by 10 percent the operating budgets of the Forest Service, the National Park Service, and the FWS. Riders were attached to various budget appropriation bills that would have prohibited the EPA from engaging in numerous regulatory functions, such as enforcing wetland protection, issuing several drinking water standards, enforcing Great Lakes water standards, and enforcing several raw sewage overflow controls. Clinton maintained that he would veto any bill that would undermine existing environmental protection.

Two proposals were of special concern to the environmental community. The first was the risk-assessment bill. This bill would have imposed risk assessments on any rules that would have an impact on the economy of at least $75 million per year. It would also provide for judicial review of such regulations. A complementary regulatory reform package in the House of Representatives would apply risk assessment, cost–benefit analysis, peer review, and prioritization standards to almost every new rule that would have an economic effect of at least $25 million. The second was a bill that proposed to give Congress the authority to review and possibly veto virtually any new federal regulation.

Despite the furor generated by these reform proposals, or perhaps because of it, very few of these proposals became law by the end of 1995. Republicans did manage to place a rider on a Defense Department appropriation bill that prohibited the listing of new species as endangered by the end of 1995; that moratorium was then extended until September 30, 1996. A budget recision bill passed during the summer of 1995 contained a rider that opened up thousands of acres of Pacific Northwest forests for salvage logging. Neither the risk-assessment bill nor the moratorium on new federal regulations managed to pass.

Some argue that the Republican Party misread the American people's intent and that it is now coming to recognize that the public does in fact support the current system of environmental protection. An article appearing in the *New York Times* on January 26, 1996,[22] reported that Republicans, increasingly concerned over political damage that might be caused by imposing deep cuts on the environment, were beginning to move away on confrontations on environmental issues; a Republican pollster disclosed that only 35 percent of the public would vote to reelect members of the House who voted to cut EPA funding.

President Clinton was reelected in 1996. Although many important environmental issues could have been holding the attention of politicians and the public as the century drew to a close, at the end of 1998 and the beginning of 1999, most people were more concerned about President Clinton's impeachment hearings.

In October 1998, several members of Congress, under the cover of the scandal, attempted to use a "stealth approach" to cutting back on environmental protection. They attached approximately 50 antienvironment riders to funding bills.[23] These riders seem to conflict with the wishes of the majority of Americans. According to public opinion polls, 70 percent of Americans consistently want the environment and wilderness areas protected. Although Republicans were generally responsible for the riders that were attached to funding bills, Republicans, in a report issued by the House Policy Committee, argued that they deserved credit for environmental protection. Democrats responded with the Miller Report, entitled "The Great Republican Environmental P. R. Campaign," arguing that Republicans were trying to "greenwash" voters.[24] Of seven key pro-environment amendments, on average, only 17 percent of the Republicans in the House voted for their passage.[25]

Toward the end of his presidency, President Clinton enacted a series of environmental regulations through executive order. These orders created national monuments, protected land from industrial interests and road building, and set up sanctuaries for wildlife. The orders particularly protected environments in several western states, Hawaii, and Florida. The impetus for these environmental protections appeared to be the Department of the Interior, which recommended several of the sites given protection by Clinton. However, because of the appearance of these rules late in the presidency, many environmentalists feared the rules would be overturned by the new president. Indeed, only hours after taking the oath of office, President Bush ordered a moratorium on the implementation of Clinton's executive orders not yet in the *Federal Registry,* including the executive order protecting 85.5 million acres of national forests from road construction and off-road vehicles. Reversals in environmental policy, such as the 2002 overturning of a Clinton executive order banning snow mobiles in Yellowstone National Park, are indicative of the Bush administration's environmental philosophy.

INCREASING USE OF "MARKET FORCES"

Beginning in the 1990s, environmental policy began to shift toward greater reliance on market forces. The term *market forces* covers a broad range of strategies. Proponents of this trend are careful to point out that the term is not a code word for deregulation. Rather, they insist, it is a way of using the market forces to encourage pollution prevention. Environmental problems can be seen as economic problems because pollution is generally an indicator of inefficiencies or market externalities that have not been factored into the costs of market transactions or the underpricing of our natural resources. Therefore, most market force solutions to environmental problems focus on fixing market failures.

One example of this type of market force incentive is the passage of "bottle bills," bills that require certain types of beverages to be sold in recyclable or reusable bottles. Consumers must pay a deposit for such bottles, which will be refunded when the bottles are returned. Consumers will be much more likely to recycle when there is a financial incentive to do so. At least nine states have such laws. Another example is what Seattle is doing in charging for refuse pickup based on poundage. If consumers pay by the pound to have their trash carted away, they will be motivated financially to reduce their trash. Pollution taxes and refundable deposits on hazardous materials are two other market-oriented incentives. Maine and Rhode Island, for example, impose refundable deposits on automobile batteries. What all these strategies have in common is that they make the polluter pay—and thus, theoretically, encourage a reduction in pollution to avoid the costs.

Other methods involve increasing product information, so that consumers are better able to choose products that are the least environmentally harmful. Increased product information can create pressure on producers to make their products more environmentally sound. The Energy Star label (discussed below) and "dolphin safe" labels on seafood products are just two examples of providing the consumer with information about their purchasing decisions.

Two of the more controversial strategies are pollution charges and marketable emissions permits, mentioned in an earlier section of this chapter. The former is an alternative to ordering plants to cut emissions by a specific amount. Instead, every unit of pollution discharged is taxed, thus giving an incentive to the firm to cut emissions. Critics, however, point out that for this scheme to work, the taxing agency would need detailed information about a company's costs to make possible the setting of fees at a level that would discourage pollution. The first major experiment in marketable emissions permits is taking place under the CAA of 1990. Described in detail in Chapter 5, this policy is designed to alleviate one of the frequent criticisms of direct regulation—that the regulations do not take into account the differences among various competitors' compliance.

Voluntary Programs

Another shift in environmental policy is toward more voluntary programs on the part of businesses to reduce pollution. Such programs include Waste Wise, Climate Wise, Water Alliances for Volunteer Efficiency (WAVE), Energy Star, 35/50, the Pesticide Environmental Stewardship Program (PESP), and the Landfill Methane Outreach Program (LMOP). These programs encourage partnerships with the regulated community as well as other organizations to demonstrate environmental leadership. LMOP, for example, works with the landfill industry to promote the use of landfill gas as a renewable energy source, preventing the emissions of methane, a greenhouse gas, into the atmosphere. As of early 2006, 490 partners have committed to work with the EPA to implement cost-effective solutions to landfill emissions. Over the past 11 years, the voluntary program prevented the release of 21 million metric tons of greenhouse gasses. This reduction is equal to removing 13.9 million cars from the road for an entire year.

One of the most successful voluntary projects is the Energy Star Program, which promotes energy efficiency for both businesses and individuals. The EPA assists manufacturers and other businesses in developing and implementing energy-efficient products and work environments. Through this partnership, energy-efficient products and homes helped to prevent 63 million metric tons of greenhouse gas emissions in 2005, the equivalent of emissions from 42 million vehicles. As a result, businesses and individuals saved over $12 billion in energy costs for the year 2005 alone.

ISO 14000

The EPA has been encouraging businesses to take a more active role in pollution prevention and environmental protection. Businesses have been responding to the challenge of the ISO 14000 series of standards, a series of international standards that cover the following topics: EMS, environmental auditing, environmental labeling, environmental performance evaluation, and life cycle analysis. The International Organization for Standardization (ISO), an organization created in 1947 to develop manufacturing, trade, and communication standards, began developing the series of environmental standards in the late 1980s. Their goal was to develop a "formula" to provide organizations throughout the world with a common approach to environmental management. Consequently, they developed the voluntary ISO 14000 standards.

Only one standard, ISO 14001, the cornerstone of the ISO 14000 standards, requires certification. A primary goal of ISO 14001 is to suggest one accepted method for companies to review and assess their EMSs. To earn the

ISO 14001 certification, a company needs to show diligent record keeping for pollution prevention and waste reduction programs to prove that they are reviewed and assessed on a defined schedule. Developing an EMS can be quite a costly and complicated process. However, an organization's stakeholders may ask that the organization obtains certification not only to demonstrate that it is making environmental considerations but also because compliance with certain ISO standards has become a necessary condition for trade with an increasing number of countries, including many European nations. These standards create a baseline against which other companies can be measured. Furthermore, the EMS can result in changes that will make the organization more cost-efficient. As of January 2006, 103,583 certifications had been issued globally, with 5,100 certifications in the United States.[26]

THE BEGINNING OF THE 21ST CENTURY

The election of George W. Bush, a champion of states' rights, property rights, and the oil industry, has caused many environmental protections, such as the CAA's New Source Review, to be removed or reduced, allowing the very pollution the law once prohibited. Some environmentalists claim that Bush has returned environmental protection to the state it was in during the Reagan era, or perhaps worse.

President Bush's cabinet appointments have been indicative of the environmental policies that have resulted from his administration. His first Secretary of the Interior, Gale Norton, supported drilling in the Arctic National Wildlife Refuge and was seen by some as sympathetic to the "wise use" movement, which is viewed by many environmentalists as an antienvironment organization. The two guiding principles of the wise use movement are "all constraints on the use of private property should be removed, including limits set for health, safety, and environmental protection" and "access to public land should be unrestricted for logging, mining, drilling, motorized recreation, and all commercial enterprise."[27] Spencer Abraham, President Bush's first Secretary of Energy, during his tenure in Congress

BUSINESS BENEFITS OF ISO 14000 STANDARDS

- Reduced cost of waste management
- Savings in consumption of energy and materials
- Lower distribution costs
- Improved corporate image among regulators, customers, and the public
- Framework for continuous improvement of your environmental performance

Source: ISO, "Business Benefits of ISO 14000." *http://www.iso.org/iso/en/iso9000–14000/ understand/basics/basics14000/basics14000_5.html* (October 12, 2006).

cosponsored a bill to abolish the department he lead and did not show support for renewable energy sources. Spencer Abraham was succeeded by Samuel W. Bodman as the Secretary of Energy, who favors opening the Arctic National Wildlife Refuge to drilling.

Bush's first EPA Administrator, former New Jersey Governor Christine Todd Whitman, was seen by many environmentalists as a moderate who was kept under the tight rein of White House conservatives. Early in her tenure, she called for controls on carbon monoxide, a greenhouse gas, but then was quickly required to endorse the administration's stance against mandatory controls for CO_2 fossil fuel utility plants. She was criticized by environmentalists for a number of her actions, including the following: opposing reinstatement of taxes on chemical feedstocks, crude oil, and corporate income to replenish the Superfund; suspending (although only temporarily) Clinton's rule that lowered the amount of arsenic allowed in drinking water; and telling people the day after the collapse of the Twin Towers that the air was safe to breathe when it was not.[28] Even though she was hardly a strong advocate for the environment, she still clashed with the administration over some policies. For example, Whitman displayed public shock over the administration's reversal on the Kyoto Protocol, suggesting she was not made part of the decision-making process. When testifying before a Senate Committee about the Defense Authorization Act, which would exempt the military from having to comply with a number of environmental regulations and roll back protections for endangered species and numerous marine mammals, she said publicly that she did not believe that any training mission anywhere was being delayed or not undertaken because of environmental laws, and she was quickly silenced by the administration. Christine Whitman resigned in 2003. Some suggested the resignation occurred because she too frequently found herself at odds with conservative members of the administration who opposed many of the EPA's policies, although her public reasons for leaving were personal. Bush appointed Mike Leavitt, former Governor of Utah, to be the next EPA Administrator. During his Senate confirmation hearings, Mike Leavitt was strongly criticized for his secret negotiations with Gale Norton to open up millions of acres of Utah wilderness to road building and development. However, he was praised for working against urban sprawl in his state.

In 2005, he left the EPA to become the Secretary of Health and Human Services and was replaced by Stephen L. Johnson. Johnson was nominated from his position as the acting Administrator of the EPA and became the first professional scientist and career EPA employee to head the agency. It remains unclear how his professional credentials and career history will influence his leadership of the EPA.

Stephen L. Johnson aside, another clear indication of the negative impact on environmental law and policy of the Bush Administration is the continuous departure of committed EPA employees. Eric Schaeffer, former director of EPA's regulatory enforcement division, quit the EPA in February 2002 and sent a withering public resignation letter to then-Administrator Christie

Whitman, citing, among other reasons, his frustration over fighting a White House "that seems determined to weaken the rules we are trying to enforce."[29] Sylvia Lowrance, an agency employee for more than 20 years who was acting Assistant Administrator of the EPA Office of Enforcement and Compliance Assurance for the first 18 months of the Bush Administration, retired quietly in July 2002, initially giving no public reason for her departure, but later voicing serious misgivings about the state of the enforcement program.[30] Three top enforcement officials at the EPA resigned or retired during the first 2 weeks of 2004.[31] One of them commented shortly after leaving, "I just didn't feel comfortable working in that environment anymore. Certainly the direction that the agency was going over the last couple years was different than what I'd experienced during my 32 years working for EPA. It was contrary to everything that I had worked for."[32] A second, the director of the air enforcement division, cited the new enforcement policy under the Bush administration, which would stop almost all work in the power plant enforcement world, as one reason he was leaving, saying that he would have stayed if he had felt there was any useful and interesting work left in the power plant enforcement area.[33] The third of that group to resign, John Suarez, the top EPA enforcement official, who left to take a job with WalMart, commented ambiguously that the EPA has "been able to provide more compliance assistance to industry than ever before."[34]

The Bush administration's 2006 budget proposal decreases EPA's budget by $300 million. This cut in funding will also reduce by 80 percent the EPA Library Network budget, which would cripple or close many of the 10 regional libraries and greatly reduce access to critical information used for enforcement and research. The libraries, used by government officials, businesses, and private citizens, houses environmental research and information that is not available elsewhere. Such policies have marked the Bush presidency as strongly opposed to environmental protection.

The League of Conservation Voters, the primary nonpartisan political voice of this nation's environmental movement, gave President Bush an "F" on the organization's 2003 Report Card on the administration's performance on environmental issues.[35] Factors contributing to Bush's failing grade included his administration's appointments, administrative and executive actions, and legislative initiatives. The Report Card faulted the Bush administration for weakening laws protecting the air and water and for taking actions to benefit timber, mining, oil and gas, and real estate development companies at the expense of the public's interest in a clean, safe, and healthy environment.[36]

At the beginning of the 21st century, environmental policy is not only a matter of political debate, it is also increasingly a matter of legal and constitutional debate. Nearly two-thirds of all legal challenges to federal environmental laws are decided on a constitutional grounds, which is really a significant change. Congressional power to regulate environmentally harmful activities, including the CAA and the CWA, is found under the Commerce Clause of Article I. As explained in Chapter 1, the scope of that power is increasingly challenged, as are Congressional powers exercised under the Supremacy Clause and the 5th and 14th Amendments where regulatory "takings" are concerned. The addition of two of President Bush's appointees to the Supreme Court, Chief Justice Roberts and Associate Justice Alito, has changed the composition of the Court in uncertain ways. The extent of Congressional power to regulate the environment will continue to come before the Supreme Court, and it remains to be seen what changes these new Justices will bring to environmental regulation.[37] Another extremely significant change we have seen in the beginning of the 21st century is a shift toward the states taking a greater role in protecting the environment. Congress and the federal government took the lead in creating our system of laws that protect the environment, but during the years of the Bush administration, we have seen the EPA becoming much less aggressive in enforcing existing regulations and promulgating more stringent standards, and we are starting to see states, both individually and as coalitions, moving in to fill what they are increasingly perceiving as a failure of the federal government to do its job in protecting the environment.

The increasingly important role that the state governments are playing in the 21st century can perhaps be most clearly seen from the fact that for the first time, during the 2006 election year, environmental groups made significant contributions and endorsements to state gubernatorial candidates who seemed to have a pro-environment agenda. In the past, these groups concentrated their resources on the federal elections because it was the federal government that was really responsible for protecting the environment. As the federal government has been gradually abdicating its role as the key protector of the environment, these groups are now shifting many resources to the new guardians of the environment, the states.

NATIONAL ENVIRONMENTAL POLICY ACT

We begin our study of environmental regulations by examining the two major policy statutes: the NEPA of 1970 and the Pollution Prevention Act of 1990. Enacted 20 years apart, these acts when contrasted give a sense of the history and future direction of our environmental policies.

NEPA was signed into law on January 1, 1970, and may be characterized as a planning statute. It does three things directly:

1. Establishes the CEQ, the federal watchdog of environmental policy
2. Requires federal agencies to take environmental consequences into account when they make certain decisions, which before NEPA, they could not do because consideration of such effects was rarely listed in agencies' enabling acts as a factor to be taken into account in agency decision making
3. Requires that an EIS be prepared for every major legislative proposal or other federal agency action having a significant impact on the quality of the human environment

COUNCIL ON ENVIRONMENTAL QUALITY

The least controversial aspect of NEPA was its first mandate: the creation of the CEQ. The CEQ is made up of three persons, one of whom is designated the chair. The role of the council is primarily advisory, mainly advising the president about environmental matters. The CEQ gathers and analyzes data, informs the president about the progress the nation is making toward cleaning up the environment, and recommends legislation that needs to be passed and issues that needs attention. Until 1995, the CEQ was required by law to use the data it gathered to publish the *President's Annual Report on Environmental Quality,* which was also made available to the public. It was once an excellent source of information about the environment. However, while the agency must still report to the president about the state of the environment, a published report available to the public is no longer required.[38]

The CEQ also helps federal agencies to meet their EIS requirements under NEPA by reviewing drafts of these statements. The CEQ establishes regulations pertaining to NEPA procedures. For example, in 1986, the CEQ amended 40 CFR 1502.22 to require the EPA to disclose when data are incomplete or inadequate to discuss potential adverse impacts fully.

The chair of the CEQ has additional duties. He or she attends meetings of the President's Domestic Policy Council when environmental matters are discussed, represents the president at international conferences, and drafts memos and executive orders related to the environment. The chair also coordinates federal agency activities involved with the World Commission on Environment Development (WCED), an offshoot of the United Nation's General Assembly that conducts research on environmental topics. The following box describes additional functions of the CEQ.

The CEQ was decimated during the 1980s. Adjusted for inflation, the CEQ's budget dropped from $4.1 million in 1975 to $700,000 by 1990, an 83 percent decline. Its staff fell from 57 in 1977 to 11 by the late 1980s.[39] With such drastic cuts in budget and personnel, it became increasingly difficult for the CEQ even to produce its mandated annual report, which continued to diminish in size, and fell several years behind schedule toward the end of the 1980s.[40]

Many had hoped that the CEQ would return to its earlier form when Bill Clinton was elected. However, President Clinton surprised many by instead moving to abolish the CEQ in February 1993 and reducing its staff from 35 to 3. In combination with this proposal, President Clinton also wanted to elevate the EPA to a cabinet-level agency, with the EPA administrator becoming Secretary of Environment. Most of the functions of the CEQ, including its functions under NEPA, would be transferred to the new Department of Environment. To ensure there was an environmental agency in the executive office of the president, Clinton proposed a new Office of Environmental Policy to be set up by executive order, not by statutory law. The head of this new office would be a deputy assistant to the president. Kathleen McGinty, a former Senate staff aide to Al Gore, was appointed to fill this new position. Among her tasks would be sitting in on meetings of the Domestic Policy Council, the National Security Council, and the Economic Policy Council.

Although the Office of Environmental Policy was established by executive order and the major positions of the CEQ were left unfilled, the House refused to pass Clinton's bill to elevate the status of the EPA and abolish the CEQ. In August 1995, Clinton finally decided to rejuvenate the CEQ, doing away with the Office of Environmental Policy, and named Kathleen McGinty as head of the CEQ. Although some environmentalists were initially worried that the 29-year-old McGinty was named to such an important position with what they perceived as little experience, she clearly demonstrated her effectiveness in her position. In the fall of 1998, she played an important role in sinking numerous budget riders to funding bills. Senior administration officials credit McGinty with the "greening" of the White House, and others credit her for the revitalization of the CEQ.[41] However, McGinty stepped down as the head of the CEQ in December 1998.

During the George W. Bush administration, the chair of the CEQ went to James Laurence Connaughton, an environmental lawyer. Connaughton

SPECIFIC FUNCTIONS OF THE CEQ INCLUDE THE FOLLOWING:

- Advise and assist the president in the development of environmental policies and proposed legislation as requested by the president
- Advise the president on national and international policies relating to the environment
- Identify, assess, and report on trends in environmental quality and recommend appropriate response strategies
- Oversee federal agency implementation of the Environmental Impact Assessment process and act as a referee for interagency disputes regarding the adequacy of such assessments
- Report annually to the president on the state of the environment through preparation of the annual Environmental Quality Report [uncertain status of this requirement]
- Provide general support and leadership for the coordination of activities of federal departments and agencies that affect, protect, and improve environmental quality
- Support and participate in the government-wide effort to reinvent environmental regulation
- Foster cooperation between the federal, state, and local governments, the private sector, and American citizens on matters of EC
- Interpret NEPA and the CEQ regulations in response to requests from federal, state, and local agencies and citizens
- Approve agency NEPA procedures and issue guidance to address systemic problems

Source: Council on Environmental Quality. *http://www.whitehouse.gov/CEQ/About.html* (November 29, 1998; site since changed, information on file with author).

previously served on a committee of the ISO that negotiates the ISO 14000 standards, discussed earlier in this chapter. Connaughton is also a member of the Council on Foreign Relations, a nonpartisan think tank addressing American foreign policy.

ENVIRONMENTAL IMPACT STATEMENT

Far more controversial than the creation of the CEQ was the requirement of the EIS. This requirement has a widespread impact on several government agencies, as well as on private firms seeking to do business under governmental agency contracts or licenses. Although the process has been criticized by many of the groups affected, most studies of NEPA's effectiveness have concluded that it has forced greater governmental awareness and more careful planning in many agencies. Figure 4-1 shows the number of EISs published by federal agencies during the years 1973 through 2004. Notice that the number of EISs steadily declined from 1973 until 1989, leveling off at approximately 500 reports annually from 1970 to 2004 (Table 4-1).

Several major issues pervade an analysis of the EIS requirement, ranging from who must file the EIS, and when, to disputes over what must be included in the statement, to whether the process is effective.

Threshold Considerations

Every time a federal agency undertakes an activity, it must decide whether to file an EIS. Filing an unnecessary EIS is a waste of time and money. Failure to file a necessary statement can be equally or more expensive if someone

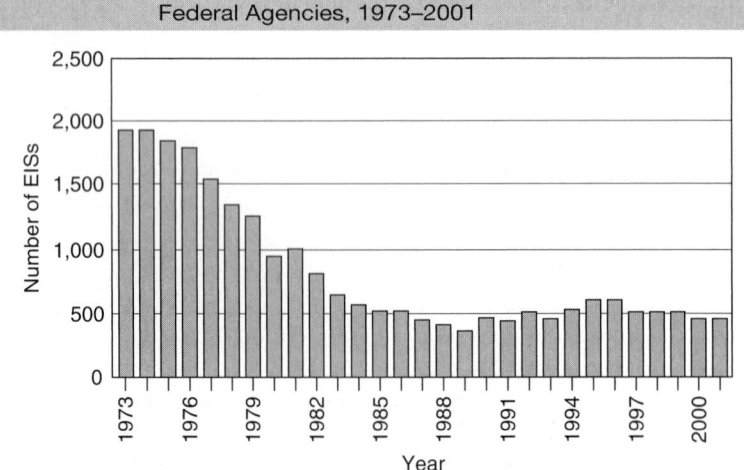

FIGURE 4-1   Environmental Impact Statements Published by All Federal Agencies, 1973–2001

Source: EPA. *http://www.epa.gov/compliance/resources/publications/nepa/ number_eis_1973_2001.pdf* (October 23, 2003).

TABLE 4-1	Environmental Impact Statements Filed 1970 Through 2004		
Year	**Draft**	**Final**	**Total**
1970–1972	—	—	5,834
1973	—	—	2,036
1974	—	—	1,965
1975	—	—	1,881
1976	—	—	1,802
1977	—	—	1,568
1978	—	—	1,355
1979	585	688	1,273
1980	440	526	966
1981	436	597	1,033
1982	359	449	808
1983	291	368	659
1984	268	309	577
1985	232	317	549
1986	216	305	521
1987	177	278	455
1988	180	252	432
1989	167	203	370
1990	228	250	478
1991	215	242	457
1992	238	275	513
1993	238	227	465
1994	247	285	532
1995	359	248	607
1996	298	304	602
1997	252	246	498
1998	280	247	527
1999	266	235	501
2000	252	221	473
2001	274	218	492
2002	284	250	534
2003	325	269	594
2004	299	298	597

Source: http://ceq.eh.doe.gov/nepa/EIS_Statistics_1970_to_2004.pdf
(October 12, 2006).

challenges the lack of an EIS and seeks an injunction. However, it is not always easy to know when an EIS is required. NEPA specifies three conditions that must be met for an EIS to be required. First, the activity must be federal. A federal activity is fairly broadly defined. If, for example, a private sector construction firm wants to construct a building that requires a government license or if the project is going to be partly financed by a government loan, the licensing or lending agency is undertaking a federal activity.

Whether an EIS is required for a federal activity depends on whether the other two criteria are met. Second, the federal activity must be major. There are no dollar guidelines as to what constitutes a major activity. The courts generally say that the activity requires a substantial commitment of resources, with resources being broadly defined to include both financial and human resources. A substantial commitment of either type of resource is sufficient.

The third criterion is that the proposed activity must have a significant impact on the human environment. The phrase significant impact on the human environment is so ambiguous that it initially generated substantial litigation. Then, in 1979, the CEQ tried to resolve some of the controversy by adopting a series of guidelines for the implementation of NEPA's procedural provisions. In these guidelines, the CEQ tried to define better what was meant by "significant impact." The CEQ stated that determining the significance of an impact necessitated examining both the context and the intensity of the action. Looking at the context was said to require consideration of both the short- and the long-term effects of the activity and looking at the impact of the activity on the local area, the region, and society as a whole.

Examining the intensity of an activity was said to involve the following ten factors:

1. Both beneficial and detrimental effects
2. The degree to which the public health and safety will be affected
3. Unique characteristics of the geographic area that may be affected by the activity
4. The degree to which the effects of the activity are likely to cause controversy
5. The degree to which the effects on the human environment are highly uncertain or unique
6. The degree to which the activity is likely to set a precedent for future actions
7. Whether insignificant effects from this activity, when combined with insignificant effects from other activities, will constitute significant effects
8. The degree to which the act may affect places of scientific, historic, or cultural significance
9. The degree to which an act may adversely affect an endangered species
10. Whether the act threatens any law designed to protect the environment[42]

Even with this "clarification" by the CEQ, it is still sometimes difficult to know whether an EIS is necessary. A demonstration of that difficulty can be made by examining two very similar cases. After reading the descriptions, try to decide whether the court in either case required an EIS.

Both cases involved the Department of Housing and Urban Development (HUD). In case 1, HUD was preparing to loan a developer $3.5 million to construct a high rise in an area of Portland, Oregon, where there were no other high rises.[43] In case 2, HUD was preparing to insure a developer's $3.7 million loan to construct a 272-unit apartment complex in Houston on a 15-acre lot.[44] Must HUD file an EIS in both cases, either case, or neither case? The court in the first case required an EIS; the court in the second case did not.

There were two primary reasons for the different outcomes. First, the activity in case 1 was major, whereas the second was not. Although both involved millions of dollars, the actual transfer of money was likely to be much greater in the first case than in the second because the former required the actual lending of money, whereas the latter was only a guarantee of a loan.[45] The only way the transfer of funds would occur would be if the developer failed to pay the loan. Because of the careful screening of candidates for insured loans, failure of repayment did not appear likely. Second, the impact of the first activity was more significant. In the first case, the use was for a unique activity, whereas in Houston, where there was no zoning as the city developed, building a housing complex was not unique, regardless of where it was.[46] There was also the possibility that building one high rise in Portland might set a dangerous precedent, leading to overcrowding in the area. Another factor, not mentioned in the statement of the case, was that there was organized opposition to the high rise in Portland.

EISs remain controversial. Newspapers frequently report conflicts between environmental groups and businesses over the need for an EIS. For example, one article described a conflict between GE and environmental groups over the building of a GE Company hangar at the airport in Harrison, New York.[47] Environmentalists argued that an EIS was necessary because the site has numerous environmental issues, such as concerns about runoff from the hangar into the area's largest water supply. GE claimed that it has demonstrated that an EIS is not necessary because "the project [did] not create an adverse impact on the environment."[48]

Two factors that may influence whether an EIS is required include the jurisdiction and the time.[49] Recall from your previous reading that most attorneys who do environmental work are aware of the fact that certain judges or courts tend to hand down more pro-environmentalist decisions than do others. In fact, in situations in which a corporation with operations in many states is being sued and the company would fall within the jurisdiction of multiple courts, the plaintiff will carefully examine rulings of all those courts, so that the case may be filed in the most environmentally friendly one.

Time may have an impact in three ways. First, although judges are not supposed to be influenced by the public, they would not be human if they were totally unaffected by public opinion. Thus, at a time when there is strong public sentiment in support of environmental protection, judges may be moved slightly toward requiring EISs in close cases. Second, during a time when the federal courts are dominated by judges appointed by a strong environmentalist president, judges may be more likely to require EISs because appointees have a tendency to have political values similar to those of the president who made the appointments. Finally, the prevailing political climate may influence federal judges who are desirous of appointments to higher courts. They may not want to displease the president and jeopardize their chances for prospective appointments.

In any situation in which the need to file an EIS is questionable, some analysis of the significance of the impact of an activity must obviously take place. If an agency decides that no EIS is necessary, although it believes others may disagree, the agency may try to protect itself by filing a Finding of No Significant Impact (FONSI). This document states the reasons why the agency believes no EIS is necessary. The FONSI is usually accompanied by an environmental assessment (EA) that provides the evidence and analysis for the agency's decision.

Once the agency decides that it needs to file an EIS, certain procedural steps must be followed. These procedures are detailed in the following section.

Procedure under the EIS Requirement

One of the major criticisms of the EIS process is related to the time-consuming nature of the procedures necessary for preparing an EIS. Initially, the agency required to file the EIS would assemble a team of specialists to prepare a draft report. In many cases, this team will consist of outside consultants, many of whom may have a vested interest in preparing positive assessments, so that they will be able to secure contracts from the agency in the future. Next, a draft version will be circulated within the agency, to be reviewed by several parties. There may frequently be disputes between reviewers who are pro-agency or pro-industry and those who are more environmentally concerned. The draft may be revised because of these initial comments.

Following the agency's completion of that draft, the document goes to the CEQ for review and comments. Then, in accordance with the APA's rules for informal rule making, the draft is published in the Federal Register for public comment. Many other agencies, including the EPA, will submit comments at this time, as will citizens' groups and business interests. The box *EPA Rating Definitions* contains the ratings the EPA uses to evaluate EISs.

EPA RATING DEFINITIONS

- *Lack of Objections* (LO)—The EPA review has not identified any potential environmental impact requiring substantive change to the proposal

- *Environmental Concerns* (EC)—The EPA has identified environmental impacts that should be avoided to fully protect the environment

- *Environmental Objective* (EO)—The EPA has identified significant environmental impacts that must be avoided to adequately protect the environment

- *Environmentally Unsatisfactory* (EU)—The EPA has identified adverse environmental impacts that are unsatisfactory from the standpoint of public health

Source: EPA. "Summary of EPA Rating Definitions." *http://es.epa.gov/oeca/ofa/rating.html* (July 22, 2001).

After the public comments have been received, a similar process will be followed for the final draft. If a draft has been severely criticized, the agency is faced with the difficult decision of whether to try to repair it or draft an entirely new document. This type of dispute can tie up an agency for weeks or months. Preparing a new draft is time-consuming and costly because all the steps have to be repeated with the new statement. However, proceeding with an inadequate EIS may lead to a successful legal challenge by parties opposed to the action. Once the agency is satisfied with its final draft, it publishes it in the Federal Register. For a routine EIS, this entire procedure may take from 6 to 9 months. Court challenges may tie up the process for a year or longer.

After publication of the final draft, the sufficiency of the draft may be challenged in court. The failure to file an EIS when required may also be challenged. This process of judicial review of the EIS has led to criticism by environmentalists. When reviewing the EIS, the court generally operates in an administrative law tradition, which means that the court will not substitute its judgment for the agencies. As long as the agency followed the proper procedures and included the requisite elements in the EIS, the court will allow the EIS to stand and the agency action to occur. Under no circumstances can a party contest the weight given by the agency to any adverse consequences listed in the statement. The court will never forbid an action on the grounds that the consequences are too severe.

Even if the court finds that the EIS was inadequate, the only remedy is a temporary injunction of agency action until a proper EIS has been filed. This limited power of the courts has led many to argue that the filing of an EIS is a "toothless" requirement. As a consequence of the court's limited remedies, a party who challenges an EIS may hope for one of three outcomes. First, the party seeking to take the action for which the EIS was required will decide to modify the project to save time or to avoid adverse publicity. Second, the delay might give the party challenging the action enough time to rally persuasive public opposition to the project. Finally, the delay may make the project too costly, so it may be dropped.

You might think that given the limited remedy available under NEPA, few challenges would be filed. However, between 1974 and 1985, roughly 120 NEPA cases were filed each year. The number of cases filed has increased since then. In 2004, there were 185 cases pending on NEPA litigation. Most cases do not result in injunctions being issued. In fact, no injunctions were granted until 1979, when the courts responded favorably to 12 of the 139 requested injunctions. From 1980 to 1985, the number of injunctions issued ranged from 8 to 21. In 2004, there were seven permanent injunctions. Of course, just because an injunction was not issued, the case was not necessarily ineffective. We do not know how many court challenges or threatened challenges led to voluntary modifications of agency plans. Sometimes, the very act of preparing the EIS causes an agency to change its plans. For example, a spokesperson for the Army COE stated that, in 1972, EISs caused the Corps to drop 24 projects temporarily, to delay 44 indefinitely, and to modify 197 significantly.

TABLE 4-2 Plaintiffs in NEPA Lawsuits 2004	
Public Interest groups	232
Individual/Citizen association	83
State government	11
Local government	21
Business groups	27
Property owners/residents	11
Indian tribes	13
Combination plaintiffs[a]	9

[a] i.e., local government and individuals; if a plaintiff type was in a combination with other plaintiff types, it was counted in the individual as well as the combination category.

Source: http://www.nepa.gov/nepa/NEPA2004LitigationSurvey.pdf (October 12, 2006).

The most frequent plaintiffs in challenges to EISs are citizens' groups and environmental groups. Table 4-2 lists the plaintiffs in NEPA lawsuits filed in 2004. The most frequent defendants tend to be the Department of Transportation, the Department of the Interior, the Army COE, and the Federal Energy Regulatory Commission (FERC).

Contents of the EIS

Whether an agency voluntarily prepares an EIS or is required to by the courts, the following elements must be contained in the document:

1. A statement of environmental impacts (positive and negative) of the proposed action
2. Any unavoidable adverse environmental impacts should the proposal be implemented
3. Alternatives to the proposal (including taking no action)
4. The relationship between short-term uses of the environment and enhancement of long-term productivity
5. Any irreversible commitments of resources

The suggested format for the EIS is given in Table 4-3.

ALTERNATIVES TO THE EIS

Environmental Assessment

An EA is a concise public document that analyzes the environmental impacts of a proposed federal action to determine the level of significance of the impacts. When an EA is completed and it is determined that there are no significant impacts, no EIS needs to be filed. If a group subsequently challenges the failure of the agency to prepare an EIS, the agency will often use the EA to demonstrate why it believed no EIS was necessary.

The EA has become so popular that more EAs are filed than EISs. It is impossible to know how many EAs are prepared because they are not

TABLE 4-3 Format of Environmental Impact Statements

Item	Length	Contents Include
1. Cover sheet	Up to 1 page	Title and locations of proposed action, locale involved, agencies, names and addresses of persons who can supply further information, relevant dates, one-paragraph abstract of statement
2. Summary	Up to 15 pages	Summary of statement stressing major conclusions, areas of controversy, and issues to be resolved
3. Table of contents		
4. Purpose and need for action		
5. Alternatives, including proposed action		Heart of the statement. Rigorous evaluation of all alternatives, including why some were eliminated from consideration, including alternative of no action, identifying agencies' preferred action, and including appropriate mitigation actions
6. Affected environment	No longer than necessary	Succinct description
7. Environmental consequence		Discussion of direct and indirect effects and their significance, energy requirements, possible conflicts with land use plans of other governmental bodies, depletable resource requirements and conservation potential of alternatives, urban quality, historical and cultural resources, and means to initiate impacts if not already discussed
8. List of preparers	Not to exceed 2 pages	Names and qualifications
9. List of agencies, organizations, and persons to whom copies are to be sent		
10. Index		
11. Appendixes (if any)		Material prepared in connection with the EIS that is analytical and relevant to any decisions to be made and substantiates any analysis fundamental to the EIS

required to be filed, but a survey of federal agencies conducted by the CEQ in 1993 revealed that approximately 50,000 EAs were being prepared annually. Some environmental groups fear that certain EAs are filed to avoid public involvement. Other groups simply see the EA as a much more efficient way to protect the environment.

Mitigated FONSI

Sometimes, an agency will discover a potentially significant environmental impact in the course of doing an EA. If the agency then proposes measures that will mitigate the adverse effects of the proposed actions, it may then conclude the NEPA process by preparing a FONSI. Increasingly, these so-called mitigated FONSIs are being used.

EFFECTIVENESS OF NEPA

In 1997, the CEQ published a report studying the effectiveness of NEPA after 25 years.[50] The report concluded that although NEPA is a success, implementation has fallen short of its goals at times. For example, companies sometimes complete the EIS after they have made their decision. In other words, they are not actually using the EIS to help make decisions regarding environmental impacts. The report also noted the increased use of EAs.

Participants in the study that led to the report stated that NEPA still takes too long and costs too much. Furthermore, they complain that the documents are too long and too technical. They view the EIS as a requirement rather than as a tool for better decision making. Despite the complaints of the study participants, NEPA has been emulated by more than 25 states and over 80 countries around the world. Following the publication of the 1997 report, the CEQ implemented the NEPA Reinvention Project. The CEQ's goals for the reinvention of NEPA are to reduce unnecessary delays, to save taxpayer money, and to promote sensible, cost-effective reform of environmental decision making. Unfortunately, there have been no published studies on NEPA's effectiveness since 1977.

In 2002, the CEQ created a NEPA Task Force to modernize the NEPA process. However, the Bush administration has been highly critical of the NEPA and has continually sought to weaken it. For example, exemption from NEPA requirements has been sought for activities by the Department of Defense. Also in 2002, the Departments of Agriculture and Interior created two exemptions to NEPA for forest management projects, including forest thinning.

POLLUTION PREVENTION ACT OF 1990

The first environmental protection laws used a very directive approach. The EPA was to establish standards, and the other agencies and businesses were to meet those standards. Many of the early regulations, as you shall see when you read about specific laws in subsequent chapters, were "command and control" (dictated standards) or end-of-pipe (using technology to treat the waste or pollutant just before it was emitted). In fact, these are still the primary types of regulations today. The Pollution Prevention Act, however, recognizes that these end-of-pipe regulations may not be enough, so we are going to have to find ways to prevent the creation of pollution in the first place.

Initially, great gains were made by using these strategies. Relatively minor investments led to dramatic decreases in pollutants. However, after 20 years of implementation of these end-of-pipe controls, it became increasingly costly to get increasingly smaller reductions of pollutants. Although $1 million might have decreased a firm's emissions of a pollutant by 80 percent, the tailpipe controls needed to decrease that pollutant by only 10 percent more might cost the firm an additional $2 million. It gradually became apparent to Congress that a new approach was necessary. That new approach was embodied in the Pollution Prevention Act of 1990, passed by Congress on October 27, 1990. In its findings, presented in Section 2 of the act, Congress stated:

> (1) There are significant opportunities for industry to reduce or prevent pollution at the source through cost-effective changes in production, operation, and raw materials use. Such changes offer industry substantial savings in reduced raw material, pollution control, and liability costs as well as help protect the environment and reduce risks to worker health and safety.
>
> (2) The opportunities for source reduction are often not realized because existing regulations, and the industrial resources they require for compliance, focus upon treatment and disposal, rather than source reduction; existing regulations do not emphasize multi-media management of pollution; and businesses need information and technical assistance to overcome institutional barriers to the adoption of source reduction practices.
>
> (3) Source reduction is fundamentally different and more desirable than waste management and pollution control. The EPA needs to address the historical lack of attention to source reduction.

The wisdom of these findings is supported by an article in the *Wall Street Journal*. According to the article, chemical companies, traditionally a group with an often-criticized record on the environment, are making a major shift and beginning to see waste as avoidable and inefficient. The more unusable by-products a process creates, the less efficient it may be. For example, at one DuPont plant, which generated 110 million pounds of waste annually, engineers adjusted their production process to use less of one raw material and slashed the plant's waste by two-thirds. The resulting savings from the change in process amounted to $1 million a year.[51]

As a result of its findings, Congress established the following policy:

> Pollution should be prevented or reduced at the source whenever feasible; pollution that cannot be prevented should be recycled in an environmentally safe manner, whenever feasible; pollution that

cannot be prevented or recycled should be treated in an environmentally safe manner whenever feasible; and disposal or other release into the environment should be employed only as a last resort and should be conducted in an environmentally safe manner.

To implement this new policy, the administrator of the EPA is required to establish a separate office within the agency to serve as administrator under the act.

The act also authorizes the provision of matching grants to states for programs to promote the use of source reduction techniques by business. Between 1989 and 2001, over $70.2 million in such grants have been awarded to support state and tribal pollution prevention programs. To collect and compile information generated by the grants and to disseminate this information, the administrator is authorized to establish a clearinghouse to serve as a center for source reduction technology transfer.

Finally, certain biennial reports are required of the administrator of the act. These reports are to include such information as analysis of grant results, identification of industries and pollutants that require priority assistance in multimedia source reduction, and evaluation of data gaps and duplication of data collected under federal environmental protection acts.

In 1993, President Clinton issued an executive order to improve pollution prevention in the federal government. The three main requirements of this order are:[52]

1. Each federal agency must develop a pollution prevention strategy that is committed to source reduction
2. Each agency must reduce total releases of toxic chemicals by 50 percent by the end of 1999
3. Each agency must establish a plan to eliminate the procurement of hazardous substances for agency use

The report notes that pollution prevention is one of the major successes of the 1990s. The EPA is working with the states to encourage businesses to prevent pollution. For example, the successes of the 35/50 Project, discussed earlier in this chapter, are attributed to the Pollution Prevention Act. One reason for the success of the act might be various pollution prevention conferences, workshops, and training sessions offered through the Office of Pollution Prevention and Toxics (OPPT). The box below provides the steps for setting up a pollution prevention program in a business.

Concluding Remarks

The primary justifications for environmental protection range from the analogy of the tragedy of the commons to the economic justifications and to the arguments from an environmental ethos. Taken together, these justifications seem to provide strong support for many of the regulatory programs you are going to be studying.

SETTING UP A POLLUTION PREVENTION PROGRAM

1. Demonstrate top management support to ensure that pollution prevention becomes an organizational goal. To demonstrate such management support, use techniques such as:
   - Circulating a written company policy on pollution prevention
   - Setting specific goals for reducing waste stream volume or toxicity
   - Designating program coordinators
   - Publicizing and rewarding successes
   - Providing employee training in pollution prevention

2. Characterize waste generation and waste management costs. Maintain a waste accounting system to track the types and amounts of wastes and hazardous constituents. The best type of system will vary for each organization. Determine the true costs associated with waste management and cleanup, including costs of regulatory oversight compliance, paperwork, materials in the waste stream, and loss of production potential.

3. Conduct periodic pollution prevention assessments to ensure that pollution prevention opportunities continue to be sought at all points in the process at which materials can be prevented from becoming waste. An assessment identifies pollution prevention options by identifying sources of pollution and waste and by looking for clean production technologies.

4. Develop a cost allocation system wherever practical and feasible to allocate the true costs of waste management to the activities responsible for generating the waste in the first place. Departments and managers should be charged "full-loaded" pollution control and waste management costs. Labor costs, liability, regulatory compliance, disposal, and oversight costs should all be included.

5. Encourage technology transfer. Consult technical manuals or EPA's clearinghouse for specific types of industry, processes, or wastes, or to review case studies that have been developed. Many successful techniques have been documented that may be applicable to your facility. Information can be obtained from federal and state agencies, universities, trade associations, and other firms.

6. Finally, review program effectiveness periodically to provide feedback and identify potential areas for improvement. Has pollution prevention become a significant part of the way you do business?

Source: EPA, "Pollution Prevention Fact Sheet: Setting Up a Pollution Prevention Program." Original EPA site no longer available, information on file with the author.

You have been introduced to various strategies that are adopted to protect the environment, such as tort law, emissions charges, marketable emissions permits, subsidies, and green taxes. In addition, the Pollution Prevention Act of 1990 encourages initial prevention and voluntary actions. However, our main approach to environmental problems continues to be direct regulation, which is the focus of the remainder of the book. Chapter 5 examines our approach to controlling air quality. We concentrate on air quality first because the CAA was the first major end-of-pipe pollution-control law, and subsequent acts for other protected resources were modeled loosely on it.

Questions for Review and Discussion

1. Explain the relationship between the tragedy of the commons and the need to control pollution.
2. Explain what a free rider is and how that concept is related to environmental law.
3. Why is tort law alone an ineffective way to control pollution?
4. Explain the advantages and disadvantages of using emissions charges and subsidies to control pollution.
5. What factors influence the development of environmental policies?
6. Explain when an EIS must be filed.
7. What must be contained in an EIS?
8. What is the purpose of the Pollution Prevention Control Act of 1990?

For Further Reading

Bellamy, Jeffrey. 2003. "Putting the Boss Behind Bars: Using Criminal Sanctions Against Executives Who Pollute — What China Can Learn from the United States." *Indian International and Comparative Law Journal 13*: 579.

Bradford, Michael. 2003. "Environmental Crimes." *South Texas Law Review 45*: 5.

Brown, Lester. 2001. *Eco-Economy: Building an Economy for the Earth.* New York: W.W. Norton & Company.

Green, Thomas, and Kristen Graham Koehler. 2003. "Environmental Crimes Update: EPA Criminal Enforcement Under the Bush Administration." *Champion* (August 27): 16.

Guha, Ramachandra. 2000. *Environmentalism: A Global History.* New York: Longman.

Hawken, Paul, et al. 1999. *Natural Capitalism: Creating the Next Industrial Revolution.* Boston: Little, Brown & Co.

Doremus, Holly. 2003. "Constitutive Law and Environmental Policy." *Stanford Environmental Law Journal 22*: 295.

Leyden, Pat. 1998. "The Price of Change: The Market Incentive Revolution in Air Pollution Regulations." *Natural Resources and Environment Journal 12*: 160.

Orts, Edward W. 1995. "Toward Reflexive Environmental Law." *Northwestern University Law Review 89*: 1227.

Vig, Norman J., et al. 2005. *Environmental Policy: New Directions for the Twenty-First Century.* CQ Press.

Yeager, Peter. 1991. *The Limits of the Law: The Public Regulation of Private Pollution.* New York: Cambridge University Press.

On the Internet

http://yosemite.epa.gov/opa/admpress.nsf/
    Contains press releases issued by the EPA
http://www.energystar.gov
    Home page of the Energystar program

http://www.whitehouse.gov/ceq
Home page of the Council on Environmental Quality
http://www.panda.org
News and information on all aspects of conservation, the environment, and sustainable development
http://www.epa.gov/opptintr/p2home/
Home page of the EPA's Office of Pollution Prevention
http://www.epa.gov/lmop/
Landfill Methane Outreach Program, an example of a voluntary program designed to reduce, and use, greenhouse gasses
http://yosemite.epa.gov/water/volmon.nsf/Home?readform
National Directory of Volunteer Monitoring Programs
http://es.epa.gov/cooperative/topics/iso14000.html
Links to ISO 14000 Industry Standards websites
http://www.lcv.org/
The League of Conservation Voters—look up congressional scorecards

Notes

1. Garrett Hardin. 1968. "The Tragedy of the Commons." *Science 162*: 1243.
2. Ibid.
3. Aldo Leopold. 1948. *A Sand County Almanac.* 1968 ed, pp 214–220. New York: Oxford University Press.
4. Ibid.
5. 287 NYS 2d 112 (1967).
6. Peter Behr. 2000. "Scientists Urge Tax on Emissions." *Washington Post* (November 16): E3. *http://www.washingtonpost.com/wp-dyn/articles/A29250-2000Nov15.html* (January 21, 2001).
7. Ibid.
8. Vanessa Houlder. 2000. "Carrying the Cost of Carbon." September 11, *http://news.ft.com/ft/gx.cgi/ftc?pagename=View&c=Article&cid=FT3F6QPF0DC&liv* (January 21, 2001).
9. Ibid.
10. *Environmental Taxes in the European Union 1980–2001. http://europa.eu.int/comm/taxation_customs/publications/other/ksnq03009_en.pdf* (November 10, 2003).
11. *New York State Green Building Initiative. http://www.dec.state.ny.us/* *website/ppu/grnbldg/index.html* (October 28, 2003).
12. Rachel Carson. 1962. *Silent Spring.* Boston: Houghton Mifflin.
13. Paul Ehrlich. 1968. *The Population Bomb.* New York: Ballantine.
14. Barry Commoner. 1972. *The Closing Circle: Nature, Man, and Technology.* New York: Knopf.
15. Norman Vig. 1990. "Presidential Leadership: From the Reagan to the Bush Administration." *Environmental Policy in the 1990's: Toward a New Agenda,* Norman Vig and Michael Kraft, editors. Washington, D.C.: Congressional Quarterly.
16. Ibid.
17. Ibid.
18. Ibid.
19. "Getting Personal." 1993. *Wall Street Journal* (January 20): R3.
20. Margaret C. Fisk. 1992. "Girding for a Change." *National Law Journal* (December 14): S1.
21. Ibid.
22. John H. Cushman, Jr. 1996. "G.O.P. Backing off from Tough Stand over Environment." *The New York Times* (January 26): A1.

23. Gregory Wetstone. 1998. "GOP Wages Stealth Attack Under the Cover of Scandal." *Sun-Sentinel* (October 1): 19A.
24. Charles Levendosky. 1998. "Ask Sea Turtles and Trees How Much They Trust GOP." *Sacramento Bee* (August 23): F5.
25. Charles Levendosky. 1998. "GOP Tries to Pass as Green." *Sun-Sentinel* (September 9): 19A.
26. ISO 14000/Insustry Standards. *http://es.epa.gov/cooperative/topics/iso14000.html* (October 14, 2006).
27. Environmental Working Group. 1993. "The Political Agenda of the 'Wise Use' Movement." *http://www.ewg.org/pub/home/clear/on_wise/afte.html* (January 30, 2001).
28. Cheryl Hogue. 2003. "EPA Whitman Calls it Quits." *Chemical and Engineering News* (May 26).
29. Pelosi Statement on Resignation of EPA Administrator Christine Todd Whitman. *http://www.democraticleader.house.gov/press/releases.cfm?pressReleaseID=90* (January 21, 2004).
30. Amanda Griscomb. "Jumping Ship at EPA." *http://www.gristmagazine.com/muck/muck010704.asp?source=muck* (January 7, 2004).
31. Jennifer B. Lee, quoting Rich Biondi. 2004. "Top Enforcement Officials Say They Will Leave EPA." *New York Times* (January 6).
32. Amanda Griscomb, note 30.
33. Ibid.
34. Ibid.
35. The League of Conservation Voters, "Bush Receives F for Environmental Issues on the LCV 2003 Presidential Report Card." *http://icv.org/News/News.cfm?ID=1658& C=26* (June 24, 2003).
36. Ibid.
37. James R. May. *Trends in Constitutional Environmental Law, TRENDS, ABA Section of Environment, Energy, and Resources,* March/April 2006.
38. See *Public Law104–66.*
39. Michael Kraft and Norman Vig, *Environmental Policies from the Seventies to the Nineties.* Washington, D.C.: CQ Press.
40. Ibid.
41. Jody Warrick. 1998. "Architect of a White House Green Machine Bids Farewell; Kathleen McGinty Reshaped Environmental Council and Probed Tough GOP Adversary in Budget Battles." *Washington Post* (October 30): A25.
42. 40 C.F.R. ñ 1508.27.
43. *Goose Hollow Foothills League v. Romney,* 334 F.Supp. 877 (1971).
44. *Hiram Clarke Civic Club v. Lynn,* 47 F.2d 421 (1973).
45. David Firestone and Frank Reed. 1983. *Environmental Law for Nonlawyers.* South Royalton, VT: Soro Press.
46. Ibid.
47. Merri Rosenberg. 1998. "Latest Issue in G.E. Bid for Hangar." *New York Times* (November 22): 12.
48. Ibid.
49. Firestone and Reed, note 45.
50. CEQ. 1997. *The National Environmental Policy Act: A Study of Its Effectiveness After Twenty-five Years.* Washington, D.C.: CEQ, Executive Office of the President.
51. Scott McMurray. 1991. "Chemical Firms Find that It Pays to Reduce Pollution at the Source." *Wall Street Journal* (June 11): A1.
52. "Executive Order 12856—Federal Compliance with Right-to-Know Laws and Pollution Prevention Requirements." *http://es.epa.gov/program/exec/12856.html* (January 21, 2004).

RESOLVING CONTROVERSIAL ENVIRONMENTAL ISSUES

- Get into the habit of identifying the issue, reasons, and conclusion of any argument you encounter. You must identify these components before you can do any evaluating. As you read the following editorial, "The Right to Pollute," identify the issue, reasons, and conclusion.
- Recall that in Chapter 3 you learned how to identify assumptions. Try to identify the assumptions in the reasoning for the following editorial. If you need help, go back and read the description of the process for finding assumptions in Chapter 3. Remember, assumptions provide a link between a reason and the conclusion. What must the author believe for the reason to lead to the conclusion?

The Right to Pollute

How should we fix our pollution problems? The best solutions are market solutions. Look at the suggested program for a system of tradable emission permits for carbon emissions. This system functions by determining a limit for total carbon emissions. Next, individual firms buy and sell the limited number of pollution licenses. This process thus reduces the total amount of carbon emissions. A panel of economists and environmentalists has estimated that using a permit approach to reduce emission levels in the United States would generate approximately $160 billion per year in new revenue. That money will reduce our pollution problems.

More than 2,000 U.S. economists agree that emission permits can solve global climate problems. This group of economists, which includes Nobel laureates, argues that the total benefits of reducing emissions would outweigh the total costs. Consequently, if the costs of a project are lower than the benefits, we should adopt that project. They have suggested that the United States could gain an additional $160 billion through the permit approach. In contrast, the cost of new technology to reduce emissions is an estimated $250 billion.

These problems seem to be solved through common sense. When costs are higher, people will buy or produce fewer goods and services. Thus, let us make the cost of pollution high. Business will therefore produce less pollution and will find ways to reduce the cost of pollution. Enter the tradable permit systems. Consider the success of the permits for the Acid Rain program. When a system achieves its goals, we need to pay attention. The permit program to reduce the acid rain problem is working; we should apply a similar program to solve other pollution problems.

Firms should be forced to pay for the costs they impose. A tradable emissions permit system would give American companies an incentive to save money by reducing pollution. Clearly, market-based solutions are the answer to our pollution problems.

CHAPTER 5
AIR-QUALITY CONTROL

When people think about air-quality problems, they often think of bumper-to-bumper traffic spewing exhaust on a freeway or steel mills with smokestacks blackening the air with soot. The first major air pollution control act, the CAA of 1970, was designed to remedy such problems. This act was passed because people no longer considered visible air pollution to be evidence of economic progress but rather saw it as a problem in need of a regulatory solution. Although this first major statutory response did significantly improve air quality, air pollution is still one of the most serious environmental problems in the United States. As recently as 2006, the EPA estimated that 60 percent of Americans live in nonattainment areas, where at least one air pollutant level exceeds federal air-quality standards.[1] Figure 5-1 shows how many people are exposed to excessive amounts of each of the criteria pollutants. You can check the precise air pollution levels where you live at http://www.scorecard.org/.

To understand the current approach to air-quality control, we first need to understand which pollutants we are trying to restrict and why we need to control them. The first section provides this information. Although these "criteria pollutants" have been the initial focus of regulation, other air-quality problems must also be remedied, and these are introduced in the second section. The third section explains the early and unsuccessful approach initially adopted to protect the air. The final section explains the current approach.

THE MAJOR AIR POLLUTANTS

Every minute of every day, vast quantities of pollutants are pouring into the atmosphere. These pollutants come from both natural and human sources and are normally cycled and destroyed through natural processes. However, the quantity of human-made pollutants has begun to overload the atmosphere's self-cleansing processes, causing damage to the environment and health problems. Although we shall discuss the primary harm caused by each individual pollutant, you should be aware that much damage also comes from the interactions of these pollutants.

The first six air pollutants we discuss are currently regulated by Congress under the CAA. They are referred to under the act as criteria pollutants. It is these criteria pollutants that were initially perceived as the major air-quality problem and were the initial focus of governmental efforts

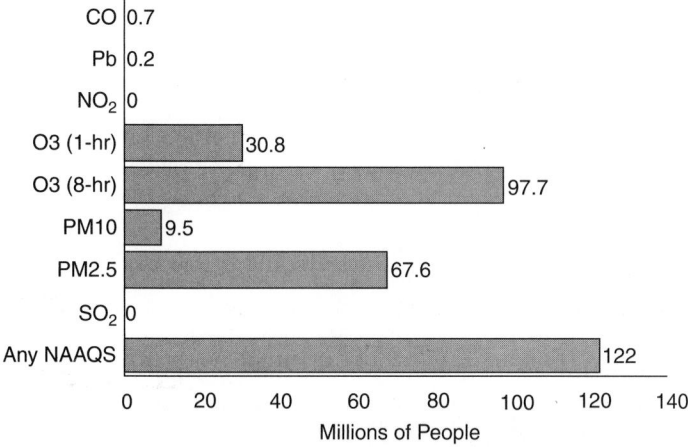

FIGURE 5-1   Number of People Living in Counties with Air Quality
Concentrations Above the Level of the NAAQS in 2005

Source: EPA Air Trends—Basic Information, *http://www.epa.gov/airtrends/sixpoll.html*
(September 3, 2006).

to improve the quality of our air. Many people still regard the regulation of
these pollutants through the establishment of ambient air-quality standards
to be the heart of air-pollution control in the United States. A brief summary of the problems caused by these pollutants is presented in Table 5-1.

SULFUR DIOXIDE

Sulfur dioxide (SO_2) is the highly corrosive gas formed when sulfur-containing
fuel is burned. It can be transported long distances in the atmosphere because

TABLE 5-1   Problems Associated with Criteria Air Pollutants

Carbon monoxide (CO)	Replaces oxygen in the bloodstream, causing angina, impaired vision, poor coordination, and lack of alertness. Contributes to formation of ozone
Lead	Damages neurological systems and kidneys
Nitrogen oxides (NO_x)	Cause lung and respiratory tract damage and contribute to acid rain and smog
Ozone	Irritates eyes, reduces lung function, increases nasal congestion, and reduces resistance to infection
Particulates	Reduce resistance to infection, irritate the eyes, ears, and throat, and cause temporary or permanent lung damage
Sulfur dioxide (SO_2)	Causes lung and respiratory tract damage and contributes to acid rain, which damages trees, buildings, vegetation, and aquatic life

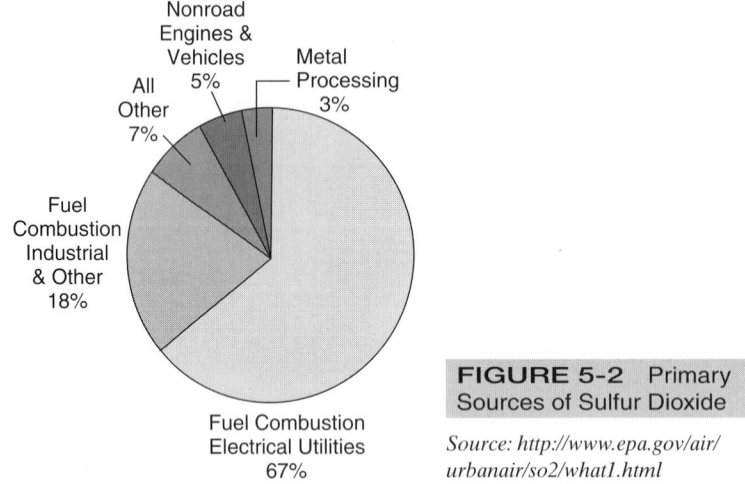

FIGURE 5-2   Primary Sources of Sulfur Dioxide

Source: http://www.epa.gov/air/urbanair/so2/what1.html

it bonds to particles of dust, smoke, or aerosols. Volcanic emissions are the largest natural source of atmospheric SO_2, although decaying organic matter and sea spray are also important. However, slightly more than half the approximately 170 million tons of SO_2 emitted globally each year come from human-made sources. The major human source of SO_2 is the burning of fossil fuels to generate electricity. The United States relies on these fuels for 90 percent of its energy needs. Figure 5-2 illustrates the primary sources of SO_2 emissions.

Since 1900, the global output of SO_2 has increased sixfold.[2] However, between 1974 and 1987, most industrial nations lowered their SO_2 emissions in urban areas through direct regulation and also by a shift away from heavy manufacturing toward burning lower-sulfur coal, and in the United States, SO_2 emissions have decreased 38 percent from 1980 to 2003.

The primary health danger from SO_2 is damage to the lungs and respiratory tract. In combination with nitrous oxide, SO_2 also contributes to the creation of acid rain, which causes harm to vegetation and buildings. Acid rain is discussed in greater detail later in this chapter.

NITROGEN OXIDES

Nitrogen oxides (NO_x) refer to two harmful gases: nitric oxide (NO) and nitrogen dioxide (NO_2). NO_x, almost immediately upon release, is converted into NO_2. On a global basis, about half of the approximately 150 million tons of NO_x emitted annually comes from natural sources, predominantly lightning and decomposing organic matter. The other half comes from human activities, with motor vehicles the largest source. Power plants and industrial emissions also make substantial contributions. Figure 5-3 depicts the sources of NO_x. Although industrialization and development have led to substantial NO_x emissions in the United States, new technology and cap and trade

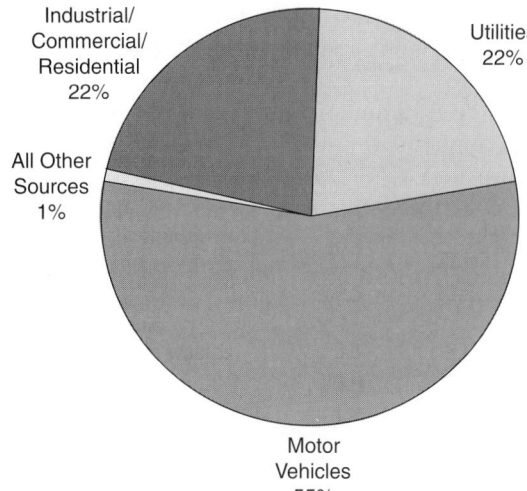

FIGURE 5-3   Manmade
Sources of Nonemissions—
2003

Source: EPA, *http://www.epa.gov/
oar/urbanair/nox/what.html*

programs have resulted in a decrease from peak discharge levels. In 2003, the
EPA recalculated previous NO_x emissions levels based on more accurate
understandings of real-world driving and determined that over the past
20 years, national emissions of NO_x have actually declined by almost 15 percent.
However, although overall NO_x emissions are declining, emissions from
some sources, such as nonroad engines, have actually increased since 1983.
To counter this growing trend, the EPA established the Clean Air Nonroad
Diesel Rule, which seeks to cut nonroad diesel vehicle emissions by 90 percent
after its effective date in 2007. Similarly, the Clean Air Interstate
Rule (CAIR) aims to reduce power-plant NO_x emission by 60 percent
before 2015.

Nitrogen oxides, like all air pollution, do not stop at state boarders.
Consequently, the EPA has required that 21 states and the District of
Columbia reduce their NO_x emissions, so downwind states do not bear the
cost of their upwind neighbors. However, EPA's attempts to reduce the
transport of NO_x emission has met some resistance; that resistance has in
fact been the source of litigation.

The primary negative health effects from NO_x mirror those of SO_2:
damage to the lungs and respiratory tract. In combination with other air
pollutants, NO_x contributes to depletion of the ozone (O_3) layer, to acid deposition, to water-quality deterioration, to smog, and to global climate change.

CARBON MONOXIDE

A third harmful gas is carbon monoxide (CO). Unlike most air pollutants,
an estimated 60 percent of CO comes from natural sources. The major

human-made source is the incomplete burning of fuels by motor vehicles. Motor vehicle exhaust is responsible for 56 percent of all CO emission in the United States and another 22 percent of CO emissions is the result of other nonroad vehicles and construction equipment. In urban areas, however, motor vehicle exhaust may account for as much as 95 percent of all CO emissions. Not surprisingly, efforts to reduce CO emissions focus on vehicle emission standards and technological advancements. Other human sources of CO include wood stoves, incinerators, and industrial processes.

Over the past 20 years, the United States, Japan, and Germany have reduced their CO emissions. In the United States, 98.7 million metric tons of CO was emitted during 1970; that amount steadily declined year after year, primarily because of automobile emission controls. Emissions fell to 61.4 million metric tons during 1987.[3] By 2006, however, 15.5 million people were still living in counties in which CO levels exceeded the federal air-quality standards.[4] Figure 5-4 identifies the counties that have not attained the CAA standards for CO as of 2006.

CO traditionally has been perceived as the least harmful of the criteria pollutants in terms of its effect on human health, but increasing evidence

FIGURE 5-4   Counties Designated Nonattainment for Carbon Monoxide

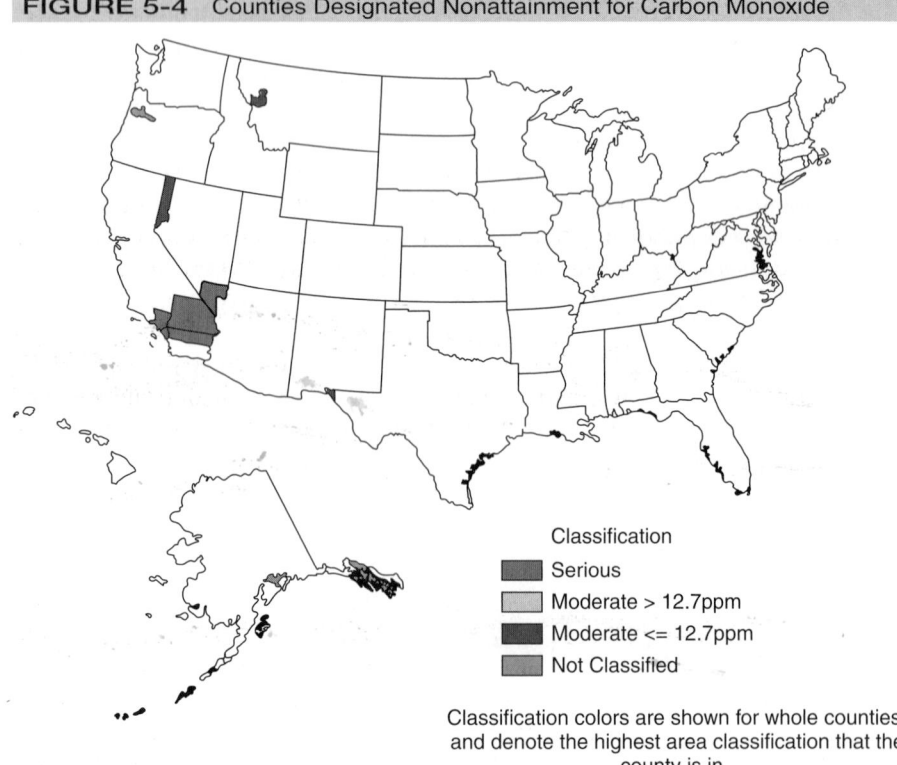

Classification

▨ Serious
▢ Moderate > 12.7ppm
▨ Moderate <= 12.7ppm
▨ Not Classified

Classification colors are shown for whole counties and denote the highest area classification that the county is in.

Source: http://www.epa.gov/air/oaqps/greenbk/mapco.html (Updated March 2006).

suggests that it does present a serious health risk. When CO is inhaled, it replaces oxygen in the bloodstream, causing angina, impaired vision, poor coordination, and lack of alertness. It may temporarily reduce one's attention span and problem-solving abilities. CO has been implicated in some accidents caused by decreased attention and reduced sensory ability. The health effects are especially severe for people who have heart and lung problems. Some animal studies have also indicated that CO can damage the central nervous system of offspring who had long-term prenatal exposure to the pollutant. CO contributes to the greenhouse effect and to the formation of O_3, itself an air pollutant.

OZONE

Some people argue that O_3 is the most intractable and widespread pollution problem. O_3, as a pollutant at low altitudes—not to be confused with the O_3 layer of the atmosphere, which actually protects life on earth from the sun's harmful rays—is not directly emitted into the air as are most of the other pollutants with which the CAA is concerned. Rather, O_3 is a gas formed when NO_x react with oxygen in the presence of sunlight, a reaction that can be enhanced by the presence of reactive hydrocarbons and other pollutants commonly found in urban environments. Chemically, O_3 is a form of oxygen that has three oxygen atoms instead of two. O_3 is the primary ingredient of smog.

We cannot measure emissions of O_3, so we examine the concentration of low-level O_3 in the air. The EPA considers the maximum safe level to be 0.08 ppm (parts per million). Concentrations vary significantly from region to region, however, and even from day to day in the same place, depending on such factors as weather and the amount of industrial activity. However, in 2003, as many as 100 million people in the United States lived in areas with unhealthy O_3 levels.[5] Because low-level O_3 is created from NO_x, efforts to reduce low-level O_3 primarily focus on reducing levels of NO_x.

O_3 causes eye irritation, nasal congestion, asthma, reduced lung function, possible damage to lung tissue, and reduced resistance to infection. O_3 harms vegetation by damaging plant tissue, inhibiting photosynthesis, and increasing plants' susceptibility to disease and drought. Short-term exposure (1–3 hours) to ambient O_3 concentrations has been linked to increased hospital admissions and emergency room visits for respiratory causes.[6]

PARTICULATES

A fifth criterion pollutant is particulates. Particulates as a pollutant refer to solid and liquid materials, varying in size from aerosol to large grit and suspended in the air. The EPA regulates both "inhalable coarse particles" (particles between 2.5 and 10 micrometers in diameter) and "fine particles" smaller than 2.5 micrometers. Particulates can be emitted directly by a source or formed in the atmosphere by the transformation of gaseous emissions. The primary human-made sources of particulates are steel mills, power plants, cotton gins, smelters, cement plants, and diesel engines. Other sources include grain elevators, demolition sites, industrial roadwork, construction work, and wood-burning stoves and fireplaces. Natural sources include soil erosion and pollen. Emissions controls have drastically reduced the amount of suspended particulates emitted into the atmosphere from human-made sources in the United States.[7] Particulates, however, are the major cause of reduced visibility in many areas in the United States. These particulates have become a significant problem in areas such as Las Vegas, Nevada, where there is a lot of continual high-volume construction.

In 2006, the EPA revised its 1997 National Ambient Air Quality Standards (NAAQSs) (discussed later in this chapter) for fine particles. The new standard reduces the 24-hour standard from 65 micrograms per cubic meter ($\mu g/m^3$) to 35 $\mu g/m^3$. The EPA estimates that this reduction will save billions of dollars in annual health costs by 2020 and is expected to prevent 2,500 premature deaths for people with heart or lung disease.[8]

The health impacts of particulates vary, depending on the particulates' size, shape, and chemistry. Fine particles pose a much greater risk to human health than do those with a diameter greater than 10 micrometers. The larger particles can be filtered out by the body's defense mechanisms, whereas the finer ones may pass through the defense mechanisms and travel into the lungs, where they may become embedded. Once in the lungs, the particulates may lead to respiratory illness or lung, or other systemic, damage. There is a demonstrated statistical correlation between high levels of particulate matter in the lungs and hospital admissions for pneumonia, bronchitis, and asthma.[9] Some particulates are carcinogenic; others may merely irritate the eyes and throat.

LEAD

The first five air pollutants were regulated as criteria pollutants under the CAA of 1970. Lead is the only pollutant to be added to the initial list of criteria pollutants, which resulted from successful litigation in *National Resources Defense Counsel v. Train* (1976). Lead emissions result primarily from burning leaded gasoline. It is also present in paints and leaded pipes.

We can see the greatest impact of regulation on pollution levels when we look at lead emissions. Human sources in the United States spewed forth 220 thousand metric tons in 1970. By 1998, this amount had fallen to 3.9 thousand metric tons.[10] These dramatic reductions resulted primarily from a prohibition of leaded gas. Today, only 13 percent of all lead emissions result from transportation sources, primarily airplanes. Metal processing is now the major source of lead emissions to the atmosphere.

Lead is of concern because it can harm the neurological system and kidneys of humans and animals. It accumulates in the blood, bones, and soft tissues and is not easily excreted. Excessive exposure to lead can cause seizures, mental retardation, and/or behavioral disorders. It can also inhibit respiration and photosynthesis in plants and block the decomposition of microorganisms.

AIRBORNE TOXINS

Another substantial group of pollutants causes both long- and short-term harm when emitted in small concentrations. Generally referred to as airborne toxins or toxic air pollutants, this group is large and not well defined, and we know relatively little about these pollutants' effects on health. Most of what we do know about their toxicity comes from studies of industrial workplaces, where these pollutants may be present in elevated concentrations, and from animal studies. There are approximately 3.7 million tons of airborne toxins released into the air each year.[11] In 2006, the EPA proposed a new rule, Control of Hazardous Air Pollutants from Mobile Sources, to reduce the amount of benzene and other toxic emissions from motor vehicles. By 2010, the EPA estimates that existing rules and regulations will reduce air toxics by one million tons from 1996 levels.

Under the most recent CAA amendments, 188 airborne toxins are currently regulated. Of these 188 pollutants, almost 60 percent are classified as known, probable carcinogens.[12] Some toxic pollutants causing great concern are benzene, primarily from chemical and plastics plants; vinyl chloride, from similar sources as those for benzene; chlorinated dioxins, from sources such as chemical processes and high-temperature burning of plastics in incinerators; asbestos; beryllium; mercury; arsenic; radionuclides; and coke oven emissions. These are the only toxic air pollutants that were regulated before the passage of the 1990 CAA amendments.

SOME SIGNIFICANT AIR-QUALITY PROBLEMS

In recent years, the focus of attention has shifted somewhat away from questioning how to control conventional and toxic pollutants to more global air-quality problems. These international issues are the concern of this section.

ACID DEPOSITION

The existence of acid deposition or acid precipitation has been known for decades. Only in recent years, however, has acid deposition been recognized as a problem. Acid deposition is a process that begins with the emission of SO_2 or NO_x. These pollutants interact with sunlight and water vapor in the upper atmosphere to form sulfuric and nitric acids, which fall to earth as "wet deposition," commonly known as acid snow or acid rain. Although acid rain is the most famous form of acid deposition, about half of the acid that falls back to earth is "dry deposition," in the form of dust, gasses, and other airborne particles. Much of the dry deposition is then washed away by heavy rains, increasing the acidity of area rivers and streams.

Acidity is measured on a pH scale that ranges from 0 to 14, with 7 being neutral, higher levels being basic, and lower levels indicating acidity. "Pure" rain, uncontaminated by human or natural sulfates, is slightly acidic, with a

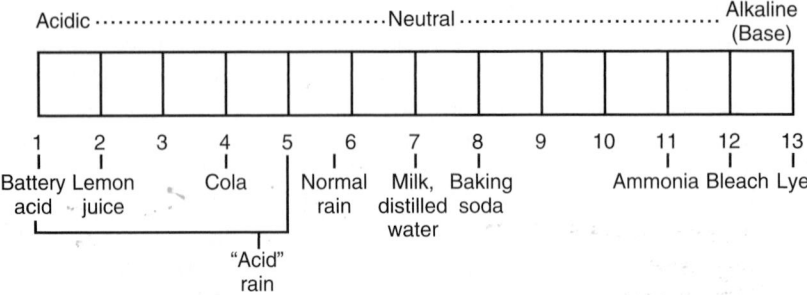

FIGURE 5-5   Acidity of Various Substances

pH of about 5.6. Figure 5-5 depicts a pH scale and shows where various substances would fall on such a scale. Acid precipitation becomes harmful when the pH levels begin to fall below 5. Rainfall with a pH level as low as 4.3 has been measured in parts of Canada and the United States.

As noted, a primary cause of acid precipitation is SO_2 emissions. According to the National Commission on Air Quality, between 75 and 90 percent of the sulfate concentration of rain falling on any state in the eastern half of the United States is attributable to sources outside those states. The export of acid gases results from the use of tall smokestacks (over 500 feet high), which use smelters and electric utilities to disperse their emissions into the upper reaches of the atmosphere (Figure 5-6). Unfortunately, the

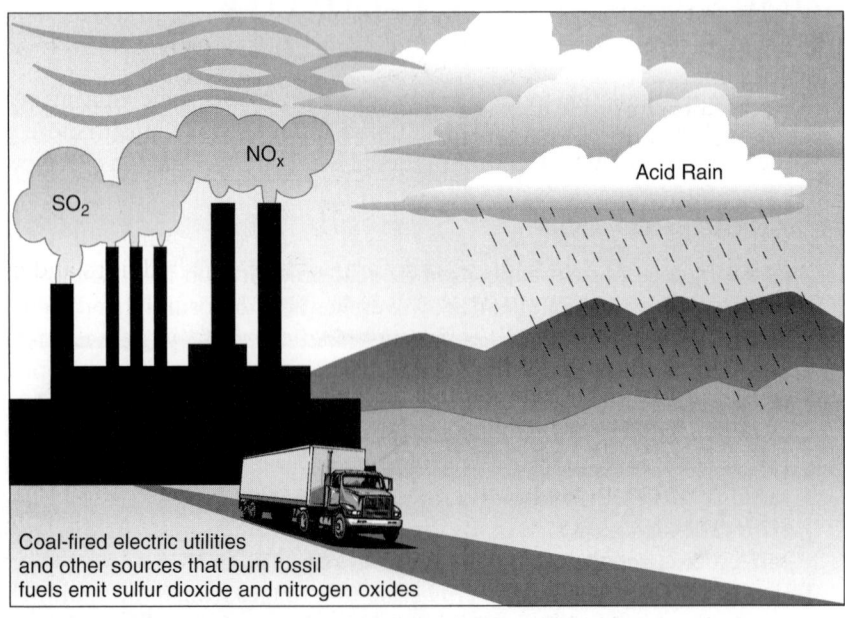

FIGURE 5-6   Process of Acid Formation

result has been to spread the acidic deposition over greater areas. Ohio, Indiana, Illinois, and Kentucky alone are responsible for nearly one-fourth of the SO_2 production in the United States, primarily from the burning of coal to generate electricity. In 2004, New York, New Jersey, and Connecticut took legal action to reduce the export of acid particulates from a Pennsylvania power company into their states. A year later, in 2005, the EPA addressed the export of acid deposition directly by instituting the CAIR, which aims to reduce air pollution the moves across state borders. CAIR applies to 28 eastern states and seeks a 70 percent reduction in SO_2 emissions and a 60 percent reduction in NO_x emissions from 2003 levels by 2015.

The extent of harm caused by acid rain depends on the amount of acid deposition in an area and the sensitivity of the area. The Midwest has alkaline-rich soils that can buffer the effects of acid rain. Lakes that lie on limestone, sandstone, or other alkaline foundations, primarily those located in the western and midwestern regions of the nation, are likewise resistant to damage from acid deposition. Regions where lakes and soils lie on granite or thin glacial tills have much lower buffering capacities and are therefore more susceptible to damage. Perhaps one of the reasons we have been reluctant to recognize the problem of acid rain is that some of its worst effects are in Europe and Canada rather than in the United States. Eighty percent of the lakes in Norway are considered dead or in critical condition, and over 300 lakes in Ontario have a pH level below 5.0. In the United States, damage to waterways seems to be concentrated along the eastern seaboard, especially in the Adirondacks.

The harmful effects of acid deposition are numerous and extensive in scope. The primary harm attributed to acid rain is damage to aquatic life, including the elimination of several species of fish and invertebrates in acidified regions. (When the pH of a lake falls below 5, most of its fish cannot survive.) Some fish taken from acidified lakes have high concentrations of mercury and other heavy metals that have been leached from the underlying soils, which makes them unfit for human consumption. Dry deposition, especially in the form of dust, is also harmful to public health. Furthermore, acid precipitation erodes stone buildings and monuments. Attempts to reduce acid deposition by reducing SO_2 and NO_x emissions are part of the CAA and are further discussed later in this chapter.

DEPLETION OF THE OZONE LAYER

We have previously discussed how O_3 is a pollutant in the air we breathe. However, in the stratosphere, which is between 9 and 30 miles above the surface of the earth, O_3 acts as a filter to help prevent ultraviolet (UV) radiation from reaching the earth. UV radiation is known to cause skin cancer in humans, to be harmful to plant life, and potentially to cause severe disruptions to the ecosystem.

There appears to be a consensus in the global scientific community about the causes and effects of O_3 depletion. Together, the United Nations Environment Programme (UNEP) and the World Meteorological Organization (WMO) issue Scientific Assessment Reports about the status of the O_3 layer. The most current report can be accessed online at http://esrl.noaa.gov/csd/assessments. Originally, the major concern was about the "hole" developing in the atmosphere over Antarctica; during the past 20 years, O_3 levels over Antarctica have dropped by more than 50 percent, as measured during the spring. The "hole" is clearly visible by satellite measurement. Greater concern, however, was aroused by a 1988 study that showed a 2 percent decline in the O_3 layer worldwide since 1969. The decline has been as much as 3 percent over some urban areas in North America and Europe, and over 3 percent over some parts of Australia, South America, and New Zealand. Further concern arose in September 2000 as the hole extended for the first time over a populated city: Punta Arenas, Chile. For 2 days, the residents of this small town were exposed to excessive levels of UV radiation, and scientists are greatly concerned that "fingers," segments separating from the O_3 hole, will further expose populated areas. In 2000, NASA data showed the O_3 hole to be larger than ever at just under 11 million square miles.

The primary causal factor for the decline in the O_3 layer is CFCs, substances for which emissions increased 28 percent from 1970 to 1985. CFCs are compounds made of chlorine, fluorine, and carbon that have been used as aerosol propellants, coolants, sterilizers, solvents, and blowing agents in foam production since their development in the 1920s. These compounds do not break down in the lower levels of the atmosphere. Instead, they rise up to the stratosphere, where they are broken down by UV light. When broken down, the chlorine reacts with O_3 to convert it back into molecular oxygen (O_2) with two atoms, thus thereby destroying the O_3 layer. What is even worse is that the chlorine molecule acts as a catalyst and moves on to destroy O_3 molecule after O_3 molecule. A chlorine atom from a single fluorocarbon molecule can destroy as many as 20,000 O_3 molecules. Seventy-five percent of the world's production of this hazardous compound is in the United States and Europe.

A second human-made compound contributing to the depletion of the O_3 layer is halon. Halons are used primarily in fire-extinguishing foams. Halons contain bromine, which also acts as a catalyst to deplete the O_3 layer. There is some evidence from laboratory tests that NO_x may also remove O_3 from the stratosphere. As you may recall, NO_x are released primarily by the burning of fossil fuels. They also come from the use of nitrogen-rich fertilizers.

In 2002, over 300 scientists from around the world drafted the UNEP report, *Scientific Assessment of Ozone Depletion: 2002*, in which an international consensus was reached as to the causes and effects of O_3 depletion. Owing to a decreased use of halogens, the report concluded, among other things, that the springtime Antarctic O_3 levels may begin to increase by 2010.[13]

HUMAN-INDUCED GLOBAL CLIMATE CHANGE

Probably, the most serious air-quality problem is human-induced climate change, sometimes called global warming. According to the Nation Academy of Sciences, the average surface temperature of the Earth has risen at least 1°F over the past centruy.[14] Furthermore, the Intergovernmental Panel on Climate Change (IPCC), a United Nations-sponsored group of scientists from over 100 countries, found that the scientific evidence points to a "discernable human influence of the global climate." Understanding human-induced climate change requires an understanding of the greenhouse effect.

The greenhouse effect occurs when CO_2, methane, CFCs, nitrous oxide, and traces of a few other gases act in a manner analogous to the glass in a greenhouse. Visible light passes through the layer of gas to the earth's surface heating it. The warmed surface then radiates energy back out toward space, but the greenhouse gases capture some of this heat, which warms the atmosphere. The greenhouse effect is necessary because, without it, Earth would be a frozen planet like Mars, with an average temperature of about 0°F. The greenhouse effect is related to climate change because of industrial processes and other human activities that increase the amount of CO_2 in the atmosphere. The IPCC's Third Assessment report in 2001 concluded that, by 2100, the average global temperature will rise between 2.5 and 10.4°F and found stronger evidence that most of the warming is attributable to human activities. The IPCC also estimates that CO_2 in the atmosphere has risen by 31 percent since 1750, to a higher level than at any time during the past 420,000 years and possibly the past million years.[15] However, there is uncertainty as to precisely how the effects of human-induced climate change will be borne out. Some parts of the Earth may warm because of the greenhouse effect, hence the term global warming, whereas certain areas of the Earth will cool, and more severe weather are likely to occur in some areas. Possible effects of human-induced climate change are discussed later.

The United States is home for only 4 percent of the population of the Earth, yet it is responsible for 25 percent of all greenhouse gases.[16] U.S. carbon dioxide emissions exceed 20 tons per capita, whereas the average for developed nations is 12 tons and for developing nations is 2 tons.[17] See Figure 5-7 to examine the greenhouse gas contributions per person from various nations.

An accelerated warming trend during the past two decades has accounted for much of this warming, as illustrated by Figure 5-8. Finally, July 1998 was recorded as the hottest of any month in almost 120 years. The average global temperature for July was 61.7°F, which was 1.26°F higher than the long-term average for July.[18] On January 7, 1999, NASA issued a report stating that researchers collecting data from around the world had concluded that global warming is occurring and that the meteorological year 1998 was the warmest on record. A scientist with the NASA Goddard Institute for Space Studies said in the report that "There should no longer be an issue about whether global warming is occurring, but what is the rate of warming, and what should be done about it."[19]

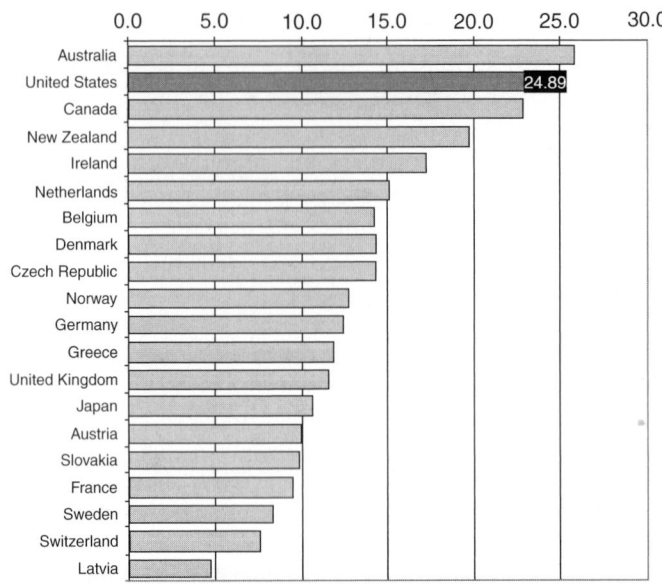

FIGURE 5-7   1998 Greenhouse Gas Emissions Per Capita (Metric Tons of CO_2 Equivalent Per Person)

Source: EPA, *http://yosemite.epa.gov/OAR/globalwarming.nsf/content/ EmissionsInternationalInventory.html* (September 20, 2006).

Possible Effects of Climate Change

A 1988 study by the American Association for the Advancement of Science predicted that an "equivalent doubling" of CO_2 will raise the average global temperature 2–5°C, with the middle and upper latitudes (including North America, Europe, and Asia) warming at twice the global average.[20] The warming could have an effect on precipitation. Some areas in the higher latitudes, such as the Soviet Union and Canada, could receive more rain and snow. Some wet tropical areas could receive more rainfall. The midwestern United States could become hotter and drier. There could also be an increase in the frequency and severity of hurricanes and other tropical storms because of increased ocean temperatures.

According to the EPA, sea levels could rise 7 feet (2.2 meters) by the year 2100 because of the expansion of water as it warms, perhaps exacerbated by the melting of land-based polar ice. See Figure 5-9, which compares polar sea ice from 1979 and 2003. Three recent cases illustrate some of the concerns arising over the potential melting of polar ice. In 2000, the Breidamerkurjökul glacier in Iceland broke apart and flowed into the lake beneath it. Although this breakup will not cause a rise in sea levels, it may drastically affect the Icelandic tourism industry. Later that same year, water was discovered at the North Pole, not ice. Some scientists predict that the polar ice cap could

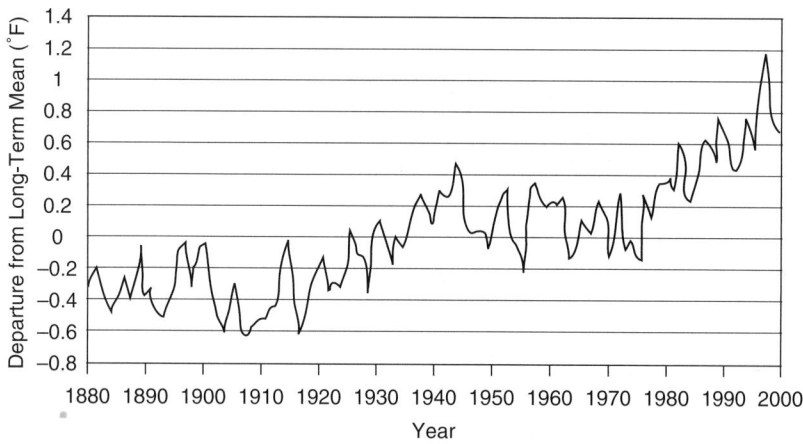

FIGURE 5-8   Global Temperature Changes 1880–2000

Source: EPA Global Warming—Climate, *http://yosemite.epa.gov/oar/globalwarming.nsf/content/climate.html* (September 25, 2006).

disappear entirely by the end of the 21st century. At the other pole, the Larsen B ice shelf on the eastern side of the Antarctic peninsula unexpectedly collapsed in early 2003, over a mere 35-day period, sending 1,300 square miles of ice, 720 billion tons, into the sea. Although it is difficult to tell at this point whether the breakage is related to human-induced climate change, there is some evidence that it may be. The National Snow and Ice Data Center reported that the area had been warming at a rate of 0.9°F per decade since the 1940s. Scientists are currently watching the other ice shelves very carefully to see whether other icebergs may break off soon.[21] According to a new study of

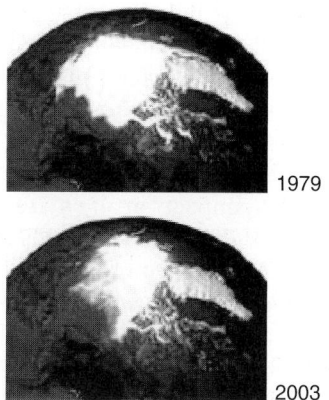

1979

2003

FIGURE 5-9   Side-by-side Comparison of Polar Sea Ice from 1979 and 2003 Courtesy of NASA

polar trends published in April 2007 in Geophysical Research Letters, climate scientists may have significantly underestimated the power of global warming from human-generated heat-trapping gases to shrink the cap of sea ice floating on the Arctic Ocean. The United Nations, in their report released in February 2007, had concluded that if emissions of heat-trapping gases such as carbon dioxide were not significantly reduced, the Arctic region could end up bereft of floating ice in summers sometime between 2050 and the early decades of the next century. However, the more recent study, which compared the observed trends with the projections made by the climate panel using the world's most advanced computer models of climate, implies that the Arctic ice may be quicker to respond to warming as concentrations of heat-trapping gases rise in coming decades. Since 1953, the area of sea ice in September has declined at an average rate of 7.8 percent per decade, whereas computer climate simulations of the same period had an average rate of ice loss of 2.5 percent per decade.[22]

A rise in sea levels will displace populations in some coastal areas around the world, from Egypt to Louisiana. Some low-lying river deltas and flood plains, where rice is currently grown, would be inundated with water and lost. However, rice paddies are also a source of greenhouse gas emissions, in the form of methane, and a shift to new methods of rice farming may help decrease emissions of methane.[22] Human-induced climate change could have an impact on forests because trees are sensitive to climate variation. If warming spreads at the faster rate projected by some scientists, many forests could be devastated. Trees now living at the warm, dry fringe of their forest habitat would face conditions for which they are unsuited and die. There could be some expansion to fringe regions previously too cold for the forests. However, this growth would be limited by the normally slow rate of seed migration or be blocked entirely by human development (roads, towns, and agriculture).

Agriculture might also be affected. Precipitation patterns could change, and much of the midwestern United States could experience long, dry summers with insufficient rain to raise traditional crops of corn and wheat. Irrigation practices might help mitigate these changes but would increase costs and disrupt current farming practices. In 1997, at the United Nations Conference on Climate Change in Kyoto, Japan, insurance executives, who seem to be persuaded by evidence for climate change, argued in favor of reducing greenhouse gas emissions because they claim that rapidly rising insurance rates will result from massive storms likely to be associated with global climate change.

According to a report of the IPCC issued in 2001, climate change is already having a "widespread and coherent impact" in all environments and on all continents.[23] On the basis of the results of observations reported in approximately 3,000 studies analyzed in the report, there is already convincing evidence of change from over 420 physical and biological systems. The report says that coral reefs in most regions could be wiped out within 30–50 years by warming oceans, which may cause coral bleaching to become an annual event. Three-quarters of the world's largest mangrove forest could be inundated, putting the Bengal tiger at risk of extinction. The Cape Floral Kingdom, in South Africa, which is home to a number of species that reside nowhere else, could be wiped out. The polar ice edge ecosystem that houses polar bears, walruses, seals, and penguins is also threatened.[24]

According to the IPCC report, the most severe impacts will be felt in developing nations, which are the least equipped to adapt. Africa is likely to experience climate change affecting its water resources and food production and causing increases in diseases. Many small island states in the Pacific and Indian oceans and the Caribbean are already experiencing coastal losses and may find themselves completely inundated with water.[25] Especially vulnerable are the Maldives, a group of approximately 1,200 islands off the coast of India.[26] Eighty percent of these islands are just 1 meter above sea level, and the director of their Ministry of Environmental Affairs is fearful that if nothing is done to reduce human-induced climate change, their people will become "environmental refugees."[27]

Industrialized nations will also suffer, however. Australia, Canada, and the United States will likely experience increased numbers of diseases such as malaria, tick-borne Lyme disease, Ross River virus, and Murray Valley encephalitis. And many areas of the world will experience heat waves that will compound the negative impacts on health from pollution in cities. Much of Europe will experience increased flooding.[28]

The purpose of this section is not to provide a definitive list of possible effects of human-induced global climate change but to suggest some of the many and diverse consequences of warming sea levels and global climate change. As noted above, one of the frightening aspects of climate change is our inability to predict with certainty exactly what changes are going to occur.

Solutions to Human-Induced Climate Change

Global warming is still perhaps one of the most controversial international issues today. Although most countries admit that global warming is occurring, nations frequently disagree about what to do to ameliorate the situation. The Kyoto Protocol, discussed in greater detail in Chapter 11, was an attempt by the global community to reduce greenhouse gas emissions by the year 2012 by an average of 5.2 percent below 1990 levels and consequently reverse the trend of warming. However, the enforcement of the treaty depended on the ratification of many developed counties, including either the United States or Russia.

In March 2001, President Bush took a major step toward encouraging the demise of the Kyoto Protocol by going back on his campaign pledge and saying that the United States was not going to be a party to the Kyoto Protocol. Other developed nations rapidly moved to criticize the U.S. position, and although representatives of many nations said that they hoped the United States could be persuaded to come back to the treaty talks, they insisted that the rest of the world go ahead and ratify the treaty even without the participation of the United States.

By pulling out of the negotiations over the treaty, the United States made it extremely difficult for the treaty to become effective because the protocol must be ratified by 55 industrial nations responsible for at least 55 percent of carbon dioxide emissions. The United States accounts for 35 percent of global emissions. Similarly, Russia, with its 17 percent of global emissions, stood in the way of the Kyoto Protocol. Seven years after the negotiation of the treaty, in 1997, the failure of either the United States or Russia cast the future of the treaty into serious doubt. Then, in late 2004, Russia provided the key signature to the treaty. The Kyoto Protocol went into effect in February 2006. As of late 2006, 166 countries that have ratified the treaty, representing nearly 62 percent of global emissions covered in the treaty. The 9 years between the drafting of the treating and its going into effect illustrates the difficulty of forging international environmental treaties.

In part, the Kyoto Protocol's slow ratification process is due to the tragedy of the commons or free rider program described in Chapter 4. All countries will benefit from the reduction of carbon dioxide emissions, yet if some countries, including the United States, are unwilling to cooperate, all may suffer in the end.

Many countries, however, began combating human-induced climate change even before the passage of the treaty. As the future of the treaty became questionable after the United States' indicated it would not ratify the protocol, other countries took the initiative to begin upholding their part of the treaty and developed their own methods of addressing climate change. The United Kingdom has required its electricity suppliers to buy up to 10 percent of their power from renewable energy sources, based on government targets, or face fines.[29] The Canadian government has set aside $500 million to combat global warming through federal purchasing of so-called green power (renewable energy), incentives for consumers to purchase green power, and a tripling in the amount of ethanol Canada produces.[30] Holland has put a program in place to reduce emissions by 80 percent over the next 40 years, whereas Germany is planning 50 percent reductions.[31]

Germany and the United Kingdom are the only countries currently on track to meet their Kyoto obligations, according to a study by the Pew Center. In perhaps one of the more interesting ideas to combat global warming, Australian scientists have dumped tons of iron into the ocean off Antarctica. This iron caused huge algal blooms that absorbed approximately 2,000 tons of carbon dioxide.[32] Although the use of iron alone will not stop global warming, it contributes to allowing oceans to absorb more carbon dioxide from the atmosphere. Other interesting proposals to stop global warming include permanently storing carbon dioxide inside certain minerals, pulling carbon dioxide out of the atmosphere and storing it in weak soils, and injecting carbon dioxide into rocks at the bottom of the ocean.[33]

Although the success of these independent programs remains to be seen, it is probable that these innovative programs will work only in conjunction with emissions reductions. For emissions reductions, the best hope environmentalists have right now is the Kyoto Protocol, despite the failure of the United States to ratify the treaty. President Bush, however, may not be the final determiner of U.S. actions with respect to climate change. Many states, angered by the Bush administration's lack of concern for global warming, have devised their own programs to limit carbon dioxide emissions. Fifteen states now require utilities to produce a portion of their power through non-polluting sources, such as wind or solar. Nine states, in 2005, and 194 cities have pledged to limit their emissions, in keeping with the intent of the Kyoto Protocol. New York and California have developed auto emission standards that go beyond what is required by the federal government. In 2006, California passed the Global Warming Solutions Act, which is similar to the Kyoto Protocol's greenhouse gas reduction plan. California, ranked 12th in global emissions, will reduce its emission by 25 percent by 2020. Such actions on the state level can have large effects on the national and global level. Because California commands such a large share of the automobile market, its emission standards could force the auto industry to build cleaner and more fuel-efficient cars or risk selling their product in California. Frustrated by the federal government's inaction on global warming, states are showing global leadership by developing their own standards to prevent increased global warming. Equally important, states are forcing the federal government to take action in regulating carbon dioxide.

In 2006, a group of 12 states, 4 local governments, and numerous private organizations brought suit against the EPA after it refused an earlier petition by the private organizations to regulate greenhouse cases, including carbon dioxide, under the CAA. The EPA held that the CAA does not authorize it to issue regulations that address global climate change, and even if it did have the authority, it was not required to exercise it.

The CAA requires that the Environmental Protection Agency "shall by regulation prescribe . . . standards applicable to the emission of any air pollutant from any class . . . of new motor vehicles . . . which in [the EPA Administrator's] judgment cause[s], or contribute[s] to, air pollution . . . reasonably . . . anticipated to endanger public health or welfare. . . ." The Act defines "air pollutant" to include "any air pollution agent . . . including any physical, chemical . . . substance . . . emitted into . . . the ambient air."

On the basis of this law, the Supreme Court ruled in 2007, in *Massachusetts v. EPA,* that greenhouse gases fall within the Act's "capacious definition of air pollutant," and therefore, EPA has the statutory authority to regulate such gasses from new motor vehicles. Furthermore, the Court held that the EPA, absent scientific evidence that "greenhouse gasses do not contribute to climate change," could not refuse to regulate greenhouse gasses under the Act. This ruling all but forces the federal government to begin regulating greenhouse gasses, and any failure on the part of the federal government to do so will undoubtedly face strong legal challenges.

This case is one of the Court's most important environmental decisions and is a major legal victory in the regulation of heat-trapping greenhouse gasses. The ruling is also important because the EPA is now more likely to approve of states' individual attempts to regulate automobile emissions. Environmentalists pleasure with the decision, however, is tempered by the fact that an EPA that is not eager to regulate these emissions can take their time in proposing standards, arguing that they are engaged in the scientific fact finding necessary to establish the appropriate standards.

INDOOR POLLUTION

Indoor pollution has recently received a lot of attention. This type of pollution occurs when airborne toxins, irritants, and other air pollutants become trapped inside buildings. The problem has been exacerbated by the construction of energy-efficient buildings. The EPA has estimated that as many as 30 percent of new and remodeled buildings have indoor air-quality problems.

Poorly ventilated buildings trap airborne pathogens, such as bacteria, fungi, and viruses; radioactive gases, such as radon; a wide range of inorganic compounds, such as lead and mercury; and organic compounds, such as formaldehyde and chloroform. Many of these harmful pollutants are caused by indoor smoking, the use of woodstoves and space heaters, chemicals on furniture finishings, and the use of cleaning solvents, wood-finishing products, and air fresheners. Figure 5-10 illustrates some of these sources of indoor pollution.

In the short run, these pollutants can cause "sick building syndrome," which is associated with runny noses; headaches; eye, nose, and throat irritations; fatigue; lethargy; irritableness; dizziness; and nausea. In the long run, they may lead to impairment of the nervous system and cancer.

Indoor pollutants are a special problem for the old and the young, who spend more than an average amount of time indoors. The average person in the United States still spends 90 percent of his or her time indoors, consequently exposing himself or herself to indoor pollutants.

One indoor pollutant discovered in the 1960s that presents a special problem because it is naturally occurring is radon. Radon is a gas emitted because of the radioactive decay of radium-226, found in a wide variety of rocks and soil. Radon enters homes through cracks in the foundation and structure and is trapped in buildings with poor ventilation. Research by the EPA in 34 states revealed that one in five homes had excessive levels of radon. When radon is inhaled, radon particles release radiation that can damage lung tissue and cause cancer. The EPA estimates that radon may be responsible for between 5,000 and 20,000 lung cancer deaths per year.

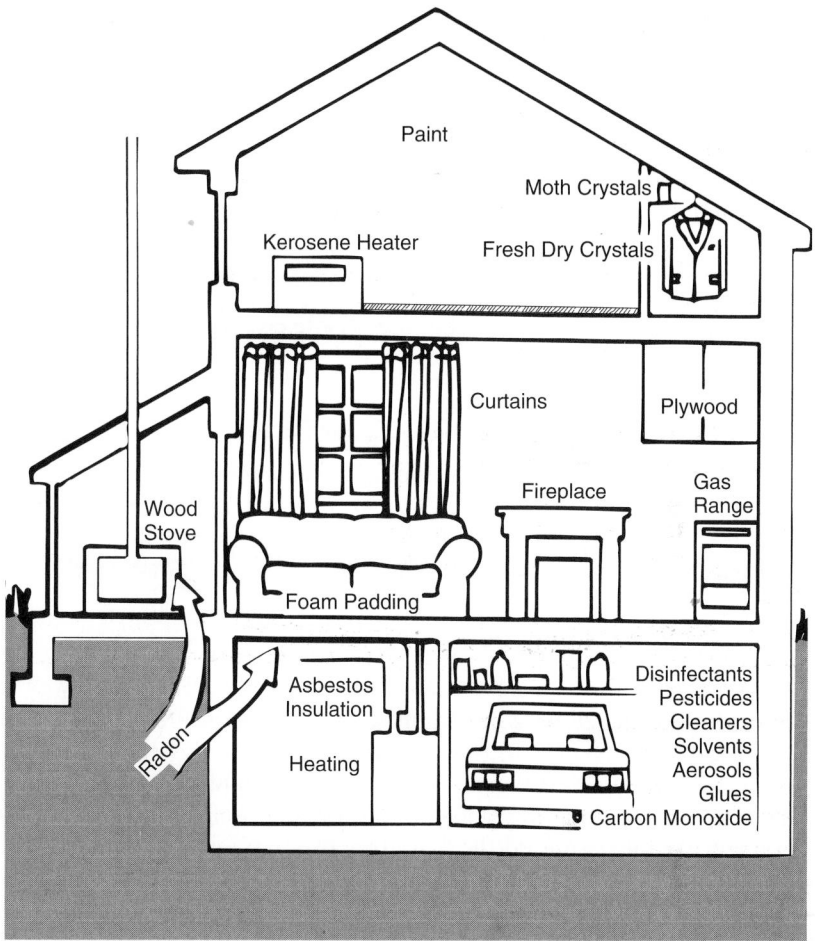

FIGURE 5-10   Air Pollution in the Home

Source: EPA. 1998. *Environmental Progress and Challenges: EPA's Update,* p 32. Washington, D.C.:
Government Printing Office.

THE INITIAL APPROACH
TO AIR-QUALITY CONTROL

Now that we understand some of the air-quality problems, we examine how
the United States has attempted to address those problems. The central legislation, and the law we focus on, is the CAA and its amendments. Although we
often think of the CAA of 1970 as the first piece of air-quality regulation,
there actually have been small amounts of regulatory activity in this area since
the late 1800s. No legislation was very effective, however, until the CAA.

　　The first air-quality laws were actually ordinances passed by the cities of
Chicago and Cincinnati in the 1880s, followed by Pittsburgh and New York

in the 1890s. These laws attempted to regulate smokestack emissions, the most visible type of air pollution. In the 1890s, the state of Ohio passed a law to regulate smoke emissions from steam boilers. Finally, in 1952, Oregon became the first state to pass a comprehensive air-pollution law and establish a state air-pollution control agency.

AIR-POLLUTION CONTROL ACT OF 1955

The main function of the first piece of federal clean air regulation was simply to provide federal money for research into air-pollution control. It authorized the surgeon general to investigate complaints of pollution problems brought by state or local governments.

MOTOR VEHICLE CONTROL ACT OF 1960

In 1960, Congress recognized that automobiles were causing air-quality problems. Motor vehicle emissions of CO, hydrocarbons, and NO_x were blamed for 60 percent of all air pollution. Congress passed the Motor Vehicle Act of 1960, which authorized research into the air-pollution effects of motor vehicles.

CLEAN AIR ACT OF 1963

The first national air-quality act was the CAA of 1963. This act, however, did not mandate any reduction of pollution. There were four major features to this act.

First, it authorized the surgeon general to conduct investigations into specific or local pollution problems at the request of any state or local government, and it permitted the Secretary of HEW, a former federal agency that was subsequently split into the Department of Education and the Department of Health and Human Services, to make such investigations on his or her own initiative if the pollution affected a state other than the state that was the source of the pollution. However, any recommendations following the investigations were advisory only; the states could ignore them.

Second, the act expanded the research and technical assistance programs established under the Motor Vehicle Act of 1955 and provided grants to state and local governments to aid them in developing and improving their control programs.

Third, it provided for the development of air-quality criteria by the secretary of HEW. These criteria were to reflect scientific knowledge of the effects of various pollution concentrations. Again, the criteria were advisory only; states did not have to adopt air-quality standards based on the information in the criteria documents.

Finally, the 1963 act provided for federal abatement of action in cases in which the health and welfare of citizens were being endangered by air pollution. The secretary of HEW could convene a conference on his or her own initiative when the pollution was interstate; it could be convened at the request of the governor for intrastate problems. The conference would issue a technical report on the problem, and the secretary would recommend an enforcement action by state or local authorities. If these actions were not taken within 6 months, the secretary (in the case of interstate pollution) or the governor (in the case of intrastate pollution) could request the U.S. attorney general to bring suit on behalf of the United States to abate the pollution. The attorney general was authorized to request only a cease and desist order, which, if not followed, could be punished as contempt of court. These conferences and their enforcement practices were cumbersome, time-consuming, and largely ineffective. From 1963 to 1970, fewer than 12 conferences were held, and only one enforcement action was brought in court.

If you take just a minute to examine the major provisions of this act, you can probably tell what the primary criticisms were. Two obvious problems were the failure of the act's standards to be mandated and its ineffective enforcement. In addition, the act did not define air pollution, stating only that the statute's purpose was to prevent and control air pollution. It is difficult to control a problem when one is not sure what the problem is. The act's limited enforcement also was hampered by a requirement that the courts take into consideration the practicability and economic and physical feasibility of stopping pollution.

Such a requirement is seen by many as defeating the purpose of the law. They argue that effective statutes must be "technology forcing," that is, they must require polluters to develop the necessary technology if it does not currently exist.

MOTOR VEHICLE AIR-POLLUTION CONTROL ACT OF 1965

This act authorized the secretary of HEW to prescribe "standards applicable to any class or classes of new motor vehicles or new motor vehicle engines." There was no express prohibition of state controls, but there was stress on the need for uniformity. This act was not particularly effective because it required that consideration be given to the economic and technological feasibility of obtaining the standards. Industry could reasonably, if inaccurately, argue that current practices were already selected on the basis of economic and technological practicalities.

1967 AIR-QUALITY ACT

The 1967 amendments to the CAA of 1963 (1967 Air-Quality Act) provided the first comprehensive federal scheme for air-pollution control. This was the first act to establish an orderly procedure for adoption and achievement by states of ambient air-quality standards. Under this act, HEW was to designate broad "atmospheric regions" in which meteorology, topology, and other factors influencing air-pollutant concentrations were similar (10 regions covering the entire nation were so designated). Next, HEW was to designate "air-quality" regions based on jurisdictional boundaries, urban-industrial concentrations, and other factors, including atmospheric areas necessary to provide adequate implementation of air-quality standards. Regions could include portions of more than one state. The purpose of the act was to create regions within which pollution could be regulated with an integrated set of controls.

Once HEW made the appropriate designations, states were required to adopt ambient air-quality standards for the air-quality regions, defining permissible concentrations of pollutants. The standards were to be based on HEW criteria documents defining adverse effects of various pollutants and describing pollution-control techniques. Standards were subject to HEW approval. If states failed to establish adequate standards, HEW could promulgate standards after a process of consultation and a public hearing. Finally, states were to adopt, subject to HEW approval, state implementation plans (SIPs) designed to ensure that the state's air would meet the ambient standards. The plan would designate sufficient limitations that would be imposed on the sources of air pollution within each region to ensure that the permissible atmospheric concentrations of pollutants were not exceeded. The means for enforcement was the conference. Under this act, federal automobile emissions controls were made preemptive of state's controls. In other words, states could not meet the standards by imposing more restrictive limits on automobile emissions.

The 1967 Air-Quality Act was a significant improvement over previous legislation. To some degree, it reflected growing awareness that purely local regulation could not control the pollution problem. Unfortunately, the act was unable to achieve rapid and effective control of air pollution. A number of reasons for its relative ineffectiveness have been proffered by academics who study regulation. Some attribute the failure to the emphasis on air-quality regions, which cut across established state and jurisdictional lines; consequently, it was difficult to obtain agreement on standards or implementation plans.

There were also numerous delays in implementing the steps of the act, such as delays by the federal government in designating regions and issuing criteria documents. States delayed adoption of plans because of a lack of personnel, information, and political will. Despite a 15-month deadline, by the spring of 1970, not one state had adopted a full-scale set of standards or an implementation plan. Another reason for the act's ineffectiveness was that, like previous air-quality regulations, this act failed to define air pollution. Reductions in pollution were less likely because the act imposed economic and technological feasibility conditions on the standards. Finally, the legislation left extensive discretion to the states.

CURRENT APPROACHES TO AIR-QUALITY CONTROL

After years of ineffective legislation, the CAA of 1970 was passed. Arguably, several factors led to the development and passage of this law. First, congressional dissatisfaction with the lack of progress was high.

Despite an increasing federal role and rising public concern, most indices showed more emissions and a decline in ambient air quality. Second, state governments responsible for enforcement of pollution-control policies were perceived as weak and vulnerable to industry "blackmail." A related concern was the fact that strict regulations in some states but not in others could put some firms at a competitive disadvantage.

Furthermore, the HEW division responsible for federal air-pollution programs was seen as lacking in zeal. It was especially sympathetic to automobile manufacturers' standards rather than forcing the industry to improve technology. Finally, political considerations may have played a role. A Democratic Congress could blame failures on the Nixon administration. Congress could mandate sweeping changes. If the timetable was unmet, Congress could blame Nixon; if it was met, Congress would take credit.

This act created a new partnership between state and federal governments, giving the states primary responsibility for directly monitoring, controlling, and preventing pollution while assigning responsibility to the EPA for establishing the standards the states must enforce, conducting research and providing financial and technical assistance to the states. When necessary, the EPA steps in to aid the states in implementation and enforcement of regulations. This act, as amended in 1976 and 1990, governs air quality today.

It is easiest to examine the act and its amendments by dividing it into five sections: national ambient air-quality standards (NAAQSs), no significant deterioration (NSD) policy, new source performance standards, mobile source emissions standards, and hazardous air toxins standards.

NATIONAL AMBIENT AIR-QUALITY STANDARDS

The centerpiece of the CAA is the NAAQSs. Under the 1970 act, the administrator of the EPA is required to determine which pollutants emanating from numerous and diverse mobile and stationary sources have an adverse impact on human health and welfare and to establish ambient air-quality standards for these pollutants. The term ambient air-quality refers to the quality of air representatively sampled from an area. To make it easier to measure and monitor air quality, the EPA divided the United States into 247 air-quality regions. Each region would have common pollution sources and characteristic weather. We can then refer to the air quality of the various regions.

The EPA initially determined that CO, SO_2, hydrocarbons, total suspended particulates, NO_2, and O_3 required regulation. The hydrocarbon standard was subsequently dropped, and lead was added. Before setting standards, the EPA prepares a criteria document for each pollutant that contains the scientific evidence of the negative health effects of each pollutant and the methods for controlling its emission. For each of these criteria pollutants, the administrator must set two standards: primary and secondary ambient air-quality standards. Primary standards are necessary to protect human health. Human health is interpreted to include the health of the most sensitive individuals, such as children and elders. Secondary standards are sufficient to protect public welfare. Public welfare includes visibility, plant life, animal life, and buildings. Some pollutants have primary standards for both long term (annual average) and short term (24 hours or less).[34]

Every 5 years, the evidence for the standards must be reviewed and new data analyzed to ensure that the standards are still valid. For example, in 1997, the EPA revised both the O_3 standard (replacing the 1-hour primary standard with an 8-hour standard) and the particulate standard. The EPA estimated that approximately 15,000 lives would be saved each year by the new particulates standard.[35] More recently, in 2006, the EPA again adopted new rules that reflect changes in data and available technology for fine particulate matter. The new rule, discussed earlier in this chapter, is also aimed at reducing health problems and reducing premature deaths.

These new standards were the subject of a significant amount of controversy when they were adopted. And their adoption led to one of the stiffest legal challenges to the CAA in its 30-year history. The American Trucking Association, joined by a powerful alliance of other industry groups, led a challenge to the agency's authority to issue the new standards that went all the way to the U.S. Supreme Court. The challengers argued that the EPA must balance the benefits to health against the anticipated high costs of compliance with the new standards. Justice Antonin Scalia wrote the decision for a unanimous court and stated that no cost–benefit requirement exists when the agency is issuing health standards under the CAA.[36] The court also rejected the argument that the delegation of authority to the EPA to issue the CAA standards was unconstitutionally vague because it did not give the EPA any basis for determining where to set the standard. The decision was not a total victory for the EPA, however, because the court, while finding no problem with the particulate standard, did direct the agency to develop a more reasonable approach for shifting from the old O_3 standard to the new one.[37] In 2002, a District of Columbia Circuit Court upheld the EPA's new clean air standards, rejecting any remaining challenges to the 1997 ambient air standards for particulates and O_3 by finding that the EPA "engaged in reasonable decision making" in establishing the new pollution levels.[38]

State Implementation Plans

Once the EPA issues the standards, in accordance with APA rule-making procedures, responsibility then passes to the states. The EPA, in coordination with the states, established air-quality regions, with each state representing at least one region. The states are required to develop SIPs that provide means for attaining the NAAQSs within the air-quality regions in the state. The states are essentially free to use any types of restriction they desire. They can impose stiff emissions controls on certain types of industrial plants and virtually no restrictions on others.

At least in theory, there are strict guidelines for the SIPs. A SIP for a criteria pollutant is to be submitted to the EPA for approval within 9 months of the date that the NAAQS is promulgated. (This deadline can be extended up to 18 months for a plan to meet the secondary standard.) The EPA must approve or reject the plan within 4 months. If an inadequate or incomplete SIP is submitted, the EPA must promulgate a plan or part thereof for the state. Or the EPA can cut off funding for highways within the state or ban construction in nonattainment areas.

As noted, SIPs are to provide for attainment of a NAAQS within 3 years of the date of its promulgation. A 2-year extension upon request of the governor is possible if the technology for certain sources is unavailable.

The Problem of Nonattainment

For the criteria pollutants described, the deadline for attainment under the 1977 amendments (after extensions) was January 1, 1987. One month after that deadline, the EPA estimated that 80 million people were living in areas that did not have healthy air. In other words, these people were living in areas where the NAAQSs had not been met. An air-quality region is defined as not in compliance when the second-highest 1-hour average concentration per day exceeds the NAAQS. Figure 5-11 demonstrates how the emissions of criteria pollutants have declined as the states attempt to meet the NAAQSs.

FIGURE 5-11   National Air Pollutant Emissions Estimates (Fires and Dust Excluded) for Major Pollutants

	Millions of Tons Per Year							
	1970	1975	1980	1985[1]	1990	1995	2000[1]	2005[2]
Carbon Monoxide (CO)	197.3	184.0	177.8	169.6	143.6	120.0	102.4	89
Nitrogen Oxides (NO_x)[3]	26.9	26.4	27.1	25.8	25.2	24.7	22.3	19
Particulate Matter (PM)[4]								
PM_{10}	12.2[1]	7.0	6.2	3.6	3.2	3.1	2.3	2
$PM_{2.5}$[5]	NA	NA	NA	NA	2.3	2.2	1.8	2
Sulfur Dioxide (SO_2)	31.2	28.0	25.9	23.3	23.1	18.6	16.3	15
Volatile Organic Compounds (VOC)	33.7	30.2	30.1	26.9	23.1	21.6	16.9	16
Lead[6]	0.221	0.16	0.074	0.022	0.005	0.004	0.003	0.003
Totals[7]	301.5	275.8	267.2	249.2	218.2	188.0	160.2	141

Notes:

1. In 1985 and 1996, EPA refined its methods for estimating emissions. Between 1970 and 1975, EPA revised its methods for estimating particulate matter emissions.
2. The estimates for 2005 are preliminary.
3. NO_x estimates before 1990 include emissions from fires. Fires would represent a small percentage of the NO_x emissions.
4. PM estimates do not include condensable PM, or the majority of PM2.5 that is formed in the atmosphere from "precursor" gases such as SO_2 and NO_x
5. EPA has not estimated PM2.5 emissions before 1990.
6. The 1999 estimate for lead is used to represent 2000 and 2005 because lead estimates do not exist for these years.
7. PM2.5 emissions are not added when calculating the total because they are included in the PM10 estimate.

By 1987, the emissions of all of the criteria pollutants had been significantly reduced from the amount emitted in 1977. Unfortunately, during 1988 and 1989, levels of O_3 and particulates had started increasing once more, and nitrogen oxide emissions had leveled. In 2005, as many as 100 million people lived in counties with O_3 concentration levels above NAASQS levels based on the 8-hour standard.[39] In 1989, 81 cities were still unable to meet all of the NAAQSs[40] and suffered no consequences for their failure to do so. In 2005, approximately 122 million Americans lived in areas that did not meet at least one of the standards for criteria air pollutants.[41] As of there were 167 nonattainment areas.[42] The map in Figure 5-12 shows these nonattainment areas.

The greatest successes were attained in meeting the NAAQSs for lead and NO_x. The most difficult problem has been the attainment of O_3 standards. The 1990 amendments to the CAA addressed the problem of O_3 nonattainment. O_3 nonattainment areas are divided into five classes, depending on the degree to which the pollutant is exceeding the standard: marginal, moderate, serious, severe, and extreme. (The only city in the

FIGURE 5-12   Counties Designated Nonattainment for Clean Air Act's National Ambient Air-Quality Standards (NAAQS)*

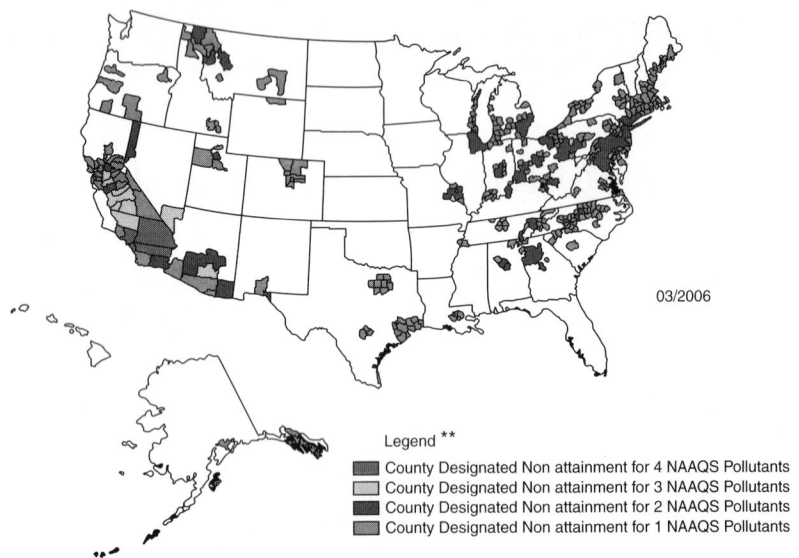

03/2006

Legend **
- County Designated Non attainment for 4 NAAQS Pollutants
- County Designated Non attainment for 3 NAAQS Pollutants
- County Designated Non attainment for 2 NAAQS Pollutants
- County Designated Non attainment for 1 NAAQS Pollutants

Guam–Piti and Tanguisson Counties are designated nonattainment for the SO2NAAQS

 * The National Ambient Air-Quality standards are health standards for lead, carbon monoxide, sulfur dioxide, ground level 8-hour ozone, and particulate matter (PM10 and PM2.5). There are no nitrogen dioxide nonattainme

** Partial counties, those with part of the county designated nonattainment and part attainment, are shown as full counties on the map.

Source: EPA, *http://www.epa.gov/air/oaqps/greenbk/mapnpoll.html* (September 28, 2006).

extreme category was Los Angeles.) Each class had a deadline for attainment, ranging from 3 years for the marginal class to 20 years for the extreme class. Interim goals were set for all classes, except marginal.

In April 2004, new standards for ground level O_3 went into effect. The new, 8-hour O_3 standard, 0.08 ppm, averaged over 8 hours, replaces the 1-hour standard that had been in place since 1979. The new 8-hour standard was originally issued in 1997, after a significant body of research showed that longer-term exposure to lower levels of O_3 can also affect human health. Implementation of the new standard was held up by a lengthy legal battle that went all the way to the Supreme Court in the previously discussed case of *Whitman v. American Trucking.*

When the new standards went into effect, governors of 31 states were told by the EPA that areas of their states did not meet these new standards. Part or all of 474 counties nationwide are in nonattainment for either failing to meet the 8-hour O_3 standard or for causing a downwind county to fail. Some 159 million people live in these areas that do not meet the new O_3 standard.[43] See Figure 5-13 to see where the new O_3 nonattainment areas are.

At the same time, it issued designations on attainment and nonattainment, EPA issued a new rule classifying areas by the severity of their O_3

FIGURE 5-13   Attainment and Nonattainment Areas in the U.S. 8-hour Ozone Standard

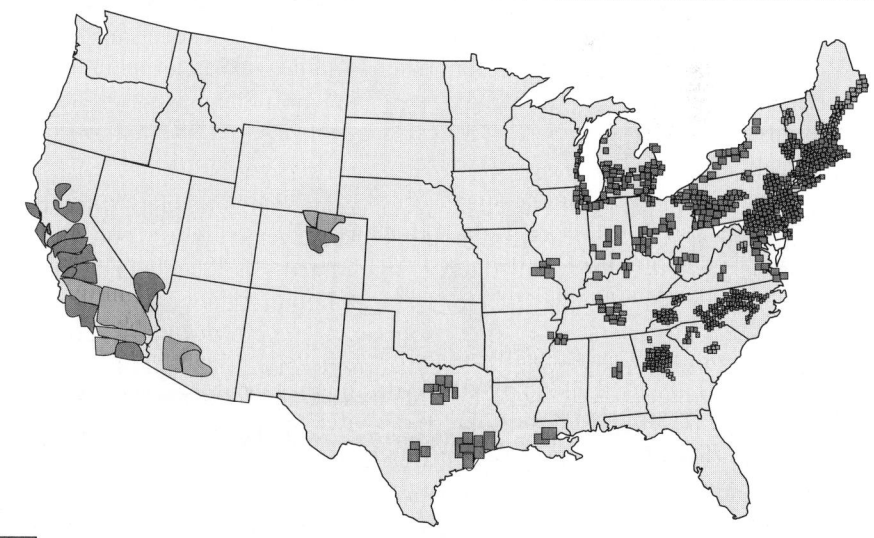

☐ Attainment (or Unclassifiable) Areas (2668 counties)
■ Nonattainment Areas (432 entire counties)
▨ Nonattainment Areas (42 partial counties)

Source: http://www.epa.gov/ozonedesignations/nonattaingreen.htm (Updated April 29, 2004).

conditions and establishing the deadline state, and local governments must meet to reduce O_3 levels. Once designations and classifications take effect on June 15, 2004, states and communities must prepare a plan to reduce ground-level O_3.

Eighteen states are meeting the new, more protective standard for O_3. EPA found no nonattainment areas in the northwest or in many of the Great Plains, Rocky Mountain, and Great Basin states. The entire population in Iowa, Minnesota, Florida, Mississippi, Vermont, Hawaii, and Alaska are breathing air that meets the new standard.

Measures that states and localities may be required to take to control O_3 pollution may include stricter controls on emissions from industrial facilities, additional planning requirements for transportation sources or other programs such as gasoline vapor recovery controls. EPA plans to work with states and local governments to help develop innovative approaches to meeting the new standard.

Deadlines for meeting the 8-hour O_3 standard range from 2007 to 2021, depending on the severity of an area's O_3 problem. For example, areas with more significant O_3 problems, such as Los Angeles, may have to apply more rigorous control measures but will have a longer time to meet the O_3 standards. Thirty areas voluntarily entered into Early Action Compacts (EACs) in 2002, agreeing to have a plan in place to reduce air pollution about 2 years sooner than required by the CAA. These communities have had their nonattainment status deferred as a result. These areas must attain the new O_3 standard no later than December 31, 2007. Areas must submit satisfactory progress reports to retain their EAC status. Three of the original 33 EAC areas did not meet their requirements (Memphis, Knoxville and Chattanooga, Tennessee) and are no longer included in the EAC program.[44]

Permit Program

One of the ways these smaller firms may be regulated is by the permit system added by the 1990 amendments. This permit system, one of the big changes imposed by the 1990 CAA amendments, is modeled after the one imposed by the CWA of 1972 for water pollutants. Under the 1990 amendments, all large and many small sources of air pollution are required to obtain 5-year permits that spell out limits on the pollutants they emit. Operating permits are issued by state and local permitting authorities. The permit program streamlines all pollution-control requirements into a single "operating permit" that covers all air pollutants.

Challenges to permits must be made in hearings before the issuance of those permits. Once a permit is issued, a "permit shield" arises. As long as a plant is operating in accordance with its permit, it cannot be in violation of the Clear Air Act.

The EPA has now approved permit programs for all 113 state, territorial, and local permitting authorities in the nation. As of 2006, there are 17,400 sources that are subject to the Operating Permit Requirements. Of that number, state and local permitting authorities have issued 16,000 permits to polluting sources.[45]

Automobile Inspection and Maintenance Program

Urban areas with populations of 200,000 or more that were classified as moderate, serious, severe, or extreme in terms of air pollution are required to have vehicle inspection and maintenance programs that meet EPA guidelines. Such programs must include annual emissions testing and enforcement through vehicle registration.

Additional programs, discussed in the section on "Mobile Source Performance Standards" also help nonattainment areas move toward attainment.

NO SIGNIFICANT DETERIORATION

Focusing on nonattainment areas sometimes causes us to overlook the fact that some air-quality regions already met or were cleaner than the NAAQS. The existence of these clean regions presented Congress with a problem. Should the air quality in these areas be prevented from deteriorating at all? Such a policy would maximize the preservation of a clean environment for future generations. Many living in clean areas, however, opposed such a policy, arguing that it would, in effect, be punishing them for not polluting. A no-degradation policy might prohibit them from bringing in substantial new industries.

Congress reached a compromise by virtue of the NSD policy. All "clean" air-quality regions were to be designated class I, II, or III. Class I air was the most pristine, and there would be only minimal increases in ambient concentrations permitted. Class II air would be allowed a moderate amount of degradation, consonant with moderate, well-controlled growth, and remain significantly cleaner than required under the NAAQSs. Class III areas would be allowed slightly more deterioration from new sources and, in some cases, allowed to degrade to the level of the secondary standards.

Originally, all clean air-quality regions were initially designated class II. The state, once it had conducted a public hearing on the matter, could petition the EPA for reclassification. The EPA generally approved requests for reclassification as long as there was no evidence that the state acted capriciously or arbitrarily. The 1977 amendments required mandatory class I designation for all international parks, natural wilderness areas and national memorial parks exceeding 5,000 acres, national parks exceeding 6,000 acres, and all areas designated class I under the 1970 act. Such areas cannot be reclassified by the EPA.

NEW SOURCE REVIEW

One of the less well-known aspects of the CAA that gained significance during the Clinton Administration was New Source Review, a requirement under the 1977 amendments. The New Source Review program essentially required that if a facility undertook a "major modification" that would cause a "significant net increase in emissions," the plant would have to meet the more stringent standards that new sources were required to meet. A "major modification" was defined as "any physical change, or change in the method of operation of a stationary source which increases the amount of any air pollutant emitted." Subsequent EPA regulations exempted "routine maintenance, repair and replacement" from the definition of a "major modification."

The NSR requirement was adopted in 1977. The existing stationary sources of pollution were not required to install the same levels of technology for controlling pollutants that the new plants had to meet. Regulators had originally assumed that most of the worst polluting facilities would be shut down relatively soon and would be replaced by new plants constructed with the most current air pollution control technology. Instead, operators retired very few plants and continued patching up the existing, heavily polluting facilities, to the detriment of the public's health. The hope was that this requirement would either lead to the retirement of ancient polluting plants or their modernization with an updating of pollution control technology.

One of the major stationary sources subject to the New Source Review program was electrical generating plants. Their owners complained that the New Source Review program was unduly burdensome and costly, and simply refused to comply with NSR requirements. Many operators attempted to avoid New Source Performance Review by arguing that all of their improvements were simply "routine maintenance." Unsurprisingly, the meaning of "routine maintenance" has been the source of much litigation.

For years, the NSR requirement was simply not enforced with respect to power plants. Under the Clinton Administration, however, the EPA began to take New Source Review seriously. In 1997, the Clinton EPA began investigating the electrical generation industry and found that many coal-burning companies were systematically violating the law regarding NSR. According to Sylvia Lowarance, the EPA's top official for enforcement and compliance from 1996 through 2002, the power companies' actions constituted "the most significant noncompliance pattern the EPA had ever found."[46] This pattern of noncompliance was particularly alarming because coal fired plants cause about 60 percent of all the US SO_2 emissions and up to 40 percent of its mercury emissions, while being the second largest source of nitrogen oxide emissions.[47] And the new scrubbers, while expensive, can cut emissions up to 95 percent.[48]

Because of their investigations, the Clinton EPA began to seek compliance from the industry, and in 1999, the Justice Department, acting upon the request of the EPA, filed several lawsuits against electrical utility companies whose power plants were allegedly responsible for emitting over two million tons of SO_2 and 660,000 tons of NO_x each year.[49] The agency had some successes. For example, the Tampa Electric Company agreed to spend more than a billion dollars on new technology at one of its Tampa Bay plants and pay $3.5 million in fines. That agreement removed 123,000 tons of pollutants from the atmosphere every year and cost the firm less than 2 percent of its 1999 profits.[50] A few other utilities followed Tampa's example but most did not.[51] Some reluctantly entered into negotiations with the EPA, but once the new EPA under the Bush administration settled in, and the new officials began sending signals that they did not favor NSR, settlements ground to a halt. According to the former head of the EPA's Civil Enforcement Division, Eric Schaeffer, the agency was over 80 percent finished with settlement agreements with several companies in 2001, and the companies just walked away from the negotiation process in response to the signals they were receiving from the new administration.[52]

In August of 2003, citing the ambiguity of the law and the need to provide industries with greater regulatory certainty, the EPA, at the urging of the White House, adopted new definitions and rules, which significantly relaxed the "new source review" provisions of the CAA under the guise of promulgating new rules that promote greater certainty when interpreting the law. For example, "routine maintenance" has been redefined to allow maintenance, upgrades, and expansions to occur without requiring new pollution controls so long as the cost of the changes do not exceed 20 percent of the cost of the entire "process unit," an ambiguous term itself. Under this new rule, major utility plant changes that cost millions of dollars and increase pollution by thousands of tons can be defined as "routine maintenance" and thus be exempt from CAA protections. The Natural Resource Defense Council estimates that this new definition alone will exempt nearly 17,000 older power plants, oil refineries, and factories from having to install pollution controls when they replace old equipment.

Environmental groups expressed strong anger toward this new rule, arguing that it will substantially harm the quality of the air, increase respiratory ailments, such as asthma, and cause thousands of premature deaths. Furthermore, a report by the General Accounting Office (GAO), the investigative arm of Congress, said that the EPA had relied not on scientific evidence but merely on anecdotal evidence from utilities to build a case for the new law. Because the changes to the New Source Review substantially weaken the CAA's ability to prevent pollution and cause many existing enforcement efforts to be dropped, 12 states (New York, Connecticut, Maine, Maryland, Massachusetts, New Hampshire, New Mexico, New Jersey, Pennsylvania, Rhode Island, Vermont, and Wisconsin) and the District of Columbia sued the Bush Administration in October of 2003 to block the changes to the New Source Review that are seen as a major rollback of the CAA and a hazard to public health.[53]

In 2005, the D.C. Court of Appeals ruled on the issue in *New York v. EPA*.[54] The court deferred to the new EPA interpretation of the New Source Review, upholding its implementation. The EPA's interpretation did not please the state petitioners or environmental groups who argued that the new standard was too narrow and allowed too many "modifications" or "routine maintenance" actions to avoid NSR requirements. However, the industrialists were not entirely satisfied by the court's deference either; they had argued that the EPA's interpretation was too broad therefore subjected too many "modifications" to the NSR.

When the new rules were being proposed, the EPA administrator claimed that the new rules would not stop any enforcement actions against utilities that had been started under the previous administration and were still ongoing, but shortly after the rules were adopted, the EPA decided to drop most of those lawsuits. The EPA enforcement chief told staff to "set aside cases not yet filed that do not violate the requirements of the new rules, which would primarily affect utility cases."[55]

Then, in 2006, on rehearing of *New York v. EPA,* the court vacated the portion of the new EPA rule that stated categorically that the replacement of components with identical or functionally equivalent components that do not exceed 20 percent of the replacement value of the process unit and does not change its basic design parameters is not a change and is within the routine maintenance exclusion.[56] The court reasoned that the new rule was clearly inconsistent with Congressional intent in passing the new source review provision of the CAA.

Thus, one of the most controversial of the Bush Administration's attempted revisions of the CAA had been undermined by the courts. While the EPA still has discretion under the statute as to when to prosecute, utilities now do not have the broad freedom to upgrade their plants that they would have had under this rule.

MOBILE SOURCE PERFORMANCE STANDARDS

Mobile source performance standards are considered one of the most successful aspects of the CAA as well as perhaps the most controversial. The mobile source performance standards are designed primarily to reduce the emissions of hydrocarbons, CO, and nitrous oxides. The reductions are controlled primarily through the Federal Motor Vehicle Control Program. Under this program, the EPA sets national emissions standards for fuel evaporation, CO, NO_x, volatile organic compounds (VOCs), and particulates. Car manufacturers must design cars to meet the standards. Since the first standards were set, there has been a running battle between the manufacturers and the EPA over whether standards are too stiff. The manufacturers have generally succeeded in getting deadline extensions, but then eventually they meet the once allegedly "unattainable" reductions.

One of the greatest successes of the EPA's regulation of mobile sources was the mandated reduction of lead content in gasoline. Beginning in 1975, the EPA started requiring the use of lead-free gasoline in new cars. By 1985, the EPA required a reduction of lead content in gasoline from an average of 1.0 gram per gallon to 0.5 gram per gallon and to 0.1 gram per gallon in 1986. In 1995, completely banned the use of leaded gasoline in all highway vehicles. Between 1980 and 1999, there was a 94 percent reduction in the levels of lead in the air. Today, the largest source of lead pollution is from metal processing plants.

Title II of the 1990 CAA amendments contained new tailpipe emissions standards, rules requiring the reformulation of gasoline, and provisions to force automobile makers to design and manufacture cars that can run on alternative fuels. Other sections of these amendments required additional controls to reduce vehicle-related smog. By 1998, manufacturers were required to have reduced the exhaust emissions of NO_x on all new vehicles by 60 percent from the 1990 levels; emissions levels of other pollutants must be reduced by 35 percent. Originally, to ensure that manufacturers met these standards, the EPA certified a prototype of each new model that had emissions controls effective up to 50,000 miles. However, in 1998, the EPA reinvented the automobile emissions certification program. Under the new vehicle emission Compliance Assurance Program (CAP 2000), manufacturers test more than 2,000 customer-owned, in-use vehicles. Shifting the certification focus from preproduction vehicles to in-use vehicles allows the EPA to ensure that vehicles are actually in compliance. Furthermore, automobile manufacturers save an estimated $55 million annually because of the program. Additional measures under the 1990 amendments included the requirement for vapor-recovery equipment on gasoline pump nozzles and mandatory automobile inspection and maintenance.

In June 1991, the EPA took one of its first steps toward implementing this act by proposing rules to mandate the sale of cleaner gasoline in the most severely polluted cities. Under these rules, by November 1992, oxygenated gasoline (gasoline blended with an oxygenate such as ethanol) was being sold during the winter in cities across the country that had CO problems.

The rules also mandated that, by January 1995, gasoline reformulated to reduce the emission of O_3-forming hydrocarbons be available for sale in the nine smoggiest cities. These cities—Baltimore, Chicago, Hartford, Houston, Los Angeles, Milwaukee, New York, Philadelphia, and San Diego—account for almost 25 percent of the country's gasoline consumption. As of July 1998, Sacramento was added to the list of the smoggiest cities, and 13 additional areas also opted to join the program in an attempt to meet CAA goals.

Prompted by consumer complaints, many of which are shared by participants in the winter oxygenated fuel program, a number of areas that voluntarily opted in are opting back out again. Consumers complained about the additional cost of the fuel—generally from $.03 to $.07 more per gallon, but sometimes as high as $.17 more.[57] Reformulated gasoline was also implicated in the large increases in gas prices seen in the Midwest in the summer of 2000. The high prices of gasoline led one state, Wisconsin, to petition the EPA for a waiver to remove itself from the program until gas prices were more reasonable. Other consumer complaints included a drop in mileage of as much as 15 percent and a fear that the fuel was damaging their engines. Finally, some motorists complained of headaches and nausea from the new fuels. The largest number of complaints seemed to come from the Milwaukee area, and when EPA officials called a special meeting about the program at a downtown hotel, over 300 angry motorists jammed the session, booing the officials and demanding that regular gas be returned to the pumps.[58]

Despite the complaints, officials from the reformulated fuels industry and the American Automobile Association believe that reformulated gasoline is one of the most cost-effective ways to reduce pollution.[59] Industry officials tend to focus on the efficiency of the fuels. They say that tests have shown a decrease of only 1–2 percent of miles per gallon (mpg) and that the fuel is not harmful to engines.[60] However, because the purpose of the EPA is to protect public health and the environment, the agency created a panel of experts who will review health issues associated with using methyl tertiary butyl ether (MTBE) and other oxygenates in fuels. For its assessment, the panel needed to:

(1) Examine the role of oxygenates in meeting the goal of clean air, (2) Evaluate each product's efficiency in providing clean air benefits and the existence of alternatives, (3) Assess the behavior of oxygenates in the environment, (4) Review any known health effects, (5) Compare the cost of production and use, and each product's availability—both at the present and in the future.[61]

MTBE accounts for about 85 percent of oxygenates added to fuels to make them cleaner. However, MTBE has been found in the drinking water of some communities and has led to a concern of groundwater contamination. And, in fact, some lawsuits brought alleging contamination of drinking water by MTBE have led to multimillion-dollar verdicts and settlements.[62] The Blue Ribbon Panel concluded that MTBE is more likely to contaminate groundwater than other gasoline components and suggested several recommendations to decrease the use of MTBE as an oxygenate.[63] The most striking of these recommendations is that Congress remove the oxygenate requirement from the CAA to ensure that MTBE use could be reduced as quickly as possible. The EPA agreed with this suggestion and proposed a legislative framework for Congress that would remove the oxygenate requirement from the CAA and replace it with a renewable fuel annual average content mandate that would preserve the clean air benefits of oxygenates but remove the health hazards of MTBE.[64] Despite the several bills that were introduced in both the House and the Senate to remove the MTBE requirement within the CAA, MTBE continues to be added to fuels. However, in 2001, the EPA began requiring all large drinking water systems, and a representative sample of smaller drinking water systems, to monitor and report the presence of MTBE.

In addition to regulating the type of fuels used in mobile sources, the government also regulates how much fuel can be used. In 1975, Congress passed the Energy Policy Conservation Act, which created the Corporate The National Highway Traffic and Safety Administration (NHTSA) and the EPA are responsible for establishing and reporting the CAFE standards. The CAFE standard is the average fuel economy for a manufacturer's passenger cars and light trucks for a model year. Cars and light trucks that weigh less than 8,500 pounds and that are sold in the United States are subject to this standard. As of 2004, all passenger cars must meet a standard of at least 27.5 mpg, whereas light trucks must exceed 20.7 mpg. The current standard for passenger cars was set in 1990 and has not changed since then. The failure to increase the CAFE standard has resulted in harsh criticism from state and environmental groups. Manufactures that fail to meet this standard must pay a penalty, and in 2002, five passenger car manufacturers failed to meet CAFE standards.[65]

THE 1990 CLEAN AIR ACT AMENDMENTS

The CAA was amended in 1990 to reflect growing concerns with certain air-quality problems. The original CAA said little about the concerns of acid rain and air toxics; the amendments to the Act in 1990 included programs to address these issues. In addition, Congress was concerned about the inability of many areas to attain the NAAQS, as discussed above. Thus, the 1990 amendments contained programs requiring the EPA to work with states in achieving air-quality goals. These programs required the EPA to issue nearly 200 regulations soon after the enactment of the amendments. The EPA was slow to promulgate these regulations, causing states to miss their deadlines in preparing SIPs. To prevent litigation and to implement the amendments as quickly as possible, the EPA used reg-neg (see Chapter 3) to solve conflicts. The two most important pieces of the 1990 CAA Amendments—the Air Toxics Program and the Acid Rain Program—are described in the next section.

1990 AIR TOXICS PROGRAM

So far, we have only discussed regulations that are directed primarily toward reduction of conventional air pollutants. Toxic or hazardous pollutants, substances that in low concentrations can cause serious long- and short-term damage to human health and the environment, are also regulated under the act. Table 5-2 lists the harms caused by some of these toxic pollutants.

Under the CAA of 1970, the EPA was given the authority to issue national emissions standards for hazardous or toxic pollutants. Unfortunately,

TABLE 5-2   Health Effects of Some Regulated Hazardous or Toxic Air Pollutants

Pollutants	Health Effects
Arsenic	Cancer
Asbestos	Various lung diseases, especially lung cancer
Benzene	Leukemia
Beryllium	Primarily lung disease; also damage to liver, spleen, kidneys, and lymph glands
Coke oven emissions	Respiratory diseases, cancer
Mercury	Damage to the brain, kidneys, and bowels
Radionuclides	Cancer
Vinyl chloride	Lung and liver cancer

Adapted from EPA. 1988. *Environmental Progress and Challenge: EPA's Update.* Washington, D.C.: Government Printing Office.

although Congress had directed the EPA to regulate toxic pollutants, of an estimated 200 air pollutants that the agency had deemed hazardous, only eight had been regulated by 1989.[66]

Frustrated by the EPA's limited regulation of air toxins, Congress included a strict new air toxins program in Title III of the 1990 amendments. The program is designed to force both large and small industrial plants to reduce significantly their emissions of 188 pollutants listed as hazardous by the EPA. The law imposes strict deadlines on the EPA, forcing the agency to issue at least 25 new rules for reducing hazardous pollutants from new and existing sources.

One of the EPA's first tasks under the new law was to designate categories and subcategories of the sources that emitted these pollutants, which the agency published on July 16, 1992. The EPA published a schedule for the issuance of standards for each category and subcategory. This schedule tells firms whether their standards will be promulgated within 2, 4, 7, or 10 years after enactment of the 1990 amendments.

For major sources—any sources that emit or have the capacity to emit either 10 tons per year of a toxic air pollutant or 25 tons of a combination of toxic pollutants—the EPA will determine the standard of maximum achievable control technology (MACT) for each toxic pollutant emitted. Instead of prescribing a specific control technology, the EPA sets a performance level based on technology or other practices used by the industry. For existing facilities, MACT is defined as the emissions reduction that the best-performing 12 percent of similar facilities have attained, assuming there are at least 30 such facilities. (If fewer than 30 facilities exist, the EPA will use the five best facilities.) For new facilities, MACT is the best emissions control any facility in that category or subcategory is achieving. For area sources, those emitting fewer pollutants than the major sources, the EPA has the discretion to order lower standards. EPA may require area sources to meet generally achievable control technologies (GACT) or management practices.

In March 1999, the EPA published its Residual Risk Report to Congress, which detailed the risks remaining for the public after the implementation of MACT standards. The EPA was directed in writing this report to make recommendations to Congress regarding legislation for the remaining risk. In the report, the EPA declined to make any recommendations to Congress regarding legislation for residual risk, stating that "the legislative strategy embodied in the 1990 CAA Amendments provides the Agency with adequate authority to address residual risks and provides a complete strategy for dealing with a variety of risk problems."[67]

One final mandate under the air toxics program was that by November 15, 1992, the EPA had to have completed an accident-prevention program including release prevention, detection, and correction requirements, such as monitoring, training, and record keeping.[68] The final rule for this program was promulgated on June 20, 1996. In it, the EPA requires industry to submit a risk management plan (RMP) that includes a hazard assessment and a prevention and emergency response program and indicates the industry's compliance with existing regulations. The RMP is intended for use by both the public and the EPA, so it must contain information on the source's registration, an executive summary, and data on compliance.

The Mercury Controversy

Mercury occurs in fossil fuels such as coal and is released into the atmosphere when those fuels are burned. When mercury particles and gases drop into water, some turn into a more toxic form known as methyl mercury, which subsequently enters the aquatic food chain and eventually ends up in humans when fish are eaten. Children born to mothers who have eaten fish may develop neurological problems from their exposure to mercury before birth. During the final days of the Clinton administration, the EPA declared mercury to be a toxic substance requiring regulation under the Air Toxics program and therefore ordered the EPA to establish the MACT standard for mercury emissions from utility plants by the end of 2003. When the order was issued, the EPA itself had acknowledged an awareness of technologies that could reduce mercury emissions from power plants by 98 percent.

As a part of the standard setting process in 2001, the EPA selected a 21-member advisory panel to make recommendations. The advisory panel asked the EPA's Office of Air and Radiation to carry out comparative studies of proposals to reduce mercury emission that would examine the effects of mercury regulation on energy markets, electricity prices, and public health. These studies, using EPA models, provide the kind of analysis the EPA typically uses to weigh alternatives when setting standards. The comparative data was never provided. Essentially, the agency's technical experts were cut out of the process of developing a major regulatory proposal.[69]

In 2003, despite the existence of data demonstrating the toxicity of mercury, and although other sectors (such as municipal waste incinerators) had already been forced to reduce their mercury emission by 90 percent, the Bush administration decided to reclassify mercury as a non-toxic pollutant, meaning it would not have to meet the stringent standards required under the Air Toxics Program. Instead, they decided to simply regulate mercury emissions as a part of their proposed "Clear Skies Initiative."[70]

In December 2003, the Bush administration's proposed rule was published in the Federal Register. The rule contained multiple paragraphs of language taken verbatim from memos provided by a national law firm that represents a number of large coal-fired utility plants, and a research and advocacy group who represents 20 power and transmission companies in a number of Western states.[71] In 2006, the proposed rule became final with few changes.

Coal-fired electrical generating plants put out about 48 tons of mercury annually. The Bush Administration's new rule will be implemented in two phases. The first would require an annual national cap on mercury of 34 tons by 2010 and the second a national cap of 15 tons by 2018. Instead of requiring every plant to meet stringent emission standards, the proposed rule would institute a cap and trading program that would allow plants to buy and sell, as well as bank, emission control credits. The first stage would automatically be met if firms installed the scrubbers and other equipment required to meet standards for nitrogen oxide and SO_2 emissions.[72]

In addition to being concerned about how the Bush administration developed the new standards, critics point out that the cap and trade program, because it is based on a national standard, will allow the continued existence of "hot spots," where there will be extremely high concentrations of mercury. The EPA's own Children's Health Advisory Committee wrote in January 2004 that "the cap and trade program, as proposed, may not address existing hot spots and may even create new local hot spots for mercury." The committee further noted that the proposal "does not go as far as feasible to reduce mercury emissions from power plants, and thereby does not sufficiently protect our nation's children."[73] Also, because firms can bank emission credits from phase 1 to use during phase 2, the lower phase 2 standard is unlikely to be met. Even the EPA is now admitting that the 70 percent reduction goal might not be met until 2025, if ever.

The original Clinton administration order would have mandated a reduction of up to 90 percent by 2008, meaning that 5 tons of mercury could have been emitted annually.[74]

States are again taking the lead for environmental protection. In 2005, nine states sued the EPA after the EPA's independent inspector general concluded that the mercury standards did not conform to the CAA because it did not require the "maximum available control technology" and that the decision was motivated by political considerations. Other states are enacting their own mercury standards. In 2006, Illinois and New York proposed their own rules to reduce mercury emissions from power plants; Illinois aims for a

90 percent reduction by 2009 and New York aims for the same reduction by 2015. Notably, however, neither state plan allows for trading of emissions credits in an effort to reduce mercury "hot spots."

ACID RAIN-CONTROL PROGRAM

One of the more noteworthy aspects of the CAA amendments of 1990 is the acid rain-control program. Accepting scientific evidence that the way to control acid rain is to reduce SO_2 emissions, Congress imposed a program of controls that would cut these emissions in half by the year 2000. To accomplish these reductions, a limited number of allowances were created under Title IV of the amendments. Each allowance authorizes its holder to emit 1 ton of SO_2 per year. The allowances are issued by the EPA using a formula specified in the statute. The first phase of reductions began on January 1, 1995, and affected 110 of the highest-emitting electricity-generating plants. The second, more stringent phase of the program went into effect on January 1, 2000, and affects a much larger number of plants. Now, the EPA will not be allowed to issue more than 8.95 million allowances annually.

Once an allowance is "used up," it is surrendered to the EPA and no longer exists. If a plant emits less SO_2 than is permitted by its allowances, the plant may sell or transfer its unneeded allowances or may "bank" them for the next year. If a plant's emissions exceed its allowance for a given year, the plant owners must secure additional allowances or face fines of up to $2,000 per ton of excess emissions, plus possible civil and criminal penalties. Violators will also face a reduction of their next year's allowances. In fact, in a precedent-setting case in 1998, Long Island Lighting Company was fined 500 tons of its SO_2 credits as part of a settlement of an enforcement action for excessive pollution from its power plants in New York.[75]

On December 3, 1991, the EPA issued proposed rules for the trading program that required over 300 pages in small type in the Federal Register. The first auction was held by the Chicago Board of Trade, on behalf of the EPA, in March 1993. Allowances to emit 150,010 tons of SO_2 were sold to bidders for prices ranging from $122 to $450 per ton. Buyers were primarily electricity-generating plants, but also present among the bidders were environmental groups who were buying the allowances simply to retire them and thereby make a small contribution to cleaning up the air a little more quickly.

However, by 1995, after 3 years of the program's operation, there was almost uniform surprise over the lack of trading going on and the low prices of the allowances. In 1995, the price fell to less than $140. Given the low price of allowances, it would have been cheaper for a significant number of plants to buy extra allowances, yet these plants instead opted for the more expensive route of installing pollution-control equipment or switching to fuel that was less polluting. In 1998, a total of 150,000 allowances were offered for sale for use in 1998, and 125,000 allowances were offered that are first usable in 2005.[76] For the 1998 allowances, the successful bid price ranged from \$115.01 to \$228.92; the average price was \$116.96. For the 7-year advance auction, the average price was \$111.05.

The number of allowances was cut back on January 1, 2000. Some people believed that utilities were stockpiling allowances in anticipation of this date and that the price of the allowances would rise as the date got closer. These predictions may have been borne out, because the price of allowances was above \$200 for the first 7 months of 1999, the only time the allowance price had exceeded \$200 since the inception of the program.[77] However, regardless of whether the utilities were stockpiling allowances, the Acid Rain Program has been extraordinarily successful. In 1999, all units subject to regulation met these obligations. As well, SO_2 emissions were 2.0 million tons (29 percent) below the allowable level for 1999.[78] Finally, activity in the trading market is beginning to increase. Although trading was flat when the program started, the number of reported traded SO_2 emissions has increased from just under 10 million in 1994 to nearly 20 million in 1999.[79]

The success of the SO_2 program in decreasing emissions has led the EPA to begin to regulate NO_x emissions. The control program for NO_x was implemented in two phases. Phase I, beginning on January 1, 1996, affected two different categories of industrial boilers that produce NO_x. The first phase gave utilities five ways to meet their emissions standards:

1. Standard emissions limitation compliance
2. Averaging emissions to comply with the standard
3. Applying for an alternative emissions limitation
4. Applying for an extension
5. Reducing early the emissions of boilers not yet regulated

Phase II of NO_x emission regulation affected the emissions of about 750 boilers compared with the fewer than 300 boilers affected by phase I.[80] For the second phase, utilities could use the first three options they had in phase I to meet EPA promulgated standards. In light of the success with the SO_2 trading program, a limited trading program for NO_x was implemented under the Acid Rain Control Program. If a utility elects to use the trading option, it must petition the EPA for the right to do so, and it must be found that the trading program would decrease emissions to a greater degree than simple compliance with the set standards. Standards from phase I of the NO_x program decreased emissions by 33 percent from 1990 emission levels; phase II standards were expected to eliminate approximately 2.06 million tons per year of NO_x emissions, yet in 2002, more than three million tons of NO_x emissions were eliminated, a reduction of 29 percent over 1990 levels and surpassing the original phase II expectations.[81]

ENFORCEMENT OF THE 1990 ACT

Whether, and to what extent, the CAA of 1990 is successful depends greatly on how the states implement and enforce the act. Many critics say that the states failed to attain the goals established by the SIPs to a large extent because, first, the states were so slow to develop and approve the plans, and second, there was much confusion about what was required from each specific source. Under the new act, whereby each source will ultimately need a permit that will specify all the regulations applicable to that source, as well as emissions limits, monitoring requirements, and maintenance procedures, there will be less confusion as to what requirements each source must meet.

Enforcement may also be strengthened because most criminal violations under the new act are now felonies; violations under the previous act were generally considered misdemeanors and were, therefore, not of much interest to the Justice Department. Under the 1990 Act, the EPA may file a civil action in a federal district court against any owner or operator of a stationary source who "knowingly violates any requirement or prohibition" in an applicable SIP or permit or violates any provision of the act. The EPA may seek a permanent or temporary injunction to obtain compliance with the SIP, permit, or law or may seek civil damages of up to $25,000 per day per violation. The EPA may also seek criminal penalties of fines or prison terms of up to 5 years against violators of the act. The agency may also issue an administrative order and impose a civil penalty of up to $25,000 per day for each day of violation if it acts within 1 year of the violation. Administrative penalties are sometimes viewed as a superior alternative simply because they are easier to obtain.

To help the EPA in its enforcement efforts, the act grants the agency the authority to award up to $10,000 to any person (excluding a government official acting in an official capacity) who "furnishes information or services which lead to a criminal conviction or judicial or administrative civil penalty" for any violation of the act.

Some enforcement efforts, however, were undermined with the Bush administration's changes to the New Source Review rules in 2003, as noted above. The changes allow coal-fired utility companies and oil refineries to expand their aging facilities beyond necessary and routine maintenance without installing new pollution reduction controls. This change could lead to 1.4 million additional tons of air pollution and jeopardize Clinton-era lawsuits that seek the installation of pollution controls after significant expansions were made on coal power. For example, the Justice Department must drop lawsuits against nine Tennessee Valley Authority power plants after they performed upgrades without installing new pollution-reduction controls. These new upgrades increased pollution by hundreds of thousand of tons, yet because the upgrades cost less than 20 percent of the entire "process unit," the increased pollution would have to be allowed.

Finally, the 1990 amendments contain provisions for suits brought by citizens. Any person can bring an action in a federal district court against state and federal officials who fail to take an action required under the law and against any source believed to be in violation of the act, a regulation, or its permit. The court may order the EPA to perform its duties and impose civil penalties;

emissions standards may be enforced. Costs of litigation may be awarded to the initiator of the citizen's suit when deemed appropriate by the court.

THE CLEAR SKIES INITIATIVE

In previous sections of this chapter, allusions have been made to President Bush's Clear Skies Initiative. These references were to ideas that the administration hoped to implement as part of a legislative package called the Clear Skies Initiative, but which he would be willing to implement in small pieces through administrative rule-making if he could not get the entire package through Congress. In essence, the initiative was to be a remake of the CAA. Existing CAA Standards for SO_2 and NO_x were to be replaced with a national new cap and trade system that would also regulate mercury emissions. The key to the effectiveness of cap and trade systems is how low the nationwide cap is. Unfortunately, while the new caps would reduce levels of SO_2 and nitrogen oxide, the new caps would allow 50 percent more of the former pollutant and 40 percent more of the latter than if the current CAA Standards were enforced.[82] The legislative Initiative was unveiled in February of 2002 and was not greeted with enthusiasm by Congress. As of April 2006, the legislative package had not been passed. And while he did manage to pass a few changes, his Clear Skies Initiative is probably dead, especially after the mid-term election of 2006.

SOLUTIONS BEYOND THE CLEAN AIR ACT

The EPA estimated that by 1990, if the CAA had not been implemented, 205,000 Americans would have died prematurely while millions more would have suffered illness.[83] In addition, from 1970 to 1990 the agency suggested that the total benefits of the programs would range from $6 trillion to $50 trillion. The actual costs of the program were $523 billion. Although much progress has occurred, some pollution-control problems are addressed by the CAA and its amendments, but others are not. Two problems that could not be addressed nationally because they are global problems requiring international solutions are depletion of the O_3 layer and global warming. Both are in fact being resolved on an international level through treaties (discussed in detail in Chapter 11), which will have the end result of substantially reducing the emissions that cause these problems.

Problems of indoor pollution likewise require a type of solution different from traditional regulation. A nontraditional approach was attempted through the 1986 Radon Gas and Indoor Air-Quality Act, which directed the EPA to implement a public information and technical assistance program. Under this act, the EPA is conducting research to try to identify and rank the risks posed by various indoor pollutants and to discover better ways to diagnose building-related diseases and correct their causes. The agency's current emphasis is on education, and it has prepared several documents offering guidance on construction of new homes and rehabilitation of old ones to reduce the risks from indoor pollution. A campaign to encourage the public to test for and repair radon problems has begun. A radon hotline has been set up, and a list of more than 1,000 EPA-approved radon contractors has been made. Meanwhile, the EPA is still exploring strategies to try to reduce the risk from radon and other indoor pollutants.

Concluding Remarks

Conventional air pollution, indoor air pollution, toxic emissions, acid rain, the greenhouse effect, and depletion of the O_3 layer are the primary air-quality problems facing the nation today. We began to address these pollution problems seriously with the 1970 CAA. This act, which has been amended twice, still provides the basic structure for attempts to improve air quality. Over the course of the past 30 years or so, some major improvements have been made in air quality, although there is still a long way to go. But with the passage of the 1990 CAA amendments, which brought more sources under regulation, imposed more stringent steps toward controlling acid rain and air toxins, provided compliance deadlines that at least appeared to be more reasonable than some imposed by the earlier CAA, and strengthened enforcement provisions, many were hopeful that our air quality would continue to improve. Since the Bush administration came to power, however, we have seen changes that do not bode well for improvements in air quality. Changes like those in new source review provide cause for alarm, although we have seen states stepping up and putting pressure on the federal government to do more to improve air quality.

Now that you understand the basic scheme for regulation of air quality, you are ready to move on to water quality. As you examine the way we protect water, try to identify those aspects of the approaches to the two different mediums that are alike and those that are different.

Questions for Review and Discussion

1. List and describe the harmful effects of the six conventional air pollutants.
2. Explain the difference between a conventional air pollutant and a toxic air pollutant.
3. What is acid deposition?
4. Why is the thinning of the O_3 layer a problem?
5. Conceptually, how did the regulation of air quality from 1970 to the present differ from air-quality legislation before 1970?
6. How is the treatment of existing air-pollution sources different from the treatment of new sources of air pollution?
7. What is the significance of an area being designated a class I air-quality control region?
8. How does the 1990 air toxins program differ from the program for controlling air toxins established under the previous Clean Air Act?

For Further Reading

Abate, Randall S. 2006. "Kyoto Or Not, Here We Come: The Promise And Perils Of The Piecemeal Approach To Climate Change Regulation In The United States." *Cornell University Cornell Journal of Law and Public Policy 15*: 369.

Goodell, Jeff. 2006. *Big Coal: The Dirty Secret Behind America's Energy Future.* New York: Houghton Mifflin.

Gutermannand, Paul E., and David H. Quigley. 2006. "Not-So-New Source Review: D.C. Circuit Signals A Return To NSR Enforcement." *The Metropolitan Counsel* April: 23.

Kessel, Anthony. 2005. *Air, the Environment and Public Health.* Cambridge: Cambridge University Press.

Gore, Al. 2006. *An Inconvenient Truth.* Emras: Rodale Press.

Joskow, Paul L., et al. 2000. *Markets for Clean Air: The U.S. Acid Rain Program.* Cambridge: Cambridge University Press.

McGarity, Thomas O. 1996. "Regulating Commuters to Clear the Air: Some Difficulties in Implementing a National Program at the Local Level." *Pacific Law Journal 27*: 1521.

May, Randolph J. "Defining Deference Down: Independent Agencies and Chevron Deference." *Administrative Law Review 58*: 429.

Reitze, Arnold W., Jr., and Sheryl-Lynn Carol. 1998. "The Legal Control of Indoor Air Pollution." *Boston College Environmental Affairs Law Review 25*: 247.

Welburn, Alan. 1988. *Air Pollution and Acid Rain: The Biological Impact.* New York: Wiley.

On the Internet

http://www.epa.gov/oar/recipes
Provides "recipes" cities and towns can use to improve air quality
http://www.epa.gov/oar/oaqps
EPA Office of Air-Quality Planning and Standards
http://www.epa.gov/airmarkets/arp/
EPA Acid Rain Program
http://www.epa.gov/acidrain/effects/index.html
The numerous effects of acid deposition can be found here
http://yosemite.epa.gov/oar/globalwarming.nsf/content/index.html
EPA's Web site on global warming
http://yosemite.epa.gov/oar/globalwarming.nsf/content/ActionsState.html
Provides information on EPA's State and Local Climate Change Program
http://www.usgcrp.gov
Provides information on the U.S. Global Change Research Program and other federal information
http://www.epa.gov/ozone/science/
The Science of Ozone Depletion
http://unfccc.int/2860.php
United Nations Framework Convention on Climate Change, providing news on international efforts to slow climate change

http://www.climatehotmap.org/
The Web site of Global Warming Early Warning Signs
http://www.epa.gov/air/toxicair/newtoxics.html
About Air Toxics, Health, and Ecological Effects
http://nadp.sws.uiuc.edu/
National Atmospheric Deposition Program—follow the link to determine the pH levels of rainfall in your area

Notes

1. *Plain English Guide to the Clean Air Act. http://www.epa.gov/oar/oaqps/peg_caa/pegcaa10.html.* See also *Criteria Pollutant Reports. http://www.epa.gov/air/oaqps/greenbk/multipol.html.*

2. CEQ. 1990. "Environmental Quality." *Twentieth Annual Report,* p 470. Washington, D.C.: Government Printing Office.

3. Ibid., 472.

4. *http://www.epa.gov/air/oaqps/greenbk/cnsum.html* (Updated March 2006).

5. EPA, *The Ozone Report: Measuring Progress Though 2003* (April 2004).

6. EPA. 2002. "Air Quality Trends Summary Report 2002." *http://www.epa.gov/air/airtrends/aqtrnd02/2002_airtrends_final.pdf* (September 22, 2006).

7. CEQ. "Environmental Quality," p 471.

8. EPA, *Final Revisions to the National Ambient Air Quality Standards for Particle Pollution (Particulate Matter). http://www.epa.gov/air/particlepollution/pdfs/20060921_factsheet.pdf* (September 30, 2006).

9. C. Arden Pope III. 1989. "Respiratory Disease Associated with Community Air Pollution and a Steel Mill, Utah Valley." *American Journal of Public Health 79*: 623.

10. Environmental Quality Statistics: US Emissions of Lead by Source. *http://ceq.eh.doe.gov/nepa/reports/statistics/tab5x7.html* (December 2, 2003).

11. EPA. 1996. "Air Toxics." *National Air-Quality and Emission Trends Report 1996,* p 63. *http://www.epa.gov/oar/aqtrnd96/chapter5.pdf* (July 22, 2001).

12. Ibid., 61.

13. *http://www.unep.org/ozone/sap2002.shtml* (December 11, 2003).

14. Committee on the Science of Climate Change, National Academy of Sciences, Climate Change Science: An Analysis of Some Key Questions (2001). *http://books.napedu/books/0309075742/html/1.html page top* (May 5, 2004).

15. IPCC. "Summary for Policymakers," p 7. *http://www.ipcc.ch/pub/spm22–01.pdf* (July 22, 2001).

16. Jeffrey Kluger. 2001. "Special Report/Global Warming." *Time Magazine 157*: 30.

17. "EU Says Ready to Sideline US in Climate Talks." April 5, 2001. *http://www.planetark.org/dailynewstory.cfm?newsid=10404&newsdate=05-Apr-2001* (July 22, 2001).

18. "Vice President Gore Announces New Data Showing July 1998 Was Hottest Month on Record," *White House Press Release* (August 10, 1998).

19. "Global Warming Is for Real, NASA Says," January 12, 1999. *http://www.enn.com/news/enn-stories/1999/01/011299/warm7_985.asp* (July 22, 2001); IPCC. "Summary for Policymakers," p 7. *http://www.ipcc.ch/pub/spm22–01.pdf* (July 22, 2001).

20. Paul C. Waggoner, ed. 1988. *Climate and Water: Report of the American Association for the Advancement of Science Panel on Climatic Variability, Climate Change, and the Planning and Management of U.S. Water Resources.* Washington, D.C.: AAAS.

21. *http://www.nsidc.com* (December 5, 2003).

22. Andrew C. Revkin, "Arctic Sea Ice Melting Faster, Study Finds", *New York Times* (May 1, 2007).

23. Andrew C. Revkin. "Debate Rises Over a Quick(er) Climate Fix." *http://www.nytimes.com/2000/10/03/science/03GREE.html* (December 16, 2000).

24. World Wildlife Federation press release. 2001. "Governments Recognize Stunning Scale of Climate Impact," February 19. (On file with author.)

25. Ibid.

26. Ibid.

27. "Maldives Says US Emissions About-face Spells Woe," April 5, 2001. *http://www.planetark.org/dailynewsstory.cfm?newsid=10405&newsdate=05-Apr-2001* (July 22, 2001).

28. Ibid.

29. World Wildlife Federation press release.

30. "Delivering Emission Reductions." *Climate Change: The UK Programme.* *http://www.defra.gov.uk/environment/climatechange/cm4913/pdf/section2.pdf* (July 22, 2001).

31. Natural Resources Canada Press Release. "Government of Canada Announces up to $500 Million for Action on Climate Change." *http://www.NRCan.gc.ca/css/imb/hqlib/200079e.html* (July 22, 2001).

32. Ross Gelbspan. "Help Me, I'm Melting!" *http://www.gristmagazine.com/grist/maindish/gelbspan092900.stm* (December 16, 2000).

33. Penny Fannin. "An Iron Key May Unlock Greenhouse." *http://www.theage.com.au/news/20000923/A12886-2000Sep22.html* (December 16, 2000).

34. "Global Air-Cleaning No Easy Task." *http://www.foxnews.com/science/100300/cleanair.sml* (December 16, 2000).

35. EPA. "Air-Quality Trends," p 7.

36. "EPA's National Ambient Air-Quality Standards: The Standard Review/Reevaluation Process." *EPA Press Release* (July 16, 1997).

37. *Whitman, et al. v. American Trucking Association, et al.,* 121 S.Ct. 903.

38. Ibid.

39. *http://yosemite.epa.gov/opa/admpress.nsf/0/35188868a47f756185256b88007ab1aa?OpenDocument.*

40. EPA, *The Ozone Report: Measuring Progress Though 2003* (April 2004).

41. Pope. "Respiratory Disease," p 471.

42. EPA, *Air Trends. http://www.epa.gov/airtrends/sixpoll.html* (September 29, 2006).

43. EPA, *Green Book, Currently Designated Nonattainment Areas for all Criteria Pollutants. http://www.epa.gov/air/oaqps/greenbk/ancl3.html* (October. 9, 2006).

44. Cynthi Bergman, EPA Issues Designations on Ozone Health Standards. *http://yosemite.epa.gov/opa/admpress.nsf/* (April 18, 2004).

45. Ibid.

46. EPA, *Air Permits. http://www.epa.gov/air/oaqps/permits/approval.html* (October 9, 2006).

47. Barcourt, Bruce. 2002. "Changing the Rules—How the Bush Administration Quietly and Radically Transformed the Nation's Clean Air Policy." *New York Times Sunday Magazine* 39, of 42 (April 4).

48. Ibid.

49. Ibid.

50. Ibid.

51. Ibid.

52. Ibid.

53. Ibid.

54. Two Studies Contradict EPA on New Rules: Changes to Boost Pollution, They Say. *Washington Post* (October 23, 2003): A2.
55. *New York v. EPA,* 413 F.3d 3 (2005).
56. Inside EPA, "EPA Retreat on NSR Enforcement Court Buoy State Legal Strategies" (November 14, 2003).
57. *New York v. EPA,* 443 F.3d 880 (2006).
58. Gary Lee. 1995. "EPA Allows Regular Gasoline as Alternative in Milwaukee." *Washington Post* (February 25): A2.
59. David Southerland. 1994. "Gas Prices Fall but Clean Fuels Issue Burns Hot." *Washington Post* (December 22): B9.
60. "EPA Announces Blue-Ribbon Panel to Review Use of MTBE and Other Oxygenates in Gasoline." *EPA Press Release* (November 30, 1998).
61. Southerland, note 59.
62. Christina Zevitas. 2001. "MTBE Settlement Could Signal Defense Success in Future Cases." *Law Week USA* (February 19): B5.
63. Achieving Clean Air and Clean Water: The Report of the Blue Ribbon Panel on Oxygenates in Gasoline (September 15, 1999). *http://www.epa.gov/otaq/consumer/fuels/oxypanel/r99021.pdf* (December 16, 2000).
64. "Legislative Principles for Protecting Drinking Water Supplies, Preserving Clean Air Benefits, and Promoting Renewable Fuels." *http://www.epa.gov/otaq/consumer/fuels/mtbe/f00011.html* (October 31, 2000).
65. David Wollin. 1991. "Air Toxins Laws Force Industries to Plan Ahead." *National Law Journal* (May 13): 256.
66. NHTSA. *CAFE Overview. http://www.nhtsa.dot.gov/Cars/rules/CAFE/overview.htm* (September 28, 2006).
67. EPA. 1999. *Residual Risk Report to Congress. http://www.epa.gov/ttn/oarpg/t3/reports/risk_rep.pdf* (December 16, 2000).
68. Wollin. "Air Toxins Laws."
69. Tom Hamburger and Alan Miller. 2004. "Mercury Emissions Rule Geared to Benefit Industry, Staffers Say." *Los Angeles Times* (March 16). *http://www.latimes.com/news/printedition/asection/la-na-mercury16mar3390999.story.*
70. Margaret Kriz. 2004. "The Next Arsenic." *National Law Journal* (February 14): 2004 WL 55305006.
71. Hamburger, note 69.
72. Kriz, note 70.
73. Hamburger, note 69.
74. Ibid.
75. Gary Gallon. 1998. Gallon Report on Climate Change. (E-mail Newsletter, On file with author.)
76. "Results of the Sixth Annual Auction of Acid Rain Allowances." *EPA Press Release* (March 27, 1998).
77. EPA Clean Air Market Programs. "Monthly Average Price of Sulfur Dioxide Allowances." *http://www.epa.gov/airmarkets/trading/so2market/pricetbl.html* (July 25, 2001).
78. EPA Clean Air Market Programs. "1999 Acid Rain Program Compliance Report." *http://www.epa.gov/airmarkets/cmprpt/arp99/index.html* (July 22, 2001).
79. Ibid.
80. Ibid. EPA Clean Air Markets Program. "Nitrogen Oxides (NO$_x$) Reduction under Phase II of the Acid Rain Program." *http://www.epa.gov/airmarket/arp/nox/phase2.html* (July 25, 2001).
81. Acid Rain Program Progress Report 2002, November 2003: 13. *http://www.epa.gov/airmarkets/cmprpt/arp02/2002report.pdf* (December 2, 2003).
82. Barcourt, note 47.
83. "New Report Shows Clean Air Benefits Significantly Outweigh Costs." *EPA Press Release* (October 21, 1997).

RESOLVING CONTROVERSIAL ENVIRONMENTAL ISSUES

- While reading the following passage, evaluate the link between each reason and the conclusion. Does each reason logically lead to the conclusion? Why or why not?
- Authors sometimes provide evidence for their reasons. Evidence may be in the form of statistics, case studies, personal testimonials, research studies, personal observations, or analogies. Identify any evidence offered in support of the reasons in the following editorial. Are there any problems with that evidence? For example, if statistics are given, can you interpret those statistics? In addition, what does it mean if the author provides no evidence for a reason?

EQUAL RIGHTS AMONG AUTOS

When asked about criteria for buying an automobile, most people will list style, color, and price. However, few people add "low-polluter" to their list of criteria for choosing a vehicle. In fact, those vehicles that are most popular are the highest polluters. Minivans, sport utility vehicles (SUVs), and light-duty pickup trucks produce higher levels of NO_x and other smog-causing gases than cars do. This higher amount of pollution occurs because these vehicles are not subject to the same strict emission standards as ordinary cars.

However, on November 5, 1998, the State Air Resources Board in California leveled the inequality between cars and SUVs by issuing more stringent emission standards that will also apply to minivans, SUVs, and light-duty trucks. SUVs currently produce one and a half to two and a half times more pollution than other vehicles. The EPA should pay attention to this valuable model as it develops new federal standards for cars, light-duty trucks, minivans, and SUVs.

Because one of every two new vehicles purchased is an SUV, air quality could truly suffer if emission standards are not tightened for these popular vehicles. As long as the EPA follows California's lead and sets higher emission standards for all vehicles, air quality should remain the same. California's standards require manufacturers to cut emissions, so that gas-powered automobiles are almost as clean as electric automobiles.

Of course, manufacturers and business groups have protested loudly against the new regulations. They claim that some models will simply not be able to meet the new standards. Although the industry has protested previous environmental regulations (e.g., fuel-economy standards), it has been wrong about compliance with those regulations. California officials believe that it will cost about $107 per vehicle to achieve the new emission standards—a small price for clean air.

The EPA should certainly follow California's lead. Air quality will be improved by higher emission standards for minivans, SUVs, and other similar vehicles.

As a student in an environmental law class, it is likely that you agreed with the author's position. However, you need to apply your critical thinking skills to any argument you encounter, especially arguments with which you agree. Perhaps you agree with the conclusion, but the author does not provide good reasons to lead you to that conclusion. You need to be able to articulate good reasons for your conclusions.

For the rest of this book, you should automatically identify the argument presented in each editorial. You will not be asked to identify the argument in the questions following each editorial. You are expected to identify the argument and then answer the critical thinking questions.

CHAPTER 6
WATER-QUALITY CONTROL

Controlling water quality means different things to different people. For instance, it includes providing good quality water in your home—knowing that when you turn on your tap, the water is safe to use for cooking, washing, and drinking without taking any special precautions. It means that local streams, lakes, ponds, rivers, and ocean coasts are places where you can safely swim, boat, and fish. It means that fish and other aquatic organisms are healthy. To the farmer, it means that water used for irrigation does not have excess amounts of salts or residuals of pesticides or pathogens. Increasingly, protecting water quality also means protecting underground aquifers, sources of groundwater vital to much of the population. To meet the need for protecting water for so many uses, a variety of complex laws and regulations have been developed.

To understand water-quality control, water-quantity control also must be understood. Many parts of the world are already severely water-stressed, particularly Africa and western Asia. Lack of freshwater is currently limiting economic growth in China, India, and Indonesia, with projections that fully two-thirds of the world's population will live in water-stressed conditions (if current consumption patterns continue) by the year 2025.[1] Often, this stress is not caused by an absolute lack of water, but by water of suitable quality not being available. Many of these water-stressed areas are adjacent to oceans, but energy is simply too expensive to make it practical to transform saltwater into useful freshwater through large-scale desalinization.

In this chapter, we first examine the basic measures of water quality and the significance of various pollutants. With that background, we turn to discussion of how water supply is controlled, focusing on the differences between the two major approaches for securing water supplies—appropriative rights and riparian rights. Finally, we examine the two federal laws, the Federal Water Pollution Control Act (FWPCA) and the Safe Drinking Water Act (SDWA), which are the most important in providing the basis of the system used in the United States to protect this vital resource.

THE MAJOR WATER POLLUTANTS

Any system for classifying pollutants must be somewhat arbitrary, particularly when concerned with water quality from a number of perspectives. Critical water-quality parameters may be very different for people and for fish, for industries and for ecosystems. By organizing pollutants into some kind of a system, enough understanding can be gained of their potential effects to see the need for a regulatory program.

PATHOGENS

Throughout the United States, there has been little worry that drinking tap water or being near surface water will lead to infectious disease. This lack of concern is not universal. The World Health Organization (WHO) reports that about 1.1 billion people have no access to an improved water supply and about 2.6 billion people have no access to an improved water sanitation system.[2] Tremendous disease and suffering result from this lack of access— worldwide, approximately 4.0 percent of all deaths and 5.7 percent of the disability-adjusted life years or DALYs (a WHO measure relating the severity of the disability to death) are associated annually with diseases attributable to unsafe water, sanitation, and hygiene.[3] About one-third of this problem occurs in Africa and another one-third in WHO's South East Asia Region-D (Bangladesh, Bhutan, Democratic People's Republic of Korea, India, Maldives, and Myanmar). Overall, 99.8 percent of deaths associated with these risks are in developing countries, and 90 percent of those dying are children.[4] WHO ranks unsafe water, sanitation, and hygiene as the sixth most important factor related to burden of disease, surpassed only by low birth rate, unsafe sex, blood pressure, tobacco, and alcohol.[5]

Ingestion of contaminated water is not the only water-quality problem. For example, about 200 million people in the world are infected with schistosomiasis, a particularly painful disease that results from exposing skin to contaminated water.[6] Mosquitoes, with a life stage dependent on surface water, are an important vector bringing disease and misery to much of the world. Mosquito-borne diseases include malaria, affecting 300 to 500 million people annually, lymphatic filariasis, infecting about 117 million people annually, and dengue fever, annually infecting approximately 50 million people.[7] The list could go on, but the point is clear—water resources and quality that are taken for granted in the United States are a major health hazard throughout much of the developing world.

Although the incidence of disease is many orders of magnitude less than in much of the developing world, the United States is not free from waterborne contamination. For example, in the 2-year period between January 2003 and December 2004, 30 disease outbreaks involving 2,760 people from 18 states were reported from contaminated drinking water. Four of the cases were linked to death. Eight of the outbreaks involved *Legionella* disease (which included the four cases linked to death), five outbreaks were caused by non-*Legionella* bacteria, two outbreaks had more than one associated etiology, one outbreak was caused by a virus, and one outbreak was caused by a parasite. Eight outbreaks were caused by chemical or toxin poisoning and the remaining five outbreaks had unknown etiology. About half of the outbreaks were associated with water not directly regulated through national drinking water protection programs under the jurisdiction of the EPA.[8] During the same period, 62 outbreaks involving approximately 2,698 people from 26 states and Guam were reported from contact with recreational waters. Gastroenteritis characterized 48 percent of these outbreaks, with another 21 percent being outbreaks of dermatitis and 11 percent being outbreaks of acute respiratory illnesses.[9]

Disease outbreaks in the United States are relatively few, but they continue to present a large-scale risk should protective systems fail. The last large-scale waterborne disease outbreak in the United States occurred in 1993 in Milwaukee from the protozoan Cryptosporidium and resulted in more than 400,000 infected individuals and approximately 100 deaths. Moreover, the large disease outbreak in Milwaukee may be seen as evidence of the vulnerability of drinking water supplies to possible terrorist attack.

The kinds of pathogens responsible for waterborne diseases include bacteria, viruses, protozoans, and parasitic worms. Bacteria are microorganisms that are ubiquitous in the environment. The human body harbors hosts of bacteria, particularly in the gastrointestinal tract. Although many bacteria are useful to our bodily functions, some are incompatible with good health. Because of the great diversity of organisms potentially found in water, it is impractical to directly monitor for each type of pathogen. Thus, groups of bacteria called coliforms are routinely monitored to indicate potential contamination of drinking water. Fecal coliforms, a subset of the coliform group, routinely have been used to monitor for pathogenic contamination of recreational waters. However, growing evidence of fecal coliforms being inadequate indicators of contamination has resulted in movement toward monitoring *Escherichia coli* and *Enterococci* as better indicators of contamination of recreational water quality.

Cholera, typhoid fever, shigellosis, and bacterial gastroenteritis are among the more important waterborne bacterial diseases; they are transmitted through contact with water contaminated by wastes from infected individuals. These diseases, characterized by severe diarrhea, can result in death (particularly in weaker individuals, such as the very young and old, or those suffering from other stressors, such as malnutrition).

Viruses are simpler organisms than bacteria. Unlike bacteria, viruses are not normal flora in the human system; only infected individuals are carriers. Viruses usually are more difficult to detect and destroy than bacteria. Infectious hepatitis and viral gastroenteritis are the primary virus-caused waterborne diseases. These diseases may be contracted from drinking water that standard tests indicate are safe from bacterial contamination; no routine and inexpensive tests are currently available to search directly for the presence of viruses.

Protozoa and parasitic worms are more complex organisms than bacteria and viruses. Backpackers have probably heard about the protozoan

Giardia lamblia and how contracting giardiasis from drinking visually pure water from apparently pristine locations can result in severe and prolonged diarrhea. The major outbreak of Cryptosporidiosis in Milwaukee resulted from the city changing its water treatment protocols to try to improve water quality. Although fatalities have occurred from *N. fowleri,* this free-living amoeba common to many surface waters only rarely causes disease. Disease incidents have been associated with swimming in warm freshwater, and inhalation (not ingestion) is the likely source of *N. fowleri* infection.

Schistosomiasis is an extremely debilitating disease in which parasitic worm larvae invade the body, develop into adults, and cause chronic inflammation and pain. It is seldom fatal itself, but it can so weaken victims as to make them susceptible to other diseases. Parasitic worms are not a major problem in the United States, but massive infections are common throughout large sections of the developing world. In the United States, flatworms are present in some freshwaters that can cause swimmers itch, a form of dermatitis caused by worm penetration of the skin. This condition is neither dangerous nor contagious, but can be very uncomfortable.

Beginning in the late 1990's, considerable media attention began focusing on a new potential pathogen, *Pfiesteria piscicida,* a dinoflagellate associated with fish kills in coastal waters. Dinoflagellates are microscopic single-celled organisms. At times, Pfiesteria, which is usually quite harmless, starts emitting a powerful fish toxin that is linked to bleeding sores or lesions. These sores may be fatal. The Pfiesteria subsequently feeds on the fish tissue and blood. Although the ecological affects of Pfiesteria can be severe, there is no conclusive evidence that consuming fish or shellfish from Pfiesteria-contaminated water will have any adverse effects on people. However, there is suspicion that swimming in infected waters may result in some memory loss, confusion, or respiratory, skin, and gastrointestinal problems. To investigate this threat, the U.S. Centers for Disease Control and Prevention (CDC), the EPA, the National Oceanic and Atmospheric Administration, the National Institute of Environmental Health Sciences, the Food and Drug administration, the Geological Survey, and the Department of Agriculture have been working with state departments of health and natural resources and universities to monitor and investigate outbreaks of Pfiesteria and the health effects on humans.

CONVENTIONAL ORGANICS

Organic chemicals come from some source related to life and have carbon as their primary structural element. These do not have to be recently living sources — petroleum, coal, and other fossil fuels are organic sources derived primarily from plants that lived millions of years ago. Pollutants from organic sources can adversely affect water quality without being directly responsible for disease. Wastes resulting from such operations as food processing, petroleum refining, and municipal wastewater treatment can result in serious disruptions of aquatic ecosystems. These wastes often have relatively large amounts of residual organic matter that can be used for energy (as food) by aquatic bacteria and other microorganisms. To use this material, dissolved oxygen is taken from the water. If the amount of food exceeds the supply of dissolved oxygen, the water turns anoxic, killing organisms such as fish. Large amounts of organic material may support substantial populations of nuisance organisms, such as filamentous bacteria (e.g., *Sphaerotilus natans*), that can clog water supply screens and that look and smell objectionable.

Large-scale contamination by organic material is typically quantified through a measure of the amount of oxygen needed for the organics to be decomposed as they are used as food. The most common of these measures are biochemical oxygen demand (BOD) and chemical oxygen demand (COD). The higher these demands, the more conventional organics exist in the water. If the oxygen demands are known and the rate of oxygen entering the water can be measured or calculated, accurate predictions can be made of the resultant oxygen content. A related measure of organic pollution is total organic carbon (TOC). This technique directly measures all organic carbon, including organic carbon that did not contribute to BOD or COD. Although it is a better measure of total organic material in the water, TOC may be less useful for evaluating the impact of organic carbon in causing oxygen depletion.

An important group of conventional organic pollutants are those identified as oil and grease. Substantial concentrations of oil and grease may be found from such diverse sources as industrial wastewater and stormwater runoff in parking lots (notice the oil sheen in the water the next time you are in a shopping center parking lot just after it starts to rain). Oil and grease is a generic measurement of those compounds resulting from a defined test procedure rather than being a measure of a specific group of chemicals. Thus, oil and grease includes a large and diverse variety of materials, ranging from extremely toxic materials, such as benzene, to benign plant waxes. Nevertheless, it is a useful measurement because of the simplicity of analysis and its use in indicating the gross level of organic pollution.

TOXIC TRACE ORGANICS

Some organic compounds are extremely toxic, presenting problems at very low (or trace) concentrations. The presence of these chemicals does not result in significant oxygen depletion, but they are of concern because of their potential direct impact on the health of humans and organisms in the ecosystem. The majority of the toxic organics of greatest concern in water are not naturally occurring but are products of chemical synthesis. Considerable work has focused on exposure and effects of such chemical groups as polychlorinated biphenyls (PCBs), polycyclic aromatic hydrocarbons (PAHs), dioxins, solvents, and pesticides. Byproducts of water treatment with chlorine and other disinfectants result in organic disinfection byproducts (DBPs) that have been linked to cancer and other adverse health outcomes. Some concern is emerging over trace levels of pharmaceutical drugs (including antibiotics) and personal care products apparently passing unchanged through human systems and appearing in measurable quantities in various waters.

Many trace organic toxicants are slow to degrade, remaining stable in the environment for extended periods. Some become concentrated in plants and animals as they move up through the food chain; low levels in water lead to medium levels in aquatic plants and relatively high levels in aquatic animals. Furthermore, the effects of contamination often are expressed only after considerable time. These characteristics greatly complicate efforts to relate exposure to effects and to understand the relationship between a given dose and a probable outcome.

The effects of trace organics on human health are variable. Many organics are thought to be carcinogens, and regulatory decisions are often made based on this risk. Other effects may include mutagenesis, teratogenesis, nervous system damage, damage to the liver and other internal organ systems, and disruption of the endocrine system. Ecological health effects from trace levels of organics are even more variable and difficult to quantify than human health effects, yet instances of harm have been documented. Perhaps one of the most well-known effects is the relationship between trace levels of dichlorodiphenyltrichloroethane (DDT) and eggshell thinning in birds (resulting in severe population crashes in a number of species because of reproductive failure).

NUTRIENTS

Unfavorable conditions caused by excess plant growth can result from organic material developing in situ, as well as from that brought in as waste. If excess fertilization occurs in a water body, photosynthesis by such organisms as algae and rooted aquatic vegetation can proceed rapidly. As the vegetation becomes increasingly luxuriant, it can become more of a problem. When vegetation dies (or at night when photosynthesis cannot occur), oxygen may be used faster than it can be replenished. Ensuing anoxic conditions destroy favorable life forms, result in objectionable tastes and odors, and encourage the growth of undesirable species.

Excessive fertilization can occur when nutrients are added to a system. The nutrients most often effective in stimulating growth are phosphorus and nitrogen. Too much pollution from nutrients, causing overfertilization and too much vegetative growth, results in a condition called cultural eutrophication. This condition can be caused by water running off well-fertilized agricultural fields, municipal wastewater containing high levels of phosphorus-based detergents and other nutrients, or wastewater from industrial and agricultural processes.

In addition to damaging ecosystems, nitrogen can directly affect public health. Excessive levels of nitrate, the form of nitrogen usually found in surface and groundwater (unless subject to gross contamination), can cause methemoglobinemia, one of the blue baby diseases. In infants, excessive nitrate in the diet reduces the capacity of blood to transport oxygen (turning the blood a bluish color), which disrupts normal development and functioning of the central nervous system.

HEAVY METALS

Another important group of toxic water pollutants are heavy metals. Substances such as mercury, cadmium, and lead are ubiquitous in our industrialized society but are extremely hazardous if not controlled properly. Similar to toxic organics, metals can present significant problems at extremely low concentrations.

Although some waters naturally have relatively high concentrations of a metal or metals, most problems with high concentrations result from discharge of industrial wastewaters or other anthropogenic sources. Heavy metals are usually in the environment at levels below that which would cause any adverse effects. To make heavy metals useful, they are mined, concentrated, and refined; residuals from this process and from the subsequent use of the refined material can result in elevated concentrations that are harmful or toxic.

Although unusual, heavy metal contamination from natural sources can severely impact public health. In Bangladesh, much of the population suffered from a surface water supply grossly contaminated with pathogens. Approximately 4.5 million shallow wells were developed throughout the country with the aid of international organizations to provide a pathogen-free drinking water. Although quite successful in reducing the risk of infectious disease, much of the groundwater obtained through these wells contain dangerously high naturally occurring levels of arsenic. Approximately 70 million people in Bangladesh using these wells are now at risk of arsenic poisoning from their drinking water.

IONIZING RADIATION

Radiation results from the decay of atoms. Atoms are composed of protons and neutrons in a nucleus surrounded by a cloud of electrons. Although most of the space in an atom is occupied by electrons, almost all of the atom's mass is in the protons and neutrons. Protons carry a positive charge and electrons carry a negative charge; so, typically, there are an equal number of protons and electrons in an atom. If an atom has an unequal number of protons and electrons, the atom has a charge and is called an ion.

Any particular element always has the same number of protons; for example, carbon always has six protons and oxygen always has eight protons. However, the number of neutrons may vary; although carbon usually has six neutrons, some carbon atoms have seven neutrons. Atoms having the identical number of protons but different numbers of neutrons are isotopes of one another. Radioactive substances have an unstable balance of neutrons and protons and emit particles and energy in changing toward more stable structures. Radioactive decay includes the emissions of alpha particles (particles containing two protons and two neutrons), beta particles (particles with a mass identical to an electron but which can be negatively or positively charged), and gamma rays (a form of highly penetrating electromagnetic radiation similar to X-rays).

Alpha and beta particles and gamma rays contain sufficient energy to ionize molecules in cells. Alpha particles have little ability to penetrate through barriers (a sheet of paper is sufficient!), but they have substantial energy to dislodge electrons from molecules and leave behind ions and free radicals (atoms that are reactive because of unpaired electrons). Because alpha particles cannot penetrate through the skin, they are a health hazard only after inhalation or ingestion. Beta particles are smaller and carry less energy, but they have better penetrating power than alpha particles. Beta particles penetrate skin sufficiently to cause burns following high exposure, although they too need to be ingested or inhaled to damage internal organs. Gamma rays can penetrate through skin to internal organs, but they contain less energy than alpha and beta particles. The health effects from ionizing radiation can include cell death and damage to the reproductive process of cells (including mutations that result in cells becoming cancerous), or they may not be observable. Keep in mind that exposure to ionizing radiation comes from many natural sources, and water typically is an extremely minor contributor to most people's total radiation dose.

OTHER MEASURES

A variety of other properties are used to characterize water and determine its most suitable uses. Mineral content is an important attribute with regard to the suitability of a water supply for agricultural use, as well as for potability. One common measure of minerals is water hardness, the sum of the dissolved calcium and magnesium. Another common measure is alkalinity, which indicates the stability of water to changes resulting from addition of acids (e.g., from acid rain).

The gross level of materials in water also can be determined in terms of solid content. Total dissolved solids are materials that cannot be easily filtered out of water. Conversely, suspended solids are contaminants that can readily be removed through filtration. An alternative measure is turbidity, which indicates the amount of solids in water that scatter light.

The pH is an important measure of water quality used in a number of applications. Either a very low pH (indicating acidic conditions) or a very high pH (indicating basic conditions) is unfavorable to most life. However, a neutral condition of pH 7 (neither acid nor base) is not synonymous with normal or good quality either. For example, noncontaminated rainwater is slightly acidic, with a pH around 5.6. Treated domestic water is commonly released from the treatment plant with a pH greater than 8.

The temperature of water also is an extremely significant factor affecting aquatic life. Many species have a fairly narrow range of tolerance to water temperatures, and changes to natural water temperature regimens can significantly influence the dynamics of an aquatic ecosystem's population. Moreover, the rate of change of water temperature can be more significant to aquatic life than just the magnitude of change. For example, the effluent from an electrical power plant may warm water, with fish and other organisms attracted to the warm areas (which may even increase rates of primary productivity and drive the local food chain). Fish migrate to the outfall slowly and become acclimated to the increased temperatures. However, when the thermal discharge is stopped (during a plant outage), the water temperatures swiftly drop. Fish and other organisms have little chance to acclimate, and large kills may result.

SOME SIGNIFICANT WATER-QUALITY PROBLEMS

Degradation of water quality can adversely affect both human health and ecosystems. Regulatory attention has been directed to both areas, although much more focus is given to pollutants that have a direct link with risks to human health.

TRACE LEVELS OF TOXIC ORGANICS

The threat of pathogens in drinking water supplies is an important issue in the United States; however, most media attention is given to chemical contamination. In particular, the relationship between chemicals used to destroy pathogens and the risk associated with the residual chemicals and their by-products remains of some concern.

Chlorine has been widely used since before the turn of the century to destroy pathogens in drinking water and is responsible for a large reduction in morbidity and mortality caused by waterborne disease. Chlorine continues to be the disinfectant of choice for domestic supplies, although by-products of disinfection may have harmful effects. These disinfection by-products, or DBPs, result from the reaction between dissolved organic compounds and chlorine or other disinfectants. Trihalomethanes (THMs) are the most well known of the DBPs. In 1979, the EPA promulgated rules restricting THM concentrations in drinking water. Standards were based on the carcinogenicity of chloroform, the THM found in most waters. As research proceeded on THMs, information also was obtained on other DBPs that form when water is chlorinated or alternative disinfectants are used. In December of 1998, five haloacetic acids (HAA5) were also regulated as part of the Stage 1 Disinfectants and Disinfection Byproducts Rule (DBPR). In December of

2005, the Stage 2 DBPR was promulgated to further strengthen requirements limiting DBPs in drinking water. These requirements focus on system
monitoring to target those parts of a drinking water distribution system most
vulnerable to high levels of DBPs.

A dilemma has emerged: disinfection remains vital to water treatment as a
method of destroying pathogens but also may result in increased risk of cancer
and other diseases caused by chemical exposure. Clearly, it is not a viable alternative to stop using disinfectants in drinking water supplies and risk massive
outbreaks of cholera, typhoid fever, and other waterborne diseases. Thus,
researchers are actively looking for alternative disinfectants and treatment
techniques that adequately destroy pathogens (for a reasonable cost) without
leaving residual concentrations of chemicals that might damage human health.

Researchers are actively investigating and regulating other organics that
may be toxic at trace levels in water. For example, organic solvents have been
found to contaminate important groundwater aquifers serving hundreds of
thousands of people in Long Island, New York, and in the San Gabriel Valley,
California, among other areas. This type of pollution is generally undetectable
by human senses, and adverse health effects occur long after initial exposure.

Considerable work is focused on the significance of trace levels of pesticides in water, particularly in the Corn, Soy, and Wheat Belt of the Midwest.
For example, the Environmental Working Group and Ohio Citizen Action
reported that in 1997 farmers used about 13 million pounds of herbicides on
corn fields and another 5 million pounds on soy fields.[10] With such large
quantities being applied to farm fields, it is not surprising that measurable
concentrations can be found in surface waters that receive agricultural
runoff. Concern is not limited to the ability of municipal water systems to
meet quality standards, but also it focuses on the adequacy of the standards.

Recent advances in analytical techniques have allowed investigation of
extremely trace levels of pharmaceuticals (including antibiotics) and hormones
in water systems and in drinking water. Pharmaceuticals and hormones may be
released in human wastes and pass untreated through conventional wastewater
treatment systems. This results in waterways containing trace but measurable
amounts of various chemicals. The significance of these chemicals in water is
extremely difficult to determine but may be important. For example, trace levels of hormones have been associated in laboratory tests with feminization of
male trout, decreased rate of testicular growth, and abnormal thyroid, fetal, and
gonad development. Problematic is the effect of these chemicals released in
natural ecosystems on native populations. Also not well understood are effects
(if any) on humans at current exposure levels. A related concern is that the
presence of antibiotics is resulting in the growth of resistant pathogenic bacteria. The U.S. Geological Survey has been monitoring surface water and groundwater throughout the United States for a variety of these chemicals and has
found that they are fairly ubiquitous in the environment. For example, a recent
study detected measurable levels of hormones and pharmaceuticals in over
80 percent of 139 streams monitored throughout the eastern United States.

Similarly, it is difficult to identify the significance of trace levels of organics such as PCBs present in aquatic sediments from drainages of many industrialized areas. In fact, there is substantial controversy over whether it is better to leave contaminated sediments in place or to dredge and remove the sediments (and potentially re-suspend the toxic chemicals). It is clear that contaminated sediments can have a serious impact on bottom-dwelling organisms, as often dramatically indicated by bottom-dwelling fish showing severe morphological impairments associated with exposure to toxic agents.

LEAD AND COPPER

Lead has been the focus of much attention as a contaminant of water. In fact, as the major sources of airborne lead are being controlled [leaded gasoline and lead-based paints (see Chapter 5)], the relative contribution of lead exposure from water may be increasing. Exposure to lead in water sufficient to cause acute effects is extremely rare. However, exposure to relatively low levels of lead for extended periods may result in an increased risk of stroke, kidney disease, cancer, and neurological damage. As chronic effects of lead continue to be evaluated, estimates of the level of lead that poses danger continues to be lowered. Recent work indicates that serious health problems may result from blood lead levels substantially lower than the 10 μg/dL standard for blood lead established by the CDC as the benchmark for intervention.[11]

Lead in a domestic water supply has two primary origins: the source water and the plumbing system. The EPA has assessed the prevalence of lead in raw (untreated) water supplies and found that about 250 surface water systems and 600 groundwater systems had water leaving the treatment plants with lead concentrations greater than 5 mg/L. This means that less than 1 percent of the public water supplies in the United States, serving a population of less than 3 percent of the 226 million people using public systems, have potential lead contamination from these sources. More concern is expressed over lead leaching into water from plumbing systems. Lead solders and fluxes used to connect copper pipes can contain up to 50 percent lead; brass and bronze alloys used in faucets and other fixtures also can contain large amounts of lead. The EPA estimates that there are about 10 million lead service lines in use in the United States, and about 20 percent of all public water systems have at least some lead service connections or lines within their distribution systems.

Copper contamination also results primarily from aggressive water leaching the metal from home plumbing, typically from copper pipes. Its health effects include problems such as stomach and intestinal distress, liver and kidney disease, and anemia. Control strategies for both copper and lead focus on limiting migration from household plumbing to the water. Most drinking water pollutants are regulated quite differently, with monitoring occurring as water leaves the treatment plant. However, concentrations of both lead and copper in drinking water received at the tap may not reflect the levels that leave the treatment plants, so the characteristics of the distribution system must be considered to ensure adequate quality.

In June 2006, the EPA proposed modifying the existing lead and copper rule governing public drinking water. These revisions include changes to the community-monitoring requirements, increased public notification of changes to treatment that can result in water with enhanced ability to corrode pipes and fixtures and release lead and copper, increased public notification of lead-monitoring results, an increased number of pipelines that must be monitored as potential sources of lead contamination, and improved delivery of information to the public when lead or copper levels exceed standards.

RADON AND OTHER RADIONUCLIDES

Interest in possible contamination by radiation has increased considerably over the past several years. Driving this interest are the disaster at Chernobyl, media attention on the development of low-level radioactive waste disposal sites, and renewed efforts to develop nuclear power plants. An important additional factor is a new awareness of radon, an invisible, odorless radioactive gas that is almost ubiquitous in its distribution. The threat to humans from radon is predominantly from airborne exposure (Table 6-1). In fact, water containing elevated radon concentrations presents a threat largely from the radon gas released when the water is exposed to the atmosphere (e.g., showering) rather than from direct consumption.

Natural surface water supplies generally carry little threat of human radiation contamination because radon volatilizes into the atmosphere. However, groundwater can have high concentrations of radon because of sustained association with uranium and radium in naturally occurring radon-emitting rock, with little chance for removal through volatilization.

TABLE 6-1	National Research Council and U.S. Environmental Protection Agency (EPA) Estimates of U.S. Cancer Deaths per Year Resulting from Radon Exposure	
Exposure Pathway	*National Research Council*	*EPA Estimate*
Inhalation of radon progeny in indoor air	18,200	13,600
Inhalation of radon progeny in outdoor air	720	520
Inhalation of radon progeny from release of radon from drinking water	160	86
Ingestion of radon in drinking water	23	100

Source: Committee on Risk Assessment to Exposure to Radon in Drinking Water, Board on Radiation Effects Research, Commission on Life Sciences, National Research Council, *Risk Assessment of Radon in Drinking Water, 1999. http://books.nap.edu/books/0309062926/html/R1.html#pagetop*

Even though relatively little information links adverse health effects to radon in water, radon limitation has become the focus of major new activities designed to protect the quality of drinking water.

COASTAL CONTAMINATION

Recognition has been growing that recreational use of the nation's beaches and adjacent recreational waters may present unreasonable risks to human health. Although the extent of this problem is not known, research has shown that it could be significant. For example, a recent study in Southern California concluded that people swimming near drains discharging stormwater were about 50 percent more likely to become ill than people swimming away from these drains. To respond to this threat, the Beaches Environmental Assessment and Coastal Health (BEACH) Act of 2000 was passed. Key elements of this act include

- a mechanism for the EPA to award grants for the development and implementation of programs to notify the public of the potential exposure to disease-causing microorganisms in coastal recreation waters;
- a program for the EPA to award grants to support microbiological testing and monitoring of coastal recreation waters;
- Amendment of Section 303 of the CWA to require by April 10, 2004, that coastal and Great Lakes states adopt the EPA's published indicators, or equivalent protection indicators, for pathogens in recreational waters adjacent to beaches with criteria at least as protective as those published by the EPA.

States failing to meet federal standards will have federal standards imposed, following promulgation of the Bacteria Rule for Coastal and Great Lakes Recreation Waters in November 2004. Federal standards can be met in one of three ways:

- adoption of the EPA-recommended criteria;
- modification of the EPA-recommended criteria to reflect site-specific conditions; or
- adoption of criteria that is "as protective as" the EPA's recommended criteria based on scientifically defensible methods

However, many states have not met these requirements nor had federal standards imposed. Changing existing monitoring programs to meet the new federal standard can be problematic to many states. The EPA requires the use of *E. coli* and *Enterococci* to monitor recreational water quality, although many states and local governments have been using, and may continue to prefer to use, fecal coliform as the measure of pathogen contamination. Clearly, it is impossible to monitor for all possible sources of pathogenic contamination, and indicators of contamination must be used as surrogate measures. The EPA has concluded that *E. coli* and *Enterococci* are the best available indicators considering both technical and economic factors, but some investigators disagree with this conclusion. Furthermore, changing monitoring requirements will result in additional expense.

Sources of beach contamination are quite diverse. Stormwater runoff, combined sewer and sanitary sewer overflows (both releasing untreated wastewater because of high levels of precipitation causing flow to exceed treatment plant capacity), malfunctioning sewage treatment plants, boating wastes, and malfunctioning septic systems are all important sources of beach water pollution. Commonly, the extent and sources of contamination to beaches are not well known, and one of the challenges to controlling pollutant discharge into recreational waters remains the identification of pollutant sources.

CONCENTRATED ANIMAL FEEDLOTS

A topic of considerable recent public interest is the environmental effect of concentrated animal-feeding operations (CAFOs) on water quality. These operations concentrate animals together, thus providing a potential for concentrating wastes and other problems associated with animal husbandry. Water-quality concerns focus on runoff from manure adversely affecting surface and groundwater. A host of other concerns including possible detrimental effects on neighboring property value, increased numbers of flies and other nuisance or disease-related insects, damage to local roads from increased truck traffic, increased dust and other air pollution, and objectionable smells all combine to make these operations local unwanted land uses (LULUs). Potential water-quality problems include manure containing nutrients supporting cultural eutrophication of neighboring surface waters, elevated nitrogen concentrations in the manure potentially causing a public health hazard to local consumers, and pathogens from the manure contaminating local water supplies. In some instances, an additional water-quality issue is that these facilities typically consume large amounts of water, which may deplete local supplies. Discussion of the regulatory response to this growing concern is provided below with reference to pollutant discharger controls.

PROTECTING WATER THROUGH GOVERNMENT ACTIONS

Many federal laws relate to water quality; however, the Federal Water Pollution Control Act (FWPCA) and the Safe Drinking Water Act (SDWA) provide most of the structure for managing water quality. They deal primarily with, respectively, ensuring the quality of surface waters and ensuring the quality of domestic supplies. To properly focus on water-quality issues, it is also important to understand how rights to use water are obtained in the United States.

WATER RIGHTS

Water rights are traditionally a state issue, with only limited involvement on the federal level. Specific policies governing rights to water reflect the tradition brought into the state by its founders and the nature of the state's water resources. Federal activity largely involves situations in which water flows through or is located across more than one state or country.

Two fundamental doctrines govern the right to use surface water. In eastern and some western states, the right to use water depends on a physical link between the water source and the user, meaning that the owner of property on the bank of a stream, river, or lake can make reasonable use of that water. This is called a riparian right. In many western states, where water is scarce, rights can be claimed for beneficial uses both adjacent to and away from water sources. Rights are prioritized with respect to time; if supply is limited, the first to acquire the right can have all the supply. Only after an earlier right has been exhausted can later rights be met. This is called an appropriative right. Groundwater traditionally has been governed differently, with the overlying landowner having rights to pump. However, this right is starting to be reconsidered because pumping can affect both neighboring users of groundwater and surface water supplies.

Riparian Rights

Riparian rights are derived from the English tradition, which in turn come from Roman law. Each owner of riparian land is entitled to receive water undiminished in quality or quantity by upstream users. This entitlement puts an obligation on each riparian landowner not to degrade the water source.

Riparian landowners in all states (including those with appropriative water laws) generally have rights to use their adjoining surface waters for such nonconsumptive uses as fishing and recreation. Within states using a riparian system to control consumptive uses, water diversion by a riparian landowner historically was restricted to domestic use. Upstream landowners could not divert water to irrigate fields, to use in mining or industry, or for any other use in which the quality or quantity of the downstream supply would be reduced.

This limitation to domestic supply prevents water-based development. To allow growth, this historic restriction has been replaced in most states by one that limits diversions to those needed for reasonable use. Under this doctrine, a riparian landowner may divert water if the use does not interfere with the legitimate use of the water by other holders of riparian rights. States individually determine reasonable use, based on such factors as the following:[12]

- Purpose of the use
- Suitability of the use to the watercourse
- Economic value of the use
- Social value of the use
- Harm associated with the use

- Practicality of avoiding the harm
- Practicality of adjusting the quantity of water use
- Protection of existing values of the water and associated land
- Equity between the water user and any injured parties.

Specific preferred uses depend on state policy, but use has generally been granted for agriculture, mining, and (historically) milling. During times of limited supply, allocation of water depends on the reasonableness of competing uses.

In states with riparian rights systems, eminent domain may be used to acquire water rights by nonriparian water companies or municipalities, who can then provide a domestic water supply. Alternatively, if a nonriparian landowner uses a water supply for a sustained and continuous period (15 years in many states), a prescriptive right may be established that allows for the continued use of that supply. Furthermore, many states with riparian rights systems also have administrative permit systems for water diversion and allocation. These administrative permits allow for diversion of water for beneficial uses to nonriparian landowners and help ensure that riparian landowners' use of water is reasonable.

Riparian rights reflect historic development patterns in wet climates, where water was usually abundant. In areas where water is scarce, riparian rights are not easily adapted to ensure that water is used to maximal benefit. Moreover, riparian rights disadvantage nonriparian land that could be productively developed if a secure water supply was available. As population continues to grow and water availability becomes more limiting, this disadvantage may become increasingly important as an obstacle to economic development. Many eastern riparian states are moving toward modification of water use policies to more fully consider public interests of using water supplies.

Appropriative Rights

Most of the western United States is drier than the East, and the water supply is much more limited. For development to occur, water must be available and long-term rights secured. The system of appropriative water rights provides mechanism for obtaining water rights as a function of water use. The use of water (such as diverting it from a stream for agriculture or industry) gives the user a right to that water supply. The earliest water users have priority for using the water supply if the supply is limited; subsequent water users have inferior rights.

Water is appropriated, and rights established, through the actual consumptive use of water. Diverting water and returning some portion to the waterway (such as returning power plant cooling water) only establishes a right to the net amount removed. If water is not used where an appropriative right exists, that right can be lost. Appropriative rights are established because of demonstrated needs; without this need, the legal right for future use is replaced by the rights of current users.

An appropriative right is not dependent on landownership but on diverting and consumptively using water for a beneficial use. Most states with appropriative systems also have statutes that govern how much water can be taken and specify beneficial uses (only Colorado maintains a pure appropriative system in which rights depend exclusively on using water).[13] Typically, agricultural, industrial, and domestic uses are all accepted as rights that may be secured.

Appropriative rights are complicated by the varying availability of water. In a wet year, all rights may be satisfied; in a dry year, many users may have unmet needs. Further complicating this issue is the need to maintain healthy aquatic ecosystems. Is it proper for appropriative users to take all of a stream's available water for human consumption and degrade or destroy the natural ecosystem? In other words, do fish have appropriative rights to the water too?

A key case demonstrating an interest in protecting the quality of waterways by limiting appropriative rights was *National Audubon Society v. Superior Court* (Mono Lake), decided by the California Supreme Court in 1983.[14] In 1940, the City of Los Angeles had appropriated for its domestic supply most of the flow of four streams draining into Mono Lake. The Audubon Society filed suit in superior court to stop diversions because of environmental damages resulting from loss of supply to the lake. Mono Lake, the second largest lake in California, is located at the base of the Sierra Nevada mountain range (east of Yosemite National Park) and receives most of its water supply from Sierra snowmelt. Because of the hot, arid climate causing rapid evaporation (leaving salts behind to concentrate), the lake is saline. Fish do not live in the lake, but many waterfowl thrive (most feeding on the abundant population of brine shrimp). By diverting flow away from the lake, the surface elevation has dropped. In addition to reducing the area of the lake, previously submerged bridges have transformed islands into peninsulas. Where island rookeries were once protected, coyotes and other predators now have access to nesting sites and young birds. Continued or increased diversion of feeder streams clearly would cause deterioration of the lake ecosystem, including a large reduction in the waterfowl population.

At issue in the case was whether appropriative rights (even those given some time ago) must consider the public trust doctrine (requiring government protection of important natural resources). The court ruled that the public trust doctrine and appropriative rights are "parts of an integrated system of water law," so both must be considered in determining appropriate use of water. This decision allows legal challenges, based on natural resource values, to state administrative decisions for water appropriation. It forces administrative decisions to include considerations of long-term resource impairment, as well as economic development. Implications to the City of Los Angeles have been that it has been forced to pump less water from this region to stabilize water levels in Mono Lake, and to re-water part of the dry

Owens Lake basin (dry because of past water diversions to Los Angeles) to prevent dust storms.

A few other states have integrated natural resource values more directly into their systems for appropriating water. For example, Montana has a statutory program that allows water to be appropriated for future uses. These future uses can include maintaining minimal flows needed to protect in-stream water quality. State agencies can establish an appropriative right for water that never is used in the traditional sense of being removed from the stream channel.

Growing water scarcity is resulting in conservation often being considered as the most viable alternative to developing additional supplies. However, strict application of the appropriative right doctrine may serve as a disincentive to conservation—lack of water use might be interpreted as release of an appropriative right. This situation is being addressed through the legislature in California. State law now specifies that "When any person entitled to the use of water under an appropriative right fails to use all or any part of the water because of water conservation efforts, any cessation or reduction in the use of such appropriated water shall be deemed equivalent to a reasonable beneficial use of water to the extent of the reduction in use."[15] Although the general intent of this legislation is to promote conservation, implementation has been difficult. Controversy remains over the definition of "conserved water" and allowable water transfers.

Two contrasting examples illustrate the remaining controversy. In 1988, the Imperial Irrigation District (IID), serving an arid agricultural region in Southern California, and the Metropolitan Water District of Southern California (MWD; serving much of the domestic need of the region) came to a water conservation and transfer agreement. The IID was under instruction from the State Water Resources Control Board (SWRCB) to cease its practice of using unlined canals to transport water for irrigation because of the tremendous loss of water through infiltration into the ground. The MWD agreed to line these canals and, in return, have rights to the conserved water. It is important to note that the MWD's rights to this conserved water occurred over rights held by the "next in line" water holder, the Coachella Irrigation District. In contrast, the El Dorado Irrigation District (EID) in Northern California also tried to transfer savings from recovery of excessive convenience losses into a greater water right. The EID was under instruction from the SWRCB to improve on the performance of Crawford Ditch, in which seepage losses exceeded 80 percent. The SWRCB ruled that this loss was so excessive as to result in forfeiture of the appropriative water. Distinguishing between these two situations was that the EID seepage provided flow to downstream users, so that reducing water losses through Crawford Ditch and consuming any of the saved water would result in decreased downstream supply. Seepage lost in the IID system was not recoverable.

Groundwater Use

Historically, groundwater use was based on land ownership. Those owning land had unlimited right to pump water from beneath their land, much as they had unlimited right to the air overlying their land. This doctrine is known as "English Rule." This approach was useful when water withdrawal was relatively low such that a landowner tapping an underlying aquifer did not substantially affect other landowners' wells, or draw down streams and other surface waters that were connected hydraulically to groundwater. However, as knowledge grew of the interrelationship between withdrawing groundwater from an individual well and the local and regional water supply (including both surface water and groundwater), restrictions began to be placed on groundwater use. These restrictions follow a reasonable use, or "American Rule" doctrine. Today, groundwater is regulated in most states as a public good with little remaining of English Rule other than practice in a few states with little problem of water scarcity (e.g., Connecticut, Georgia, and Mississippi). This regulation is done largely at the state and local levels. Although the federal government has extensive control over surface water resources, there is not a parallel for groundwater. Groundwater not affecting navigable waters of the nation generally is not seen as under federal constitutional jurisdiction. The federal government may have some ability to regulate groundwater linked hydraulically to surface water, but this ability has not been thoroughly exercised or tested in court. The federal government has largely deferred groundwater issues to state law.

Most states control groundwater as a public good subject to state regulation. For example, in Oregon, anyone intending to use groundwater must obtain a water right permit from the state Water Resources Department. Exceptions to this permit rule are for small uses such as individual homes pumping no more than 15,000 gallons per day and for watering lawns and noncommercial gardens no larger than one-half acre. A balance is sought between allowing individuals to extract water for their personal use and larger commercial uses that could affect water availability to others. Colorado uses a somewhat different approach to groundwater control, requiring a permit (from the State Engineer's Office) to drill all wells (other than test wells). The permit is granted if the new well will not injure water supply of existing users. Thus, the Colorado system more fully depends on appropriative water rights, with earlier users of groundwater having priority over those later seeking to withdraw from underground supplies. Similarly, California's Water Code provides that "all water within the State is property of the People of the State, but the right to the use of water may be acquired by the right of appropriation."[16] Very much a current regulatory issue in many states is the definition of reasonable use, particularly when groundwater will be transported off of overlying land. For example, *Michigan Citizens for Water Conservation (MCWC) v. Nestlé Waters North America* raises the question of the right of a private company to harvest groundwater, bottle it, and sell it out of the watershed. A Michigan trial court ruled that taking groundwater outside the watershed cannot reduce the flow of or have negative impacts on the connected hydrologically connected riparian water. This ruling was overturned by the court of appeals, on the basis of Michigan precedent having established a reasonable-use balancing test between competing water users. This case is now (2006) proceeding to the Michigan Supreme Court, and its decision may set important president between competing groundwater and riparian uses.[17]

It is important to note that the current system for managing groundwater in the United States has resulted in overdrafting in many areas (withdrawing groundwater at a faster rate than it is replenished). As groundwater is depleted, hydraulically connected surface water may lose its supply. For example, groundwater pumping has resulted in degradation or drying of approximately 90 percent of Arizona's once perennial desert streams, rivers, and riparian habitats. Lowering of groundwater aquifers also has occurred and had detrimental affects in wet areas, such as the periodic drying of the Ipswich River north of Boston because of groundwater pumping by suburban homes. There are many more examples, but the important conclusion from available data is that throughout the United States groundwater is being mined rather than used in a sustainable way.

PROTECTING SURFACE WATER QUALITY

Until relatively recently, protecting water quality was not a major concern of the federal government. Historically, federal involvement was largely defined by three acts. The Rivers and Harbors Act of 1899 provided limited protection of water quality through restrictions on discharge that would present obstacles to navigation. The Public Health Service Act of 1912 provided for federal investigation of water pollution affecting public health. The Oil Pollution Act of 1924 prohibited discharge of oil into coastal waters. These acts were not broadly interpreted or widely enforced, so they had little impact on water quality.

With a growing population and increasing rate of waterborne disease, the need for a more active federal role became evident. During the 1930s and 1940s, federal money was used to help states and cities construct wastewater treatment plants. In 1948, the Federal Water Pollution Control Act (FWPCA) was passed, formalizing government obligations for the control of water pollution. State governments maintained primary responsibility, with the federal role focusing on providing financial assistance and research support through the U.S. Public Health Service.

The 1956 and 1965 amendments to this act strengthened the role of the federal government but left primary responsibility with the states. Increasing funding granted by the federal government for construction of local wastewater treatment plants was important. The 1965 amendments [also known as the Water Quality Act (WQA)] moved federal responsibility from the Public Health Service to the newly created Federal Water

Pollution Control Administration. The 1965 amendments also represented a compromise in the face of clearly deteriorating water quality throughout the nation. Industry opposed federal standard setting as an obstacle to business, and states opposed an increased federal presence in an area traditionally left to them. Yet, something had to be done. These amendments permitted the federal government to establish water-quality standards if states refused to establish their own. However, an effective and enforced set of standards was not developed, and water quality continued to diminish.

During the late 1960s, a series of events turned public attention toward the deteriorating environment and led to a public demand for action. Two of the most dramatic incidents occurred almost 2,500 miles apart: one in Ohio and the other in California. In June 1969, the Cuyahoga River near Cleveland caught fire! Clearly, this river was little more than an industrial sewer, with oily waste concentrating sufficiently to turn a major waterway into a fire hazard. Soon thereafter, more than 250 million gallons of crude oil leaked from an oil-drilling operation offshore of Santa Barbara, California. The media gave substantial coverage to both events, and pictures of dead, oil-coated waterfowl, sea otters, and other wildlife crowded the front pages of newspapers. The public was ready to support major changes.

In response, Congress passed the Federal Water Pollution Control Act (FWPCA) of 1972 over the veto of President Nixon. It mandated major changes in the way water quality would be controlled in the United States and provided the basis for water-quality programs used today. Three subsequent acts made substantial amendments to the FWPCA: the Clean Water Act of 1977 (CWA), the Water Quality Act of 1987 (WQA), and the Oil Pollution Act of 1990. These amendments followed the basic principles established in the 1972 act and have resulted in a complex and comprehensive system of water pollution control.

A strong federal role is now integral to our system of water-quality protection. Ambitious water-quality objectives are clearly established for the nation: "The objective of this Act is to restore and maintain the chemical, physical and biological integrity of the Nation's waters." Note that water-quality goals include more than maintaining a safe drinking water supply. Specific reference is made to providing for "the protection and propagation of fish, shellfish and wildlife, and . . . recreation in and on the water." Thus, all waters of the nation are required to be fit for fishing and swimming.

To protect water quality, restrictions could have been set on pollutant dischargers (assuming that if sufficient restrictions are applied, the water body will be protected) or ambient quality standards could have been established (with restrictions imposed to control pollutant sources or other conditions if the ambient standards are not met). The law adopted both approaches, although the majority of the regulatory activity has focused on controlling individual dischargers.

Pollutant Discharger Controls

All discrete point sources of discharge into surface water, such as factories, pulp and paper mills, food-processing plants, and municipal wastewater treatment plants, are required to obtain a discharge permit. In addition, permits are required of municipal and industrial stormwater systems and concentrated animal feeding operations (CAFOs). Over 400,000 sources are now regulated by these permits nationwide.[18] These permits are administered through the National Pollution Discharge Elimination System (NPDES) process, and dischargers must follow specifications of their NPDES permits. Effluent limitations are dependent on the type of pollutant, type of discharger, and characteristics of the local watershed. In setting these limitations, three broad categories of pollutants are identified: conventional, nonconventional, and toxic. Requirements also vary depending on whether the discharge is a new or existing source. Furthermore, municipal wastewater treatment plants must meet standards somewhat different from those required for other dischargers.

The least stringent level of control is imposed on existing dischargers of conventional pollutants, requiring only that best conventional pollutant control technology (BCT) standards are met. Only five conventional pollutants are specified; biochemical oxygen demand (BOD), total suspended solids, pH, and fecal coliform were established in the 1977 amendments, and the EPA subsequently added oil and grease.

In setting BCT standards, the EPA is required to consider the relationship between the costs of pollution control and the derived benefits; these costs must then be compared with the cost of compliance at wastewater treatment plants. In addition, the EPA is required to consider "the age of equipment and facilities involved, the process employed, the engineering aspects of the application of various types of control techniques, process changes, nonwater-quality environmental impact (including energy requirements), and such other factors as the Administrator [of the EPA] deems appropriate."[19]

Toxic and nonconventional pollutants must be controlled by using the best available technology economically achievable (BAT), a more rigorous standard than BCT. Nonconventional pollutants are anything not included in these other two categories that still may pose a threat to water quality (such as thermal pollution). To help identify toxic pollutants, a list of 65 toxic chemicals, known as priority pollutants, was developed by the EPA.[20] This list includes individual chemicals and chemical groups. However, effluent standards are not restricted to these 65 chemicals or chemical groups. In establishing effluent limitations, the EPA can establish specific chemical standards in response to the particular types of chemicals used by that industry. For example, the new source performance standards for steam electric power-generating facilities identify a priority pollutant list of 126 specific chemicals (not chemical groups) for which none should be detectable (following specified techniques) in cooling tower blowdown effluent.[21]

BCT standards "shall include consideration of the reasonableness of the relationship between the costs of attaining a reduction in effluents and the effluent reduction benefits derived," whereas BAT standards require only that standard determination "shall take into account the cost of achieving such effluent reduction." This reduced requirement for cost assessment has resulted in the EPA establishing BAT standards primarily based on health criteria. The 1977 amendments to the Act specify that effluent standards for toxic pollutants consider

> the toxicity of the pollutant, its persistence, degradability, the usual or potential presence of the affected organisms in any waters, the importance of the affected organisms and the nature and extent of the effect of the toxic pollutant on such organisms, and the extent to which effective control is being or may be achieved under other regulatory authority.[22]

The FWPCA and its subsequent amendments do not specifically identify a system for setting standards. The EPA established standards for existing industry based on industrial classifications, assuming that plants performing similar functions should have similar effluent limitations. However, this approach was challenged. E. I. Du Pont de Nemours and Company claimed that the EPA was required to establish effluent standards uniquely for each plant, being responsive to plant-specific conditions. The U.S. Supreme Court decided that it would be impractical to do so (estimating that there were more than 42,000 dischargers) and that the legislative intent of the Act would best be upheld by allowing for control based on industry class. However, standard setting must include sufficient flexibility to allow for some variation for individual plants.[23]

New sources are subject to more rigorous effluent limits than existing sources, based on the belief that it is cheaper to minimize effluent pollutants if environmental controls are considered during plant design than it is to retrofit existing facilities. New sources include major modifications to existing facilities, as well as new construction. Effluent limits for new sources are based on consideration of an entire process rather than the BAT and BCT approach, which requires pollution controls to be imposed following waste generation (commonly known as end-of-pipe treatment). As specified in the FWPCA, standards must consider

> control of the discharge of pollutants which reflects the greatest degree of effluent reduction which the Administrator determines to be achievable through application of the best available demonstrated control technology, *processes, operating methods, or other alternative* including, where practicable, a standard permitting no discharge of pollutants [emphasis added].

Congress listed 27 pollution sources in the FWPCA for which the EPA was required to develop performance standards. The EPA was also given the authority to add to this list; 34 sources subsequently are identified in the NPDES Primary Industry Categories list.[24] The EPA is required to periodically review new source requirements and make amendments reflecting changes in technology and economic conditions.

The system for controlling effluent from public wastewater treatment plants [called publicly owned treatment works (POTWs)] differs slightly from that of other dischargers. POTWs must meet effluent standards characterized by waste receiving "secondary treatment." EPA initially defined secondary treatment to effectively limit compliance to communities using activated sludge technology meeting rigorous performance standards. This requirement was subsequently viewed as excessive in many situations, particularly where small POTWs were discharging into waters capable of rapidly assimilating the wastewater. Moreover, it was viewed as economically impractical and ecologically unnecessary for many small communities. Therefore, these requirements were modified.

A system also is in place to control industrial discharges of pollutants into municipal sewage. Industry must pretreat their wastewater to meet quality standards. These standards are designed to prevent the introduction of pollutants into sewers that will interfere with the operations of a POTW, including the use or disposal of its sludge, or that will pass through the treatment works. These standards also are intended to improve opportunities for recycling and reclaiming municipal and industrial wastewater sludges. Discharges are prohibited that do the following:[25]

- Create a fire or explosion hazard in the sewers or treatment works
- Are corrosive (with a pH <5.0)
- Obstruct flow because of solids or viscous materials
- Upset the treatment processes
- Increase the temperature of wastewater entering the treatment plant to more than 104 F
- Add mineral, nonbiodegradable cutting, or petroleum oils that pass through or interfere with the treatment process
- Result in the presence of toxic gas vapors or fumes that may cause acute worker health and safety problems
- Are trucked or hauled to discharge points not designated by the POTW

These regulations also are intended to ensure that the hazardous waste management system is not circumvented through the use of municipal sewers.

Most of the regulatory burden for the pretreatment program is on local POTWs. More than 1,500 POTWs have sufficient industry in their wastesheds to be required to have a pretreatment program. Each POTW is required to identify all industrial sources and the volume and characteristics of industrial discharge in its wasteshed. With the use of this information, limits on problem dischargers are imposed to protect the POTW; this program requires the POTWs to expend considerable resources (in industrialized communities) to ensure that pretreatment requirements are met. Currently, about 30,000 significant industrial users of municipal sewers are being regulated under a pretreatment program.[26]

In contrast to the pretreatment program, most aspects of the water-quality regulatory system are largely controlled at the state and federal levels. The NPDES system is administered through the EPA; however, similar to many environmental statutes, most states have assumed active management responsibilities (only Alaska, Idaho, Massachusetts, New Hampshire, and New Mexico do not have an approved NPDES regulatory program) with the EPA maintaining an oversight role. National effluent and pretreatment standards have been promulgated for 57 industry types (Table 6-2). However,

TABLE 6-2 Industry Types for Which Effluent Guidelines and Standards Have Been Promulgated

Aluminum forming	Metal finishing
Asbestos manufacturing	Metal molding and casting
Battery manufacturing	Metal products and machinery
Carbon black manufacturing	Mineral mining and processing
Canned and preserved fruits and vegetables processing	Nonferrous metals forming
Canned and preserved seafood processing	Nonferrous metals manufacturing
Cement manufacturing	Oil and gas extraction
Centralized waste treatment	Ore mining and dressing
Coal mining	Organic chemicals, plastics, and synthetic fibers
Coil coating	Paint formulating
Concentrated animal-feeding operations	Paving and roofing
Copper forming	Pesticide chemicals
Dairy products	Petroleum refining
Electrical and electronic components	Pharmaceutical manufacturing
Electroplating	Phosphate manufacturing
Explosives manufacturing	Photographic
Ferroalloy manufacturing	Plastics molding and forming
Fertilizer manufacturing	Porcelain enameling
Fruits and vegetables processing	Pulp, paper, and paperboard manufacturing
Glass manufacturing	Rubber processing
Grain mill manufacturing	Sugar processing
Gum and wood chemicals manufacturing	Soaps and detergents manufacturing
Hospital	Steam electric manufacturing
Ink formulating	Textile mills
Inorganic chemicals	Timber products manufacturing
Iron and steel manufacturing	Transportation equipment cleaning
Landfills	Waste combustors
Leather tannin and finishing	
Meat products	

Source: U.S. Environmental Protection Agency, Subchapter N, Effluent Guidelines and Standards. 2003. *http://www.epa.gov/docs/epacfr40/chapt-I.info/subch-N.htm*

facilities not associated with a specific category must meet general discharge requirements intended to protect water quality.

The rule for controlling effluents from CAFOs is somewhat different from other NPDES industry-specific rules, with requirements on feeding operations extending beyond control of effluents discharged in discrete pipes. This rule was developed late in the NPDES process, being signed on December 22, 2002, following a long period of controversy and development. The rule reflects a cooperative approach involving the EPA and the U.S. Department of Agriculture (USDA). Reflecting their work to develop a unified national strategy to minimize the water quality and public health impacts of feeding operations, they published a draft Unified National Strategy for Animal Feeding Operations on September 21, 1998. The final rule purports to reflect a balance between support of the agriculture industry and the risk of animal-feeding operations damaging water resources (primarily through pollution with animal manure). A separation of regulatory responsibility is made on the basis of the operation size (Table 6-3). All large CAFOs are required to have an NPDES permit and to develop and implement a nutrient management plan. Medium feeding operations are required to be permitted as CAFOs if they have a manmade ditch or pipe that carries manure or wastewater to surface water or if the animals come directly into contact with surface water running through their confined areas. Small operations are generally unregulated by the NPDES process. However, both medium and small operations can be regulated as CAFOs should the permitting authority identify them as significant contributors of pollution.

The WQA included requirements for implementing a regulatory program to address stormwater discharge from industrial and municipal stormwater sources. The program was divided into two implementation phases to deal first with those dischargers who presented the most severe threat to water quality and to allow flexibility in developing appropriate limitations on other dischargers based on water-quality impact. The phase I program was promulgated in 1990. Under phase I, NPDES permits are required for large (population greater than 250,000) and medium (population 100,000 to 250,000) municipal areas. Each regional office of the EPA has considerable latitude regarding appropriate permit requirements for individual municipalities.

Phase II of the stormwater control program was published in 1999. The phase II program covers all small municipal separate storm sewer systems (MS4s) located in urban areas. Exceptions can be made to exclude urban MS4s or to include nonurban MS4s by the NPDES-permitting authority. Operators must design control programs that reduce the discharge of pollutants to the maximum extent practicable (MEP), protect water quality, and satisfy the appropriate water-quality requirements of the CWA. Six elements must be included in the MS4 programs: public education and outreach, public participation/involvement, illicit discharge detection and elimination, construction site runoff control, postconstruction runoff control, and pollution

TABLE 6-3 Regulatory Definitions of Concentrated Animal-Feeding Operations (CAFOs)

Animal Sector	Large CAFOs	Medium CAFOs[a]	Small CAFOs[b]
	Size Thresholds (number of animals)		
Cattle or cow/calf pairs	1,000 or more	300–999	<300
Mature dairy cattle	700 or more	200–699	<200
Veal calves	1,000 or more	300–999	<300
Swine (weighing over 55 pounds)	2,500 or more	750–2,499	<750
Swine (weighing <55 pounds)	10,000 or more	3,000–9,999	<3,000
Horses	500 or more	150–499	<150
Sheep or lambs	10,000 or more	3,000–9,999	<3,000
Turkeys	55,000 or more	16,500–54,999	<16,500
Laying hens or broilers (liquid manure-handling systems)	30,000 or more	9,000–29,999	<9,000
Chickens other than laying hens (other than liquid manure-handling systems)	125,000 or more	37,500–124,999	<37,500
Laying hens (other than liquid manure-handling systems)	82,000 or more	25,000–81,999	<25,000
Ducks (other than liquid manure-handling systems)	30,000 or more	10,000–29,999	<10,000
Ducks (liquid manure-handling systems)	5,000 or more	1,500–4,999	<1,500

[a]Must also have a manmade ditch or pipe that carries manure or wastewater to surface water, or the animals come into contact with surface water that passes through the area where they are confined.
[b]Never a CAFO by regulatory definition but may be designated as a CAFO on a case-by-case basis based on being a significant contributor of pollutants.
Source: U.S. EPA National Pollution Discharge System (NPDES). *Animal Feeding Operations.* http://www.epa.gov/npdes/pubs/sector_table.pdf

prevention/good housekeeping. These small systems were required to obtain an NPDES permit by March 10, 2003.

Facilities discharging in municipal stormwater sewers and falling into one of eleven industrial categories also must obtain an NPDES stormwater permit (Table 6-4). The EPA developed a Multi-Sector General Permit (MSGP-2000) to specify permit conditions, which includes development and implementation of a stormwater pollution prevention plan. However, use of this permit expired on October 31, 2005, and has not yet been replaced with a new, approved permit. Facilities with this expired permit are being required to continue to operate under their existing permit conditions, including their stormwater pollution prevention plans. EPA has indicated that it is likely to finalize the new Multi-Sector General Permit (MSGP-2006) by the end of 2006.

TABLE 6-4	Municipal Industrial Categores Requiring NPDES Stormwater Permit
Category 1:	Facilities with effluent limitations
Category 2:	Manufacturing
Category 3:	Mineral, metal, oil and gas
Category 4:	Hazardous waste, treatment, or disposal facilities
Category 5:	Landfills
Category 6:	Recycling facilities
Category 7:	Steam electric plants
Category 8:	Transportation facilities
Category 9:	Treatment works
Category 10:	Construction activity
Category 11:	Light industrial activity

Construction is treated differently than the other industrial categories. An operator of a proposed construction site of one acre or more must submit to the permitting authority a Notice of Intent and prepare a Stormwater Pollution Prevention Plan (SWPPP). This Plan must include[27]

• Diversion of stormwater away from disturbed or exposed areas of the construction site
• Installation of Best Management Practices (BMPs) to control erosion and sediment and manage stormwater
• Regular site inspections and proper maintenance of BMPs, especially after rainstorms
• Revision of the SWPPP if site conditions change if BMPs are not effective
• Minimization of the exposure of bare soils to precipitation
• Maintaining a clear construction site.

The operator also must evaluate potential impacts on endangered and threatened species, and on designated critical habitats that could be affected by the proposed construction.

Ambient Water-Quality Control

In addition to a nationally based system of discharge control based on industry types, a second regulatory strategy is based on ambient water quality. Subject to federal review, states are required to establish water-quality standards for intrastate waters. These water-quality standards must specify the designated use of the water body (e.g., recreation, water supply, aquatic life, or agriculture), criteria to protect the designated use, and an antidegradation policy. Furthermore, states are required to evaluate their water quality biennially. The most current report compiled nationally by the EPA of these state water-quality data documents much of the nation's water being out of compliance with the intent of the CWA. Of the assessed surface water throughout the United States, only 61 percent of the river and stream miles, 54 percent of the lake acres, 49 percent of the estuarine square miles, and 22 percent of the Great Lakes shoreline miles fully support water-quality standards. Furthermore, most surface water is not being evaluated following the biennial regulatory requirement, with only 19 percent of the river and stream miles, 43 percent of the lake acres, 36 percent of the estuary square miles, and 92 percent of the Great Lakes shorelines miles having been evaluated for 2000.[28] The EPA is now revisiting how it compiles data among the states to more reliably characterize national water-quality conditions using consistent techniques among the states.

Much of the failure to meet water-quality standards is caused by nonpoint source or diffuse pollution. In contrast to pipes discharging point sources of wastewater that can be controlled through NPDES permits, nonpoint source pollution originates from many scattered small sources. For example, many automobiles leaking small amounts of oil and grease are a major source of nonpoint pollution to urban watersheds. Even though municipalities are now required to have NPDES permits governing their stormwater, it is obviously impractical to require every automobile to have its own permit as a polluter. Section 303 of the CWA requires that both point and nonpoint sources of pollution be considered in protecting surface waters. Total Maximum Daily Loads (TMDLs) must be established for each surface water reflecting its particular vulnerability and designated use. States are required to implement comprehensive programs so that the total discharge into waters, from both point and nonpoint sources, does not result in a violation of water-quality standards. Even though all states now have an EPA-approved nonpoint source quality assessment and management program, surface waters throughout the nation continue to fail to meet water-quality objectives. In particular, agricultural nonpoint sources are known to contribute the majority of the pollution responsible for degrading assessed rivers and streams, and lakes (agriculture is the leading source of impairment to almost 50 percent of the impaired assessed river miles and to about 40 percent of the impaired assessed lake acres).

Section 319(h) of the CWA provides a mechanism for the EPA to help states implement their nonpoint source management programs through a funding program. The EPA has published four volumes of success stories (in 1994, 1997, 2002, and 2005) highlighting innovative and effective approaches to nonpoint source control.[29] Yet, in reviewing the statistics above, it is clear that substantial water-quality problems remain throughout the nation relating to nonpoint source pollution. Although the 319 program has resulted in approaches demonstrably successful in improving water quality, the handful of projects supported annually by the EPA is of insufficient magnitude to clearly move the nation forward in attaining water-quality standards. Voluntary compliance with nonpoint source pollution control measures appears insufficient to restore and protect, at least in the short-term, the quality of surface waters adversely impacted by nonpoint pollution.

Penalties for Violation

Civil and administrative penalties (some quite severe) may be assessed against violators of FWPCA regulations (and subsequent amendments). "Knowing endangerment," whereby someone places another person in imminent danger, carries a maximum penalty of 15 years imprisonment and a $250,000 fine ($1 million for organizations). "Negligent violations" carry a maximum penalty of $27,500 a day; continued operation of a process not meeting standards could quickly become expensive. The EPA also may seek civil penalties, including injunctive relief and fines. The EPA may issue administrative orders directly but will pay a fine if these orders are not followed.

Citizen suits are authorized for anyone adversely affected by a discharger. Provisions are included that allow payment of the plaintiff's attorney fees, making it more practical for individuals or local groups to seek relief against major companies. Citizen suits provide individuals the opportunity to seek civil remedies against dischargers or to force the EPA to take action against dischargers or otherwise meet its legal responsibilities for protecting water quality. Remedies can include fines and adoption of compliance schedules.

PROTECTING GROUNDWATER QUALITY

Groundwater does not have identical regulatory protection as surface water. Much of the control of groundwater quality (as well as groundwater usage) occurs at the local and state level, although a variety of national laws influence groundwater quality. In particular, the CWA and the SDWA have provisions that specifically address protection of groundwater quality. Section 102 of the CWA provides that "the [EPA] administrator shall . . . prepare or develop comprehensive programs for preventing, reducing, or eliminating the pollution of the navigable waters and ground water and improving the sanitary condition of surface and underground waters." In response, the EPA has developed a program to work with the states in preparing Comprehensive State Ground Water Protection Programs (CSGWPPs). The CSGWPPs are envisioned as mechanisms to facilitate interaction among the states, tribes, and local governments to comprehensively protect groundwater. However, by 1999, the EPA had approved CSGWPPs for only 11 states, perhaps indicating that groundwater quality protection has not been a priority concern in many states.

Under authority of the SDWA and its amendments, several programs have been implemented that may help protect groundwater useful as a drinking water supply. The Underground Injection Control Program (UIC) was established in the SDWA and gave the EPA authority to control intentional injection of fluids underground. This power was granted because underground injection of wastes for disposal and injection of water or other fluids to enhance recovery of oil and gas both can lead to contamination of aquifers used for drinking water supplies. Technical regulations for state programs to control underground injection were published by the EPA in 1980, although it was not until the 1981 amendments to the SDWA that delegation of regulatory control was authorized to the states. It is of interest that specific mention was made in these amendments that this authority was not to interfere with the production of oil and gas unless needed for the protection of drinking water sources. The federal program for controlling injection has continued to evolve. On the basis of the responsibility provided in the Hazardous and Solid Waste Amendments (HSWA) of 1984 (see Chapter 8), the EPA published special regulations for deep wells injecting hazardous waste. These regulations include a requirement for well operators to demonstrate that hazardous waste will not be released from the well's injection zone for at least 10,000 years or will be rendered nonhazardous by natural processes. In 1999, the EPA expanded its UIC program to provide regulations and guidance governing shallow wells discharging nonhazardous wastes. Examples of shallow wells include discharge from large septic tanks, stormwater drywells, agricultural drainage wells, aquaculture waste disposal wells, spent brine return flow wells, and geothermal electric power wells.

The Sole Source Aquifer Protection Program provides additional protection to groundwater through establishing a federal role for aquifers that provide more than 50 percent of the local population with its primary source of drinking water. Established in the SDWA and reauthorized in the 1996 amendments, individuals, communities, and organizations may petition the EPA for protection of their sole source drinking water supply. If a project potentially affecting a sole source aquifer has federal involvement (e.g., through permit authority or financing), the EPA may review and approve the project. For example, in 1998, a gas station and convenience store being constructed in Idaho over a sole source aquifer, and receiving federal financial assistance, adjusted its plans based on the EPA's recommendations. These adjustments included obtaining certification for its gasoline storage tanks, installing grassed retention basins for treating stormwater runoff, and installing an underground oil/water separator tank capable of treating large petroleum spills.

The 1986 amendments to the SDWA established the wellhead protection program as another mechanism to protect groundwater. This program requires each state to identify areas around public water supply wells in which contaminants could infiltrate into groundwater and to manage potential contamination sources to minimize this risk. Building on this program is the Source Water Assessment Program established in the 1996 amendments to the SDWA. States are required to evaluate the sources of their drinking water supplies with respect to potential contamination sources and susceptibility to contamination and to make this information widely available. Source waters include untreated water from streams, rivers, lakes, and underground aquifers that are used to supply private wells and public drinking water. Individuals may obtain information on their municipal system's source water quality from their local consumer confidence report (see the following section on drinking water).

Although substantial federal regulation governs groundwater quality, most of the application of regulatory protections on groundwater supplies occurs at the state and local levels. State regulatory programs may exceed federal requirements and can focus on site-specific conditions. However, groundwater contamination also continues to occur from a number of sources. Often, contamination is from diffuse local sources, making control difficult. For example, local septic systems largely remain under the purview of local governments. Most rural homeowners use septic tanks and leach fields to dispose of their wastewater into the ground, with aquifers ultimately receiving much of this waste. A tradition of rural independence of private land use has resulted in relatively little control of these systems, with failure and contamination of groundwater common. In particular, this source of contamination presents a threat to rural residents who depend on local aquifers for their drinking water supplies, and who have virtually no regulatory protection governing personal use of wells.

PROTECTING DRINKING WATER QUALITY

Historically, drinking water protection has been the responsibility of individual states, not the federal government. The quality of drinking water was governed by local and state boards of health or was not governed at all. The role of the federal government was limited largely to providing research grants, loans for development of treatment works, and technical assistance, and to being involved in interstate and international quality issues.

In 1974, the SDWA was passed in response to a growing concern over contamination of domestic supplies with synthetic organic chemicals and other pollutants. The statute required the development of national domestic water-quality standards. It also provided for the protection of groundwater supplies, the source of domestic water for about 50 percent of the U.S. population.

This act was intended to protect public water supply systems and to ensure that they supply potable water free from biological, chemical, and physical contamination. Nonpublic systems, such as wells supplying individual homes, are not protected. In remote areas, there are usually few sources of contamination, which leaves local supplies safe for consumption. However, as rural areas suburbanize, with population density increasing (often accompanied by increasing dependence on local septic systems with wastes infiltrating into groundwater or discharging to surface waters), the potential for contamination of local sources has increased. Many users of individual water supplies may be unaware of the vulnerability of their system and may never test or otherwise ensure the adequacy of their drinking water.

Public water systems subject to SDWA requirements are defined as systems that have at least 15 service connections or serve 25 or more people for at least 60 days annually. Consequently, homes and businesses served by individual wells (common in rural areas) are not regulated. Public water supply systems are further separated into three categories: community systems, nontransient noncommunity systems, and transient noncommunity systems.

A community public water system supplies water to the same population year-round. A nontransient noncommunity public system supplies water to at least 25 of the same people at least 6 months per year, but not year-round. Good examples are schools, factories, office buildings, and hospitals with their own water systems. Public transient noncommunity water systems provide water in places where people do not remain for long periods, such as campgrounds and service stations. Furthermore, specific standards or compliance schedules are often based on the size of the community system.

The SDWA required the EPA to develop National Interim Primary Drinking Water Regulations to protect human health and "secondary standards" to protect the aesthetic quality of drinking water. Interim standards were required to be proposed by March 1975, with final standards adopted by September 1977. The EPA could not meet this ambitious schedule and by 1986 had adopted interim standards on only 23 contaminants.

Amendments to the SDWA made in 1986 provided a new timetable for establishing water-quality standards and expanded the number of contaminants to be considered. For contaminants that may have an adverse effect on human health, the EPA is responsible for developing (concurrently) Maximum Contaminant Level Goals (MCLGs) and Maximum Contaminant Levels (MCLs). MCLGs are nonenforceable health goals; they are levels at which no adverse health effects should occur. MCLs are enforceable standards set as close to MCLGs as possible, but they take into account the feasibility of achieving standards based on available technology and the costs of treatment. Congress required that the 83 contaminants listed in the Advanced Notice for Proposed Rule Makings of March 4, 1982, and October 5, 1983, have MCLGs and MCLs established. Seven substitutes to this list are allowed, and the EPA has exchanged seven of the original chemicals with seven organic contaminants suspected to be carcinogens. Although not able to complete this work by the legislative deadline, the EPA was successful in establishing needed standards by 1992.

In addition to the contaminants specified by Congress in the SDWA amendments, the EPA was required to develop a list of contaminants needing regulation to protect the quality of drinking water. This "drinking water priority list" (DWPL) contained an additional 77 substances or groups of substances for which MCLs and MCLGs needed to be developed.

Substantial amendments again were made to the SDWA in 1996. The DWPL was replaced by a drinking water contaminant candidate list (CCL), and the EPA is required to prepare this list every 3 years. This list identifies contaminants that the EPA is considering for future regulation and for priority drinking water research, occurrence monitoring, and health advisory guidance. Unlike the DWPL, there is no responsibility to develop MCLs or MCLGs for contaminants on the CCL. Beginning in August 2001, the EPA must select at least five contaminants from the CCL every 5 years to determine whether they should be regulated in drinking water. On March 2, 1998, the EPA published in the Federal Register a list of 60 contaminants

(50 chemicals and 10 microbes) for the CCL. In July 2003, the EPA reported that it had sufficient information on nine of these contaminants (eight chemicals and one microbe) to make the regulatory determination that these contaminants do not impose enough risk to drinking water to regulate through development of drinking water standards. Almost 2 years later, the EPA published a second CCL containing the 51 contaminants for which no determination had yet been made from the original list.

Rather than trying to develop standards independently, the EPA has been involving the regulated community (and other individuals with interest and expertise) directly in the rule-making process. This process of negotiated rule making is viewed as the most practical approach to this complex regulatory issue. For example, regulating DBPs requires consideration not only of the health effects of residual chemicals but also of the effects associated with alternative disinfection practices and the costs to the community of new forms of water treatment. Between 1992 and 1993, the EPA conducted a formal negotiation to develop a consensus-based standard. The standard was proposed on July 29, 1994. A final DBP rule was issued December 16, 1998, becoming effective February 16, 1999. In addition to setting standards for DBPs (in particular, THMs and HAAs), it requires changes to the treatment processes of many systems independent of DBP levels in plant effluent. These treatment requirements are included to reduce DBP formation downstream of the water treatment plant in the community distribution system.

The 1996 SDWA amendments direct the EPA to be actively involved with interested parties. In response, the National Drinking Water Advisory Council, originally chartered under the SDWA of 1974, has actively provided advice and recommendations on drinking water issues. Topics that have been addressed by the Council include consumer confidence reports, benefits of developing regulations for drinking water, CCL and contaminant occurrence, state revolving funds for drinking water, operator certification guidelines, public right-to-know about drinking water issues, regulation of high-risk shallow disposal systems (class V injection wells), small drinking water systems, and source water assessment and protection. At the time of publication, the Council has only one working group. This group is called the Water Security Working Group, and is developing recommendations for both water and wastewater utilities.

In addition to focusing on water treatment, the 1996 amendments address protection of source water quality. Each state's Source Water Assessment and Protection (SWAP) Program must include a definition of a watershed, an inventory of potential contamination sources, and identification of the vulnerability of public water supplies. The SWAP Program is intended both to increase public participation and to provide an additional line of defense in protecting drinking water quality. It is interesting to note that passage of this provision may reflect an inadequacy of the CWA to fully protect waters designated as drinking water supplies.

The national primary drinking water standards currently in effect are available on the Internet (see URL address at the end of the chapter). The review of these standards is required by the EPA at least every 6 years, with the first 6-year period beginning with the passage of the 1996 amendments to the SDWA. In July 2003, EPA announced that it had completed reviewing 69 National Primary Drinking Water Regulations (NPDWRs) that were established before 1997. These 69 NPDWRs include 68 chemical NPDWRs and the Total Coliform Rule (TCR). None of the 68 chemical standards were determined to need revision. However, the TCR is being reconsidered, with proposed rule making and final action currently scheduled for June 2006 and June 2008, respectively. Completion of the next comprehensive review of standards is targeted for 2008 and will include all standards (including the 68 for which no revision was determined) promulgated through 2002.

Three revised drinking standards have become effective in 2006. The level of permitted arsenic was reduced from 50 to 10 mg/L. This revision was first proposed for 2001 but was met with substantial resistance, particularly from smaller utilities who believed that the new standard was impractical from the perspective of the expense of the system modifications needed to meet the proposed standard. The Long Term 2 Enhanced Surface Water Treatment Rule (LT2 rule) requires additional monitoring and protection from pathogens such as Cryptosporidium and other microorganisms that might become a problem as systems work to reduce their concentration of disinfection byproducts (DBPs). The Stage 2 Disinfectants and Disinfection Byproducts Rule is intended to work with the LT2 rule in guarding against pathogen contamination while also limiting adverse affects of DBPs. Changes in monitoring requirements begin for larger systems in 2006, but full implementation is expected to take up to 10 years.

The number of regulated contaminants has grown, with current standards having been promulgated for 87 contaminants. In some cases, rather than meeting specific water-quality standards determined by monitoring, an assumption is made that specific standards will be met if the appropriate treatment technology is used. For example, the EPA's Surface Water Treatment Rule requires surface water systems, or groundwater systems influenced by surface water, to use disinfection and filtration to control for pathogens such as viruses and protozoans at the 99.9 percent kill or inactivation level. However, direct measurements of destruction are not required.

Compliance and enforcement responsibility is intended for the state level, an approach common to most federal environmental programs. State programs must be at least as stringent as the federal specifications. Community systems are monitored by water utilities, following a plan approved by the state (or the EPA if the state does not have primacy). Monthly monitoring requirements are based on the system size, with larger systems taking more samples. Noncommunity systems can be monitored quarterly, although local conditions may necessitate additional sampling.

The rapidly expanding requirements for drinking water-quality control are imposing an enormous burden on water purveyors. In addition to the expense of monitoring, water systems may have to be modified to meet new requirements. The EPA is authorized by the SDWA to enforce regulations by administrative orders and to collect administrative penalties for noncompliance. However, this authorization does not deal with the fundamental question of securing financial resources needed to meet these new requirements.

Individuals may sue public water systems in federal court for failure to meet required standards. Individuals will learn of failures because administrators of water systems are required to notify their service communities of MCL violations. Following the traditional requirements for citizen suits, individuals must first give 60 days' notice to the EPA, state, and alleged violators before pursuing court action. Notification must come after the event has occurred. This requirement is not directly useful as a preventive tool; however, repeated notification should effectively demonstrate a pattern of failure. Individuals can then respond by pursuing legal remedies, working through the political system to upgrade services, or by personally seeking alternative supplies.

Further enabling public participation to influence water quality is the obligation established in the 1996 amendments for water purveyors to provide an annual consumer confidence report for their service area. Information required in this report is shown in Table 6-5. Contaminant presence must be reported even if measured in concentrations below regulatory standards (e.g., although fluoride is usually added to public drinking water supplies as an aid in preventing dental caries, its presence as a potential contaminant must be reported because an overabundance of fluoride is associated with health problems). The public now has ready access to comprehensive water-quality

---

TABLE 6-5 Consumer Confidence Report Requirements

Identification of the lake, river, aquifer, or other sources of the drinking water

A brief summary of the susceptibility to contamination of the local drinking water source, based on the source water assessments that states are completing over the next 5 years

How to get a copy of the water system's complete source water assessment

The level (or range of levels) of any contaminant found in local drinking water, as well as the environmental protection agency (EPA) health-based standard (maximum contaminant level) for comparison

The likely source of that contaminant in the local drinking water supply

The potential health effects of any contaminant detected in violation of an EPA health standard and an accounting of the system's actions to restore safe drinking water

The water system's compliance with other drinking water-related rules

An educational statement for vulnerable populations about avoiding Cryptosporidium

Educational information on nitrate, arsenic, or lead in areas where these contaminants are detected above 50 percent of the EPA's standard

Phone numbers of additional sources of information, including the water system and the EPA's Safe Drinking Water Hotline (800-426-4791)

Source: U.S. EPA Office of Water. 1998. *Consumer Confidence Reports, Final Rule.* Washington, D.C.: Government Printing Office. Publication no. EPA 816-F-98-007.

information in their communities through consumer confidence reports and through on-line reporting.

Response to Terrorism Threats

A recently identified threat to water systems is from terrorism. Water may be contaminated with biological, chemical, or radioactive agents, or water systems may be physically destroyed or damaged. Obtaining hazardous agents may not be difficult. A number of pathogenic bacteria, viruses, and protozoan can be recovered from natural sources or easily cultured and grown. Toxic chemicals may be purchased or synthesized, and radioactive material is not universally secure. The effectiveness of conventional treatment has not been studied with regard to many of the agents that may have potential for terrorist use. Some of these agents are well known to be tolerant of chlorine disinfection (e.g., anthrax spores and cryptosporidium oocysts) and other conventional forms of treatment. Although dilution provides some protection (in large systems, an obstacle to contamination of treatment works or source water would be the delivery of the agents in sufficient quantities), small systems or parts of systems may present a smaller obstacle to attack. For example, introduction of agents within a distribution system, downstream of storage facilities and treatment systems, may provide an effective way to distribute an agent within a neighborhood. The simplest method of upsetting water delivery may be through physical disruption of a water system with conventional explosives. Disruption of the water supply infrastructure would cripple any modern community.

The Public Health Security and Bioterrorism Preparedness and Response Act of 2002 requires activities at the national, state, and local levels to help the public health community respond to the threat of terrorist activities. Included in the Act are elements to help protect drinking water systems. Every community water system that serves a population of greater than 3,300 persons must conduct a vulnerability assessment of the system, submit the assessment to the EPA, and certify that the system has completed or updated an emergency response plan. The timetable for completing this work is very short, as summarized in Table 6-6.

TABLE 6-6 Timetable for Municipal Water System to Submit Vulnerability Reports and Certify Emergency Response Plans

Systems Serving Population of	Certify and Submit Vulnerability Assessment (VA) by	Certify Emergency Response Plan
100,000 or greater	March 31, 2003	Six months following the completion of the vulnerability assessment
50,000–99,999	December 31, 2003	
3,301–49,999	June 30, 2004	

Source: U.S. EPA Water Infrastructure Security webpage. *http://www.epa.gov/safewater/security/community.html* (December 3).

Vulnerability assessments must consider the susceptibility of the water supply (both surface water and groundwater) and the transmission, treatment, and distribution systems to terrorist attacks. Risks to the surrounding community resulting from attacks on the water system also must be documented. The assessment must include a qualitative estimate of the likelihood of attack and an evaluation of available countermeasures. Risk reduction and emergency response plans need to consider business practices that provide a security-related culture (e.g., through policies, procedures, and training), modern system components that enhance overall system performance while providing protective system redundancies, and security systems for detecting and responding to attacks.

Concluding Remarks

Our system governing the use and quality of water is more mature than many areas of environmental law and regulation. Water is one of the basic needs of life, and we have a history of concern coincident with the development of population centers and large pollution sources.

We experienced a period when many important water systems were substantially degraded. Now, gross contamination of surface water has been greatly reduced throughout the United States, although much of the nation's waters remain impaired and insufficiently evaluated. Major discrete, or point source, dischargers are governed by a regulatory system that is generally effective, although the major sources of degradation to the nation's estuaries continue to come from point source dischargers. Progress is continuing on difficult questions regarding how to manage diffuse, or nonpoint, sources of pollution and toxic materials. Nonpoint source pollution from agriculture has been identified as the major source of contamination currently adversely impacting water quality in streams, rivers, and lakes, and it presents a difficult regulatory challenge. We also are facing a situation in which water is becoming an increasingly expensive commodity because of the costs involved in treatment and because of an increased demand. We are consuming groundwater at a much faster rate than it is being replenished, which is resulting in a diminishing supply and increased costs of use. Growing populations heavily dependent on groundwater may lead to critical water shortages in the future.

Substantial interest has risen over the past several years concerning possible inadequacies of drinking water-quality standards. In particular, trace levels of pesticides and DBPs, and pathogen contamination have arisen as possible problem areas. Standards have expanded to include treatment and source water protection specifications in addition to limiting concentrations of discrete pollutants. The EPA is actively engaged in comprehensively reviewing and modifying drinking water-quality standards, assisted through processes designed for substantial input by affected communities. Yet, as clearly seen by the boom in the bottled drinking water industry, the public's faith in the quality of the municipal drinking water system is not high. Water quality currently is a very active and controversial regulatory area in which issues of expense and relative risk will play major roles in driving future rule making.

Questions for Review and Discussion

1. Why is cultural eutrophication a problem?
2. Describe the difference between conventional and toxic organics. Compare the relative amounts of each allowed in water.
3. Why are DBPs allowed by law to be present in water, even though they may be carcinogens?
4. The majority of the waterborne diseases reported in the United States originated from drinking water wells. Reflecting our regulatory framework governing drinking water, why might this be non-surprising?
5. What is the difference between riparian and appropriative water rights? Under what conditions are each of these most suited?
6. Why have the courts ruled that saving water through implementation of a conservation plan may not result in a recoverable appropriative right?
7. Is there any meaningful societal difference between a company withdrawing and bottling groundwater from an aquifer for out-of-region sales from that of a farmer using groundwater to grow crops? Is there any difference to the regulatory system governing these two activities?
8. Is the federal water-quality control program designed to focus on protection of public health or environmental quality?
9. How does the regulatory burden differ for a discharger into a sanitary sewer compared to a discharger into natural water?
10. Review one of the success stories of the 319 programs to control nonpoint pollution (see list of useful Web sites). What do you think was the driving force that allowed this activity to be successful, whereas in general nonpoint source control remains problematic?
11. How could consumer confidence reports be used to influence community decisions regarding water source control and treatment?
12. If a community finds it impractical to meet increasingly stringent standards for a drinking water pollutant (e.g., arsenic), should it be able to retain existing standards? In your response, consider the opportunity costs for a community investing in expensive upgrading of its water treatment system.

For Further Reading

Getches, David H. 1997. *Water Law in a Nutshell.* St. Paul, MN: West Publishing.

Glennon, Robert J. 2002. *Water Follies: Groundwater Pumping and the Fate of America's Fresh Waters.* Washington, D.C.: Island Press.

Pontius, Frederick. 2003. *Drinking Water Regulation and Health.* New York: Wiley-Interscience.

Resiner, Marc. 1986. *Cadillac Desert: The American West and Its Disappearing Water.* New York: Viking.

Sax, Joseph L., Robert H. Abrams, Barton H. Thompson, and John D. Leshy. 2000.

Legal Control of Water Resources. St. Paul, MN: West Publishing.

Young, Herbert C. 2003. *Understanding Water Rights and Conflicts.* Denver: BurgYoung Publishing.

On the Internet

http://www.awwa.org/
    Home page of the American Water Works Association
http://www.epa.gov/epahome/media.htm#water
    EPA's media projects and programs page
http://www.epa.gov/OGWDW/
    EPA's Office of Ground Water and Drinking Water home page
http://www.epa.gov/safewater/dwinfo.htm
    On-line consumer confidence reports for public water systems throughout the United States
http://www.epa.gov/water/
    EPA's Office of Water home page
http://www.epa.gov/nps/Section319III/pdf/319_all.pdf
    Section 319 Success Stories Volume III: The Successful Implementation of the Clean Water Act's Section 319 Nonpoint Source Pollution Program
http://www.epa.gov/esd/chemistry/pharma/index.htm
    Pharmaceuticals and Personal Care Products (PPCPs) as Environmental Pollutants
http://www.epa.gov/safewater/mcl.html
    National primary and secondary drinking water regulations
http://www.epa.gov/safewater/security/index.html
    Water infrastructure security information
http://waterdata.usgs.gov/nwis/qw
    U.S. Geological Survey Water Quality Data for the Nation
http://www.wef.org/
    Home page for the Water Environment Federation
http://www.epa.gov/owow/nps/watershed_handbook/
    Draft EPA publication Handbook for Developing Watershed Plans to Restore and Protect Our Waters

Notes

1. World Health Organization (WHO) et al. 1997. *Comprehensive Assessment of the Freshwater Resources of the World.* Geneva, Switzerland.

2. World Health Organization (WHO)/Unicef Joint Monitoring Programme for Water Supply and Sanitation. 2004. *Water for Life:*

Making it Happen. Geneva, Switzerland.

3. A. Prüss, D. Kay, L. Fewtrell, and Jamie Bartram. 2002. "Estimating the Burden of Disease from Water, Sanitation, and Hygiene at a Global Level." *Environmental Health Perspectives* 110(5): 537–542.

4. World Health Organization (WHO). *World Health Report 2002.* Geneva, Switzerland.

5. World Health Organization (WHO). *World Health Report 2003.* Geneva, Switzerland.

6. United Nations Environment Programme, United Nations Children's Fund, World Health Organization. 2002. "Children in the New Millennium: Environmental Impact on Health." *http://www.unep.org, http://www.unicef.org,* and *http://www.who.int.*

7. World Health Organization (WHO). 1996. *Climate Change and Human Health,* ed. A. J. Michael et al., Table 4.1, p 75. Geneva, Switzerland.

8. Liang, J. L, et al. 2006. "Surveillance for Waterborne-Disease Outbreaks Associated with Drinking Water and Water Not Intended for Drinking – United State, 2003–2004." *MMWR Surveill Summ.* 55(SS12) (December 22): 31–58.

9. Dziuban E. J. 2006. "Surveillance for Waterborne-Disease Outbreaks Associated with Recreational – United State, 2003–2004." *MMWR Surveill Summ.* 55(SS12) (December 22): 1–24.

10. Environmental Working Group and Ohio Citizen Action. 1998. *Full Disclosure, What Ohioians Need to Know to Clean Up Their Water.* Washington, D.C.

11. Canfield, R. L., C. R. Henderson, D. A. Cory-Slechta, C. Cox, T. A. Jusko, and B. P. Lanphear. 2003. "Intellectual Impairment in Children with Blood Lead Concentrations Below 10 mg per Deciliter." *New England Journal of Medicine* 348(16): 1517–1526.

12. D. H. Getches. 1984. *Water Law in a Nutshell, 58.* St. Paul, MN: West Publishing.

13. L. Rice and M. D. White. 1987. *Engineering Aspects of Water Law.* New York: Wiley.

14. *National Audubon Society v. Superior Court,* S.F. No. 24368, Supreme Court of California, 33 Cal. 3d 419; 658 P. 2d 709; 1983 Cal. LEXIS 152; 189 Cal. Rptr. 346; 21 ERC (BNA) 1490; 13 ELR 20272, February 17, 1983.

15. Cal Water Code § 1911.

16. Cal Water Code § 102.

17. *Mich. Citizens for Water Conservation v. Nestle Waters N. Am., Inc.,* No. 254202, No. 256153, Court Of Appeals Of Michigan, 269 Mich. App. 25; 709 N.W. 2d 174; 2005 Mich. App. LEXIS 2940, June 14, 2005, Submitted; November 29, 2005, Decided.

18. U.S. Environmental Protection Agency, Office of Water, A Strategic Plan. 2001. FY 2001 and Beyond, Protecting the Nation's Waters Through Effective NPDES Permits. Washington, D.C.: EPA-833-R-01–001.

19. Federal Water Pollution Control Act, § 304 (b)(4)(B) (1972).

20. 40 C.F.R. § 401.15.

21. 40 C.F.R. § 423.15.

22. Federal Water Pollution Control Act § 307(a)(3)(2) (1977).

23. *E. I. DuPont Nemours and Company v. Train,* 430 U.S. 112 (1977).

24. 40 C.F.R. § 122 App. A.

25. 40 C.F.R. Part 403.

26. Environmental Protection Agency, Office of Wastewater Management. 1999. *Introduction to the National Pretreatment Program.* Publication no. EPA 833-B-98-002. Washington, D.C.: Government Printing Office.

27. Environmental Protection Agency. *Does Your Construction Site Need a Stormwater Permit? A Construction Site Operator's Guide to EPA's Stormwater Permit Program.* *http://www.epa.gov/npdes/pubs/ sw_cgp_brochure.pdf*

28. U.S. EPA Office of Water. *National Water Quality Inventory 2000 Report.* August 2002, EPA-841-R-02-001.

29. U.S. EPA Office of Water. 2005. Section 319 Success Stories EPA 841-F-05-004S. *http://www.epa.gov/ owow/nps/success319/pdf/319_all.pdf*

RESOLVING CONTROVERSIAL ENVIRONMENTAL ISSUES

What Lurks Behind That Faucet

As we begin the 21st century, it seems only fair to be able to answer a simple question: "Is the water safe to drink?" But we cannot.

Go to any department store and choose among the many types, sizes, and prices of devices designed to clean your drinking water. What do these devices do? Will they make the water safer, do they do nothing but add cost and inconvenience to your water supply, or do they actually add to your risk? Bypass these questions by going to the supermarket and buying bottled water. But where does this water come from? Who checks it for safety, and does it present you less risk than water from your tap? How do you make the best choice about your drinking water?

The U.S. EPA's Office of Enforcement and Compliance Assurance is responsible for ensuring the compliance of the regulated community with federal environmental statutes. Its recent report on 2000 compliance with the SDWA should add some insight. Let's see what this report says:

- Seventy-five percent of all public water systems neither reported violations of health-based standards nor significant violations of monitoring and reporting requirements
- Ninety-four percent of America's public water systems reported no violations of any health-based drinking water standards
- Most violations were significant violations of monitoring and reporting requirements rather than violations of health-based drinking water standards
- Only 2 percent of public water systems served more than 10,000 people and provided service to 75 percent of all uses. But violations at a few large systems potentially could affect large populations
- Ninety-four percent of public water systems served 3,300 or fewer people. Most violations of drinking water standards occurred at a small system

These statistics can be used both to support and to refute the idea that our water is safe. Let us see how they could be used to advance either position.

1. The EPA may take pride in 94 percent of all public water systems having no violation of any health-based standards. Is this the same thing as saying that 94 percent of all people using water from public systems have no risk from their drinking water? What if the 6 percent of the public water systems having a risk include New York, Los Angeles, and Chicago? What if all of the 6 percent of these public water systems with violations were among those serving fewer than 3,300 people? If you knew that the 6 percent of violations were all in small systems, how would you evaluate the overall performance in the United States of our government programs? If you happened to live in one of these small cities with violations, how would you evaluate the programs?

2. Critics of our water protection programs might argue that 25 percent of the public systems had either reported violations of health-based standards or significant violations of monitoring and reporting requirements. They might conclude that this failure puts one of four systems at risk to the consumer. Do you think that our water is of sufficiently poor quality that a reasonable risk

estimate is one of four? Do you know anyone who ever got sick from drinking water in the United States? Careful selection of statistics can promote a point of view. When critiquing an argument that uses statistics, be sure to consider precisely what the statistics mean. For example, if a facility provided perfectly pure water, but forgot to report on its performance in removing turbidity, would it be part of this 25 percent? Would this indicate a real threat to drinking water quality?

In addition to using statistics to promote a point of view, it is interested to examine opinions based on ethical values. Based on the following short essay, what might you conclude about the consistency of values shown by the farming community? How would you describe the prevailing values?

Should the Farmer and the Cowman be Friends? (with apologies to Rodgers and Hammerstein)

Tremendous pressure is being put on elected officials in much of the country in response to the growth of CAFOs. The EPA has responded through development and implementation of rules and regulations, most of which are strongly criticized as being insufficient for protection of public and environmental health. Concerns about water include direct effects of contamination of water with pathogens and with elevated levels of nitrogen. Other concerns include smells, flies, destruction of country roads because of the increased truck traffic, decreased property values, and a shift in a way-of-life away from the family farm.

Many of the objections to CAFOs are coming from their neighbors, fellow agriculturalists. Yet, farming has been shown to be the predominant source of contamination to rivers and lakes throughout the country. Much of the contamination is simply from soil erosion-added sediments to surface water. Additional concerns derive from the heavy use of pesticides characteristic of modern agriculture. The farming community has been very strong (and many say very successful) in limiting the role of government with respect to imposing environmental controls. Agriculture in the United States can help feed the world—"let the free market work without environmental constraints!"

Unsurprisingly, legislative review reveals that many rural agricultural areas have political preferences supportive of minimizing the role of government. However, it is this same group of farmers who are often calling the loudest for controlling of CAFOs through strong government intervention programs. Is this argument legitimate? Ethical? Do you see solutions that make sense for rural, agricultural areas to best provide food for the nation and the world and protect the local environment?

CHAPTER 7
CONTROLLING TOXIC SUBSTANCES

In 1948, Swiss chemist Paul Muller received the Nobel Prize in medicine for discovering the insecticidal properties of DDT. Through its use to control mosquito populations, DDT saved untold lives from malaria. But within 10 years, this insecticide had produced so many adverse effects that it was banned, or its use was severely restricted in several parts of the world.[1]

The experience with DDT is just one example of the potential risks and benefits of the chemical age in which we live. It also points out the primary problem the U.S. legal system faces in trying to regulate such substances. Many substances that are developed end up having extremely harmful effects; natural chemicals, of course, may be equally or more toxic than many artificial ones. The legal system's main problem, therefore, is trying to find a way to encourage the development and use of helpful chemicals while preventing inadvertent, widespread use of chemicals with toxic effects. This chapter and Chapter 8 explore the regulatory schemes that have been developed to help identify toxic substances and manage their use and disposal.

This chapter begins with a discussion of toxicity. Then federal regulation of toxic substances under the TSCA; the FIFRA; and the Federal Food, Drug, and Cosmetics Act (FFDCA) are explained. The last section discusses the use of tort law to control toxic substances or at least to provide compensation for harm resulting from exposure to them.

IDENTIFICATION OF POTENTIALLY TOXIC SUBSTANCES

Toxic substances are regulated by a wide variety of environmental laws, as summarized in Table 7-1. In Chapters 5 and 6, on air pollution and water pollution, you were introduced to some of these regulations. This chapter focuses on the two main laws that regulate potentially toxic substances used in commerce. Before we examine these specific laws, however, we need to know what the term *toxic substance* means. Generally, toxic refers to something that is directly poisonous to humans. However, nowhere in the TSCA does Congress specifically define the term; in fact, in none of the acts that regulate potentially toxic substances is the term defined. Instead, some acts, such as the FWPCA, list certain substances that must be regulated as toxins; and other statutes focus on

TABLE 7-1   Environmental Laws Regulating Toxic Substances

Statute	*Regulated Substances*
Asbestos Hazard Emergency Response Act	Asbestos
Clean Air Act	Hazardous air pollutants
Clean Water Act	Hazardous water pollutants
Comprehensive Environmental Response, Compensation, and Liability Act	Hazardous waste
Federal Food, Drug, and Cosmetics Act	Pesticide residues
Federal Insecticide, Fungicide, and Rodenticide Act	Pesticides
Marine Protection Research and Sanctuaries Act	Toxic waste
Occupational Safety and Health Act	Toxic substances in the workplace
Resource Conservation and Recovery Act	Hazardous waste
Safe Drinking Water Act	Pesticides and other hazardous substances
Toxic Substances Control Act	Toxic substances used in commerce

the risk of harm imposed by certain substances that makes them subject to regulation as toxins.

Many substances regulated as toxins have certain characteristics that make their regulation especially urgent. For example, extremely low doses of a potentially toxic substance can produce adverse effects in humans, animals, or plants. A conventional pollutant may be harmful in parts per million, whereas a toxic pollutant may be harmful in parts per trillion. In addition, the harmful effects of a toxic substance may not show up for decades after the exposure. Furthermore, potentially toxic substances may bioaccumulate. If, for example, the toxin is in the water, that substance may accumulate in the bodies of fish so that it would be much more heavily concentrated in the fish than it would be in the surrounding water. Another closely related characteristic is that toxic substances often persist, that is, they take a long time to break down biologically. Or when they do break down, their degradation produces toxic by-products.

SCIENTIFIC UNCERTAINTY

One of the biggest problems with environmental regulation, and especially the regulation of toxic substances, is that of scientific uncertainty. We can see the smog hanging over the skyline and feel it burning our eyes, but we can neither see nor taste the DDT bioaccumulating in the fish we just ate. Although there are ways to determine when a chemical in a set dosage is harmful, there is no test that can prove beyond a doubt that a chemical will not cause any harm to human health or the environment. There is always the potential for harm in a little higher concentration or in a slightly more prolonged exposure.

So, how is a regulatory agency to determine whether a chemical is "safe"? Although they regularly struggle with this issue, the courts have not come to a definitive conclusion. They have not specified precisely what degree of evidence of harm is necessary for a substance to be banned or regulated, but they have said that assessing risk and determining how to regulate involve not only factual evidence but also policy considerations. In *Ethyl Corporation v. United States EPA*,[2] a case involving regulation of a conventional pollutant under the CAA, the court said:

> Undoubtedly certainty is a scientific ideal—to the extent that even science can be certain of its truth. But certainty in the complexities of environmental medicine may be achievable only after the fact, when scientists have the opportunity for leisurely and isolated scrutiny of an entire mechanism.
>
> Awaiting certainty will often allow for only reactive, not preventative regulation. Petitioners suggest that anything less than certainty, that any speculation, is irresponsible. But when statutes seek to avoid environmental catastrophe, can preventative, albeit uncertain decisions legitimately be so labeled?

Thus, the courts have tended not to hold the EPA to a rigorous standard of proof when determining when a substance can be regulated.

The District of Columbia Circuit Court, in *Lead Industries Association, Inc. v. EPA*,[3] even went so far as to say that "feasibility and cost" were irrelevant when the EPA was determining a reasonable margin of safety to protect the public health. However, in *NRDC v. United States EPA*,[4] the same court, in considering the regulation of a hazardous air pollutant, stated that an "ample margin of safety to protect human health" does not have to mean "risk free"; there can be an "acceptable" risk to health.

Still, despite the courts' lack of assistance, agencies such as the EPA and the OSHA must determine acceptable risk. They generally do so by using the processes of risk assessment and risk management.

RISK ASSESSMENT

Risk assessment is generally defined as the process of characterizing the potentially adverse consequences of human exposure to an environmental hazard. Risk assessment is a necessary preliminary step to risk management, the process by which policy choices are made once the risks have been determined. To understand the process that agencies go through to make these assessments, we can examine the scientific basis for risk assessment.

As noted earlier, one of the risks a potentially toxic substance may pose is that of carcinogenicity. In deciding whether to regulate a chemical in a manner that would sustain judicial scrutiny, an agency may undertake risk assessment. The four-step process detailed in the following sections would be typical of such an assessment. This process was first described and recommended in 1983 by a committee of the National Research Council.[5]

Hazard Identification

Four types of information are generally used at the hazard identification stage of risk assessment: comparisons of molecular structures (there is almost unanimous acceptance of this approach within the scientific community), short-term studies, animal bioassay data, and epidemiological studies.

An initial step that may lead to further identification of a potential carcinogen is the comparison of a substance's physical and chemical properties with those of a known carcinogen. These comparisons are primarily useful in setting priorities concerning which substances most urgently need further investigation. Short-term studies of the effects of the substance on single-celled animals may be the next step. If exposure causes mutation, this result is generally an indicator that a substance is likely to be carcinogenic, and thus further studies are warranted. Because these short-term studies are quick and relatively inexpensive, they provide a good screening device.

The most commonly used data to support regulation of a substance as a carcinogen are obtained from animal bioassays. To support a finding of carcinogenicity, scientists usually look for consistently positive results in both sexes and in several strains and species. Higher incidences at higher doses are also considered important. Although animal bioassays are important, they are viewed cautiously. There are several fundamental biological similarities among all mammals, and so we can expect similarities in response to chemical toxicity. Usually, in cases in which human and animal responses can be compared, these similarities are borne out. Thus far, all human carcinogens (except possibly arsenic) have also been shown to be capable of causing cancer in some (but not all) animal species. Usually, but not always, the same sites of the bodies of both humans and animals are most vulnerable to the carcinogen. Benzidine, for example, is most strongly linked to bladder cancer in dogs and in humans, but to liver cancer in rats. So we rely on animal tests, but cautiously.

Another question with respect to animal bioassays is whether it is ethical to use animals to test for carcinogenicity. Increasingly, people are organizing to protest the use of animals in research.

Epidemiological data that show a positive association between exposure to an agent and disease are considered the most convincing evidence about human risk. This evidence, however, is generally very difficult to obtain because the number of people exposed to any particular hazard may be low, exposures may be confounded by exposures to other substances, and the latency period may be uncertain. Even if these problems did not exist, we still would not want to risk waiting to regulate until people had been exposed to the potentially hazardous substance.

Dose–Response Assessment

Once the hazardous substance has been identified, the next step is to determine the response of humans to various levels of exposure. In a limited number of cases, sufficient epidemiological data are available to allow extrapolations from the exposures observed in the studies. A problem with such extrapolations, however, is that the general population may contain some people, such as children and the elderly, who are more sensitive than the people in the studies.

Because epidemiological data are not generally available for most substances that are being assessed, dose–response assessment usually requires assessments of animal studies. One problem with these studies is that the amount to which the animals are exposed in the tests for hazard identification is much higher than the doses to which humans would generally be exposed. Scientists have developed a number of mathematical models to predict risks to humans exposed to lower doses. Adjustments must also be made to account for differences in size and metabolic rates.

Exposure Assessment

The third step in the process is to determine which populations would be exposed to the chemical and the dosages to which they would be exposed. Although in rare cases, especially more structured sites such as workplaces, exposures may be directly measured, more typically, exposure data must be estimated.

When a community's exposure is being assessed, the ambient concentrations of chemicals to which people are exposed are calculated on the basis of emission rates, assuming that transport and conversion processes are known. For some chemicals, no data are available and estimates of exposures must be made. When chemicals are present in food or absorbed when a consumer product is used, the exposure assessment is even more complicated because of people's different dietary and personal habits. Part of the exposure assessment process also involves ascertaining which groups would be exposed to the substances. Some groups, such as children or pregnant women, might be especially susceptible. Exposure of a group to a mixture of potential carcinogens also requires consideration, although such calculations are nearly impossible to make.

Risk Characterization

The final step, the estimate of the magnitude of the public health problem, requires no further scientific knowledge or concepts. At this stage, the value judgments of the assessors are most likely to come into play. Because of the general deference the courts give to decisions made by the agency involved, following such a procedure as the one just described would give the agency's rule a strong chance of being upheld. Remember that the courts tend to look most carefully at the procedures that agency decision makers follow.

Since the 1950s, global economic activity has quadrupled,[6] and manufacture of synthetic organic chemicals has grown dramatically from a tiny, specialty enterprise to a huge, powerful industry. Organic compounds or chemicals, by definition, are those containing carbon, which bonds easily with itself and other elements. Scientists have learned to take advantage of carbon's unique properties to create hundreds of thousands of new chemical compounds and thus new consumer goods. Between 1945 and 1985, there was a 15-fold increase in the production of synthetic organic chemicals, from 6.7 to 102 million tons per year.[7] Worldwide, more than 70,000 chemicals are in everyday use,[8] and approximately 1,500 new ones are added every year.[9] There is no reason to believe this growth will cease, because people are always searching for something "better," and chemicals provide much of the hope for that improvement.

Creation of this plethora of synthetic organic substances is, unfortunately, not without risk. As we know all too well, the toxic effects of a chemical may not become known until several years after people are exposed to the substance. This long latency period, during which hundreds of thousands of people may be exposed, is one of the main problems of some toxic substances. Other problems were mentioned previously, such as their tendency to bioaccumulate and the fact that sometimes very small amounts may cause tremendous harm. The main problem the legal system faces is trying to find a way to encourage the development and use of helpful chemicals while preventing inadvertent, widespread use of chemicals with toxic effects.

Pesticides, substances designed to eradicate pests such as rodents, insects, fungi, bacteria, and weeds, are a special category of toxic substances. Over 1 billion tons of pesticide products are used each year in the United States.[10] In 2001, annual expenditures by users of pesticides totaled $11 billion.[11] The agricultural sector accounts for 76 percent of total pesticide usage in the United States.[12] Table 7-2 summarizes some of the common uses of pesticides. Undoubtedly, their use has increased crop yields worldwide. However, there are also a number of problems associated with these substances. First of all, because they are toxic, they have the capacity to harm not only targeted pests but also humans and wildlife. Approximately 165 pesticidal chemicals classified by the EPA are known, probable, or possible carcinogens.[13] A related problem is that only a small percentage of the pesticide actually reaches the target pests; the rest may contaminate the soil and drinking water.

Another problem associated with pesticide use is that a given pesticide does not retain its effectiveness for long. Although a pesticide may be highly effective at first, some of the targeted pests, the strongest ones, will survive and breed. Through natural selection, a newer, stronger strain of the pest that is resistant to the pesticide will evolve, resulting in lower crop yields again until some new, stronger pesticide is developed, one that is potentially more dangerous not only to the pests but also to the environment in general.

TABLE 7-2   Some Pesticides Taken Off the Market

Pesticide	Use	Concerns
Aldrin	Insecticide	Oncogenicity
Chlordane (agricultural uses; termiticide uses suspended or canceled)	Insecticide/termites, ants	Oncogenicity; reductions in nontarget and endangered species
Compound 1080 (livestock Coyote control, collar retained; rodenticide use under review)	Rodenticide	Reductions in nontarget and endangered species; no known antidote
Diazinon (agricultural uses retained)	Insecticide	Bird kills, other wildlife
Dibromochloropropane (DBCP)	Soil fumigant, fruits, and vegetables	Oncogenicity; mutagenicity, reproductive effects
Dichlorodiphenyltri-chloroethane (DDT) and related compounds	Insecticide	Ecological (eggshell thinning); carcinogenicity
Dieldrin	Insecticide	Oncogenicity
Dinoseb (in hearings)	Herbicide/crop desiccant	Fetotoxicity; reproductive effects; acute toxicity
Dursban (certain agricultural uses retained)	Insecticide	Blurred vision, memory loss
Endrin (avicide use retained)	Insecticide/avicide	Oncogenicity/teratogenicity; reductions in nontarget and endangered species
Ethylene dibromide (EDB)	Insecticide/fumigant	Oncogenicity; mutagenicity, reproductive effects
Heptachlor (agricultural uses; termiticide uses suspended or canceled)	Insecticide	Oncogenicity, reductions in nontarget and endangered species
Kepone	Insecticide	Oncogenicity
Lindane (indoor smoke bomb canceled; some uses restricted)	Insecticide/vaporizer	Oncogenicity, teratogenicity, reproductive effects, acute toxicity; other long-term effects
Mercury	Microbial uses	Cumulative toxicant causing brain damage
Mirex	Insecticide/fire ant control	Nontarget species; potential oncogenicity
Silvex	Herbicide/forestry, rights-of-way, weed control	Oncogenicity, teratogenicity; fetotoxicity
Strychinine (rodenticide uses and livestock collar retained)	Mammalian predator control, rodenticide	Reductions in nontarget and endangered species

(continued)

TABLE 7-2 *(cont.)*		
Pesticide	*Use*	*Concerns*
2,4,5–T	Herbicide, forestry, right of way, weed control	Oncogenicity; teratogenicity; fetotoxicity
Toxaphene (livestock dip retained)	Insecticide, cotton	Oncogenicity; reductions in nontarget species; acute toxicity to aquatic organisms; long-term effects on wildlife

The remaining sections of this chapter discuss how some of the problems created by potentially toxic substances are addressed through federal regulation and state common law.

TSCA

The primary federal law designed to regulate toxic substances is the TSCA, passed in 1976. The EPA OPPT is responsible for the implementation of the TSCA. Three significant policies are set forth at the beginning of the TSCA:

1. Data on environmental effects of chemicals must be developed by industry
2. Government must have adequate authority to prevent unreasonable risk of injury to health or the environment, particularly imminent hazards
3. Government authority must be exercised so as to not "impede unduly or create unnecessary barriers to technology while fulfilling the primary purpose of the Act"

The policy statement may sound attractive; in fact, it contains language that both environmentalists and *laissez-faire* businesspeople may embrace. Unfortunately, it is a policy statement full of ambiguity, promoting the often conflicting goals of ensuring environmental safety and encouraging technological development. Many people, however, believe this conflict will always exist because we do want a safe environment, yet we also want the benefits new chemicals may bring, and the act does the best possible job of balancing these conflicting objectives. It is still unknown whether many chemical substances are toxic, as they are often not put through a rigorous testing process.[14] As you read the following sections on how the act regulates both new and existing chemicals, ask yourself whether the law does indeed perform a good balancing act.

Treatment of Old Chemicals

When we examine the structure of the act, we see that TSCA can be divided into two parts: treatment of old chemicals and treatment of new chemicals. By 1979, the EPA had compiled an inventory of all chemicals commercially used or produced in the United States between January 1975 and July 1979, as required by TSCA.

Once the inventory was completed, the Interagency Testing Committee had to categorize all chemicals as high priority or not. Information used to determine whether a chemical is high priority comes from manufacturers and importers and is updated every 4 years. Putting a chemical on the high-priority list means that the chemical is subject to further investigation and testing. High priority goes to those chemicals suspected of causing cancer, mutation, or birth defects.

Under TSCA, no more than 50 chemicals can be listed as high priority within a 12-month period. Every 6 months the list is revised. Once the EPA has placed a chemical on the list, the agency has 12 months to assess the risk of the chemical or to issue testing rules if it has insufficient data to assess risk. Using a hybrid form of rule making, the EPA must publish these testing rules within reasonable time limits. The publication must include the purpose of the tests and the methods to be used. Test results must be published in the *Federal Register.*

Unfortunately, according to the U.S. National Research Council, the EPA currently has over 48,000 chemicals on its inventory of toxic substances and has no information on the toxic effects of 79 percent of them. Less than one-fifth have been tested for short-term effects, and less than one-tenth for long-term (e.g., carcinogenic), reproductive, or mutagenic effects.

Treatment of New Chemicals

The centerpiece of the EPA's regulation of new chemicals is the pre-manufacturing notice (PMN), sometimes referred to as a "section 5 notice." The PMN must be submitted 90 days in advance of the manufacture or importation of any new chemical for sale or use in commerce. In fiscal year 2002, the EPA received 1,471 PMN submissions from industry for new chemicals.[15] This notice must contain a significant amount of information about the chemical, including its chemical name; chemical identity; molecular structure; trade names or synonyms; by-products resulting from its manufacture, processing, use, or disposal; intended categories of use by function and application; and the estimated maximum quantity to be manufactured or imported during the first year of production and for any 12-month period during the first 3 years. Details about the manufacture of the product that must be contained in the notice include the site where the chemical will be manufactured, processed, or used by the manufacturer, as well as information about worker exposure and releases to the environment. Perhaps the most important information in the notice, however, are the test data. The notice must contain all available test data related to the impact of the new chemical on human health and the environment, including effects resulting not only from use of the substance but also from its manufacture, processing, distribution, and disposal. If some of the data were obtained from scientific journals, citations of the journal articles must be included. Any new data gathered or generated subsequent to submission of the PMN must be given to the EPA.

Within 5 days of receipt of the PMN, the EPA must publish a notice in the *Federal Register* containing the name of the new chemical, its intended use, and the test data submitted by the manufacturer to demonstrate that the chemical does not present an unreasonable risk of harm to health or the human environment. Within 45 days, the EPA must act to limit the amount to be produced, sold, or processed; prohibit the sale or manufacture of the chemical; or require further testing and temporarily enjoin the manufacture or sale until the data are provided. In taking action, the EPA must select the "least burdensome control." If no action is taken, the manufacturer is free to use the new chemical after the 90-day period has expired.

Environmentalists are highly displeased with the PMN program for several reasons. First, by 1983, stop or limit orders had been issued for only 13 of 2,300 chemicals. It is highly unlikely that only 13 chemicals had insufficient testing done to ensure their safety. Of course, those who quote that statistic often ignore the fact that several hundred chemicals were actually withdrawn by the manufacturer rather than risk EPA disapproval. Second, the statute is considered weak because it requires only known data to be reported; there is no requirement for testing. Some argue that this requirement discourages thorough testing. If a firm is fearful of a certain side effect, it may simply not test for it. Of course, firms reject this criticism, arguing that fear of civil liability to persons harmed from a toxic substance provides them with the incentive to perform the necessary tests.

A 1995 Office of Technology Assessment study of PMNs showed that 67 percent had no toxicity data; the other 85 percent had only limited data. Where were the EPA temporary injunctions for insufficient testing?

Although there have been many concerns about the PMN requirement, severe penalties are possible for noncompliance. For example, in 1996, the EPA proposed that Safety-Kleen Corporation be fined $1.8 million for alleged improper sales of a recycled oil product.[16] The EPA alleged that the Elgin firm sold an asphalt extender before filing a PMN. Furthermore, in 1997, in the first case involving criminal charges filed by the EPA for violating reporting requirements of TSCA, Futura Coatings admitted to manufacturing over 54,000 pounds of three different novel chemicals between 1991 and 1993 without filing PMNs with the EPA.[17] The company was fined $350,000. And more recently, in 2002, Transcontinental Gas Pipe Line Corporation agreed to pay a $1.4 million civil penalty and to clean up soil and groundwater contamination after it disposed of waste in violation of TSCA. The contamination, involving improper disposal of PCBs, stretches along a pipeline that runs through 12 states, from Texas to New York.[18]

But, it is not just environmentalists who criticize the PMN process. Chemical firms are also critical. They say the procedure is expensive and requires unnecessary red tape. After all, the firms argue, they would not produce unsafe chemicals, because if they did, they would be liable in tort for negligence. These situations are not like water or air pollution, they claim, where causation is difficult to prove. There will not be the potential anonymity created by 50 dumpers; only one manufacturer made the product that caused the injury. Because chemicals affect so many people, the liability would be enormous.

In light of some of the weaknesses of the TSCA, Americans should be happy that the European Union is moving to strengthen its regulation of toxic substances. Their new regulatory scheme, described in the International Regulation of Toxic Substances section of this chapter, fills in some of the gaps in regulation under the TSCA.

FIFRA

Not all potentially toxic chemicals are regulated primarily under TSCA. The first toxic substances to arouse public concern (herbicides, insecticides, fungicides, and rodenticides) are all commonly referred to as pesticides and are regulated primarily under the FIFRA, passed in 1947. Because of the sheer volume of pesticides used in the United States—over 1.2 billion pounds in 2000 and 2001, accounting for more than 20 percent of total world pesticide use[19]—their regulation is extremely important. And the use of pesticides seems destined to increase as we plant more genetically engineered (GE) crops. According to a report issued in November of 2003 by the Northwest Science and Environment Policy Center, during the first 3 years of their use, GE crops required fewer pesticides, but in the last 3 years, over 73 million more pounds of pesticides were applied on GE acres. Many farmers have had to spray incrementally more herbicides on GE acres to keep up with shifts in weeds toward tougher-to-control species, along with the emergence of genetic resistance in certain weed populations.[20] See Figure 7-1 for a breakdown of these percentages by type of pesticide.

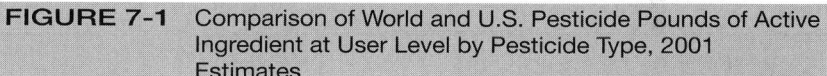

FIGURE 7-1   Comparison of World and U.S. Pesticide Pounds of Active Ingredient at User Level by Pesticide Type, 2001 Estimates

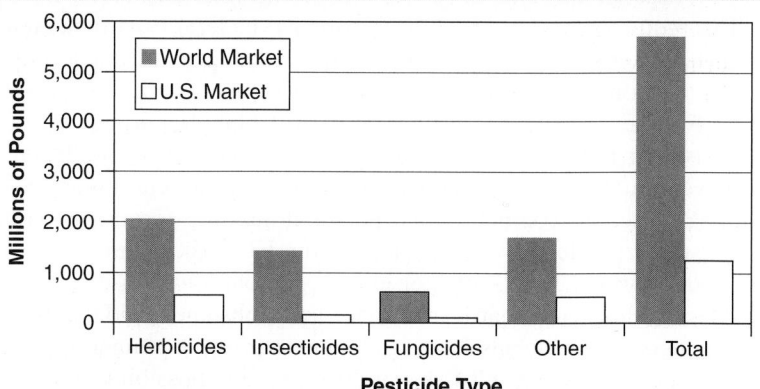

Source: EPA. *2000–2001 Pesticide Market Estimates: Usage. http://www.epa.gov/oppbead1/pestsales/01pestsales/market_estimates2001.pdf*

Registration Under FIFRA

For the purposes of FIFRA, all pesticides (aside from a small number of exclusions) must be registered and properly labeled before they can be distributed in the United States. As of 1999, approximately 20,000 such products had been registered by the EPA.[21] Pesticides are registered with the PA's Office of Pesticide Programs (OPPs). In 2004, 78 new pesticide products were registered, 35 were amended, and 14 products were cancelled.[22]

When a pesticide is to be registered, data showing its impact are submitted to the EPA. The EPA will register the pesticide when four factors exist:

1. The pesticide's composition is such as to warrant the proposed claims for it
2. Its labeling complies with the act
3. The pesticide will perform its intended function without unreasonable risks to people and the environment (taking into account economic, social, and environmental costs and benefits of the pesticide)
4. When used in accordance with commonly used practice, the pesticide will not cause unreasonable risk to the environment

An obvious question arises with respect to these factors: What is unreasonable risk? Originally, risk referred primarily to carcinogenicity. Today, however, the EPA also examines reproductive, immunological, and neurological effects of the pesticide, as well as its impact on groundwater and on the growth and reproduction of wildlife and fish. The EPA, when determining unreasonable risk, weighs the economic, social, and environmental costs and benefits of the pesticide. In other words, if there are few or no substitutes available to do the same job, a greater risk to human health might be considered more reasonable than if there were numerous alternatives available. Some people criticize this standard as being insufficiently protective of health and the environment, noting that most other risk-based environmental standards are lessened only because of a lack of technology.

A second question arises with respect to what constitutes a proper label. This requirement dates back to the original Federal Environmental Pesticide Control Act of 1947, which was simply a labeling act. Today, a proper label is one that contains the warnings necessary to prevent injuries to persons and the environment. The EPA is trying to improve labels, particularly through the Consumer Labeling Initiative (CLI), a voluntary effort to "foster pollution prevention, empower consumer choice, and improve consumer understanding of safe use, environmental and personal health information on household consumer product labels."[23] In 1996, the EPA asked individual consumers about existing labels on indoor insecticides, outdoor house and garden pesticides, and household hard-surface cleaners. Consumers said that they struggled to understand the labels. In an attempt to improve consumer understanding of pesticide labels, the CLI is investigating the possibility of standardized environmental information on product labels, similar to standard nutrition labels on food products. The first project of CLI, launched March 6, 2000, is known as Read the Label FIRST!, a massive consumer education project, with campaign materials that can be received and distributed by anyone. Several reports have been made on the issue since that time, and voluntary guidelines have been set up; however, there is no requirement that companies must follow. Consumers can go to http://www.epa.gov/pesticides/label/, where they can run their cursor over various parts of a generic label, and pop-ups will explain how to interpret various parts of a pesticide label.

A pesticide can be registered for general or restricted use. General use is by far the most desired form of registration. In essence, a general-use pesticide meets the standards set by the EPA and can be sold to anyone in any quantity. Restricted-use pesticides have the potential to have an unreasonable impact. However, these unreasonable effects can be mitigated or prevented if the use and/or sale of the pesticide is restricted in some manner—hence the term *restricted use.*

The most common restriction is to limit use to certified applicators who take a test. Use is defined by the statute as application of the pesticide by or under the supervision of a certified applicator. This definition leaves a lot of room for abuse. Another problem with this restriction is that it contains an exception for private applicators: If the pesticide is used only on one's own land, a private applicator has to take the courses only and not the test. This exception assumes that those private applicators will be very knowledgeable and careful. Other possible restrictions include a limit on the frequency of use of the pesticide or to locations in which the substance can be sold or applied. The pests that may be targeted and the amount used per application can also be limited.

Under the 1988 amendments to FIFRA, the EPA is required to expedite its review of applications for pesticides that meet one of two criteria. The first standard is when the pesticide is identical or substantially similar in composition and labeling to a currently registered pesticide (often referred to as a "me too" application). Alternatively, the pesticide may be one that differs in composition and labeling from a currently registered pesticide only in ways that would not significantly increase the risk of adverse environmental effects.

Registration lasts 5 years. If the EPA receives no request for renewal within 30 days before the end of registration, notice of impending cancellation is published in the *Federal Register.* The manufacturer has 30 days within which to protest the cancellation, or the registration terminates.

The EPA does not always grant registration for 5 years. Sometimes it grants only conditional registration. Conditional registration is given when certain required data are not submitted and two conditions exist:

1. The pesticide and proposed use are substantially similar to a currently used pesticide (i.e., they have similar active ingredients) or differ in ways that would not substantially harm the environment
2. No significant harm or risk of unreasonable adverse effects would result from the pesticide's use

If the active ingredient of the pesticide is not currently being used, conditional registration can be granted for the time needed to generate and submit the required data, not to exceed 1 year. Again, there must be no unreasonable risk (considering costs and benefits), and the granting of the conditional registration must be in the public interest.

If registration is denied, the EPA notifies the applicant of the reasons for denial. The applicant has 30 days to correct the condition (e.g., improper label) that led to the denial. If no correction is made, the notice of denial will be published in the *Federal Register*, along with the reasons for denial. Within 30 days, the applicant may seek an EPA hearing and administrative review of the denial.

Reregistration

The 1988 amendments to FIFRA created the reregistration scheme. This scheme applies only to pesticides registered before November 1984 because in general these pesticides do not meet today's health and safety standards for pesticides' active ingredients, particularly those of the Food Quality Protection Act (FQPA), which will be discussed later in this chapter. The EPA requires data from these pesticides to be reviewed before it will grant reregistration. There are 612 reregistration cases for the EPA to consider; of these cases, 66 percent have been completed, meaning that the products are being reregistered, voluntarily canceled, or deregulated.[24]

Cancellation of Registration

As noted, if a pesticide manufacturer does not request renewal of the registration before the end of the 5-year period, the process for termination of registration automatically begins. Sometimes, however, the EPA may move to cancel a registration earlier. This action for cancellation will occur whenever the EPA obtains information that an existing pesticide may present an unreasonable risk. The EPA will then undertake an intensive review of the pesticide. If it believes the risk is unreasonable, the agency will issue a notice of intent to cancel registration. (Table 7-2 identifies some pesticides that have been removed from the market through this process.) Interested parties, generally users and manufacturers, then have 30 days to contest the cancellation by requesting a hearing. If no such request is made, cancellation is effective. If the cancellation is challenged, there must be a hearing to determine whether the registration should be canceled.

There has been a whole series of opinions resulting from litigation between the EPA and the Environmental Defense Fund (now Environmental Defense) concerning the issue of who should have the burden of proof in cancellation hearings. The resultant case law has established that once the EPA issues a notice of cancellation, a presumption arises in favor of cancellation. Issuance of the notice is presumed to mean that a substantial question of safety exists that requires suspension in the absence of proof by the manufacturer that the risk is minimal or that the countervailing benefits outweigh the risks. Once the EPA has obtained evidence that one mode of exposure is hazardous, the presumption also arises that all modes of exposure are hazardous.

If a manufacturer contests a cancellation, the hearing process can be extremely time-consuming, often taking up to 2 years. During this time, the pesticide will continue to be sold. Many believe that in light of the presumption in favor of cancellation, it seems irrational to allow the continued production and sale of the pesticide until the final outcome of the cancellation proceedings has been determined.

There is an important exception to this time-consuming process. Suspension can be immediate if the continued use of the pesticide presents an imminent hazard. When evidence of an imminent hazard comes to light, the administrator of the EPA can issue a notice to the manufacturer of the pesticide that use of the pesticide is being suspended. Findings as to the imminent hazard must be included with the notice. The manufacturer then has 5 days within which to request an expedited hearing before the suspension. If no hearing is requested, the suspension will take place at the end of the 5-day period.

One even stronger action the EPA administrator can take is an emergency suspension. If the administrator determines that an emergency exists, he or she may order an immediate suspension of all use, sales, and distribution of the pesticide. The manufacturer, however, is entitled to an expedited hearing to determine whether the suspension was appropriate. As you might guess, emergency suspension has been exercised only a few times.

An interesting issue that arises with respect to cancellation is about what should be done with pesticides that have had their registrations canceled. The EPA has the authority to allow the sale and use of existing stocks "under such conditions and for such uses as will not unreasonably adversely affect the environment." In many cases, as long as they can use their stock, manufacturers do not protest cancellation. This ability to get an easy cancellation makes it tempting for the EPA to go along with such an arrangement.

Another problem that arises with the cancellation of a registration for a pesticide that has been in use for a long time is that the manufacturer, retailers, and end users may have large supplies of the pesticide on hand. Under the original act, the EPA indemnified, or reimbursed, the holders (manufacturers and users) of the pesticide for the costs of the canceled/suspended products, plus disposal of the pesticide if requested, and established standards for its disposal. This provision of the act proved costly. For example, in 1986, the EPA spent $1.5 million on an untested chemical method to neutralize the pesticide ethylene dibromide (EDB). Unfortunately, this process released toxic vapors into the air, requiring the EPA to find another way to dispose of it. The 1988 amendments to FIFRA modified this indemnification provision. Consequently, only farmers and other end users are now entitled to indemnification. Under certain extraordinary circumstances, Congress may make a specific line-item appropriation to reimburse a manufacturer or retailer. Otherwise, the retailer or other nonend user may seek reimbursement from the seller/manufacturer.

The seller/manufacturer may avoid this liability only by notifying the buyer in writing at the time of the sale that there will be no reimbursement.

Once a pesticide is suspended, the EPA must notify foreign governments through the State Department, providing them with reasons for cancellation and alternatives to the canceled pesticide. However, the pesticide can still be sold to foreigners, leading to one of the criticisms of FIFRA. There seems to be something problematic about saying that a pesticide is too harmful to be sold at home, yet it can be sold abroad. Even if there were no concern about exposure to others, many foreign growers are using those pesticides on crops that will eventually be exported to the United States. This so-called circle of poison is a major issue in environmental ethics today.

Change of Use Registration

If the EPA decides to change use registration, it must publish its intent to do so 45 days in advance in the *Federal Register*. The registrant may request a hearing. If a pesticide is classified for restricted use, the registrant may petition the EPA for a change any time. Before any pesticide to be used on a food or feed crop is registered, the EPA must follow one more step. The agency must establish a "tolerance" to pesticide residue. Both locally grown and imported crops are randomly tested to ensure that these tolerances are not exceeded.

Worker Protection Standard Program

In an attempt to reduce the number of pesticide-related illnesses and injuries, in 1992 the EPA established the Worker Protection Standard (WPS) program. The WPS program contains regulations protecting employees on farms, forests, nurseries, and greenhouses from exposure to agricultural pesticides. Examples of these requirements include protection during

---

WHAT IS A PESTICIDE?

All the following common products are considered pesticides:

- Cockroach sprays and baits
- Insect repellents for personal use
- Rat and other rodent poisons
- Flea and tick sprays, powders, and pet collars
- Kitchen, laundry, and bath disinfectants and sanitizers
- Products that kill mold and mildew
- Some lawn and garden products, such as weed killers
- Some swimming pool chemicals

Source: EPA, Office of Pesticide Programs. *http://www.epa.gov/opp00001/whatis.htm* (July 25, 2001).

pesticide application, use of personal protective equipment, and training for pesticide safety. One of these requirements explicitly states that protective eyewear and other simple safety measures would reduce substantially the number of pesticide-related illnesses and injuries. Violations of these requirements can lead to serious fines. In June 2003, the EPA issued an administrative complaint seeking the largest penalty ever proposed under the WPS program. In its case against David Petrocco Farms, Inc., EPA is proposing a civil penalty of $231,990 for 229 violations of FIFRA's WPS. The alleged violations included not centrally displaying pesticide safety, emergency, and application information for its workers in 2001 and, 1 year later, after having received a warning, still not correcting the problem.[25]

Enforcement

The EPA requires manufacturers to keep records showing the quantity sold, date of delivery, and recipient for all pesticides sold. On presentation of credentials and a written reason for inspection, including whether a violation is suspected, the manufacturer or retailer of pesticides must allow an inspection of its facility. Samples may also be taken following the same procedures. The inspection must be prompt, with a receipt given for samples taken.

If there is a violation of FIFRA, the EPA or state agriculture department must notify the defendant of the civil or criminal proceedings in writing, thereby giving that party an opportunity to be heard orally or in writing before the agency's filing charges.

For minor violations, when it is in the public interest, the EPA may simply give a written warning to the violator. A warning is likely to be used if the violation occurred despite due care and did not cause significant harm to the environment. A stop sale, use, or removal order may also be issued. Or a seizure order may be obtained in federal court. Civil penalties under FIFRA are up to $5,000 per violation by a registrant, wholesaler, distributor, or retailer and up to $1,000 per violation by private user/applicator. Factors the EPA uses to determine the penalty include a comparison of the size of the fine with the size of the business, the effect a fine would have on the violator's ability to stay in business, and the gravity of violation. A private user may use as a defense a guarantee from the seller that the pesticide is lawfully registered.

Criminal penalties may be imposed when there are knowing violations of the act. These fines are up to $25,000 for a firm and $1,000 for a user or applicator. Officials of the firm may also receive up to a 1-year jail sentence, and private users may be required to serve up to 30 days in jail. For example, in 1998, Lee Poole was sentenced to a 2-year prison term and payment of $2,189,000 in restitution for federal emergency cleanup costs.[26] Despite two previous enforcement actions taken against Poole for improper and unlicensed use of methyl parathion, Poole once again illegally sprayed methyl parathion in homes in February 1996. Furthermore, in 2000, Chempace Corporation of Toldeo, Ohio, was charged with 99 violations of FIRFA, which were primarily for the selling of unregistered pesticides. The case was ruled in favor of the EPA, and Chemspace was ordered to pay $92,193.[27] In 2003, Hing Mau, Inc., was fined $7,920 for selling a pesticide not registered with FIFRA, in violation of FIFRA. The product was immediately removed from the shelf. The penalty was small because the unregistered chemical, naphthalene, caused little harm to human health in the time that it was illegally sold from stores.[28]

FFDCA

The FFDCA aids in the regulation of pesticide use by requiring the administrator of the EPA to establish tolerance levels for concentrations of pesticide residues on commodities consumed in the United States. In establishing these limits, the administrator is to consider "the necessity for the production of an adequate, wholesome, and economic food supply." Tolerances are enforced by the FDA for most foods and by the USDA's Food Safety and Inspection Service (USDA/FSIS) for meat, poultry, and some egg products. Theoretically, violations will be caught by the EPA through inspections and by the FDA in its routine sampling program. A problem with relying on the FDA, however, is that less than 1 percent of fruits and vegetables are inspected. In addition, not all pesticides are tested for. Tests take an average of 28 days; by then, the food is often sold. The shipment from which a sample has been taken is supposed to be held; unfortunately, it rarely is.

The EPA is responsible for regulating all pesticide products, whereas the FDA is responsible for regulating food packaging. For some products, the EPA's role overlaps with the FDA's responsibilities to regulate food packaging. For example, new technology uses oils as an "insect repellent" within food packaging. In an attempt to streamline food-packaging regulations, in 1998 the EPA transferred regulatory authority for nonpesticidal components of food packaging to the EPA. Without this rule, the EPA would be required to evaluate each component of food packaging. However, with the rule, the EPA can focus on pesticidal components of packaging while the FDA regulates nonpesticidal components.[29]

FQPA

Numerous inconsistencies between FIFRA and FFDCA led to the passage of the FQPA in 1996. The FQPA, amending both major pesticide laws, established a more consistent, protective regulatory scheme. This act creates a single, health-based standard for all pesticide residues in food. Under the FQPA, the EPA must be able to conclude with "reasonable certainty that no harm will result from aggregate exposure to each pesticide from dietary and other sources." In addition, when reviewing existing or new tolerances, the FQPA requires the EPA to explicitly address risks to children and infants. The act also established a more favorable regulatory environment for the use of lower-risk chemicals in agriculture. Figure 7-2 shows the numbers for

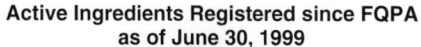

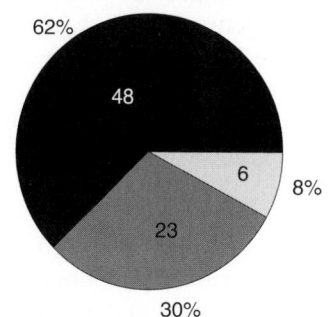

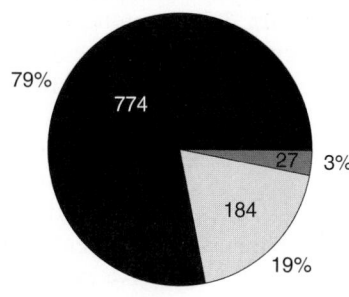

| Safer (Conventional Reduced Risk and Biopesticides) | Conventional | Antimicrobial |

FIGURE 7-2 Lowered Pesticides Risks because of FQPA

Note: Percentages may not add to 100 because of rounding.

Safer Active Ingredients: Active ingredients are the substances in a pesticide that prevent, destroy, repel, or mitigate a pest. Since FQPA was enacted, the EPA has registered 48 active ingredients that are considered "safer" than conventional pesticides, representing 62 percent of the total number of active ingredients registered.

Safer New Uses: "Uses" are the specific crop(s) or other site(s) where a pesticide product can be used. One active ingredient can have many different uses. Since FQPA was enacted, the EPA has approved 774 new uses that are considered "safer," representing 77 percent of the total new uses approved.

Source: EPA, Office of Prevention, Pesticides, and Toxic Substances. *Implementing the Food Quality Protection Act: Progress Report. http://www.epa.gov/oppfead1/fqpa/fqpareport.pdf* (February 5, 2001): 4.

new active ingredients and new uses registered since the passage of the FQPA. Of the new active ingredients, 62 percent are considered safer than conventional pesticides; of the new uses, 77 percent are considered safer than conventional uses. Furthermore, the act requires that by 2006, all existing tolerances be reviewed to ensure they meet the requirements of the new health-based standard. Through this reassessment process, in 1998 the EPA investigated 1,400 tolerances and revoked 874 tolerances for pesticide residues.[30] In 2000, the reassessment process for chlorpyrifos, commonly known as Dursban, resulted in an agreement between the EPA and Dursban's manufacturer to stop production of the chemical for home, lawn, garden, and termite uses and to significantly lower the pesticide residues on foods eaten by children, including grapes, tomatoes, and apples. Later that same year, diazinon, another pesticide from the organophosphate family, had its use severely restricted. Uses of diazinon indoors will be completely eliminated, but use will be retained for approximately 40 crops. Both these restrictions resulted from the stricter regulatory scheme of the FQPA.

Finally, under FQPA, pesticides must now be tested for endocrine disruption potential. Endocrine disruptors are certain chemicals that may modify (slightly or severely) the functioning of human and wildlife hormone systems. Thus, endocrine disruptors have the potential to cause problems with development, behavior, and reproduction. The lack of data showing effects of endocrine disruptors on humans led Congress to request that the EPA develop a way to test chemicals for endocrine disruption potential. Conventional tests looking for chemical toxicity "may be inadequate to determine whether these substances interact with specific components of the endocrine system." In August 2000, the EPA issued its Report to Congress on the Endocrine Disruptor Screening Program.[31] This report detailed the different screening tests the EPA is planning to use to determine whether a substance may cause hormonal problems in humans. Validation for the use of these tests began in 2001, and in September 2005, the EPA set forth the procedures based on levels of human exposure that would be used to select the first 50–100 chemicals to be tested.[32]

PESTICIDE ENVIRONMENTAL STEWARDSHIP PROGRAM

As explained in Chapter 4, the EPA attempts to find ways to encourage voluntary actions that improve environmental quality. One such approach to controlling the risk associated with pesticides is the PESP. The voluntary program was developed in 1994 by the EPA, USDA, and FDA as a means toward pesticide risk reduction through improvement in the use of existing conventional pesticides as well as research into alternatives, technologies, and practices that reduce the pesticide risk to both humans and the environment. Grants are made available to research and develop methods adoptable by both agricultural and nonagricultural users of pesticides. For example, natural compounds, such as fine clays, have been found to control pests without harming the environment. Participants, or partners, in the program are asked to develop a strategic approach focusing on long-term goals, and the EPA provides a liaison to assist in achieving those goals. In 2003, the EPA reported that 79 percent of strategies involve reducing overall pesticide use and 70 percent adopt the use of reduced-risk alternatives to conventional pesticides.[33]

PROGRESS UNDER THE ACTS

The EPA believes that progress in reducing risk from pesticides has been considerable. Since the enactment of FIFRA, registrations of 34 potentially hazardous pesticides have been canceled, and 60 toxic inert ingredients have been eliminated from use. Levels of persistent pesticides in humans have declined significantly. A National Pesticide Telecommunications Network has been established. By calling the network's toll-free number (800-858-PEST), you can obtain general information about the use and disposal of pesticides and how to recognize and manage pesticide poisoning.

Not everyone is convinced that pesticide regulation is as effective as it could be, however. Increasingly, FIFRA is coming under fire for one of the protections it offers pesticide manufacturers. Under FIFRA, manufacturers do not have to list on their labels the specific inert ingredients, those ingredients that function only to preserve the active, pest-killing ingredients or make them easier to apply. All they have to cite is the broad-term inert ingredients and the percentage of the total ingredients made up of inert ingredients. This incomplete labeling provides confidentiality for manufacturers to make it more difficult for competitors to discover their formulas.

The problem with confidentiality protection is that many of the inert ingredients are among the most toxic substances, including phenol, toluene, and chlorobenzene, and all have been linked to birth defects, liver and kidney damage, or nervous system disorders. Others are suspected carcinogens. The consumer who buys these pesticides for home and garden use has no way to find out what these inert ingredients are because the EPA is required to keep them confidential. This confidentiality requirement is particularly troublesome because in many instances the inert ingredients constitute 80 to 90 percent of the total ingredients.

However, in response to the growing concern about inert ingredients, the EPA began to investigate these ingredients in 1997. The OPPT's Structure Activity Team has evaluated 1,700 chemicals used as inert ingredients in pesticide formulations, and these evaluations will be used to help support reclassification determinations.[34]

INTERNATIONAL REGULATION OF TOXIC SUBSTANCES

As noted earlier in this chapter, use of chemicals and pesticides has increased dramatically over the past 50 years. Strict regulation of pesticides and other chemicals in the United States and other industrialized nations has often resulted in banned or severely restricted chemicals being exported to developing nations, which generally lack the infrastructure to use these chemicals in any sort of safe manner. Tales are often told of farmers spraying DDT without protective gear or of young children being poisoned because their parents neglected to put pesticides out of the child's reach. A common theme in the use of pesticides by developing countries is that these countries often do not know when a chemical has been banned from use.

Because the exportation of banned pesticides results in a large potential risk, not only for the importing country, but also for the world, the United Nations and the Food and Agriculture Organization (UN/FAO) jointly worked to create a voluntary "right to know" procedure, implemented in 1989. This voluntary procedure involved three simple steps. A country acting to ban a pesticide would report such a ban to the UN/FAO. The UN/FAO would then report to importers of this product that the product has been restricted or banned. The importing nation notifies the UN/FAO of its intent either to cease or to continue receiving the product. Should the importing country wish to stop using the product, the UN/FAO ensures that such a product is not imported to the country.

ROTTERDAM CONVENTION

As international environmental concern continued to grow, countries met in 1992 for the Rio Summit, explained in further detail in Chapter 11. At the summit, many countries adopted Agenda 21, the 19th chapter of which called for the development of a legally binding version of the voluntary "right to know" procedure. Thus, the FAO and the UNEP began negotiations of such an instrument, with the conclusion and signing of the treaty in 1998. This treaty, known as the Rotterdam Convention on the Prior Informed Consent Procedure for Certain Hazardous Chemicals and Pesticides in International Trade, or simply PIC, creates such a legally binding instrument by requiring parties to report their banned chemicals to the PIC Secretariat, which then performs similar functions to those performed by the UN/FAO under the voluntary procedure.

In addition to advising the Secretariat, however, PIC parties must also provide export notification, one of the strongest aspects of the treaty. When a chemical is banned or severely restricted in the exporting country (and is not already listed as a chemical subject to the PIC), the exporter must notify the importing country of this decision before the first export made after the final banning act. The chemical or pesticide may not be exported until the importing country indicates its receipt of the export notification and specifies a desire to continue receiving the product. PIC also creates labeling criteria for exporting parties of banned or severely restricted products. Labels on banned or severely restricted chemicals and pesticides must indicate the risks to human health and to the environment. For chemicals and pesticides intended for occupational use, a safety data sheet must be included. A country may voluntarily choose to label as risky those chemicals and pesticides that it exports but that are not banned or severely restricted in the home country. As discussed above, the United States already has an export notification procedure for pesticides banned under FIFRA; the EPA must notify foreign governments of the abolishment of the pesticide. PIC requires such a procedure of all parties and requires that importing countries indicate their desire to continue to receive shipments, a step forward in international trade in pesticides.

PIC currently includes 24 banned pesticides, 6 severely restricted pesticides, and 11 industrial chemicals; however, more pesticides and chemicals are expected to be evaluated and added to the list of restrictions.[35] As of November 2003, 73 countries had signed the convention and 51 had ratified it.[36] Having received the 50th ratification, the treaty went into effect on February 24, 2004. Although the United States has not yet ratified PIC, its ratification would not prove really have any significant consequences for the United States because U.S. requirements are already stricter than those of the treaty. Another international convention aimed at protecting the environment from toxic and hazardous chemicals is the Basel Convention on the Control of Transboundary Movements of Hazardous Waste and Their Disposal. This convention, entering into force in 1992, seeks to minimize the generation of hazardous waste and to reduce the movement of hazardous waste by disposing of the waste near the source. This important convention is discussed in greater detail in Chapter 11.

REGISTRATION, EVALUATION, AND AUTHORIZATION OF CHEMICALS

Treaties are not the only international source of environmental protection. In 2007, Americans received additional protection from exposure to toxic chemicals not because of anything the United States' government did but because of the passage by the European Union Parliament of the world's most stringent law aimed at protecting citizens from toxic chemicals. The law protects American consumers because it applies to chemicals used in products sold in the European Union, and because so many American companies' products are also exported to the European Union, the companies will be forced to comply with the new standards, so their products can continue to be both sold in the United States and exported.

The new legislation, called REACH or Registration, Evaluation, and Authorization of Chemicals, will force industries to register and submit health and safety data for approximately 30,000 toxic chemical substances and replace the most hazardous ones with safer alternatives. Approximately 1,500 of the most hazardous ones may be banned or restricted, including some compounds used in electronics, furniture, toys, cosmetics, and other everyday items.

The law became effective in June and be phased in over 11 years. The new program will be overseen by a new central regulatory authority, the European Chemicals Agency, based in Helsinki, Finland.

TOXIC TORTS

Increasingly, common-law tort cases are being used to seek compensation for persons injured or killed because of exposure to toxic substances. A wide variety of theories are used to seek recovery in such cases; the most common are negligence and strict product liability. Often, these cases are referred to as toxic torts, regardless of which theory of liability is being used. In most cases, a plaintiff will bring an action attempting to prove both these theories of liability. This approach is reasonable because this area of the law is very unclear, and it is often difficult to know which theory one will be able to prove.

THEORIES OF RECOVERY

Negligence

To prove a cause of action based on negligence, the plaintiff must prove the following: that the defendant owed a duty of care to the plaintiff, that the defendant failed to meet this duty of care, that this failure to meet the duty of care caused the injury to the plaintiff, and that the plaintiff did indeed incur a compensable injury. The duty of care that a manufacturer generally has is a duty not to expose others to an unreasonable risk of harm. This duty may entail such specific actions as properly testing chemical substances for their potentially harmful effects. In many toxic tort cases, the duty that the defendant is alleged to have failed to live up to is a duty to warn the plaintiff of known or knowable dangers resulting from specific uses of the product.

A typical explanation of what a plaintiff needs to demonstrate in a toxic tort case can be seen in a Maryland judge's statement of what the plaintiffs had to prove in the 1984 case of *Chevron Chemical Company v. Ferebee.*[37] Ferebee had been exposed on numerous occasions over a 3-year period to the pesticide paraquat, manufactured by the Chevron Corporation. Ten months after his last exposure, he developed severe lung fibrosis. During the course of the trial, he died, leaving his family to carry on the lawsuit.

In explaining why he found in the plaintiff's favor, the judge said that the plaintiff had the burden of proving, by a preponderance of the evidence, the following elements:

1. That paraquat proximately caused Ferebee's illness and death
2. That paraquat is inherently dangerous
3. That Chevron knew, or should have known, at the time it sold paraquat, used by Ferebee, that the chemical was inherently dangerous
4. That the resulting duty to provide an adequate warning of the danger was not met
5. That the inadequacy of the warning proximately caused Ferebee's illness and death

Strict Product Liability

A special form of strict liability, strict product liability, is most often applicable in cases involving consumers injured by products containing toxic substances. Strict liability, as a general theory of tort liability, requires the plaintiff to demonstrate that the defendant was engaged in an abnormally dangerous activity that caused the plaintiff's harm. The Restatement (Second) of Torts, Section 402A, sets out the theory of strict product liability as follows:

1. One who sells any product in a defective condition, unreasonably dangerous, to the user or consumer or to his property, is subject to liability for the physical harm thereby caused to the ultimate user or consumer or to his property, if
   a. the seller is engaged in the business of selling such a product, and
   b. it is expected to reach the consumer without substantial change in the condition in which it is sold.

2. The rule stated in Subsection (1) applies although

   a. the seller has exercised all possible care in the preparation and sale of his product, and

   b. the user or consumer has not bought the product from or entered into any contractual relation with the seller.

When looking at the definition of strict product liability, one might naturally ask, "When does a defective condition become 'unreasonably dangerous'?" Because tort law is state law, the precise definition varies from state to state, but most courts rely on one of two tests. The first is the "consumer expectations" test. If a product is more dangerous than the reasonable consumer would expect it to be, then it is unreasonably dangerous. The second test is the feasible alternative test. The court asks whether there was some other, less dangerous, reasonably feasible alternative available, but the manufacturer chose not to use it. When applying this test, the manufacturer looks at such factors as the utility of the product, the availability of substitutes, the obviousness of the danger, the role a warning label could have played, the avoidability of danger with careful use, and the viability of eliminating the danger without impairing the usefulness of the product. For example, a knife is dangerous, but it would not be considered unreasonably dangerous to the consumer who got cut using it because the danger is obvious, and the utility would be lost by eliminating the danger.

PROBLEMS IN ESTABLISHING CAUSATION

Regardless of the theory of liability used, the plaintiff must establish that the defendant's conduct caused the plaintiff harm. Proof of causation in toxic tort cases is extremely difficult, for a number of reasons. First, it may be difficult to prove that the chemical in question causes the harm that has resulted, usually cancer, leukemia, or birth defects. Medical science cannot fully explain the causes of many of these diseases. Often, there are multiple causative factors. Animal studies may be used, but these usually involve higher doses than those received by the plaintiff. Then the issue may also be raised of whether one can extrapolate between species. Epidemiological studies may be used, but these are often unavailable or considered inconclusive.

A few courts have even allowed causation to be proved without statistical evidence. In *Chevron Chemical Company v. Ferebee,* the appellate judges upheld a jury verdict for which the evidence for causation came solely from the testimony of two expert medical witnesses who based their conclusions about causation on their examination of the victim. The court stated that "as long as the basic methodology employed to reach a conclusion is sound, such as the use of tissue samples, standard tests, and patient examination, product liability law does not preclude recovery until a 'statistically significant' number of people have been injured or until science has had the time and resources to complete sophisticated laboratory studies of the chemical." Not all courts, however, have been equally liberal.

Even if the plaintiff establishes a link between the chemical and the harm, it may still be difficult to demonstrate that the particular exposure to the defendant's chemical caused the plaintiff's specific injury, especially when there are a number of factors that could have caused the plaintiff harm. For example, asbestos may cause lung disease, but what if the victim is also a chain smoker?

The problems associated with establishing causation in toxic tort cases are discussed in great detail in a district court opinion in the case of *Allen v. United States,*[38] a case that arose from the federal government's bomb testing at a Nevada test site between 1951 and 1953. Plaintiffs, all of whom had resided in southern Utah, northern Arizona, and southeast Nevada, claimed to have suffered leukemia or cancer because of exposure to radioactive fall-out from the bomb tests. Plaintiffs alleged that the government was negligent in conducting the open-air testing, failing to monitor the results, failing to warn people who were in danger of the hazards, and failing to inform such persons of what they could do to minimize their risk from the testing.

In addressing the difficulty of proving that the defendant's action definitely caused the harm, the court stated that if the plaintiff could not establish a cause-in-fact connection, the plaintiff should attempt to establish the most exclusive factual connection between the injury and the defendant. If the defendant's conduct can be found to be a "substantial factor," it may then be judged to be a legal cause. With respect to the particular facts of the case before it, the judge wrote:

> Where a defendant who negligently creates a radiological hazard which puts an identifiable population group at increased risk, and a member of that group at risk develops a biological condition which is consistent with having been caused by the hazard to which he has been negligently subjected, such consistency having been demonstrated by substantial, appropriate, persuasive, and connecting factors, a fact finder may reasonably conclude that the hazard caused the condition, absent persuasive proof to the contrary offered by the defendant.

The judge went on to quote from the Restatement (Second) of Torts, § 433, as to what factors would be relevant:

> The following considerations are in themselves or in combination with one another important in determining whether the actor's conduct is a substantial factor in bringing about harm to another: (a) the number of other factors which contribute in producing the harm and the extent of the effect which they have in producing it, (b) whether the actor's conduct has created a force or series of forces which are in continuous and active operation up to the time of the harm, or has created a situation harmless unless acted upon by other forces for which the actor is not responsible, and (c) lapse of time.

The court then went on to discuss the problems related to the use of statistics to demonstrate a causal link, saying that in a case in which a plaintiff tries to establish a factual connection between a particular "cause" and a delayed, nonspecific effect, such as cancer or leukemia, the strongest evidence of the relationship is likely to be statistical in form.

> Where the injuries are causally indistinguishable, and where experts cannot determine whether an individual injury results from culpable human cause or nonculpable natural causes, evidence that there is an increased incidence of injury in a population following exposure to a defendant's risk-creating conduct may justify an inference of causal linkage between the defendant's conduct and the plaintiff's injuries . . . whenever there is an increase of observed cases of a particular cancer or leukemia over the number statistically expected to normally appear, the question arises whether it may be rationally inferred that the increase is causally connected to the specific human activity.

The court then went on to describe the scientists' use of the concept of statistical significance, by which they generally mean that the odds of the event occurring because of random chance are equal to or less than one in 20; some researchers use an even more stringent standard of one in 100 or less. The court was highly critical of the statisticians' requirement of 95 percent probability and added that the problems of this stringent requirement are exacerbated when the exposed population is fairly small, as is the case with most toxic exposures. The court said that statistical evidence, when combined with other evidence, could "supply a useful link in the process of proof." In discussing the evidence, "the value of the available statistical data concerning radiation and cancer in offsite communities is not confined by arbitrary tests of 'statistical significance'." The court said that whether causal inferences should be drawn that will carry the case to the additional issues of risk, scope of duty, and culpable breach of duty (e.g., negligence) is a question of judgment resting in part on policy. The court must determine those risks for which the defendant should be held responsible. Thus, the courts are not going to define causation as rigorously as the scientist might, but they cannot clearly articulate the lesser standard of proof they will require.

ENTERPRISE LIABILITY

An additional problem that sometimes arises in toxic tort cases occurs when the exposure was several years before the injury and the toxin was produced by multiple manufacturers. Because of the time lapse, the plaintiff is unable to identify exactly which manufacturer produced the substance to which he or she was exposed. Because of the requirement of establishing the link between the defendant's action and the plaintiff's injury, this lack of knowledge might at first appear to be an insurmountable obstacle. However, some courts thought that to leave a plaintiff in a situation like this would be unfair. So, in the case of *Sindell v. Abbott Laboratories,*[39] the court fashioned the concept of enterprise, or market share, liability, whereby a manufacturer that produced a defective product that was sold interchangeably with other brands of the same product could be held responsible for that percentage of the plaintiff's injuries proportionate to the market share the defendant had at the time of the plaintiff's exposure to the product.

In the Sindell case, the plaintiffs' mothers had taken DES (diethylstilbestrol) during pregnancies that had occurred before the drug was banned. The drug caused cancer and other side effects in the plaintiffs. The 11 defendants had collaborated in testing, promoting, and marketing the drug, and none of the plaintiffs could identify the specific manufacturer of the drugs their mothers had taken, to a large extent because doctors prescribed the drugs generically and pharmacists filled prescriptions with whichever brands they had on hand.

The court said, in setting out the novel market share theory:

> In our contemporary complex industrialized society, advances in science and technology create fungible goods which may harm consumers and which cannot be traced to any specific producer. The response of the courts can be either to adhere rigidly to prior doctrine, denying recovery to those injured by such products, or to fashion remedies to meet these changing needs. . . .
>
> The most persuasive reason for finding that the plaintiff states a cause of action is . . . as between an innocent plaintiff and negligent defendants, the latter should bear the cost of the injury. . . .
>
> From a broader policy standpoint, defendants are better able to bear the cost of injury resulting from the manufacture of a defective product.

Thus, the courts removed a potential hurdle that could arise in many toxic tort cases because of the latency of many effects.

PUNITIVE DAMAGES

In most toxic tort cases, regardless of the theory of liability on which the action is based, the primary goal of the plaintiff is to recover compensatory damages, damages designed to place the plaintiff in the position he or she would have been in if the tort never occurred. Such damages include payment for doctor bills, lost wages, property damages, and pain and suffering. In addition, plaintiffs may also seek punitive damages when the defendant's conduct may be described as "willful and wanton" or "extremely egregious." Punitive damages are designed, as their name implies, to punish the defendant for his or her wrongful conduct and to provide a strong deterrent to others who might consider engaging in similar activities. In the toxic tort area, punitive damages may also serve to provide an incentive to encourage private citizens to sue to ensure compliance with environmental regulations.

To meet the goals of deterrence and punishment, the amount of punitive damages awarded in tort cases is based primarily on the wrongfulness of the defendant's act and the resources of the defendant. The more egregious the act, the more substantial is the award. The more resources the defendant has, the more substantial the award must be for it to have any punitive effect.

In recent toxic tort cases, defendants have tried to argue that punitive damages should not be awarded in cases in which a substantial number of potential plaintiffs have been harmed or when the tort occurred in the distant past. Probably the most well-publicized case is *Fischer v. Johns–Manville Corporation*.[40] The trial court awarded Fischer punitive damages based on an exposure to asbestos that had occurred 40 years before the lawsuit. The defendant, on appeal, raised several arguments as to why punitive damages were inappropriate. First, the defendant argued that the remoteness of the claim made the award unfair because at the time the conduct occurred, different social values might have made the conduct less egregious than the same conduct would appear today. The court dismissed that argument, finding that Johns–Manville's conduct, "knowingly and deliberately" subjected the plaintiff and other asbestos workers to serious health hazards with utter disregard for their safety and wellbeing, would have been regarded as equally egregious back then.

The defendant then argued that different officers and managers committed the tort, so punishing the corporation today was unfair. The court likewise did not buy this argument, pointing out that although the officers and managers may have changed, Johns–Manville was the same corporate entity. Officers and managers are merely agents of the corporation. Besides, a goal of punitive damages is general deterrence, which will still be accomplished regardless of who is in command.

The court also did not accept the argument that punitive damages were unfair to innocent shareholders. After all, the shareholders benefited from the misconduct in the past, so it was only fair that they now share in the associated losses. Finally, the argument that mass punitive damages could lead to a corporation's inability to pay later claimants because the firm would have lost all its assets caused slightly more concern on the part of the court. However, the court did not believe this potential problem was insurmountable. First, a defendant could introduce evidence at trial of having paid large punitive damage awards in previous cases so that the jury could take those payments into account when deciding whether to assess punitive damages. Second, if any punitive damage award were so high as to make financial disaster imminent, the defendant could file a motion for remittitur, which is a request for damages to be reduced.

Thus, it appears that if a plaintiff can overcome the tremendous burden of proving causation, recovery of punitive damages in toxic tort cases is possible. This threat of potentially unlimited punitive damage awards may provide some incentive for makers of potentially toxic chemicals to test their products more carefully.

Concluding Remarks

The federal regulatory scheme has been designed both to remove existing toxins from the market and to prevent the introduction of new toxins into commerce. Private law also plays a part in regulating toxins. If someone has been harmed by a toxic chemical, he or she can file a toxic tort case, based on either negligence or strict liability. Recovery through such an action will be difficult, although not impossible.

This chapter has focused on toxic chemicals in commerce. We now turn to an examination of toxics in another form—waste—in Chapter 8.

Questions for Review and Discussion

1. Explain the process of risk assessment.
2. Explain the statutory scheme for the regulation of existing toxic chemicals.
3. Evaluate the criticisms that might be made of TSCA's regulation of new chemicals.
4. List the criteria for registration of a pesticide under FIFRA.
5. Explain why general-use registration is superior to restricted-use registration.
6. Explain how and when a pesticide's registration may be canceled.
7. Explain two theories of liability on which a plaintiff exposed to a toxic substance might base a lawsuit.
8. What is the rationale for allowing a private party to recover punitive damages in a toxic tort case?

For Further Reading

Block, Alan, and Frank Scarpitti. 1985. *Poisoning for Profit.* New York: William Morrow.

Brennan, Troyen A. 1988. "Causal Chains and Statistical Links: The Role of Scientific Uncertainty in Ultrahazardous Substance Litigation." *Cornell Law Review* 73: 469.

Brodeur, Paul. 1985. *Outrageous Misconduct: The Asbestos Industry on Trial.* New York: Pantheon Books.

Brown, Michael. 1987. *The Toxic Cloud.* New York: Harper & Row.

Craner, Carl F. 1993. *Regulating Toxic Substances: A Philosophy of Science and the Law (Environmental Ethics and Science Policy Series).* New York: Oxford University Press, Inc.

Cross, Frank B. 1997. "The Consequences of Consensus: Dangerous Compromises of the Food Quality Protection Act." *Washington University Law Quarterly* 72: 1155.

Farber, Daniel A. 1987. "Toxic Causation." *Minnesota Law Review* 71: 1219.

(Note) 1986. "Toxic Tort Litigation and the Causation Element: Is There Any Hope of Reconciliation?" *Southwestern Law Journal* 40: 909.

Love, Dennis. 2006. *My City Was Gone.* New York: Harper-Collins.

Pretty, Jules. 2005. *The Pesticide Detox: Towards a More Sustainable Agricultural.* London: Earthscan.

Rahm, Dianne. 2002. *Toxic Waste and Environmental Policy in the 21st Century United States.* North Carolina: McFarland & Co.

Winston, Mark. 1997. *Nature Wars: People vs. Pests.* Cambridge: Harvard University Press.

On the Internet

http://cfpub.epa.gov/ncea/cfm/nceawhatnew.cfm
What's new at the National Center for Environmental Assessment
http://www.epa.gov/opprd001/registrationkit
Contains forms and information necessary to register a pesticide
http://www.epa.gov/oppt/pubs/opptabt.htm
Office of Pollution Prevention and Toxics
http://books.nap.edu/books/0309071402/html/index.html
Toxicological Effects of Methyl Mercury—Report tracing the risk assessment process for methyl mercury
http://www.epa.gov/opptintr/labeling/pubs/campaign.htm
EPA's Read the Label FIRST! Campaign
http://scorecard.org/
Displays toxic releases from industrial facilities in your area
http://www.epa.gov/tri/
EPA's Toxic Release Inventory (TRI) Program
http://www.nrdc.org/health/pesticides/default.asp
Contains studies on the effects of pesticides and reports on government pesticide regulation

Notes

1. Sandra Postel. 1987. "Diffusing the Toxics Threat: Controlling Pesticides and Industrial Waste." *Worldwatch Paper 79* (Worldwatch Institute): 5.
2. 541 F.2d 1 (D.C. Cir. 1976) (en banc).
3. 647 F.2d 1130 (D.C. Cir. 1980).
4. 824 F.2d 1146 (D.C. Cir. 1987).
5. Joseph V. Rodricks. 1992. *Calculated Risks: Understanding the Toxicity and Human Health Risks of Chemicals in* *Our Environment.* Cambridge: Cambridge University Press.
6. Postel, "Diffusing the Toxics Threat," 7.
7. Ibid.
8. Ibid., 8.
9. United Nations Environment Programme. 2004. *The Environment in the News. http://www.unep.org/cpi/ briefs/Brief25Feb04.doc* (September 10, 2006).

10. EPA, Office of Pesticide Programs. *The EPA and Food Security.* http://www.epa.gov/pesticides/citizens/securty.htm (July 25, 2001).

11. *EPA. 2000–2001 Pesticide Market Estimates.* http://www.epa.gov/oppbead1/pestsales/01pestsales/ (July 11, 2006).

12. Ibid.

13. Lynn Goldman. 1998. "Chemicals and Children's Environment: What We Don't Know About Risks." *Environmental Health Perspectives 106* (Suppl 3).

14. United Press International. "Commercial Chemicals Safety Unknown." (August 2006) http://www.upi.com/ConsumerHealthDaily/view.php?StoryID=20060808-034510-1446r (September 14, 2006).

15. EPA. *Office of Pollution Prevention and Toxics Annual Report, FY 2002 (January 2003).* http://www.epa.gov/oppt/ar02/progress02a2.pdf (July 11, 2006): 7.

16. "Safety-Kleen Objects to EPA Fine." *Chicago Tribune* (August 10, 1996): N1.

17. "Futura Pleads Guilty." *Chemical Week* (February 5, 1997): 54.

18. EPA. *Civil Enforcement.* http://www.epa.gov/compliance/resources/cases/civil/mm/transco.html (December 8, 2003).

19. EPA. *2001–2001 Pesticide Market Estimates: Usage.* http://www.epa.gov/oppbead1/pestsales/01pestsales/usage2001.html (July 11, 2006).

20. "Biotech and Pesticide Use." *Multinational Monitor* (December 2003), 4.

21. EPA. *Office of Pesticide Programs Biennial Report for FY 1998 and 1999 (December 1999).* http://www.epa.gov/oppfead1/annual/98-99/98-99annual.pdf (December 6, 2000): 11.

22. EPA. *Promoting Safety for America's Future, Office of Pesticide Programs, FY 2004 Annual Report.* http://www.epa.gov/oppfead1/annual/2002/2002annualreport.pdf (December 7, 2003), 31.

23. EPA, Office of Prevention, Pesticides, and Toxic Substances. *Fact Sheet: Consumer Labeling Initiative.* http://www.epa.gov/opptintr/labeling/factsht.pdf (December 6, 2000).

24. EPA, Office of Pesticide Programs. *Status of Pesticides in Registration, Reregistration, and Special Review (Rainbow Report)* (Spring 1998), 63.

25. EPA Cites Five Colorado Growers for Failure to Comply with Agricultural Worker Regulations. http://www.pestlaw.com/x/press/2003/OPP-20030605B.html (December 12, 2003).

26. "Criminal Prosecutions: Sentences." *National Environmental Enforcement Journal* (December 1997–January 1998).

27. EPA. 2000. *Chemspace Corporation.* http://www.epa.gov/eab/disk11/chempace.pdf (September 10, 2006).

28. http://www.epa.gov/aljhomep/orders/hingmau7-id.pdf (December 7, 2003).

29. EPA. 1999. *Pesticide Program Highlights from FY 1998.* Washington, D.C.: Government Printing Office.

30. EPA. *Office of Pollution Prevention and Toxics Annual Report.*

31. EPA. *EDSP Chronology.* http://w9w.epa.gov/scipoly/oscpendo/reporttocongress0800 (September 10, 2006).

32. EPA. *Endocrine Disruptor Screening Program: Report to Congress.* http://www.epa.gov/scipoly/oscpendo/reporttocongress0800.pdf (July 25, 2001).

33. EPA. *Promoting Safety for America's Future, Office of Pesticide Programs, FY 2002 Annual Report.*

http://www.epa.gov/oppbppd1/PESP/ strategies/strategy_intro.htm (December 7, 2003), 39.

34. EPA, Office of Pesticide Programs. "EPA, and FDA Streamline Food Packaging Regulations." *http://www. epa.gov/pesticides/citizens/foodfyi.htm* (March 1998).

35. PIC. "Test of the Convention" (September 2004). *http://www.pic.int/*

en/ViewPage.asp?id=104#III%20 Annex (September 10, 2006).

36. PIC. "Signatures and Ratification" (February 2004). *http://www.pic.int* (July 11, 2006).

37. 736 F.2d 1529 (D.C. Cir. 1984).

38. 588 F.Supp. 247 (D. Ct. Utah 1984).

39. 26 Cal.3d 588, 607 P.2d 924 (1980).

40. 103 N.J. 643, 518 A.2d 466 (1986).

RESOLVING CONTROVERSIAL ENVIRONMENTAL ISSUES

- In the following essay, what evidence does the author offer in an attempt to persuade you? Evaluate the worth of that evidence.

- Authors often leave out important information from their arguments. There are many reasons why someone might omit information from an article. For example, the author might be limited by the space allotted for the article. Time constraints also lead to missing information. However, sometimes an author might intentionally leave out information. In any case, missing information will often influence your decision to accept or reject an author's conclusion. Thus, you should ask questions that will help you think about counterarguments. If someone disagrees with the author's argument, what reasons and evidence does that person offer? Does the author think about any counterarguments? You might also want to ask a question about the short-term and long-term omitted effects of the conclusion advocated or opposed. Now you can try to identify missing information yourself.

EPA Too Cautious With Pesticides

The FQPA directs the EPA to consider pesticide exposures of infants and children. The EPA is supposed to identify cases in which children are more sensitive than adults. Furthermore, under the FQPA, the EPA must reevaluate its past decisions about pesticides in food. Although the FQPA seems like a good idea, we should be concerned about the implementation of the FQPA. The EPA is simply being too cautious. Why?

The EPA is exaggerating the risks associated with pesticides instead of using scientific data. The EPA is simply doing a lot of guesswork. Their guessing has resulted in the EPA's consideration of the removal of many pesticides from the market.

Although I understand that the EPA's overall interest is in protecting human health, they are making conservative assumptions that provide us with an enormous margin of safety. For example, the EPA may determine that a pesticide used on peaches is unsafe because they assume that a grower is using the highest level of pesticide possible, the pesticide residues are the highest possible, and the consumer eats several peaches a day for 25 years. Clearly, consumers are not going to eat several peaches a day for 25 years! The EPA is simply exaggerating the risks. Analyses conducted by various researchers have demonstrated that residue levels in humans are extremely low.

What are the consequences of exaggerating the risks associated with pesticides? The EPA makes regulatory decisions regarding the use of pesticides. Using exaggerated risks to make decisions can force growers to stop using effective pesticides. The use of less-effective pesticide products could increase. Workers applying the product could face greater health risks. Pests would develop greater resistance to the less-effective products. Consequently, food quality and production will be decreased.

The EPA simply needs to make realistic assumptions regarding pesticides. Because they are being overly cautious, our food supply will likely suffer.

CHAPTER 8
WASTE MANAGEMENT AND HAZARDOUS RELEASES

Chemicals and other agents that exhibit hazardous properties are widely used throughout modern society. As discussed earlier, regulatory programs are in place governing the introduction of these agents into commerce (in particular, see Chapter 7). However, these regulatory programs are not sufficient to ensure that chemicals are used or disposed of properly. Thus, major regulatory programs have emerged to maximize resource use, manage resulting hazardous and non-hazardous wastes, and provide remedies when hazardous wastes are released into the environment in inappropriate ways. These programs contribute to both prevention and response-encouraging proper management but providing remedies for the inevitable failures of management systems.

In 1976, the U.S. Congress adopted the Resource Conservation and Recovery Act (RCRA). For the first time, the federal government was actively taking responsibility for promoting the proper disposal of hazardous and non-hazardous wastes and the recovery and reuse of wastes as resources. However, as with other environmental management strategies, progress has been slow. Today, we still have unresolved questions of how to implement reasonable waste management (not just disposal) strategies that are economically and technologically feasible yet fully protect human health and the environment.

Major federal efforts governing release prevention and remediation of hazardous material releases did not start until 1980 with the passage of the Comprehensive Environmental Response, Compensation, and Liability Act (CERCLA). CERCLA provides a complex regulatory system dealing with a continuum of activities ranging from spill prevention through final cleanup of contaminated sites.

This chapter proceeds chronologically, first discussing waste control and RCRA, and then proceeding through CERCLA and hazardous material management. Throughout this chapter, consider that a regulatory distinction often is made between hazardous wastes and hazardous materials. Remember that this distinction is not clear and that the regulatory structures often overlap.

WASTE CONTROL TECHNIQUES

When you throw something away, where is "away"? In the United States, away often means putting it in the ground (in a landfill), where it is stored indefinitely. However, using landfills as the primary waste management tool has many disadvantages. Waste entering a landfill may be, or become, hazardous and migrate from the site to the groundwater, surface water, or air. Material placed in landfills as waste probably has lost its potential use as a resource (although there is some interest in mining landfills to recover heavy metals and other resources). Furthermore, people do not want landfills in their neighborhoods. Landfills typically decrease property values and are perceived of as a threat to health and quality of life. As the amount of waste increases and available open space decreases, it becomes increasingly difficult to find acceptable sites for landfill development.

Rather than throwing waste in the ground (which often minimizes short-term costs to the generator), it is better to prevent it from being generated (which often minimizes long-term costs to society). Reducing waste generation at its source (source reduction) is the highest priority in the EPA's waste management strategy. When practical, the best strategy to manage waste is never to produce it. After production, reuse of the material is the preferred management strategy. Taking an old computer (perhaps too slow or memory limited to meet industrial needs) and giving it to an elementary school (where only simple programs are used) provides an excellent example of reuse solving a waste problem.

Recycling also can be an effective management tool, although it is less preferable than source reduction or reuse. Recycling typically is a reprocessing of a waste product to recover its inherent resource value. For example, recycling of aluminum cans entails recovering the aluminum to manufacture new cans. Not only does this keep aluminum cans out of landfills, but it reduces the need to mine for new aluminum. Keep in mind that recycling usually (although not always) requires more energy and other resources than reuse. Refilling (reusing) plastic detergent bottles is a more environmentally friendly activity than recycling them, although it is rarely done (at least in the United States). The municipal waste management systems in the United States tend to focus more on recycling than on reuse or waste reduction. In contrast, some interesting governmental requirements in parts of Europe promote reduction and reuse—it will be important to monitor and evaluate the success of these programs compared with U.S. recycling programs.

Various methods are available to change waste into less hazardous forms, reduce it in quantity, or otherwise cause desirable transformations. For example, non-toxic organic waste may be degraded biologically. This can take forms such as reapplying yard waste to land as compost. An example dealing with hazardous waste would be an acidic waste that is neutralized and transformed into waste without hazard potential. Waste transformation can reduce the quantity or hazardous characteristics of the waste, and sometimes both.

Resource recovery also can take the form of incineration, in which some of the potential energy of a waste can be captured as heat or transformed into electricity. However, this form of resource recovery has less potential to fully maximize the resource value than a reprocessing (recycling) process. Often the goal of incineration is limited to waste destruction (particularly when destroying hazardous waste), and no attempt is made to harness the waste's potential energy. Substantial concern exists about the by-products of incineration, which may include toxic chemicals such as dioxins in the exhaust gases. Ashes resulting from incineration also may cause disposal problems, particularly if the waste material contains substantial quantities of heavy metals. Although incineration has more potential for productive use or final destruction of waste than does landfilling, incineration may be no more desirable than landfilling (historically the worst legal waste management option) because of incineration's relatively high costs and potential environmental impacts.

Traditionally, waste management has been a local issue. When consumer goods were scarce and people did not live in large communities, the relatively small quantities of waste being produced presented little threat. However, the industrial revolution led to growing urban centers and increased amounts of waste material. Individuals could no longer easily dispose of their waste without threatening the health of their communities. Beginning in the late 1800s, cities began to assume some responsibility for waste collection and disposal to counter this threat to public health. By 1880, 43 percent of U.S. cities provided some form of garbage collection.[1]

Both the generation and the recovery of municipal solid waste increased between 1960 and 1988. However, the overall rate of growth was much higher than the increased rate of recovery. Concurrent with this growth in waste was a growing concern that waste management practices were inadequate. In developing RCRA, the Subcommittee on Transportation and Commerce of the U.S. House of Representatives indicated that 48 major cities were projected to have insufficient landfill capacity by the year 1982.[2] A 1986 EPA study indicated that 45 percent of all operating municipal landfills would reach capacity by 1991.[3] Furthermore, the annual municipal waste stream was estimated to grow to 216 million tons by the year 2000.[4] It was becoming increasingly apparent that something needed to be done.

In 1989, the EPA published a national strategy for municipal solid waste management. Three goals were identified:

1. Increase source reduction and recycling
2. Increase disposal capacity and improve secondary material markets
3. Improve the safety of solid waste management facilities

The first two goals deal with issues pertaining to waste quantities: How to reduce generation and how to provide enough capacity to properly manage waste. The third goal recognizes that municipal solid waste properly managed from a regulated perspective still may retain substantial environmental and health risks. The EPA strategy clearly states that the current municipal waste management system is inadequate and that major changes are needed.

Following passage of this strategy, waste generation continued to increase. The EPA reported that there were more than 209 million tons of municipal solid waste generated in 1996 (4.3 pounds per person per day!), an increase of about 29 million tons from 1988. More recently, the rate of

increase has slowed (Figure 8-1), with the per capita generation of municipal solid waste steady at about 4.5 pounds per day since the late 1990s.[5] The
rate of waste recovery has been slowly but steadily increasing, and exceeded
30 percent for this first time in 2003 (Table 8-1). It is unclear if any of the
success in recycling is occurring at the expense of source reduction programs. For example, ever-increasing quantities of waste paper are being generated, more is being recycled, but an environmentally preferable option
would be to produce less. Some commodities with large recycling potential
have experienced decreases in the rate of recycling, most notably aluminum
and glass. It may be of interest to look at the contents of the waste stream
and conjecture what strategies might be best in minimizing future municipal
solid waste problems. Waste management practices of 2003 put about 55.4
percent (131 million tons) of the municipal waste stream into landfills, 14.0
percent (33 million tons) into incinerators, and the remaining 30.6 percent
(72 million tons) into recycling.[5]

Providing for the proper management of hazardous waste, a particular
kind (or subset) of solid waste, also presents major challenges to the legal and
regulatory system. Before 1975, government paid little attention to hazardous
waste; only 25 states even had hazardous waste programs. There was no

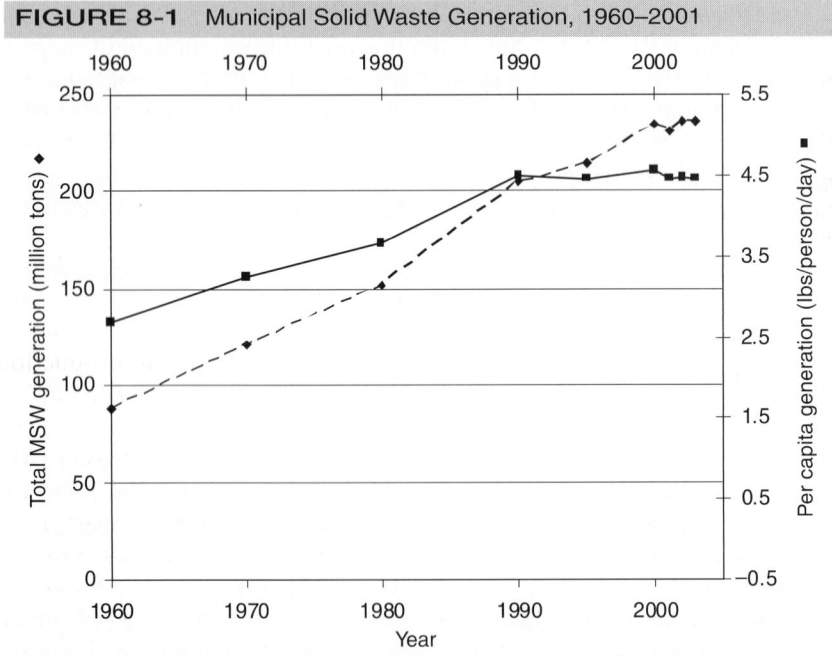

FIGURE 8-1 Municipal Solid Waste Generation, 1960–2001

Source: EPA Office of Solid Waste and Emergency Response. 2005. *Municipal Solid Waste Generation, Recycling and Disposal in the United States 2003 Facts and Figures.* Washington, D.C.: Government Printing Office. Publication no. 530-F-05-003. *http://www.epa.gov/msw/pubs/msw05rpt.pdf*

TABLE 8-1 Generation and Recovery of Materials in Municipal Solid Waste, 1998 and 2001

Waste Constituent	Weight Generated (million tons)		Weight Recovered (million tons)		Percent of Generation	
	1998	2003	1998	2003	1998	2003
Aluminum	3.1	3.2	0.9	0.7	27.9	21.4
Food wastes and paper for composting	22.1	27.6	0.6	0.8	2.6	2.7
Glass	12.5	12.5	3.2	2.4	25.5	18.8
Miscellaneous inorganic wastes	3.3	3.6	*	*	*	*
Other materials	3.9	4.3	0.9	1.0	23.1	22.7
Other nonferrous metals	1.4	1.6	0.9	1.1	67.4	66.7
Paper and paperboard	84.1	83.1	35.0	40.0	41.6	48.1
Plastics	22.4	26.7	1.2	1.4	5.4	5.2
Rubber and leather	6.9	6.8	0.9	1.1	12.5	16.1
Steel	12.4	14.0	4.3	5.1	35.1	36.4
Textiles	8.6	10.6	1.1	1.5	12.8	14.4
Wood	11.9	13.6	0.7	1.3	6.0	9.4
Yard trimmings	27.7	28.6	12.6	16.1	45.3	56.3
Total municipal solid waste	220.1	236.2	62.4	72.3	28.4	30.6

* Less than 5,000 tons or 0.05 percent.

Sources: EPA Office of Solid Waste and Emergency Response. 2005. *Municipal Solid Waste Generation, Recycling and Disposal in the United States 2003 Facts and Figures.* Washington, D.C.: Government Printing Office. Publication no. 530-F-05-003. *http://www.epa.gov/msw/pubs/msw05rpt.pdf* and Environmental Protection Agency. 2001. *Office of Solid Waste and Emergency Response, Municipal Solid Waste in the United States, 1999 Facts and Figures.* Washington, D.C.: Government Printing Office. Publication no. EPA530-R-01-014. Data tables. *http://www.epa.gov/epaoswer/non-hw/muncpl/pubs/99tables.pdf*

consistency among states regarding these limited programs, so companies faced different requirements depending on where they were doing business.

The significance of the problem of hazardous waste production has never been clear. There have been numerous "official estimates" of the volume of hazardous waste production in the United States, but none are conclusive. Perhaps more importantly, estimates of quantity do little to identify the resultant risk. The EPA estimated that 235,473,584 tons of hazardous waste had been generated nationally in 1993, from a total of 22,615 generators. More recent estimates indicate substantially less waste— data from 2001 indicate the generation of "only" 30,176,118 tons from a total of 17,694 large quantity generators.[6] Table 8-2 shows the 10 states with the greatest hazardous waste generation. It is important to note, however, that measures of gross quantities of waste generation cannot be used as reliable estimates of the magnitude of environmental risk. For example, Kentucky ranks third nationally in terms of hazardous waste generation but 20th in terms

TABLE 8-2   Ten States with Greatest Generation of RCRA Hazardous Waste, 2003

State	Thousands of Tons Generated	Percentage of National Total	Number of Generators
Texas	6,585	21.8	756
Louisiana	4,560	15.1	347
Kentucky	2,441	8.1	305
Mississippi	2,004	6.6	314
Ohio	1,800	6.0	1,040
Alabama	1,252	4.1	232
New Jersey	1,236	4.1	626
New York	1,130	3.7	1,339
Illinois	1,125	3.7	917
Indiana	988	3.3	589

Source: EPA. 2005. *Office of Solid Waste and Emergency Response, The National Biennial RCRA Hazardous Waste Report* (Based on 2003 Data). Washington, D.C.: Government Printing Office. Publication no. EPA530-R-03-007.

of numbers of generators. On the other extreme, more generators are in California (2514) than in any other state although it only ranks 16th in terms of total hazardous waste generation (445,317 tons). Is risk higher in a state characterized by a few, large generators or in a state characterized by many, smaller generators? Moreover, it is surprisingly difficult to provide meaningful long-term measures of generation. For example, the EPA changed its original listing methodology and now excludes from its listing of RCRA hazardous waste generation those hazardous wastes received from off-site for storage/bulking and subsequently transferred off-site for treatment or disposal, and those hazardous wastes that are stored, bulked, and/or transferred off-site with no prior treatment/recovery, fuel blending, or disposal. This change exemplifies the difficulty of determining trends because past analysis often considers a different universe of data than what is currently being used. Although many states have changed considerably in their relative ranking of hazardous waste generation through several generations of accounting, it may be significant to note that Texas has consistently accounted for the largest source of hazardous waste generation.

Quantifying risk from hazardous waste may be unnecessary; simply knowing that the risk is substantial was sufficient for Congress to demand (through RCRA and its subsequent amendments) a national hazardous waste management program. We began to understand by the early 1970s that our industrialized society was producing large amounts of hazardous waste and that much of it was being managed improperly. Locations became widely known where improper disposal of hazardous waste had caused, or had the potential to cause, severe health problems. We now have a comprehensive regulatory system that manages and limits at least some of the risks from wastes.

MUNICIPAL SOLID WASTE

RCRA establishes the framework for a national system of solid waste control. Subtitle D of the Act is dedicated to non-hazardous solid waste requirements, whereas Subtitle C focuses on hazardous solid waste. Remember that solid waste includes solids, liquids, and gases; it is defined in RCRA as

> any garbage, refuse, sludge from a waste treatment plant, water supply treatment plant, or air pollution control facility and other discarded material, including solid, liquid, semi-solid, or contained gaseous material resulting from industrial, commercial, mining and agricultural operations, and from community activities.[7]

Note that it must be discarded material to be considered waste. Thus, if economics warrant the purification of an industrial by-product for reintroduction into a process, then that material may not be a waste. The same by-product will be a waste if the recycling economics are less favorable. Some material is specifically excluded from being classified as solid waste, including domestic sewage sludge, industrial discharges that are point source discharges regulated under the Clean Water Act, irrigation return flows, and radioactive waste regulated by the Nuclear Regulatory Commission (NRC).[8]

RCRA directs most of the responsibility for active municipal solid waste management to state and local governments. The federal role is to set nation-wide standards, to provide technical and financial assistance, and to provide regulatory oversight and enforcement. States are encouraged to seek primacy over their solid waste programs. The EPA maintains an active management role for states unwilling or unable to assume responsibility for their own programs.

Resource conservation is specified as an important goal of the Act, although most attention has focused on waste disposal. A key condition is that "no reasonable probability of adverse effects on health or the environment" results from solid waste disposal practices. A facility meeting this requirement is called a *sanitary landfill,* whereas a facility failing to provide this protection is classified as an open dump.

In 1984, Congress passed RCRA amendments called the *Hazardous and Solid Waste Amendments* (HSWA) of 1984. Each state (with an approved program) is required to prepare a solid waste management plan. These plans must include methods for encouraging resource conservation or recovery. Each state also must implement a permit program for its solid waste management facilities that receive hazardous waste. Thus, sanitary landfills, which accept such waste as household hazardous waste, must have a permit and meet federal design and operational standards. Substantial flexibility is allowed in the federal standards, however, to allow states to develop specific criteria best suited to the local situation.

Existing regulations had been found to be inadequate, in part, because hazardous wastes from small-quantity generators and households could be disposed of (legally) as part of the municipal waste stream. Rather than trying to limit the types of waste introduced into sanitary landfills to exclude all waste with hazard potential, the EPA elected to require additional landfill controls inhibiting off-site migration. On October 9, 1991, the EPA promulgated its final rule on municipal solid waste landfills (MSWLFs), specifying criteria for sanitary landfills. These regulations increase requirements on landfill construction, operations, monitoring, and closure. However, they do not duplicate requirements on hazardous waste landfills (specified in Subtitle C of the Act), contrary to the expectations of a number of commentators to the proposed rule. Interest in having MSWLFs meet the same criteria as hazardous waste landfills is based on concern that the two types of disposal facilities share a common potential for damage to human health and the environment.

In establishing the new rules, the EPA requires MSWLFs to meet requirements more stringent than previously demanded but less stringent than required for hazardous waste landfills. This distinction is based on the EPA's determination that MSWLFs intrinsically represent a lesser threat than hazardous waste landfills and because the language of the statute and congressional record allow such a distinction. The EPA argued that the congressional intent of distinguishing between levels of protection at hazardous waste landfills and MSWLFs is evident in RCRA language. For hazardous waste landfills, standards shall be those "necessary for protection of human health and the environment." However, for a facility to be classified as a sanitary landfill, it must show only "no reasonable probability of adverse effects on health or the environment." Reasonable probability is interpreted as allowing a less severe standard (which may include economic considerations) than allowed for hazardous waste landfills.

The philosophy behind landfill design is that the landfills must prevent movement of any of the waste constituents away from the site (Figure 8-2). Landfills must be lined with either plastic or clay (usually both) as a barrier to waste migration. Liquids must be minimized because if liquids build up inside a facility, they result in a force (hydraulic head) that pushes dissolved waste products through the barriers. To keep out water from rain and runoff, closed facilities must have surface liners of the same type as that used on the bottom

FIGURE 8-2 Municipal Solid Waste Landfill

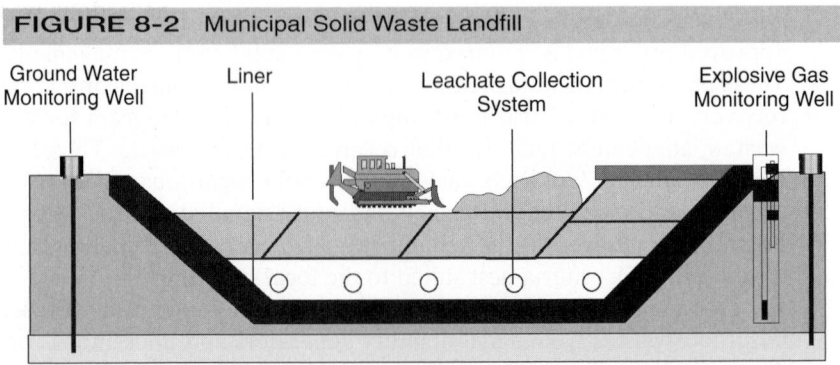

Ground Water Monitoring Well   Liner   Leachate Collection System   Explosive Gas Monitoring Well

Source: USEPA RCRA Orientation Manual January 2006. EPA530-R-06-003

and sides. Leachate collection systems must underlie the landfills to facilitate collection of residual liquids (leachate) that percolate through the waste. In the resulting oxygen-deficient, dry environment, little degradation of waste occurs. Modern landfill design effectively preserves the wastes. Closure plans must ensure that landfills will not fail (allow leakage from the site) for an extended period. A 30-year postclosure care period is specified in the federal rule, although either a reduction or an extension is allowed depending on local conditions.

These regulations effectively result in the long-term storage of waste in landfills rather than the waste being degraded. Concern is emerging that after the postclosure care period, water will inevitably leak into landfills. Formation of hazardous waste by-products and migration from the sites would occur after owners and operators no longer have responsibility. Some efforts are beginning to provide long-term waste stabilization by pumping leachate back into the landfill—the water enhances biological and chemical waste degradation and provides an inexpensive waste destruction system. In some designs, air is also provided to the landfill to further stimulate degradation. In this "bioreactor" landfill, degradation occurs during the active site-monitoring period when a responsible party is available to actively manage and remediate the facility. Long-term storage in a non-reactive containment landfill presents a risk of later failure when responsibility for control probably would need to revert to the government. Regulatory flexibility has been provided to a few demonstration bioreactors to research the potential of this approach for solid waste management.

The EPA identifies four tools that it uses to encourage the states to ensure that their state solid waste management plans comply with federal guidelines. The simplest is the denial of federal funding or technical assistance to non-compliant states. The EPA may seek injunctive relief when solid waste disposal presents an imminent threat to health or the environment, although this authority is somewhat limited because Congress wanted municipal solid waste problems to be solved through local efforts.[9] However, the EPA's power to intervene directly is enhanced by its ability to use hazardous waste enforcement authority in states that do not provide a permit program for MSWLFs receiving household hazardous waste or hazardous waste from conditionally exempt small-quantity generators (generators producing less than 100 kg of hazardous waste per month).[10]

The fourth enforcement tool is the citizen suit. Any citizen may bring suit against any government agency or individual alleged to be violating any requirement of the law or the state plan. Suits can be brought against the EPA for failure to perform required duties, as well as for violations of specific facility requirements.[11]

In addition to its regulatory role, the EPA advocates a number of voluntary waste management approaches to encourage government and industry to reduce waste generation and dependence on landfills. Information on these approaches can be found in its Office of Solid Waste home page Web site (provided at the end of this chapter). An interesting federal opportunity, led by the EPA, to encourage recycling is the Comprehensive Procurement Guideline Program authorized under Section 6002 of RCRA and strengthened by Executive Order 13101 (signed September 14, 1998). The EPA is required to designate products that are or can be made with recovered materials. Federal procuring agencies are then required to purchase those products with the highest recovered material content level practicable. However, it is important to remember that, although federal efforts have been supportive, local and state efforts predominate in providing innovative solid waste management tools to communities and businesses.

HAZARDOUS WASTE

Identification

For material to be regulated as a hazardous waste, first it must be found to be a solid waste or a combination of solid wastes. RCRA then specifies that solid waste meeting the following criteria will be considered hazardous waste:

1. Waste that causes or significantly contributes to an increase in mortality or an increase in serious irreversible or incapacitating reversible illness; or
2. Waste that poses a substantial present or potential hazard to human health or the environment when improperly treated, stored, transported, disposed of, or otherwise managed

The definitions of hazardous waste and solid waste clearly reflect the intent of Congress but are too non-specific to incorporate directly into a regulatory program. Subsequently, the EPA developed language to provide specific direction in determining whether materials need to be regulated as solid and hazardous wastes. The EPA originally defined solid waste in 1980 as "any garbage, refuse, sludge, or any other waste material" except for material specifically excluded from consideration. Difficulty with this definition arose because other waste material was interpreted to mean material that sometimes is discarded, by anyone in a similar industry, after serving its original purpose. This interpretation led to confusion regarding the status of intermediate products that were used for later processes and to difficulty in comparing processes to determine when similar materials were sometimes discarded. The EPA expanded and simplified its definition of solid waste in 1985 to include any discarded material not exempted from such classification. Discarded material consists of material disposed of in landfills, injection wells, or other facilities where the waste is placed in land or water such that there is potential for migration away from the site. It also includes material that is burned or incinerated and many materials that are recycled.

Recycled materials pose a difficult problem for regulation. Recycling hazardous material is more desirable than disposing of it as waste, but recycling also may present threats to human health and the environment that need careful control. Removal of management obligations through conversion of hazardous wastes into recyclable materials might prove valuable as a recycling incentive system but also might be misused as a mechanism to avoid regulatory control. The EPA addresses this issue by exempting three kinds of materials (that ordinarily would be considered solid waste) from the definition of solid waste (and thus potentially hazardous waste) based on its subsequent use: (1) directly in a production product, (2) as a direct substitution for a commercial product, or (3) if it is returned to the production process as a feedstock. In all three cases, the material must be used without reclamation. Non-exempted wastes for which some resource value is recovered, such as by incineration and energy recovery, remain classified as solid wastes.

Hazardous wastes are identified either by characteristic or by listing. It is the responsibility of the generator to determine whether it is producing solid waste and whether the solid waste has a hazardous waste characteristic of ignitability, corrosivity, reactivity, or toxicity. (Notice that toxicity is only one of the characteristics for hazardous waste—many people incorrectly use toxic waste synonymously with hazardous waste.) Solid waste must be evaluated for ignitability, corrosivity, and toxicity following specific EPA-designated test procedures. Ignitability is the characteristic of catching fire.[12] Most ignitable wastes are liquids (e.g., organic solvents and oils), although solids that can catch fire spontaneously or through friction or moisture absorption and burn vigorously also are included. Solid wastes are considered hazardous because of corrosivity if their pH is equal to or greater than 12.5 (a strong base) or their pH is equal to or less than 2 (a strong acid), or if they have the ability to corrode steel under prescribed conditions.[13]

Toxicity may be the most difficult characteristic to assess. Almost everything is toxic in great enough concentrations, so the regulatory definition cannot include all potentially toxic wastes. The EPA had to develop a definition useful as an indicator of potential toxicity, rather than one directly related to all plausible toxic agents. Waste is evaluated for toxicity by conducting a testing procedure that somewhat simulates conditions found in a landfill.[14] Liquids in a landfill usually are acidic, a condition favorable to the leaching of many heavy metals and other materials from solids. Because liquids are more mobile than solids, the risk of migration of toxics away from landfills is greatly enhanced when they are solubilized. The required test procedure, called the *Toxicity Characteristic Leaching Procedure* (TCLP), puts the solid waste in a liquid acidic solution under rigidly defined operating conditions. At the end of the test period, the acid is tested for 32 organic and eight inorganic chemicals. If any of those chemicals are found at concentrations above regulatory levels, that waste is classified as hazardous because of its toxicity potential.

Reactive wastes are those that are unstable under normal conditions and can form toxic fumes or explode.[15] It is difficult to develop a specific (and safe!) test procedure that adequately tests reactivity; therefore, the EPA has promulgated a narrative description of reactivity characteristics to assess waste rather than requiring the generator to perform a particular test procedure.

Solid wastes also are considered hazardous wastes if the EPA has them listed on one of the four lists it developed to identify hazardous waste. Determining whether a particular waste stream belongs on an EPA hazardous waste list is made by the EPA, with the generator responsible for looking at the lists to determine if its waste is included. A source-specific list identifies wastes from specific industrial processes (such as petroleum refining) in which operation is known to produce wastes of known hazards (K-wastes). A non-source-specific list contains hazardous wastes commonly found from various sources, such as degreasing solvents (F-wastes). Discarded commercial chemical products are identified on the final lists, which include off-specification chemicals, containers, and spill residues (P- and U-wastes). P-wastes are acutely toxic at low dose. Although U-waste may also be toxic, they also have other hazardous characteristics such as ignitability or corrosivity.

Listed hazardous waste may be delisted from a particular facility. To accomplish this, the facility must demonstrate through petition that the waste does not meet the criteria for which it was listed, does not exhibit any other hazardous waste characteristics, and does not pose a threat to human health and the environment by being hazardous for any other reason. For example, a K-waste that is listed for the characteristic of being ignitable may be delisted if the waste stream from that particular facility is not ignitable because a different solvent is used than the norm for that industry. The EPA reports that between 1980 and 1999, 136 waste streams from 115 different facilities were delisted. Electroplating waste (F006) was the most common waste delisted, with 45 million tons of waste having been excluded from management as hazardous waste.

Certain solid waste is exempt from being classified as a hazardous waste. These exemptions include household waste, mining overburden returned to the mine site and other waste resulting from the extraction and processing of ores and minerals, utility waste from coal combustion, waste from exploration drilling for oil and natural gas, cement kiln dust waste, and waste from the growing and harvesting of crops, or raising of animals, returned to the soil as fertilizer.[16]

To prevent waste generators from trying to manage hazardous waste by dilution, listed hazardous waste mixed with non-hazardous waste is classified as hazardous waste and must be managed following hazardous waste regulations. Mixing of a hazardous waste with a non-hazardous waste is effectively discouraged because the mixing will simply result in a larger hazardous waste stream requiring active (and expensive) management. In contrast, a mixture of characteristic hazardous waste and non-hazardous waste that no longer has the hazardous characteristic (e.g., an acid waste mixed with a basic waste to form a neutral waste) will lose its hazardous waste designations.

Cradle to Grave

Passage of RCRA means that hazardous waste now needs to be tracked and managed from the point of generation (cradle) to its ultimate fate in the environment (grave). The generator is responsible for identifying whether a material is a waste and whether the waste is hazardous. The generator must ensure that the waste is handled appropriately even after it leaves the generating facility.

Each generator must obtain an identification number from the state agency responsible for maintaining the hazardous waste program (or the EPA if the state does not have primacy for the program). Waste being sent off-site must be listed by the generator on a waste manifest. The waste is characterized following a numerical coding system developed by the EPA. The manifest also contains information on the waste quantity and identifies the generator, transporter, and receiving facility. The generator also must certify that efforts have been taken to minimize the waste quantity and associated hazard. On the manifest, the generator's signature must follow a required statement certifying that efforts have been taken to minimize the waste quantity and associated hazard.

Generators using off-site waste management facilities must provide the hazardous waste transporter with a manifest to accompany the waste. The manifest is then provided by the transporter to the waste treatment, storage, or disposal facility (TSDF) that checks to ensure that the waste can be properly handled at that facility. Also vital is physically checking the waste to make sure it is the same as designated on the manifest. A copy of the manifest is returned to the generator, who is supposed to ensure that it has not been changed. The generator should know that the waste has arrived in an unaltered state at the intended designation, with any problems reported to the appropriate agency in an "exception report." The generator is required to retain a copy of the manifest for at least 3 years, although most generators will retain them indefinitely.

The EPA recently modified the Uniform Hazardous Waste Manifest, with the use of the new manifest required on September 5, 2006. The January 2001 proposed standards for a new manifest included the ability to complete, sign, and transmit manifests electronically. However, the EPA decided that technical problems currently prevented this option but would continue to investigate this option for possible adoption at a later time.

It is important to remember that although hazardous waste generators have substantial obligations under RCRA, if they do not treat, store, or dispose of waste they do not have to obtain a permit. Because permit requirements can be burdensome (see the following section), many facilities eliminate or avoid practices that would turn them into a TSDF.

The evolution of disposal requirements being applied to ever-smaller hazardous waste generators reflects an interesting dynamic between Congress and the EPA. Early in the RCRA program, the EPA decided that its resources were insufficient to effectively control all generators. In response, it exempted those facilities generating less than 1,000 kg of hazardous waste per month from almost all hazardous waste management requirements, concluding that this was a reasonable method of optimizing available resources because the great majority of the risk from hazardous waste would come from the relatively few large generators. Congress did not condone this practice and subsequently required in HSWA that the EPA also regulate small-quantity generators (generating between 100 and 1,000 kg of hazardous waste per month). Only conditionally exempt small-quantity generators, producing less than 100 kg of hazardous waste per month, now escape the RCRA waste management regulatory burdens. Hazardous waste from these conditionally exempt small-quantity generators may continue to be legally deposited in municipal landfills (although municipal landfills are under no obligation to accept such waste).

Permits

All hazardous waste TSDFs are required to obtain a permit. Congress recognized a problem when implementing a permit requirement: If all TSDFs submitted their applications at the onset of the program, the EPA would not have the resources to provide timely permit review. Therefore, a system was specified to allow TSDFs to operate under an interim permit until obtaining a final permit.

All TSDFs in existence on November 19, 1980, that had submitted a Part A application were given an interim permit. The Part A application contains only basic information, including the facility location, estimates of waste quantities, and waste management practices. This information was quite unreliable and of limited value. To obtain a final permit, a Part B permit application needs to be approved by the EPA. Part B permit applications require substantially more operational and organizational detail than Part A permits and may run several volumes in length for major facilities. Part B applications were submitted only after the EPA requested them from individual facilities. This policy was established to maintain submission of permit applications at a rate coincident with the EPA's ability to provide permit review. However, Congress did not agree with this approach because few final permits were being issued. After the program's 1980 inception, only 24 facilities (out of about 8,000) had been issued final permits by July 31, 1983.[17] Twenty of these permits had been issued to storage facilities. From the more significant waste management units, only one landfill and three incinerators had been issued permits. Congress tried to replace the EPA's program of calling up final permit applications at the EPA's convenience by setting a schedule for permit issuance. Land disposal facilities were required to submit by November 8, 1988, incinerators by November 8, 1989, and other facilities by November 1992. However, the EPA was unable to meet this schedule.

Subsequently, the EPA set a specific goal under the Government Performance and Results Act (GPRA) to have 80 percent of all existing TSDFs in compliance with permitting or closure standards by 2005 (Subobjective February 5, 2004). In July 2003, the EPA reported that a total of 2,752 facilities were in the TSDF system. Of these, 2,242 (81 percent) were fully permitted or had met closure requirements, with 510 facilities (19 percent) not yet in full compliance. The EPA has met its goal for 2005 on a national level although not in every state or region. Shown on Figure 8-3 are the percentage of fully permitted facilities on a regional basis through mid-2006.

New TSDFs must obtain a permit before they begin operating. The permitting process is quite complex. First, an informal public meeting is held in which the facility is described, including identification of waste management practices and wastes that will be handled. The public is given the opportunity to ask questions and make suggestions. Following this meeting, the permit application, including both Part A and Part B, is submitted. After receipt of the permit application, the state-permitting agency (or the EPA in states that do not have an approved RCRA program) provides an opportunity for public review and comment and reviews the permit for completeness. If it is complete, review begins for satisfying technical requirements. Either a notice of intent to deny or a draft permit will follow this review, depending on the acceptability of the facility. The decision is made public, and, in the case of a positive decision, the draft permit is made available for public review. The permitting agency must respond to public comments and produce a final decision. The owner and the operator of the proposed facility have the right to appeal an adverse decision through the EPA's Environmental Appeals Board. Further remedy is available through judicial review of the final permit decision. This process is intended to provide substantial opportunity for public involvement through the permitting process and a reasonable expectation that a project proponent can be successful in obtaining a permit and beginning operation. However, in addition to the formal permitting process, proponents typically also must anticipate the Not In My Backyard (NIMBY) syndrome, in which local residents will strongly contest any land use perceived as potentially risky regardless of regulatory controls.

In October 2005, a new permitting approach became available to facilities that store or treat hazardous waste in tanks, containers, and containment buildings. These facilities have available to them a "standardized permit" that

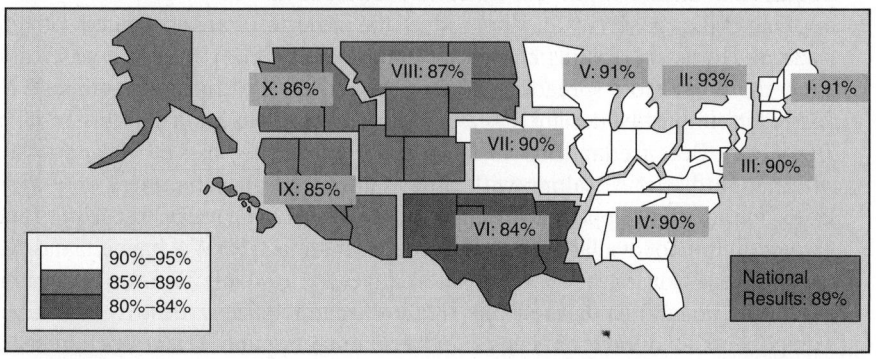

FIGURE 8-3   Percentage of Treatment, Storage, and Disposal Facilities with Final Permits or Meeting Closure Requirements

X: 86%   VIII: 87%   V: 91%   II: 93%   I: 91%
VII: 90%   III: 90%
IX: 85%   VI: 84%   IV: 90%

90%–95%
85%–89%
80%–84%

National Results: 89%

Source: EPA Regional Program Permitting Progress. *http://www.epa.gov/epaoswer/hazwaste/permit/charts/charts.pdf*

is intended to streamline the permitting process. The EPA estimates that between 870 and 1,130 facilities will be able to use this new standardized permitting approach, with a potential cost savings of more than $3 million. In May 2006, additional changes were finalized regarding paperwork associated with TSDF permitting. The EPA estimates that the reduced paperwork requirements will result in an annual savings of between $2 million and $3 million. These regulatory initiatives demonstrate the complexity of the permitting process resulting in relatively small changes resulting in meaningful cost savings. However, these saving are very small compared with the overall costs of the permitting program (from the perspectives of both the regulated and the regulatory communities).

Facility Standards

All TSDFs are governed by EPA minimum standards, which may be further refined (but not weakened) by individual states. Specific design, construction, and operating standards have been established for hazardous waste facilities with containers, tanks, surface impoundments, drip pads (designed to catch preservation chemicals dripping from wood), containment buildings, waste piles, land treatment units, landfills, incinerators, corrective action for solid waste management units, hazardous waste munitions and explosives storage, and miscellaneous units.[18] Interim standards have been established for thermal treatment units, chemical, physical and biological treatment units, and underground injection wells.[19] These standards are technically complex, so their complete discussion is inappropriate in a book on environmental law. It is vital to recognize, however, that those responsible for a TSDF must follow these standards precisely.

Before RCRA, the federal system had little impact on disposal practices. Hazardous waste commonly was disposed of in landfills that were not designed for long-term containment of their hazardous constituents. Now, landfills must be highly engineered units providing redundant barriers to waste migration. Furthermore, a comprehensive monitoring program is required to ensure that these barriers are effective.

Landfilling generally does not reduce the intrinsic hazard associated with the hazardous waste. Landfills keep people and wildlife away from the waste and keep the waste from spreading to uncontrolled parts of the environment. The landfill itself must be designed as a facility that retains its hazardous potential in perpetuity. Because landfills do not destroy waste, they can be viewed as the alternative of choice (along with other land disposal techniques) only after determining that opportunities for waste reduction, reuse, recycling, and treatment are not available or are not practical. In fact, HSWA banned land disposal of hazardous waste for which alternatives are available. Before a hazardous waste can be landfilled, it must be treated to immobilize or destroy hazardous components. Dilution is not considered a treatment option. This restriction probably has been quite influential in diverting a meaningful portion of the hazardous waste stream to other management options (including waste reduction).

An elaborate procedure must be followed to close a hazardous waste landfill or a section of a landfill.[20] A written closure plan is part of a facility application, although it may be modified during the active life of the landfill. Technical requirements include capping the top with another liner to ensure that water does not infiltrate the site. Groundwater monitoring must continue, and the site must remain secure from people or animals. However, perhaps the most important part of the entire closure process is that someone must remain identifiable as being responsible for a facility, with financial resources available to remedy any problems.

The owner or the operator of a facility must provide an appropriate instrument guaranteeing long-term financial ability to manage the site, even after it has been closed. This instrument may be a trust fund, surety bond, letter of credit, insurance policy, or financial worth test. This financial guarantee became necessary because a past practice of some unethical operators was to charge for waste disposal services but then dump waste illegally and inexpensively. The company would go bankrupt before the practice was discovered, so it could not be forced to pay to clean up the mess. In the meantime, the company owners and operators, having already taken the money for the waste disposal, were not easily found or held culpable.

Standards for TSDFs other than landfills also require redundant protection systems to guard against the release of hazardous waste. For example, new hazardous waste storage tanks must have secondary containment systems that will contain a leak from the primary tank. The standards consider release into multiple environmental media, including air emissions. These standards have added considerable cost to the management of most hazardous wastes, providing incentive for waste reduction, reuse, and recycling.

Reflecting the maturing and emphasis of the hazardous waste management regulatory program and the large amounts of waste associated with resource extraction, a relatively small fraction of the waste stream is landfilled. Deep well or underground injection is the method used for the majority of waste disposal (see Chapter 6 for discussion of potential impact on drinking water and related controls). However, this does not mean that the risks from these primary management techniques are proportionately greater than those posed by the other management methods. Between 1999 and 2003, the amount of hazardous waste managed under RCRA has increased in many categories (Table 8-3). Although a substantial reduction in hazardous waste generation occurred following passage of RCRA and other federal laws, it will be interesting to observe if waste quantities will continue to increase with the impact of a new system becoming fully integrated into management decisions. Obviously, the surest way to minimize risk from hazardous waste is to limit its generation, but these requirements and other EPA directives have not resulted in a declining volume (although unknown is if without these regulations the increase in generation would have been greater). Again, care must be taken when comparing data among years because of differences in counting systems.

TABLE 8-3   RCRA Hazardous Waste Management Methods Used in 1999 and 2003

Management Method	Thousands of Tons Managed		Percentage of Total Tons Managed		Number of Facilities	
	1999	2003	1999	2003	1999	2003
Deepwell/underground injection	16,043	14,479	61.0	34.4	46	42
Energy recovery	1,542	1,468	5.9	3.5	99	103
Incineration/Surface Impoundment	2,159	1,273	8.2	3.0	151	162
Landfill	1,410	1,676	5.4	4.0	60	72
Other disposal	1,399	3,349	5.3	8.0	39	128
Stabilization	1,337	748	5.1	1.8	84	156
Fuel blending	1,100	916	4.2	2.2	104	116
Metals recovery	720	1,152	2.7	2.7	88	159
Solvents recovery	368	263	1.4	0.6	111	523
Other recovery	158	729	0.6	1.7	46	85
Sludge treatment	48	557	0.2	1.3	16	78
Land treatment/ application/farming	30	28	0.1	0.1	7	14
Other treatment	—	7,746	—	18.4	—	461
Aqueous Organic Treatment	—	5,584	—	13.3	—	98

Source: EPA. *Solid Waste and Emergency Response [5305W], National Analysis, The Preliminary National Biennial RCRA Hazardous Waste Report (Based on 1999 Data).* EPA530-R-01-009 (Washington, D.C.: Government Printing Office, June 2001) and National Analysis, The National Biennial RCRA Hazardous Waste Report (Based on 2003 Data).

ENFORCEMENT OF RCRA

HSWA greatly expand the scope of criminal liability for RCRA violations. The key to criminal liability is that the violator must have committed the act knowingly; no such requirement is necessary for civil action. Criminal actions can result in fines and imprisonment. Individuals can be penalized up to 5 years in jail and $5,000 per day for (1) transporting waste to a non-permitted facility; (2) treating, storing, or disposing of waste without a permit; (3) omitting information or making false statements on a label, manifest, report, permit, or interim status standard; (4) generating, treating, storing, or disposing of hazardous waste without meeting RCRA's reporting and record-keeping requirements; (5) transporting hazardous waste without a manifest; and (6) exporting a hazardous waste without the permission of the receiving country. A much more severe penalty, up to 15 years in prison and a $250,000 fine for an individual, or a $1 million fine for a company, can be imposed for transporting, treating, storing, disposing of, or exporting waste in such a way to impose an imminent danger of serious bodily injury or death.

The EPA also may take civil action to obtain compliance with RCRA. Civil penalties for Subtitle C non-compliance violations can be up to $27,500 for each day of violation. The EPA may seek injunctive relief in court or issue compliance orders directly. Failure to comply with administrative orders may result in a company losing its hazardous waste permit. Failure to comply with monitoring and analysis orders carries a penalty of up to $5,500 per day for non-compliance. An individual responsible for imminent and substantial endangerment also may be fined up to $5,500 per day.

States (or the EPA in states without primacy over their hazardous waste programs) are required to inspect all privately operated TSDFs at least once every 2 years. (Federal and state-operated TSDFs must be inspected annually.) This requirement was made part of HSWA because of the lack of an effective existing monitoring program; companies could take the gamble not to comply because there was a good chance they would not be discovered.

RCRA also established a right for individuals to bring citizen suits against alleged violators or against the EPA for alleged failure to meet its responsibility. However, citizen suits are prohibited when dealing with the siting and permitting of a TSDF, when the EPA is prosecuting an action, when the EPA or the responsible state is conducting a remedial action, or when the responsible party is carrying out the approved remedial action.

Before leaving this section on enforcement, consider why an elaborate program for controlling hazardous waste is needed. Before RCRA, companies frequently disposed of waste by using inexpensive techniques. Complying with hazardous waste regulations imposes a substantial financial burden which may result in a company's product or service becoming economically non-competitive (or in substantially reducing the profit margin). One response to these new burdens is to ignore them. Firms may gamble that illegal practices will not be detected, or, if they are, that the penalties will be less onerous than the compliance costs.

Much of the rationale for imposing criminal sanctions and having a strong enforcement program is to make illegal practices more expensive than compliance. Criminal penalties may be particularly effective because the expense of a possible jail sentence—in terms of personal lifestyle costs— would deter most people much more than would a personal or company fine.

Consider the recent situation of the Simpson Construction Company of Cleveland, Tennessee.[21] The company president and the foreman pleaded guilty on January 30, 2001, to RCRA violations associated with burning hazardous solvent and paint wastes in a pit at the company's facility. Maximum sentencing may include up to 3 years' imprisonment for the company president and up to 1 year's imprisonment for the foreman. The company has also agreed to pay $867,321 in fines and funding of remediation and supplemental environmental projects and to develop and implement an environmental compliance plan. The penalties associated with non-compliance are severe—and perhaps will have an impact on the decision makers of other companies contemplating non-compliance. Because compliance costs continue to grow, the expense of non-compliance must keep pace to maintain the effectiveness of waste management programs. Ultimately, we will measure success of the current regulatory programs by the magnitude of future problems resulting from today's hazardous waste management practices.

CERCLA: AN OVERVIEW

The key law that brought active federal government involvement to emergency response, site remediation, and spill prevention is the Comprehensive Environmental Response, Compensation, and Liability Act of 1980 (CERCLA, or the Superfund Act). Congress intended CERCLA to be comprehensive in its coverage, encompassing both prevention of and response to uncontrolled hazardous substance releases. The Act deals with environmental response, providing mechanisms for reacting to emergency situations and to chronic hazardous material releases. In addition to establishing procedures to prevent and remedy problems, it establishes a system for compensating appropriate individuals and assigning appropriate liability. It is designed to plan for and respond to failures in other regulatory programs and to remedy problems resulting from action taken before the era of comprehensive regulatory protection.

EMERGENCY RESPONSE PLANS
AND RIGHT TO KNOW

To begin our discussion of hazardous material releases, we examine the requirement to plan for emergencies, including consideration of prevention. The federal program requiring comprehensive community planning was established in the Emergency Planning and Community Right-to-Know Act of 1986 (EPCRA), which was passed as part of the Superfund Amendments and Reauthorization Act of 1986 (SARA).

SARA Title III is organized into three subtitles. Subtitle A covers emergency planning, Subtitle B specifies hazardous chemical reporting requirements, and Subtitle C describes how the public will have access to facility information.

State and local governments are required to develop emergency response and preparedness plans. Every state must have an emergency response commission. Each commission must appoint local emergency response-planning committees and designate emergency-planning districts. Each committee must include, at minimum, representatives from "elected State and local officials; law enforcement, civil defense, firefighting, first aid, health, local environmental, hospital, and transportation personnel; broadcast and print media; community groups; and owners and operators of facilities subject to the requirements of this subtitle."[22] This requirement makes the local committees fairly large and cumbersome but also ensures that all affected parties will be represented.

Each local planning committee was required to have prepared by October 17, 1988, its comprehensive emergency response plan. At a minimum, these plans are designed to determine what extremely hazardous substances are located in or pass through a community, who is responsible for them, what resources are available to deal with spills, how spill information will be communicated so that the correct response is taken, and how the entire system has been integrated so that it will work. Ideally, much of this planning will be preventive in nature.

Substantial burden is placed on facilities that use extremely hazardous substances. The EPA has published a list of extremely hazardous substances with associated threshold-planning quantities. Any facility that has any of these substances in more than the designated quantity must notify the state planning commission and the local planning committee that it is subject to provisions of this law. Note that there is a duplicative effort required of the facility because there is not (by law or regulation) a uniform reporting system to ensure that a single report will be transmitted to all involved agencies.

Facilities also are required to report to the local committee, the state commission, and the local fire department if they have any chemicals regulated under OSHA's hazard communication standard in quantities of 10,000 pounds or more. For each reportable chemical, the facility must submit either a material safety data sheet (MSDS) or a list of the reportable chemicals providing the following information:[23]

1. The chemical or common name of each chemical
2. A list of the hazardous chemicals grouped by hazard category; whether the chemical can be considered an "immediate health hazard," chronic health hazard (including carcinogens), fire hazard, hazard from sudden pressure release (such as explosives and compressed gases), or a chemical reactive
3. Identification of any hazardous component of each chemical as identified on the MSDS

Ordinarily, the chemical list and associated information will be more useful than receiving MSDSs for all chemicals. These lists are intended to identify critical information in an organized fashion. MSDSs typically provide such an overwhelming amount of detail as to make them difficult to interpret for pertinent emergency planning and response information.

In addition to this initial reporting requirement, facilities must report annually on the quantities and locations of their hazardous chemicals.[24] To meet "Tier I" requirements, this information must include the following:

1. An estimate of the maximum amount of hazardous chemicals in each category at any time during the year (these estimates do not have to be made on a chemical-by-chemical basis, only by category)
2. An estimate of the average daily amount of chemicals in each category present at the facility during the year
3. The general location of chemicals in each category

Local committees, state commissions, or local fire departments can also request Tier II information. Although the Tier I data-reporting requirements identify categories of chemicals and their general locations, Tier II requirements identify individual chemicals by names and report their specific locations and storage conditions. Companies may elect to protect trade secrets by withholding specific names and locations of chemicals from public reporting. However, community planning agencies must have access to specific names and locations if they request it. The EPA has available an electronic form for submitting Tier II information.

Another list of chemicals is used as the basis for reporting on the presence of toxic materials. Facilities with chemical use greater than threshold quantities on the Toxic Chemicals Subject to Section 313 of the Emergency Planning and Community Right-To-Know Act of 1986 (EPCRA) list must report to the EPA annually. In addition to information identifying the facility, and chemical use at that facility, the report must document the annual quantity of the toxic chemical entering each environmental medium. The EPA collects this information and maintains a national toxic chemical inventory available to the public. Facilities within the manufacturing sectors (SIC codes 20–39) or certain industrial facilities (SIC code 10, except for SIC codes 1011, 1081, and 1094; SIC code 12 except for SIC code 1241 and extraction activities; and SIC codes 4911, 4931, 4939, 4953, 5169, 5171, and 7389) are obligated to report, and the information is compiled by the EPA. A Toxic Release Inventory (TRI) is made available electronically over the Internet by the EPA, giving communities a simple tool to examine the risk from chemicals in their neighborhoods. This information has sparked interest in many communities about the activities of local industry. As these data are released by the EPA and reported by local media, many companies have been faced with a local population outraged by the vast quantities of toxic chemicals being discharged regularly as part of their normal operating practices. A common response has been for these companies to implement programs to reduce chemical release. Thus, voluntary reduction in chemical release has resulted from public pressure encouraged by regulatory reporting requirements.

New laws and regulations that followed the passage of EPCRA expand on prevention, response, and disclosure requirements. The CAA amendments of 1990 require many facilities to prepare risk-management plans, effectively supplementing EPCRA emergency planning provisions. Minor changes have been made to these rules in 2004 including a requirement to update facility risk-management plans within 6 months of a reportable accident (previously this may have taken as long as 5 years to be added as part of the regular updating of the risk-management plan). Toxic release inventories have been expanded by requirements of the Pollution Prevention Act of 1990 to also include recycling and source reduction activities. In 1994, the EPA added 286 chemical and chemical categories to the list required for Section 313 reporting. The list currently includes 581 individually listed chemicals and 30 chemical categories. However, the EPA is also allowing an alternative threshold for small businesses to reduce the burden of Section 313 reporting.

Following the attack on the World Trade Center and Pentagon on September 11, 2001, the EPA took part in the emergency response through monitoring of indoor and outdoor air. However, EPA is being criticized by many for their work as not providing proper guidance to emergency response and clean-up personnel, perhaps resulting in substantial chronic health hazards. Some authority for an active EPA role in planning for and responding to terrorist attacks clearly falls within EPCRA, as well as other elements of CERLCA and the Clean Water Act as amended by the Oil Pollution Act of 1990. However, EPA does not have clear statutory authority to establish and enforce health-based regulatory standards for indoor air.

FEDERAL RESPONSE TO CONTAMINATED SITES

Before CERCLA, the federal government had little ability to take an active role in responding to a hazardous material spill or to a site contaminated with hazardous material. CERCLA provided both the necessary authority and a funding mechanism to respond to these types of situations.

Two types of responses are identified in CERCLA: removal actions and remedial actions. Removal actions are intended to stabilize or clean up a hazardous site that poses an immediate threat to human health or the environment. Remedial actions are intended to provide permanent remedies. Removal actions may not eliminate the need for remedial actions because chronic problems may be ignored while providing immediate protection.

The universe of chemicals regulated by CERCLA is much broader than that regulated under RCRA. CERCLA includes RCRA hazardous wastes and hazardous substances designated under the Clean Air Act, the

Clean Water Act, and the Toxic Substances Control Act. CERCLA also requires the EPA to maintain an additional list of substances not included in these other acts that present a potential threat to human health and the environment.

The Hazardous Substances Response Trust Fund, or Superfund, was established in the 1980 legislation to provide a mechanism for the federal government to finance its emergency response and remedial response activities and to recover costs. This was a fund of $1.6 billion, 87.5 percent of which was obtained from the petroleum and chemical industries, with the remaining 12.5 percent coming from general federal revenues. The EPA could use these funds to cover its own costs, or the costs involved with work it orders, in responding to an immediate threat. This fund was intended primarily as a rotating fund, with costs incurred in cleanup recovered from the responsible parties.

Congress increased the Superfund to $8.5 billion dollars as part of the SARA of 1986. Although the petroleum and chemical industries continued to finance much of this fund ($2.75 billion and $1.4 billion, respectively), corporate income taxes also provided $2.5 billion. The remainder of the fund came from general federal revenues ($1.25 billion), interest ($0.3 billion), and recovery of cleanup costs ($0.3 billion). If recoveries from potentially responsible parties (PRPs) are insufficient, additional funds may be authorized. For example, in 1992, the Superfund received an additional $1.75 billion in federal money. In 1994, authorization was extended by an additional $5.1 billion. More recently, funding of this program has shifted to general tax revenues. In 1995, Congress did not renew the tax on industry that contributed to the fund, and in 2003, the fund was exhausted. This is a major shift in philosophy for providing clean-up funds, with revenue now coming from general tax dollars if not available through recovery from PRPs.

REMOVAL ACTION

Following release of a "reportable quantity" of a hazardous substance, notification must be given to the state emergency response commission, the local emergency response committee, and the National Response Center (operated by the Coast Guard). Typically, fire and police departments also will be notified. Chemicals for which notification must be made include both the approximately 800 substances identified as part of the CERCLA legislation from hazardous waste sites and 360 extremely hazardous substances identified as part of the EPRCA. Under CERCLA, reportable quantities of chemicals were originally established as 1 pound, but the EPA has been adjusting those quantities to reflect the relative risk of the spilled substances. Five reporting levels have been established at 1, 10, 100, 1,000, and 5,000 pounds.[25] In addition, the Department of Transportation regulations require reporting spills if the spill results in hospitalization or death, damage exceeds $50,000, pathogens or radioactive materials are involved, the area is evacuated for more than 1 hour, or the operational flight pattern of an aircraft is altered. Supporting the work of the National Response Center is the National Response Team, a group of 16 agencies cochaired by the EPA and the Coast Guard. This team has the responsibility of providing information about spills, planning for emergencies, and training for emergencies (but it does not respond directly to incidents).

Following a spill or notification of an immediate danger posed by an abandoned hazardous waste site, the EPA can implement a removal action. These actions are limited to situations in which there is an immediate threat to human health or the environment. Each action is limited to 12 months and $2 million (before the passage of SARA, these limits were 6 months and $1 million), although extensions can be granted. An example of a removal action is a collection of leaking drums of explosive material. Local governments responding to a hazardous material emergency may receive up to $25,000 in reimbursement per incident from the EPA.

Removal actions are not meant necessarily to provide permanent solutions. This means that the EPA may take actions that provide immediate protection and then leave, even though substantial hazards remain. Once immediate contact is prevented, the threat becomes chronic rather than acute. Because there are so many sites that present chronic risks, the EPA must follow an elaborate procedure to prioritize them (see the following section on remedial response).

The EPA identifies among the successes of its removal program the protection of more than 49 million people from health hazards stemming from the release of hazardous substances, providing over 200,000 people with a safe supply of drinking water when their drinking water became contaminated, and moving 40,000 people from the vicinity of very dangerous sites.[26] However, it is important to keep in mind that following removal of the acute problem, remediation needs typically remain. The removal program is designed to deal exclusively with emergencies, not long-term environmental problems.

If the EPCRA of 1986 is effective, the need for direct federal involvement in spill cleanup and hazardous substance removals should be significantly reduced. However, evaluating this effectiveness is quite difficult. Rather than looking at the spill incidents occurring before and after the passage of EPCRA, the evaluation should project the incidents that may have occurred without the legislation. Moreover, in evaluating the effectiveness of these programs, you may want to consider the incentives that a spiller might have in not reporting an incident.

REMEDIAL RESPONSE

Before CERCLA, only common law remedies applied to most sites where hazardous substances had been released and presented a threat to human health and the environment. At many sites, there were a host of uncertainties regarding the nature of the threats and the potentially responsible parties. No one seemed to be accountable for determining what kinds of materials were present, how effectively materials were contained, the effects of human exposure to the leaking chemicals, or the long-term effects on the environment. Thus, there was little being done to remove the threat to human health and the environment, or to provide remediation from these sites.

Congress realized that a system was needed to prioritize the sites potentially needing remediation and required the EPA to develop appropriate criteria. The EPA responded with a hazard-ranking system by which sites were evaluated on the basis of relative risk to human health and the environment (note that there was no attempt to quantify the actual risk). This is necessarily a complex task because of the many routes by which harm may occur. Four scores are determined on the basis of potential exposure through the four major routes: surface water, groundwater, air, and soil. Sites scoring high enough on this ranking system are included on the National Priorities List (NPL). Scoring high with regard to only one environmental medium is usually sufficient to result in inclusion on the NPL. Only NPL sites are eligible for EPA remedial action. However, the EPA is not obligated to pursue sites on the NPL in any particular order. Thus, the EPA site selection for implementing remedial action is a very political process as well as a technically demanding one.

The process for remediation begins with site identification, followed by a preliminary assessment. Sites are identified from a number of sources, including formal identification processes run by the states. Individuals may play an important role in identifying potential sites. A preliminary assessment is done by collecting readily available site information and determining the relative level of risk. If the risk is acute and substantial, emergency response (removal action) may be initiated. At the other extreme, this preliminary assessment may reveal little threat and no further need for investigation. However, if a potential is seen for the site presenting a significant long-term risk, a site inspection is conducted, including sampling of environmental media. Results are used to produce a hazard-ranking system score, with sufficiently high scoring sites (in January 2001 a score of 28.50 or higher) eligible for inclusion on the NPL.

Once a site on the NPL has been selected for remediation, a formal process must be followed to determine and implement appropriate actions. A Remedial Investigation/Feasibility Study (RI/FS) is done first. The RI is done to characterize site conditions, to determine the nature of the waste, to assess the risk to human health and the environment, and to conduct tests that evaluate the potential performance and cost of possible treatment technologies. Key issues include the extent of contamination, migration offsite, and potential for human and environmental exposure. The FS includes development of a series of specific remediation alternatives, including specification of costs, technical feasibility, and environmental impacts. RI and FS are done concurrently because site data are critical in developing appropriate remedial alternatives. RI/FS are expensive; in 1992, the average cost reported by the EPA was approximately $1.35 million for each site.

On the basis of an RI/FS, a Record of Decision (ROD) is written in which the EPA documents and justifies the selection of a particular cleanup option. Public comments and concerns should be a part of the ROD, which is a public document. On the basis of the ROD, project remediation enters the remedial design/remedial action (RD/RA) phase. Technical specifications for cleanup remedies and technologies are designed (RD) and construction and site cleanup commence (RA). Following completion of remedial activities, sites are placed on the Construction Completion List, signifying completion of remedial activities. To be included on this list, a finding must be made that

1. Any necessary physical construction is complete, whether or not final cleanup levels or other requirements have been achieved
2. Further response action should be limited to measures that do not involve construction (e.g., institutional controls)
3. The site qualifies for deletion from the NPL

CERCLA provides little guidance on how the EPA should determine the level of removal during a site cleanup. SARA provides the EPA more direction in determining suitable removal levels during a remedial response by providing that cleanups must be protective of human health and the environment, be cost-effective, and use permanent solutions (including treatment and resource recovery) as much as is practicable. Land disposal is discouraged. However, even within the framework established by SARA, it is difficult to determine appropriate cleanup levels for specific sites. Removal of all of a contaminant is virtually impossible, exceedingly expensive, and may involve analytical measurements beyond technical abilities. The EPA regulations promulgated in 1990 include detailed information to provide more direct guidance, but they may have resulted in a loss of useful site-specific flexibility.

The Superfund can be used to finance remedial response (in addition to emergency response, as described earlier). Again, the intended use of the fund is to allow activity to begin before potentially responsible parties are identified. In addition, if no (financially solvent) PRP can be identified, work may be completely financed from the fund. Ultimately, PRPs should replenish most of the fund, although initial recoveries from PRPs were far lower than initially anticipated. Between 1980 and 1989, responsible parties agreed to contribute approximately $642 million toward cleanups at 441 sites. The pace of recovery increased in 1990, with the EPA reporting recovery of more than $1 billion from private parties. The EPA reported in its 2005 annual summary of its Superfund program that more than $1.1 billion was committed by private parties for cleanups.[27]

The EPA may use the Superfund to engage in a cleanup while it is negotiating with PRPs and later recover its costs. Alternatively, the EPA may issue an administrative order or go through the courts to force responsible parties to pay directly for site cleanup. Typically, cleanup settlements reflect months or years of negotiations among the EPA and responsible parties to determine appropriate solutions and division of financial responsibility. The EPA encourages parties to decide on their own the proper allocation of responsibilities, as long as their settlement covers all costs. Obviously, this is often difficult, and the EPA must become involved. One big problem in negotiating is that there is great uncertainty about responsibility (the percentage of the problem that is due to each company's waste). Another important complication is that frequently companies that are now insolvent may have contributed significantly. The EPA may use Superfund dollars to cover their portion of the cleanup, although it is not required (or even encouraged) to do so. However, the EPA has shown great reluctance to accept a settlement for less than 100 percent of the total cleanup costs.

PRPs may be legally identified as responsible for waste cleanup even if they have relatively little involvement with the site difficulties. These parties can include present and past owners and operators of the site, transporters of the substances to the site, and generators who produced the substances. Joint and several liability is assigned, meaning that a responsible party may be assigned all, or any part, of the liability. Thus, if a company provided only a tiny fraction of the hazardous substances to an NPL site (but perhaps was the most financially solvent of the potentially responsible parties), the EPA would be acting within its authority to assign the total cleanup costs to that company. Of course, that company could then pursue through the courts cost recovery from the other sources of the hazardous substances. Liability is also retroactive, meaning that companies are responsible for their hazardous substances regardless of the time of disposal (or if they were in compliance with existing laws). Strict liability also applies, meaning that even if a company met all requirements existing at the time of disposal, problems occurring today still put them under the purview of CERCLA.

The definition of a potentially responsible party has been very broadly interpreted by the courts to expand the net of those who could be held liable. For example, in *United States v. Carolawn Chemical Company*,[28] the district court held that a chemical company that had held title to a hazardous waste disposal site for only 1 hour could be held liable under the Act as an owner and operator. The court in that case rejected the chemical company's claim that they had not really been an owner but had merely been a "conduit" in the transfer of title to the site. Other unlikely candidates also have been held responsible as owners under the Act. In *United States v. Burns,*[29] a district court in New Hampshire found the trustee of a realty trust liable as an owner. And, in a widely discussed case, *United States v. Fleet Factors Corporation,*[30] the court held that a lender holding a security interest in a corporation that owns a contaminated site may be liable if that lender is able to "affect hazardous waste disposal decisions" at the site.[31]

The EPA has provided a mechanism for eliminating liability for owners whose interest in a facility is only financial and does not involve site management. This protection to lending institutions largely applies to "involuntary" acquisitions of property rather than active participation in decisions involving the facility or hazardous material. Future liability also may be limited by obtaining a "covenant not to sue" or by agreement to a *de minimis* settlement. A PRP that contributed relatively little of the material causing the hazardous condition of a site may enter into an agreement in which it makes a relatively small settlement. As part of this *de minimis* settlement, the EPA may agree that this party will not be responsible for future liability for activities needed beyond those already specified in the ROD. Because the PRP will not be responsible for future activities, the EPA will agree not to sue them in the future for cost recovery. These arrangements are intended to allow relatively quick and complete settlement for companies that had little to do with a site and allow concentration of effort on the parties responsible for the majority of the problem. The EPA reports that as of October 1998, the Superfund enforcement program had reached settlements with more than 14,000 small parties, 66 percent of these since 1994.[32]

A decision by the Third Circuit Court in *U.S. v. Alcan Aluminum Corp.*[33] may result in an additional mechanism for industry to remove liability from involvement in a hazardous waste site. In this case, the court ruled that *Alcan Aluminum* must be given an opportunity to demonstrate the portion of harm it was responsible for, rather than having the court indiscriminately impose joint and several liability. If this case serves as a precedent, companies may become less concerned about the status of the disposal sites accepting their wastes as long as the ultimate fate and impact of their wastes can be clearly identified.

Another liability issue is whether an officer of a corporation responsible for dumping waste at a site may be held personally liable. In the 1985 case of *United States v. Mottolo,*[34] the court held the president of a chemical company personally liable, stating that those persons who actually arranged for or disposed of a hazardous waste under the Act did not need to be owners to be held responsible. Thus, we can see that the court is attempting to extend liability broadly to ensure that the Superfund will be at least partially replenished.

The regulatory and court's general pattern of assigning liability to industry may seem totally inequitable at first, because companies with very little involvement in a problem may face substantial financial obligations. However, keep in mind that if a responsible party cannot be found, the burden falls back on the taxpayer. Probably more important is that these liability burdens provide substantial incentive to the generating facilities to ensure that hazardous substances are properly disposed of. Thus, in addition to regulatory agencies checking on performance, companies exporting their wastes also have substantial incentive to ensure the proper management of TSDFs. This system brings both industry and government expertise to the task of TSDF inspections.

Citizen suits permit individuals to sue the government, any company, or individual for alleged violations of SARA.[35] Cases will be heard in the district court in the district where the alleged violation occurred or in the district court for the District of Columbia if the case is against the government. However, to allow time for compliance, no action may begin until at least 60 days after the plaintiff has notified the federal and state governments and the alleged violator of the intent to prosecute. Substantial opportunity and requirement for public involvement is built into this process; the EPA can give grants for up to $50,000 to public groups to hire appropriate people to help them understand the key issues. Obviously, this also makes data available to anyone who wishes to pursue litigation. CERCLA does not replace common law liability for personal injury or death under applicable principles of toxic tort laws, as discussed in Chapter 7.

Although the Superfund Program has undergone substantial modification since its origin, with the EPA reporting substantial progress, it still faces severe criticism. Following CERCLA's passage in 1980, the EPA's activities affecting remedial cleanup clearly was quite slow. By 1986, only eight sites had been remediated, and the entire Superfund had been spent. This obviously was not the intent of Congress, so it included in SARA a schedule for work to begin at NPL sites. The EPA responded by increasing its pace for remediation. By December 1994, the EPA reported that 279 NPL sites had been included on its "Construction Completion List." However, as sites continue to be discovered and evaluated, the size of the NPL continues to grow. For example, effective January 17, 1995, there were 1,088 General Superfund sites and 154 sites in the Federal Facilities Section. An additional 46 sites had been proposed, resulting in a total of 1,288 final and proposed sites. In 1997, the NPL had grown to include 1,405 sites.[36] Of all the listed sites, only 178 had been deleted from the NPL by October 8, 1998.[37] By the end of 2000, the EPA reported that it had accomplished 757 complete constructions, with 417 constructions underway, 61 facilities with design underway, 39 facilities with the remediation being selected, 178 facilities being studied, and another 50 facilities with work yet to begin.[38] Construction on an additional 47 sites was completed during the 2001 fiscal year. In 2004, the total number of NPL sites was 1,242, with 54 additional sites proposed for inclusion on the list.[39] In 2005, the EPA reported that remedial work had been completed at 966 sites and that the number of NPL sites had increased to 1498.[27]

Obviously, a substantial amount of cleanup has taken place. However, concern remains that there are many additional sites yet to be identified and remediated. During the Clinton Administration, the EPA went on record as supporting a revised Superfund law that would make major changes in many aspects of the regulatory program.[40] Although there has not been legislative activity directed at making substantial revisions, in response to continuing concern a Superfund Subcommittee was created in June 2002 to work with the EPA in identifying future directions for the Superfund. This subcommittee focuses its work on three areas: the NPL, complex and expensive sites (megasites), and measurement of program progress. Criticism of the effectiveness of the Superfund Program (from both the business and the environmental communities) remains active, and many would welcome amended Superfund legislation.

BROWNFIELDS

An unintended adverse consequence of joint and several liability potentially affecting industry is reluctance to site facilities in preexisting industrial sites. This hesitancy often conflicts with local and state land-use policies that promote retention of an active industrial zone to prevent economic stagnation or depression. Furthermore, industry locating in traditionally non-industrial areas often presents other problems, including the elimination of farmland, destruction of wilderness, or conflict with residential land uses. In response, some states are attempting to entice industrial development by reducing the liability associated with site redevelopment. It is of interest that this may be reverting the liability burden back to the taxpayer, in direct opposition to the rationale behind the federal assignment of responsibility.

The EPA has encouraged redevelopment of contaminated urban sites and has been promoting its Brownfield Economic Redevelopment Initiative. This initiative attempts to help communities revitalize abandoned contaminated property. The EPA provides funding for assessment of demonstration pilot programs (up to $200,000 over 2 years), training for residents affected by brownfields to facilitate cleanup, and a revolving loan fund to capitalize loans (up to $500,000 over 5 years) for environmental cleanup. Through the year 2000, the EPA has awarded funding for more than 360 Brownfield Assessment Demonstration Pilots. These pilots have been used for "testing redevelopment models, directing efforts at removing regulatory barriers, and bringing together community groups, investors, lenders, developers and other affected parties to address brownfield issues."[41] In 2006, the EPA is administering a "Brownfields Assessment, Revolving Loan Fund, and Cleanup Grants" Program with an estimated funding of $72 million to include approximately 200 agreements.

An excellent example of brownfield reclamation through coordinated activities of government and industry is the construction of a new manufacturing plant by Daimler/Chrysler to produce Jeeps in Toledo, Ohio. The new plant was constructed on a parcel of land secured by Toledo (in part by evoking eminent domain). The City invested about $75 million in the site, including funding for land acquisition, road construction, and environmental remediation. Assisted by the environmental cleanup and financial benefits, Daimler/Chrysler agreed to develop this site, and production on a new model of Jeep began at this facility in 2001.

Liability remains a key concern to those interested in redeveloping a brownfield site. The EPA may agree to a covenant not to sue a prospective developer for existing site contamination, relieving at least part of the liability concern. An EPA-generated archival list of more than 31,000 sites shows locations where there has been federal investigation of contamination, but no interest in pursuing Superfund activity. Again, this helps alleviate concerns about future liability from past contamination.

Federal legislation was proposed but failed in 2000 which would have made about $150 million in grants available annually to state brownfield programs and to provide liability exemptions for firms conducting cleanups. In 2001, the Brownfields Revitalization and Environmental Restoration Act of 2001 was introduced to "amend the Comprehensive Environmental Response, Compensation, and Liability Act of 1980 to promote the cleanup and reuse of brownfields, to provide financial assistance for brownfields revitalization, to enhance State response programs, and for other purposes." This bill failed. Finally, in 2002, the Small Business Liability Relief and Brownfields Revitalization Act was passed by Congress. The Administration subsequently announced various federal commitments to encourage brownfield revitalization. Funding of up to $850 million over the next 5 years for state, tribal, and local brownfields programs is to be provided by the EPA. The U.S. Economic Development Administration, the U.S. Department of Housing and Urban Development, the U.S. Department of the Interior, the U.S. Department of Justice, and the U.S. Department of Labor are charged with prioritizing brownfield communities within their respective grant mechanisms. The National Oceanic and Atmospheric Administration is identified as the lead agency for an interagency project renovating brownfields at ports and harbors. The U.S. Army Corps of Engineers is charged with developing eight brownfields pilot projects within its "Urban Rivers Initiative." Broad federal involvement also is encouraged through the formation of a federal 22-agency partnership (Table 8-4).[42] It should be interesting to monitor these initiatives to learn if they provide assistance to local development useful in reversing current trends of abandoning many industrial core areas.

TABLE 8-4   Federal Agencies Identified as Federal Brownfields Partners[43]

- Appalachian Regional Commission
- Department of Agriculture
- Department of Commerce
- Department of Defense
- Department of Education
- Department of Energy
- Department of Health and Human Services
- Department of Housing and Urban Development
- Department of Interior
- Department of Justice
- Department of Labor
- Department of Transportation
- Department of Treasury
- Department of Veterans Affairs
- Environmental Protection Agency
- Federal Deposit Insurance Corporation
- Federal Housing Finance Board
- General Services Administration
- Small Business Administration

UNDERGROUND STORAGE TANK PROGRAM

A program related to emergency planning, although of different regulatory origin, is the underground storage tank (UST) program. RCRA's Hazard and Solid Waste Amendments of 1984 (HSWA) provided the framework for a regulatory program designed to help prevent releases from underground storage tanks (USTs). Most of the USTs in the United States store gasoline. However, other flammable industrial chemicals (such as degreasing solvents) have traditionally been stored underground to minimize fire hazards. Various early estimates put the number of regulated tanks at 1.5 to 2 million, with somewhere between 10 and 30 percent of them leaking. Following more than two decades of federal regulatory control, only about 650,000 regulated tanks are estimated to remain, perhaps reflecting in part the removal of tanks that are uneconomical to maintain meeting regulatory requirements.

Leaks in USTs can contaminate important groundwater supplies and cost millions of dollars to remediate (even partially). One area that has experienced major problems is the Silicon Valley in Santa Clara County, California, a hub of the semiconductor industry. In the 18-month period beginning in April 1980, IBM, Hewlett Packard, Intel, Advanced Micro

Devices, and Fairchild all reported tanks leaking organic solvents. These solvents moved to drinking water wells; one well near Fairchild had one organic solvent, 1-1-1-trichloroethane or TCA, at concentrations 29 times the state action level. Cleanup of the groundwater in Silicon Valley will cost millions of dollars and may never be successfully completed. Obviously, the best remedy to this problem would have been prevention.

A comprehensive program for managing USTs has emerged. Although HSWA requirements demand EPA leadership and involvement, program implementation with owners and operators of private underground tanks is done through state and local programs. Federal rules serve as minimum standards. For example, the federal regulatory program tank and leak detection standards specify that new tanks must have spill and overflow protection devices. The tanks must meet performance standards designed to ensure that the stored material will not cause corrosion. Because responsibility for these programs is being taken over by the states, actual requirements may be more stringent than these federal minimums. Existing tanks had until December 1998 to meet the new tank standards. This can be accomplished by installing a liner, or cathodic protection, against corrosion. Spill and overflow protection and a leak detection system also must be installed. Tanks that store hazardous substances (other than petroleum products) must have extra protection against release of those hazardous substances. This may be accomplished through a secondary containment system, a double-walled tank, or an external liner. These devices are intended to keep any release of the inner tank contained, whereas the leak-detection system signals that the inner tank has lost its integrity. The EPA has developed technical guidance documents identifying acceptable methods to meet these requirements.

A significant burden is placed on the owner/operator of a tank to ensure that adequate financial resources are available to respond to a leak. Financial responsibility can be demonstrated through insurance, a letter of credit, a trust fund, a surety bond, or a state-managed financial assurance device. Large facilities, handling more than 10,000 gallons of petroleum per month, must have at least $1 million of coverage per occurrence. All other facilities must have $500,000 coverage per occurrence.

These regulatory requirements impose a substantial financial burden on a tank owner/operator. To encourage compliance is the threat of both criminal and civil penalties. Federal law establishes a penalty of not more than $10,000 per tank per day for failing to comply with UST standards or submitting false information. Moreover, local and state programs could impose greater penalties. A recent federal case vividly demonstrates the potential for imposition of substantial penalty for non-compliance. Tanknology-NDE International, Inc., was sentenced in federal district court in Austin, Texas, in October 2002 to pay a criminal fine of $1 million and restitution of $1.29 million for the costs of retesting falsely tested underground storage tanks. Tanknology pleaded guilty to falsifying storage tank testing at various federal facilities, including those of the U.S. Department of Defense, the U.S. Postal Service, and the National Aeronautics and Space Administration.

The EPA completed a comprehensive review of its UST Regulations in 1998.[43] Five factors were considered:

1. The continued need for the program
2. The nature of complaints or comments about the program
3. The program's complexity
4. The extent of the program's overlap, duplication, or conflicts with other government rules
5. The degree that technology, economics, and other factors have changed since the program was developed

The EPA's findings were that the program continues to be important and that the December 22, 1998, deadline for compliance with underground tank requirement is appropriate. The State of Florida recommended to the EPA that the program be expanded to require secondary containment of all UST systems, but the EPA ruled that this would impose an unnecessary cost in situations where corrosion protection and leak detection is sufficient. Florida also recommended that the UST program be expanded to include above-ground tanks, but the EPA responded that it has no regulatory authority to do this. The EPA also found that the regulations are sufficiently clear to be understandable to the regulatory community, including small owners and operators (such as individuals who own gasoline stations). Problems were not identified with redundancies or conflicts with other regulatory programs, and the period of review of these regulations appears to be appropriate. The EPA's findings that these regulatory requirements were not unreasonable perhaps is best documented by having had only a single agency submit comments during the review period.

The UST program clearly has reduced contamination from leaking USTs. About 1.5 million substandard USTs have closed and others have been retrofitted. Over 300,000 cleanups have been completed and more than another 400,000 initiated. However, problems with leaking tanks remain. To further assist efforts to limit contamination from these sources, the EPA announced on October 23, 2000, four initiatives to enhance the underground tank program. The UST brownfields initiative is designed to provide federal assistance and funding to help remediate brownfields housing abandoned or closed USTs. A second initiative is designed to improve compliance with current UST laws and regulations. The EPA reported that about 21 percent of the 683,000 active USTs in the United States are out of compliance with spill, overfill, and corrosion-protection requirements, with 28 percent not meeting the leak-detection requirements.[44] A third initiative is intended to hasten cleanups from tanks that have already leaked. The final initiative is to better define the effectiveness of the UST regulatory program.

The problem of adequately measuring a regulatory system's performance is vividly demonstrated in the UST Program. The EPA and state and local governments can point to widespread compliance with standards designed to ensure that chemicals in underground tanks do not leak. Yet, the EPA's Blue Ribbon Panel for Reviewing the Use of MTBE and Other Oxygenates in Gasoline concluded, in part, that "there continue to be reports of releases [of gasoline additives] from some upgraded systems, due to inadequate design, installation, maintenance, and/or operation."[45] The physical presence of components of gasoline in groundwater provides the ultimate measure of regulatory system performance—regulations designed to prevent leaks are not always preventing leaks. This outcome measure may indicate important deficiencies in the regulatory program including its implementation and enforcement. The continued presence of gasoline components in groundwater also has triggered substantial debate about appropriate gasoline additives and possible trade-offs between better burning fuels with fuels that have less potential for dispersal in groundwater. Less visible are discussions of new regulatory programs and approaches to overcome deficiencies in the helpful but currently incomplete control offered through the current UST program.

The Energy Policy Act (EPAct) of 2005 included the Underground Storage Tanks Compliance Act of 2005, which contained several amendments to HSWA to further strengthen the control of USTs. These amendments include

- All tanks not inspected since December 22, 1998, must be inspected by August 8, 2007,
- Following completion of the inspection of tanks that had not been inspected since December 22, 1998, all regulated tanks must be inspected very 3 years,
- Training guidelines and requirements must be developed for operators who operate and maintain federally regulated UST systems,
- New or replaced tanks and piping within 1,000 feet of an existing community water system or an existing potable drinking water well must be secondarily contained, and
- New dispenser systems within 1,000 feet of an existing community water system or an existing potable drinking water well must have under-dispenser spill containment.

It is too early to evaluate the effectiveness of these amendments in preventing leaks of hazardous materials from USTs, although the passage of the Act demonstrates clear recognition of the need for greater regulatory control.

Concluding Remarks

Waste management practices in the United States have changed remarkably over the past 30 years. A complex and comprehensive system now governs the fate of waste, with incentives to reduce generation and recycle rather than "dispose" through permanent storage on the land or in the water. Nevertheless, much of our waste stream continues to be put in landfills, and this quantity may be slowly increasing. Although modern landfills should be effective in containing wastes, even several layers of plastic and clay liners will not last forever. Thus, modern technology may be only deferring liability problems into the future.

It is clear that progress has been made in providing protection from the unintended release of hazardous materials; it is equally obvious that these releases still occur. In addition to the CERCLA and UST provisions, efforts to reduce hazardous waste generation and to properly manage waste following RCRA provisions are important in minimizing risk from hazardous materials. CERCLA followed RCRA because initial concerns focused more on hazardous wastes than on hazardous materials; much of the public probably still views hazardous waste as presenting the larger threat. The regulatory community recognizes the need to protect the public and the environment from all agents that have a substantial potential to cause harm.

The nation's brownfields present both an opportunity and a challenge to revitalize the urban core. Leadership must come from the local and state level, and the federal government has promised to support these efforts through a variety of mechanisms. Although not part of the specific mandate of the EPA, programs that provided jobs to the inner cities while reducing demands for energy and infrastructure to accommodate long commutes to the suburbs would have far-reaching benefits in addition to providing a cost-effective approach to managing hazardous waste.

The current regulatory framework governing wastes and hazardous materials continues to be challenged as overly complex, expensive, and cumbersome. Yet, major changes to this framework neither have been made over the past decade nor are on the horizon of the federal legislative agenda. However, waste and hazardous material management have become—at least to some extent—an integral part of most industrial practices. This may be enough to prevent or greatly reduce the likelihood of disastrous outcomes similar to those that we are only now remediating. Furthermore, programs at the local and state levels, prompted through community awareness, may drive additional improvement in management programs although doing little about regulatory complexities.

Interesting will be to see how the growing attention being given to issues surrounding resource use affects these regulatory programs. Already, it is apparent that global climate change and energy use will be issues dominating environmental, and perhaps political, agendas as we enter the 21st century. Certainly, improved use of resources not only holds promise for easing the burden of waste management but also can contribute to reducing greenhouse gas emissions and dependence on fossil-fuel-based sources of energy. The past decade has been one of relatively little regulatory activity governing resource conservation—an optimist might conclude that this means that tremendous opportunity remains to help solve the major environmental threats facing the planet.

Questions for Review and Discussion

1. What is the best solution to the growing problem of waste production?
2. Should laws exclude hazardous wastes from households and small-quantity generators from regulation?
3. Should there be a different level of protection at hazardous waste landfills from that at sanitary landfills? What is the EPA's opinion?
4. How should long-term liability best be controlled from landfills that prohibit rapid degradation of waste?
5. Why is CERCLA commonly referred to as Superfund? Was this appropriate when the law was passed? Is this appropriate now?
6. What obstacles does the regulated community face in responding to notification requirements of SARA Title III?
7. What groups must be represented in emergency planning? Are there other groups that should be represented?
8. What type of approach would be useful for evaluating the effectiveness of EPCRA in preventing hazardous substance spills?
9. What is the difference between a removal action and a remedial action?
10. How much involvement must a company or an individual have with a hazardous substance to be considered a PRP under CERCLA?
11. Should a company renovating a brownfields site be able to have guaranteed immunity from CERCLA liability? What are the advantages and disadvantages of providing this immunity?
12. Is the Brownfield Economic Redevelopment Initiative going to help or hinder protection and restoration of environmental quality? What do you suspect are the views of the pertinent interest groups (e.g., industrial organizations, environmental groups, the EPA)?
13. USTs meeting UST regulatory requirements are still failing. New requirements have recently been added to strengthen the UST regulatory program; Do you think that these new requirements will be adequate? Are there other additional actions that should be taken?

For Further Reading

Applegate, J. S., and J.G. Laitos. 2005. *Environmental Law: RCRA, CERCLA, and the Management of Hazardous Waste.* New York: Foundation Press.

Cunningham, S. 2002. *The Restoration Economy: The Greatest New Growth Frontier: Immediate & Emerging Opportunities for Businesses, Communities & Investors.* Williston, VT: Berrett-Koehler.

Environmental Law Institute. 1998. *An Analysis of State Superfund Programs:*

50-State Study, 1998 Update. Washington, D.C.: Environmental Law Institute.

Hall, R. M., Jr., et al. 2001. *RCRA Hazardous Wastes Handbook.* 12th ed. Knoxville, TN: Abs Group Inc.

McDonough, W., and M. Braungart. 2002. *Cradle to Cradle: Remaking the Way We Make Things.* New York: North Point Press.

Porter, R. C. 2002. *The Economics of Waste.* Baltimore, MD: Resources for the Future.

Probst, K. M, D. M. Konisky, R. Hersh, M. B. Batz, and K. D. Walker. 2001. *Superfund's Future: What Will It Cost?* Baltimore, MD: Resources for the Future.

Rafson, H. J., and R. N. Rafson, eds. 1999. *Brownfields: Redeveloping Environmentally Distressed Properties.* New York: McGraw-Hill.

Shah, K. 1999. *Basics of Solid and Hazardous Waste Management Technology.* Englewood Cliffs, NJ: Prentice-Hall.

Sullivan, T. F. P., et al. 2003. *Environmental Law Handbook.* 17th ed. Knoxville, TN: Abs Group Inc.

Wagner, T. 1999. *The Complete Guide to the Hazardous Waste Regulations: RCRA, TSCA, HMTA, OSHA and Superfund.* 3rd ed. New York: Wiley.

On the Internet

http://www.atsdr.cdc.gov/
    Agency for Toxic Substances and Disease Registry home page
http://www.epa.gov/enviro/
    EPA's "Envirofacts Data Warehouse" provides a source to multimedia environmental data
http://www.epa.gov/epaoswer/general/orientat/
    The EPA's RCRA Orientation Manual 2006
http://www.epa.gov/superfund/
    The EPA's Superfund information site
http://www.epa.gov/swercepp/
    The EPA's Office of Emergency Management home page
http://www.epa.gov/superfund/programs/er/hazsubs/supers.htm
    Description of the EPA's Superfund Response Program
http://www.epa.gov/superfund/sites/query/basic.htm
    EPA National Priorities List query form
http://www.epa.gov/swerust1/
    The EPA's Office of Underground Storage Tanks home page
http://www.epa.gov/swercepp/tier2.htm
    Provides access to EPA's Tier II electronic reporting
http://www.epa.gov/triexplorer/introduction.htm
    Provides information on the toxic release inventory program and access to the chemical list
http://www.epa.gov/msw/msw99.htm
    Provides year 2005 facts and figures on municipal solid waste in the United States
http://www.epa.gov/osw/catalog/cat17.pdf
    Catalog of EPA hazardous and solid waste publications
http://www.epa.gov/brownfields/partners/2005_fpg.pdf
    The EPA's Brownfields Federal Programs Guide, 2005 Edition

Notes

1. L. Blumberg, and R. Gottlieb. 1989. *War on Waste: Can America Win Its Battle with Garbage?* Washington, D.C.: Island Press.

2. Subcommittee on Transportation and Commerce, Committee on Interstate and Foreign Commerce, U.S. House of Representatives, Resource Conservation and Recovery Act of 1976, 94th Congress, second session; Waste Control Act of 1975; Hearings on H.R. 5487 and H.R. 406 Before Subcommittee on Transportation and Commerce, 94th Congress, first session (1975).

3. EPA. 1986. *Office of Solid Waste, Survey of Solid Waste (Municipal) Landfill Facilities.* Washington, D.C.: Government Printing Office.

4. EPA. 1988. *Office of Solid Waste and Emergency Response, Report to Congress, Solid Waste Disposal in the United States.* Washington, D.C.: Government Printing Office. Publication no. EPA 530-SW-88-011B.

5. EPA. 2005. *Office of Solid Waste and Emergency Response, Municipal Solid Waste Generation, Recycling, and Disposal in the United States: Facts and Figures for 2003.* Washington, D.C.: Government Printing Office. Publication no. EPA-530-F-05-003.

6. EPA. 2005. *Office of Solid Waste and Emergency Response, The National Biennial RCRA Hazardous Waste Report (Based on 2003 Data).* Washington, D.C.: Government Printing Office. Publication no. EPA530-R-03-007

7. Title 42—The Public Health and Welfare, Chapter 82—Solid Waste Disposal.

8. 40 C.F.R. 261.4(a).

9. 42 U.S.C. 6073.

10. P.L. 898-616, 302.

11. 42 U.S.C. 6972.

12. 40 C.F.R. 261.21.

13. 40 C.F.R. 261.22.

14. 40 C.F.R. 261.24.

15. 40 C.F.R. 261.23.

16. 40 C.F.R. 261.4(b).

17. Government Accounting Office. 1983. *Interim Report on Inspection, Enforcement, and Permitting Activities at Hazardous Waste Facilities.* Washington, D.C.: Government Printing Office.

18. 40 C.F.R. 264, subparts I–O, S, X.

19. 40 C.F.R. 265, subparts I–R, W.

20. 40 C.F.R. 264, 3008.

21. *EPA Press Release.* "Tennessee Firm and Officers Plead Guilty to Illegal Waste Disposal" (February 22, 2001). *http://yosemite.epa.gov/opa/admpress. nsf/b1ab9f485b098972852562e7004dc68 6/373b0ed73c465e9e852569fb0079ed02? OpenDocument.*

22. Emergency Planning and Community Right-to-Know Act 301 (1986).

23. Emergency Planning and Community Right-to-Know Act 311 (1986).

24. Emergency Planning and Community Right-to-Know Act 312 (1986).

25. EPA. *Emergency Response Program, Hazardous Substances Release, Reporting Triggers. http://www. epa.gov/superfund/programs/er/ triggers/haztrigs/rqover.htm.*

26. EPA. *Emergency Response Program, Superfund Emergency Response, Program Accomplishments. http://www.epa.gov/superfund/ programs/er/hazsubs/accomps.htm.*

27. EPA. *Annual Superfund Data Shows Continuing Cleanup Progress. http://www.epa.gov/superfund/news/ pr_112205.htm*

28. 21 Environmental Reporter Cases 2124 (D.S.C. 1984).

29. No. C-88-94-L (D.N.H. 1988).

30. 901 F.2a 155 (11th Cir. 1990), cert. denied, 111 S.C5.752 (1991).

31. Ibid., 1557.

32. EPA. *Emergency Response Program Office.*
33. 25 ELR 21556.
34. 605 F.Supp. 898 (D.N.H. 1985).
35. SARA, Sec. 310.
36. EPA. *Superfund Cleanup Figures 1998.* http://www.epa.gov/superfund/whatissf/ mgmtrpt.htm.
37. EPA. *Sites Deleted from the NPL.* http://www.epa.gov/superfund/sites/ npl/npldel.htm.
38. EPA. *Emergency Response Program Office.*
39. EPA. *National Priorities List.* http://www.epa.gov/superfund/sites/ query/basic.htm.
40. EPA. *Superfund Reauthorization Principles.* http://www.epa.gov/ superfund/action/congress/princple.htm.
41. EPA. 2000. *Solid Waste and Emergency Response [5105], Brownfields Economic Redevelopment Initiative.* Washington, D.C.: Government Printing Office. Publication no. EPA 500-F-00-241.
42. EPA. *Brownfields Economic Redevelopment Initiative Fact Sheet.* http://www.epa.gov/swerosps/bf/ html-doc/econinit.htm.
43. 5 U.S.C. 610.
44. EPA. *Office of Solid Waste and Emergency Response, UST Program Facts.* http://www.epa.gov/oust/ pubs/ustprogramfacts.pdf.
45. EPA. *Office of Underground Storage Tanks. Four UST Program Initiatives.* http://www.epa.gov/swerust1/ initiati.htm.

RESOLVING CONTROVERSIAL ENVIRONMENTAL ISSUES

HAS SUPERFUND TURNED THE CORNER?

The Superfund Program and the EPA have received intense criticism for spending enormous amounts of money and yet failing to protect public health and the environment. Since 1980 many changes have been made, and the EPA reports that the Superfund Program is now working well. The following "Summary of Significant Accomplishments" was published by the EPA at *http://www.epa.gov/superfund/action/process/numbers05.htm*

SUPERFUND SUMMARY OF SIGNIFICANT ACCOMPLISHMENTS

EPA's Superfund Program

- obligated $524 million to perform construction and postconstruction activities and to conduct and oversee emergency response actions
- obligated $404 million in appropriated funds, State cost-share contributions, and PRP settlement resources for construction and postconstruction projects
- obligated $120 million to conduct more than 400 emergency response and removal actions to address immediate and substantial threats to communities
- obligated nearly $70 million in appropriated funds, State cost-share contributions, and PRP settlement resources for 17 new construction projects ranked by the National Risk-Based Priority Panel at 15 NPL sites
- conducted or oversaw 665 ongoing construction projects (by EPA, PRPs, and federal facilities) at 422 sites.

Federal facilities accounted for 220 of these ongoing projects
- completed construction phase of cleanup at 40 sites across the country for a total of 966 or 62% of the sites on the NPL
- listed 18 new sites on the NPL and proposed 12 sites for the NPL
- obligated more than $214 million in appropriated funds, State cost-share contributions, and PRP settlement resources to conduct and oversee
  - site assessments and investigations
  - selection and design of cleanup plans
  - support for State, Tribal, community involvement activities, and other activities.
- selected final cleanup plans at 39 sites, including five federal facilities sites. This brings the cumulative total of sites with final cleanup plans to approximately 70% of 1498 NPL sites
- conducted 247 5-Year Reviews, including 27 Reviews at federal facilities sites. These Reviews are conducted to ensure that protective measures for waste that has been secured on-site remain intact
- deleted 18 sites, including one federal facility, and partially deleted five sites from the NPL
- In 2005, EPA participated on 131 active Restoration Advisory Boards (RABs) and Site Specific Advisory Boards (SSABs) at Department of Defense (DOD) or Department of Energy facilities (DOE), respectively, on the NPL. RABs and SSABs provide a forum for concerned stakeholders and community members to provide input on DOD's and DOE's

environmental activities at individual facilities

- underscoring EPA's commitment to the "polluter pays" principle, the Agency secured private party-funding commitments of more than $1.1 billion in Fiscal Year 2005. Of this amount, PRPs agreed to conduct more than $857 million in future response work and to reimburse EPA for $248 million in past costs

1. The U.S. EPA is making a case for having made significant progress in the Superfund Program. In Chapter 7, you learned about problems with missing infor mation. What additional information would help you better evaluate the progress of the Superfund program?
2. Statistical information is given to support the EPA's position. At the end of Chapter 6, you learned about problems with statistics. Do these statistics about Superfund make a clear case for the Program's success? Are there any problems with these statistics as the EPA presents them?

Although the EPA touts its successes it has many critics, and these critics come from multiple perspectives. For example, Senator James Inhofe (R-Oklahoma), former chairman of the Committee on Environment and Public Works, has said in his opening statement to a hearing for "The Range Readiness and Preservation Initiative of the Department of Defense" (a proposal to limit the military's obligations under several major environmental laws) that

Trial lawyers too are interested in full employment. For example, these lawyers swear blind allegiance to the much maligned and tragically flawed CERCLA/Superfund Act. It is no coincidence that the CERCLA/Superfund Act is commonly called the "Lawyers'

Full Employment Act" due to the fact that so much money goes to lawyers, including government lawyers, and so little actually goes to clean our water and soil. With so many twisted and convoluted regulatory procedures, and particularly eco-regulatory procedures, we have created the world's largest maze complete with an invasive species to run through the maze–the trial lawyer.

Senator Inhofe, widely viewed in the environmental community as being among the most environmentally unfriendly members of the U.S. Senate, obviously does not think highly of our regulatory system for managing wastes. Yet, many in the environmental community agree with the Senator regarding the effectiveness of current regulatory programs. For example, the Sierra Club states on one of its web pages (*http://www. sierraclub.org/toxics/superfund/report04/*) that

The Bush administration's failure to protect Americans' health from toxic waste pollution is documented in this new report on the Superfund toxic waste cleanup program released today by the Sierra Club. The report breaks down state-by-state the Superfund sites across the country where human exposure to toxic pollution and groundwater pollution is either not under control or where insufficient data on threats exist.

The report is based on Environmental Protection Agency (EPA) performance indicators that show that the task of protecting people's health and water supplies from toxic chemical contamination is far from complete.

The report finds that human exposure to health-threatening chemicals is not under control at 111 Superfund sites. At another 199 Superfund sites, EPA has insufficient data to determine if migration of groundwater pollution is under control.

Americans are paying twice: once with their health and again with their taxes. There is a better way. The Bush administration could help solve these health threats and tax burden by supporting the polluter-pays principle to recreate a stable funding source for the Superfund program.

Two very different perspectives, from opposite sides of the political/environmental spectrum, seem to agree that the Superfund Program is not working as well as it should. The EPA, responsible for implementing and enforcing this program, may even be agreeing that more progress would be better. In its concluding remarks pertaining to its annual accomplishments, it noted that

Superfund faces constraints: 1) In Fiscal Year 2005, 50 percent of Superfund obligations for construction and post-construction activities went to 11 sites,

and 2) Due to EPA's priority to fund ongoing work, less funding was available for new construction projects, and EPA did not have enough resources to fund 9 new construction projects evaluated by the National Priority Panel and that were ready for construction.

1. You learned about ethical norms involved in reasoning. Describe the ethical norms of the Senator and the Sierra Club with respect to the Superfund program and extrapolate to consider their views on the role of government.

2. Consider the final statements of the EPA with regard to Superfund constraints. Suggest ways to reconcile the program with respect to the views expressed by Senator Inhofe, the Sierra Club, and the EPA. Identify the type of outcome data that would satisfy the demands of each.

CHAPTER 9
ENERGY

This chapter examines energy law and policy, the area of law that attempts to manage energy needs. As we enter the 21st century, developing a coherent energy policy for the United States will be increasingly important. The U.S. consumption of energy accounts for approximately one-forth of all energy produced in the world; maintaining this level of consumption will become more difficult as energy resources are depleted. Adding to the troubles of resource depletion is the worldwide rise in demand for energy. As China and India continue to industrialize and expand at high rates, the worldwide demand for energy also increases. This overall increase in energy demand further taxes the nonrenewable sources of energy this planet has to offer. A symptom of this growing demand for energy is that although the United States appears to be using less energy than in the past, as our share of energy consumption has diminished, the overall amount of energy consumed by the United States has not decreased significantly. Rather, India, China, and other countries have started using more energy, thus decreasing our overall percentage of energy used. For example, whereas the United States accounts for approximately 23 percent of world energy consumption, China constitutes 11 percent of worldwide energy consumption.[1] India, far from being the third highest energy-consuming country, is now up to 3 percent of worldwide energy consumption.[2]

Many argue we should change our consumption patterns; such change is highly unlikely to occur absent some cataclysmic event. Some people also view our dependency on foreign countries for vast amounts of our energy supply as a national security hazard. Development of renewable energy is one solution to end our reliance on nonrenewable sources of energy and on foreign countries, but this area has its problems as well. As you can see, energy law and policy is therefore very complex. Further complicating issue are the heat waves experience around the United States over the last few years. States nationwide have been setting record high temperatures. In fact, almost every state in the United States reached temperatures at least in the 1990s for close to 2 weeks in the summer of 2006. With the increased temperatures come increased energy usage as households and businesses turn up the air conditioning in an attempt to escape the heat. However, the problem is energy use skyrockets as air conditions are running longer and working harder to maintain the cooler temperatures. Given the worldwide increase of energy use, as well as the weather's increasing effect upon energy consumption, national energy policy is more important than ever.

ENERGY POLICY: A HISTORICAL OVERVIEW

The U.S. energy policy has been anything but consistent. We seem to bounce back and forth from complacency to crisis to complacency, at least with respect to aspects of energy policy designed to ensure that the nation's demand for energy can be met. Early in 2001, it appeared that we were heading into another crisis as gasoline prices increased to almost $2.00 per gallon in some states, and California began experiencing rolling power blackouts. After the terrorist attacks of September 11, 2001, there was a strong push to decrease our energy dependency on foreign countries and to increase domestic oil production. However, after President Bush made his "Mission Accomplished" address on May 1, 2003 regarding American operations in Iraq, the push to decrease oil-based energy dependency subsided with promises of greater oil availability. These promises did not come to fruition, and gas prices continued to rise, occasionally surpassing $3.00 per gallon.

As you examine energy policy, you should be aware of the major conflict in philosophies that underlies our shifting policies. On the one hand, the belief in unlimited resources or unlimited technological developments tends to encourage the full development of energy resources. On the other hand, the view that energy is a limited resource favors policies that encourage conservation and demand reduction.

Before the 1970s, energy policy received little consideration. Although the possibilities of nuclear energy had begun to be explored, we were still complacently relying on what seemed to be an unlimited access to worldwide stores of fossil fuels: coal, petroleum, and natural gas. In fact, in 1900, coal provided 90 percent of the energy in the United States. By 1970, petroleum and natural gas each provided about 35 percent. Coal still remained a significant source, however, providing about 23 percent of our energy. Figure 9-1 illustrates the consumption, production, and importation of petroleum from 1950 to 2004.

THE CRISIS BEGINS

Not until 1973 did the phrase energy crisis enter the American vocabulary. The "crisis," which would last until 1978, began in October 1973, when the United States was importing 38.8 percent of its daily petroleum consumption. The Organization of Petroleum Exporting Countries (OPEC) voted to cut its oil production by 5 percent monthly until Israel made fundamental changes in its Arab policies. The day after that vote, Saudi Arabia, OPEC's major producer, cut its oil exports by 10 percent and ended all petroleum shipments to the United States until the Nixon administration altered its pro-Israel policies. The loss of two million barrels of oil a day shocked Americans into suddenly recognizing how dependent we had become on foreign oil. The loss also forced Americans to recognize what political, economic, and military risks this dependence entailed. From an environmental standpoint, the situation was a crisis because if the oil shortage continued for long, the United States might be

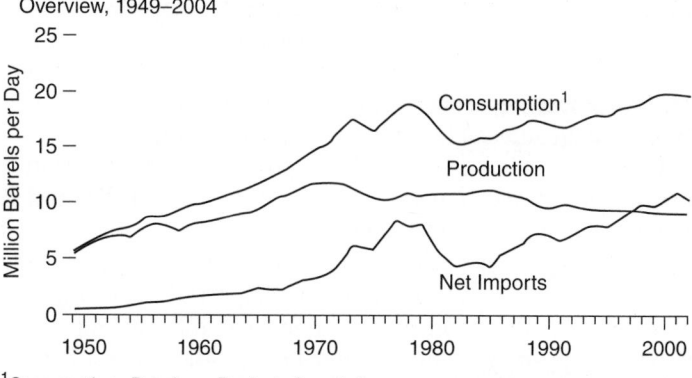

Overview, 1949–2004

¹Consumption = Petroleum Products Supplied

FIGURE 9-1   Consumption, Production, and Importation of Petroleum

When U.S. domestic supply of petroleum peaked at 11.7 million barrels per day in 1970, net imports stood at 3.2 million barrels per day. As domestic supply declined, consumption grew. In 1998, for the first time, net imports surpassed domestic supply. In 2004, domestic supply was 5.4 million barrels per day and net imports were 12.9 million barrels per day.

Source: Energy Information Administration. *Annual Energy Review 2004. http://www.eia. doe.gov/emeu/aer/pdf/aer.pdf* (July 10, 2006).

compelled to increase greatly its mining of coal, with potentially disastrous ecological consequences.[3]

In response to the OPEC oil embargo, Nixon took the first steps in the U.S. history toward comprehensive national energy planning. He established the Federal Energy Office (FEO) within the White House staff in late 1973. The next year, he established the Federal Energy Administration, which was given the authority to initiate federal policy and take whatever steps the White House deemed necessary for national energy needs. Congress, likewise, contributed to a developing national energy policy by creating the Energy Research and Development Administration (ERDA) to consolidate all federal energy research in a single agency.

Until his forced resignation in 1974, Nixon continued to urge legislation designed to increase the federal role in energy management. He proposed laws restricting public and private energy consumption, providing unemployment insurance for those who lost jobs because of the energy crisis, temporarily relaxing air pollution standards for automobile emissions and power plants, and imposing a windfall profit tax to keep companies from making excess profits by rapidly increasing energy prices. He used powers granted to him by Congress to impose mandatory allocations of selected fossil fuels, as well as to set up an allocation program and price guidelines for crude oil and petroleum.

By the end of Nixon's term, he and Congress had also instituted national daylight savings time and the 55-mile-per-hour speed limit as conservation efforts. They had funded new federal programs for research into solar energy and had encouraged private development of nuclear energy. Nixon had also invented Project Independence, a hastily crafted program designed to ensure that, by the end of the decade, the United States would be able to meet all of its own energy needs. Many of the proposals were technologically infeasible, and some were contradictory.

The energy crisis continued through the Ford administration, with Ford submitting a package of measures in his 1975 Energy Policy and Conservation Act, focusing on programs designed to give flexibility to the administration in handling energy problems. This act established the strategic petroleum reserve, the purpose of which is to minimize the impact of an oil importing crisis like the one in 1973. President Carter came into office making energy policy his number one priority. A month after taking office, he set forth his National Energy Plan (NEP), organized around four broad objectives:

1. To centralize federal energy planning through institutional reform
2. To achieve greater energy efficiency through selective use of market forces and a major expansion of federal regulatory policy
3. To increase rapidly federal spending on research and development of new technology for energy conservation and productivity
4. To ensure environmental protection and social equity would be important in these new programs[4]

Over 200 separate proposals were considered by Congress in relation to NEP. Many were defeated, and the program was perceived by many as hastily constructed and too complex. But by the end of his term, Carter had made some significant changes in federal energy policy: The Department of Energy (DOE) had been created, domestic gas and petroleum prices had been decontrolled, increased government funding had been provided for federal research and development for new energy technologies, and more environmental safeguards on energy use had been established.

A RETURN TO COMPLACENCY

Reagan's victory signaled the end of the energy crisis, at least as perceived by the executive and the general public. In his first NEP, Reagan informed the public that the forecast for energy supplies was not as bad as some had thought; there were going to be no more "wars on energy." Reagan's program of regulatory relief was going to be applied to energy policies as well as to other regulatory actions. Within a few years, energy policy had been dramatically altered. There was a return to the preembargo days of abundant energy. This new philosophy continued through the Bush administration.

Reagan tried to abolish the DOE, but Congress would not go along with him and he had to be content with reducing the agency's authority. He slashed the budget of the Office of Strip Mining, weakening its ability to enforce regulations. His secretary of state attempted to lease more public land on the OCS and in federal wild areas for energy exploration than had been leased in the entire period before Nixon's election. Funding for energy conservation programs and research for renewable sources of energy, such as solar and wind power, was slashed.

By mid-1985, energy no longer appeared in public opinion polls as a major concern. Conservation of energy was no longer a concern by the late 1980s; in 1989, Ford Motor Company brought back the V8 engine in its Mustang, an act representative of the return of the gas-guzzling "muscle cars." By 1990, Americans were no longer interested in energy-efficient houses; many developers had quit building them because of a lack of demand. In 1986, residential energy demand had exceeded industrial demand for the first time. By the end of Reagan's term, funding for research and development of renewable energy sources had fallen to 18 percent of 1980 levels, and federal tax credits for the use of these alternative energy sources had expired.

A BRIGHT SPOT: THE ENERGY POLICY ACT

There were some indications that the 1990s might see a renewed interest in a national energy policy. The 1990 invasion of Kuwait, which made Americans again aware of the danger of dependence on foreign oil, may have served as a partial stimulus. In February 1991, then-President Bush introduced his National Energy Strategy (NES), an attempt to achieve roughly equal measures of new energy production and conservation. The NES focused on five main categories: energy security, energy and economic efficiency, future energy supplies, environmental quality, and expanding scientific research and education. A follow-up report on the NES indicated that considerable progress had been made in the implementation of NES initiatives. Some of the major accomplishments cited in this report include creating the U.S. Advanced Battery Consortium, developing ethanol from biomass and waste, upgrading a DOE research facility to the National Renewable Energy Laboratory, and developing the National Technology Initiative.[5] However, this study was released only 1 year after the introduction of the NES, and further assessment is difficult because of the change in the administration in 1993. The GAO was less optimistic about the success of the NES. In testimony before Congress in 1991, the GAO noted that development of the NES was not as open to the public as it should have been, used optimistic macroeconomic assumptions in its models, and claimed the CAA amendments of 1990 as a part of the NES, thereby making it difficult to determine which positive effects could be attributed to the CAA amendments and which to the NES.[6]

As part of the implementation of the NES, President Bush issued an Executive Order on Federal Energy Management in April 1991.[7] If fully implemented, the order was projected to save taxpayers up to $800 million in annual energy costs and cut federal energy consumption by the equivalent of up to 100,000 barrels of oil per day.[8] The three primary elements of the order are as follows:[9]

1. Energy use in federal buildings must be reduced to 20 percent below 1985 levels by 2000
2. Gasoline and diesel use in government fleets of 300 or more must be reduced to 10 percent below 1991 levels by 1995
3. All federal agencies must secure the largest practicable number of alternative fuel vehicles by the end of 1995

The success of this executive order was borne out in 2000, when the DOE announced that reduction in energy use had been achieved—and a year early! Reducing energy use to 20 percent below 1985 levels by 1999 has saved taxpayers over $19 billion since 1985, with $2 billion of that in 1999 alone, and has reduced greenhouse gas emissions by 2.4 million metric tons since 1985.[10]

The issuing of these initiatives by then-President Bush culminated in the signing of the EPAct of 1992. The EPAct addresses energy issues such as alternative fuels, electric vehicles, renewable energy, coal, global climate change, reduction of oil vulnerability, energy and the environment, and energy and economics. The EPAct is somewhat revolutionary in that it marks a serious attempt to structure the U.S. energy policy. The act established several different programs and requirements for federal, state, and municipal governments and the private sector. The EPAct was very ambitious; it

- required uniform labeling of alternative fuels and alternative fuel vehicles;
- established low-interest loans for private sector small businesses for the purpose of converting to alternative fuels;
- required that vehicles acquired by federal and state government in 1999 and 2000, respectively, must be at least 75 percent alternative fuel vehicles;
- promoted increasing reliance on renewable energy;
- established a Director of Climate Protection at the DOE as well as a Global Climate Change Response Fund to be used in global efforts on climate change;
- created programs to study methods of increasing energy efficiency;
- established the Spark M. Matsunaga Renewable Energy and Ocean Technology Center to research renewable energy and energy storage;
- promoted advanced mathematics and science education for underprivileged and first-generation college students.

The EPAct is a comprehensive and complex law that attempts to provide a coherent energy policy for the United States.

One of the interesting provisions of the EPAct is a clause allowing for mortgage incentives on energy-efficient homes. These energy-efficient mortgages (EEMs), originated under President Carter, but little used, allow homeowners to receive a slightly larger mortgage than they would have been able to based on their risk as an investment, provided that the increased mortgage is used for energy improvements in the home.[11] The EPAct improves EEMs by ensuring that energy bills will decrease enough to allow homeowners to be able to pay the increased mortgages.[12] The pilot program, implemented by the Department of HUD, was so successful that it was extended nationwide.[13]

The impact of the EPAct is difficult to ascertain. In 2006, the United States was importing around 60 percent of its daily petroleum consumption, an increase over the 35 percent that was imported in the 1970s, and still a national security hazard. The United States is certainly vulnerable to disruptions in oil supply by our foreign suppliers, while the EPAct held as one of its main goals the reduction of oil vulnerability. Domestic oil production is decreasing; in 2004, the U.S. production was at its lowest level in over 50 years, producing 5.4 million barrels per day, and was not expected to increase significantly, if at all. Only about 6 percent of the U.S. energy supply in 2004 came from renewable sources and our per capita energy consumption continued to increase.[14] Figure 9-1 traces the production, import, and consumption of petroleum since 1950.

A "VOLUNTARY" ENERGY POLICY

President Clinton issued Executive Order 12902, which was then superseded by Executive Order 13123, to promote energy efficiency in the federal government. Executive Order 13123, issued on June 3, 1999, had the following major goals.[15]

1. Reducing greenhouse gas emissions from federal agency energy use to 30 percent below 1990 levels by 2010
2. Reducing energy consumption of federal agencies to 30 percent below 1985 levels by 2005 and 35 percent below by 2010
3. Installing 20,000 solar energy systems in federal facilities by 2010

The Clinton administration's energy policy mainly centered on the reduction of energy use, explicitly through voluntary programs. Examples of these programs include Energy Star (including the former Green Lights program) and Methane Outreach. Both programs fall under the direction of the EPA's Atmospheric Pollution Prevention Division. The mission statement of this division is to improve building energy and office equipment efficiency. Energy Star, through its promotion of energy-efficient household products and home-building techniques, in 2005, saved the equivalent of 4 percent of the 2005 electricity demand and prevented greenhouse gas emissions equivalent to removing 23 million cars from the road. In addition, over $12 billion dollars were saved in energy costs because of voluntary compliance with Energy Star's guidelines. Concerning the use of alternative fuels, the EPA's Green Power Partnership is a voluntary program encouraging the use of green power in homes and offices. As part of the EPAct of 1992, tax credits can be awarded for use of green power.

During the Clinton administration, automobile manufacturers were encouraged to develop alternative fuel vehicles through the voluntary Partnership for a New Generation of Vehicles, collaboration between manufacturers and government agencies such as the DOE, EPA, Department of Transportation, and the Office of Science and Technology Policy. Other voluntary programs, such as the LMOP and the Million Solar Roofs Initiative, are described later in the chapter.

TRANSPORTATION

Transportation accounted for more than 27 percent of all energy consumption in the United States during 2004. Furthermore, in 2002, 4.4 trillion miles were logged on American roadways. Although the need for energy-efficient means of transportation would seem to be an essential component in the development of a national energy policy plan, the United States too often favors less energy-efficient transportation policies.

When gas prices surged in 2005 and 2006, reaching over $3.00 a gallon in some states, some people blamed the rise in gas prices on reformulated gasoline, some people on the war in Iraq, others on OPEC, and still others on a conspiracy by the U.S. oil companies. Another source of the rise in energy prices was BP's (British Petroleum) closing of a significant portion of the Alaskan pipeline. In 2006, when significant corrosion was found in the Alaskan pipeline, BP announced it would probably have to close a portion of the Alaska pipeline for repairs, which lead to an immediate spike in the price of barrels of oil, and thus of gasoline.[16] At the time this book was published, the fate of the Alaska pipeline was still undecided.

Although the reasons for such high gas prices are difficult to determine, the response to this oil crisis is far more interesting. The two previous energy crises resulted in the creation of a U.S. energy policy, increased use of small cars, the imposition of speed limits nationwide, and other conservation measures. Conservation, however, seemed far from the minds of the American public during the energy crisis of 2006. There was no call to use smaller cars nor to reinstitute the 55-mile-per-hour speed limit Clinton lifted in late 1995. Instead, public officials talked about increasing domestic gas production by drilling in the Arctic National Wildlife Refuge and the Gulf of Mexico. It seems that instead of asking the public to reduce its energy consumption, the Bush administration and others preferred to find ways to allow people to keep their high-consumption lifestyles. The Bush administration's energy plan, which focuses on greater production of petroleum rather than the reduction of energy consumption, demonstrates the preference for more oil over reduced consumption. Perhaps the best example of attitudes toward energy consumption is our lawmakers' great reluctance to force auto manufacturers to increase their fuel efficiency standards.

As part of the Energy Policy and Conservation Act of 1975, car and light truck manufacturers are required to meet the CAFE standards. The CAFE standards remain the best method to increase vehicle fuel efficiency; however, powerful lobbying by the auto industry has kept fuel standards from increasing. In 2001, when Congress required the NHTSA to issue a fuel-economy standard for the 2004 model year for pickup trucks, minivans, and SUVs (Sport Utility Vehicle), the NHTSA decided not to raise the standard of 20.7 miles per gallon, a standard that has changed little in the past 20 years. However, the fuel-economy standards for model years 2005 to 2007 for pickup trucks, minivans, and SUVs are scheduled to be 21.0, 21.6, and 22.2 miles per gallon for each year, respectively.

The fuel standards for passenger cars have not changed since the 1980s. Despite advancements in technology that would allow for a considerable increase in the fuel standard without significant consequence to the performance of the vehicle, fuel standards remain at 27.5 miles per gallon for passenger cars. For example, the 2004 model hybrid Honda Civic gets 46 miles per gallon (51 on the highway), which is 45 percent better fuel efficiency than most other sedan model cars.

NATIONAL ENERGY POLICY PLANS

The DOE has been crafting National Energy Policy Plans since its creation. National energy policy plans under the second Bush administration have focused on greater reliance on fossil fuels. Environmental regulations have been changed to allow greater fossil fuel exploration and ease energy production and distribution, including the opening of many public lands for oil and natural gas drilling, as well as allowing environmentally harmful coal-mining practices, such as mountain top removal. Through the Bush administration's tax policies, oil, gas, and nuclear energies have received large tax incentives, whereas alternative-fuel sources have received less government assistance. Such an emphasis could have been expected given the make up of Bush's Energy Department transition team, which consisted of 54 members representing the coal, oil and gas, nuclear power, uranium mining, and electrical industries, one energy efficiency expert, one public interest representative, and no renewable energy experts.[17]

George W. Bush's 2002 budget showed his intent to encourage continued heavy reliance on fossil fuels, because it contained $150 million for research on cleaner methods for burning coal, while slashing funding for renewable energy sources, such as solar, wind, and biomass energy, more than 50 percent from the previous year's allocation.[18] He also indicated a definite preference for increasing the supply of energy over increasing efficiency and encouraging conservation by cutting by 35 percent the Doe's share of the multiage "Partnership for a New Generation of Vehicles," a program that aims to develop a small passenger car that can get as much as 85 miles per gallon.[19]

President Bush's budget for fiscal year 2007 further demonstrates his position regarding energy in the United States. Instead of increasing the funds for the Industrial Technologies Program (ITP), a program that saves the U.S. $7 of energy for every $1 the program spends, President Bush cut the ITP budget to one-third of its 2005 level. In fact, President Bush's budget for 2007 cuts energy efficiency programs by 16 percent, which when adjusted for inflation is more akin to a 30 percent budget cut from its 2002 funding. Instead of focusing on energy efficiency and reliable power production, President Bush has opted to allocate $1.2 billion over 5 years for a hydrogen-fuel program. However, energy efficiency proponents argue ITP is far more efficient at saving oil, and in fact, ITP has already saved more oil to date than the proposed hydrogen-fuel program will save by 2025 if the hydrogen-fuel program is even successful.[20]

In early 2001, Bush established a cabinet-level energy task force, headed by Vice President Cheney, to prepare a report on which Bush could base his energy policy for the United States. Bush's NES, the 163-page report prepared by the task force, was unveiled on May 18, 2001. The White House energy report concluded that the United States was facing the worst energy shortages since the oil embargos of the 1970s and contained 105 recommendations. As expected, the plan was heavily weighted toward increasing supply, rather than decreasing demand.

Many aspects of the report are highly controversial. For example, the report orders the DOJ and the EPA to review their enforcement of pollution laws in light of their potential to discourage refinery expansion, although at least half of the nation's 152 oil refineries are estimated to be violating air pollution laws. Other questionable aspects of the plan include opening up Alaska's Arctic National Wildlife Refuge for oil and gas drilling, reexamining the moratorium on offshore drilling for natural gas, speeding up the building of nuclear power plants, reviewing the prohibitions on the reprocessing of spent fuel from nuclear power plants, building more pipelines to carry oil and natural gas, reviewing all public lands to determine whether they should be open to energy development, giving the FERC the power to take private land to build electricity transmission lines, and increasing subsidies to the coal, oil, and gas industries. The plan also includes more than $10 billion worth of tax credits over 10 years for conservation and energy development, but about half of those credits already exist or were previously proposed in the president's budget. The largest credit, $4 billion, is aimed at spurring sales of hybrid gas–electric cars.[21]

The report was immediately embraced by the natural gas, electric, oil, nuclear, and coal interests. However, it sparked outrage on the part of environmental groups, who fear that the plan will lead to huge increases in the use of coal, oil, and other fossil fuels that contribute to global warming and will increase air pollution by reducing enforcement of the CAA. Some Congresspersons were sufficiently concerned about the report, and the influence that the energy industry had on its drafting, that they asked the GAO to determine which business interests participated in closed-door meetings with Cheney's task force. In their request to the GAO, Representatives John Dingell (D-MI) and Henry Waxman (D-CA) wrote, "It is our understanding that the task force has conducted a number of meetings . . . and some, if not all, of these meetings have included exclusive groups of non-governmental participants—including political contributors—to discuss specific policies, rules, regulation, and legislation."[22]

After several years of lower court challenges requesting that the Bush administration release documents pertaining to those in attendance at Cheney's energy task force meetings, in 2004, the Supreme Court agreed to hear Cheney's arguments for keeping private those task force papers. Cheney argued he does not have to disclose the names of those from whom he or the President sought advice. However, environmentalists suspected the major energy companies had a large influence in the development, and even wording, of the administration's national energy policy.

   The Supreme Court ultimately reversed the Court of Appeals dismissal of the government's legal claims and remanded the case back to the Court of Appeals for additional consideration. On remand, the Court of Appeals found the plaintiffs failed to establish a clear duty owed to them by the government under the Federal Advisory Committee Act.[23] Furthermore, the Court of Appeals argued no nonfederal member of the commission voted or exercised a veto over the plan. Therefore, if any role was served by nonfederal employees, it was strictly an advisory one and does not subject the task force to Freedom of Information Act claims.[24] Subsequently, White House documents revealed that energy executives did meet with the Cheney task force in 2001. The documents revealed that executives from Sonoco, Shell Oil Co., Exxon Mobile Corp., and B.P. America Inc. all met with the task force while the task force was working on creating the national energy policy.[25]

   Questions about the influence of the fossil fuel interests arise in part because the drafters of the energy plan seemed to completely ignore a report by scientists at this country's national laboratories, completed just before the Bush administration took office, that projected enormous energy savings if the government would take aggressive steps to encourage energy conservation in homes, offices, cars, and power plants.[19] Although the Bush administration claims that the United States needs to build a power plant every week for the next 20 years to keep up with demand and that large increases in production of coal and natural gas are necessary to fuel the plants, the studies detailed in the report contradict the administration's claims.[26] The report stated that a government-led efficiency program that emphasized research and incentives to adopt new technologies could reduce the growth in demand for electricity by 20 percent. One of the studies, prepared by the Pacific Northwest National Laboratory, found that the federal government, which is the largest user of energy in the country, could reduce its energy consumption by one-fifth. Securing this reduction would require an investment of $5.2 billion, but the resultant energy savings would reduce the government's annual energy bill by almost $1 billion, thereby making not only environmental, but also economic, sense.[27]

   Despite the possibilities for consumption reductions through increased efficiency programs, however, it appears that under President Bush, the United States will continue in its role as a major consumer of energy. The Energy Tax Incentive Act, signed into law in 2005, did provide some tax credits for energy-efficient vehicles. However, the rules for qualification were very complicated, meaning that most people would not be able to figure out the applicable credit amounts on their own. Furthermore, the credits for two of the most attractive qualifying vehicles are phased out after a manufacturer has sold over 60,000 vehicles. It also included a tax credit for residential energy improvements, but this tax credit has a lifetime limit of $500, so it is probably not going to have a major impact.

   In mid-2006, both houses of Congress passed somewhat different versions of an energy bill. But with midterm elections approaching, the two houses were unable to agree on a compromise version. At the time the book went to press in mid-2007, a new energy bill had not yet been passed.

In 2007, however, President Bush did announce his new energy proposals, which included a plan to reduce U.S. gasoline consumption by 20 percent in 10 years, in part by requiring suppliers to include 35 billion gallons of alternative fuels in the nation's vehicle fuel supply by 2017, up from the current 5 billion gallons. Bush also called for Congress to give him new authority to set vehicle fuel-economy rules but rejected bipartisan calls for Congress to set new fuel-economy rules.

Bush was not the only one, however, with ideas for an energy policy. Also in 2007, a bipartisan group of senators and representatives introduced House and Senate Concurrent Resolutions calling for a new national renewable energy goal—25 percent of the nation's energy supply from renewable sources by 2025, the so-called 25 × '25 goal. The House version was introduced with 22 co-sponsors and the Senate with 25. The measure introduced to Congress has no real specifics, but simply directs the committees to debate and take action that would reduce U.S. dependence on foreign oil, expand the development and use of biofuels and other alternative fuels; reduce the risks of global warming, diversify and build more secure, efficient, and environmentally friendly energy supplies and technologies; reduce the burden of rising energy prices on consumers; eliminate tax "give aways" and prevent energy price manipulation. However, the originators of the 25 × '25 goal have developed an action plan that contains specific policy recommendations that would enable the United States to attain that goal. The plan can be found at http://www.25x25.org/index.php?option=com_frontpage&Itemid=1, which is the home page for 25 × '25.

While the implementation of the 25 × '25 plan at this point is uncertain, one thing that is certain is the implementation of some new energy-efficieny standards. New energy-efficiency standards for 22 appliances will be set over the next 4.5 years under an agreement settling a lawsuit brought against the Energy Department by the Natural Resources Defense Council, consumer groups, and 15 states. The settlement agreement was reached in late 2006.

In the next sections, we look at where all of this controversial energy is used. Then, we examine the types of energy we have to choose from, along with the problems of each and the temporary solutions arrived at. Although it may seem strange to examine each type of energy independently when we need a strategy combining all of them, you will see that as a nation we have indeed chosen to treat each independently—and perhaps that is part of our inability to establish a coherent energy policy.

ENERGY CONSUMPTION AND PRODUCTION

One of the reasons that lack of a coherent, long-term energy policy is problematic is that, as a nation, we have extremely high energy demands, consuming about one-fourth of the world's energy production. Although the U.S. population grew 93 percent from 1949 to 2004, our energy consumption grew 233 percent during the same period, which is a 58 percent increase in per capita energy use. From 1973 to 2004, our total energy consumption increased by 33 percent.[28] Consumption of energy is consistent with our high standard of living, large land mass, low population density, and historically abundant, relatively low-cost energy resources. The great demand for energy can be understood a little better if we examine the four economic activities that place the greatest demands on our energy resources: residential, commercial, industrial, and transportation. Figure 9-2 depicts demand for energy in the United States.

Because of the large number of single-family dwellings, the relative spaciousness of these dwellings, relatively small average family size, a desire for heating and cooling systems to maintain uniform indoor temperatures year round, and a wide range of labor-saving devices, the U.S. energy use per dwelling is among the highest in the world. Residential energy use currently accounts for 21 percent of total primary energy demand. More than 64 percent of that use is for heat and hot water; approximately 30 percent is used to run major appliances. One compact fluorescent lamp, used by one person over a lifetime, can save nearly a ton of carbon dioxide emissions from the atmosphere and save the consumer money.

Commercial energy use is primarily for heating and cooling commercial buildings. Approximately one-third of the nation's energy demands come from industry. Eighty-eight percent of that demand can be traced to the six most energy-intensive industries, including steel, paper, and chemical. Finally, transportation of goods and people accounts for over one-fourth of

FIGURE 9-2   Energy Consumption by End Use

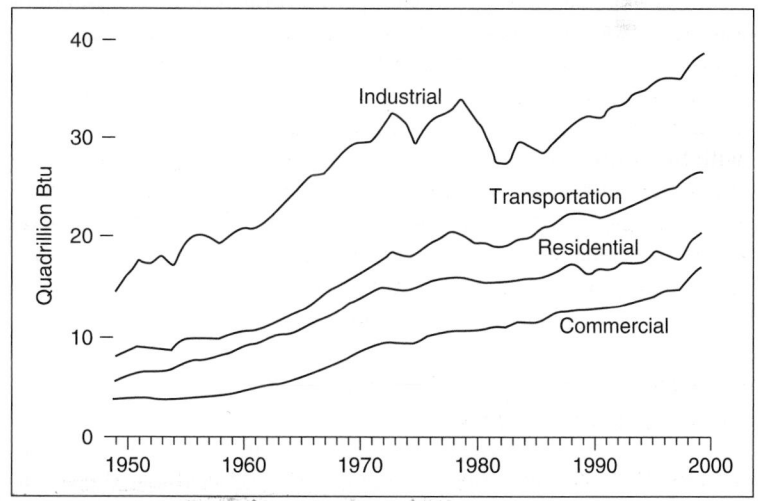

Source: DOE. *Total Consumption by End-Use Sector: 1949–2004. http://www.eia.doe.gov/ emeu/aer/pdf/aer.pdf* (July 12, 2006).

energy consumption. Most of this energy comes from the petroleum used to power automobiles, planes, trains, ships, and trucks.

From 1949 to 1973, the demand for energy in the United States more than doubled. However, from 1973 to 1991, consumption increased by only 10 percent. Still, the 2001 National Energy Policy, developed by the Bush administration, calls for the construction of 1,300–1,900 new power plants over the next 20 years, or 60–90 new power plants per year, to keep up with the projected energy demand of the United States. Production of energy has generally been regulated by federal and state governments, particularly the generation of electricity. Because utilities constitute what many would call a natural monopoly (i.e., left to develop on their own), electricity providers would naturally merge into one provider; federal and state governments have a role to play in ensuring that energy prices are not as high as they would be in a monopoly situation. However, calls for deregulation of the energy industry have been heard and, in some cases, been heeded. These calls for deregulation generally stem from the idea that, with competition, energy prices will decrease and lead to better results for consumers. In addition, consumers will be able to choose their energy provider with deregulation, something they are unable to do now because generally only one utility provides electricity for a given area. As noted in Figure 9-3, nearly 50 percent of states have restructured the way they provide electricity, deregulating their energy provisions in some way, and other states and cities are looking into deregulation.

Perhaps the most notorious recent example of a deregulation fiasco is that of California in 2001. California deregulated its energy production in 1996, but not fully. Although wholesale prices were deregulated, the state of California capped retail prices to ensure that consumers would be able to afford to purchase electricity. However, as wholesale prices increased, utilities were unable to pass along these costs to consumers, because of the caps on retail prices, and energy blackouts ensued all over the state of California in early 2001. California's largest utilities found themselves on the brink of bankruptcy because of the high cost of energy, and conservation became necessary for the state's 33 million residents. However, some of those residents found themselves in a much better situation than their neighbors. In Ukiah, a small city in northern California, about 100 residents have been generating their own power since the 1970s.[29] Off the energy grid, these people use different forms of renewable energy to generate their own power and are constantly aware of how much power they have and how much they are using.[30] In light of the energy problems in California, their actions appear especially perceptive.

In part because of the California energy crisis, and its potential to spread to other states, President Bush established the new cabinet-level task force to deal with energy policy for the United States as a whole, which was discussed in the previous section. According to the Bush administration, demand for energy is outstripping supply and new sources of energy must be found.[31] The task force was mandated to explore new sources of energy, including developing alternative energy, opening up the Arctic National

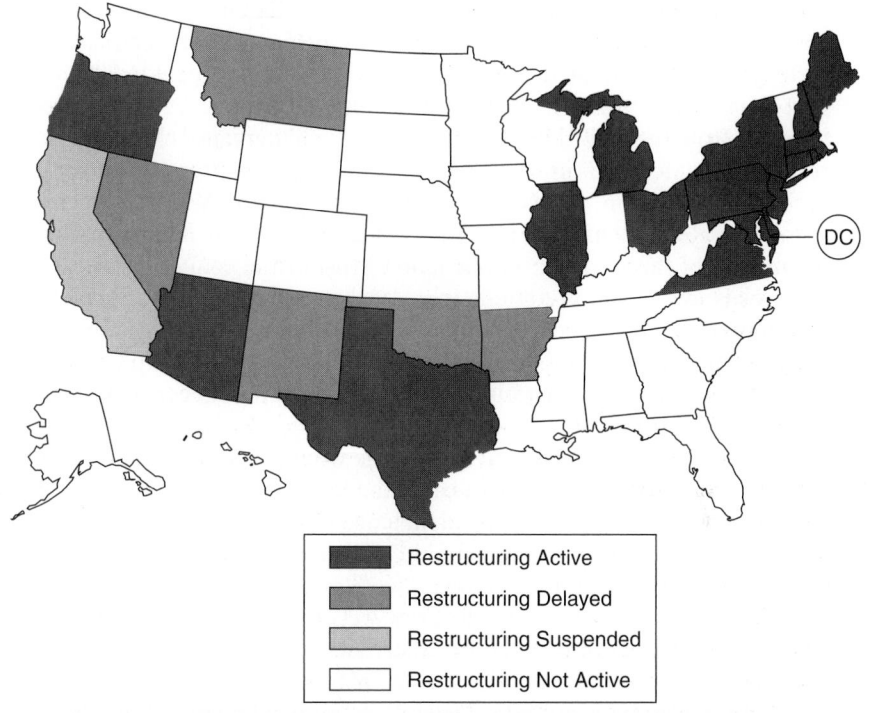

FIGURE 9-3   Status of State Electric Industry Restructuring Activity

Source: DOE Energy Information Administration. "Status of State Electric Industry Restructuring Activity as of February 2003." *http://www.eia.doe.gov/cneaf/electricity/chg_str/regmap.html* (December 11, 2003).

Wildlife Refuge for drilling, and finding more reliable supplies of oil. The task force, however, made no recommendations for solving California's immediate problems with energy shortages or higher-than-ever gas prices.

As most readers are well aware, production of energy occurs through many different energy sources, including fossil fuels, water, and "renewable" forms of energy. Although fossil fuels are the most common energy source for the United States, interest in renewable forms of energy seems to be on the rise and may increase even more with the lessons learned in California. In the following sections, we examine the alternative ways to satisfy our voracious demand for energy.

COAL: THE OLDEST ENERGY SOURCE

Coal is this nation's most plentiful fossil fuel, constituting approximately 90 percent of the U.S. hydrocarbon reserves. At one time providing over 90 percent of our energy needs, today coal supplies about 25 percent. At present rates of consumption, we have sufficient reserves to last approximately

200 years. Coal is extremely important because it is used to generate 50 percent of the nation's electrical power; however, the percentage of electricity generated by coal seems to be decreasing, slipping below 50 percent in 2002 for the first time since 1979.[32] In 2004, coal production was 1,112 million tons, a decrease from the record high in 2001 of 1,128 million tons.[33] Most of the coal reserves are located in three regions of the country: the seven-state Appalachian region, the Midwestern plains, and the Western plains and grasslands. Roughly half the coal reserves are in the West, and approximately 60 percent of those are on public lands. Most of the coal on these western reserves is low in sulfur content; most of the coal in the eastern reserves is privately owned and has high-sulfur content. Because of the tightened sulfur dioxide emission standards that took effect in 2000, as part of phase 2 of the CAA Amendments, the majority of coal production now occurs in the West, as illustrated by Figure 9-4.

Because coal is so plentiful and its use would therefore reduce the U.S. dependence on foreign oil and because an increase in coal production could increase employment, every president since Nixon has, in some way, sought to increase our reliance on coal. Congress has also jumped on the bandwagon for greater use of coal.

Under the 1978 National Energy Act, five statutes were passed by Congress, which were designed to increase our dependence on coal. The most significant of these was the Power plant and Industrial Fuel Use Act (PIFUA).[34] This act required certain electrical power generating plants and major fuel-burning installations to switch from oil or gas to coal. The DOE was authorized to require facilities, both individually and by category, to convert to coal or other alternative fuels when two conditions were met: (1) the conversion was financially feasible and (2) the facilities had the

FIGURE 9-4   Areas of Coal Production in the United States, 1949–2004

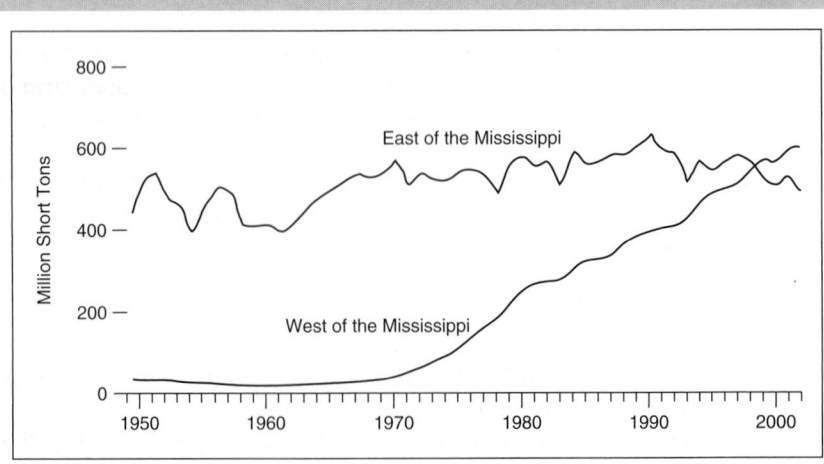

Source: DOE. *Annual Energy Review: 1949–2004. http://www.eia.doe.gov/emeu/aer/pdf/aer.pdf* (July 12, 2006).

technical capability to be converted without substantial physical modifications or reductions in capacity. Individual plants in categories subject to conversion were to be granted permanent exemptions if the plant would have difficulty, because of its location, in getting access to alternative fuels. In addition, conversion would not be required if it would cause a violation of any state or federal environmental regulations. The EPA was charged with making sure that no proposed conversions would result in NAAQS violations.

More recently, changes to the New Source Review (discussed in Chapter 5) proposed by the Bush administration in 2003 encourage greater dependence on coal by removing many of the costly requirements for pollution control upgrades in older coal-fired power plants. As the administration removed such requirements on the nation's coal-fired power plants, it also earmarked $2 billion for research and development of "clean coal" technology. Through these mixed signals, one message comes across unimpeded by contradiction: coal, as a major source of America's power supply, is here to stay.

PROBLEMS WITH COAL

Given the plentiful nature of coal and its positive impact on employment, one may wonder why the United States does not more wholeheartedly endorse a policy that emphasizes the use of coal. The reason is that a number of environmental problems are associated with the use of coal, especially the high-sulfur coal of the eastern reserves. Recall the discussion of acid rain in Chapter 5 and that one of the major factors in acid rain is sulfur dioxide emissions. Increased use of coal, especially high-sulfur coal, may increase acid deposition.

Out of the entire electric industry, some estimate that coal-fired power plants contribute 96 percent of sulfur dioxide emissions, 99 percent of mercury emissions, 93 percent of nitrogen oxide emissions, and 88 percent of carbon dioxide emissions. Such pollutants significantly contribute to the deterioration of public health, especially in the development of respiratory ailments such as asthma.[35]

Another one of the major problems associated with the use of coal is that coal mining can have disastrous environmental effects, especially strip or surface mining. Roughly 44 percent of the western coal and 18 percent of the eastern coal reserves are accessible by strip mining. There are three basic types of surface mining: contour mining, area mining, and open pit mining. Figure 9-5 compares underground to surface mining in the United States.

Contour mining, also commonly referred to as Mountaintop removal, is the main type of mining used in Appalachia. The miner excavates a portion of the hillside where the coal seam intersects the surface. Then, the soil that covers the seam is stripped off, following the seam along the contour as far into the mountain as possible. The excess dirt unearthed to reveal the coal is thrown downhill from where the coal is removed.

In flat or rolling terrain, area mining is used. The earth is stripped off the coal and piled up to one side in a ridge along the area from which the coal has been removed.

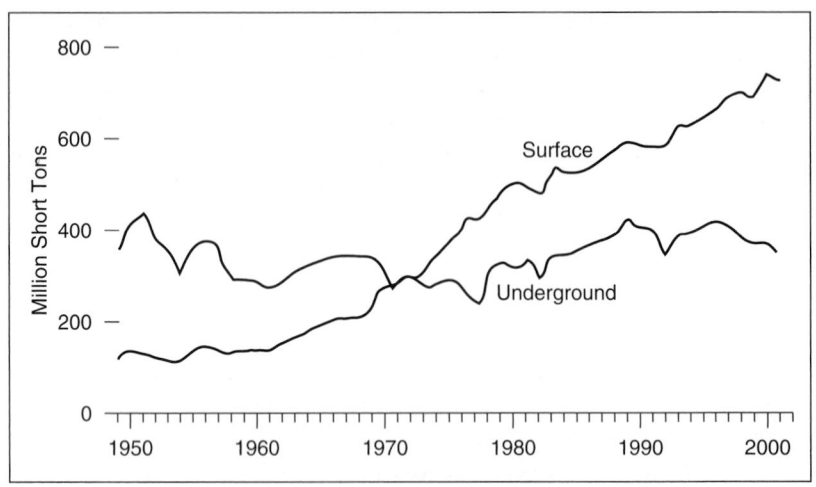

FIGURE 9-5   Coal Production from 1949 to 2004

Source: DOE. *Annual Energy Review: 1949–2004. http://www.eia.doe.gov/emeu/aer/pdf/aer.pdf* (July 12, 2006).

Open pit mining is similar to area mining except that the area from which the coal has been stripped is much deeper than the thickness of the land that was stripped off, so the stripped-off land, called the overburden, is not thick enough to replace the coal that was removed; consequently, a deep depression is left.

If unregulated, the results of strip mining are acres of barren, sterile land. Unregulated strip mining may cause soil erosion, pollution of streams from mining runoff, destruction of the land for agricultural purposes, destruction of ecosystems, and loss of habitat for numerous species. By some estimates, more than 1.5 million acres in more than 30 states have been disturbed by strip mining, and more than a million of these acres remain abandoned wasteland, no longer claimed by those who took the coal and no longer productive.[36] More than 1,200 miles of streams have been buried or destroyed, and over 1,000 more acres are being ravaged each week by further mining.

In 2003, the EPA released an EIS on Mountaintop Removal coal mining, detailing many of the harmful environmental effects to the surrounding ecosystems.[37] Yet, despite the EIS, the Bush administration continues to encourage strip mining practices by allowing mining waste to cover over streams and creeks, in violation of the CWA. New rules and regulations finalized in 2004 by the EPA make it easier for companies to receive permits allowing for greater valley fill.

Given these disastrous environmental consequences, why has strip mining remained such a viable activity? The answer lies to a large extent in the fact that surface mining is much cheaper, less labor-intensive, more efficient, more profitable, and safer than underground mining.

Strip mining practices, however, are increasingly being challenged in court. Using the CWA, citizen and environmental groups are working to stop the more environmentally harmful practices of strip mining. In a recent challenge, Federal Judge Hayden overturned a Bush administration rule that allowed strip mining refuse to be dumped over waterways. Unfortunately, in 2003, the Fourth Circuit Court in Virginia overruled Hayden's decisions, reinstating the rule.[38]

REGULATION OF THE MINING INDUSTRY

In an attempt to contain some of the disastrous consequences of strip mining, Congress passed the Surface Mining Control and Reclamation Act (SMCRA) of 1977. Vetoed twice by President Ford and strongly opposed by the mining industry, the act was finally signed into law by President Carter. The primary objective of the act, as indicated by its name, was to force the mining industry to return the land from which it stripped the coal to a level of productivity equal or superior to its condition before mining.

The act contains very strong provisions that were extremely pleasing to environmentalists; but the implementation of the act, from an environmentalist's perspective, has been a disaster. Under the act, a number of environmental protection performance standards were established, regulating a broad range of activities, including the removal, storage, and redistribution of topsoil; silting and erosion control; and drainage and protection of water. These standards were to be implemented in two stages: an interim and a permanent phase.

The interim standards were published in 1977 and require mine operators to meet standards that include restoring the land to its prior or a superior condition, returning the land to its original contour, segregating and preserving topsoil, minimizing disturbance of the hydrologic balance in the mined area, and revegetation. Permanent regulations for all performance standards were published in 1979. These have not yet been adopted by all states because of a provision providing that the final regulations will be enforceable when the state adopts a permanent program. This program may contain equal or more stringent provisions than the federal regulations provide. Special, more stringent performance and reclamation standards were to be established under the act for mining on alluvial valley floors in arid and semiarid regions, on prime farmland, and on steep slopes. Mining was to be prohibited on land deemed unsuitable for mining.

A new executive agency, the Office of Surface Mining Reclamation and Enforcement (OSM), was created within the Department of the Interior to enforce the act. To ensure that this agency was not captured by the mining industry, the OSM could, by statute, employ only individuals from other agencies who had no association with any authority, program, or function intended to promote the use or development of coal. The primary means of enforcing the SMCRA is through a permit system that can be administered by the states if they adopt programs for enforcing the act that are at least as stringent as the federal program.

Although the SMCRA reads like a strong piece of environmental regulation, its effectiveness is highly questionable. The act has been fraught with problems from the beginning. Under the Carter administration, many strong regulations were drafted, a number of which were vehemently opposed by the mining industry. One of the industry's most common arguments was that the OSM exceeded its authority to establish performance standards for mine sites when it set standards for both the types of controls to be used and the standard of performance to be met. It also argued that standards were too rigid and did not allow for enough local flexibility.

Industry's complaints were heeded shortly after the Reagan administration came to power. Under the auspices of Interior Department Secretary James Watt, approximately 90 percent of the regulations promulgated under the Carter administration were rewritten. The OSM also underwent massive downsizing, making serious enforcement of the law almost impossible. The OSM also suffered from instability at the top; in its first 8 years, it had six acting directors.

The OSM's record of enforcement, especially under the Reagan administration, has been abysmal and has subjected the agency to congressional investigations and litigation by environmental groups. In 1983 and 1984, congressional hearings revealed that state enforcement was inadequate in several states in light of evidence that mining activities were causing severe environmental deterioration. There was, obviously, a strong incentive for states not to enforce the regulations strictly. Compliance was costly, so mining companies in states with loose enforcement would be at a competitive advantage.

Enforcement of the mining laws and regulations continues to suffer under the Bush administration. Before becoming Interior Department Secretary in 2001, Gale Norton opposed SMCRA and publicly argued that it is unconstitutional. In 2002, the Ohio Valley Environmental Coalition, composed of seven citizen and environmental groups opposed to strip mining practices, sent a letter to Secretary Norton, listing grievances against the OSM for failure to enforce the law. Secretary Norton did not increase enforce while she was with the Department of the Interior. In May 2006, Dirk Kempthorne became the new Secretary of the Interior, and he too has shown no intention of altering this pattern of nonenforcement in the near future.

In 1984, in response to a lawsuit brought by a number of environmental groups, the Department of the Interior agreed to establish a computerized system to monitor mine operators that violated the act and prevent them from obtaining permits in the future. The settlement also allowed plaintiffs to monitor the Interior Department's enforcement actions. This settlement took place at a time when there were about 1,700 cease and desist orders against violators that had never been enforced.[39] In 1985, a House Government Operations subcommittee cited the OSM for failing to collect more than $150 million in fines for violation of the SMCRA.[40] What is incredible about the OSM's inaction is that approximately $72 million of the fines were fully processed, undisputed, and unappealable.[41]

The lack of enforcement of SMCRA brought 88 homeowners and an environmental group in West Virginia to sue state surface mining officials after they continually granted permits allowing mountaintop removal coal mining in violation of SMCRA. In *Bragg v. Robertson,*[42] the plaintiffs sued the state for minimal compliance with SMCRA, arguing that the law requires the state to "establish a nationwide program to protect society and the environment from adverse effects of surface coal mining operations."[43] The district court found that mountaintop removal mining practices were impossible to reconcile with SMCRA and therefore had to be terminated. Two years later, in 2001, the Fourth Circuit Court of Appeals overturned the district court's decision, allowing the practices of mountaintop removal to continue. Similar court challenges in recent years, including those using the CWA to prevent harmful mining practices, have met strong resistance in higher courts.

Clearly, the SMCRA is not the success for which its advocates had hoped. There is some evidence that the act has helped maintain environmentally safe conditions in some states, such as Montana, Pennsylvania, and Wyoming,[44] but in states such as West Virginia and Kentucky, minimal enforcement means minimal impact.[45] Some people, however, question whether the act's overall objective can actually be accomplished, even with the most vigorous enforcement program. Some scientists believe that the disruption of subsurface hydrology and the drainage of acids and salts that occurs during mining may cause irreparable damages.[46] In light of all the controversy over the potential environmental destruction resulting from strip mining, it is no wonder that another problem with the use of coal is the extent to which the federal government should lease exploration and mining rights to coal companies. Remember that over half the coal reserves in the western states are on public lands.

Under the Mineral Leasing Act of 1920, the secretary of the interior may lease federal lands to private companies for oil, gas, and mineral exploration and production. Until the 1960s, very few leases were sought for energy production. There was a slight increase in interest in leases for coal production during the 1970s. During the Reagan administration's tenure, however, Secretary of the Interior James Watt announced his intention to increase lease sales from the Carter administration's 771 million tons of new coal to 2.2 billion tons. In 1982, the Department of the Interior received almost $55 million in bids on almost 1.6 million acres of reserves, the largest coal lease sale in the U.S. history. Some congressional Democrats fiercely opposed the leases, as did the governors of many western coal states. Some congressional staff reports alleged that the leases were being offered for far less than fair market value.

Because of the controversy, Watt appointed a special panel to study federal coal-leasing policies. The panel called the Linowes Commission, after its chairman, concluded that the government had offered too many leases, many at less than fair market value. The commission recommended that the Department of Interior revises its schedule of leases to respond better to changes in the coal market. Shortly before the commission issued its report,

Watt resigned. Since his resignation, other interior secretaries have been less eager to lease federal coal reserves.

The Coal Lease Amendment Act of 2003, had it been passed by Congress, would have amended the Mineral Leasing Act of 1920 "to provide for the development of coal resources," in greater quantities.[47] The amendment, which served the Bush administration's energy plan, would have repealed the 160 acre limitation on coal leases, allowing for more federal land to be leased to a single company. Furthermore, the amendment would have repealed the requirement for financial assurance to the federal government for certain coal leases, and the Secretary of the Interior would have had the power to suspend the payment of royalties to the federal government from coal companies. Such changes to the Mineral Leasing Act could have significantly increased the United States' level of coal production and subsequently increased the country's reliance on coal as an energy source. The Amendment was sent to committee in February 2003 and appears to have had no further action taken since then.[48]

PETROLEUM AND NATURAL GAS

Since 1955, petroleum and natural gas have been the primary sources of energy for the United States, supplying over two-thirds of our energy needs. In 2005, the U.S. oil production totaled 5.1 million barrels each day.[49] Petroleum has been a chief energy source primarily because of its low cost. Natural gas is a fossil fuel that, like petroleum, burns cleanly and efficiently, producing few pollutants. It constitutes about 30 percent of domestic energy production. Approximately one-fourth of this domestic production satisfies about 40 percent of residential energy needs. To combat national security concerns, President Bush ordered the Strategic Petroleum Reserves (SPR) filled to their capacity at 700 million barrels by 2005, temporarily protecting the United States if foreign oil were to become unavailable. The SPR reached its capacity on August 17, 2005. A mere 2 weeks later on August 31, 2005, Hurricane Katrina hit the Golf coast crippling a number of U.S. oil refineries. The President used part of the SPR to keep gas prices down and help the damaged refineries. As of November 14, 2005, the SPR constituted the largest emergency oil reserves with 684 million barrels of oil.[50]

Natural reserves of natural gas in the United States, however, are not extensive. In the mid-1980s, known reserves of natural gas were sufficient to last for 20–40 years at then-current rates of consumption. Today, the United States has 192.5 trillion cubic feet of proven natural gas reserves. The proven reserves in the U.S. constitute 3 percent of the world's supply of natural gas, ranking the U.S. at sixth in the world for proven reserves.[51] Petroleum and natural gas share common problems, primarily related to production and transportation.

ONSHORE DEVELOPMENT PROBLEMS

Production and transportation of petroleum and natural gas necessitate large refineries and terminals, as well as miles of pipelines. Construction of these facilities often causes conflicts over land use. Many times, the terminals and refineries are near coastal areas, which many people believe should be preserved as natural areas or used only for recreation. The environmental balance in these areas is delicate, and many fear disruption of this balance from the construction. There are those who are fearful of spills at these facilities. Even though large spills are not common, their environmental consequences can be devastating. For example, in 1988, a storage tank in Pennsylvania collapsed, spilling more than a million gallons of diesel fuel into the Monogahela River, causing an oil slick that eventually spread into the Ohio River and caused the disruption of numerous communities' drinking water systems. Large numbers of birds and other wildlife were also killed by the spill.

Fears about pipeline ruptures causing similar ecological disasters have made it difficult for firms to obtain permission to construct pipelines to transport oil across land. More than 325,000 miles of pipeline across the United States require constant checks and maintenance to prevent major spills. The 700-mile Alaskan Pipeline, for example, was constructed only after great controversy. Additional segments of that pipeline, from Port Angeles, Washington, to Clearbrook, Minnesota, generated so many disputes that ultimately the project was canceled.

OFFSHORE DEVELOPMENT PROBLEMS

Even more controversies have been generated over offshore development, primarily in conjunction with the federal leasing of land in the OCS for energy exploration. The federal government, primarily through the Department of the Interior, exercises authority over the approximately 1.1 billion acres of the continental shelf beginning three miles from the coastline and extending 10–12 miles farther offshore. As custodian of this public land, the government leases some of it to private firms for exploration and production of oil. To ensure that states have some say in the development of submerged land off their shores and to help ensure that multiple interests are taken into account when leasing decisions were made, Congress passed the Outer Continental Shelf Leasing Act (OCSLA).

As amended in 1978, OCSLA requires the secretary of the interior to establish a 5-year leasing program that includes as many details as possible about plans for leases during that time. Details include the time, location, and sizes of leases that the secretary believes are necessary to meet the nation's energy needs. In developing the leasing plan, the secretary is to take into account four basic principles. First, the OCS must be managed in a manner that reflects a balancing of economic, social, and environmental values. The impact of exploration on the marine, coastal, and human environment must be taken into account. Second, choice of locations for development must be based on an equitable sharing of developmental benefits and environmental risks among the various regions, with special attention given to the laws, goals, and policies of the affected states as communicated by their governors to the secretary.

Third, in selecting timing and location of leases, the secretary must balance the potential for environmental damage, the potential for the discovery of oil and gas, and the potential for adverse impacts on the coastal zone. Finally, the federal government must receive fair market value for the land.

The steps for developing the leasing program are laid out by the act. When initially drafting the program, the secretary of the interior must "invite and consider suggestions" from governors of any states that might be affected by the leasing program. The proposed program finally drafted must then be submitted for comments to the governors of the affected states. If any governor makes any suggestions that the secretary denies, the reasons for the denial must be provided, in writing, to the governor.

The next step is publication of the proposed program in the *Federal Register.* Any interested parties, including representatives of the affected states, have 90 days to submit written comments to the secretary. The secretary will then forward the proposed program, along with the comments, to Congress and the president. If any suggestions from a state were not incorporated, the secretary must include an explanation for rejecting the state's advice.

Sixty days after submitting the proposed program to the president and Congress, the secretary may finally approve the program. Anyone who participated in the administrative process that led to the adoption of the leasing program and who will be adversely affected by it then has 60 days to challenge the program in the Circuit Court of Appeals for the District of Columbia. When reviewing the actions of the secretary, the court must take the secretary's findings as conclusive if supported by substantial evidence on the record. After the process of judicial review has been completed, the secretary of the interior will then propose and conduct competitive bidding lease sales. Once land has been leased, lessees submit to the secretary their exploration plans, followed by development and production plans. Throughout these stages, the secretary must still operate in accordance with the four principles described previously.

President Reagan's Interior Secretary James Watt caused a great deal of controversy by suggesting that all OCS lands might be open for leasing. The actual program he proposed was not so dramatic, but still it offered almost one billion acres of OCS land for oil and gas leasing from 1982 to 1987. His program was challenged in a combined action brought by eight environmental groups and several state and local governments. Their primary claim was a lack of balance among the competing factors of potential for environmental damage, hydrocarbon discovery, and adverse coastal effects. The legality of Watt's plan was upheld, but the next secretary of the interior, William Clark, feeling pressure from Congress, removed some areas from the program and canceled some leases. Congress helped prevent some leasing along the coasts by denying appropriations for the administration of the program. The 1987 to 1992 plan, finally approved in 1985 by Secretary of the Interior Donald Hodel, removed from planned leasing 650 million of the 1.4 billion acres Watt had proposed. However, other new areas that had previously been protected were proposed under Hodel's plan. Some of these controversial areas include the fishing area of Georges Bank off the New England coast and other sensitive areas off the Pacific and Atlantic coasts.

In 1990, George W. Bush signed an executive memorandum placing a 10-year moratorium on the issue of new leases for the OCS. The moratorium was then extended to 2012 by President Clinton. However, in 2003, the Senate voted to allow the Interior Department to perform exploratory drilling to inventory oil and natural gas reserves on the entire OCS. Such exploration could significantly harm some of the most sensitive coastal waters, which were once protected regions of the OCS. In addition, new discoveries of oil or natural gas on the OCS could pressure law makers to issue leases in environmentally fragile areas of the OCS. In fact, in the summer of 2006, both the House and the Senate voted to expand drilling into the OCS in the Gulf of Mexico. Later that year, a compromise version of the two bills was passed by both the House and the Senate. That legislation, the Gulf of Mexico Energy Security Act, requires Interior to lease acreage in two areas: the so-called "181 Area," comprising 2 million acres in what's considered the Central Gulf and another 580,000 acres in the Eastern Gulf; and the "181 South Area," another 5.8 million acres in the Central Gulf.[52]

On April 30, 2007, President Bush proposed a broad 5-year plan to open up 48 million acres along the outer continental shelf to oil and gas drilling. The plan would allow the leasing of millions of acres along the coasts of Alaska and Virginia, environmentally sensitive areas that were formerly protected. The plan faced some Congressional opposition, and at press time, the outcome of the plan was not certain. By executive order, Bush removed the morotorium that Clinton had placed on drilling on the OCS until 2012, removing one potential obstacle to his plan for drilling on the OCS. The program faces uneven support in Congress, and some of its opponent describe it as a very aggressive plan, in terms of giving the oil industry what they want and paying very little attention to environmental concerns. At the time the book went to press, the plan was still awaiting Congressional approval.[53]

OCSLA is not the only law designed to ensure a balanced development of coastal and subcoastal lands. The Coastal Zone Management Act (CZMA) aids in this process by providing financial assistance for states that develop and administer management programs that achieve a balance between energy development and environmental and coastal zone factors. The NEPA also comes into play, because leasing is a major federal activity. Therefore, the secretary of the interior generally will have to prepare an EIS when proposing a lease sale. Many times, in fact, environmental groups will challenge an EIS as a way to at least delay proposed lease sales.

OIL SPILLS

One of the worst problems associated with oil and petroleum, or at least the one that captures the public's attention, is oil spills. The United States uses over 250 billion gallons of oil and petroleum products each year, while producing an average of 125 billion gallons of crude oil and other petroleum products.[54] With the large amount of oil produced and imported, the potential for an oil spill is significant. In March 1989, when the Exxon Valdez ran aground, it dumped 11.2 million gallons of oil into Alaska's Prince William Sound. Since that gigantic spill, there have been several other spills. In Scotland's Shetland Islands, for example, in 1992, the oil tanker Braer ran aground in hurricane force winds while carrying 25 million gallons of light crude oil. Other smaller spills have occurred since these two huge spills, almost on a yearly basis. Two oil spills in 1993 dumped a total of 728,000 gallons of oil into the environment in Tampa Bay, Florida, and Fairfax County, Virginia. In addition, in Indiana in 1997, a break in a 22-inch Marathon Oil pipeline resulted in the discharge of 470,000 gallons of crude oil. More recently, the Tasman Spirit ran aground in 2003 off the coast of Karachi spilling over 25,000 tons of crude oil, killing marine life for miles. On average, only 30 percent of all birds and mammals exposed to oil spills survive longer than a year.

The U.S. Coast Guard is charged with cleaning up oil spills and has developed expertise on the issue after being involved in so many cleanups. At any oil spill, either the local Coast Guard or the EPA acts as coordinator of the cleanup, and each Coast Guard district has plans on how to perform an oil spill cleanup.[55] Many of the techniques we use to mitigate the impact of oil spills were developed by the Coast Guard, including "hazardous material detection devices, spill containment equipment, oil dispersant chemicals and removal skimmers."[56] The Coast Guard has also worked on preventing oil spills through drug and alcohol testing of crews, licensing procedures, spill-prevention training, improvements in cargo vessel safety, and improved oil on-loading and off-loading methods.[57]

The Coast Guard also performs some of the investigative work on oil spills, such as in 1975 when a "mystery" oil spill occurred. The Coast Guard took samples of the spilled oil and of oil from vessels in the area to compare and attempt to determine the culprit. After checking more than 200 vessels and 50 samples, the Coast Guard found the guilty party, resulting in a $10,000 fine for the company.[58] The Coast Guard was also a key figure in cleaning up the oil spill in the Galapagos Islands on January 16, 2001. The oil tanker Jessica dumped more than 170,000 gallons of diesel oil over an area of 488 square miles, damaging the unique Galapagos wildlife and creating concern that the oil may destroy algae at the bottom of the ocean and disrupt the food chain.

To reduce the harm from oil spills when tankers run aground, break up in heavy weather, or collide with other vessels, President Carter issued an executive order in 1976 requiring all tankers over 20,000 tons that sailed in American waters to be fitted with double hulls and bottoms by

1982—a proposal the Coast Guard had suggested as early as 1973. When the double hull requirement was not met by 1990, Congress passed the Oil Pollution Act of 1990, discussed later in this section. This act mandated that all ships have double hulls within 25 years. Shipowners argue that the expense is too great considering the low likelihood of a wreck; and these costs, they add, would have to be passed on to the consumers. However, the EPA created a program designed to prevent oil spills. The program encourages companies to prevent, prepare for, and respond to oil spills. For example, the EPA requires owners or operators of certain oil storage facilities to prepare spill-prevention plans that detail the facility's spill-prevention and spill-control measures. The Oil Spill Program has reduced the number of spills to less than one percent of the total volume handled each year.[59]

Oil spills in conjunction with production of oil on the OCS are also a concern. The 1978 amendments to OCSLA impose strict liability for cleanup costs and damages resulting from OCS activities on owners and operators of offshore facilities and vessels carrying oil from such facilities. Liability is limited to $250,000 for a vessel and $35 million plus government removal costs for a facility. The act also created the Offshore Oil Spill Pollution Protection Fund, which pays for all losses that cannot be covered by the responsible parties. The fund receives its income from a per-barrel tax imposed on purchasers of OCS oil.

Additional liability was also imposed by the CWA. Section 311 held vessel operators strictly liable for cleanup costs incurred by the government unless the operator can prove that the cause of the spill was an act of God, an act of war, an act or omission of a third party, or negligence of the federal government. Government removal costs under this act include restoration or replacement of natural resources damaged or destroyed by the spill. Damages were limited, however, to $125,000 for inland barges, $250,000 for other vessels, and $50 million for onshore and offshore facilities. The limits would not apply if the accident were caused by "willful negligence or willful misconduct within the privity and knowledge of the owner."

Liability of responsible parties was broadened by the Oil Pollution Act of 1990, which replaces the foregoing liability provisions. Under this new law, each responsible party, defined as owners and operators of vessels, onshore facilities, or pipelines, is liable for removal costs, damage to natural resources, damages for injury to or economic losses from destruction of real or personal property, and lost profits because of the injury or destruction of any real property, personal property, or natural resources. The measure of damages to natural resources was clearly spelled out under the act. It includes the cost of restoring, rehabilitating, rejecting, or acquiring the equivalent of the damaged resources; the diminution of value of those resources pending restoration; and the reasonable cost of assessing those damages.

Liability limits under the Oil Pollution Act were increased to $10 million for ships weighing more than 3,000 gross tons and $75 million for owners of offshore facilities. Limits are inapplicable if the spill is caused by gross negligence, willful misconduct, or a safety violation. The act also established a $1 billion oil spill trust fund.

In 2003, the Norwegian container ship Star Evviva was fined $2.5 million in both civil and criminal fines for leaking 24,000 gallons of heavy crude oil 35 miles off the coast of Charleston in 1999.[60] The fines will be paid into the oil spill liability trust fund to pay for future oil spills. The crew members of the ship who failed to follow safety regulations were investigated for further criminal violations of the CWA and the Migratory Bird Treaty Act, because over 200 loons were consequently killed from the oil spill. In May 2000, the captain and chief engineer of the ship were indicted on criminal violations, but both have subsequently fled and become fugitives.[61]

Finally, part of the 1990 Oil Pollution Act banned the Exxon Valdez, which dumped 11.2 million gallons of oil, from ever sailing into Prince William Sound again. The amendment to the Oil Pollution Act does not explicitly name the Exxon Valdez. Instead, "vessels that have spilled more than 1,000,000 gallons of oil into the marine environment after March 22, 1989" are banned from entering the sound.

While most attention is given to preventing and cleaning large oil spills that occur during production or transportation of the oil, the largest amount of oil and gas enters the environment through runoff. A new research study done by the Nation Academy of Sciences in 2002 reports that over 11 million gallons of oil seep into the environment every 8 months because of road and surface runoff.[62] This runoff is the equivalent of the Exxon Valdez spilling oil into the nation's waterways every 8 months. The report also says that although the runoff is more dispersed than a concentrated spill, low concentrations of oil continually entering the nation's waterways does have a large environmental impact. Perhaps more attention will be given in the future toward finding solutions for harmful runoff, just as attention has been given to alleviating the causes and dangers of the more renowned oil spills.

NUCLEAR ENERGY

Nuclear energy once offered a dream of cheap, unlimited electrical power. In many people's opinion, that dream has now been dimmed as numerous problems have developed during the past 40 years of attempts to harness nuclear power to satisfy energy needs. As originally conceived, uranium ore would be mined, processed, used in nuclear reactors, reprocessed, and used again in nuclear reactors—all in a continuous, closed cycle. The cycle did not work that way, however, leading to perhaps the most serious problem of nuclear energy: nuclear waste.

HISTORY OF NUCLEAR ENERGY DEVELOPMENT

Development of nuclear energy as a fuel really began in the mid-1950s. The federal government invested a great deal of money to subsidize early research and development. To encourage industry further in developing nuclear power, Congress even passed the Price–Anderson Act in 1957 to limit liability for any nuclear reactor accident. By 1975, the high point for nuclear energy, 56 commercial reactors had been built, 69 were under construction, and there were plans for 111 more. By 1986, 95 nuclear reactors were licensed and operating. Then came the near-catastrophe of Three Mile Island, which alerted the public to the potential risks of nuclear accidents and also called attention to many other problems in the nuclear industry. The core meltdown at Chernobyl, in the Soviet Union, further turned public opinion away from nuclear energy.

As of July 2006, 103 commercial reactors were generating electricity in the United States,[63] providing 19 percent of the country's electricity.[64] In contrast, other countries, such as France, rely on nuclear power for 78 percent of their power needs.[65] Half the generators in the United States are scheduled to be closed down between 2005 and 2015; the remainder will be shut down by 2075. No new reactors have been ordered since 1979, so at the end of the 20th century, it seemed conceivable that nuclear energy as a source of power would be only a memory by the year 2075. But with the election of George W. Bush, the outlook for nuclear energy changed. The NEP, developed by Vice President Cheney in 2001, said nuclear power should account for a higher percentage of U.S. electricity than the then current level of 20 percent. Cheney, calling for an increase in the number of power plants nationwide, said that "some of those ought to be nuclear."[66] And President Bush's 2007 budget allocated $250 million for the Global Nuclear Energy Partnership (GNEP), a partnership with nations that have advanced civillian nuclear energy programs that is organized to develop and deploy innovative, advanced reactors and new methods to recycle spent nuclear fuel. The administration believes that GNEP also will help resolve nuclear waste disposal issues. On the basis of technological advancements that will be made through GNEP, the volume and radio-toxicity of waste requiring permanent disposal is supposed to be reduced. Despite their confidence in the importance of nuclear energy for our nation's future, administration officials have not set a specific goal as to how much energy should come from nuclear generation or how many additional plants would be built.

In December 2005, the NRC certified the development of a new type of reactor known as an Advanced Passive (AP) Reactor. Six separate locations in the United States are vying for the new reactor, and there is a chance at least one will be built within the next 5 years.[67] Congress's $3.1 billion on tax credits offered to the nuclear power industry in 2005 has helped to encourage the development of more nuclear power plants.[68]

Regardless, as of now, no plans have been approved for new reactors or new power plants. Nuclear power plants still face public disapproval, high closing costs, and expensive safety concerns. Given the large downsides and the lack of clear steps forward, the future of nuclear power in the United States is still uncertain.

PROBLEMS WITH NUCLEAR ENERGY

A major problem with the nuclear industry is safety. Many of the materials and designs currently in use in reactors have failed safety tests, and many reactor parts have aged faster than projected. A 1988 survey by the GAO revealed that one-third of the plants it inspected had prematurely deteriorating pipes; consequently, the GAO recommended inspection of pipes at all facilities. Horror stories abound about mismanagement and incompetence of managers and technicians in the industry. Those within the industry, however, point out that, in terms of accidents, the nuclear industry has a good safety record.

Although not environmentally related, per se, the nuclear industry has been beset with economic problems. Costs were underestimated, and many of the facilities completed during the 1980s and early 1990s were 500–1,000 percent over budget. The licensing procedures caused costly delays in startups, with many plants taking 4–8 years to obtain all the necessary permits.

The most troublesome problem with nuclear energy, perhaps, is nuclear waste. Four types of wastes are created, all of which present problems. First are the high-level radioactive liquids created during the reprocessing of reactor fuels. More than 100 million gallons of these highly dangerous wastes currently are being stored in temporary containment facilities in New York, North Carolina, Idaho, and Washington. Second, stored along with the high-level wastes are transuranic wastes. These are by-products of reactor fuel and military waste processing. Some have a half-life of over 200,000 years. The most well known of these dangerous by-products is probably plutonium-239, with a half-life of 24,000 years. A third category is spent nuclear fuel, which is currently being stored in cooling ponds at reactor sites. Many of these ponds are nearly full. This category of waste was never expected to be so large, because this spent fuel was supposed to have been recyclable. Unfortunately, the necessary technology for recycling did not develop. More than 63,000 metric tons of this waste is expected to exist by 2010. Finally, there are low-level radioactive wastes. This category includes items such as clothing, tools, and equipment that have become radioactive through exposure at reactors. These wastes are currently being stored at repositories in South Carolina, Washington, and a limited number in Utah.

As the nuclear industry was developing, those in the industry assumed they would discover the technology to reprocess and then safely contain the waste. When the technology did not develop, the industry was, and still is, unprepared to handle all the hazardous wastes. A major problem is finding permanent sites to dispose of the waste. The next section will give a more in-depth look at the problems of nuclear waste storage.

Not only is waste disposal a problem, but the cost of decommissioning these plants now appears to be much higher than anticipated. In 1993, the first nuclear plant began to be taken apart for decommissioning. That relatively small plant, located at Fort St. Vrain, in Colorado, cost $224 million to build in the 1970s; it is now being taken apart at a cost of $333 million. The NRC requires utilities to put aside up to $130 million for each of their nuclear plants to cover the costs of dismantling them. Not only is this amount apparently going to be far less than needed, the NRC estimates that the total amount that utilities have set aside falls far short of even this inadequate sum. To make matters still worse, many plants are wearing out far earlier than their projected 40-year life span, after having never consistently produced the low-cost energy they were designed to produce. Closed plants now operate an average of 12.7 years. Table 9-1 lists the nation's oldest nuclear power plants. Since 1960, more than 70 power reactors in the United States have been retired. Currently, at least 14 nuclear plants have closed and are being mothballed until a lower-cost method of dismantling them can be developed. The NRC will allow plants to sit idle for up to 60 years before the owners must dismantle them. However, maintaining, inspecting, and securing a closed nuclear facility can cost up to $10 million a year. A new method of disposing of a nuclear facility is simply to sell the entire power plant, often to a foreign buyer. Thirty countries have at least one power plant.

TABLE 9-1   The Nation's Oldest Nuclear Power Plants

Plant	Location	To Be Retired
Oyster Creek	Lacey Township, NJ	April 2009
Nine Mile Point 1	Scriba, NY	August 2009
R. E. Ginna	Ontario, NY	September 2009
Dresden 2	Morris, IL	December 2009
H. B. Robinson 2	Hartsville, SC	July 2010
Monticello	Monticello, MN	September 2010
Point Beach 1	Two Creeks, WI	October 2010
Millstone 1	Waterford, CT	October 2010
Dresden 3	Morris, IL	January 2011
Palisades	Covert, MI	March 2012

Source: Adapted from Paul Hoversten. 1998. "Nuclear Plant up for Grabs in Going Out-of-Business Sale." *USA Today* July 13. 4A.

REGULATION OF THE NUCLEAR INDUSTRY

The Atomic Energy Act of 1954 is the primary legislation that gives the federal government the authority to protect human health and the environment from excessive exposure to radiation. The agency responsible for regulating the nuclear industry is the NRC. Created in 1978 to replace the old Atomic Energy Commission, the NRC issues licenses for the construction and operation of nuclear facilities, as well as for the possession, use, handling, and disposal of nuclear wastes. The NRC has generally been staffed by people who believe in nuclear energy and is cited by some as an example of a captured agency.

In 1979, after the accident at Three Mile Island, the Kemeny Commission was established to investigate the accident. Chief among the commission's findings was that to prevent similar accidents in the future, changes would be necessary in the organization, procedures, practices, and attitudes of the NRC. The commission felt that the NRC had grown too firmly convinced that nuclear plants were sufficiently safe. The NRC was too preoccupied with regulations and equipment and was not paying enough attention to human factors. Workers were not being well trained to respond to equipment malfunctions, especially severe or multiple malfunctions. The commission said that the NRC was not paying enough attention to the ongoing process of ensuring nuclear safety.

In 1980, in partial response to the accident at Three Mile Island and the Kemeny Commission's report, Congress passed Public Law 96–295. The law provided funding to train additional federal inspectors who would be stationed at nuclear power plants. The law also required the agency to draw up a plan for agency responses to nuclear accidents, as well as to issue new regulations to improve safety at reactors.

However, these additional federal inspectors and improved safety regulations failed to catch a grave oversight at the Davis-Besse nuclear plant, near Toledo, Ohio. An engineer first noticed corrosion on the reactor's lid in early 2000 and reported it to the NRC along with color photographs of the corrosion. Not until 2002, during a routine maintenance inspection, did inspectors find the reactor lid bulging under immense pressure, leaving only a dangerously thin piece of stainless steel to prevent a major nuclear accident. In 2003, a 29-page report was issued by the NRC's inspector general, finding instances of flawed communication, inept assessments, and wrong assumptions. It is not yet clear what changes, if any, will result from these potentially dangerous NRC oversights.

Aside from the regulation of the nuclear plants themselves, many regulations oversee the proper disposal of nuclear waste. The Nuclear Waste Policy Act of 1982 was passed to resolve the problem of siting and developing permanent repositories for high-level nuclear waste. By 1985, the DOE was to nominate five sites. After extensive public hearings, the president was to make a recommendation to Congress. If the site were approved by the selected state or Congress, the DOE was to apply to the NRC for a repository license. Until the permanent facility was established, an interim storage program was to be maintained.

Nomination of three sites—volcanic rock in Nye County, Nevada, salt beds in Deaf Smith County, Texas, and basalt deposits at Hanford Reservation in Washington—led to an uproar among local citizens. In 1987, Congress, perhaps in frustration over the political opposition created by the site-selection process, passed legislation directing the DOE to examine a site in Yucca Mountain, Nevada.

The proposal to make Yucca Mountain a nuclear waste repository is an enduring controversial issue. Many scientists argue that Yucca Mountain has the following features that may make it suitable for a nuclear waste repository. First, it is in a remote location and far away from a large population center. Second, the dry climate—less than 6 inches of rainfall each year—is a favorable condition. Finally, Yucca Mountain has an extremely deep water table—800–1,000 feet below the level of the potential repository.

However, environmental and consumer organizations want Yucca Mountain to be disqualified from consideration as a nuclear waste repository. They argue that the rapid water travel times to the nearest wells that supply drinking water require the energy secretary to disqualify the site. Yet, as of 2004, the DOE has spent over $6 billion on research studies of Yucca Mountain, and it contends that the site remains the safest option for long-term nuclear waste disposal. Consequently, in 2001, the Secretary of the DOE formally recommended the site to President Bush, who approved the secretary's recommendation in 2002. Nevada Governor Guinn voiced the State's official disapproval of Yucca Mountain as the nation's nuclear waste repository. Despite strong objections from the State of Nevada and some environmental groups, Congress approved the site in 2002, allowing the DOE to move forward in acquiring the necessary permits and licenses from the NRC. There have been multiple delays in the Yucca Mountain Project, including the discovery in early 2005 that certain employees working on the project may have falsified documentation required by the NRC.[69] Despite this discovery, the DOE reported in July 2006 that they plan to submit a license application for the nuclear waste repository at Yucca Mountain by June 30, 2008.[70] The earliest projected date for receipt of nuclear waste is now March 31, 2017.[71]

Environmental regulation of the nuclear industry is extremely complex. The EPA has the authority to regulate high-level nuclear wastes, setting standards for radioactive emissions to protect the environment and human health. With the possible development of the Yucca Mountain site, controversy has ensued over whether the NRC or the EPA should regulate nuclear wastes. Some in Congress believe that the EPA would set standards that would be impossible to reach, particularly for ground-water concentrations, whereas some scientists believe they could in fact meet any standards set by the EPA. In 2000, Congress passed a bill that would have placed the NRC in charge of Yucca Mountain standards and limited the role of the EPA. This bill was vetoed by President Clinton, and the attempt at an override was unsuccessful. The division over whether the NRC or the EPA should be the agency to develop standards for Yucca Mountain is simply one of many issues that need to be resolved in the regulation of the nuclear industry.

RENEWABLE FUELS

Coal, natural gas, and oil are fossil fuels—fuels formed from decaying prehistoric plants and animals. Because the so-called traditional fuels present a number of environmental problems—and they are bound to be depleted someday—many argue that the government needs to encourage more research into renewable fuels, sources of energy that are continuously renewed. The renewables most heavily used today include hydropower, solar power, wind, biomass, and the burning of waste for steam. In 2004, renewable energy provided 6 percent of total energy consumption. Of this percentage, 45 percent of the energy came from hydropower.[72] Briefly, these sources offer the benefits of generally being less polluting and being available domestically, so they reduce dependence on foreign oil. Figure 9-6 depicts the percentage of renewable fuels being used today.

FIGURE 9-6   Renewable Energy in 2004

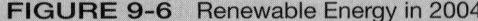
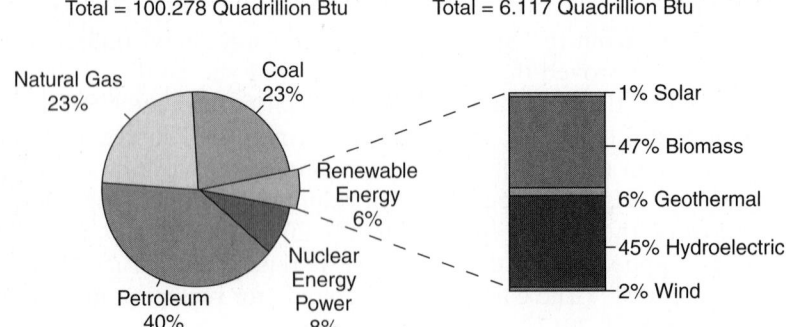

This pie chart shows that renewable energy consumption made up 6 percent of total U.S. energy consumption which was 100.3 quadrillion Btu in 2004. Hydroelectric energy provided 45 percent of renewable energy consumption, whereas nonhydroelectric energy sources collectively provided the remaining 55 percent.

Source: DOE. Energy Information Administration. June 2006. "The Role of Renewable Energy Consumption in the Nation's Energy Supply, 2004." *http://www.eia.doe.gov/cneaf/solar.renewables/page/rea_data/rea_sum.html* (August 1, 2006).

HYDROPOWER

The most popular of the renewable energy sources is hydropower (i.e., the power to generate electricity from running water). Hydropower is very inexpensive and produces no air pollution. In 2006, hydropower from dams generates about 9 percent of the electricity used in the United States.[73] Of the 76,000 dams in the United States, more than 2,500 are used to generate power.[74] Increasingly, environmental groups have been raising concerns about the environmental effects of dams, such as the impact they have in the West on the survival of certain kinds of endangered fish. In 1997, the first ever dam decommissioning without the owners' consent occurred on the Kennebec River in Maine, because of environmental impacts. In addition, in 1999, after extensive litigation initiated by an environmental group, the court ordered the closing of a dam because of its environmental impact. Particular controversy has ensued over four dams on the Snake River in the northwestern United States. These dams have led to the near destruction of salmon on the river, but they also provide a good deal of hydroelectric power to the surrounding area. From 1999 through August 2005, at least 185 dams have been removed.[75]

In an attempt to mitigate some of the environmental harm caused by dams, engineers have installed fish ladders or fish elevators to some dams, so that fish, such as salmon, can swim upstream without being harmed or blocked by the dam. Screens, and other diversion techniques, are also being installed on many dams to prevent fish from entering the turbine intakes. Fish, however, are not the only aquatic life harmed by dams. The quality of water downstream from a dam is often unhealthy to all aquatic life because of low dissolved oxygen levels in the water. To ensure that the aquatic life has the necessary oxygen levels downstream, some damns are now installing aeration equipment. Although efforts are being made to make dams more environmentally friendly, the environmental damage caused to surrounding ecosystems by damming a waterway cannot easily be remedied.

Dams are licensed by the FERC. The 1986 Electric Consumers Act requires the FERC to give environmental and recreational factors equal weight with power generation when granting and reviewing licenses. FERC, with these regulations and the Kennebec River dam decommissioning bolstering the decision, is now "willing to consider" the value of existing dams when the time comes for relicensing.[76]

Global concern over the environmental and social effects of dams resulted in the creation of the World Commission on Dams. The commission issued its report on dams in late 2000, with a less than favorable view of existing dams. The commission found that although dams have been beneficial, these benefits have often been outweighed by social and environmental costs, specifically because dams have led to an "irreversible loss of species and ecosystems."[77] For example, China is currently building the Three Gorges Dam on the Yangzi River, which will be the world's largest hydro-electric dam upon its completion in 2009. The dam, over 1.5 miles long and 600 feet high, has attracted international criticism because it requires the resettlement of 1.2 million people and destroys one of China's rarest ecosystems. The dam is expected to create a reservoir 400 miles long and hundreds of feet deep, yet its supporters claim that the dam will produce the electric equivalent of 18 nuclear power plants.

Similar to nuclear power, however, the future of dams, both in the United States and in the world remains uncertain.

SOLAR ENERGY

The sun can provide energy in different ways. Solar energy can be used at one centralized location to create electricity, or it can be used in individual residences or commercial buildings to satisfy energy needs directly. Because solar energy requires sunshine, it is obviously not a source that could satisfy anyone's energy needs completely. Places where there is sufficient sunlight year-round to justify construction of a solar energy plant are extremely limited. Currently, California and Texas are the only states with utilities generating solar power. In 1999, solar electricity generation by utilities in these two states totaled just over 3 gigawatt-hours. Ninety-seven percent of this generation came from California. Generally, utilities use solar thermal technology to generate solar power. Solar thermal plants use trough collectors to focus sunlight onto pipes that carry a synthetic oil-based heat-transfer fluid. When heated, this oil creates the steam that drives a turbine to generate electricity.

Solar energy systems used at individual sites are generally referred to as passive or active. Passive solar energy is a matter of designing a structure, so that it will become a solar collector. For example, you would have big south-facing energy-efficient windows that would capture the heat of the sunlight. Active systems are ones that use moving parts to generate energy for heating, producing hot water, and sometimes even powering air-conditioning. Active systems generally use some sort of collector to absorb the sunlight and transfer its heat to some other medium for distribution or storage.

The legal system can encourage or discourage the use of solar energy, primarily through the funding of research into solar energy and through the tax system—directly by providing tax breaks for installing solar technologies or indirectly by increasing taxes on the use of fossil fuels. For example, in 1977, Congress provided a tax break for homeowners who installed solar technology; this tax break ended in 1984. During that time, about 924,000 homeowners claimed the tax break. When Carter was president, he saw great merit in solar technology research and funded it accordingly. When Reagan came into office, he saw no need for government support of an energy technology that did not appear to offer much of an opportunity for profit to the private sector and drastically reduced funding.

In 1997, in part to encourage the market for solar energy, President Clinton announced the Million Solar Roofs Initiative, a program to install solar energy systems on one million U.S. buildings by 2010. The Million Solar Roofs Initiative will reduce greenhouse gas and other emissions. President Clinton committed the federal government to install the solar energy systems on 20,000 federal buildings by 2010. As of 2004, 71 state and local partnerships had already committed 900,000 solar energy systems, an encouraging sign that the Million Solar Roofs Initiative may be successful.[78]

Another innovative solar energy program is the DOE's Brightfields Initiative. Many inner cities suffer from the problem of industrial "brownfields," discussed in Chapter 8. The Brightfields Initiative redevelops these brownfields through the incorporation of solar energy, revitalizing the community and providing a source of renewable energy for it. Chicago has already begun to create a brightfield that will eventually provide solar energy to all Chicago public schools, in addition to participating in the Million Solar Roofs Initiative by installing solar panels on school roofs.[79]

WIND ENERGY

Another form of renewable energy, which, again, can be used in only appropriate climates, is energy from the wind. In California, wind produces enough power for over 500,000 homes. Renewed interest in wind power in the United States began in the late 1990s. In 2005, wind's generating capacity expanded by 36 percent reaching a record high of 9,149 MW.[80] Over 15,000 wind power turbines were in place across the nation in 2001, and this number continues to grow. By the start of 2006, thirty states contained commercial wind farms.[81] Currently, New York produces 280 MW of wind energy a year, with an additional 235 MW planned.[82] Furthermore, GE, which currently supplies 60 percent of the wind turbines used in the United States, has sold out orders for new wind turbines through 2007.

The Cape Wind Project, five miles off the coast of Cape Cod, Massachusetts, is expected to be completed and operational in 2009.[83] When complete, the offshore wind farm will generate up to 420 MW of electricity with 130 wind turbines, which can replace up to 113 million gallons of oil per year. However, this is not the first offshore wind farm. Currently, wind farms exist off the coasts of many European countries, including Sweden and Denmark, with Denmark setting the goal to meet 50 percent of its energy needs from wind turbines by 2030. Although the Cape Cod windfarm has the potential to produce large amounts of wind energy, it is not without some controversy. The Nantucket Sound, where the Cape Cod wind farm will be located, is home to a number of people as well as a tourist destination. Those who live or vacation there, including many members of the Kennedey family, claim the windmills will ruin their view of the ocean and serve as an eye sore. Although many of these people are environmentalists and support wind energy, they have a problem with it being in their proverbial back yards.[84] The controversy appears to be less about wind energy and more about the location of the wind farm. This controversy over the windfarm has led to legislation in Congress to allow governors the power to veto proposed energy plans such as the Cape Cod windfarm.[85] Ultimately, Congress reached a compromise, and the Coast Guard, not the Massachusetts governor, has the power to alter, or even stop, the Cape Wind project.

Wind energy is a small but rapidly growing market, and its use has already generated some controversy. The fields of generators create noise and are viewed by some people as an eyesore. In addition, bird enthusiasts have approached the use of wind power with caution because of concern that the rapidly rotating windmill blades may kill birds. However, power lines have also killed many birds, particularly raptors. Recent statistics indicate the effect of wind turbines on bird populations is negligible. Windplant-related bird fatalities account for less than one percent of the number of bird fatalities from collisions with man-made objects.[86] Furthermore, per turbine deaths are less than the average of per communication tower deaths, as well as far below the number of birds killed each year by power lines.[87]

BIOMASS ENERGY

Biomass conversion simply means burning organic matter to generate energy: agricultural waste, municipal garbage, grains, animal manure, and wood. Wood is currently the largest source of human biomass power. Burning wood creates pollution problems, but other biofuels are much cleaner than fossil fuels. Agricultural wastes are also burned to produce electricity. As air pollution standards become more stringent, use of these alternative fuels becomes more desirable.

The EPA's LMOP works with landfills to capture methane gases generated from landfill waste and use it as an energy source. This program is especially important because if the methane gas from landfills is not captured, then the greenhouse gas is vented into the atmosphere. For every one million tons of waste in the landfill, 1 MW of electricity can be generated from the methane given off during decomposition. In December 2005, about 395 landfill gas projects were operational not only providing approximately 9 billion kilowatt-hours of electricity per year but preventing the release of 21 million tons of carbon equivalent into the atmosphere, which is the same as removing 14.9 million cars from the road for an entire year.

The DOE is embarking on some biomass energy projects in its BioPower Program. Funding from this program helped the McNeil Generating Station in Burlington, Vermont, create a biomass gasifier "capable of producing enough fuel gas to produce 12 MW of electricity, generating it more efficiently, and with less pollution, than conventional boiler/turbine technology."[88] This gasifier will allow many different types of biomass fuel to be used, including sawdust and other wood residues that are generally sent to landfills.[89] Continued funding of renewable fuel programs may spawn other technologies that will allow biomass energy to generate a significant portion of U.S. energy needs.

GEOTHERMAL ENERGY

Geothermal energy refers to the use of heat trapped within the earth. Technically, it is not a renewable fuel, but it is often thought of as one because it is such a vast source. The most common form of geothermal energy is hydrothermal energy. Naturally occurring hot water reservoirs are tapped for their energy. Low to moderate temperature (68–302°F) geothermal resources are widespread in the United States and are used to provide direct heat to homes and industry. High temperature (above 302°F) resources are present primarily in the West for electric power generation.

HYDROGEN FUEL

The latest development in energy technologies is that of hydrogen fuels. Although hydrogen will not be ready for use anytime soon, developments in hydrogen technologies have made it one of the cleanest fuels. Hydrogen is currently derived from methane and petroleum, but with improved technologies, it could be derived from water, biomass, and other renewable sources. Hydrogen can be used for various energy purposes, including as a fuel for conventional vehicles and alternative vehicles and as a replacement for natural gas heating and cooling systems. As part of his energy policy, President Bush planned to allocate $1.2 billion toward making hydrogen a competitive source of energy, both in electric generation and as a source of fuel in vehicles. Although additional research is needed, it remains to be seen if hydrogen fuel will replace fossil fuels in the near future, as many environmentalists hope.

Concluding Remarks

Energy policy, although often not thought of as part of traditional environmental law, is important to environmental conditions. We need energy, and although some say that the United States uses more than its share, our consumptive behaviors are not likely to change soon.

Therefore, the best the law can do is to try to regulate use of energy in ways that allow us to extend the life of current resources and not create environmental damage through the extraction and use of those resources.

Questions for Review and Discussion

1. Identify and differentiate between the energy policies (if any) of the Nixon, Ford, Carter, Reagan, George H. W. Bush, Clinton, and George W. Bush administrations.
2. Why has the EPAct been called an ambitious piece of legislation?
3. Explain why we have come to rely so heavily on coal as an energy source at so many times in our history.
4. Explain the main problems associated with coal as a fuel and how we try to solve those problems.
5. Explain the primary problems associated with petroleum as a fuel and how we try to solve those problems.
6. Explain the primary problems associated with nuclear energy as a fuel and how we try to solve those problems.
7. What are the main sources of alternative, or renewable, energy?
8. Which alternative energy source do you believe will see the most development? Justify your answer.

For Further Reading

Byrne, John, and Daniel Rich, eds. 1992. *Energy and Global Environmental Change.* New York: Transaction Publishers.

Hall, Charles, et al. 1992. *Energy and Resource Quality: The Ecology of the Economic Process.* Boulder: University of Colorado Press.

Lewis, Neal H. 2006. "Interpreting the Oracle: Licensing Modifications, Economics, Safety, Politics, and the Future of Nuclear Power in the United States." *Albany Law Journal of Science & Technology 16* : 27.

Mane, Christopher. 1991. *Green Rage.* Boston: Little Brown.

Martha M. Roggenkamp, Anita Ronne, Catherine Redgwell, and Inigo del Guayo. 2001. *Energy Law in Europe: National, EU and International Law and Institutions.* London, UK: Oxford University Press.

Munasingne, Mohan. 1990. Energy Analysis and Policy. Stoneham, MA: Butterworth-Heinemann.

Park, Patricia. 2002. *Energy Law and the Environment.* New York: Taylor and Francis.

Smolin, Michael J. 2005. "Bioethics Symposium: Biofuels and the New Energy Economy: Challenges and Opportunities for Energy Alternatives for Transportation in the United States." *Cumberland Law Review 36*: 479

Tomain, Joseph P. 2005. "Bioethics Symposium: Biofuels and the New Energy Economy: Smart Energy Path: How Willie Nelson Saved the Planet." *Cumberland Law Review 36*: 417.

Wilson, Andrew C., et al. 1997. "Tracking Spills and Releases: High-Tech in the Courtroom." Tulane Environmental Law Journal 10: 371.

On the Internet

http://www.converger.com/
Tools for Resource Policy in the Public Interest
http://www.newsdata.com
Indexes information on electrical and natural gas energy production
http://www.eia.doe.gov
Energy Information Administration—Official Energy Statistics from the U.S. government
http://www.eere.energy.gov/
The DOE Office of Energy Efficiency and Renewable Energy Network
http://www.damsreport.org
A downloadable version of the report by the World Commission on Dams
http://www.eere.energy.gov/brightfields/
Information about the Brightfields Initiative
http://geoheat.oit.edu/dusys.htm
Interactive map of geothermal energy projects around the United States
http://www.pvpower.com/pvhistory.html
A good source for information on solar energy (photovoltaic power) in history
http://www.climnet.org/resources/resources.htm#euenergy
Climate Network Europe's Web site, which has pages on European Union energy and greenhouse gas issues
http://www.ornl.gov/ORNL/Energy_Eff/CEF.htm
At this address, you will find the Department of Energy report detailing the savings that the United States could attain from energy efficiency programs
http://www.energystar.gov/
The EPA's Energy Star Program
http://www.epa.gov/lmop/index.htm
The EPA's Landfill Methane Outreach Program
http://www.citizenscoalcouncil.org/index.htm
Citizen Coal Council and information on Mountaintop Removal coal mining
http://www.netl.doe.gov/scng/publications/NG_SDPrimer_v7.pdf
Department of Energy, Natural Gas Fundamentals

Notes

1. Energy Information Administration. "Energy Info Card." July 2005. *http://www.eia.doe.gov/neic/brochure/infocard01.htm* (August 11, 2006).
2. Ibid.
3. Bureau of the Census. 1989. *Statistical Abstract of the United States,* p 563. Washington, D.C.: U.S. Department of Commerce.
4. Walter A. Rosenbaum. 1987. *Energy, Politics, and Public Policy,* p 6. Washington, D.C.: Congressional Quarterly.
5. Department of Energy. 1992. "Executive Summary." *National Energy Strategy: Powerful Ideas for America One Year Later,* pp 2–4. Washington, D.C.: National Technical Information Service.

6. Judy England-Joseph, Associate Director of the Energy Issues, Resources, Community and Economic Development Division, U.S. General Accounting Office, Testimony Before the Subcommittee on Regulation, Business Opportunities, and Energy of the House Committee on Small Business, "Has the National Energy Strategy Been Short-Circuited?" April 8, 1991.

7. Council on Environmental Quality. 1992. *Environmental Quality: The Twenty-Second Annual Report,* p 80. Washington, D.C.: Government Printing Office.

8. Ibid.

9. Ibid.

10. "Federal Buildings Reduce Annual Energy Use by 20 Percent and One Year Early." *DOE Press Release,* April 20, 2000. *http://www.eren.doe.gov/ femp/newsevents/doe_0420002.html* (January 15, 2001).

11. Dan R. Williams and Larry Good. 1994. *Guide to the Energy Policy Act of 1992,* p 92. Lilburn, GA: Fairmont.

12. Ibid., 89.

13. Department of Housing and Urban Development. 1995. "Mortgagee Letter 95–46," October 6. *http://www. hudclips.org/sub_nonhud/cgi/nph-brs. cgi?d=MLET&s1=(95-46)[no]& op1=AND&l=100&SECT1=TXT_HI TS&SECT5=MLET&u=./hudclips.cgi &p=1&r=1&f=G* (January 18, 2001).

14. Energy Information Administration. *Annual Energy Review 2004. http://www.eia.doe.gov/emeu/aer/pdf/ aer.pdf* (July 11, 2006).

15. William J. Clinton, Executive Order 13123. 1999. "Greening the Government Through Efficient Energy Management," June 3. *http://www.eren.doe.gov/femp/ aboutfemp/exec13123.html* (January 15, 2001).

16. Reuters. "BP Near Crucial Alaska Decision." August 11, 2006. *http://www. nytimes.com/reuters/business/business- energy-bp-prudhoe.html* (August 11, 2006).

17. The Bush Administration's Energy Transition Team. *http://www. sdeartntimes.com/et0301S27.html* (April 03, 2001).

18. Dave Morantz. 2001. "President Unveils Energy Blueprint: Bush Tours an Iowa Biomass Facility After Proposing Expanded Oil and Gas Drilling and Added Nuclear Power." *Omaha World-Herald* (May 18): 1.

19. John J. Fialka. 2001. "Gore Projects to Conserve Energy Are Cut, as Focus Swings to Coal." *The Wall Street Journal* (?xml:namespace prefix = st1 ns = "urn:schemas-microsoft-com: office:smarttags") (April 10): A24.

20. Mark Clayton. "Bush Energy Plan Whacks Conservation." *The Christian Science Monitor,* May 31, 2006. *http://www.csmonitor.com/2006/0531/ p02s01-uspo.html* (July 11, 2006).

21. Ibid.

22. Timothy Gardner. "U.S. Policymakers Want Probe of Cheney's Energy Panel." *Reuters News Service,* May 21. *http://www.planetark.org/dailynews- story.cfm?newsid=10889* (July 29, 2001).

23. 5 U.S.C. App. § 3.

24. *In re:* Cheney, 406 F.3d 723 (2005).

25. Dana Milbank and Justin Blum. 2005. "Document Says Oil Chiefs Met with Cheney Task Force." *Washington Post* (November 16): A1.

26. Joseph Kahn. 2001. "U.S. Scientists See Big Power Savings from Conservation." *New York Times* (May 6): 1.

27. Ibid.

28. Energy Information Administration. *Annual Energy Review 2004. http://www.eia.doe.gov/emeu/aer/pdf/ aer.pdf* (July 11, 2006).

29. Patricia Leigh Brown. 2001. "Home-Grown Energy's Time to Shine." *New York Times,* January 24. *http://www.nytimes.com/2001/01/24/national/24GRID.html* (July 29, 2001).
30. Ibid.
31. "White House Forms Energy Task Force, but Offers California Scant Hope of Aid," January 29, 2001. *http://www.cnn.com/2001/US/01/29/power.woes.03/index.html* (January 30, 2001).
32. DOE Energy Information Administration. "U.S. Electric Power Industry Net Generation, 2004." *http://www.eia.doe.gov/cneaf/electricity/epa/figes2.html* (July 12, 2006).
33. DOE Energy Information Administration. "Table 7.1: Coal Overview, Select Years, 1949–2004." *http://www.eia.doe.gov/emeu/aer/pdf/aer.pdf* (July 12, 2006).
34. 42 USCA §§ 8301–8433 (1978).
35. Sierra Club. *http://www.sierraclub.org/cleanair/factsheets/power.asp* (July 12, 2006).
36. Walter A. Rosenbaum. 1991. *Environmental Politics and Policy.* 2nd ed. Washington, D.C.: Congressional Quarterly.
37. Mid-Atlantic Mountaintop Mining. *Environmental Impact Statement.* *http://www.epa.gov/region3/mtntop/eis.htm* (December 20, 2003).
38. This letter can be found at *http://www.ohvec.org/press_room/press_releases/2002/07_31.html#letter* (December 20, 2003).
39. Rosenbaum. Energy, Politics, and Public Policy.
40. Ibid.
41. Ibid.
42. 72 F.Supp2d 642 (1999), 2001 WL 410382 (4th Cir. 2001).
43. 30 U.S.C. § 1202 (a).
44. Rosenbaum. *Environmental Politics and Policy* 264.
45. Ibid.
46. Ibid., 265.
47. H.R. 794, 108th Congress, 1st Session.
48. The Library of Congress. *Legislative Information on H.R. 794. http://thomas.loc.gov/cgi-bin/bdquery/z?d108:HR00794:@@@L&summ2=m&* (July 30, 2006).
49. DOE Energy Information Administration. "Basic Petroleum Statistics." July 2006. *http://www.eia.doe.gov/neic/quickfacts/quickoil.html* (August 2, 2006).
50. DOE Energy Information Administration. "United States Energy Data, Statistics, and Analysis—Oil, Gas, Electricity, Coal." *http://www.eia.doe.gov/emeu/cabs/Usa/Oil.html* (July 30, 2006).
51. DOE Energy Information Administration. "United States Energy Data, Statistics, and Analysis—Oil, Gas, Electricity, Coal." *http://www.eia.doe.gov/emeu/cabs/Usa/NaturalGas.html* (July 30, 2006).
52. David Ivanovich. "Proposal Would Expand Offshore Drilling, Houston Chronicle." *http://www.chron.com/disp/story.mpl/business/4757152.html* (April 27, 2007).
53. Edmund L. Andrews. "Administration Proposes New Energy Drilling." *New York Times* May 1, 2007.
54. EPA. 2006. "Oil Spill Program Overview," March 9. *http://www.epa.gov/oilspill/overview.htm* (August 2, 2006).
55. Donald Canney. "The Coast Guard and the Environment." *http://www.uscg.mil/hq/g-cp/history/h_environment.html* (December 29, 2000).
56. Ibid.
57. Ibid.
58. Ibid.
59. EPA, note 54.

382 Part II ◆ The Environmental Laws

60. South Carolina Department of Natural Resources. "Construction of Oil-Spill Response Facility for Waterbirds Underway." *http://www.dnr.sc.gov/news/Yr2006/june19/june19_oil.html* (July 30, 2006).

61. United States Coast Guard. "The Trail of Environmental Crimes." *Winter 2004–2005. http://www.uscg.mil/hq/gm/nmc/pubs/proceed/winter-proce04_05/ENVIRO%20CRIMES%202005.pdf* (July 30, 2006).

62. National Academy of Sciences. *http://www4.nas.edu/news.nsf/isbn/0309084385?OpenDocument* (December 20, 2003).

63. World Nuclear Association. 2006. "World Nuclear Power Reactors 2005–2006 and Uranium Requirements," July 24. *http://www.world-nuclear.org/info/reactors.htm* (July 30, 2006).

64. Ibid.

65. World Nuclear Association. "French Nuclear Power Program." May 2006. *http://www.world-nuclear.org/info/inf40.htm* (July 30, 2006).

66. Bob Davis. 2001. "Bush Energy Plan Increases Reliance on Nuclear Power." *The Wall Street Journal* (April 9): A3.

67. Paul Guinnessy. "Stronger Future for Nuclear Power." *Physics Today,* February 2006. *http://www.physicstoday.org/vol-59/iss-2/p19.html* (August 11, 2006).

68. Ibid.

69. U.S. Department of Energy. 2005. "Statement from Secretary of Energy, Samuel Bodman," March 16. *http://www.energy.gov/news/1601.htm* (July 30, 2006).

70. United States Department of Energy. 2006. "DOE Announces Yucca Mountain License Application Schedule," July 19. *http://www.ocrwm.doe.gov/info_library/newsroom/documents/ym-schedule-2006.pdf* (July 30, 2006).

71. United States Department of Energy. 2006. "Yucca Mountain Repository Schedule," July 19. *http://www.ocrwm.doe.gov/info_library/newsroom/documents/CtrSchedule.pdf* (July 30, 2006).

72. Department of Energy, Renewable Energy Annual 2004. June 2006. *http://www.eia.doe.gov/cneaf/solar.renewables/page/rea_data/rea_sum.html* (July 30, 2006).

73. Environmental Protection Agency. 2006. "Clean Energy: Electricity from Hydropower," July 19. *http://www.epa.gov/cleanrgy/hydro.htm* (July 30, 2006).

74. American Rivers. "Dam Removal: Frequently Asked Questions," June 2005. *http://www.americanrivers.org/site/DocServer/FAQ_on_Dam_Removal.pdf?docID=2981* (July 30, 2006).

75. American Rivers. 2005. "56 Dams in 11 States to be Removed in 2005," August 24. *http://www.americanrivers.org/site/News2?page=NewsArticle&id=7733&news_iv_ctrl=1129* (July 30, 2006).

76. Bruce Babbitt. 1998. "Dams Are Instruments Not Monuments." *Speech,* July 8. Washington, D.C.: FERC Distinguished Speakers Series. *http://www.doi.gov/news/archives/speeches&articles/fercnote.htm* (January 30, 2001).

77. World Commission on Dams. 2000. "Executive Summary." *Dams and Development: A Framework for Decision-Making,* November 16: xxxi. *http://www.damsreport.org/docs/report/wcdexec.pdf* (January 30, 2001).

78. Department of Energy. "How Are We Doing?" *http://www.eren.doe.gov/millionroofs/goals.html* (January 30, 2001).

79. "Schools Going Solar: Chicago's Brightfields Solar Initiative Benefits City Schools." *http://www.ttcorp.com/upvg/schools/sgs99rei.htm* (December 16, 2000).

80. Earth Policy Institute. 2006. "Wind Energy Demand Booming," March 22, 2006. *http://www.earth-policy.org/Updates/2006/Update52.htm* (August 1, 2006).
81. Ibid.
82. American Wind Energy Association. 2006. "New York State Wind Energy Development," July 25. *http://www. awea.org/projects/newyork.html* (August 1, 2006).
83. Cape Wind. "Project Timeline." *http://www.capewind.org/article26.htm* (August 1, 2006).
84. CBS News. 2003. "Storm over Mass. Windmill Plan." June 29, 2003. *http://www.cbsnews.com/stories/2003/06/26/sunday/main560595.shtml* (August 11, 2006).
85. Jason Szep. 2006. "Cape Cod Debates First Offshore Wind Farm." April 27. *http://www.planetark.com/dailynewsstory.cfm/newsid/36155/story.htm* (August 12, 2006).
86. Mick Sagrillo. 2003. "Putting Wind Power's Effect on Birds in Perspective." *http://www.awea.org/faq/sagrillo/swbirds.html* (August 1, 2006).
87. Ibid.
88. "Biomass in Use." *http://www.eren.doe.gov/biopower/basics/ba_inuse.htm* (December 16, 2000).
89. Ibid.

RESOLVING CONTROVERSIAL ENVIRONMENTAL ISSUES

- Once you have identified the issue, reasons, and conclusion in the following essay, identify any ambiguous wording or missing information, as discussed in Chapters 1 and 7.
- Authors sometimes commit logical fallacies when they make their arguments. Logical fallacies take many forms. Here, you will only learn about the most common forms. The first type of logical fallacy is when authors make hasty generalizations. That is, the author may write only about a specific occurrence but will apply her conclusions to all other similar occurrences. Another type of logical fallacy is an emotional appeal, whereby the author uses the reader's emotions to detract him from the argument being made. Authors sometimes commit an ad hominem fallacy, meaning that the author will attack the person, rather than her ideas. Another type of logical fallacy is when authors attribute causation to two items related only by correlation. An infamous example of this fallacy is the relationship between lunar cycles and women's menstrual cycles. Because both cycles are about the same length, 27–28 days, many people used to believe that lunar cycles caused women's menstrual cycles, when they are, of course, only correlated. These are simply a few of the many logical fallacies an author could commit. Do you see any examples of these in the following editorial or examples of any other logical fallacies you may know about?

OIL IS THE BEST FORM OF ENERGY

The United States is, arguably, the most developed country in the world. Our economy is soaring, industry is booming, and resources are abundant. The incredible growth of the United States since its settlement by the British is due to the discovery of oil. Oil has allowed us to grow; it has created industries, appliances, and objects that most Americans could not live without. Recently, environmentalists have called for funding of alternative energy through federal grants. Such handouts are a poor use of taxpayer money, which will be wasted in the development of these inefficient forms of energy.

Oil is an incredibly efficient source of energy; in fact, it is the most efficient source to date. Such high efficiency means that oil is a very economical source of energy, providing a lot of "bang for the buck." Other forms of energy are simply not as efficient as oil and, therefore, not as cheap.

Predictions of the decline of oil have not been borne out. It was not that long ago that environmentalists were claiming oil would only last until 1950, and then until 1990, and then until 2010. The truth is that oil is plentiful. Estimates of reserves by geologists continue to grow larger, both for U.S. untapped oil and for that of foreign countries. Doomsday scenarios, such as those created by environmentalists, are simply not coming true.

In addition, many environmentalists claim that the development of alternative energy is necessary because oil production and consumption are polluting the environment. Yet, the environmental regulations placed on both the producers of oil and on items that use oil have made oil an environmentally friendly fuel. Car manufacturers are nearing the point where noxious emissions will be a thing of the past, and other emissions of pollutants from oil have been regulated. Oil is not polluting our environment any longer.

Money for the development of alternative energy essentially amounts to corporate welfare. If these technologies are viable, then they will be produced by the market without government intervention. The subsidization of alternative energies proves that alternative energy is only a dream for now, while oil is still an abundant, efficient resource that will last for generations to come.

Now read the opposing editorial. Answer the same critical thinking questions and then decide which editorial makes a better argument.

FUNDS FOR ALTERNATIVE ENERGY NEEDED

Oil is a depletable resource and the world will run out of oil within this century. To safeguard the United States against an energy crisis, technologies for alternative energy must be developed now, so that alternative energy will be a viable source of energy in the future. Government funding for alternative energy is absolutely necessary if the United States is to continue its energy consumption uninterrupted.

Many greedy oil companies with short-term memories have decried government funding for alternative energy, conveniently forgetting that oil production itself has been subsidized through tax credits for research and development and write-offs for unproductive wells. Alternative energy needs subsidies to become competitive with large oil companies.

Alternative energy is generally renewable, meaning that such energy is unlikely to be depleted. In addition, alternative energy does not have a negative impact on the environment, generating no air pollution or hazardous waste, as the production of fossil fuels does. The use of alternative energy follows the path of our ancestors; harnessing the sun's energy has been the method of people throughout history. The use of photovoltaic cells now is equivalent to the way people used the sun to provide their energy in the past.

Finally, using alternative energy will reduce our reliance on volatile foreign nations. Oil importation has become a matter of national security. We must have energy to run our economy, yet we cannot count on foreign countries to supply us with the oil we need. Alternative energy means fewer wars, fewer dead soldiers, and more reliance on domestic forms of energy. All areas of the United States could produce and consume at least one of the many forms of alternative energy, thereby ending the influence of foreign countries on our energy supplies. Funds for alternative energy must be put in place now; our children's future depends on it.

CHAPTER 10
NATURAL RESOURCES

No nation seems more endowed with natural resources than the United States—abundant water, fertile soil, a benign climate, an incredible variety of plant and animal species, and stores of energy resources, including natural gas, coal, oil, and uranium. Yet, these resources are not unlimited. Without careful management, many will become depleted or destroyed. This chapter focuses on how we protect these important natural resources by examining U.S. policies with respect to preservation of land, protection of coastal areas and wetlands, and the protection of plant and animal species.

PROTECTING PUBLIC LANDS

As the preceding chapter has revealed, use of one of our major energy resources—fossil fuels—often comes into conflict with alternative uses of one of our most important natural resources, the land. This section focuses on a particular segment of land resources—public lands. When examining the laws developed to regulate our public lands, it is important to remember that, historically, the purpose of these laws was to preserve the land for sustained exploitation.

More than half a billion acres of public lands are managed by federal agencies. Many conflicts arise over the appropriate use of these lands. Some argue that we should take a purely economic view of the use of public lands. If the Sierra Club is willing to pay more for Yellowstone National Park, for example, then it should have it to preserve for nature lovers' enjoyment. But if the strip-mining companies will pay more, then perhaps the best disposition of the land is to sell it to the strip-mining companies.

In response to this purely economic standpoint, the school of conservation arose with a view toward using resources wisely. There are two branches of this school: utilitarians and preservationists. Utilitarians tend to focus more on using resources, whereas preservationists want to preserve wilderness areas just as they are. Utilitarians believe resources should be used, but used sustainably (i.e., used in a way that will sustain them for future generations). Utilitarians have an instrumental view of nature; its purpose is to serve humans. Preservationists, on the contrary, view nature as having an inherent value. For preservationists, nature has a value beyond the value given to it by humans that creates a need to preserve natural areas. Both preservationists and utilitarians tend to be especially concerned about protecting certain types of land, namely, forests and wilderness.

FORESTS

Forests are complex ecosystems, made up of interdependent communities of plants, animals, and microbes. Forests are one of the nation's largest sources of biodiversity, and they are essential for maintaining healthy ecosystems throughout the United States and the world. They are vital because they serve to regulate climate, reduce air pollution, absorb the greenhouse gas carbon dioxide, provide wildlife habitats, prevent erosion, and filter over two-thirds of the country's fresh water supply. Forests also provide humans with recreational opportunities, timber, minerals, food, and raw materials for pharmaceuticals.

There are numerous types of forests from the scrub forests of the arid interior West to the lush forests on the coasts. A major concern today is the declining amount of forested land in the United States. Obviously, when the nation was young, forests were cleared with abandon. In the early part of the century, approximately 50 million acres were lost yearly. But even during the 1970s and 1980s, many acres of forestland were lost. Many were cleared for agricultural use because of a rapid growth of agricultural exports during that period. Despite consequent recognition of the need to protect these areas, their acreage loss has been slowed, but not halted. The EPA in 1990 estimated a further decline of 4 percent by 2040. This figure represents an annual decline of half a million acres per year, an improvement over the decline of 1.5 million acres per year from 1970 through 1987. In addition, 2002 was the third worst fire year on record, with over seven million acres of forest lost to wildfire compared with the 3.8 million acres of forests burned in 2003. Yet, despite the grim predictions and historical decline in forest acreage, the Forest Service announced in a recent report that forestland area actually increased 1 percent during the last decade. Most recent calculations have the United States gaining, counting tree plantation growth, close to 393,000 acres annually.[1] Today, forests cover 749 million acres, or about 33 percent, of the United States.[2]

Of particular concern is the loss of a special type of forest, old-growth forests. Old-growth forests contain trees that are hundreds, even thousands, of years old—great stands of Douglas firs and giant sequoias and redwoods. Some of the firs are up to 300 feet tall. These old-growth forests are considered valuable by conservationists because they contain a much greater diversity of plant and animal species than do younger, so-called secondary forests. In 1992, only about 15 percent of the old-growth forests that once covered the United States remained, and some conservation groups fear that at current rates of cutting, most of the old-growth forests of the United States will be gone within 15–20 years. Currently, the United States has the seventh worst loss of old-growth forest in the world. Between the years 2000 and 2005, the United States lost an average of approximately 532,000 acres.

One of the causes of the rapid depletion of forestland is a process known as clear-cutting. Clear-cutting occurs when a logging firm moves into a 25- to 50-acre area and cuts down every tree in that area. Clear-cutting is favored by the timber industry over the alternative, selective cutting of individual trees in a forest, for several reasons. With selective cutting, the company must search through the forest to identify small groups of single intermediate or mature trees to be cut. This method, which preserves a "whole" forest with trees of multiple ages, is extremely expensive and time-consuming. Clear-cutting is cheaper and requires less skill. Fewer roads must be built into the area, and replanting is relatively easy. In addition, the company knows that in a given number of years it can come back and reharvest a huge acreage of relatively similar size trees. Clear-cutting does not require a great amount of planning.

When clear-cutting was initially proposed, some thought it would be ecologically superior. After all, it left some areas of forest completely undisturbed. Soon, however, problems began to materialize. First, removal of big swatches of trees affects the ecological balance in the adjacent areas. If the clearing is done on sloped land, there can be extreme erosion problems: flooding from melting snow and heavy rains, and landslides. From an aesthetic viewpoint, it is ugly. Today, an estimated two-thirds of the annual timber harvest is done by clear-cutting. Consumer pressure may help limit the extent of clear-cutting with the formation of the global Forest Stewardship Council (FSC). This council certifies that wood products are harvested in a sustainable and environmentally friendly manner from the forest to store shelves.[3] Concerned consumers can then purchase FSC-labeled products with the confidence that such products were created by adhering to FSC's forestry management standards. Currently, approximately 22,598,933 acres of U.S. forests were certified by the FSC as of late 2006.[4] However, this total represents only a portion of our forests; clear-cutting is still a widely used practice. The various rules and regulations governing clear-cutting, and logging in general, are discussed later in this chapter.

RANGELANDS

Much of public land is rangeland, because the definition of rangeland is broad and encompasses diverse ecosystems. The wet grasslands of Florida, mountain meadows, and the desert shrubs of the dry West are all examples of rangelands that span throughout the country. Of the nation's 770 million acres of rangeland, the Bureau of Land Management oversees over 158,894,262 acres, whereas the Forest Service manages approximately 104 million acres, about half of which is timbered. Other federal agencies that manage public rangelands are the EPA, the U.S. Soil Conservation Service, U.S. Fish and Wildlife Service (FWS), and the National Park Service. The primary issue with respect to rangeland is the extent to which such land should be leased to farmers for grazing.

Grazing on private rangelands costs ranchers between $6.50 and $12.00 per head of cattle per month. By contrast, however, ranchers are charged only $1.35 per head of cattle per month to graze on federal rangelands. This low cost is because ranchers are heavily subsidized by the federal government, costing the U.S. Treasury between $20 and $150 million per year. Many critics argue that the cost to the federal government is too high, considering that only 3 percent of U.S. beef comes from federal rangelands. Consequently, there is a question about the extent to which grazing should be viewed as the dominant use of these lands, especially when the land is to be managed under a multiple-use concept (described in the next section).

Specific legislation directing the use and management of federal rangelands is discussed in the following section.

REGULATION OF PUBLIC LANDS

No comprehensive statutory scheme for regulation of public lands exists, and management of these lands is fragmented among a number of agencies housed under different departments, which have different directives and land management philosophies. The primary agencies responsible for land management are the Bureau of Land Management, the FWS, the Forest Service, and the National Park Service. In addition, the Department of Defense is responsible for managing six million acres of forestland. The map in Figure 10-1 illustrates where the national forests, parks, and grasslands are located.

The Bureau of Land Management, within the Department of the Interior, is responsible for managing approximately 261 million acres of public lands, of which 55 million are forestlands. Another Interior Department agency, the FWS, manages approximately 95 million acres, 16 million of which are national forestlands. The Forest Service, in the Agriculture Department, manages 193 million acres of forestland, and the National Park Service manages 93 million acres.

The management activities of these agencies are directed by diverse statutes. To discuss all of them would take an entire book, so our discussion will be limited to the most influential laws affecting the management of public lands, starting with the earliest laws, so that you can follow the historical development of policies for public lands.

Initially, the attitude of the federal government toward public lands was "sell and develop." Early homestead acts conveyed large tracts of public lands to farmers and ranchers who were willing to develop those lands. The Mining Law of 1872 provided that anyone who discovered a valuable mineral deposit (excluding oil, gas, coal, and oil shale) on public land could obtain a mining claim on that land; further provisions of the act allowed the miner also to obtain title to the land on which the claim was located, hence encouraging mining of formerly public lands.

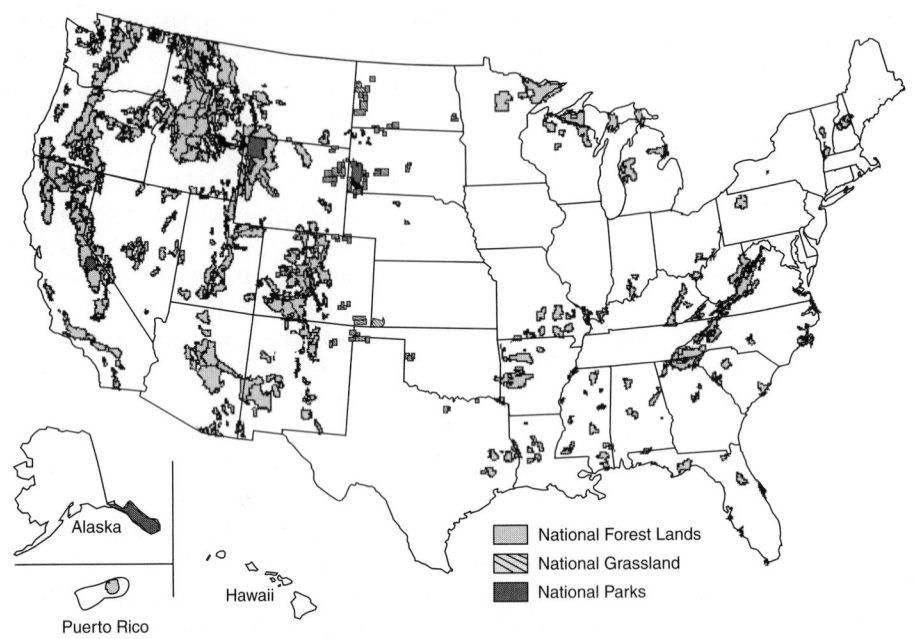

FIGURE 10-1   Map of the National Forests, Parks, and Grasslands

Source: U.S. Forest Service. *http://www.fs.fed.us/land/staff/lar/nfsmap.htm* (June 27, 2006).

The president was first authorized to set aside land for national forests by The Forest Reserve Act of 1891.[5] An 1897 statute declared the purposes for establishing such forests were to be water control and "a continuous supply of timber."[6] In 1920, the exploitation of land for the extraction of oil and gas was encouraged by the Mineral Leasing Act of 1920, described in Chapter 9.

In more recent years, land-use regulation took on a less singularly developmental tone. In 1960, Congress passed the Multiple-Use Sustained Yield Act.[7] This act provides that national forests should be managed to fulfill a multiplicity of purposes: outdoor recreation, timber, and provision of wildlife habitats. No particular weight is given to any of these uses by the act.

In 1964, Congress passed what many preservationists consider one of the most significant pieces of legislation for the protection of land—the Wilderness Act, the law that created the National Wilderness Preservation System. The act defines a wilderness as having four characteristics. First, there has been no noticeable human impact on the land. Second, the area offers opportunities for solitude or primitive recreation. Third, the area consists of at least 5,000 acres or a sufficient size to make preservation possible. Finally, although this characteristic is not mandatory, the area has ecological, geological, or other value. The act itself specifies certain areas to be designated wilderness and other forests to be reviewed for consideration as wilderness in the future. Under this law, once land is designated wilderness, its use is sharply restricted. The agency administering the land must preserve the "wilderness character" of the area and make sure that the area is devoted to "the public purposes of recreational, scenic, scientific, education, conservation, and historical use." Unless specifically provided for by statute, no commercial enterprises or permanent roads may be constructed in any wilderness area. An exception in the act, however, provided for the continuation of mining in wilderness areas until 1983. By the middle of 2006, 106,619 million acres had been designated wilderness under the National Wilderness Preservation System.

The Wilderness Act has generated some concern over the issue of where land is being protected. Because the Wilderness Act was passed primarily with the preservation of the West in mind, the Eastern Wilderness Areas Act was passed in 1975 to add 16 new lands to the system from the eastern half of the United States. However, today only four million acres of the 106 million acres in the National Wilderness Preservation System are east of the 100th meridian.[8] This disparity stems from the fact that the Wilderness Act strongly suggests the proposed area to be at least 5,000 acres, a difficult number to obtain in the populous east. The act also requires that the area be "untrammeled by man," which is also nearly impossible in the early-settled East. To correct this "imbalance," the Eastern Wilderness Act of 1998 (H.R. 1567) was introduced in the 105th Congress to amend the Wilderness Act. This bill called for wilderness areas to be at least 500 acres, allowing more land in the eastern part of the United States to be proposed for wilderness designation.[9] The bill would also allow areas that could eventually qualify as wilderness through natural reclamation to be designated as such.[10] However, federal agencies felt the bill would be redundant, because areas under 5,000 acres are allowed if they are of sufficient size to make preservation possible. The bill did not make it to the House floor.

In 1976, greater protection for public lands was encouraged by the Federal Land Policy and Management Act. This act requires the secretary of the interior, when managing the public lands, to take any action necessary to "prevent unnecessary or undue degradation of the lands."[11] This act also requires the Bureau of Land Management to prepare land management plans for the 450 million acres of land it administers.[12] Similar management plans for national forests were required of the secretary of agriculture in legislation passed by Congress in 1974, 1976, and 1978.[13] The National Forest Management Act of 1976, for example, is the primary statute directing the Department of Agriculture's administration of the National Forests. The act requires detailed resource management plans based on multiple-use and sustained-yield principles.

Because much of the federal rangelands are classified as National Forest land, they are managed and regulated under legislation pertaining to all National Forest land. However, two pieces of legislation are directed specifically toward the management of all federal rangelands. The Forest and Rangelands Renewable Resource Planning Act of 1974 and the Public Rangelands Act of 1978 govern the various uses of these public lands. The latter mandates that the rangelands be managed as to be "productive as feasible for all rangeland values,"[14] which includes maintaining healthy grazing land for cattle as well as the management of the wild horses and burro populations on the land so that their numbers do not become harmful to the rangeland ecosystem.

In 1998, the Omnibus National Parks and Public Lands Act (H.R. 4570) was introduced into the House. Representative Jim Hansen (R-UT) combined numerous small bills into one big bill. This bill included a provision for the privatization of natural parkland. Parcels of land within the C&O Canal National Historic Park could have been sold and leased. In addition, the bill included a provision that would have transferred 666 acres of parkland to the Miccosukee Tribe for permanent use. Finally, the act contained several provisions that would have created exceptions to the Wilderness Act. Although the act failed to pass in the House, the controversial idea that the government should privatize parkland is not dead, and we may see similar attempts in the future.

Although the Clinton administration attempted to provide greater protections to public lands and restrict their use by the mining and timber industries, President Bush views such an approach as unfair to the mining and timber industries and found ways to open up more public lands to industry. He also reduced the federal role in management of public lands and turned more of the decision making over to state and local authorities. To achieve his goals, he overturned a number of the actions that were undertaken by the Clinton administration. For example, the Bush administration attempted to repeal the Roadless Area Conservation Rule, which barred virtually all road building, logging, and mining on 58.5 million acres of national forest. The U.S. Appeals Court, however, upheld the rule in 2002, handing a major setback to timber and mining interests. In 2003, the Bush administration overturned a Clinton era policy, reinstating grazing policies on federal rangelands that led to overgrazing and other unsustainable practices. Similar actions, such as allowing increased logging in the Sierra Nevada, Tongass, and the Northwest, signify for environmentalists a regression of previous policy achievements.

One area where the Bush administration disagrees sharply with the Clinton administration is over the creation of national monuments. President Clinton sought to seal a legacy in environmental protection by creating or expanding 22 national monuments during his presidency, providing additional protections for over a million acres of federal land in the West. The 1906 Antiquities Act allows presidents to create national monuments to protect historical landmarks and structures and "other objects of historic or scientific interest." The amount of land to be protected is restricted to the "smallest area compatible with proper care and management of the objects to be protected." Designation of an area as a national monument allows the president to ban new logging and mining in the area, as well as to restrict the use of off-road vehicles and grazing. Existing uses are generally allowed to continue. In an unprecedented act, President Bush in 2002 allowed energy exploratory drilling on 1,900 acres of not previously leased land within the Canyons of the Ancients National Monument. However, before exploration could begin, environmentalists filed suit in court and the judge temporarily halted further action. The parties to this precedent-setting case settled outside of court.

Although the Antiquities Act had been used 102 times before Clinton's presidency, the act has become extremely controversial since his second term in office. During 2000 and 2001, six bills were proposed to amend or repeal the act. The act is viewed by its supporters as a powerful land conservation tool that empowers the president to unilaterally protect lands that are threatened because of congressional inaction or proposed congressional actions. They believe the act provides a mechanism for necessary and decisive executive action, while protecting the public with a provision that enables Congress to legislatively alter or revoke any national monument designation.

Opponents of the legislation view it as allowing the fate of public lands to be decided without mandated public input. They argue that the act allows a president to end many people's last hopes for earning high wages because it makes the areas off limits for new mining and timber operations in the monument area. This debate continues, unresolved, in both Congress and the courts, yet the outcome will undoubtedly have significant ramifications for the future preservation of public lands.

One of the more difficult regulatory challenges concerning public lands is the creation and management of forest fire prevention. In recent years, record wildfires have ravaged public lands and caused the destruction of many human developments. During the first 10 months of 2006 alone, 4.5 million acres of forests in the west burned. Yet, fire prevention is not as simple as preventing all fires, because many ecosystems within our National Forests depend and thrive on the occasional fire as a source of rejuvenation. Mismanagement and fear of wildfires have allowed an unhealthy buildup of flammable underbrush over many years. Over 20 million acres of national forests are susceptible to fire and require brush and tree thinning to prevent forest fires from growing to an ecologically unhealthy size. However, environmentalists are fearful that the much-needed thinning might serve as an excuse for unneeded logging.

The Healthy Forests Restoration Act of 2003, which is the first major forest management legislation in over 25 years, was signed by President Bush in the name of fire prevention. However, many environmentalists claim that the legislation allows for logging of old-growth trees and in healthy forests that are fire resistant. Furthermore, the legislation undermines portions of the Endangered Species Act (ESA) (discussed later in this chapter) by foregoing environmental studies before trees and forests are cut down. It is clear that the Act is reducing some of the requirements that must be met before logging in certain forests; the question is what

TABLE 10-1	Key Provisions of the Healthy Forests Restoration Act of 2003

- provides authority for expedited vegetation treatments on certain types of Forest Service and Bureau of Land Management lands that (1) are at risk of wildland fire, (2) have experienced windthrow, blowdown, or ice-storm damage, (3) are currently experiencing disease or insect epidemics, or (4) are at imminent risk of such epidemics because of conditions on adjacent land
- provides expedited environmental analysis of HFRA projects
- provides administrative review before decisions are issued on proposed HFRA projects on Forest Service lands
- contains requirements governing the maintenance and restoration of old-growth forest stands when the Forest Service and Bureau of Land Management carry out HFRA projects in such stands
- requires HFRA projects on Forest Service and Bureau of Land Management land to maximize retention of larger trees in areas other than old-growth stands, consistent with the objective of restoring fire-resilient stands and protecting 'at-risk' communities and Federal lands
- requires collaboration between Federal agencies and local communities, particularly when Community Wildfire Protection Plans are prepared
- requires using at least 50 percent of the dollars allocated to HFRA projects to protect areas adjacent to communities at risk of wildland fire
- requires performance to be monitored when agencies conduct hazardous fuel reduction projects and encourages multiparty monitoring that includes communities and other diverse stakeholders (including interested citizens and Tribes)
- encourages courts to expedite judicial review of legal challenges to HFRA projects
- directs that when courts consider a request for an injunction on an HFRA-authorized project, they balance the short- and long-term environmental effects of undertaking the project against the effects of taking no action

Source: http://www.healthyforests.gov/initiative/legislation.html

effects those changes will have. Examine the summary of what the act does in Table 10-1 and just consider the impact each of those items might have. Of course, only after the law has been in effect for a few years will we really know whether this legislation will restore the much-needed ecological balance in our nation's forests or simply increase revenue to the timber industry. And as the pie chart in Figure 10-2 illustrates, only 33 percent of the forests are owned by the federal government, which means that only 33 percent of the forests are covered by the above regulations.

Some legislators did not feel that the Healthy Forests Restoration Act went far enough, and so they proposed follow-up legislation, the Forest Emergency Recovery and Research Act. As of November 2006, this bill had not yet been signed into law, but its advocates were working for its adoption. Advocates of the legislation say it is necessary to allow for more rapid clean up of forest areas that have been hit by some sort of natural disaster, such as a hurricane. The version of the bill passed by the House would require the Forest Service and the Bureau of Land Management to formulate generic

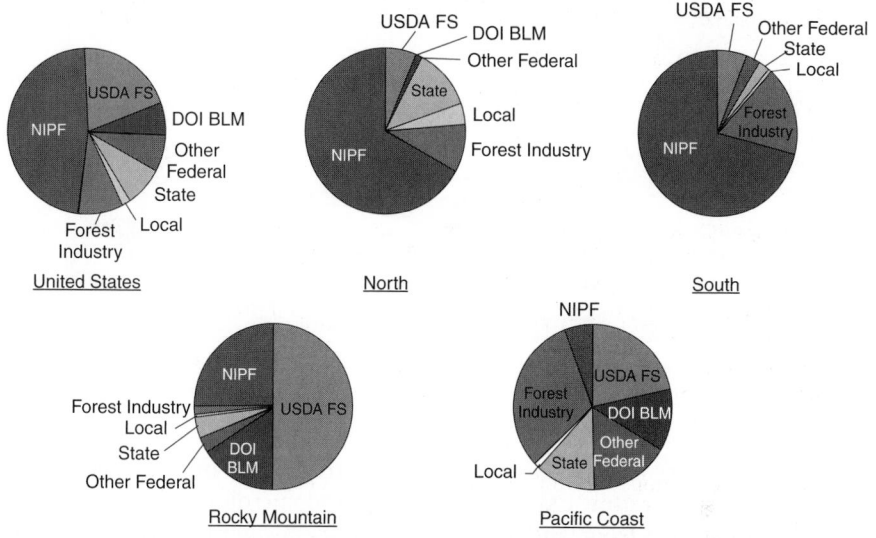

FIGURE 10-2 Ownership of Forests in the United States

Note: NIPF is Nonindustrial private forest owners.

Source: U.S. Forest Service National Sustainability Report—2003. *http://www.fs.fed.us/research/sustain* (August 20, 2006).

guidelines for timber sales that could be put into effect immediately after a fire, insect infestation, storm, or other major disaster. The bill also would require forest managers to come up with a plan within 30 days for how much timber to sell, which would be followed by a 90-day public comment period. The measure would not limit court challenges to timber sales. Environmentalists oppose the new legislation on grounds that under the Healthy Forest Act, managers of forests already have flexibility after a disaster, and that this law will allow unanalyzed salvage timber sales, new road building, including in roadless areas, and projects that threaten water supplies without any true, legally reviewable analysis of alternatives.

WETLANDS, ESTUARIES, AND COASTAL AREAS

Although the need to regulate public lands has been recognized to some extent since the late 1800s, preservation of wetlands, estuaries, and coastal areas is of more recent vintage. A wetland is an area of land covered with water all or part of the year. Wetlands are any of the following: bogs, bottomland hardwoods, fens, mangrove swamps, marshes, swamps, prairie potholes, playa lakes, pocosins, vernal pools, and wet meadows. When covered with saltwater, these areas are known as coastal wetlands; when covered with freshwater, they are inland wetlands. The wet tundra that covers 58 percent of Alaska is also a wetlands. Figure 10-3 depicts the typical features of a wetland.

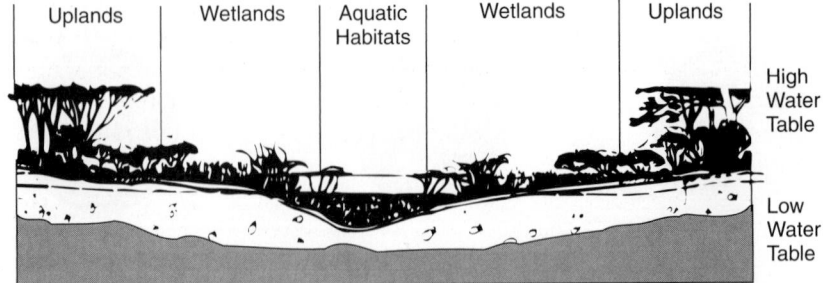

| Uplands | Wetlands | Aquatic Habitats | Wetlands | Uplands |

High Water Table

Low Water Table

FIGURE 10-3   Identifying Features of Wetlands

Source: Council on Environmental Quality. 1989. *Environmental Trends,* p 97. Washington, D.C.: Government Printing Office.

An estuary is a coastal area where the freshwater of rivers and streams mixes with seawater. Estuaries, and the land surrounding them, serve as transition places from land to sea, and from freshwater to seawater. Familiar examples of estuaries include San Francisco Bay, Puget Sound, Chesapeake Bay, Boston Harbor, and Tampa Bay.[15]

Coastal wetlands, as their name suggests, are found along the Atlantic, Pacific, Alaskan, and Gulf coasts. They make up about 30 percent of the wetlands and 16 percent of the coastline. Figure 10-4 shows the types of coastal wetlands, the regions where they are located, and the states with the greatest coastal wetlands acreage. Although they are viewed by many as useless homes

FIGURE 10-4   Wetland Area Compared to the Total Land Area of the Coterminous United States, 2004

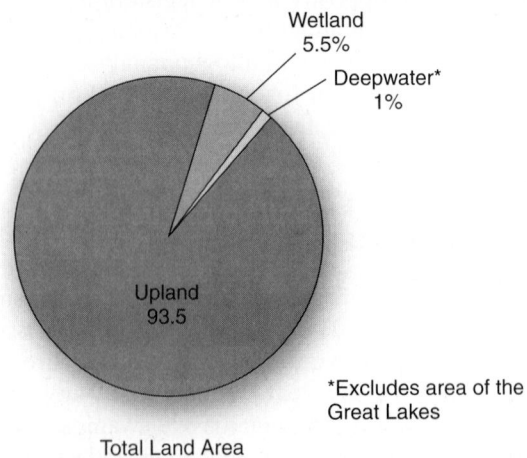

Wetland 5.5%

Deepwater* 1%

Upland 93.5

*Excludes area of the Great Lakes

Total Land Area

Source: Fish and Wildlife Service. "Status and Trends of Wetlands in the Coterminous United States 1998–2004." *http://wetlandsfws.er.usgs.gov/status_trends/national_reports/trends_2005_report.pdf* (October 1, 2006).

for mosquitoes, coastal wetlands are one of the most productive ecosystems in the world. They provide a habitat for numerous plant and animal species, including a number of endangered species. Roughly 70 percent of the nation's commercial seafood is spawned in coastal wetlands. Coastal wetlands also dilute water pollutants, thereby helping to improve the quality of the adjacent water.

Both coastal wetlands and estuaries help prevent erosion of coastlines. When hurricanes and tropical storms hit coastlines, estuaries and wetlands help to absorb the impact of the waves. Inland wetlands, commonly referred to as bogs and marshes, are important as habitats for a number of fish (most inland sport fish spawn in inland wetlands), waterfowl, and wildlife. Inland wetlands also help to prevent riverbank erosion and flooding.

BENEFITS OF WETLANDS

Enumerating the many benefits, in both ecological and economical terms, is difficult because the ecology of wetlands is so diverse. However, most wetlands provide the following benefits, although this list should not be seen as inclusive of all the benefits of maintaining healthy wetlands. First, they provide food and habitat for many species, including numerous species of migratory birds. Although wetlands account for only 5 percent of land area in the continental United States, they are home to over 31 percent of the nation's plant species. From an economic perspective, 75 percent of all fish caught commercially, and 80–90 percent of all fish caught recreationally, find salt marshes and estuaries as essential habitats for their spawning and development. Second, they are among the most biologically productive natural ecosystems in the world; consequently, they are vital to the survival of various plants and animals and surrounding ecosystems. Third, wetlands serve to control shoreline erosion. They also help to improve the quality of drinking water and prevent flooding by intercepting surface runoff and removing it. One acre of wetland can store 1.5 million gallons of floodwater. The U.S. Army COE, for example, found that by protecting wetlands near Boston, Massachusetts, they could save $17 million in flood damages. Fourth, they provide natural products for human use. Fifth, they provide various opportunities for recreation and education.

DESTRUCTION OF WETLANDS

Wetlands were once plentiful in the United States, but since the 18th century, over half of them have been lost, with some states losing up to 80 percent of their wetlands. From the mid-1950s to the mid-1970s, wetlands in the lower 48 states were lost at a rate of approximately 458,000 acres per year. Figure 10-5 shows the percentage of wetlands acreage lost between the 1780s and the 1980s. From the 1970s to the 1980s, this loss fell to approximately 290,000 acres per year.[16] In the next decade, wetlands were lost at a

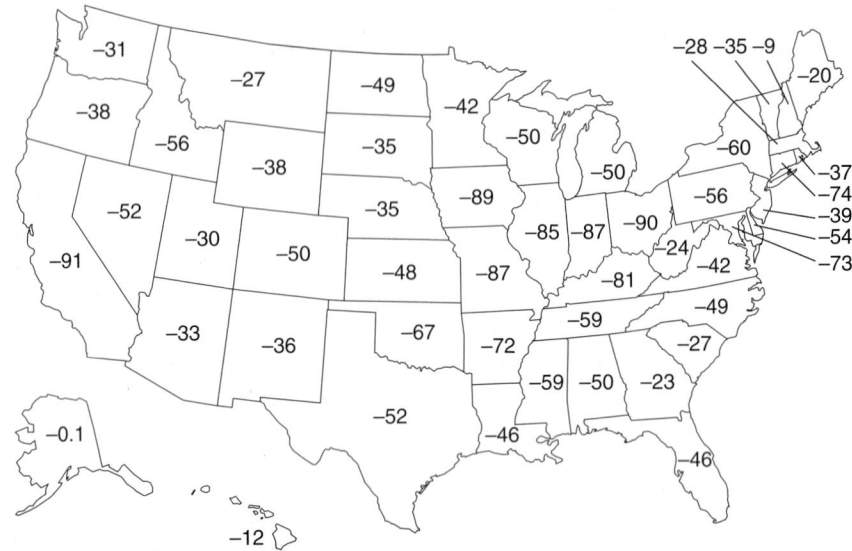

FIGURE 10-5   Percentage of Wetlands Acreage Lost, 1780s–1980s

Twenty-two states have lost at least 50 percent of their original wetlands. Seven states—
Indiana, Illinois, Missouri, Kentucky, Iowa, California, and Ohio—have lost over 80 percent of
their original wetlands. Since the 1970s, the most extensive losses of wetlands have been in
Louisiana, Mississippi, Arkansas, Florida, South Carolina, and North Carolina.

Source: Mitsch and Gosselink. *Wetlands.* 2nd Edition, Van Nostrand Reinhold, 1993.

rate of about 58,500 per year.[17] Alaska's wetland losses have not been as
severe, with only about 1 percent being lost. However, in coastal areas
around major cities, losses have been about 50 percent.[18] Because of
wetland destruction, many species are struggling to survive; over a third of
endangered species in the United States live in wetland habitats.

Coastal wetlands and estuaries are being lost in part because of the
development spurred by increasing coastal populations. Almost half the
country's population in 1990 lived in coastal counties, which make up only
11 percent of the nation's total land. By the year 2010, this coastal population of 110 million is projected to grow to 127 million. Not only are wetlands
being filled in for development, but runoff, including sewer overflows, is also
polluting these fragile areas. The denser the population, the more severe the
pollution problem becomes. Forty-three of the one hundred and forty-six
known hypoxic zones are in U.S. costal waters.[19] These are areas where
depletion of oxygen is so severe that fish leave and other animals eventually
suffocate.

Loss of inland wetlands can be attributed primarily to filling in the
wetlands for agricultural use. Additional losses are due to a desire to develop
wetlands for industrial or residential use. Regulations seeking to prevent these
and other causes of wetland destruction are discussed in the next section.

REGULATIONS TO PRESERVE COASTAL AREAS, ESTUARIES, AND WETLANDS

A number of regulations and federal programs have been implemented to preserve wetlands and coastal areas. Preservation of wetlands is in some ways more difficult than protecting wilderness and forest areas because many of the wetlands are on private property. As a result, the majority of preservation efforts use grants and matching funds to allow local and state governments the opportunity to purchase and protect their wetlands from private landowners. However, many federal regulations do exist to preserve and protect the nation's various wetlands.

The main regulatory tool for preserving wetlands is Section 404 of the CWA. This provision requires that any landowner seeking to add dredged or filled material to a wetland must receive a permit from the Army COE or risk being subject to both civil and criminal penalties. To obtain such a permit, the landowner must demonstrate that they have (1) taken steps to avoid wetland impacts where practical, (2) minimized potential impacts to wetlands, and (3) provided compensation for any remaining, unavoidable impacts through activities to restore or create wetlands, and that the activity is in the public interest. In many states, the landowner must also comply with state regulations governing wetlands. If the landowner cannot demonstrate that the destruction of any portion of wetland is necessary and that there are not reasonable alternatives, then a permit is not granted. However, since the CWA went into effect in 1979, the EPA has only denied 11 of the more than 150,000 permit applications.[20]

COMMERCE CLAUSE RESTRICTIONS ON WETLANDS PRESERVATION

When Congress created the CWA, the act regulated "navigable waters." The CWA, like many environmental laws, derives its authority from the commerce clause of the Constitution (discussed in Chapter 1), meaning that the act can only regulate intrastate wetlands in so far as they affect interstate commerce. The meaning of "navigable waters" is a matter of some dispute, and the COE's definition of "navigable waters" included intrastate waters when changes to these waters would affect interstate commerce. The COE has been regulating intrastate waters pursuant to this definition of "navigable waters." The COE attempted to clarify this definition in 1986 under what has been termed the Migratory Bird Rule. Under this rule, the COE regulates intrastate waters, including isolated wetlands, based on whether the waters provide habitat for migratory birds.

Migratory bird habitats fall under the commerce clause, according to the COE, because bird watching is a popular activity that generates revenue and supports interstate travel and tourism. So long as an intrastate wetland or estuary provided a habitat for migratory birds, COE and the EPA could regulate that wetland under Section 404 of the CWA.

The regulatory power of the CWA began to change, however, when in 1994 a consortium of Chicago municipalities applied for a permit under Section 404 to convert an isolated wetland into a solid-waste disposal site. This isolated wetland had developed over a period of 30 years, after the site had been abandoned. Although the COE initially determined that it had no jurisdiction over the site, it later reversed this determination after finding that the wetland provided habitat for over 120 bird species. In keeping with the Migratory Bird Rule, described above, the COE would not grant the permit to the municipalities, because a waste disposal site would disrupt the habitat of the migratory birds. The municipalities took the COE to court, and after several legal battles, the municipalities won their case in 2001.

The Supreme Court decision in *Solid Waste Agency of Northern Cook County v. United States Army COEs*[21] (a 5–4 split) is a serious setback to wetlands protection. This decision invalidates the Migratory Bird Rule and scales back wetlands' protection by the COE to only those wetlands that are adjacent to navigable waters or to the tributaries of navigable waters.[22] After notice of the ruling, many states were scrambling to protect wetlands that no longer had federal protection. Each state has several isolated wetlands that it will now have to protect under state legislation if the state still wants the wetlands to be protected. One state particularly worried about the status of its wetlands' protections is Wisconsin. Wisconsin's wetlands' protections are based on the authority given to the COE in the CWA; without jurisdiction by the COE, the state of Wisconsin also has no jurisdiction to protect the wetlands.[23] In response, the state of Wisconsin created new wetlands legislation in 2001 with a unanimous vote in both houses of the state legislature.

The limitations set forth in Solid Waste Agency were further upheld in the 2006 Supreme Court case, *Rapanos v. United States.*[24] In *Rapanos,* a divided court (5–4) appears to have further limited the jurisdiction of the COE over waters under the CWA. The Court's opinion, written by Scalia and joined by Roberts, Thomas, and Alito, held "the waters of the United States" limits the COE's jurisdiction to relatively permanent flowing bodies of water, such as streams, rivers, lakes, and oceans. According to the plurality opinion, temporary bodies of water or those that are loosely connected to major waterways are not under the COE's jurisdiction, and thus are not protected under the CWA. Scalia also argues the Act's use of "navigable waters" clearly indicates jurisdiction is not to extend to temporary bodies of water, or those that do not directly contribute a continuous, and significant amount of water to a navigable-in-fact waterway. Had Justice Kennedy, the other justice who voted to send the case back to the lower court, agreed with the reasoning of Scalia, this new, much more restrictive standard would be applied in all future cases and significantly reduce the federal government's authority over wetlands.

Justice Kennedy, however, wrote a separate, concurring opinion. Justice Kennedy, much like the opinion in Solid Waste Agency, focused primarily on the "significant nexus" language of the CWA. Kennedy urges the Court to consider the "significant nexus" in terms of the goals and purposes of the CWA. The CWA is intended to preserve the integrity of national waterways, and therefore, waters in question should be evaluated based upon the impact these waterways have on national waterways. Accordingly, Justice Kennedy proposes a case-by-case analysis based upon environmental impact to determine whether the "significant nexus" is met to allow a waterway to fall within the COE's jurisdiction. Because the Court's main opinion did not have a majority of the Court's support, the lower courts were not given much guidance. Most commentators assume that, in the future, courts will apply the test suggested by Kennedy because his test does not really change the existing law significantly; it just requires the Army COEs to prove that the nexus exists in each individual case, rather than their being able to simply assume that this nexus exists.

MARINE PROTECTION, RESEARCH, AND SANCTUARIES ACT

The 1972 Marine Protection, Research, and Sanctuaries Act allows the National Oceanic and Atmospheric Administration to designate specific areas as marine sanctuaries. Such sanctuaries are the marine equivalent to national parks, and they are to have protective management of their recreational, ecological, historical, educational, and aesthetic values. Figure 10-6 shows where existing and proposed marine sanctuaries were located as of 2006, including the Northwestern Hawaiian Islands Marine National

FIGURE 10-6   National Marine Sanctuaries Directory

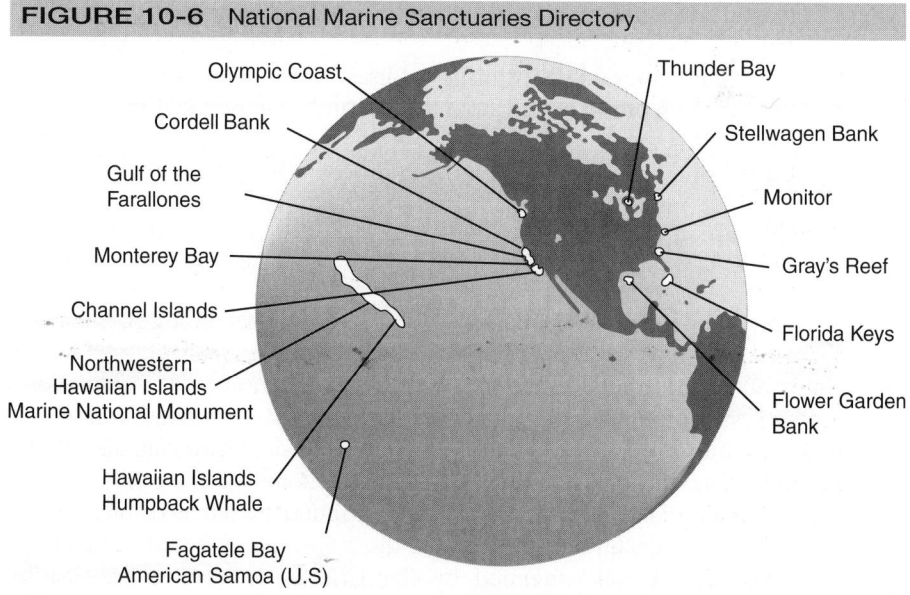

Source: Sanctuaries Web Group. *http://www.sanctuaries.nos.noaa.gov/* (June 2006).

Monument approved by President Bush in June 2006, and provides a description of some of them. The Northwestern Hawaiian Islands National Monument is the largest marine-protected area in the world, covering 84 million acres and providing a home to 7,000 species of birds, fish, and marine mammals, at least a quarter of which are unique to Hawaii. A report by the American Association for the Advancement of Science indicates that marine reserves are crucial to conserve both biodiversity and fisheries.[25] A marine reserve is different from a marine sanctuary because sanctuaries allow a certain amount of extractive activity. The main conclusion of the report was that marine reserves will replenish the seas and that although fishers may lose certain areas in which to fish, they will benefit in other areas because of replenishment.[26]

COASTAL ZONE MANAGEMENT ACT

In 1972, to encourage the prudent management and conservation of the coastal zone, defined as state land near the shorelines of the coastal states and the coastal waters extending to the outer limits of the U.S. territorial sea, Congress passed the CZMA. The act, like the NEPA, is a planning statute. Under CZMA, the federal government will provide matching funds to a coastal state, including Great Lakes states, to assist the state in developing a management plan for its coastal lands and waters. CZMA specifies nine elements that must be included in the plan. Some of the more substantive elements include

- a definition of what will constitute permissible land uses within the coastal zone that will have direct and significant impact on coastal waters
- broad guidelines on the priorities of uses in particular areas
- a description of the organizational structure to implement the proposed management plan
- a definition of beach and a planning process for protection of and access to public beaches and other public coastal areas of environmental, recreational, historical, aesthetic, ecological, or cultural value
- a planning process for studying and controlling erosion

The plan must give full consideration to ecological, cultural, historical, and aesthetic values, as well as to needs for economic development. The National Oceanographic and Atmospheric Administration (NOAA) reviews the plans submitted by the states. If the plan is approved, the state will receive additional funds to administer the plan. Approval of a state plan also means that any federal activity within the state's coastal zone must be consistent with that state's management plan "to the maximum extent possible." As an incentive, funding can be withdrawn if the state fails to adhere to its plan. In 1990, CZMA was amended by the Coastal Zone Reauthorization Amendment Act to require each state to develop a nonpoint source pollution-control program. Recall that one of the major problems along the coasts is nonpoint source pollution.

COASTAL WETLANDS PLANNING, PROTECTION, AND RESTORATION ACT OF 1990

Similar to the CZMA, the Coastal Wetlands Planning, Protection, and Restoration Act (CWPRA) of 1990 allows the U.S. FWS to work with coastal states in the restoration, enhancement, or acquisition of coastal wetlands through the use of matching funds. Today, over 40,000 acres of coastal wetlands have been restored, enhanced, or acquired because of $32 million in grants, which have been awarded to 23 states. Priority in awarding grants is given to states that demonstrate a dedication to preserving and enhancing their current coastal wetlands. In addition, restoration plans consistent with the National Wetlands Priority Conservation Plan are also given priority.

New Jersey, for example, through the use of CWPPRA, purchased 153 acres in Cape May, completing a crucial link between existing protected coastal wetlands, used as a stopping point for tropical bound migratory birds.

THE CONVENTION ON WETLANDS OF INTERNATIONAL IMPORTANCE ESPECIALLY AS WATERFOWL HABITAT

In 1975, the first modern global environmental treaty on conservation and wise use of resources was entered into force.[27] Commonly called the Ramsar Convention, this international treaty, with 152 parties as of 2006, has had an impact on ensuring the existence of wetlands. Each party to the convention must designate at least one wetland in its country as a candidate for the "Ramsar List," a list of wetlands of international importance. Currently, 1,609 wetlands are on the Ramsar List, covering an area of more than 360 million acres.[28] Twenty-two of the wetlands on the Ramsar List are in the United States.[29] Once a wetland is designated as being of international importance, the country must take steps to conserve and protect that wetland. Each party must also consider wetlands conservation in its national land-use planning and must support training in wetlands management and research.

"SWAMPBUSTER" PROVISIONS OF THE 1985 FOOD SECURITY ACT

Many people argue that one of the most effective measures for protecting wetlands, particularly inland wetlands, has been what is commonly referred to as the "Swampbuster bill." This provision was an attempt by Congress to slow the conversion of wetlands to agricultural land. It provides that any persons who produce crops on wetlands that were converted after December 23, 1985, will be ineligible for most federal farm benefits. The Swampbuster bill, in conjunction with Section 404 of the CWA, is credited with slowing the loss of swampland from 500,000 acres per year in the 1960s and 1970s to less than 60,000 acres per year in late 1990s. The Department of Agriculture Research Service estimates that between 5.8 and 13 million acres of wetlands are currently protected from becoming farmland because of the swampbuster bill, which has the additional hidden benefit of preventing crop prices from being further depressed.

Amendments were added to the bill in 1990 and 1996, allowing for certain wetlands to be drained for farmland under "minimal effects," meaning that the wetland was small enough not to have widespread effects. The amendments are said to add flexibility to the swampbuster provision, and as of yet, the amendments have not significantly reduced the effectiveness of the bill in preserving wetlands.

NATIONAL ESTUARY PROGRAM

The National Estuary Program was created by the CWA Amendments of 1987. The program is run by the EPA's Office of Water to develop comprehensive conservation and management plans to protect estuaries of national significance. Such estuaries are nominated by the governor of a state for inclusion in the National Estuary Program. After the development of the comprehensive conservation and management plan, the EPA may make grants to states or other local areas to help in the estuary's protection. Currently, there are 28 estuaries in the program, including nine in the Northeast, six in the Southeast, seven on the Gulf of Mexico, and six on the West coast. These estuaries include such areas as Long Island Sound, Puget Sound, and Tampa Bay.

"NO-NET-LOSS" POLICY

In August 1989, President Bush announced a no-net-loss of wetlands policy. The policy, however, has been criticized by many as sounding better than it actually is. Much of the policy involved improving funding with respect to existing nonregulatory wetlands programs, such as the North American Waterfowl Management Plan, which was designed to help restore declining waterfowl populations by the acquisition and restoration of wetlands that provided breeding grounds and resting areas for these waterfowl.

Bush's policy of no-net-loss of wetlands was mitigated by the fact that no-net-loss really meant except when the loss was "unavoidable." If the loss were unavoidable, the developer had the option of creating roughly the same amount of wetlands elsewhere. This option completely overlooks the significance of a loss in a particular area. In addition, if the loss were "insignificant," a clearly vague term, then no replacement would be necessary. Finally, in a move many believed was clearly directed toward Alaska, replacement was unnecessary if it would be impractical to create more. The no-net-loss policy did not initially live up to its name; between 1986 and 1997, 644,000 acres of wetlands were lost.[30]

Evaluating the progress we are making on protecting wetlands is compli-cated, however. In 2001, reports by both the National Academy of Sciences and the GAO confirmed the ineffectiveness of the no-net-loss policy, concluding that wetland replacement projects overwhelmingly fail and that federal agen-cies inadequately enforce the policy. Responding to these reports, the current Bush administration in early 2003 revised the no-net-loss policy, emphasizing the quality of restored wetlands over the quantity. Focus was given in the policy revisions to how and where the replacement wetlands are created and not the number of wetland acres created, with the hope being that even if we continued to have a net loss of wetlands, there would be an overall ecological gain.

Two more recent studies have given us both encouraging and discourag-ing news. In the FWSs' report to Congress, *Status and Trends of Wetlands in the Conterminous United States 1998 to 2004*,[31] the agency reported that there were an estimated 107.7 million acres of wetlands in the conterminous United States in 2004 (Table 10-2). Ninety-five percent of the wetlands were freshwa-ter wetlands and 5 percent were estuarine or marine wetlands. This figure represents an overall a net gain of 191,750 acres of wetlands and other waters, for an annual increase of wetland areas of 32,000 acres annually, which is the good news. This study was the first one to report a net gain in wetlands.[32]

TABLE 10-2 Change in wetland area for selected wetland and deepwater categories 1988–2004. The coefficient of variation (CV) for each entry (expressed as a percentage) is given in parentheses

Wetland/Deepwater Category	Estimated Area, 1998	Estimated Area, 2004	Change, 1998–2004	Change (In Percent)
Marine	130.4 (20.2)	128.6 (20.5)	−1/9 (68.7)	−1.4
Estuarine intertidal non-vegetated[a]	594.1 (10.7)	600.0 (10.3)	5.9 *	1.0
Estuarine intertidal vegetated[b]	4,604.2 (4.0)	4,571.7 (4.0)	−32.4 (32.7)	−0.7
All intertidal wetlands	5,328.7 (3.8)	5,300.3 (3.8)	−28.4 (48.6)	−0.5
Freshwater non vegetated[c]	5,918.7 (3.7)	6,633.9 (3.5)	715.3 (12.8)	12.1
Freshwater ponds[d]	5,534.3 (3.7)	6,229.6 (3.5)	695.4 (13.1)	12.6
Freshwater vegetated[e]	96,414.9 (3.0)	95,819.8 (3.0)	−495.1 (35.0)	−0.5
Freshwater emergent	26,289.6 (8.0)	26,147.0 (8.0)	−142.6 *	−0.5
Freshwater forested	51,483.1 (2.8)	52,031.4 (2.8)	548.2 (56.1)	1.1

(continued)

TABLE 10-2   *(cont.)*

Wetland/Deepwater Category	Area, In Thousands of Acres			
	Estimated Area, 1998	Estimated Area, 2004	Change, 1998–2004	Change (In Percent)
Freshwater shrub	18,542.2 (4.1)	17,641.4 (4.3)	−900.8 (34.2)	−4.9
All freshwater wetlands	102,233.6 (2.9)	102,453.8 (2.8)	220.2 (77.3)	0.2
All wetlands	107,562.3 (2.7)	107,754.0 (2.7)	191.8 (89.1)	0.2
Deepwater habitats				
Lacustrine^e	16,610.5 (10.4)	16,773.4 (10.2)	162.9 (76.2)	1.0
Riverine	6,765.5 (9.1)	6,813.3 (9.1)	47.7 (68.8)	0.7
Estuarine subtitdal	17.680.5 (2.2)	17.717.8 (2.2)	37.3 (40.8)	0.2
All deepwater habitats	41,046.6 (4.6)	41,304.5 (4.5)	247.9 (51.7)	0.6
All wetlands and deepwater habitats^{a,b}	148,618.8 (2.4)	149,058.5 (2.4)	439.7 (31.3)	0.3

*Statistically unreliable.

^{a}Includes the categories: Estuarine Interlidal Aquatic Bed and Estuarine Intertidal Unconsolidated Shore.

^{b}Includes the categories: Estuarine Interlidal Emergent and Estuarine Intertidal Shrub.

^{c}Includes the categories: Palustrine Aquatic Bed, Palustrine Unconsolidated Bottom and Palustrine Unconsolidated Shore.

^{d}Includes the categories: Palustrine Aquatic Bed, Palustrine Unconsolidated Bottom.

^{e}Includes the categories: Palustrine Emergent, Palustrine Forested and Palustrine Shrub.

Percent coefficient of variation was expressed as (standard deviation/mean) × 100

Source: Fish and Wildlife Service. "Status and Trends of Wetlands in the Coterminous United States 1998–2004." *http://wetlandsfws.er.usgs.gov/status_trends/national_reports/trends_2005_report.pdf* (October 1, 2006).

However, despite the net gains realized from restoration and creation projects, human-induced wetland losses continued to affect the trends of freshwater vegetated wetlands, especially freshwater emergent marshes which declined by an estimated 142,570 acres. Tidal salt marshes and shrub swamps continue to be lost at significant levels. Another problem is that the claim that there has been "no net loss of wetlands" can be somewhat deceptive because the reason for the net gain is largely because of an increase in ponds, lakes, and other "deepwater habitats," as the report points out. These ponds include ornamental lakes for residential developments, stormwater detention ponds, wastewater treatment lagoons, aquaculture ponds, and golf course water hazards.[33]

A close look at the study reveals that there was a net loss of more than half a million acres of naturally occurring wetlands. Salt marshes decline by 5,540 acres, the same rate of loss they suffered from 1985 through 1997. Freshwater emergent wetlands declined by 142,570 acres and freshwater shrub wetlands declined by 900,800 acres during the time of the study. The net increase in pond acreage during that time was 700,000 acres.[34] And, as the report illustrates, some regions of the country still have losses that exceed gains. For example, the Great Lakes states and rapidly developing urban areas continue to show net losses.[35]

At the end of 2006, the CEQ released its progress report on President Bush's 2004 pledge to expand the number of wetlands. According to this report, during the period from 2004 to 2006, 588,000 acres of wetlands were restored or created, 563,000 acres were improved, and 646,000 were protected. The administration's goal is to add one million acres of new wetlands and improve the quality of one million acres between 2004 and 2009.[36]

ESTUARY RESTORATION ACT OF 2000

The Estuary Restoration Act (ERA) was passed as part of the larger Estuaries and Clean Waters Act of 2000. The goal of the ERA is to restore one million acres of estuary habitat by the year 2010. An Estuary Habitat Restoration Council was established under the act to recommend to the secretary of the army areas for restoration projects. The council is also

MAJOR CAUSES OF WETLAND LOSS AND DEGRADATION

Human activities

- Drainage
- Dredging and stream channelization
- Diking and damming
- Tilling for crop production
- Logging
- Mining

- Construction
- Runoff
- Air and water pollutants
- Changing nutrient levels
- Releasing toxic chemicals

Natural threats

- Erosion
- Subsidence
- Sea-level rise

- Droughts
- Hurricanes and other storms

Source: Welcome to the National Marine Sanctuaries. *http://www.sanctuaries.nos.noaa.gov/oms/oms.html* (December 16, 2000).

responsible for developing a comprehensive strategy for estuary habitat restoration that includes incentives for public and private partnerships, includes the provision of healthy ecosystems, and ensures equitable geographic distribution of selected projects.

PROTECTION OF THE GREAT LAKES

Water is not often thought of as a natural resource, yet water is necessary for life. North America is endowed with the largest bodies of freshwater in the world: the Great Lakes. The Great Lakes contain one-fifth of the world's freshwater but are constantly besieged by pollution from excessive population, industry, and recreation. Although often taken for granted, particularly before 1960, the Great Lakes are an international treasure that must be protected. Chapter 6 discussed the importance of laws protecting water quality. However, laws such as the CWA and the Safe Drinking Water Act apply only to the United States, whereas the protection of the Great Lakes requires the joint effort of the United States and Canada.

In 1909, the Boundary Waters Treaty was adopted by the two nations to protect waters common to both countries. This treaty established the International Joint Commission (IJC), a six-member commission dedicated to studying boundary waters, particularly the Great Lakes, and fostering cooperation between the United States and Canada. The role of the IJC was subsequently strengthened by the Great Lakes Water Quality Agreements (GLWQA) of 1972 and 1978. Every other year, the IJC releases a report on the status of the Great Lakes. In 2000, the IJC released its tenth biennial report on water quality, indicating that both nations had a long way to go to achieve the goals of the GLWQA. The IJC made strong statements in its report about the inability of the two nations' governments to live up to their obligations under the agreements, stating that both governments had neither committed the funding nor taken appropriate actions to improve the quality of the Great Lakes.[37] In 2004, in the IJC's twelfth annual report, the Commission acknowledged both countries were making improvements. However, the IJC also states the countries need to do much more to ensure a safe, healthy, and functioning environment in the Great Lakes water.[38]

One of the most pernicious problems affecting the Great Lakes is the introduction of toxic substances to their waters. In 1997, the United States and Canada agreed to what is known as the Great Lakes Binational Toxics Strategy with the goal of the virtual elimination of substances such as aldrin, chlordane, and DDT from the Great Lakes basin. The IJC's tenth report questioned the viability of the strategy because of a lack of adequate data. The commission recommended that an inventory of air emissions be established along with emission reduction scenarios to strengthen the integration and priority-setting components of the strategy.[39] Although Lake Erie is no longer foaming with detergent suds nor smelling of sewage, and some life has found its way back into the lake, it appears that the United States and Canada have a long way to go to protect these important sources of freshwater.

WILD AND SCENIC RIVERS SYSTEM

Rivers have wildlife, historic, recreational, and scenic values, among others. Congress recognized such values with the passage of the Wild and Scenic Rivers Act in 1968. The preface to this act contains Congress's vision of a new river policy for the United States:

> It is hereby declared to be the policy of the United States that certain selected rivers of the Nation which, with their immediate environments, possess outstandingly remarkable scenic, recreational, geologic, fish and wildlife, historic, cultural, or other similar values, shall be preserved in free-flowing condition, and that they and their immediate environments shall be protected for the benefit and enjoyment of present and future generations. The Congress declares that the established national policy of dam and other construction at appropriate sections of the rivers of the United States needs to be complemented by a policy that would preserve other selected rivers or sections thereof in their free-flowing condition to protect the water quality of such rivers and to fulfill other vital national conservation purposes.[40]

The original act placed segments of eight rivers in the system, which now encompasses an additional 148. The segments of rivers in the system total nearly 11,300 miles. Each section of a river that is classified under the Wild and Scenic Rivers Act is designated as a wild, scenic, or recreational river area. A wild river area is one that represents primitive America, accessible only by trail. Rivers accessible by roads are classified as scenic rivers and rivers that are readily accessible by road or railroad and have undergone some development are classified as recreational river areas. The Wild and Scenic Rivers Act is more akin to the Multiple-Use Sustained Yield Act than the Wilderness Act. Rivers designated as wild, scenic, or recreational under the act are not removed from use. Development and compatible uses of the river area are allowed and "change is expected."[41]

ENDANGERED SPECIES

In 1973, Congress recognized that the wide variety of plants and animals in the United States do indeed constitute an important natural resource, and it passed what has since become one of the most controversial, and some say most effective, pieces of environmental legislation ever enacted: the ESA. In setting forth its findings to justify the ESA, Congress declared that[42]

1. various species of fish, wildlife, and plants in the United States have been rendered extinct because of economic growth and development untempered by adequate concern and conservation
2. other species of fish, wildlife, and plants have become so depleted in numbers that they are in danger of or threatened with extinction
3. these species of fish, wildlife, and plants are of aesthetic, ecological, educational, historical, recreational, and scientific value to the Nation and its people

Congress went on to state that the purpose of the ESA was to provide a means to preserve the ecosystems in which endangered species survive, to provide a program to conserve such species, and to enter into appropriate treaties for species protection on an international level. Thus, the ESA has both a national focus and an international one. This chapter discusses the national aspect; Chapter 11 addresses the international aspect.

Under the ESA, the secretary of the interior is required to list species of animals and plants that are both threatened and endangered, a task that he has delegated to the FWS and the National Marine Fisheries Service (NMFS). A species can become threatened or endangered because of a number of factors: "present or threatened destruction, modification or curtailment of its habitat or range; overutilization for commercial recreation, scientific, or educational purposes; disease or predation, the inadequacy of existing statutory mechanisms; or other natural or man-made factors affecting its continued existence."[43] As of October 2006, 1,311 species of plants and animals in the United States were listed as threatened or endangered; 279 are on a list of candidates for listing, meaning that they have been proposed for being added to either the threatened or endangered list, but no action has yet been taken to list them.

Figure 10-7 illustrates the number of species designated as threatened or endangered by state. Of all the species that have ever been listed, only 42 have been delisted. Of these, 17 were delisted because of recovery, 9 were delisted because of probable extinction, and 16 were delisted for other reasons. Once a species is listed as endangered, it cannot be "taken" (i.e., it cannot be harassed, harmed, pursued, hunted, shot, wounded, killed, trapped, captured, or collected). Violation of the prohibition against taking can result in criminal sanctions.

A major issue under the ESA until the summer of 1995 was the definition of harm. The secretary of the interior interpreted "harm" in the definition of a "taking" under the act to mean "an act which actually kills or injures wildlife. Such act may include significant habitat modification or degradation where it actually kills or injures wildlife by significantly impairing essential behavior patterns, including breeding, feeding or sheltering."[44] This broad interpretation of harm was challenged by a plaintiff that included citizens' groups, lumber companies, and lumber trade associations. The plaintiff argued that Secretary Babbitt had exceeded his authority by

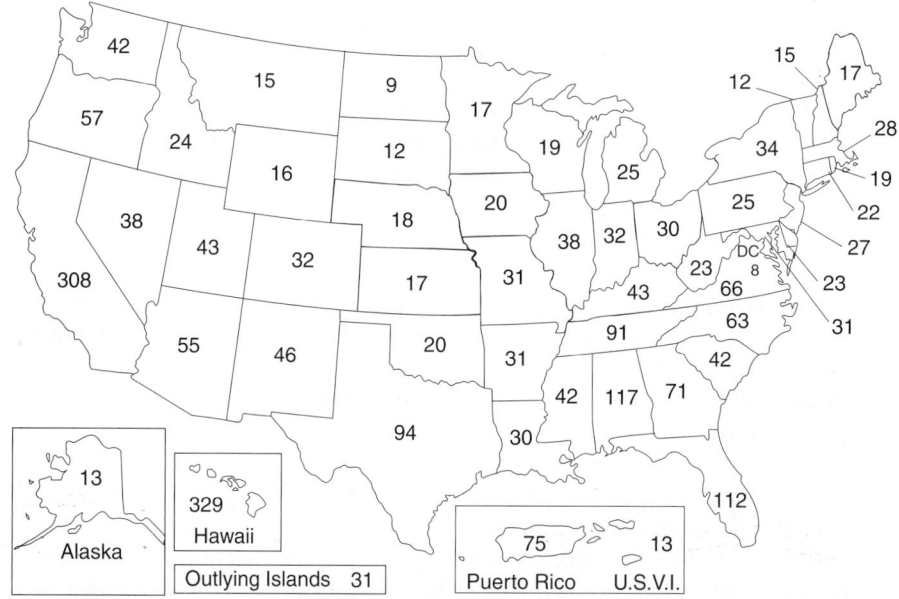

FIGURE 10-7   Endangered Species by State. Total U.S. species is 1,006. Numbers are not additive, a species often occurs in multiple states.

Source: Fish and Wildlife Service. *http://ecos.fws.gov/tess_public/StateListing.do?state=all* (accessed 11/05/2006).

issuing that definition of harm because the ESA had excluded habitat modification from the specific list of prohibited actions that constituted "takings" of species.[45] In July 1993, environmentalists received a temporary victory when the court of appeals upheld the secretary's broad interpretation. However, in an unusual move, the circuit court subsequently agreed to rehear the appeal and this time ruled that the secretary's interpretation was in fact not a reasonable interpretation of the statute.[46]

In the summer of 1995, however, the U.S. Supreme Court, in a 6–3 decision, overturned the court of appeals decision and ruled that the secretary's interpretation was in fact reasonable. Thus, the broad interpretation of harm stands, and a private property owner may not develop or use his or her land in a way that modifies the habitat of an endangered or threatened species to such an extent that the species may die because the habitat modification or degradation will impair essential behavior patterns.

Although this Supreme Court decision was a significant victory for environmentalists, it was considered a major setback by property rights advocates. Some believe the decision may have helped motivate more property rights advocates to put pressure on Congress to pass legislation to reduce the power of the ESA.

The ESA was supposed to have been reauthorized in 1993; however, a lack of consensus as to whether it needed to be strengthened, weakened, or significantly modified led Congress to simply fund the act for another year with the hope of making necessary modifications in the act in 1994. That year saw much debate over a broad range of bills, yet ended once again in simply refunding the act for another year. A third year of unresolved debate over the future of the ESA occurred in 1995. This debate continued through 1998. Because the bill has not yet been authorized, numerous instances occur that weaken the protection of endangered species. First, states and private sector entities can enter into Candidate Conservation Agreements (CCA). These agreements give the states and private entities responsibility for protecting species. More importantly, they prevent species from being listed. Second, parties may obtain permits for the "incidental take" of listed species. Parties must construct Habitat Conservation Plans (HCP), which allow projects to cause harm to endangered species habitats, provided that the landowner takes some action to make up for the harm to the habitat. By the end of 2006, the FWS had approved 593 HCPs, 452 of which are current, and 141 that have expired.[47] The FWS and NOAA jointly issued an administrative rule called "no surprises," which assures property owners who have these incidental take permits that they will not be subject to additional land use restrictions for that species, even if circumstances arise in which action would need to be taken. However, the FWS does retain the right to revoke the incidental take permit, thereby nullifying the protections. Third, landowners and the FWS can enter into voluntary agreements called "Safe Harbors." Landowners agree to conserve listed species by improving the land in such a manner as to increase the species' population, without the burden of increased restrictions on these improvements. Should the landowner desire to change the improvements made to the land, thereby reducing the increased population, there will be no penalty for that landowner under the ESA provided that the land remains in at least the condition it was in before the original improvement.

Although much of the focus of the debate over the ESA reauthorization is on the impact of the act on private property owners who might own land on which an endangered species resides, perhaps an equally important aspect of the ESA is Section 7, which requires all federal agencies to take actions necessary to ensure that activities authorized, funded, or carried out by them do not jeopardize the continued existence of endangered or threatened species. This section of the act has ended up being a powerful tool to protect the habitat of endangered species, which many environmentalists believe is the key to protecting the species. So powerful is this section that many accuse environmentalists of using, or abusing, it to prohibit developments they primarily oppose for other environmental reasons.

There is no doubt that because many habitats are on public lands, this law also helps regulate the use of public lands and protect old-growth forests and wilderness areas. Most Americans probably became aware of the controversy over protection of old-growth forests as well as endangered species because of the application of the ESA in a highly publicized case involving the northern spotted owl.

The controversy began during the late 1980s, when the Forest Service, charged with perpetuating vertebrate species native to the national forests, discovered through its research that the population of the northern spotted owl was shrinking because of the destruction of its forest habitat by logging. The Forest Service recognized that if the spotted owl were placed on the endangered species list, a virtual cessation of logging in the Northwest could be mandated. So the agency proposed setting aside 550 spotted owl habitats in Oregon and Washington, along with 200 areas in northwestern California. Each habitat area consisted of approximately 2,200 acres of old-growth forest. The plan was criticized immediately by environmentalists, who claimed that this was insufficient habitat area.

After discussing in its findings of fact the importance of logging, and the record of violations by the FWS, the court acknowledged the likelihood of irreparable harm from continued logging: the extinction of a species. The court then discussed the balancing of equities necessary in an environmental case and issued an injunction ordering the Forest Service to come up with a plan to preserve the species by March 5, 1992, and to prohibit the selling of further logging rights in spotted owl habitats until it was in compliance with the law.

That same year the situation became more complex: the issue became more than "owls versus jobs." Environmental groups sought to have the Pacific Yew, the bark of which provides an extract that can be used in a potent drug to fight cancer, listed as an endangered species. The tree, one of the slowest-growing species in the world, is found exclusively in old-growth forests. In June 1990 after considerable controversy, and under court order, the FWS listed the northern spotted owl as a threatened species under the ESA. This precipitated a massive publicity campaign by the timber industry, forecasting the loss of thousands of jobs.

On February 26, 1991, the federal district court once again ruled that the FWS had violated the law. This time, it had violated the ESA by failing to designate critical habitat with the listing of the spotted owl, and it had failed to comply with the deadline of September 30, 1990, for adopting a plan for ensuring the owl's survival. The Audubon Society then filed an action seeking a permanent injunction against any further sales of logging rights in northern spotted owl habitat until the Forest Service adopted guidelines and regulations to ensure that a viable population of the species would be maintained in the forest.

Subsequently, an interagency team of federal, state, and university representatives met to develop a plan for the recovery of the species. In January 1992, the FWS adopted regulations designating 6.9 million acres in Oregon, Washington, and California critical habitat for the owls. Thus, a tentative resolution was reached. Loggers were allowed to exercise the logging rights they had previously obtained, but future logging right sales, at least in a limited area, were temporarily halted.

The controversy continued into 1993, when President Clinton called a special summit for affected interests to try to discuss the ongoing controversy. This summit resulted in the creation of the Northwest Forest Plan, a policy for the long-term management of forested lands in the Northwest. However, controversy over protection of the spotted owl and old-growth forests continued even after the publication of this decision. The controversy will never really end because the timber industry may always return to argue that logging in this or that area will not adversely affect the owl's habitat. As well, the battle has left many citizens in the Northwest bitter toward the government and environmentalists.

Perhaps a compromise reauthorization bill will be reached at some point in time. In May 1995, the National Research Council of the National Academy of Sciences released a report on the ESA that had been requested by members of both congressional parties 4 years before. The report concluded that the ESA is "critically important" and "based on sound scientific principals," but changes are needed in the way biological populations and habitats are designated. The most dramatic change recommended in the report is to permit federal officials to designate "survival habitat" for species immediately on their designation as threatened or endangered. This designation would prevent further losses. The report also stated that "habitat protection is essential not only to protect those relatively few species whose endangerment is established, it is also in essence a preemptive approach to species conservation that also in essence can help to avoid triggering the provisions of the ESA." The report also encouraged the protection of "distinct populations."

Another document that may have an impact on Congress as it deliberates over the proposals for reauthorization is the House Republican Policy Committee's principles for reauthorization, which it adopted in August 1995. These principles include

- using accurate, "nonpoliticized" science in the listing process and implementation process
- allowing for social and economic considerations in the conservation plan process
- using incentives to encourage private property owners to enhance habitat and protect species
- compensating property owners "when practical use of their land has been taken from them"
- enhancing the state and local role in endangered species protection

Of course, these principles are by no means shared by all members of the House of Representatives, but the setting forth of these principles seem to be reflected in one particular proposed reauthorization bill.

Two bills were strongly considered in 1998. The Kempthorne bill (S. 1180), the bill that had the greatest chance of being passed, claimed to seek a middle ground between property owners and environmentalists. In contrast, the Miller bill (H.R. 2351) also sought to find a balance between environmental and property interests, but it gave priority to at-risk species and emphasized recovery instead of economic interests.

The bills were different in several ways. First, the Kempthorne bill contained many private property-friendly provisions, such as the "no surprises" provision, which requires each conservation plan developed to include a clause that allows the permittee to avoid any future costs and any additional restriction on land use. This provision would extend the "no surprises" protection already established by administrative law. Furthermore, the Kempthorne bill required the secretary to prioritize plans to minimize conflict with private property. Although both bills claimed to find a balance, the Kempthorne bill more often yielded to property interest and weakened protection of endangered species. Miller stated, "The Kempthorne bill may save the ESA, but it will not save any endangered species."

The Kempthorne bill received support from the Clinton administration as well as the secretary of the interior, but it was opposed almost universally by environmental groups. Near the end of the session, an attempt was made to pass the Kempthorne bill as a rider to an appropriations bill. Although it did not pass, similar bills came up for discussion in the 106th Congress. The Landowners Equal Treatment Act of 1999 would have required any federal action on private property to occur only with the permission or compensation of the landowner. The Property Owners Protection Act of 1999 would not have allowed any information obtained without the consent of the property owner to be used in protecting endangered species. The Stop Taking Our Property Act of 1999 sought to prohibit the federal government from requiring property owners to mitigate the impacts of past activities. None of these bills ever reached the floor.

Proposals for amending the act continue to be made each year and generally die before getting out of committee. For example, in 2003, Senator Craig Thomas introduced the Endangered Species Listing and Delisting Process Reform Act of 2003, which would have amended the ESA of 1973 to require the secretary of the interior to use data that are empirical or have been field tested or peer reviewed in any case in which such act requires the secretary to use the best scientific and commercial data available in the determination of a species for inclusion on the endangered or threatened species list. It would have also required the secretary to determine that a species is an endangered or threatened species only if there is sufficient biological information to support recovery planning for the species.[48] The bill did not get out of the Committee on Environment and Public Works. Because this bill would have made it more difficult to get a species listed, many environmentalists were relieved that it did not pass. Altogether, eight bills were introduced in either the House or the Senate in 2003 which would have directly amended the ESA, but none got out of the committee to which they were referred.

In September 2005, the House of Representatives passed H.R. 3824. H.R. 3824 would have severely hindered environmental protections to critical habitats for endangered species; provided an exemption to the pesticide industry to avoid wildlife safety regulations; as well as given large amounts in government funds to large developers and gas companies that do not harm or kill threatened or endangered species. The Senate never passed a similar bill, so H.R. 3824 did not become law.

In 2007, word leaked out that the Fish and Wildlife Service was considering making some changes in the regulations used to implement the Endangered Species Act and that a number of the proposed regulatory changes were similar to some of the provisions of the failed legislative proposals. As of the time the book went to press, however, none of these changes had been formally proposed.

THE GLOBAL EXTINCTION CRISIS

The rate at which species are disappearing from the planet has increased tremendously as humans have increased their technological capacity and exploration of the earth. In fact, some biologists have equated the extinctions occurring today as equivalent to those experienced during the age of the dinosaurs. Species extinction is occurring at about 50 times the normal background rate, with 816 extinct species in the past 500 years; humans have been blamed for this increase.[49] The variety of species, also known as biodiversity, aside from generating food and medicine, provides a number of services that are necessary for life on this planet: decomposition of wastes, nitrogen fixation in soil, disease reduction in crops, and water filtration, to name only a few.

Current estimations of global endangered and extinct species are startling. Table 10-3 outlines the threatened species for several areas around the world. In the international arena, species are classified as threatened when they are either critically endangered, endangered, or vulnerable.[50] From Table 10-1, it is obvious that every part of the world is dealing with the extinction crisis; however, some parts are more critical than others. The island of Madagascar, off the coast of Africa, is home to a great wealth of biodiversity, but it, tied with Vietnam, has the most critically endangered and endangered primates.[51] Madagascar is also the home to the world's four most endangered primates. Brazil has the largest number of threatened (critically endangered, endangered, and vulnerable) birds at 124 species, and Indonesia has more threatened mammals than any other area at 146 species.[52] Ecuador, with 1,832 threatened plant species, has nearly triple the number of the next closest country.[53]

Leading causes of extinction include habitat loss or degradation, exploitation, and the introduction of nonnative invasive species. For instance, in the United States, the disappearance of natural grasslands and

TABLE 10-3 Threatened (Critically Endangered, Endangered, and Vulnerable) Species by Region, 2000

Region	Mammals	Birds	Reptiles	Amphibians	Fish	Mollusks	Other Invertebrates	Plants	Total
North Africa	79	66	39	7	96	0	32	8	327
Sub-Saharan Africa	782	605	177	329	983	175	277	2,339	5,667
Antarctica	3	56	0	0	4	0	0	0	63
East Asia	175	274	55	125	153	28	32	541	1,383
North Asia	72	79	9	0	45	1	54	8	268
South and Southeast Asia	654	651	240	319	443	29	122	2,326	4,784
West and Central Asia	274	344	112	19	279	7	80	187	1,302
Europe	300	379	55	27	519	206	470	160	2,116
Mesoamerica	136	133	78	493	220	9	59	859	1,987
North America	59	100	30	54	186	275	313	244	1,261
South America	346	611	103	664	247	69	35	3,022	5,097
Oceania	191	415	114	64	287	280	131	611	2,093

Adapted from IUCN. "Summary Statistics: Threatened Species: Threatened Species: Country Totals by Taxonomic Group." The 2006 IUCN Red List of Threatened Species. http://www.iucnredlist.org/info/tables/table5 (July 7, 2006).

their transformation into forested areas has been linked to a decline in the number of endemic bird species, while contributing beneficially to migrant bird species by creating woody habitat.[54] The World Conservation Union (IUCN) estimates that approximately 24 percent of all mammal species and 12 percent of bird species will face extinction during the 21st century.[55] In a sobering report, the IUCN notes that "human and financial resources must be mobilized at between 10 and 100 times the current level to address this crisis."[56] Chapter 11 discusses some of the international treaties designed to protect species and slow extinction rates.

Concluding Remarks

Resource protection, although often not thought of as part of traditional environmental law, is important to environmental conditions. Therefore, legislation has attempted to protect the forests, rangelands, wetlands, and estuaries. We have even come to recognize species of plants and animals as natural resources and are according them protection under the ESA. When we think about issues of resource protection, however, it makes no sense to think in terms of national resources alone. Resource protection is really a global issue, as you will realize when reading Chapter 11.

Questions for Review and Discussion

1. What is an old-growth forest, and why are such forests important?
2. Explore the changing view of public land regulation.
3. What are wetlands, and why are they important?
4. Why might the recent Supreme Court decision on Section 404 undermine wetlands protection?
5. Explain the purpose of the CZMA.
6. Describe several of the programs that may undermine endangered species protection.
7. Explain the similarities and differences between Section 7 of the ESA and the EIS requirement of NEPA.
8. Why is the global loss of species important?

For Further Reading

Ashworth, William. 1987. *The Late, Great Lakes: An Environmental History.* Detroit: Wayne State University Press.

Daily, Gretchen, ed. 1998. *Nature's Services: Societal Dependence on Natural Ecosystems.* Washington, D.C.: Island Press.

Gustanski, Julie. 2000. *Protecting the Land: Conservation Easements Past, Present, and Future.* Washington, D.C.: Island Press.

Meyers, Gary. 1995. "Of Woodchips, Wildlife, and Wetlands: A New Ecological Ethic for a Planet in Crisis." *Environmental and Planning Law Journal 12*: 211.

Nash, Roderick. 1967. *Wilderness and the American Mind.* New Haven, CT: Yale University Press.

Pederson, William F. 2004. "Using Federal Environmental Regulations to Bargain for Private Land Use Controls." *Yale Journal on Regulation* 21 (Winter): 1.

Ruckelshaus, William D., et al. 1997. "The Endangered Species Act and Private Property." *Land and Water Law Review* 32: 479.

Ruhl, J. B. 1998. "While the Cat's Asleep: The Making of the 'New' ESA." *Natural Resources and Environment* 187 (Winter): 187–205.

Sutherland, William J., and David A. Hill. 1996. *Managing Habitats for Conservation.* New York: Cambridge University Press.

Vaughn, Ray. 1995. "State of Extinction: The Case of the Alabama Sturgeon and Ways Opponents of the Endangered Species Act Thwart Protection for Rare Species." *Alabama Law Review* 46: 569.

On the Internet

http://www.fws.gov
United States Fish and Wildlife Service
http://www.sierraclub.org/policy/conservation/index.asp
Sierra Club conservation policies
http://restoration.nos.noaa.gov/htmls/era/era_act.html
Web site for the Estuary Restoration Act
http://www.oceanconservancy.org/dynamic/home/home.htm
The Ocean Conservancy
http://hawaiireef.noaa.gov/welcome.html
Information on the progress of declaring the Northwestern Hawaiian Islands Coral Reef Ecosystem Reserve a National Marine Sanctuary
http://www.bishopmuseum.org/bishop/HBS/endangered
Web site of Hawaii's Endangered and Threatened Species
http://www.redlist.org
2000 IUCN Red List of Threatened Species
http://ipl.unm.edu/cwl/fedbook/statute_frame.htm
Federal Wildlife and Related Laws Handbook
http://www.wetlands.com/
The Wetlands Regulation Center
http://www.healthyforests.gov/initiative/legislation.html
This website provides government information about the Healthy Forests Initiative
http://www.whitehouse.gov/ceq/wetlands_200604.pdf
Read "Conserving America's Wetlands 2006, A Report to Congress from the CEQ" here
http://wetlandsfws.er.usgs.gov/status_trends/national_reports/trends_2005_report.pdf
Read "Status and Trends of Wetlands in the Coterminous United States 1998–2004" here

Notes

1. Rhett A. Butler. "United States Has Seventh Highest Rate of Primary Forest Loss." *http://news.mongabay.com/ 2005/1116-forests.html* (November 16, 2005).

2. U.S. Forest Service. *National Report on Sustainable Forests—2003. http://www.fs.fed.us/research/sustain/* (December 23, 2003).

3. Forest Stewardship Council. "Certificates in the United States." *http://www.fscus.org/certified_ companies/?num=20* (June 26, 2005).

4. United Nations Development Programme, United Nations Environment Programme, World Bank, and World Resources Institute. *World Resources: 2000–2001,* p 253. Washington, D.C.: World Resources Institute.

5. 16 USCA § 471.

6. 16 USCA § 475.

7. 16 USCA § 528–31.

8. House Committee on Resources. "Bill Designed to Preserve Valuable Lands in Eastern States." *Press Release,* November 5, 1997. *http://resources committee.house.gov/press/1997/ 110597pe.htm* (March 6, 2001).

9. Ibid.

10. Ibid.

11. 43 USCA § 1732(b).

12. 43 USCA § 1701–1784.

13. 16 USCA § 1601 et seq.

14. 43 USCA § 1901.

15. EPA, Office of Water. "National Estuary Program: What Is an Estuary?" *http://www.epa.gov/ owow/estuaries/about1.htm* (January 10, 1998).

16. CEQ. Twenty-Fifth Report, 193–194.

17. Thomas E. Dahl. 2000. Status and Trends of Wetlands in the Conterminous United States 1986–1997, p 34. *http://training.fws.gov/ library/Pubs9/wetlands86-97_lowres.pdf* (June 28, 2006).

18. CEQ. Twenty-Fifth Report, 194.

19. Janet Larsen. The Earth Policy Institute. June 16, 2004. "Dead Zones Increasing in World's Costal Waters. *http://www.earth-policy.org/Updates/ Update41.htm* (June 28, 2006).

20. Understanding the Clean Water Act. *http://www.cleanwateract.org/pages/ c7.cfm* (June 28, 2006).

21. 120 S.Ct. 2711, 2000.

22. Ibid.

23. "DNR Official Blasts High Court." 2001. *Wisconsin State Journal* (January 11): B3.

24. 2006 U.S. LEXIS 4887 (2006).

25. Nancy Baron and Valerie Holford. "Leading Marine Scientists Release New Evidence that Marine Reserves Produce Enormous Benefits Within Their Boundaries and Beyond: 150 Leading Marine Scientists Call for the Immediate Establishment of Networks of Marine Reserves to Replenish Depleted Seas." *Press Release,* February 17, 2001. *http://www. eurekalert.org/pub_releases/2001-02/ S-Lmsr-1602101.php* (June 28, 2006).

26. Ibid.

27. The Ramsar Convention Bureau. "What is the Ramsar Convention on Wetlands?" *http://www.ramsar.org/ about_infopack_2e.htm* (February 12, 2001).

28. The Ramsar Convention on Wetlands. *http://www.ramsar.org/* (June 28, 2006).

29. Ibid.

30. Dahl. "Status and Trends," 69.

31. Fish and Wildlife Service. "Status and Trends of Wetlands in the Coterminous United States 1998–2004." *http:// wetlandsfws.er.usgs.gov/status_trends/ national_reports/trends_2005_report.pdf* (October 1, 2006).

32. Ibid.

33. Ibid.

34. Ibid.

35. Ibid.
36. Council on Environmental Quality, A Report to Congress: Conserving America's Wetlands: 2006. *http://www.whitehouse.gov/ceq/wetlands_200604.pdf*
37. "IJC Advises U.S. and Canadian Federal Governments that Greater Efforts Are Needed or Great Lakes Agreement May Fail." *Press Release. http://www.ijc.org/comm/10br/en/release10en.html* (March 7, 2001).
38. International Joint Commission. 12th Biennial Report on Great Lakes Water Quality, September 2004. *http://www.ijc.org/php/publications/html/12br/english/report/* (July 5, 2006).
39. International Joint Commission. "Persistent Toxic Substances." Tenth Biennial Report on Great Lakes Water Quality, June 29, 2000, 28. *http://www.ijc.org/comm/10br/en/indexen.html* (March 8, 2001).
40. 16 USCA § 1271.
41. National Park Service. "Wild and Scenic Rivers." *http://www.nps.gov/rivers/index.html* (June 28, 2006).
42. 16 USCA § 1531.
43. 16 USCA § 1533.
44. 50 C.F.R. Sec. 17.3 (1994)
45. Sweet Home Chapter of Communities for a *Great Oregon v. Babbitt,* 1 F.3d 1 (D.C. Cir. 1993).
46. 17 F.3d 1463, 1464 (1994).
47. *http://thomas.loc.gov/cgi-bin/bdquery/z?d108:SN00369:@@@D&summ25m&*
48. *http://ecos.fws.gov/tess_public/SummaryStatistics.do*
49. World Conservation Union. "Confirming the Global Extinction Crisis." *Press Release,* September 28, 2000. *http://www.iucn.org/redlist/2000/news.html* (February 5, 2001).
50. Ibid.
51. Environment News Service. "Extinction Forecast for One-Quarter of All Primates." April 7, 2005. *http://www.ens-newswire.com/ens/apr2005/2005-04-07-03.asp* (July 5, 2006).
52. World Conservation Union. 2006. "Table 5: Threatened Species in Each Country." *IUCN Red List of Threatened Species. http://www.iucnredlist.org/info/tables/table5* (July 5, 2006).
53. Ibid.
54. Ecological Society of America. "As the Grasslands Change and Disappear, What Happens to the Birds?" *Press Release,* January 25, 2001. *http://esa.sdsc.edu/pr012501.htm* (February 7, 2001).
55. World Conservation Union, note 49.
56. Ibid.

RESOLVING CONTROVERSIAL ENVIRONMENTAL ISSUES

- In the following essays, identify the issue, reasons, and conclusion and then identify the assumptions that link the reasons and the conclusion. Are these assumptions justified? Do you see any problems with the assumptions?
- What important information is missing from the following argument? In other words, what information could help you make a decision regarding the worth of this argument? One way to identify missing information is to ask yourself the following question: "What questions would I ask the author if I had the chance?" If you need help, review the discussion at the end of Chapter 7 regarding missing information.

BAN ON SNOWMOBILES BEST POLICY FOR YELLOWSTONE

A federal judge made the right decision to block the Bush administration's plan to overturn a Clinton era policy, which gradually phases out the use of snowmobiles in Yellowstone National Park over a 3-year period. On any given day, over 1,100 snowmobiles run throughout the park spewing pollution into one of the world's most unique environments. According to the National Park Service, air pollution has reached such unhealthy levels in the park that on numerous occasions park rangers have had to wear respiratory masks.

The Clinton plan allows for only 490 snowmobiles per day in 2004, leading to a total ban by 2005. By contrast, the Bush plan would allow for the continuation of high numbers of snowmobiles but would mandate a reduction in pollution by 2005. However, pollution is not the only damage snowmobiles inflict on Yellowstone.

Noise pollution from the snowmobiles disturbs the peace of the pristine environment and scares away wildlife, such as bison and elk. The disruption to sensitive wildlife, caused by snowmobiles, cannot easily be solved except by a total ban on the intrusive vehicles.

When creating the National Park Service, Congress mandated that the park resources be left "unimpaired for the enjoyment of future generations." Snowmobiles, however, pollute the air, ground, and silence of Yellowstone, and that if continued, will irrevocably impair the ability of future generations from enjoying the pristine and unique environment. The federal judge recognized that the best way to preserve Yellowstone for future generations was to allow for the gradual phaseout of snowmobiles.

Now read the opposing editorial. Answer the same critical thinking questions and then decide which editorial makes a better argument.

BAN ON SNOWMOBILES UNNECESSARY

A federal judge was wrong to overturn the Bush administration's attempt at a more reasonable regulation of snowmobiles in Yellowstone National Park than the Clinton era policy of gradually phasing out snowmobiles. By reinstating the Clinton administration's policy, snowmobiles will be a thing of the past in our National Parks, denying the personal freedom and enjoyment to thousands of people who regularly use snowmobiles in Yellowstone. Furthermore, the total ban will cause economic hardships on those whose livelihoods depend upon renting and selling snowmobiles in the Yellowstone area.

The Bush plan would require a reduction in pollution from snowmobiles by

2005. Environmental complaints of pollution should be quelled by such a significant reduction. Snowmobiles can also be made to be quieter than they are now. Reducing the amount of both pollution and noise emitted by snowmobiles allows their use to continue without significant harm to the environment.

Snowmobiles provide an economic boost to towns such as West Yellowstone, and the eventual ban on snowmobiles will leave many without jobs. The concern for the environment is important, but so is the concern over providing economic safety and jobs to people in the Yellowstone area.

The Bush plan would allow for snowmobiles to continue providing jobs while reducing pollution in the park.

The National Park Service was created by Congress to "promote" and "provide for the use and enjoyment" of our natural resources. Snowmobiles allow thousands of people to use and enjoy the national park every year. Even with consideration of environmental issues, the federal judge was wrong to ban the use of snowmobiles because as quieter and less polluting technology becomes available, the environmental impact of snowmobiles will lessen.

CHAPTER 11
INTERNATIONAL ENVIRONMENTAL LAW

Thus far, we have been examining the environmental law of the United States. Environmental protection, however, if it is to be truly effective, must have an international dimension.

THE NEED FOR INTERNATIONAL ENVIRONMENTAL LAW

Over the past two decades, there has been growing recognition of the need for international environmental law, primarily because of an increasing awareness of the severity of certain worldwide environmental problems. These problems are discussed first. Figure 11-1 shows the key environmental issues in various regions of the world, contrasted with the concern for the trends in each region. The next section explains the unique nature of international law, followed by descriptions of the sources of environmental law and the primary institutions that carry out those laws. The final sections address how international environmental law is attempting to remedy some specific environmental problems and speculate about the future of international environmental law.

OVERPOPULATION

One of the most severe problems in the world today is overpopulation. Just look at the numbers of people living in the various cities around the world listed in the graph in Figure 11-2! This problem necessitates an international solution because without a worldwide solution, extremely adverse consequences will result. The threat of overpopulation was set forth originally in the now famous book of Thomas Robert Malthus, *An Essay on the Principle of Population.*[1] Published in 1798, Malthus's work argued that population, which grows geometrically, will eventually outstrip food production, which grows arithmetically, resulting in mass starvation. Although Malthus's timetable for disaster may have been disrupted by unanticipated agricultural developments, many believe that the ultimate impact of those developments is simply to delay the point at which our inability to provide sufficient foodstuffs will occur.

FIGURE 11-1 Key Environmental Issues by Global Environment Outlook Project (GEO) Region

	Land	Forests	Biodiversity	Freshwater	Coastal and marine	Atmosphere	Urban areas	Disasters
Africa	• Degradation and desertification • Inappropriate and inequitable land tenure	• Deforestation • Loss of forest quality	• Habitat degradation and loss • Bushmeat trade	• Variability of water resources • Water stress and scarcity • Access to safe water and sanitation • Deteriorating water quality • Wetlands loss	• Coastal area erosion and degradation • Pollution • Climate change and sea-level rise	• Air quality • Climate variability and vulnerability to climate change • Floods and drought	• Rapid urbanization • Solid waste • Water supply and sanitation • Air pollution	• Drought • Floods • Armed conflict
Asia and the Pacific	• Land degradation • Desertification • Land use change	• Forest degradation • Deforestation	• Habitat loss • Forest loss and degradation • Alien species	• Water scarcity • Pollution	• Degradation of coastal and marine resources • Pollution due to mining and coastal development	• Air quality • Ozone depletion • Greenhouse gas emissions and climate change	• Air pollution • Waste management • Water supply and sanitation • Solid waste	• Floods • Drought • Volcanoes • Earthquakes
Europe	• Land use • Soil degradation, sealing and contamination • Soil erosion	• Loss of natural forests • Forest degradation • Sustainable forest management	• Agricultural intensification • Genetically modified organisms	• Water quantity and quality • Policy and legislative framework	• Coastal erosion • Pollution	• Air pollution • Stratospheric ozone depletion • Greenhouse gas emissions	• Air quality • Noise pollution • Solid waste	• Storms and floods • Earthquakes • Human-caused disasters
Latin America and the Caribbean	• Land degradation • Land tenure	• Deforestation • Forest degradation	• Habitat loss and degradation • Overexploitation of resources and illegal trade	• Decreasing water available per capita • Water quality	• Habitat conversion and destruction • Pollution • Overexploitation of fisheries	• Air pollution • Ozone depletion • Air quality	• Solid waste • Water supply and sanitation • Air quality	• Drought • Hurricanes • Floods • Earthquakes • Spills of hazardous substances
North America	• Land degradation • Pesticides	• Forest health • Old growth forests	• Habitat destruction and degradation • Bio-invasion	• Groundwater • Great Lakes water quality	• Conversion of fragile ecosystems • Overexploitation of marine resources • Pollution	• Stratospheric ozone depletion • Greenhouse gases and climate change	• Urban sprawl • Ecological footprint	• Floods and climate change • Forest fires
West Asia	• Land degradation • Rangeland deterioration	• Degradation • Overexploitation • Sustainable forest management	• Habitat degradation and loss • Overexploitation of species	• Increasing water demand • Overexploitation of groundwater • Water quality	• Coastal development and urbanization • Overexploitation of resources • Marine pollution	• Air pollution • Ozone-depleting substances • Climate change	• Land conversion • Solid waste	• Drought • Oil discharges • Armed conflict
Polar	• Degradation • Erosion • Climate change	• Boreal forest issues • Threats to forest tundra	• Climate change • Ozone depletion • Overexploitation	• Alien species • Pollution	• Overexploitation of fisheries • Pollution • Climate change	• Stratospheric ozone depletion • Long-range air pollution • Climate change	• Sanitation and waste	• Floods • Oil discharges • Pest invasion

Source: UN. State of the Environment and Policy Retrospective, 1972–2002. *http://www.unep.org/geo/geo3/english/pdfs/chapter2-0_intro.pdf* (January 15, 2004).

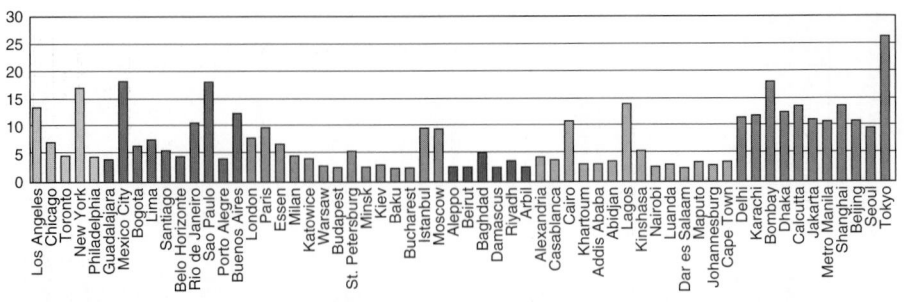

FIGURE 11-2   Population (In Millions) of Some of the Largest Cities in the World, by Region

Source: UNEP. Global Environmental Outlook 3. *http://www.grida.no/geo/geo3/english/pdfs/ synthesis.pdf* (January 10, 2004).

Added to this original concern, and more important to stimulating the development of international environmental law, is the effect that a larger population has on the overall ability of the planet to sustain life. More people use more energy, more land, and more water. This greater use of resources may lead to their depletion. A huge influx in population also creates more pollution. Burning wood and low-sulfur coal contributes to the buildup of carbon monoxide. Rapid urbanization, occurring in most Third World nations today, leads to massive traffic jams, overcrowded slums, and clogged waste disposal systems, all of which degrade the environment. Infrastructure created for the automobiles that urbanization and Western influence made ubiquitous have led to the destruction of cropland around the world, creating concern over the possibility of feeding an ever-expanding population.[2]

Some social scientists, most notably Julian Simon, believe that population growth is good for humanity, primarily because human intellect is our most valuable resource: The more people, the greater the intellect pool from which society can draw. Those who do not believe there is a population problem point out that whenever apparently fixed resources become scarce, we seem to figure out a way to replace them. For example, when horse-powered transportation became a problem, we developed the railroad and the motor car. When trees became scarce in the 16th century, we learned to burn coal. Hence, it could be argued from history that every apparent shortage is just a stimulus for the development of new resources, new resources that in the long run may be cheaper than the old ones.[3]

Whether we agree with those who see increased population as a blessing or a curse, we can all agree that the population of the planet is increasing at an unprecedented pace. Overall, the world's population is increasing by over 86 million people each year. The United Nations (UN) predicts that global population will peak at 11 billion in 2200. The recent growth in population is illustrated in Figure 11-3.

millions

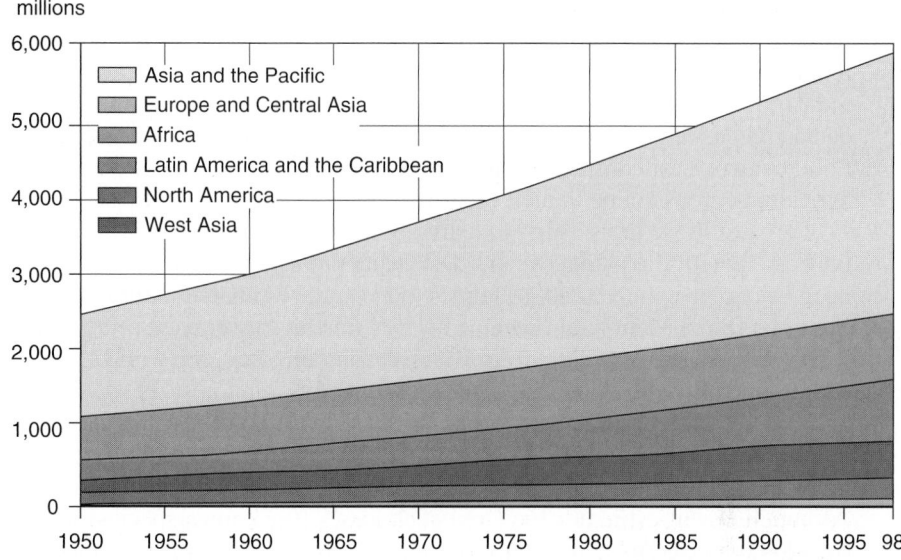

FIGURE 11-3   World Population Growth

Source: UNEP. GEO-Overview 2000. *http://www-cger.nies.go.jp/geo2000/ov-e/ioe2.htm* (January 10, 2004).

Perhaps, as a society, we have always been able to handle increases in population and increasing demands on resources, but it is only logical that a breaking point must be reached. For years the air managed to cleanse itself, but then its self-cleansing properties were overcome by excess pollutants. The same phenomenon occurs with bodies of water. Many fear that despite our successes in the past, we are nearing the carrying capacity for Earth. A recent atlas compiled by the American Association for the Advancement of Science shows that population is having a severe impact because humanity is "showing signs of overreaching itself, of threatening key resources on which we depend."[4]

Regardless of whether we perceive population increases as nearing crisis levels, certainly the fact that an increasing number of people are using common resources means that we are more likely to interfere with one another's use of these resources. Hence, there is a need for an international body of law to respond to questions regarding use and abuse of the global environment.

LOSS OF BIOLOGICAL DIVERSITY

Although some see overpopulation as the preeminent global problem today, others consider loss of biological diversity an even greater problem. Scientists have classified approximately 1.75 million living species, of which more than half are insects and nearly one-sixth are plants.[5] No one knows how many millions more exist that have not been classified. The more we learn about these diverse species, the more we discover ways that they can improve and maintain our lives. Some plants and animals provide food, medicine, and industrial raw materials. For example, over 40 percent of prescription drugs contain chemicals originally derived from wild species. Other species provide flood control, pest control, and natural recycling of waste. Ninety percent of agricultural crops are pollinated exclusively by insects.

Yet, just as we are starting to learn about many of these species and how they can benefit the planet, we are destroying them. Some 1,600 species have been becoming extinct at 50–100 times the average estimated natural rate. At least two-thirds of all land-dwelling species inhabit the tropical rain forests, which are being rapidly destroyed. The Amazon rain forest, the world's richest collection of biological diversity, lost 37 percent of its rain forests between 1990 and 2000.[6] As the rain forests are being destroyed, so are the species that inhabit these areas. Estimates of species loss vary, and it would be impossible to know the precise figure, but they range from 4,004 to 17,500 species per year. Although recent estimates have put such losses (for known species) at just over 1,000 species, it is important to remember that a species is not generally listed as extinct until it has not been seen for 50 years.[7] Therefore, species that became extinct in the 1990s would not be recognized as such until after 2040. In Madagascar, the Philippines, and Haiti, approximately 20 percent of the bird and mammal species are threatened.[8] However, in Mauritius, an island in the Indian Ocean, almost 40 percent of birds and mammals are classified as threatened.[9] The species of island nations are more vulnerable to extinction because many are unique and cannot escape to another area when faced with a threat. For the Hawaiian islands, close to 90 percent of birds are missing, endangered, extinct, or known from bones only.[10]

The greatest losses are occurring in tropical forests, where most of the various species reside. These losses are occurring because increases in population, endemic poverty, the need for fuel wood, and the failure to use sustainable agricultural methods have led to massive clearing of these forests. Essentially, it is human activity that destroys habitats and leads to the loss of species.

THE GLOBAL COMMONS

The term *biosphere* refers to the thin shell where the atmosphere, hydrosphere, and lithosphere connect; in this context life and its products exist. The biosphere constitutes a symbol of the unity and interrelationships of living things and their physical setting. The biosphere calls to mind a complementary relationship between humans and the physical environment. That environment is not viewed primarily as a set of independent, strictly bounded territories but, rather, as one related unit, divided if at all, into natural components—air, water, and land—each having interactive relationships with one another and with humans. Space travel permitted the first real view of Earth as a biosphere. From outer space we could see Earth as a single, unitary whole, set against the blackness of the universe. When we view Earth as a biosphere, we can see that the air, water, and land are interconnected and, in fact, represent a sort of global commons.

Obviously, the oceans and seas constitute a major part of the global commons. Problems associated with the destruction of these shared resources are potentially numerous: human health may be placed directly at risk by contamination of seafood, the reproductive cycles of species of animal life may be disrupted, human health may also be adversely affected because of direct contact with polluted water, and the aesthetic qualities of coastal environments may be destroyed. About 40 percent of the global population lives within 100 kilometers of the coastline, and about one billion people depend on fish as their primary source of protein.[11] Furthermore, according to one estimate, one billion to 2.4 billion people will live in water-scarce countries by 2050.[12]

Potential destruction of the ocean environment comes primarily from three sources: ocean shipping, land-based pollution, and the dumping of wastes into the oceans. The primary problem caused by marine shipping is pollution created by marine oil. Ninety percent of this oil is from standard ship operations, deballasting, and tank washing. Only about 10 percent results from tanker accidents, although it is these accidents that tend to generate the greatest publicity. Recall from Chapter 6 that water pollution from land-based activities can be point or nonpoint source. The same two categories apply to pollution of oceans. Point source discharges occur when manufacturers along a coast discharge insufficiently treated or untreated water directly into the ocean. Nonpoint source pollution comes primarily from runoff from cropland, urban areas, and construction and mining sites. Wastes being dumped at sea include sewage sludge, industrial waste, and dredge spoils. These wastes may contain a plethora of heavy metals, synthetic chemicals, and other toxic materials. Ocean dumping of low-level radioactive waste was a problem at one time, but it no longer is.

Forestlands are another component of the global commons. Forests provide sinks for carbon dioxide absorption, slowing the rate of global climate change. Yet, agricultural lands have replaced 20–30 percent of the world's forests.[13] However, agricultural lands are becoming decreasingly productive because of poor farming practices that have degraded soil, which increases concern over the ability of nations to feed their populations.[14] In addition, agricultural lands require a high level of maintenance and large quantities of water, causing water tables to fall.[15] With the world's population expected to increase by 25 percent by 2020, the need for forestlands to be converted to agricultural lands may become more pressing.

Air is another important part of the global commons. Because of air currents, substances one country emits into the atmosphere are likely to travel to other countries. The three primary global problems associated with air (described in Chapter 5) are acid deposition, depletion of the ozone layer, and the greenhouse effect.

ENVIRONMENTAL DISASTERS
AND TRANSBOUNDARY POLLUTION

During the past 20 years, a number of dramatic environmental disasters have made people recognize the potential that our advanced levels of technology have for allowing one nation to wreak havoc on the environment worldwide. These catastrophes make it clear that no nation, regardless of the precautions it takes, can protect its environment by itself. Some of these disastrous incidents include nuclear accidents such as the Chernobyl incident in the Soviet Union and the nearly catastrophic Three Mile Island accident in the United States. Others are the industrial accident in Sevesko, Italy, and the Exxon Valdez oil spill in Alaska. The combined effect of these incidents has been to make people question whether there should be some international agreement on how to respond to such disasters when they arise and, even more importantly, how to prevent their occurrence.

Transboundary pollution, on the contrary, has been around for years. Transboundary pollution generally arises in two ways. First, pollution is generated in one area and transported a great distance before falling to earth in another nation. A typical example would be when a U.S. firm uses tall stacks to disperse air pollutants, which causes the air pollutants to settle in Canada. The second type of transboundary pollution occurs when two or more nations border on a common resource and one nation pollutes the common resource to the detriment of the other. An example would be Mexico's dumping sewage into the Tijuana River, resulting in damage to wells and crops in California.

Solutions to these wide-ranging problems are being sought through international environmental law. Before we examine international environmental law *per se*, however, we need to understand how international law in general compares with domestic law.

THE NATURE OF INTERNATIONAL LAW

International law is unlike any other area of law in that there is disagreement over whether indeed there can even be a body of law known as international law, and if there is, what those laws are. There is no international superlegislature to establish these laws and no effective international mechanism with enforcement authority.

International law is generally viewed as being derived from two sources: treaties and other agreements freely entered into by nation-states and principles derived from long-standing practices. Laws from treaties are referred to as conventional laws; those from long-standing practice are called customary laws. The primary actors in the international law system are the nation-states, as represented by their governments. Intergovernmental agencies also play an important role in the international law system, as do nongovernmental organizations (NGOs). In addition, individuals and corporations are sometimes participants.

Enforcement is where international law presents the greatest difficulty. The Security Council of the UN is most often viewed as the primary source of enforcement of international law. The council has limited executive authority to enforce the provisions of its charter and to maintain peace and security. However, it does not have any enforcement authority over international law in general. It is also limited because it requires unanimity of all of its members before it can act.

The UN has established an International Court of Justice. However, the impact of this court has been limited by the fact that it decides only cases submitted by parties who agree to be there. The parties between whom there is the greatest disagreement are, therefore, unlikely to go before the court because they will not agree to submit their dispute. Thus, arguably, the parties who need the court the most will be the least likely to use it. In some cases, the court has the authority to issue advisory opinions only, which may be, and frequently are, freely ignored.

Given the ineffectiveness of these sources of enforcement, parties have sometimes turned to the courts of the nation-states to seek enforcement of international law. As long as the court will assume jurisdiction, this approach may be the most effective. (This approach is discussed in somewhat greater detail later in the chapter.)

SOURCES OF INTERNATIONAL ENVIRONMENTAL LAW

As noted in the preceding section, international law comes from both treaties and practices. International environmental law, likewise, draws from these two sources. Its conventional law comprises some 20 multilateral treaties governing environmental issues and more than 275 bilateral agreements that contain references to environmental issues.

CONVENTIONAL LAW

Conventional international environmental law can trace its roots back to the UN Conference on the Human Environment in Stockholm in 1972. This 2-week meeting produced the Stockholm Declaration of the conference, which was subsequently adopted by the 17th session of the UN General Assembly by a vote of 114–0, with 10 abstentions. This document contained 26 principles, an action plan consisting of 109 recommendations, and a resolution on institutional and financial arrangements. The topics covered by the principles included fundamental human rights (Principle 1), management of human resources (Principles 2–7), the relationship between development and the environment (Principles 8–12), planning and demographic policy (Principles 13–17), science and technology (Principles 18–20), state responsibility (Principles 21–22), respect for national environmental standards along with the need for state cooperation (Principles 23–25), and the threat of nuclear weapons to the environment (Principle 26).[16]

The principles are important because they consolidated the existing rules of international environmental law while also providing guidance for the future of this body of law. Principle 21 is a good example of the tone of these principles and also reflects a recognition by the drafters of the existence of a body of international environmental law. Principle 21 reads as follows:

> States shall cooperate to develop further the international law regarding liability and compensation for the victims of pollution and other environmental damage caused by activities within the jurisdiction or control of such states to areas beyond their jurisdiction.

A second important agreement, the world charter for nature,[17] was adopted by the UN General Assembly in 1982, by a vote of 111–1, with the United States casting the only dissenting vote. The charter contains a preamble and 25 principles. The first five are general principles. Principles 6 through 13 provide detailed rules for planning and management of the natural environment. Finally, principles 14 through 25 contain implementation rules that specify obligations for members of the international community.

CUSTOMARY LAW

Customary law is defined by Article 38 of the statute of the International Court of Justice[18] as having its source in state practice, in the "general principles of law that are recognized by civilized nations, and in the judicial decisions and teachings of respected jurists." Think of customary law as analogous to common law in the U.S. legal system.

Four basic principles seem to have evolved as customary international environmental laws. These customary laws are reinforced by treaty provisions. Attempts to codify these customary rules have been undertaken by two private organizations: the International Law Association and the International Law Commission (ILC).

A first principle is that of good neighborliness—the rule that no state is entitled to use its land in a way that would infringe on the rights of others. This principle, often cited in its Latin form, *sic uter tuo alienum non laedas,* can be viewed as an international application of the U.S. common law of nuisance, discussed in Chapter 4. The doctrine of good neighborliness seems to have been initially granted its status as a customary law in the Trail Smelter arbitration.[19] Trail Smelter arose from a situation in which sulfur dioxide fumes from a smelter in Trail, British Columbia, were damaging farmland and crops in the state of Washington. The United States complained to Canada in 1927. After years of negotiations, Canada accepted liability and agreed to arbitrate the issue of damages. In 1941, the decision was handed down that contains the often-quoted principle of good neighborliness as applied to transboundary pollution: "Under principles of international law, as well as the law of the United States, no state has the right to permit the use of its territory in such a manner as to cause injury by fumes to another country or to the properties or persons therein where the case is of serious consequence and the injury is established by clear and convincing evidence." This decision is sometimes criticized because of two require-ments that limit the rule's application: the description of the consequences as serious and the standard of clear and convincing evidence.

Further support for this customary law can be found in several treaties that incorporate the principle of good neighborliness. For example, the preamble to the Charter of the UN states the desire of member states to "live together in peace with one another as good neighbors." Article 74 of the same document encourages member states to conduct their social, economic, and commercial policies in accordance with "general principles of good neighborliness."

A second principle is the duty of due diligence—the obligation to pro-tect the rights of other states. In the environmental area, this duty has been extended to mean a duty to use due diligence to prevent and abate pollu-tion. This principle has not been interpreted as an absolute prohibition on pollution but, rather, as a mandate that the state take the measures expected under "good government" to prevent pollution.

Another important principle is that of the equitable utilization of shared resources—the requirement of the reasonable use of shared resources. The obvious question that arises with respect to this principle is how one decides whether a use is reasonable. In fact, if one decides that reasonable use may be derived from past practice, one may in fact be sanctioning the very activities that gave rise to the environmental problems in the first place.

This customary law of equitable utilization was first set out in the River Oder case.[20] In that case, the Permanent Court of International Justice laid down the rule by stating that "this community of interest (of riparian states) in a navigable river becomes the basis of a common legal right, the essential features of which are the perfect equality of all riparian states in the use of the whole course of the river."

This principle was reinforced by its inclusion in the Helsinki Rules.[21] Article IV states: "Each basin state is entitled, within its territory, to a reasonable and equitable share in the beneficial uses of the waters of an international drainage basin." The Helsinki Rules attempt to provide some guidance as to what is considered reasonable use by listing some factors that should be taken into account: geographic and climatic conditions, social and economic needs of the neighboring states, comparative costs of alternative ways to satisfy those needs, availability of the technological means to reduce the impact on the environment, and the practicality of compensation as a means of adjusting the burden. The rules do not suggest any order of impor-tance for these factors, indicating that their relevance depends on the indi-vidual circumstances of each case.[22]

A final principle is the duty to inform and cooperate. The duty to give prior notice is recognized in such often-cited cases as the Corfu Channel case.[23] This case arose when two British warships traveling through the Corfu Channel, part of Albania's water, were damaged by mines that had been placed there by the Germans. Albania was believed to have, at minimum, knowledge of the mines. The International Court of Justice, in ruling that Albania had to compensate the British for the damage to property and life, stated that "the obligations incumbent upon the Albanian authorities consisted in notifying . . . the existence of a minefield in Albanian territorial waters and in warning the approaching British warships of the immediate danger to which the minefield exposed them."

Adoption of the duty to inform is evidenced by this principle's inclusion in many treaties. For example, Article XXIX of the Helsinki Rules recommends that states "furnish any other basin state the interests of which may be substantially affected, notice of a proposed construction or installation which would alter the regime of the basin."[24]

INSTITUTIONS THAT EFFECTUATE AND INFLUENCE INTERNATIONAL ENVIRONMENTAL LAW

UNITED NATIONS

The most influential intergovernmental organization in the development of international environmental law is the UN, which was established in 1945. Its primary bodies include the General Assembly, the Security Council, and the Economic and Social Council. Technically, all the UN can do is make recommendations; the individual members must adopt their own policies. However, the articulation of treaties and policies by the UN is a powerful first step toward the worldwide adoption of environmental policies. The UN also sponsors several programs that have a significant impact on international environmental law.

UN Environmental Program

The UN Environmental Program (UNEP) is a special body created by the UN General Assembly, which has done much to effectuate worldwide environmental policies. Created at the same time was the Environmental Fund. Both UNEP and the Environmental Fund were mandated by Resolution 2997 (XXVII) in 1972 to effectuate the action plan set forth in the Stockholm Declaration.

UNEP's structure has three distinct entities: the Governing Council, the Environment Secretariat, and the Environment Fund. The Governing Council comprises delegates from the 58 member states who are elected on a rotating basis by the General Assembly. The main responsibilities of the Governing Council are to promote international cooperation in environmental matters and to provide general policy guidance for the direction and coordination of environmental programs within the UN system. The council also annually reviews and approves the allocation of money from the Environment Fund. Every year the council receives from the executive director, the state of the environment report, which it uses to identify environmental issues and to decide on future initiatives. The Governing Council reviews the impact of environmental policies on developing countries, as well as promotes contributions to program formulation and development from the scientific and other communities. The council reports UNEP's activities to the General Assembly through the Economic and Social Council, with special attention being paid to questions of coordination and to the relationship of environmental policies and programs within the UN system to overall economic and social policies and priorities.

The Environment Secretariat is composed of approximately 200 people and is headed by UNEP's executive director, who is elected by the General Assembly. The tasks of the secretariat include coordinating environmental programs in the UN system and reviewing and evaluating their effectiveness, providing advisory services for promotion of international cooperation, advising intergovernmental bodies of the UN system on environmental programs, and administering the Environment Fund.

The Environment Fund receives about $5 million in funds annually from the UN to cover operating expenses, but it relies on voluntary contributions from governments to build up funds to be used for financing initiatives taken within the UN and to sponsor many of their programs of general interest that are described in the following paragraphs. In 2003, the Environmental Fund received $47.3 million in voluntary contributions from 110 countries.

UNEP's mandate is to assess, monitor, and protect the human environment by seeking solutions to pollution and human-made contamination, promoting environmentally sound economic and social developments in urban and rural areas. UNEP is primarily a catalyst and coordinating agency. As such, it collaborates with other environmental agencies, as well as runs some of its own programs.

The Division of Early Warning and Assessment (DEWA) is one of the most important UNEP programs. DEWA is responsible for analyzing the state of the global environment and assessing global and regional trends. DEWA also provides policy advice and early warning information on environmental threats. In 1995, UNEP established the Global Environment Outlook Project (GEO) as a clearinghouse for information from DEWA and other UNEP and non-UNEP organizations. GEO reports provide an in-depth look at the state of the global environment, including recommendations on policies and actions. A component of DEWA is the Global Resource Information Database (GRID). This project began in 1985 to assimilate and reference data geographically from a wide variety of sources, including satellite observations. In the United States, the GRID office is run by the U.S. Geological Survey out of Sioux Falls, South Dakota.

The Regional Seas Programme is one of UNEP's most successful endeavors. This program involves more than 140 states and territories through 13 regional programs. The Programme fosters cooperation among nations sharing coastal areas and encourages the development of regional agreements to address water issues from waste to development. These

..its provide UNEP's main legal, financial, and administrative ...nework for protecting the marine environment.

UNEP also engages in a wide range of cooperative ventures with other organizations such as the International Council of Scientific Unions. For example, UNEP publishes the International Register of Potentially Toxic Chemicals, which provides detailed information and policy proposals for more than 80,000 chemicals.

World Commission on Environment and Development

The WCED (sometimes referred to as the Brundtland Commission) was created by the General Assembly of the UN in the fall of 1983 to formulate long-term strategies to attain sustainable development by the year 2000 and beyond. The prime minister of Norway was named chair; the prime minister of the Sudan was named vice-chair. These two appointed the remaining 21 members, with more than half being from developing nations.

On October 13, 1984, the newly organized WCED met and adopted a mandate to re-examine critical issues of environment and development and formulate innovative, concrete, and realistic action proposals to address them, strengthen international cooperation on environment and development, and assess and propose new forms of cooperation that can reshape existing economic patterns and influence policies and events in the direction of needed change; and raise the level of understanding and commitment to action on the part of individuals, voluntary associations, businesses, institutions, and governments.[25]

The major accomplishment of WCED was the publication of _Our Common Future_. The report was based on data gathered from public hearings in a dozen cities around the world and information from several advisory panels. The report concluded that "humanity has the ability to make development sustainable—to ensure that it meets the needs of the present without compromising the ability of future generations to meet their own needs."[26]

The idea of sustainability has become an important one to the environmental community. In 1993, former USSR President Mikhail Gorbachev founded Green Cross International "to help create the conditions for a sustainable future by cultivating a more harmonious relationship between humans and the environment."[27] Since its founding, Green Cross International has been active in 30 countries, including the United States, and has developed five program areas: creation of an Earth Charter for adoption by nations, mitigation of environmental damage from wars, prevention of water conflicts and desertification, promotion of decreasing energy consumption and greater resource efficiency, and development of environmental education.[28] Other groups, in conjunction with Green Cross International, have been working on the Earth Charter, and a draft text of the charter has been prepared. The draft text endorses four principles: respect and care for the community of life, ecological integrity, social and economic justice, and democracy, nonviolence, and peace. The charter was approved by The United Nations Educational, Scientific and Cultural Organization (UNESCO) in 2000.[29]

WORLD BANK

The World Bank is one of the primary sources of funding for projects in developing countries. As such, it has the potential to play an extremely influential role in environmental policies worldwide.

Before the mid-1980s, environmental factors were not a consideration in the World Bank's lending decisions. In fact, many have criticized the bank for lending money without considering the social impacts of the projects (e.g., lending money for projects that led to deforestation and to governments that do not care about indigenous tribal minorities). In 1987, however, the bank was reorganized and an environmental department was established. As a result, potential borrowers were asked to prepare an environmental issues paper for each loan they wished to obtain. The contents of these papers were to be considered when loans were being made.

In 1989, the impact of potential environmental effects was given even more prominence by an operational directive on EAs of proposed projects. Now, when a project is being considered, a preliminary screening is done by the environmental department of the World Bank. The project is rated according to its potential impact on the environment. Category A has the greatest potential, so it would require that a full EA be done by the potential borrower. Category B would require only limited assessment of specific impacts. Category C would not necessitate any assessment because it is unlikely to have environmental impacts. Category D does not require any assessment because the environment is the focus of the project. Not only are these assessments taken into account when the bank is considering action on loan requests, but a summary of the project's environmental impact is included in a supplement to the bank's monthly operational summary, the main document the bank uses to convey its future plans to interested parties. From 1990 to 2000, 210 projects were classified as Category A and 1,006 projects were classified as Category B.[30] Thus, projects requiring a full EA or an environmental analysis totaled between 30 and 67 percent of the total annual lending volume of the World Bank.[31]

Recognizing the need to do more to address environmental issues, the World Bank adopted several policies in the 1990s. However, no comprehensive framework existed for determining the environmental viability of projects until 2001, when the World Bank adopted its final strategy on incorporating EC into funding decisions. The goal of this strategy is "to promote environmental improvements as a fundamental element of development and poverty reduction strategies and actions."[32] To reach this goal, the World Bank will institute country-level environmental analyses to assess environmental trends and priorities. Strategic EAs will be used in the early portions of the decision-making process to assist in analyses. The World Bank will also work to improve the environmental outcomes of adjustment lending. Determinations of country-level environmental assistance will be based on "a diagnosis of environmental priorities and management capacity, country demand, and consistency with the [country assistance strategy]."[33]

In 2001, the Bank initiated an Extractive Industries Review to analyze its involvement in funding oil, mining, and gas projects, after receiving numerous complaints about the impact of these projects. They issued their final report in November 2003. The report recommended increasing support for renewable energy (RE) projects and downgrading extractive projects. It also recommended that a number of measures be taken with the mining and gas projects that the World Bank was financing. These measures included more transparency in revenue flows, revenue sharing with local communities, measuring projects' success based on their effect on poverty, and more rigorous controls over mine and other waste.[34] The report is non-binding, but has been the catalyst for significant changes in the Bank's lending policies.

A report in 2005 outlines the changes, the progress made, and sets guidelines for future investment strategies.[35] The lending institutions within the World Bank Group now have specific guidelines in the Social and Environmental Policy and Performance Standards. Most of the standards are currently in place; however, some standards faced proposed revisions in late 2005 and expect to be implemented in 2006. These standards require proof of significant broad community support, with more stringent guidelines when the project has potential effect on indigenous peoples. The guidelines also clarify the criteria required to prohibit investment in certain areas to protect biodiversity and critical habitats. The Extractive Industries Transparency Initiative (EITI) requires open access to financial records of significant projects and will apply to all projects by 2007.

The 2005 implementation report also outlines investment goals for future projects. RE and Energy Efficiency (EE) are priorities for investment, and accounted for $748 million in FY2005.[36] The World Bank Group has set a goal of increasing the investment in RE and EE 20 percent annually from 2005 to 2010. The goal is to "vigorously" pursue RE and EE initiatives to promote sustainable economic growth by reducing energy costs.

GLOBAL ENVIRONMENT FACILITY

Although the World Bank provides funding for projects in developing countries, the Global Environment Facility (GEF) finances projects focusing on environmental protection. The GEF was established in 1991 and later modified in 1994 to finance actions in four globally critical areas: biodiversity loss, climate change, degradation of international waters, and ozone depletion.

Members of the GEF (currently totaling 176) meet every 4 years to replenish the GEF fund. In 2002, a total of $3 billion was pledged to the GEF by 32 countries.[37] In August, 2006, the same countries pledged $3.13 billion dollars at the Third GEF Assembly.[38] The Council of the GEF is made up of 16 representatives from less-developed nations, 14 representatives from more-developed nations, and two representatives from transition economies. All decisions on funding are made by a consensus of the GEF Council. Some projects receive matching grants from both public and private organizations. The GEF is the only international financial institution with an open door policy toward NGOs; indeed, many GEF-funded projects are carried out through partnerships with NGOs.

Since its creation, the GEF has funded more than 1,300 projects in 140 countries.[39] The majority of these projects address the issues of biodiversity loss and climate change. The GEF also holds an important role as the funding mechanism for some environmental treaties. The Convention on International Trade in Endangered Flora and Fauna, the Framework Convention on Climate Change, and the Montreal Protocol, all discussed later in this chapter, fund their projects through the GEF.

EUROPEAN UNION

The EU is a group of 25 European nations set to grow to 27 nations in 2007. Their overall objective is to do away with internal tariffs among member states and to create uniform external tariffs to be applied to nonmember states. The EU wants to "level the economic playing field" among member states and achieve the free movement of goods, capital, and people across member states' borders. See Table 11-1 for a list of the member states of the EU.

The EU has been given the authority, by its member states, to negotiate treaties that directly bind the members without further ratification by members' separate legislatures. The EU consists of a council, whose members are

TABLE 11-1 Nation-States of the European Union	
Belgium (1958)	Finland (1994)
France (1958)	Estonia (2004)
Germany (1958)	Latvia (2004)
Italy (1958)	Malta (2004)
Luxembourg (1958)	Slovakia (2004)
Netherlands (1958)	Cyprus (2004)
Denmark (1973)	Czech Republic (2004)
Ireland (1973)	Hungary (2004)
United Kingdom (1973)	Lithuania (2004)
Greece (1981)	Poland (2004)
Portugal (1986)	Slovenia (2004)
Spain (1986)	Bulgaria (2007)
Austria (1994)	Romania (2007)
Sweden (1994)	

ministers from the member nations, a commission, and a parliament, which is made up of representatives directly elected by member states. The commission proposes legislation, and the council adopts it after receiving input from the parliament. The legislation passed by the EU is in two forms—regulations and directives. Regulations have the force of a national law and are directly enforceable in each nation's court. Directives are broader and bind nations to ends that are to be achieved.

The EU [then being a much smaller unit, comprised of only six member states, and known as the European Community (EC)] first began to address environmental policy explicitly in 1972, influenced to a great extent by the Stockholm Conference. Legislation is adopted in accordance with the EU's environmental action program. The program, which has been redefined four times since its inception, establishes principles in accordance with which environmental legislation is to be adopted. Eleven principles have been established; the following are typical examples of those principles: Activities in one nation should not cause deterioration of the environment of another, and the effects of environmental policies in member states should take into account the interests of developing nations. By 2002, the EU had adopted more than 300 pieces of environmental legislation. These regulations cover a broad range of environmental issues, from drinking water standards to limits on sulfur dioxide emissions for controlling acid rain.

From the perspective of those concerned about environmental issues, one of the biggest concerns about the expansion of the EC into the EU and its continued growth is the impact that joining the EU has on environmental regulation of member states. Remember that the objective of the EU is to remove trade barriers among member states. What this means in terms of environmental protection is that no state can set up environmental standards that would keep another member state from competing in its markets or keep its firms from competing in other states' markets. The problem from an environmentalist's perspective is that the northern EC states have traditionally had much more stringent environmental regulations than have the southern European states. Many fear that what will happen as the states unify their laws is that the southern European states will block the northern European states from imposing their more stringent requirements on the entire community and may in fact have to reduce some of their own standards.

The EU also acts as negotiator for its member states in negotiations for treaties (often referred to as conventions) with nonmember nations. As a representative of many nations, the EU has greater clout than any single nation would have. Although the EU is an active and influential participant in these treaty negotiations, it does not actually bind member states to most conventions; member states independently determine whether they will become signatories to such agreements. In some cases, however, member states do give the EU the authority to bind them to a proposed treaty. When given such authority, the EU has even greater power at the negotiating table.

ADDRESSING SPECIFIC INTERNATIONAL ENVIRONMENTAL PROBLEMS

In this section, we examine how international environmental law attempts to solve some specific problems. Treatment of these problem areas relies on both customary and conventional law, neither of which is very satisfactory. Customary law is plagued by the uncertainty of its principles. Treaties, because they require agreement of parties with conflicting interests, are often very weak, imposing few absolute rights or obligations. Both types of law are victims of the overall problem of weak enforceability.

TRANSBOUNDARY POLLUTION

Transboundary pollution occurs when pollution generated in one nation is transported to another nation, or when two countries share a common resource and one contaminates that resource to the detriment of the other. Establishing an international law for transboundary pollution is difficult because of two conflicting perspectives on state sovereignty. One is a concept of absolute sovereignty, under which a nation is free to do whatever it wishes with resources within its boundaries. Most nations denounce this absolutist position, but, still, in practice, it describes many nations' behavior. The opposing view is that of absolute territorial integrity. This view holds that no state may engage in activities that would in any way damage the territory of another nation.

The development of international environmental law regarding transboundary pollution can be seen as an attempt to find a way to recognize these two competing notions of territoriality. The current tentative resolution of this conflict seems to be that the rights emanating from territorial sovereignty imply a reciprocal duty to take into account the impact of one nation's behavior on other nations. Recognition of the need to incorporate both concepts of territoriality is perhaps best exemplified by Principle 21 of the Stockholm Declaration, which reads as follows:

> States have, in accordance with the Charter of the United Nations and the principles of international law, the sovereign right to exploit their own resources pursuant to their environmental principles, and the responsibility to ensure that activities within their jurisdiction or control do not cause damage to the environment of other states or areas beyond the limits of national jurisdiction.

Finding a definitive statement of the law of transboundary pollution is not easy. In Restatement (Third) of the Foreign Relations Law of the

United States, we find the following statement of liability for transboundary pollution:

§ 902 INTERSTATE CLAIMS AND REMEDIES

1. A state may bring a claim against another state for violation of an international obligation owed to the claimant state or to states generally, either through diplomatic channels, or through any procedure to which the two states have agreed
2. Under Subsection (1), a state may bring claims, *inter alia* for violations of international obligations resulting in injury to its nationals or to other persons on whose behalf it is entitled to make a claim under international law

Because of the confusion surrounding the issue of liability of nations for transboundary pollution, the UN General Assembly requested that the ILC report on liability for transboundary pollution when the acts giving rise to the injury were not illegal, *per se.* (The ILC is a body of the UN composed of 35 representatives that are elected by the General Assembly according to geographic location.) The conclusions reached by the ILC seem to reflect what we have seen as the principles of customary international environmental law.

Four duties appear to be imposed on nations: to prevent transboundary harm, to inform other nations of accidents that might cause transboundary harm, to enter into negotiations to attempt to develop a convention to determine how the situation should be handled, and, if no convention can be adopted, to negotiate in good faith with respect to the rights and obligations of the parties. When harm has resulted, liability should be determined by considering a number of factors, including the amount of damage, the degree of control exercised by the responsible state, the reasonableness of the parties' conduct, and the relative costs of preventing the injury.

Air Pollution

Today it is common knowledge that air pollution generated in one region of the world can end up hundreds or even thousands of miles from the point of generation. Acid rain, discussed in Chapter 5, is a particularly egregious form of one nation's use of its resources having an impact on another nation's enjoyment of theirs. The first international legally binding instrument to deal with the problems of transboundary air pollution was the Convention on Long Range Transboundary Air Pollution (LRTAP), signed in 1979. The impetus for LRTAP came from Europe, when it was discovered that emissions from countries in continental Europe were damaging lakes and other bodies of water in the Scandinavian countries.

The text of LRTAP is actually quite short, with broad and somewhat fuzzy objectives. The fundamental principles of the treaty include protecting humans and the environment from air pollution by limiting, reducing, and finally preventing long-range transboundary air pollution, developing policies and strategies to combat air pollution, and sharing information on methods of air pollution reduction. After the entry into force of LRTAP in 1983, several additional protocols were developed to strengthen LRTAP and make its objectives more concrete.

The Helsinki Protocol of 1987 dealt with the emissions of sulfur compounds. Parties to the Helsinki Protocol agreed to reduce their national annual emissions of sulfur by 30 percent of 1980 levels by 1993. The necessity of additional reductions in sulfur emissions was to be determined by the individual countries. The Oslo Protocol, entered into force in 1998, further refined the Helsinki Protocol by developing an effect-based approach to reductions in the emissions of sulfur compounds. Parties to the protocol find themselves with different emissions reductions quotas based on various criteria. The Sofia Protocol called for parties to reduce emissions of nitrogen oxides to below 1987 levels by 1994 and to develop national emissions standards on nitrogen oxides for new sources of nitrogen oxide emissions. The United States chose to use 1978 as the level below which to reduce its nitrogen oxide emissions rather than the 1987 level.[40] The Geneva Protocol addressed the problems of VOC emissions by calling on parties to reduce VOC emissions by 30 percent of 1984–1990 levels by 1999. The Aarhus Protocol dealt with heavy metal emissions by requiring parties to reduce emissions of cadmium, lead, and mercury below 1990 levels. A second Aarhus Protocol, adopted on the same day, reduces emissions of persistent organic pollutants (POP) for parties, with the objective of ultimate elimination of such pollutants. Both Aarhus Protocols entered into force in late 2003. A LRTAP Convention report issued in 2004 points out that there is evidence of reductions in both heavy metal emissions and POPs, but long-term effects of the protocols will require long-term studies.[41]

The most recent addition to LRTAP is the Gothenburg Protocol, signed November 30, 1999, which sets emissions limits by the year 2010 for sulfur, nitrogen oxides, VOCs, and ammonia. This protocol has been viewed as particularly important because of its impact on reducing the amount of particulates in the air and the acidification of bodies of water. One estimate is that areas of severe acidification in Europe will be reduced by 84 percent and areas of excessive eutrophication will be reduced by 35 percent, whereas decreases in particulates will result in approximately 47,500 fewer premature deaths in Europe alone.[42] Although 31 countries signed the initial protocol in 1999, it did not enter into force until May 17, 2005, when Portugal became the 16th signatory to ratify. Currently, there are 20 countries, including the United States, that are party to the Gothenburg Protocol.[43]

Hazardous Waste

Another transboundary pollution problem presents itself in the form of hazardous waste. Chapter 8 discussed the regulations surrounding hazardous waste disposal in the United States, but hazardous waste disposal in the international community presents even larger problems. Many more-developed countries find it more convenient to ship their wastes to less-developed countries so that the more-developed country does not have to deal with the hassles of proper disposal. In addition, many countries are running out of storage space for hazardous waste. The main source of international law for hazardous wastes is the Basel Convention on the Control of Transboundary Movements of Hazardous Wastes and Their Disposal. This convention entered into force in 1992 and currently has 168 parties. Although the United States did sign the convention, it has not yet ratified it and is, therefore, not a party to the convention. The United States, Haiti, and Afghanistan are the only signatories that have not ratified the convention.[44]

The objectives of the Basel Convention are threefold: to minimize the generation of hazardous wastes, to dispose of such wastes as close to the source as possible, and to reduce the movement of hazardous wastes.[45] For this convention, hazardous wastes are those wastes that are toxic, poisonous, explosive, corrosive, flammable, eco-toxic, or infectious. Parties may indicate that they will not accept certain forms of hazardous wastes if exported to them, and other parties must respect this decision. In addition, importing parties are bound not to accept hazardous waste if they feel such waste could not be properly disposed of in their country. Special protection for developing countries was provided in the text of the Basel Convention as the parties recognized that many less-developed countries do not have the capabilities to accept hazardous waste for disposal. Parties to the Basel Convention may not export hazardous wastes for disposal to areas south of 60°S latitude. All parties to the Basel Convention must dispose of hazardous wastes in an "environmentally sound manner." The convention defines this phrase as management that takes "all practicable steps to ensure that hazardous wastes or other wastes are managed in a manner which will protect human health and the environment against the adverse effects which may result from such wastes."[46]

One major concern is dismantling and recycling of ships. Ship recycling can recover hundreds of tons of steel that can be reused. However, large ships can contain tons of PCBs, asbestos, old fuel oil, and other hazardous materials. Towing the ships across international waters poses a large environmental risk, because the ships are in poor physical condition. Furthermore, the ships may be dismantled over water, as opposed to a dry dock. The ship-dismantling industry was based in Europe in the 1970s, but increasing costs to meeting environmental and occupational safety requirements caused the industry to move to Asia.[47] Now, most ship dismantling takes place in India, China, Bangladesh, Pakistan, and Turkey. There are frequent violations to the Basel Convention guidelines for ship dismantling. The Basel Action Network and Greenpeace, among other environmental groups, wage legal battles against shipowners who violate the guidelines. There is also concern regarding environmental justice: shipowners from wealthy countries have their ships dismantled in poorer countries, and the toxic waste becomes the environmental problem of the poorer country.

Recent additions to the Basel Convention include the Basel Ban Amendment that prohibits the export of any hazardous wastes from the EU, countries in the Organization for Economic Cooperation and Development (OECD), and Liechtenstein. There is controversy regarding when it will enter into force. Originally 82 countries were present when the Basel Ban was adopted in 1995, and it was determined that three-fourths of the parties present need to ratify the amendment before it enters into force. Currently, the 62 countries required have ratified the amendment. However, in 2004, the UN Office of Legal Affairs determined that ratification is dependent upon three-fourths of all of the signatories of the original Basel Convention. That would require 126 countries of the total 168 signatories. Just before publication, the issue is still unresolved and the Basel Ban is still not in force.[48]

Another addition to the Basel Convention is the 1999 Protocol on Liability and Compensation, developed in response to concerns over the inability to pay for damages. It establishes rules concerning liability and compensation for damages caused by accidental spills of hazardous waste during importation, exportation, or disposal. This protocol is not yet in force. Currently, 13 parties have ratified it, and under previous guidelines only seven more parties would be required to put the protocol into force. However, how the conflict regarding the Basel Ban ratification is resolved could affect when and how the Liability Protocol comes into force.[49]

As the book is going to print, the Basel Convention is planning to meet in Nairobi, Kenya, for the Eighth meeting of the convention. During the next 10 years, the Basel Convention will emphasize enforcement of the commitments agreed to by parties and the minimization of hazardous waste generation.[50] The convention will promote the use of cleaner technologies, monitor illegal waste trafficking, assist developing nations with their commitments, and develop centers of technology transfer between countries.[51] Convention of the Party: The agenda will focus on appropriate management of electronic wastes, including end of life computers and other electronic equipment, and will establish best practice guidelines.

Persistent Organic Pollutants

POPs are a particularly problematic form of pollution. These compounds resist degradation, bioaccumulate, are highly toxic to both people and animals, and have the ability to travel long distances. POPs have been linked to nervous and immune system damage, reproductive and developmental disorders, and various forms of cancer. For instance, DDT, although never used at either of the poles, can be found in the tissues of penguins. Both LRTAP and the Basel Convention address POPs, as does the Rotterdam Convention, discussed in Chapter 7, but these conventions address POPs only secondarily and in relation to their main focus. Recognizing the need for a treaty on POPs, UNEP started negotiations for such a treaty in 1998. The signing of the Stockholm Convention on

POPs took place in May 2001 and went into force in 2003 with a $20 million gift from Canada to help developing countries reduce POPs. There are currently 151 signatories, and 133 have ratified and are party to the convention. The United States has signed but not ratified this convention.[52]

The POPs' Convention has sent an encouraging message to the environmental community, because the final text included references to the polluter pays principle and the need for precautionary measures in the environmental arena, and prohibited or severely restricted the production and use of nine of the most harmful POPs: aldrin, chlordane, dieldrin, endrin, heptachlor, hexochlorobenzene, mirex, PCBs, and toxaphene. DDT use has been restricted to disease vector control for health in countries that suffer from outbreaks of malaria, with the ultimate goal being the elimination of DDT production and use. Parties must work to minimize total anthropogenic releases of POPs also with the goal of ultimate elimination. Parties must also take appropriate measures to deal with the disposal of waste containing POPs such that the waste is handled in an environmentally sound manner and the POP content is destroyed or transformed irreversibly.

CHOICE OF FORUMS

A question may arise when considering how countries address what they view as harm caused to them by another country: Where should such a case be brought? Earlier we made reference to the fact that one of the problems of international law is its lack of an effective forum for both dispute resolution and the subsequent enforcement of any judgment that may be obtained. That problem is reaffirmed in our examination of the alternative forums in which transboundary pollution disputes may be brought.

Whenever one thinks of resolving a transboundary pollution dispute, the first forum that comes to mind is the International Court of Justice. The International Court of Justice has the jurisdiction to decide cases that are submitted to it. In addition, the court may render advisory opinions at the request of the General Assembly or any other competent body of the UN. One obvious problem is that when one party is the transgressor, that party is obviously going to be reluctant to submit the dispute to the court. If the court is asked to render a nonbinding advisory opinion, the effect of that advice is likely to be nil, especially if the opinion suggests the payment of reparations. The rarity of disputes coming before this forum is reflected by the low number of opinions rendered by this court. From 1946 to 2003 only 104 cases were submitted, resulting in 63 judgments, more than 300 orders, and 25 advisory opinions.[53]

Even if a judgment is rendered, enforcement is difficult. The UN Security Council can, "if it deems necessary, make recommendations or decide upon measures to be taken to give effect to the judgment."[54]

However, because of the uncertainty of this clause, the Security Council has been reluctant to take action under it. Therefore, states have felt fairly free simply to ignore the judgments of the International Court of Justice.

Perhaps the most effective forum for resolution of these disputes is the court of the nation in which the harmful conduct took place. The major problem addressed by this approach is that there exists an effective means of enforcement. The power of the state lies behind the judgment. This approach, however, is most likely to be effective when the victim state is suing a private party residing in the offending state rather than actually suing the state itself.

The UNEP Draft Principles of Conduct express a preference for the use of national courts for the resolution of transboundary pollution problems. Principle 14 provides as follows:

> States should endeavor, in accordance with their legal systems and where appropriate, on a basis agreed by them, to provide persons in other states who have been or may be adversely affected by environmental damage resulting from the utilizations of shared resources with equivalent access and treatment in the same judicial and administrative proceedings and make available to them the same remedies as are available to persons within their own jurisdiction who may have been or may be similarly situated.

The UN OECD, in its 1977 Recommendation for Implementation of a Regime of Equal Right of Access and Non-Discrimination in Relation to Transfrontier Pollution, reflects a similar view. The OECD recommends that equal access to information be given to foreign nations, as well as equal access to all public authorities, courts, and administrative agencies. In private treaties, some nations are adopting this equal access approach with respect to transboundary pollution. One example of such a treaty is the Convention on Protection of the Environment, the so-called Nordic Convention, entered into by Sweden, Denmark, Finland, and Norway. Article 3 of the convention provides that any person who is affected or may be affected by a nuisance caused by environmentally harmful activities in another contracting state shall have the right to bring before the appropriate court or administrative authority of that state the question of the permissibility of measures to prevent damage and to appeal against the decision of the court or administrative agency to the same extent and on the same terms as a legal entity of the state in which the activities are being carried out.

An alternative forum to the courts themselves is the use of international arbitration. To make the decision binding, disputants enter into a compromise or agreement that sets forth the subject matter of the dispute, the method for selecting the arbitration panel, and the procedures to be followed during the arbitration. Again, however, because of the need for an agreement to arbitrate, the most hotly contested cases may not come before

the arbitrator. In addition, once the award is made, if one of the parties disagrees with the award and refuses to comply, there is no mechanism for
enforcement.

A final, and perhaps most common, way of resolving conflicts arising
out of transboundary pollution is diplomacy. Diplomatic solutions are
generally compromises brought about through negotiations between the
countries in conflict. Frequently they are aided by representatives from an
international or regional organization, so that the procedure for resolution
in fact becomes a form of mediation.

THE GLOBAL COMMONS

Recall that the global commons refers to those areas of Earth that cannot
easily be partitioned and those resources that belong to no one but preserve
and maintain the lives of us all. If we all simply use the commons without
taking care to preserve it, the global commons will be destroyed. The primary problems associated with the global commons have been discussed
earlier in this chapter. Here, we consider attempts to solve some of these
problems. As you will see, the primary approach has been through multilateral treaties.

Destruction of the Ozone Layer

Although this problem has been considered a national problem, it is, in
fact, global in nature. The United States could totally ban the use of ozone-
destroying CFCs, but if other nations did not follow suit, the ozone layer
would still be destroyed. We cannot separate "our" portion of the ozone
layer.

The worldwide response to ozone depletion has been remarkably swift.
On September 16, 1987, 24 nations and the EC signed the Montreal
Protocol on Substances That Deplete the Ozone Layer. The primary objec-
tives of the treaty were as follows:

1. In 1987, to hold increases of ozone-depleting CFCs and halons to
   10 percent of 1986 levels
2. Within 4 more years, to reduce the production of CFCs and halons to
   80 percent of 1986 levels
3. By July 1, 1999, to reduce CFC and halon production to 50 percent of
   1986 levels

The protocol provided an exception for developing countries. The
treaty also provided that there would be no trade in controlled substances
with any nation not a party to the treaty. A Montreal Protocol Multilateral
Fund was also set up in conjunction with the treaty. This fund provides aid to
assist developing nations in the transition from ozone-depleting chemicals.
At a June 1990 meeting in London, the parties to the protocol agreed to
phase out CFCs, carbon tetrachloride, and nonessential uses of halons by
the year 2000 and the use of methyl chloroform by 2005.

Between November 23 and 25, 1992, representatives from the over 100 signatories to the Montreal Protocol held the Fourth Meeting of the Parties to the Montreal Protocol on Substances That Deplete the Ozone Layer. Ultimately, the parties agreed to speed up the dates for reduction of CFCs. They agreed that by 1994, there would be reduction of CFC production by 75 percent of 1986 levels, and a complete elimination of CFC production by January 1, 1996.

At that meeting, representatives agreed that there was a need to look closely at the substances being used as substitutes for CFCs. Most frequently used are hydrochlorofluorocarbons (HCFCs), which are not as harmful to the ozone layer as CFCs, but they do contain some chlorine and do destroy some of the stratospheric ozone. They are, therefore, not a permanent solution to the CFC problem. Some parties argued that the main goal is to eliminate the use of CFCs as quickly as possible; therefore, HCFCs need to be available as a "lesser of two evils" alternative until a better substitute can be developed.

Others argued that there already were better alternatives available, but as long as HCFCs could be used, there would be no motivation to invest in technologies to use the alternative substances. In the end, the parties agreed to

1. cap the use of HCFCs in January 1996 at a level equal to the sum of their use in 1989
2. subsequently reduce their use of HCFCs by 35 percent by 2004, by 65 percent by 2010, by 90 percent by 2015, by 99.5 percent by 2020, and by 100 percent by 2030

The late date of the final phaseout can be seen as evidence of the power of those who want to continue using the HCFCs as long as possible, primarily the United States. The United States was particularly concerned about being able to continue to use HCFCs because they play an important role in air-conditioning of big buildings.

After that meeting, there was pressure to add methyl bromide as a controlled, ozone-depleting substance. Methyl bromide is an insecticide that is primarily used to fumigate stored produce and grain, soil, and structures. Many believe that the scientific evidence of methyl bromide's ozone-depleting effects is undeniable. By far, the greatest production of that chemical is in North America, where approximately 42 percent is produced. Europe produces roughly 29 percent and Asia 22 percent.

At the 1995 meeting on the protocol, representatives agreed to phase out the use of methyl bromide in industrialized nations entirely by 2012 and to gradually phase out its use during the 15 years before that deadline. Use in developing nations was frozen in the year 2002 at annual levels equivalent to the average of the annual volume of domestic use from 1995 through 1998. Representatives also agreed to look at this issue again at the 1997 meeting. Many environmental organizations were upset by the failure of the 149 parties to the protocol to take more urgent action when, according to a UN report, the quickest and most efficient way to reduce future ozone loss would be to ban the use of this pesticide. Some scientists estimate that the chemical is 50 times more destructive to the ozone layer per atom than are CFCs.

Under the CAA, the United States was already required to phase out the domestic use and production of methyl bromide by the year 2001. However, President Clinton asked Congress to amend the CAA in such a way as not to require the complete phaseout of the insecticide until the date mandated under the Montreal Protocol. The argument of Clinton and the EPA (and, many would argue, the agribusiness interests) was that there is no guarantee that an adequate substitute for all of the chemical's uses would be found by the year 2002, and if the United States is required to cease use of this chemical before other nations are, it will put the United States at a competitive disadvantage. Other nations, however, including Austria, Finland, and Sweden have eliminated their major use of methyl bromide.

Opponents of extending the deadline argued that the effects on the ozone layer clearly justify the early deadline and that the best way to ensure that substitute products are found is by having firm, early deadlines and creating a definite market for the substitutes. Some argued that if industry had spent as much time and money on research as it did on lobbying to change the law, substitute products would already have been found. They also pointed out that farmers throughout the world were already using innovative alternatives to methyl bromide.

In October 1998, Congress attached a rider to the Fiscal Year 1999 Appropriations bill that amended the CAA to change the date of the methyl bromide phaseout. The phaseout plan scheduled gradual reduction of use: 50 percent of the 1991 level, then 70 percent in 2004, and 100 percent in 2005. These changes were meant to "harmonize" the U.S. phaseout of methyl bromide with the Montreal Protocol phaseout schedule. However, the EPA reports that methyl bromide is still being used in agriculture under "critical use" exemptions for those in agriculture who claim they have no "technically or economically feasible alternatives." Applications for critical use is steadily decreasing, as well as the inventory of methyl bromide currently held by U.S. companies, but use will be allowed by the EPA until at least 2008.[55]

Then, in 2003, the Bush administration requested broad exemptions from the ban on methyl bromide for use on strawberry fields, golf courses, and by honey producers. An international panel approved the exemption request because possible substitutes did not yet exist to replace methyl bromide. Many environmentalists are fearful that too many exceptions and delays might undermine the treaty in the future.[56]

A few weeks before the 1998 meeting on the Montreal Protocol, scientists reported the largest Antarctic ozone "hole" ever recorded—equal to an area more than 25 times the size of Egypt. This discovery probably weighed heavily in the minds of delegates for the parties to the protocol. At the 1998 meeting, parties faced the new challenge of making policies to protect the ozone layer consistent with the ongoing efforts to reduce climate change.

Gases that are used as ozone-safe replacements for CFCs contribute to global warming and are thus targeted under the 1997 Kyoto Protocol for reduction. (The Kyoto Conference will be discussed in greater detail later in the chapter.) The parties agreed to strengthen measures to close down CFC production facilities. Furthermore, the parties considered the problem of noncompliance. The GEF will continue to assist countries that have not yet met the benchmark standards; however, stricter measures will be imposed in the future.

Human-Induced Climate Change

The problem of human-induced climate change (global warming) was discussed briefly in Chapter 5. Figure 11-4 depicts the contributions of various nations to global warming. As you can see from the figure, carbon dioxide is the primary contributor to global warming, and the United States is a primary source. In May 1992, the problem of greenhouse gas emissions was first addressed globally by the signing of the 1992 United Nations Framework Convention on Climate Change by representatives of 154 nations. This treaty attempted to reduce the level of emissions of greenhouse gases (carbon dioxide, methane, and nitrous oxide) by developed nations back to 1990 levels by the year 2000. Signatories to the treaty agreed to set up a procedure for monitoring scientific advances so that modifications could be

FIGURE 11-4 Regional Contributions to Global Warming

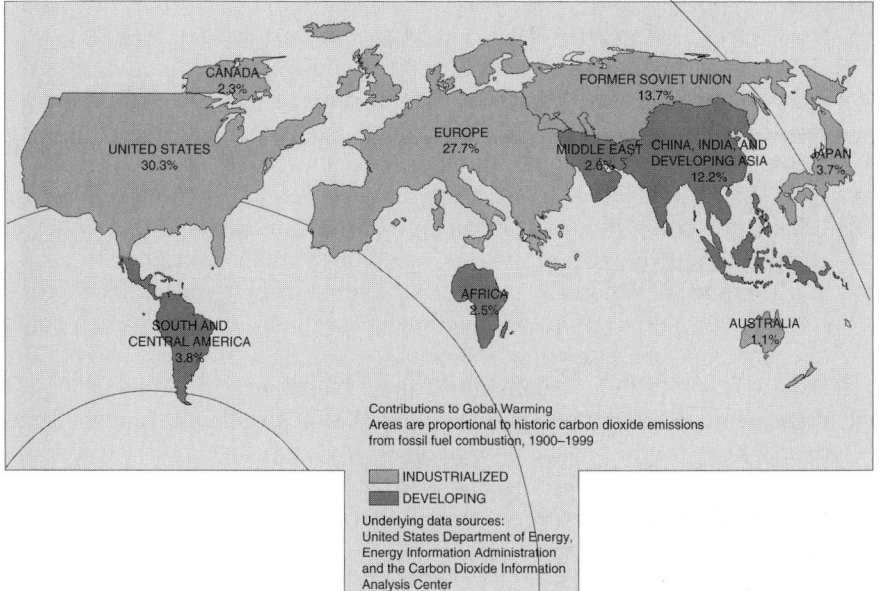

Source: World Resource Institute. *http://www.wri.org/climate/contributions_map.html* (January 15, 2004).

undertaken if necessary. Developing nations were to adopt policies to limit the increase in their emissions, although these emissions will still increase substantially, and developed nations will provide financial and technical aid to developing countries.

This treaty was actually much less stringent than originally proposed; many environmentalists argued that the treaty had been gutted by the United States. President Bush had used this treaty for leverage to bargain with other nations at the Earth Summit in Rio (discussed later in this chapter), where the treaty was one of the main focuses. Bush agreed to attend this major international conference on the environment only if stipulations in the original treaty that absolute curbs on carbon dioxide levels would be enforced were removed. Consequently, the treaty signed by President Bush in late 1992 created a nonbinding goal of reducing green house gas emissions and went into effect in March of 1994.

Since the ratification of the treaty, the signatories have met annually to evaluate and create methods of slowing human-induced climate change. The most famous of these meetings, in Kyoto, Japan, in 1997, produced the legally binding Kyoto Protocol, discussed in the following section.

Recent projections suggest that most expanded production will come from coal, oil, and natural gas, especially in rapidly growing countries such as China and India. If current practices continue, renewable energy sources, such as solar and wind energy, are expected to provide only 2–4 percent of global energy supplies from 1990 to 2020. Consequently, these energy projections suggest that greenhouse gases will continue to increase.[57]

Kyoto Protocol

Even though countries agreed to limit gases thought to cause climate change at the United Nations Conference on Environment and Development's (UNCED) Rio Summit in 1992 discussed in further detail below, many nations were falling short of the target to reduce emissions by 2000. In an attempt to address this noncompliance, representatives of 150 countries met in Kyoto, Japan, in late 1997, to create a measure legally committing developed nations to bring down their emissions to certain levels by specific dates. The parties to the convention agreed that developed countries would have a legally binding commitment to reduce their collective emissions of six greenhouse gases by an average of 5 percent from 1990 levels by 2008–2012. Sweden, central and eastern Europe, and the EU would reduce emissions by 8 percent. The United States, Canada, Hungary, Japan, and Poland would reduce emissions by 6 percent, whereas Russia, New Zealand, and the Ukraine would be expected to stabilize their emissions. Some countries, such as Norway, Australia, and Iceland could increase their emissions. "Demonstrable progress" must have been made by 2005. Each country's emission targets must be met by 2008–2012.

The protocol was opened for signature on March 16, 1998, and entered into force when ratified by at least 55 countries, which account for at least

55 percent of global emissions. In 2004, Russia ratified the treaty, and the Kyoto Protocol become effective on February 16, 2005.

As of 2006, 166 countries, accounting for 61 percent of global emissions, have ratified the protocol, including the EU, Canada, Japan, China, Brazil, and India. Although the United States signed in November 1998, the Bush administration indicated that the United States would not ratify the treaty.

One component of the Kyoto Protocol allows international emissions trading. In addition, the protocol contains a component called "Clean Development Mechanism." This mechanism allows companies in the developed world to use emission reductions from project activities in developing countries to contribute to their compliance with greenhouse gas reduction targets. However, one of the more controversial components of the protocol is the fact that the developing countries are not bound to emission targets.

In November 1998, delegates met in Buenos Aires to establish deadlines for finalizing work on the Kyoto mechanisms as well as compliance issues and policies. They established an action plan with timetables. Hope for more progress in nailing down the specifics of the Kyoto Protocol centered on the November 2000 Conference of the Parties at the Hague. The press kit for the event identified five "crunch" issues that this conference needed to decide: operating practices of flexibility mechanisms, such as the clean development mechanism mentioned above, clearer definition of sinks, framework for North–South cooperation, programs for adversely impacted countries, and rules for determining compliance with the protocol.[58] Obviously, these are important issues that many countries feel must be decided before they will sign the protocol. However, the tension between the United States and the EU could not be resolved during the 2-week conference, and the talks ended in failure; many felt the United States and the EU were to blame.

In July 2001, delegates returned to work on the Kyoto Protocol in another conference in Bonn, Germany. Just a few months before this conference, President Bush indicated that the United States would not ratify the protocol because it was "fatally flawed," as described in Chapter 5. Perhaps, because of U.S. opposition and the need to ensure that the entire treaty did not collapse, delegates in Bonn were able to agree on a more detailed protocol. With the United States only a side consideration, Japan emerged as the key player in the negotiations because it is the largest economy after the United States. The new protocol requires 38 industrialized nations to reduce their combined annual carbon dioxide emissions to 5.2 percent below 1990 levels by 2012 or face reducing emissions by even larger amounts in the period after 2012. The new agreement clarifies the emissions trading process but also allows nations to take credits for planting trees to absorb carbon dioxide rather than forcing them to actually reduce emissions.

The protocol must be approved by the most-polluting countries, which is difficult without the United States. However, the 36 developed nations that supported the new language emit more carbon dioxide combined than the

United States does.[59] To some, the success of this conference proved that the EU can and will lead the world when the United States refuses to do so.[60]

In 2003, Russia created serious doubt in the Kyoto Protocol's future when President Putin's economic advisor signaled that Russia would not ratify the treaty. Putin then announced that Russia may ratify the treaty, but only if it proves to be in their best interest. Because the United States has indicated it will not ratify the protocol, Russia's ratification was necessary for the protocol to go into effect, because Russia accounts for 18 percent of global emissions.

Enforcement of the Kyoto Protocol by the United Nations Framework Convention on Climate Change is most demanding of developed countries. Failure to meet emission standards requires the offending country to make up the difference plus an additional 30 percent.[61] The Kyoto Protocol is also discussed in detail in Chapter 5.

Marine Pollution

As with most global commons problems, the primary approach to protecting the oceans and seas has been through the use of treaties, with one of the more important treaties being the 1982 Convention on the Law of the Sea. Restatement (Third) of Foreign Relations Law of the United States, Part VI, the Law of the Environment (1988), reiterates some of the important aspects of this convention. Pollution control is particularly important in oceans. Experts at the world's first Marine Mammal Science Conference said pollution, not hunting, threatens whales most. Record levels of human-made pollution are threatening some species with extinction.

Section 603, State Responsibility for Marine Pollution, obligates a state to "adopt laws and regulations to prevent, reduce and control any significant pollution of the marine environment that are no less effective than generally accepted international rules and standards," and to "ensure compliance with the foregoing by ships flying its flag, imposing adequate penalties on the captain or owner of the ship that violates such rules." Part (2) of Section 603 provides that "a state is obligated to take, individually and jointly with other states, such measures as may be necessary, to the extent practicable under the circumstances, to prevent, reduce, and control pollution causing or threatening to cause significant injury to the marine environment."

Remedies for marine pollution caused by violating Section 603 are given in Section 604, which provides that any state responsible to another state for violating Section 603 is subject to general interstate remedies "to prevent, reduce, or terminate the activity threatening or causing pollution and to pay reparation for the injury caused." The state must ensure that a remedy is available through its legal system "to provide prompt and adequate compensation or other relief for an injury to private interests caused by pollution of the marine environment."

This section gives coastal states the additional authority to detain and institute proceedings against foreign states navigating its territorial seas and violating one of the state's antipollution laws or violating international antipollution laws that resulted in a discharge that caused or threatened a major injury to the state. A port state may institute proceedings against a foreign ship that voluntarily entered its port for "a violation of that states anti-pollution laws . . . if the violation occurred in the port state's territorial sea or exclusive economic zone"; or for "a discharge in violation of applicable international anti-pollution rules and standards that occurred beyond the limits of national jurisdiction of any state." A port state also has the obligation, as far as practicable, under Section 604(c), to investigate whether a ship that voluntarily entered its port was responsible for a discharge in violation of applicable antipollution rules and standards, when asked to do so either by the states in whose waters the discharge allegedly occurred or by the flag state.

Another important international treaty dealing with marine pollution is the International Convention for the Prevention of Pollution from Ships of 1973, as modified by its protocol of 1978, and generally referred to as the Marine Pollution (MARPOL) Convention. The convention is divided into six sections, called annexes, with each attempting to regulate a different potential problem: pollution by oil (Annex I), noxious liquid substances carried in bulk (Annex II); harmful substances carried in packages (Annex III), ship sewage (Annex IV), and ship garbage (Annex V); and air pollution from ships (Annex VI). Annexes I and II have been ratified by 127 countries and thereby regulate nearly 97 percent of the world's merchant fleet. Annex III has been ratified by 110 countries, regulating nearly 80–84 percent of world tonnage. Annex IV, ratified by 95 countries as of early 2004, went into force in September of 2003, regulating 53 percent of world tonnage. Annex V has been ratified by 115 countries, regulating approximately 90 percent of world tonnage. Annex VI, the newest annex to the convention, had been ratified by only 12 countries as of 2004 and is not yet in force. Many of the treaty's directives involve standards for design and equipment. For example, Annex I requires ballast tanks of all oil-carrying vessels to be strategically located around the outer periphery of the hull of the vessel. Discharges are also regulated under the MARPOL Convention. For example, oil tankers may discharge no more than 60 liters of oil per mile, and discharges must take place at least 50 miles from land. Under the convention the disposal of plastics at sea is completely prohibited. The disposal of other types of garbage is restricted to certain distances from land. Domestic garbage cannot be dumped within 3 miles of land, and if it is to be dumped within 12 miles, it must first be sent through a grinder.

Ocean dumping is regulated by the London Convention on the Prevention of Marine Pollution by Dumping of Wastes and Other Matter, effective since December 29, 1972. This treaty prohibits the deliberate dumping of high-level radioactive waste at sea. Other compounds that parties may wish to dump are divided into annexes and regulated accordingly: Matter from Annex I cannot be dumped. Matter listed in Annex II can be dumped only with a "special permit," the criteria for which are specified in Annex III. All matter not mentioned in Annexes I or II may be dumped with a prior general permit.

Land-based pollution, in general, is simply regulated by the state of origin. Article 207 of the UN Law of the Sea Convention, however, does oblige parties to adopt necessary laws to prevent and control land-based sources of marine pollution.

By 1991, the United States had ratified three additional treaties that are important for protecting the marine environment. The first was the International Convention on Oil Pollution Preparedness, Response, and Cooperation; this treaty establishes a worldwide network of expertise and resources to prevent and respond to oil spills. The second treaty, the 1989 Salvage Convention, provides compensation for persons who take steps to preserve the environment while salvaging a ship or cargo at sea. The third treaty was the International Convention on Standards of Training, Certification, and Watch Keeping for Seafarers, which sets standards for ship officers and crew so that accidents will be less likely to occur.

PRESERVATION OF BIOLOGICAL DIVERSITY

The primary way that we are attempting to preserve biological diversity is through treaties. See Table 11-2 for a listing of some of these treaties.

Convention on International Trade in Endangered Species of Fauna and Flora

The Convention on International Trade in Species of Endangered Wild Fauna and Flora (CITES) has been characterized by some as "perhaps the most successful of all international treaties concerned with the conservation of wildlife."[62] Ratified by 164 nations as of 2004, the treaty is designed to prohibit the international trafficking in wildlife species and products that are endangered. Under CITES, species are listed under Appendices I, II, and III. Appendix I species are endangered, and trade in these species will be authorized under only the most extraordinary circumstances. Appendix II contains species that are not now threatened with extinction but may become so if traded. Appendix III consists of species that a nation protects within its jurisdiction and is seeking the cooperation of other nations to protect that species from exploitation. Only under extremely strict conditions specified in CITES can a listed species be traded. Enforcement is left to the signatory parties.

Although CITES looks good, the problem with it lies in its enforcement, which is almost nil. Studies of enforcement of the treaty have found that most inspectors in signatory nations are not trained well enough to be able to enforce the treaty.

In the United States, CITES is implemented through the Endangered Species Act, which many call the most stringent environmental statute in the world. As explained in Chapter 10, it prohibits the import, export, sale, or

TABLE 11-2 Treaties That Help Preserve the Global Commons and Biological Diversity

Treaty	Purpose
Convention on Regulation of Antarctic Mineral Resource Activity	Regulate exploitation of mineral resources in Antarctica
Declaration on Arctic Environmental Protection	Encourage cooperation in areas of pollution, marine environmental protection, emergency response, conservation of flora and fauna, and research and monitoring in the Arctic
Convention for the Protection of the Environment in the South Pacific	Encourage cooperation in addressing water treatment programs, management of coastal zones and wastes, lagoon and coral reef restoration, and climate change issues
International Whaling Convention	Phase out commercial whaling by 1986, except when meat and products are used for local consumption by aborigines
Treaty for Amazonian Cooperation	Obtain agreement among eight countries with territories in Amazon to balance economic growth and environment protection
Convention in International Trade in Endangered Species	Prohibit international trade of endangered plants and animals
United Nations Convention on Biodiversity	Stimulate the transfer of technology and sharing of benefits of technology to preserve biodiversity

shipment of any endangered or threatened species in the course of a commercial activity, as well as the possession of any species taken in violation of the act. Only with a special permit can one cause any harm to an endangered species or its habitat. The act is enforced by the U.S. FWS with respect to animals and by the Animal and Plant Health Inspection Service with respect to plants.

Today, 1,006 domestic species are listed in the act as threatened or endangered. Another 279 are candidates for listing, and four species are proposed for candidate status. The FWS is continuously studying the species list and updates the list on the service Web site daily. In addition, during 1995, Congress placed a moratorium on the listing of new species, as mentioned previously. Since the law's passage, 17 species have recovered because of being protected; nine listed species have become extinct.[63]

The act is up for reauthorization and is generating considerable debate. Some argue that there is not enough money to save all species, as the act tries to do, and that under the new law certain species should be targeted so that the money can be used more efficiently to save the targeted species. Many argue that the way the decision as to what biological species or sub-species are to be preserved must be revised. Currently, subspecies and even distinct populations of subspecies may be listed. This issue was raised when the preservation of one of 25 subspecies of the red squirrel halted the construction of an observatory. Some people are even arguing that the species-by-species approach is wrong; instead, they argue, the focus should be on creating and preserving habitats. Given all these conflicting views, it should be an interesting reauthorization process.

Man and the Biosphere Program

UNESCO has tried another approach to preserving our biological diversity. In 1976, UNESCO's Man and the Biosphere (MAB) program became operational. Participating countries create and protect biosphere reserves—protected areas designed to combine conservation and sustainable use. In the center of a reserve is a core area where there is minimal disturbance of an ecosystem characteristic of a major type of natural environment. This core is surrounded by a buffer zone in which activities are managed in ways that will help protect the core. Outside the buffer zone is the transition area, which combines conservation and sustainable activities such as forestry and recreation. There are currently 440 biosphere reserves in 97 countries. The United States established its first reserve in 1974 and now has 47.

Debt for Nature Swaps

One new way to try to protect diversity is an innovative contractual arrangement called debt for nature swaps. In simplest terms, a debt for nature swap occurs when conservation parks or sustainable use areas are set aside and legally protected by a foreign government in exchange for which a portion of that country's foreign debt is canceled. An intermediary group, generally a conservation organization, facilitates the swap by paying off the debt at a deeply discounted rate.

The first such debt for nature swap occurred in Bolivia in 1987. Conservation International (CI), a nonprofit organization, obtained a $100,000 grant from the Frank Weeden Foundation, a charitable organization in California that donates money exclusively to environmental causes. CI used this grant to purchase $650,000 of discounted Bolivian debt from a Swiss bank. In exchange for the $650,000 face-value debt from CI, the Bolivian government agreed to establish three conservation and sustainable use areas consisting of 3.7 million acres, adjacent to an existing biosphere reserve.

Three conservation organizations are most frequently involved in swaps: CI, the Nature Conservancy, and the World Wildlife Foundation. Of the first 22 swaps, these organizations engineered 19 of them, raising $17 million in private funds to retire $99 million worth of debt through these first swaps. To date, approximately $1 billion in funding has been generated to aid the environment and relieve Third World debt in 30 countries.[64]

The typical debt for nature contract attempts to achieve its environmental goals by specifying the environmental activities that are to be undertaken by the host government. Many include provisions allowing the conservation organization to undertake specific activities on the newly protected area. The debtor nation is usually required to set aside a specific fund of money to be used in managing the protected area.

These projects seem to have potential, but, again, the major problem is their enforceability. The developing country may mismanage the funds set aside for protecting the area. The host country may simply be incompetent and not manage the area appropriately. Or, in some less stable nations, the government that agreed to the swap may be overthrown and the new government unwilling to carry out the contract.

If the host country breaches the agreement, the organization that retired the debt may always sue for breach of contract in the host country. That country's willingness to rule against its own government is somewhat unlikely, however. Alternatively, the conservation group may hold out the threat of refusing to carry out any further swaps with the nation in question if compliance is not attained. Another possibility is to include in the contract a provision that if compliance by the host country is lacking, that country becomes liable to the conservation organization for the amount of debt retired by the organization.

Another problem with the debt for nature swaps is that their use on a large scale may be impossible. Part of the reason why these swaps can be done is the willingness of banks to discount debt. Banks may do so when they feel they will never get full payment anyway. But their willingness to discount loans is not unlimited.

Despite these potential problems, many believe debt for nature swaps are an important tool for retaining biodiversity. First, when successful, land that otherwise might have been developed is set aside. Second, deforestation in areas other than the swapped region should be prevented because one of the reasons for deforestation is that developing countries are often forced to exploit their natural resources to service their debt. Third, the economies of Third World nations have been found to benefit significantly from the nature swaps. Without the massive debt, much exploitation may be unnecessary. Because of the success of the program throughout the 1990s, the UN is expanding the program into new areas, most recently setting up funds in Africa. Because swaps are new, it is too early to speculate as to their effectiveness. For now, we can only wait and see.

MADRID PROTOCOL

The Protocol on Environmental Protection to the Antarctic, also known as the Madrid Protocol, was created in 1991 to designate Antarctica as a natural reserve, preserve the unique biodiversity, and to prevent further environmental degradation. The protocol entered into effect in 1998 and governs activities that take place in Antarctica. For example, the protocol requires the preparation of environmental impact assessments, waste management plans, prevention of marine pollution plans, and an environmental emergency plan before any activity is approved. As of 2006, 32 countries, including the United States, are party to the protocol, which has been claimed a success in preventing harm to the biodiversity of the Antarctic.

THE FUTURE OF INTERNATIONAL ENVIRONMENTAL LAW

RIO SUMMIT

From June 1 through June 12, 1992, delegates from more than 120 nations met in Rio de Janeiro for the UNCED, commonly referred to as the Rio Summit. With 2 years of negotiations leading up to the summit, the participants in the meeting had established a lofty goal for themselves: to agree on a set of principles and conventions to set the world on a new environmental course, and perhaps someday eradicate the pollution that is threatening our planet.

Although there is no consensus on the real impact, if any, of the summit on worldwide environmental policies, some participants are claiming that it has already been a success because, if nothing else, the 2 years of preparation brought the idea of sustainable development—progress without destruction of the environment—before hundreds of officials from developing nations. Others applauded the creation of a UN Sustainable Development Commission, modeled on the Human Rights Commission, which will use public criticism and pressure to hold governments accountable for achieving the goals laid out at the summit.

Five documents came out of the summit. Whether the agreements will have any long-range impact on international environmental law depends on the agreements' ratification and enforcement.

Agenda 21

Agenda 21, an 800-page blueprint for sustainable development, covers a diverse range of issues, including hazardous waste, human health, ocean pollution, and advancement for women. The heart of this document is a program of aid to Third World nations to help them clean up their pollution and replant their forests, at an estimated cost of $125 billion per year. In 2002, the UN's Economic and Social Council reviewed the implementation of Agenda 21 and reported a gap in four areas of implementation. First, efforts to create sustainable development have been fragmented and continually fall short of set goals. Second, the unsustainable levels of consumption have not significantly been altered since the delegates first met in 1992. Third, the policies and approaches to finance, investment, and technology concerning sustainable development lack overall coherence. Finally, the financial resources needed to better implement Agenda 21 have not been forthcoming, and Third World debt continues to worsen.[65] However, despite these implementation problems, Agenda 21 remains a valid and important plan for international progress for some of the most important international issues of the 21st century.

Rio Declaration

The Rio Declaration is a 6-page statement containing 27 principles that calls for a link between environmental protection and development, spelling out the "rights" of poor nations to develop in responsible ways. This document was designed to encourage new levels of cooperation among states.

Biodiversity

The agreement that aroused the most debate in the United States was the biodiversity agreement, the United Nations Convention on Biological Diversity. This treaty requires signatory nations to establish policies to slow the loss of plant and animal species. Developed nations with technology will cooperate with nondeveloped nations that have the diverse species of rain forest flora and fauna to develop new pharmaceuticals. President Bush created an uproar among environmentalists by opposing the treaty on the grounds that it would not adequately protect biotechnology and other patents and would excessively regulate the biotechnology industry. He also argued that the treaty was unnecessary because the U.S. Endangered Species Act was already providing much greater protection than would be provided under this treaty. When President Clinton took office, he said that he would sign the biodiversity treaty, and on June 30, 1993, he did so, after having drawn up interpretive language that he claimed would protect U.S. patents.

The battle for ratification of the treaty in the House and Senate, however, has been a long one. As of 2004, the treaty still had not been ratified. Its primary opponents initially came from organizations of cattlemen and ranchers, who feared that signing the treaty would make it more difficult for Congress to weaken the Endangered Species Act. Additional opposition came from firms in the biotechnology industry, who feared loss of some of their patent rights, although they have since changed their position and now support ratification of the treaty. Although the treaty still awaits ratification in the United States, it went into effect for parties on December 29, 1993. As of 2004, 188 nations and the EU have ratified the convention.

In 2000, parties agreed to an addition to the convention known as the Cartagena Protocol on Biosafety. The main purpose of the protocol was to address the growing concern about genetically modified organisms and biotechnology. The Biosafety Protocol ensures that countries have the necessary information before deciding to allow such organisms into their nation and establishes a clearinghouse of information on genetically modified organisms. Environmentalists were pleased with the text of the Biosafety Protocol because it made several references to the need for a precautionary approach by parties. As of mid-2004, 135 countries have signed the Biosafety Protocol and 103 have ratified it. The United States is not one of the signatories.

Forest Protection

A statement of principles called for sustainable forest management and asked nations to avoid excessive cutting of trees.

It was clear from the meeting that some changes from all nations are going to be needed if Rio's agreements are to be successfully ratified and implemented. Poor nations tended to place all blame for the world's woes on developed nations and asserted that the polluters should pay developing countries to protect their ecosystems. Clearly, the World Bank, the primary distributor of money to developing nations, will have to do a better job of integrating environment and development in its investments. Only time will tell, however, whether the world will be able to live up to the forest management goals set forth at the Rio Summit.

Climate Change

As discussed earlier in this chapter, the industrialized nations, including the United States, agreed to reduce emissions of greenhouse gases to 1990 levels by the year 2000. Developing nations are to develop policies to control their emissions. By the end of 2000, there were 186 parties to the convention, which entered into force on March 21, 1994. The convention agreed upon at the Rio Summit was followed by the Kyoto Protocol, discussed previously, which now faces an uncertain future.

ENVIRONMENTALISM AND TRADE

Traditionally, the only treaties environmentalists really worried about were those designed to address specific environmental problems, such as the treaties we have examined in this chapter. Increasingly, however, some environmental groups are beginning to see the value of having input into international trade agreements, although not surprisingly, not all environmental organizations agree about how environmental interests can best be protected through these treaties.

The negotiations of two treaties designed to make trade freer—the 103-nation General Agreement on Tariffs and Trade (GATT) [initially negotiated almost 50 years ago and strengthened by several renegotiations, culminating in the formation of the World Trade Organization (WTO)] and the North American Free Trade Agreement (NAFTA)—have caught the interest of environmentalists. One issue that negotiators must resolve is the potential conflict that arises when a nation's "green" laws have an adverse effect on commerce. For example, Germany passed a law requiring that all packaging be recyclable. Because other nations do not require recyclable (and, thus, more expensive) packaging, an extra burden is placed on foreign competitors that do not do a significant amount of business in Germany yet would probably, for efficiency, have to change the packaging of their products or leave the market.

The key provision of GATT related to this issue is the statement that nations have the right to enact any environmental, health, and safety laws they choose, as long as the laws are "necessary" and are the "least trade-restrictive" way of resolving the problem. In addition, NAFTA requires that the laws be based on "scientific principles" and "risk assessment." Because U.S. laws are often based on political compromise as well as science, one can see how some of this nation's laws might not meet these standards.

In fact, the United States has already lost two environmental law battles under GATT. GATT disputes are resolved by a GATT panel of trade judges. In 1991, such a panel ruled that the United States violated GATT by banning the importation of tuna caught in the type of net that kills dolphins, a ban required by the Marine Mammal Protection Act. Fortunately, the United States and Mexico, the nation challenging the ban, reached a settlement satisfactory to both. But this adverse ruling was sufficient to alarm many environmentalists, as was the similar ruling in 1993 against a U.S. boycott of tuna caught by fishing methods that killed dolphins.

A subsequent ruling in a 1994 case, however, is cited by some as evidence that environmentalists need not fear the strengthening of GATT under the recently negotiated WTO. In 1993, the EU challenged the 1975 CAFE standards established under the CAA, as well as a 1978 "gas guzzler" tax on automobiles that taxed those vehicles that had a fuel efficiency of less than 22.5 miles per gallon. These laws hit the German Mercedes-Benz corporation particularly hard. The laws were held not to violate the GATT.

Mickey Kantor, U.S. trade representative at the time, saw the decision as evidence that the GATT's trade rules can be compatible with environmental protection.[66] Likewise, the director of the Yale Center for Environmental Law and Policy said that the decision "shows GATT is learning to accommodate ecological concerns."[67] However, the director of the Natural Resources Defense Council was not convinced by that decision that the agreement would not ultimately be used to bar enforcement of more stringent environmental laws.

As noted above, the GATT has undergone a number of revisions. The most significant round of negotiations, known as the Uruguay Round, was completed in 1993. This round of negotiations established the WTO, which became operational on January 1, 1995. Additional negotiations in 1994 led to the formation of the Committee on Trade and the Environment, which will operate under the auspices of the WTO. Many environmentalists saw the creation of this committee as a significant improvement in the treatment of environmental analysis under the GATT/WTO. However, there was still a great deal of concern about the wisdom of entering into this agreement.

Ralph Nader questioned the wisdom of entering into an agreement that gives substantial legislative, executive, and judicial authority, including the authority to impose sanctions to an international body in which the United

States would have equal voting power with every other nation and no veto power. Never before had the United States entered a comparable international organization without having either veto power or weighted voting.[68]

Another concern raised by Nader and many others was the wisdom of entering into an agreement with a mandate based on the supremacy of trade matters over consumer, worker, and environmental safeguards, an arrangement under which countries could not be in violation by treating the environment too harshly, but they could be subject to trade sanctions for being too protective of the environment.[69]

Some people, including Senator Max Baucus (D-MT), argue that for purposes of trade, lax environmental regulation should be seen as a governmental subsidy because it will be cheaper to produce products when a firm does not have to meet stringent environmental standards. Therefore, many argue, nations with strict environmental standards should be able to place a duty on goods made under relaxed regulations to increase their price to what it would have been without the subsidy. His position, however, is a minority position among those who negotiated the WTO.

A key issue during the Uruguay Round was that of dispute resolution. The final mechanism for dispute resolution under the agreement is viewed by many environmentalists as being inferior to the method for resolving environment/trade conflicts under NAFTA. Under the Dispute Settlement Understanding, a three-person arbitration panel hears the claim and issues a report that contains its decision. If both parties accept this report, it becomes the final decision. The parties, however, have the option of appealing the decision to the Settlement Body. A final appeal may be made to the Appellate Body (the "Supreme Court" of the WTO), and if it still upholds the decision, the party must comply with the ruling or face trade sanctions, which have not as yet been determined.

In terms of the procedures, there are a few aspects of the process that are not seen as favorable by many environmentalists. For example, although the arbitration panel may request information and technical advice from any source it deems appropriate, disputing parties cannot unilaterally call on experts to present information to the panels. An even greater concern in challenges that an environmental regulation adversely affects trade is that the burden of proof lies with the party seeking to defend the regulation. (This burden is the opposite of that included in the NAFTA provisions.)

The opportunity to examine how these processes work came up sooner than many had anticipated. On January 17, 1996, in the first complaint brought before the body since it came into existence on January 1, 1995, a WTO panel ruled against the United States in a challenge brought against the U.S. EPA's rules for implementing the Reformulated Gasoline Program. The regulations at issue required foreign refiners to use EPA baseline data for calculating necessary reductions in certain fuel components, whereas U.S. refiners could opt to use their own data rather than the more stringent EPA data. The EPA had said that it needed to require the foreign firms to use EPA data because those firms did not keep sufficient records to allow them to use their own data. Not requiring them to use EPA data could lead to the importation of a reformulated gasoline that is less clean than what can be expected from U.S. refiners.

Mickey Kantor was not happy with the ruling and promptly declared that a WTO ruling has no force under U.S. law, although he did indicate an intent to appeal. Regardless of the outcome of the appeal, this first ruling does not bode well for those concerned about protecting the environment. Trade officials were more concerned about Kantor's reaction, saying that a rejection of a ruling of the WTO by Washington would send a negative signal regarding U.S. intentions regarding the WTO.

In May 1996, the WTO's appeals board upheld the decision by WTO's dispute-settlement board that the U.S. rule on reformulated gasoline imports discriminates against foreign refiners. The United States had 30 days to decide whether to revise the regulation, to pay compensation, or to accept trade retaliation from nations injured by the rule. In June 1996, the United States reluctantly accepted the WTO's ruling on the EPA's reformulated gasoline rule, and the EPA was given 2 years to revise the rule.

The controversy over the potentially harmful effect of the WTO on the environment continued when in April 1998 a WTO panel ruled against a U.S. import ban on shrimps caught in nets that were not fitted with turtle excluder devices (TEDs). The WTO rules have been interpreted to mean that a country cannot discriminate solely on the method in which the good was produced, which the United States was seen to be doing in this case. The ruling dealt a serious blow to efforts to save the critically endangered turtles, 100,000 of which drown in shrimp nets each year.

The latest turn of the debate on trade and environment issues has been concern over the relationship between the WTO and multilateral environmental agreements (MEAs). MEAs include agreements such as the Montreal Protocol and CITES, discussed earlier in this chapter. Many MEAs contain trade provisions, such as restrictions on trade in endangered animals in CITES and restrictions on trade in hazardous waste in the Basel Convention. Many environmentalists fear that the WTO may try to set itself as superior to MEA provisions, rather than viewing the MEAs as having equal status with the WTO. If a dispute arises and both countries are party to the MEA, then there is no cause for concern about WTO preemption. However, if a dispute arises between a party to an MEA and a nonparty, then the nonparty may claim that the MEA poses trade barriers. Here is where the concern lies: the WTO may undermine the trade provisions of MEAs by claiming they pose unfair barriers to trade. Some environmentalists have urged the WTO to end the concern over this issue by amending Article XX (the exemption article) to include MEAs. No move has yet been made by the WTO to amend this article.

However, the WTO is addressing the issue of trade and environment through some of its programs. In October 1999, the WTO Secretariat released a report on trade and the environment, indicating that sound policies at both the national and the international level are necessary to protect the environment and that "trade would unambiguously raise welfare if proper environmental policies were in place."[70] This report claims that the key to harmonization of trade and the environment is cooperation.[71] In fact, as this report sees it, trade is not really the issue that is harming environmental policy; environmental policy itself is what must be changed. The authors of the report argue that the real necessity is "to reinvent environmental policies in an ever more integrated world economy so as to ensure that we live with ecological limits."[72] Just as countries have negotiated trade rules for cooperation, so should countries now establish environmental rules for cooperation.[73] Although the report perhaps clarifies certain issues with regard to trade and the environment, the concern over the status of MEAs *vis-à-vis* the WTO has not yet been addressed.

The concern of environmentalists over the relationship of MEAs to trade agreements is perhaps justified in light of a recent decision. Canada, which is part of NAFTA, is also a party to the Basel Convention; the United States is not. To meet its obligations under the Basel Convention, Canada banned the export of PCB wastes to reduce trafficking in hazardous wastes. An Ohio company specializing in the processing of PCB wastes, S. D. Myers, sued Canada under NAFTA, claiming the ban broke NAFTA rules. Although Canada removed the ban before the dispute, S. D. Myers wanted compensation for revenues lost while the 15-month ban was in place. A NAFTA tribunal upheld the claim of S. D. Myers and, in 2002, ordered Canada to pay damages to the sum of $8.2 million. This decision seems to place compliance with NAFTA above compliance with the Basel Convention. Canada has indicated that it may ask for a court review of the ruling (NAFTA has no appeals process). Environmentalists, fearful of the precedent the case may set, have since filed submissions to NAFTA outlining errors made by the tribunal against the government of Canada.

Concluding Remarks

This chapter clearly demonstrates that many of our major EC—acid rain, the greenhouse effect, transboundary pollution, and the loss of biodiversity—are really global problems. World population is growing at an unprecedented rate, and this increase in population only exacerbates these problems. International environmental agreements appear to be the best approach to solving these problems. As we see how these treaties work, we may begin to understand the extent to which we may be able, through international cooperation, to solve the most pressing environmental problems. We can also continue to try innovative ideas such as the debt for nature swaps. The United States is a small part of a complex biosphere; thus, we must remember that we cannot solve our environmental problems in isolation.

Questions for Review and Discussion

1. Identify four major problems that international environmental law needs to address.
2. Discuss the two primary sources of international law.
3. Why does international law tend to be ineffective?
4. Explain the four primary principles of customary international environmental law.
5. How does UNEP function?
6. Explain why it has been difficult to establish a satisfactory way to handle transboundary pollution problems.
7. What are the purposes and provisions of the Montreal Protocol?
8. Explain how international law is addressing the problem of pollution of the oceans and seas.

For Further Reading

Charnovitz, Steve. 1997. "A Critical Guide to the WTO's Report on Trade and Environment." *Arizona Journal of International and Comprehensive Law* *14*: 341.

Costanza, Robert, et al. 1995. "Sustainable Trade: A New Paradigm for World Welfare." *Environment* (June): 16.

McLarty, Taunya L. 1995. "The Applicability of NEPA to NAFTA: Law, Politics, or Economics?" *Maryland Journal of International Law and Trade 19*: 121.

Meier, Mike. 1997. "GATT, WTO, and the Environment: To What Extent Do GATT/WTO Rules Permit Member Nations to Protect the Environment When Doing so Adversely Affects Trade?" *Colorado Journal of International Environmental Law and Policy 8*: 241.

Ovink, B. John. 1995. "Transboundary Shipments of Toxic Waste: The Basel and Bamako Conventions: Do Third World Countries Have a Choice?" *Dickenson Environmental Law Journal 13*: 281.

Rebovich, Donald. 1992. *Dangerous Ground: The World of Hazardous Waste Crime.* New Brunswick, NJ: Transaction Publishers.

Wagner, Rodney. 1990. "Doing More with Debt for Nature Swaps." *International Environmental Affairs 2*: 160.

Wirth, David A. 1995. "The Rio Declaration on Environment and Development: Two Steps Forward and One Back, or Vice Versa?" *Georgia Law Review 29*: 599.

World Commission on Environment and Development. 1987. *Our Common Future.* New York: Oxford University Press.

On the Internet

http://www.ciel.org
    Center for International Environmental Law
http://www.usgcrp.gov/usgcrp/links/assessments.htm
    Major National and International Assessments of Global Environment Issues
http://sedac.ciesin.columbia.edu/entri/index.jsp
    Environmental Treaties and Resource Indicators (ENTRI)
http://info.worldbank.org/etools/bspn/index.asp
    Webcasting for Development: View World Bank Events
http://www.earthcharter.org
    The Earth Charter Initiative

http://europa.eu.int/index.htm
  Information regarding the European Union
http://www.pewclimate.org
  Pewcenter Global Climate — A Review of Climate Change and Ozone Depletion
http://www.usgcrp.gov/usgcrp/links/focusarealinks.htm
  Focus Areas of the U.S. Global Change Research Program
www.fiacc.net
  Web site on "Future International Action on Climate Change Network" maintained
by The Federal Environmental Agency, Germany (UBA) and Ecofys Germany
http://www.unesco.org/mab/index.shtml
  Home page of the Man and the Biosphere Program
http://www.law.pace.edu
  Pace Virtual Environmental Law Library containing much international information
http://www.law.georgetown.edu/journals/gielr/index.html
  Georgetown International Environmental Law Review
http://unfccc.int/kyoto_mechanisms/compliance/introduction/items/3024.php
(October 15, 2006)
  A good source for information about enforcement of the Kyoto Protocol

Notes

1. Thomas R. Malthus. 1798. *An Essay on the Principle of Population, as it Affects the Future Improvement of Society* (London: J. Johnson).
2. Lester R. Brown. "Paving the Planet: Cars and Crops Competing for Land." *http://www.worldwatch.org/chairman/issue/010214.html* (March 3, 2001).
3. Julian Simon. 1990. "Population Growth Is Not Bad for Humanity." *National Forum* 70 (Winter): 12.
4. "AAAS Atlas Shows Human Impact on Environment." *http://www.aaas.org/news/atlas.html* (March 3, 2001).
5. Nigel E. Stork. 1999. "The Magnitude of Global Biodiversity and Its Decline." *The Living Planet in Crisis: Biodiversity Science and Policy,* eds Joel Cracraft and Francesca T. Grifo, 6. New York: Columbia University Press.
6. UNEP. *State of the Environment and Policy Retrospective, 1972–2002. http://www.unep.org/geo/geo3/english/pdfs/chapter2-3_forests.pdf* (January 10, 2004).
7. Stork. "Magnitude": 25.
8. World Wildlife Fund. *Living Planet Report 1998. http://panda.org/living planet/lpr/index.htm* (July 30, 2001).
9. Ibid.
10. Stork. "Magnitude": 27.
11. United Nations Development Programme, United Nations Environment Programme, World Bank and World Resources Institute. 2000. *World Resources 2000–2001,* p 70. Washington, D.C.: World Resources Institute.
12. "Executive Summary." 1996. *World Resources Report 1996–97,* p xii. Washington, D.C.: World Resources Institute.
13. World Resources Institute. "New Study Reveals that Environmental Damage Threatens Future World Food Production." *Press Release* (February 14, 2001). *http://www.wri.org/press/page_agroecosystems.html* (March 3, 2001).
14. Ibid.
15. Ibid.

16. Louis Sohn. 1973. "The Stockholm Declaration on the Human Environment." *Harvard Journal of Environmental Law 14*: 423.
17. GA Res. 37/7, 37 UN. GAOR SUPP. (No. 51) at 7, U.N. DOC. A/37/51 (1982).
18. I.J. Acts and Documents 77 (1978).
19. "Trail Smelter Arbitration." 1983. *Encyclopedia of Public International Law Installment 2*: 267–280.
20. P.I.C.J. Ser. A. No. 23 at 27 (1929).
21. International Law Association. 1966. "Comment to Article IV, Helsinki Rules on the Uses of Waters of International Rivers." *Report of the Fifty-Second Conference,* p 487. London: International Law Association.
22. Ibid., comment to Article X: 497.
23. I.C.J. Reports (1949): 4.
24. International Law Association. 1966. "Legal Aspects of the Conservation of the Environment." *Report of the Fifty-Second Conference.* London: International Law Association.
25. World Conference on Environment and Development. 1987. *Our Common Future 58,* U.N.Doc. UNEP/GC.14/13.
26. World Commission on Environment and Development. 1987. *Our Common Future.* New York: Oxford University Press.
27. Green Cross International. "General Presentation." May 2000. *http://www.gci.ch/GreenCrossFamily/presentation.html* (March 8, 2001).
28. Ibid.
29. Green Cross International Activity Report 2003–2005. *http://www.greencrossinternational.net/docs/Activity%20Report0305.pdf* (November 6, 2006).
30. World Bank. 2001. "Lessons from World Bank Experience." *Making Sustainable Commitments: An Environment Strategy for the World Bank,* p 17. *http://www.worldbank.org/environment/* (July 30, 2001).
31. Ibid.
32. World Bank. 2001. "Executive Summary." *Making Sustainable Commitments: An Environment Strategy for the World Bank,* p iii. *http://www.worldbank.org/environment* (July 30, 2001).
33. Ibid.: vi–viii.
34. "Stop Banking on Coal." *Multinational Monitor* (December 2003): 4.
35. Implementation of the Management Response to the Extracive Industries Review, December 9, 2005. *http://www.bankwatch.org/documents/implementationreport_eir_2005.pdf* (November 4, 2006)
36. Ibid.
37. Global Environment Facility. "What Is the Global Environment Facility?" *http://www.gefweb.org/What_is_the_GEF/what_is_the_gef.html* (January 12, 2004).
38. Global Environment Facility. *http://www.gefweb.org/* (last visited October 21, 2006).
39. Supra see note 37.
40. "Protocol Concerning the Control of Emissions of Nitrogen Oxides." *http://www.unece.org/env/lrtap* (February 15, 2001).
41. Report of the Working Group on Effects of the Convention on Long-Range Transboundary Air Pollution, 2004. *http://www.unece.org/env/wge/WorkingGroupOnEffects2004.pdf* (November 4, 2006).
42. "Protocol to Abate Acidification, Eutrophication and Ground-level Ozone." *http://www.unece.org/env/lrtap* (February 15, 2001).
43. *http://www.unece.org/env/lrtap/status/lrtap_s.htm* (November 4, 2006).
44. Basel Convention. *http://www.basel.int/ratif/frsetmain.php* (October 21, 2006).
45. United Nations Environment Programme. "Basel Basics." *http://www.basel.int/pub/basics.html* (February 15, 2001).

46. "Basel Convention on the Control of Transboundary Movements of Hazardous Wastes and Their Disposal." *http://www.basel.int/ text/con-e.html* (February 15, 2001).

47. Greenpeace Shipbreaking. *http://www.greenpeaceweb.org/ shipbreak/whatis.asp* (November 5, 2006).

48. Basel Action Network. *http://www. ban.org/*

49. Basel Convention. *http://www.basel.int/ ratif/frsetmain.php* (November 5, 2006).

50. UNEP. "Basel Basics."

51. Ibid.

52. *http://www.pops.int/documents/ signature/signstatus.htm*

53. International Court of Justice. "List of Cases Brought Before the Court Since 1946." *http://www.icj-cij.org/icjwww/ idecisions.htm* (July 30, 2001).

54. Richard Levy. 1987. "International Law and the Chernobyl Accident, Reflections on an Important but Imperfect System." *Kansas Law Review 36*: 81.

55. Environmental Protection Agency *http://www.epa.gov/ozone/mbr/ index.html*

56. Andrew Kevkin. 2003. Panel Endorses U.S. Exemption on Ozone Pact. *The New York Times,* October 21.

57. "Executive Summary." 1996. *World Resources Report 1996–97,* p xiii. Washington, DC: World Resources Institute.

58. United Nations. "Press Kit: The Hague 2000." *http://cop6.unfccc.int/ pdf/presskc6e2.pdf* (March 8, 2001).

59. Andrew C. Revkin. 2001. "178 Nations Reach Climate Accord; U.S. Only Looks On." *New York Times,* July 24. *http://www.nytimes.com/2001/07/24/ science/24CLIM.html?searchpv= day07* (July 31, 2001).

60. Ibid.

61. UNFCC, *http://unfccc.int/ kyoto_mechanisms/compliance/ introduction/items/3024.php* (October 15, 2006).

62. John Heppes and Eric McFadden. 1987. "The Convention on International Trade in Endangered Species of Wild Fauna and Flora: Improving the Prospects for Preserving Our Biological Heritage." *Boston University International Law Journal 5*: 22.

63. U.S. Fish and Wildlife Service Endangered Species. *http://www.fws.gov/endangered/*

64. United Nations Development Programs, Department-for-Environment Swaps 2003. *http://www.surf-as.org/Papers/ Dept-for-environment%20swaps% 20Sep03.pdf* (January 15, 2004).

65. United Nations, Economic and Social Council. Implementing Agenda 21, report issued 2002. *http://www. earthsummit2002.org/es/updates/ default.htm* (January 15, 2004).

66. Timothy Noah. 1994. "GATT Backs Fuel Efficiency Rule, Recognizing U.S. Environmental Laws." *Wall Street Journal,* October 3.

67. Ibid.

68. Ralph Nader. 1994. "WTO Means Rule by Unaccountable Tribunals." *Wall Street Journal,* August 17.

69. Ibid.

70. World Trade Organization. "Trade Liberalization Reinforces the Need for Environmental Cooperation." *Press Release* (October 8, 1999). *http://www.wto.org/english/tratop_e/ envir_e/stud99_e.htm* (March 3, 2001).

71. Ibid.

72. Ibid.

73. Ibid.

RESOLVING CONTROVERSIAL
ENVIRONMENTAL ISSUES

- What evidence does the author offer to lead to her conclusion? On the basis of this evidence, are you persuaded by the author's argument? What evidence would persuade you?
- We asked you one critical thinking question. Ask yourself another critical thinking question, using the skills you have learned. Choose a question that offers the strongest critique of the argument. Ask yourself the question and then offer an answer.

The editorial below provides many opportunities to practice your critical thinking skills. Before you answer the following questions, think about the critical thinking skills you learned throughout the book. You learned to identify the components of an argument. You can identify ambiguous words, ethical norms preferred by authors, and assumptions. You learned the importance of identifying and evaluating evidence. You have also learned to look for missing information. Finally, you learned some of the many logical fallacies.

Amend the WTO

Environmentalists who are at all concerned about the future of our planet should work to change the WTO. Recent rulings by the WTO have undermined environmental protections to the detriment of human health and the future we are leaving our children. One recent egregious example of the WTO's ability to undercut a country's environmental protections is the WTO's decision in the shrimp–turtle case.

The United States banned the importation of shrimp caught in ways that harm endangered sea turtles. This ban was applied both to U.S. shrimpers and to shrimpers abroad. For shrimp to be acceptable for market in the United States, the shrimp had to be caught in nets that use TEDs. These devices ensure that sea turtles will not be brutally killed by shrimp nets. India, Malaysia, Pakistan, and Thailand sued the United States under WTO rules stating that TEDs constituted an unfair barrier to trade. The WTO, full of antienvironment capitalists who would create freer trade even at the expense of human life, of course ruled that the U.S. ban constituted an unfair trade barrier.

Democratically instituted rules have been overturned by a supranational body that is accountable to no one. The U.S. rules were implemented on both U.S. and foreign shrimpers; How can this constitute a trade barrier? The WTO is just hypersuspicious and views any environmental rule as a threat to trade; witness the decision in the dolphin–tuna case. In fact, the WTO is really hypocritical. Production methods are regulated by parts of the agreement, including the fact that countries can decline goods produced by prison labor without this ban being construed as a barrier to trade. The WTO apparently recognizes the moral issues surrounding prison labor but refuses to see that environmental rules fall under the same category.

It will not be long before this race to the bottom threatens everything we hold dear. If we care about the environment and the human race, we should work to change the WTO. Every time an environmental rule prohibits certain behavior, it should not automatically be ruled a trade barrier. In fact, if all countries would work together to implement the same environmental standards, we would not have the problem created by the U.S. requirement for the use of TEDs. However, because such cooperation is unlikely to happen, at a minimum, the WTO should be revised to include concerns for environmental regulations. Only then will we see a sustainable world that we can feel proud to pass down to our children.

Now read the following editorial. Apply the same critical thinking questions to this editorial. Which argument do you think has more worth?

Process and Production Methods Cannot be Regulated

Environmentalists have angrily struck out at a recent decision by the WTO that a U.S. ban on shrimp caught without TEDs constituted an unfair barrier to trade. Yet, many important issues have been ignored by environmentalists in their hasty desire to condemn the WTO. One of these issues is the difficulty of regulating process and production methods (PPMs).

The U.S. ban was applied to PPMs. Basically, the United States stated that only shrimp caught in a particular way would be acceptable for the U.S. market. This ban flies in the face of global commitment to freer trade. The idea that like products cannot be discriminated against is one of the fundamental tenets of a free-trade regime. Shrimp are shrimp, regardless of the method by which they were caught. Once we allow countries to regulate on the basis of PPMs, trade barriers will be erected everywhere.

As well, if countries can begin to specify exactly how goods should be produced, then countries without those technologies will be at a severe disadvantage. Environmentalists often claim to look out for the poor and for less-developed nations, but allowing regulation of PPMs will certainly not help these countries. Once a rich nation such as the United States says that some good must be produced in a certain way, less-developed nations are already at a disadvantage in trade compared with areas such as the EU that probably already have the technology. The purpose of free trade is to make countries better off. By allowing less-developed countries to engage in trade, new markets are opened and new money can begin to improve the welfare of people in the country. Regulation of PPMs would send us back to the days of isolationism, and less-developed countries would be hurt the most.

Free trade provides benefits to everyone. Through specialization and the theory of comparative advantage, countries that trade can have more of the goods they want than if trade did not happen. Obviously, more goods mean that people are better off and can have a higher standard of living. Is not this the world we want to leave to our children?

APPENDIX

ABBREVIATIONS AND ACRONYMS

AAA	American Arbitration Association
ACO	Administrative Consent Order
ADR	Alternate Dispute Resolution
AEC	Atomic Energy Commission (now NRC)
ALJ	Administrative Law Judge
AP	Advanced Passive
APA	Administrative Procedures Act
AQCR	Air Quality Control Regions (CAA)
BAT	Best Available Technology or Best Available Technology Economically Achievable
BCT	Best Conventional Control Technology
BDAT	Best Demonstrated Available Technology
BDT	Best Available Demonstrated Control Technology
BLM	Bureau of Land Management
BMP	Best Management Practices
BNA	Bureau of National Affairs
BPT	Best Practicable Control Technology Currently Available
CAA	Clean Air Act
CAFE	Corporate Average Fuel Economy
CAIR	Clean Air Interstate Rule
CAP	Compliance Assurance Program
CCA	Candidate Conservation Agreements
CCL	Contaminant Candidate List
CEQ	Council on Environmental Quality (executive office of the president)
CERCLA	Comprehensive Environmental Response, Compensation, and Liability Act
CFC	Chlorofluorocarbons
CFR	Code of Federal Regulations
COE	Corps of Engineers
CRA	Congressional Review Act
CSGWPP	Comprehensive State Ground Water Protection Program
CSI	Common Sense Initiative
CWA	Clean Water Act
CZMA	Coastal Zone Management Act
DALY	Disability-Adjusted Life Years
DDT	Dichlorodiphenyltrichloroethane
DEQ	Department of Environmental Quality
DEWA	Division of Early Warning and Assessment

DNR	Department of Natural Resources
DOA	U.S. Department of Agriculture
DOI	U.S. Department of Interior
DOJ	U.S. Department of Justice
DOT	U.S. Department of Transportation
DWPL	Drinking Water Priority List
EA	Environmental Assessment
EAB	Environmental Appeals Board
EAC	Early Action Compact
EC	European Community
ECRA	Environmental Cleanup Responsibility Act
EDB	Ethylene Dibromide
EDF	Environmental Defense Fund
EEM	Energy-Efficient Mortgages
EIS	Environmental Impact Statement
EITI	Extractive Industries Transparency Initiative
ELR	Environmental Law Reporter
EMS	Environmental Management System
EO	Executive Order
EPA	U.S. Environmental Protection Agency
EPCRA	Emergency Planning and Community Right to Know Act
EPCRTKA or EPCRA	Emergency Planning and Community Right to Know Act
ERC	BNA Environmental Reporter—Cases
ERDA	Energy Research and Development Administration
ESA	Endangered Species Act
FDA	U.S. Food and Drug Administration
FEPCA	Federal Environmental Pesticide Control Act
FERC	Federal Energy Regulatory Commission
FHWA	Federal Highway Administration
FIFRA	Federal Insecticide, Fungicide, and 2nd Rodenticide Act
FLPMA	Federal Land Policy and Management Act
FMCS	Federal Mediation and Conciliation Service
FOE	Friends of the Earth
FOIA	Freedom of Information Act
FONSI	Finding of No Significant Impact (NEPA)
FR	*Federal Register*
FRCP	Federal Rules of Civil Procedure
FRE	Foundation for Research on Economics and the Environment
FSC	Forest Stewardship Council
FTC	Federal Trade Commission
FWPCA	Federal Water Pollution Control Act (CWA)

FWS	Fish and Wildlife Service
GACT	Generally Achievable Control Technologies
GAO	General Accounting Office (congressional)
GPRA	Government Performance and Results Act
GRID	Global Resource Information Database
HCP	Habitat Conservation Plan
HEW	Health, Education, and Welfare
HRS	Hazard Ranking System (CERCLA)
HSWA	Hazardous and Solid Waste Amendments (of 1984)
HUD	Housing and Urban Development
ICC	Interstate Commerce Commission
ICJ	International Court of Justice (The Hague)
IGO	Intergovernmental Organization
IJC	International Joint Commission (U.S.-Canada)
ILM	International Legal Materials
IPM	Integrated Pest Management
IPCC	Intergovernmental Panel on Climate Change
ISC	Interagency Scientific Committee (ESA)
ISO	International Organization for Standardization
ITP	Industrial Technologies Program
IWC	International Whaling Commission
LAER	Lowest Achievable Emissions Rate
LMOP	Landfill Methane Outreach Program
LRTAP	Long-Range Transboundary Air Pollution
MACT	Maximum Available Control Technology
MCL	Maximum Contaminant Level (CWA)
MCLG	Maximum Contaminant Level Goals
MEP	Maximum Extent Practicable
MSGP	Multi-Sector General Permit
MTBE	Methyl Tertiary Butyl Ether
NAAQS	National Ambient Air Quality Standards
NAM	National Association of Manufacturers
NCP	National Contingency Plan (Superfund)
NEJAC	National Environmental Justice Advisory Counsel
NEP	National Energy Plan
NEPA	National Environmental Policy Act of 1969
NEPPS	National Environmental Performance Partnership System
NES	National Energy Strategy
NESHAP	National Emissions Standards for Hazardous Air Pollutants
NFMA	National Forest Management Act
NGO	Non-Governmental Organization
NHTSA	National Highway Traffic and Safety Administration

NMFS	National Marine Fisheries Service
NOAA	National Oceanographic and Atmospheric Administration (Department of Commerce)
NPDES	National Pollutant Discharge Elimination System (CWA)
NPDWR	National Primary Drinking Water Regulations
NPL	National Priority List (Superfund)
NPS	National Park Service
NRC	U.S. Nuclear Regulatory Commission or (state) Natural Resources Commission
NRDC	National Resources Defense Council
NSD	No Significant Deterioration
NSPS	New Source Performance Standards (Air)
NWF	National Wildlife Foundation
NWQS	National Water Quality Standards (CWA)
OCS	Outer Continental Shelf
OCSLA	Outer Continental Shelf Leasing Act
OMB	Office of Management and Budget (executive offices of the president)
OPEC	Organization of Petroleum Exporting Countries
OPEI	Office of Policy, Economics, and Innovation
OPM	Office of Personnel Management
OPP	Office of Pesticide Program
OPPT	Office of Pollution Prevention and Toxics
OSHA	Occupational Safety and Health Act, Occupational Safety and Health Administration
OSWER	Office of Solid Waste and Energy Response
OTA	Office of Technology Assessment (congressional)
PCB	Polychlorinate biphenyl
PEL	Permissible Exposure Limit
PERC	Property and Environmental Research Center
PESP	Pesticide Environmental Stewardship Program
PIFUA	Powerplant and Industrial Fuel Use Act
PMN	Premanufacturing Notice
POP	Persistent Organic Pollutants
POTW	Publicly Owned Treatment Works (CWA)
PRP	Potentially Responsible Party (Superfund)

PSD	Prevention of Significant Deterioration
RAB	Restoration Advisory Boards
RCRA	Resource Conservation and Recovery Act
RMP	Risk Management Plan
SARA	Superfund Amendment and Reauthorization Act
SCS	U.S. Soil Conservation Service
SDWA	Safe Drinking Water Act
SEC	Securities and Exchange Commission
SIP	State Implementation Plan (CAA)
SMCRA	Surface Mining Control and Reclamation Act
SPR	Strategic Petroleum Reserves
SSAB	Site-Specific Advisory Board
Superfund	Trust Fund for Clean-ups Under CERCLA
SUV	Sport Utility Vehicle
SWDA	Solid Waste Disposal Act
TCLP	Toxicity Characteristic Leaching Procedure
TCR	Total Coliform Rule
TMDL	Total Maximum Daily Load
TRI	Toxic Release Inventory
ToSCA or TSCA	Toxic Substances Control Act
TRO	Temporary Restraining Order
TSD	Treatment, Storage, and Disposal (CERCLA)
TVA	Tennessee Valley Authority
UNEP	United Nations Environmental Programme
USDA	U.S. Department of Agriculture
USFS	U.S. Forest Service
UST	Underground Storage Tank
WAVE	Water Alliances for Volunteer Efficiency
WCED	World Commission on Environment Development
WHO	World Health Organization
WMO	World Meteorological Organization
WPS	Worker Protection Standard
WQA	Water Quality Act
WQS	Water Quality Standards (CWA)

INDEX

Aarhus Protocols, 443
Abbreviations, 473
Abraham, Spencer, 146–147
Acid deposition, 175–177
Acid rain, 175–177
  Europe, 177
Acid rain-control program,
  207–208
Acidity, 175–176
Acronyms, 473
Adjudication, 96–100
  citizen rewards, 99–100
  corrective orders, 98
  minimum standards, 97
  noncompliance penalties, 99
  process, 97
Administrative agencies,
  89–126. *See also* specific
  agencies
  adjudication, 96–100
  administrative activities,
    100–101
  administrative law judge
    (ALJ), 90
  Brownfields partners, 327
  "captured", 95
  creation, 90
  executive vs. independent,
    106–107
  functions, 90–101
  hot lines, 100, 101
  hybrid, 107
  independent, 100, 102,
    106–107
  interagency cooperation,
    116–118
  limits on powers, 101–106
  responsibilities, 91
  rule making, (*See* also Rule
    making (agency)), 90–100
  as source of law, 14, 46
Administrative law judge
  (ALJ), 90
Administrative Procedure Act
  (APA), 91
  agency adjudication, 96–100
  rule making, 90–96
Advanced Micro Devices,
  327–328
Advanced Passive (AP)
  Reactor, 367

Adversary system, 52–59
  actors, 60–62
  attorney-client privilege, 60
  criticisms, 52–53
  dual system, 54
  federal, 55
  state, 55, 57
  subject matter jurisdiction,
    57–59
  venue, 59
Affirmative defense, 71
AFL-CIO v. *OSHA*, 104–105
Agencies. *See* Administrative
  agencies
Agenda 21, 460–461
Agriculture, 182
Agriculture, Department of,
  See U.S. Department of
  Agriculture (USDA)
Air conditioners, 137
Air pollutants, 168–175
  airborne toxins, 175
  carbon monoxide, 171–173
  lead, 174
  manmade sources of
    nonemissions, 171
  nitrogen oxides, 170–171
  ozone, 173
  particulates, 173–174
  sulfur dioxide, 169–170
Air pollution. *See also* Clean
  Air Act; Pollution
  indoor, 186–187
  international law, 442–443
  levels, on website, 168
Air toxics program, 1990,
  203–205
Airborne toxins
  1990 air toxics program,
    203–205
  health effects, 175
Air-Pollution Control Act of
  1955, 188
Air-Quality Act of 1967,
  189–190
Air-quality control, 168–216.
  See also Clean Air Act
  1990 Clean Air Act amend-
    ments, 203–210
  additional solutions,
    210–211

Clear Skies Initiative, 210
  current approach, 190–203
  initial approach, 187–190
  major air pollutants,
    168–175
  problems, 175–187
  standards, 185
Air-quality problems,
  175–187
  acid deposition, 175–177
  climate change (global
    warming), 179–186
  indoor pollution, 186–187
  ozone layer depletion,
    177–178
Alaskan Pipeline, 346, 361
Alexander, Rita, 67
Allen v. United States, 286
Allowances. *See* Emissions,
  trading
Alpha particles, 224
Alternative Dispute
  Resolution (ADR), 83
Alternatives to EIS, 158–160
Ambient water-quality control,
  244–246
American Arbitration
  Association (AAA), 81
American Association for the
  Advancement of Science,
  402, 427
  global warming, 180
  marine reserves, 402
  overpopulation, 414,
    426–427
American Automobile
  Association, 202
American rule (ground-
  water), 235
American Trucking
  Association, 192
*An Essay on the Principle of
  Population*, 424
Animal bioassays, 264
Answer, 70, 71, 72
Antarctica, 178, 184,
  459–460
Antibiotics, 222, 226
Antiquities Act of 1906,
  392–393
Appeals, 78, 79

478

Appellate courts, 77–79, 94
Appellate procedure, 77–79
Appropriative water rights,
    232–234
Aquifers, 247
Arbitration, 80–82
Arctic National Wildlife Refuge,
    142, 146, 147, 346, 348
Area mining, 355
Army Corps of Engineers
    (COE)
  environmental impact
    statement (EIS), 157
  environmental responsibili-
    ties, 119
  NEPA lawsuits, 158
  no-net-loss rule, 113
  wetlands, 32, 397
Arsenic, 204
Asbestos Hazard Emergency
    Response Act, 262
Atomic Energy Act of
    1954, 370
Atomic Energy
    Commission, 107
Atoms, 223
Attorney, 60
Attorney-client privilege, 60
Attorneys, 60
Audit Policy, 26–29
Audubon Society, 413
Automobile emissions
  inspection program, 197
  performance standards,
    200–203
Automobiles, alternative-fuel,
    201, 344, 350

Babbitt, Bruce, 410–411
Bacteria, 219
Basel Action Network, 444
Basel Ban Amendment, 445
Basel Convention on the
    Control of Transboundary
    Movements of Hazardous
    Waste, 283, 444
BAT (best available technology
    economically achievable)
    standards, 238–239
Baucus, Max, 110, 464
BCT (best conventional pollu-
    tant control technology)
    standards, 238
Beach. See Coastal waters
Beaches Environmental
    Assessment and Coastal
    Health (BEACH)
    Act, 229
Bengal tiger, 183

Bennett v. Spear, 67
Benzidine, 264
Best available technology
    economically achievable
    (BAT), 238
Best conventional pollutant
    control technology
    (BCT), 238
Best Management Practices
    (BMPs), 244
Beta particles, 224
Beyond a reasonable doubt, 16
Bill, 6–7, 9
Bioassays, 264
Biochemical oxygen demand
    (BOD), 221, 238
Biodiversity, 456–459,
    461–462
  Convention on International
    Trade in Species of
    Endangered Wild Fauna
    and Flora (CITES),
    456–457
  debt for nature swaps,
    458–459
  international law, 456–459
  loss of, 427–428
  Man and the Biosphere
    (MAB) program, 458
  Rio Summit, 460
Biomass energy, 376–377
BioPower Program, 377
Bioreactor landfill, 303
Biosafety Protocol, 461–462
Biosphere, 428
Blackmun, Harry
  interstate waste disposal, 34
  standing, 66
Blue baby disease, 223
Bodman, Samuel W., 147
Boomer v. Atlantic Cement
    Company, 133
Bottle bills, 144
Bottled water, 259
Boundary Waters Treaty of
    1909, 408
Braggs v. Robertson, 359
Breidamerkurjokul
    glacier, 180
Briefs, arbitration, 80
Brightfields Initiative, 375
Bromine, 178
Browner, Carol M., 43,
    108, 110
Brownfield Economic
    Redevelopment Initiative
    Brightfields Initiative, 325
  underground storage tank
    (UST) program, 327–330

Brownfields, 325–327
Brundtland Commission, 436
Brzonkala v. Morrison, 32
Bureau of Land Management,
    120–121, 388, 389
Burford, Anne (Gorsuch), 108
Bush, George H.W.
  biodiversity treaty, 461
  climate change treaty,
    451–452
  energy policy, 343–345
  EPA, 108, 141
  limitations on administrative
    agencies, 103
  offshore drilling, 348
  wetlands, 404
Bush, George W.
  energy policy, 347–350
  environmental enforcement,
    17, 23
  environmental policy,
    146–149
  EPA, 113
  executive orders, 13
  forest fire prevention, 393
  hazardous waste
    manifests, 307
  hydrogen fuel, 347
  Kyoto Treaty, 12
  methyl bromide, 450
  mining policy, 356–359
  national monuments, 392
  New Source Review (NSR),
    113–114, 146
  nuclear energy, 367
  offshore drilling, 363
  petroleum reserves, 360
  public lands, 392–395
  signing statements, 13
  standing, 66
  wetlands, 404
  Yucca Mountain, 371–372

C&O Canal National Historic
    Park, 392
Cabinet-level agencies, 107
CAFE (corporate average fuel
    economy) standards, 113,
    203, 346
California
  auto emissions standards, 185
  energy crisis, 352
  oil spill, 139, 237
Canada
  acid rain, 176
  climate change measures, 184
  Great Lakes protection,
    408–409
  Trail Smelter arbitration, 432

Candidate Conservation
    Agreements (CCA), 412
Canyons of the Ancients
    National Monument, 393
Cape Floral Kingdom, 183
Cape Wind Project, 375–376
Carbon, 266
Carbon dioxide
    containment, 184
    emissions, 185
Carbon monoxide, 171–173
"Carbon tax", 137
Carcinogens, risk assessment,
    264, 265, 266
Cars. See Automobile
    emissions; Automobiles,
    alternative-fuel
Carson, Rachel, 139
Cartagena Protocol on
    Biosafety, 461–462
Carter, Jimmy
    coal-leasing, 359
    energy policy, 342
    energy-efficient mortgage
        (EEM), 344–345
    oil spills, 364
    solar energy, 375–376
    surface mining, 358
Case (controversy), 69
Case law, 9-11. See also Law(s)
Cattle grazing, 389, 392
Causation, 285–287
Center for American
    Progress, 114
Centers for Disease Control
    (CDC) blood lead
    standard, 227
Challenge, peremptory, 75
Chemical oxygen demand
    (COD), 221
Chemical Waste Management,
    Inc. v. Hunt, 34
Chemicals. See also Organic
    chemicals
Cheney, Dick
    energy task force, 348–349
    EPA, 113
    nuclear energy, 367
Chernobyl, 228, 367
Chevron Chemical Company v.
    Ferebee, 284, 285
Children's Health Advisory
    Committee, 206
Chlorine, 178, 222, 225
Chlorofluorocarbons (CFCs)
    green taxes, 136–137
    Montreal Protocol, 12
    ozone layer depletion, 177
Chlorpyrifos, 279
Circuit courts of appeals, 55

Citizen suits, 246
Citizens for a Better
    Environment (CBE),
    67–68
Citizens of Overton Park v.
    Volpe, 104
Citizenship, diversity of, 57, 58
City of Philadelphia v. New
    Jersey, 33–34
Civil law, 15–16. See also Law(s)
Civil liability/penalties, 23–25
Civil litigation. See also
    Litigation
    alternatives to, 79–84
    appellate procedure, 77–79
    case or controversy, 69
    discovery, 72–73
    pretrial, 70–74
    pretrial motions, 72
    ripeness, 69–70
    service (of summons), 70–71
    standing, 63–69
    steps, 63–79
    summary judgment, motions
        for, 73
    threshold issues, 63–70
    trial, 74–77
Civil procedure, rules of, 63
Clark, William, 361, 362
Clean Air Act
    of 1963, 188–189
    1967 amendments, 190–191
    of 1970, 203
    1990 amendments, 203–210
    1990 enforcement, 208–210
    airborne toxins, 175
    automobile inspection, 197
    benefits, 210
    citizen rewards, 99–100
    coal production, 354, 356
    criteria pollutants, 168, 174,
        191, 193, 194
    environmental racism,
        141, 142
    judicial power, 90
    legal challenges, 148, 192
    marketable emissions
        permits, 136, 144–145
    methyl bromide, 450
    mobile source standards,
        201–203
    national ambient air quality
        standards (NAAQSs),
        174, 191–192
    New Source Review, 198–200
    no significant deterioration
        (NSD), 197
    nonattainment, 193–196
    penalties for violations of,
        42–43

    permit program, 196–197
    state implementation, 190
    sulfur dioxide trading,
        207–208
    zinc mine emissions, 106
Clean Air Interstate Rule
    (CAIR), 171
Clean Air Nonroad Diesel
    Rule, 171
Clean Development
    Mechanism, 453
Clean Water Act (CWA)
    of 1977, 237
    coastal waters, 236, 363
    environmental racism, 41
    estuaries, 396, 397, 398, 404,
        407–408
    groundwater, 246–248
    liability for oil spills, 365
    penalties for violations,
        19–23
    wetlands, 33
Clear Skies Initiative, 210
Clear-cutting, 387–388
Climate change, 179–186,
    451–452,
    possible effects, 180–183
    regional contributions to
        global warming, 451
    Rio Summit, 462
    temperatures, 180, 339
Climate Wise, 145
Clinton, William J.
    biodiversity treaty, 461
    Council on Environmental
        Quality (CEQ), 150–151
    energy policy, 345
    environmental justice, 42
    EPA, 24
    executive orders, 13, 42, 143,
        150, 162, 345
    Kempthorne bill, 415
    mercury, 205
    methyl bromide, 450
    national monuments,
        143–144
    New Source Review
        (NSR), 198
    northern spotted owl, 413
    offshore drilling, 363
    public lands, 392
    solar energy, 375
    source reduction, 162
    Superfund, 325
    Yucca Mountain, 372
Closing arguments, 77
Closing Circle, The, 139
Coal, 353–360
    areas of production, 354
    leasing policies, 359–360

problems, 355–357
production amounts by
method, 356
regulation of industry,
357–360
Coal Lease Amendment Act
of 2003, 360
Coastal waters
contamination, 236
offshore drilling, 363
Coastal wetlands. *See* Wetlands
Coastal Wetlands Planning,
Protection, and
Restoration Act of
1990, 403
Coastal Zone Management
Act (CZMA) of 1972, 363,
402–403
Coliforms, 219
Command-and-control
regulation, 137
Commerce, 31
Commerce clause, 31–35
state regulation and, 33–35
wetlands and, 32–33,
399–401
Commerce clause restrictions,
399–401
Common law, *See also* Law(s)
Common Sense Initiative
(CSI), 110
Common Sense Initiative
(CSI) (EPA), 110
Commoner, Barry, 139
Community survey (jury
selection), 75
Compact fluorescent lamp, 351
Compensation, 36–37
Competitiveness Council, 141
Complaint, 70
Compliance, 25-26
conflict between state/
federal laws, 30
drinking water quality, 251
EPA compliance assistance
centers, 100
order, 97
Compliance Assistance
Centers, 100–101
Compliance Assurance
Program (CAP 2000), 201
Comprehensive Environmental
Response, Compensation,
and Liability Act
(CERCLA). *See* Superfund
Act (CERCLA)
Comprehensive Environmental
Response, Compensation,
and Liability Act
(CERCLA), 97

Comprehensive Procurement
Guideline Program, 304
Comprehensive State Ground
Water Protection Program
(CSGWPP), 246
Concentrated animal feeding
operations (CAFOs),
230, 238
Concurrent jurisdiction,
57, 58
Concurring opinion, 78
Conference, pretrial, 74
Congress. *See also* Legislative
branch
administrative agencies, 90
committees and sub-
committees, 8
legislative power, 31
*Congressional Quarterly
Weekly*, 7
Congressional Record, 10
Congressional Review Act
(CRA), 103–104
Connaughton, James
Laurence, 151–152
Conservation Foundation, 108
Conservation International
(CI), 458
Conservationists, 120, 387
Constitution
commerce clause, 31
due process clause,
36–37
equal protection clause, 41
executive branch, 3, 12
federal preemption, 30
federalism, 29–30
Fifth Amendment, 36–37, 38
Fourteenth Amendment, 36,
37, 41
Fourth Amendment, 35–36
judicial branch, 9–11
legal principles, 29–47
Ninth Amendment, 44
right to environmental
protection, 43–47
supremacy clause, 30
takings clause, 37–43
Constitutional Convention, 29
Construction Completion List,
321, 324
Consumer Labeling Initiative
(CLI), 272–273
Consumer Products Safety
Commission, 119
Contaminant candidate list
(CCL), 249
Contour mining, 355
"Contract with America", 142
Controversy (case), 69

Convention on International
Trade in Species of
Endangered Wild Fauna
and Flora (CITES),
456–457
Convention on Long Range
Transboundary Air
Pollution (LRTAP), 442
Convention on Protection of
the Environment, 447
Convention on the Law of the
Sea, 454
Conventional law, 431–432
Conventional organics,
220–221
Copper, 227–228
Coral reefs, 182
Corporate average fuel
economy (CAFE)
standards, 113
Corporate Environmental
Enforcement Council, 27
Corporations
Fourth Amendment,
35–36, 94
lobbyists, 5
Corrective order, 98
Cosmetics. *See* Federal Food,
Drug, and Cosmetics Act
(FFDCA)
Cost-benefit analysis, 13, 102
Costle, Douglas, 108
Council on Environmental
Quality (CEQ),
150–152
functions, 150, 151
limitations by executive
branch, 102
NEPA report, 158, 160
Counsel. *See* Lawyers
Counterclaim, 70, 72
Court cases
AFL-CIO v. *OSHA*, 104–105
Allen v. United States, 286
Bennett v. Spear, 67
*Boomer v. Atlantic Cement
Company*, 134
Braggs v. Robertson, 359
*Chemical Waste Management,
Inc. v. Hunt*, 34
*Chevron Chemical Company
v. Ferebee*, 284, 285
*Citizens of Overton Park v.
Volpe*, 104
*City of Philadelphia v. New
Jersey*, 33
Dolan v. Tigard, 40
*Ethyl Corporation v. United
States EPA*, 263
federal question, 57, 58

Court cases (*continued*)
Fischer v. Johns-Manville Corporation, 289–290
Friends of the Earth (FOE) v. Laidlaw Environmental Services, 68
Hodel v. Virginia Surface Mining and Reclamation Association, Inc., 31
Houlton Citizen's Coalition v. Town of Houlton, 35
Huish Detergents, Inc. v. Warren County, KY, 35
Illinois Central Railroad Co. v. Illinois, 45
Kelo v. London, 41
Lead Industries Association, Inc. v. EPA, 263
Liijan v. Defenders of Wildlife, 65
Lucas v. South Carolina Coastal Council, 38
Marbury v. Madison, 11
Massachusetts v. EPA, 185–186
Michigan Citizens for Water Conservation v. Nestle Waters North America, 235
National Audubon Society v. Superior Court (Mono Lake), 233
National Resources Defense Council v. Train, 174
Nat'l Parks Conservation Ass'n v. Manson, 68–69
New York v. EPA, 200
NRDC v. United States EPA, 263
Paepke v. Building Commission, 45–46
Palazzolo v. Rhode Island, 40
Rapanos v. United States, 400
Scientific Assessment of Ozone Depletion: 2002, 178
Sierra Club v. Morton, 65–66
Sindell v. Abbott Laboratories, 288
Solid Waste Agency of Northern Cook County v. United States Army Corps of Engineers, 400
Steel Co. v. Citizens for a Better Environment, 67–68
Tanner et al. v. Armco Steel et al., 44
United States v. Alcan Aluminum Corporation, 323
United States v. Burns, 323
United States v. Carolawn Chemical Company, 322
United States v. Fleet Factors Corporation, 323
United States v. Hayes International Corporation, 25
United States v. Mottolo, 323
United States v. Park, 25
United States v. Students Challenging Regulatory Agency Procedures (SCRAP 1), 66
Whitman v. American Trucking, 195
Whitney v. United States, 39
Court reporter (stenographer), 73
Courts
dual system, 52–59
federal, 55
geographical boundaries, 56
jurisdiction, 57–59
state, 55, 57
venue, 59
Criminal law, 15–16. *See also* Law(s)
Criminal penalties, 16–23
Criminal prosecutions. *See* Environmental criminal prosecutions
Criminal Task Force Investigation Division, 117
Cross-examination, 76, 92, 93
Cryptosporidium, 219
Customary law, 432–434
Cuyahoga River, 237
CWA (Clean Water Act). *See* Clean Water Act (CWA)

Daimler/Chrysler, 326
Damages
permanent, 134
punitive, 288–290
Dams. *See* Hydropower
David Petrocco Farms, Inc., 277
Davis-Besse nuclear plant, 370
DDT (dichlorodiphenyl-trichloroethane), 222, 261, 262, 446
Debt for nature swaps, 458–459
Defendant, 70, 71–72
Defenders of Wildlife, 5
Defense, affirmative, 71, 72
Defense Authorization Act, 147
Defense Department, 143
Department of Agriculture, 121
Department of Agriculture Research Service, 404
Department of Energy (DOE), 107
biomass energy, 376–377
Brightfields Initiative, 375
Carter Administration, 358
nuclear waste sites, 371–372
Reagan Administration, 358
Department of Health, Education and Welfare (HEW), 107
Department of Housing and Urban Development (HUD), 154–155
energy-efficient mortgage (EEM), 344
environmental impact statement (EIS), 154–155
Department of Justice (DOJ)
criminal prosecutions, 16–25
Environmental Crimes Unit, 16–17
Land and Natural Resources Division, 16–17
lawsuits against utilities, 198–199
Department of Labor, 121
Department of the Interior, 118–121
Clinton administration, 144
coal-leasing, 346
NEPA lawsuits, 155, 158
standing, 65, 68
surface mining, 345
Department of Transportation, 107, 314
hazardous material release, 314
NEPA lawsuits, 158
Deposition, 73
Deregulation, of energy industry, 352
Diazinon, 267
Dichlorodiphenyltrichloroethane (DDT), 222
Diffuse pollution, 245
Dingell, John, 348
Dinoflagellates, 220
Direct examination, 76
Direct regulation, 137
Directed verdict, motion for, 76
Disability Adjusted Life Years (DALYs), 218
Discharge, 238–245
Discovery, 72–73
Disinfectants, 187, 222
Disinfectants and Disinfection Byproducts Rule, 225–226
Disinfection by-products (DBPs), 225, 251
Dismissal, for cause, 67, 349
Dissenting opinion, 78

Dissolved solids, 224
District courts, 54, 55, 56, 59
Diversity of Citizenship
Division of Early Warning
and Assessment
(DEWA), 435
Dolan v. Tigard, 40
Domestic Policy Council, 150
Dose-response assessment, 265
Drinking water
consumer confidence
reports, 252
contaminant candidate list
(CCL), 249
priority list (DWPL), 249
protection, 248–253
terrorism threats, 253
types of public systems,
248–249
"Drinking water priority list"
(DWPL), 249
Dry deposition, 175, 177
Due diligence, 433
Due process clause, 36–37
DuPont, 99, 161
Dursban, 267, 279
Duty to inform and
cooperate, 433

E. coli, 229–230
E. I. Du Pont de Nemours and
Company, 239
Early Action Compacts
(EACs), 196
Earth Charter, 436
Earth Day, 139
Earth First!, 5
Eastern Wilderness Areas
Acts, 391
Ecology, 131
Economic Policy Council, 150
Effluent standards,
238–239, 240
Ehrlich, Paul, 139
Electric Consumers Act of
1986, 373
Elgin, 270
Elias, Allen, 23
Emergency Planning and
Community Right-to-
Know Act of 1986
(EPCRA), 314
Emissions
1970–2005, estimates
automobile, 172, 186, 190,
197, 201
charges, 134, 135–136
trading, 136
Emissions charges, 134, 135–136
Enabling legislation, 90

Endangered species, 409–418
convention on international
trade, 439, 456–458
global extinction crisis,
416–418
number per state, 411
prohibition of listing, 143
threatened species by
region, 417
Endangered Species Act of
1973, 409–416
definition of "harm", 410
environmental organizations
and standing, 63–66
Healthy Forests Restoration
Act, 393–394
listing and delisting bill, 415
penalties for violations, 16–25
standing for animals, 67
Endangered Species Listing
and Delisting Process
Reform Act of 2003, 415
Endocrine disruptors, 279–280
End-of-pipe regulation, 137
Energy, 339–385. *See also*
individual energy sources
coal, 353–360
consumption and production,
350–353
nuclear energy, 366–372
petroleum and natural gas,
360–366
renewable fuels, 372–377
sources, 353–377
Energy policy, 339–350. *See
also* individual presidents
1973 energy crisis, 340–342
Bush (George H.W)
Administration, 343–345
Bush (George W.)
Administration, 347–350
Clinton Administration, 345
EPAct of 1992, 344–345
historical overview, 340–350
National Energy Policy
Plans, 347–350
Reagan Administration,
342–343
transportation, 346–347
Energy Policy Act (EPAct), 330
Energy Policy Act of 1992, 380
Energy Policy and
Conservation Act of
1975, 342
Energy Research and
Development
Administration
(ERDA), 341
Energy Star, 145
Energy-efficient buildings, 186

Energy-efficient mortgage
(EEM), 344–345
English rule (groundwater), 235
Enterococci, 219, 229–230
Enterprise liability, 287–288
Enviromentalism and trade,
462–466
Environment Programme
(UNEP), 434–436
Environmental Appeals Board
(EAB), 97
Environmental assessment
(EA), 156
Environmental auditing, 26–29
elements of successful
program, 26
privilege, 27–28
Environmental cases
recent fines, 19–20, 22
recent prison sentences,
20–22
Environmental compliance, 314
Environmental concerns
(EC), 141
Environmental criminal
prosecutions
civil liability/penalties, 23–25
criminal prosecutions, 16–23
increased enforcement,
responding to, 25–29
Environmental Defense Fund
lobbying, 5
pesticide cancellation
hearings, 274–275
Environmental disasters, 430
*Environmental Equity:
Reducing Risk for All
Communities*, 42
Environmental ethic, 131–132
Environmental Fund, 434, 435
Environmental impact
statement (EIS), 152–160
alternatives to, 158–160
contents, 158
court challenges, 157–158
EPA rating definitions, 156
format, 159
number published by federal
agencies, 152
procedures, 156–158
threshold considerations,
152–156
Environmental Law Institute, 61
Environmental laws. *See* Law(s)
Environmental management
system (EMS), 113
Environmental organizations
campaign spending, 5
Ronald Reagan and, 139–140
standing, 63–67

Environmental policy. *See also*
  individual acts
  1970s, 139
  1980s, 139–140
  1990s, 140–144
  direct regulation, 137
  early 21st century, 146–149
  emissions charges, 135–136
  environmental ethic, 131–132
  evolution, 138–149
  free rider problem, 130–131
  green taxes, 136–137
  ISO 14000, 145–146
  market forces, 144–145
  marketable emissions
    permits, 136
  National Environmental
    Policy Act, (*See* also
    National Environmental
    Policy Act (NEPA)),
    149–160
  origins, 138
  pollution as externality, 131
  Pollution Prevention Act,
    160–162
  subsidies, 134–135
  tragedy of the commons,
    129–130
  voluntary programs, 145
Environmental Protection
  Agency (EPA)
  adjudication, 96–97
  administrative law judges
    (ALJ), 115
  air pollution levels, 168
  audits, 26–29
  budget, 24–25,
  challenges of rules, 94
  citizen rewards, 99–100
  creation, 107,
  criminal enforcement trends,
    16–18, 23–25
  Criminal Task Force
    Investigation Division, 117
  Environmental Appeals
    Board (EAB), 97
  Environmental Equity
    Workgroup, 42
  environmental justice,
    42, 43, 444
  Fourth Amendment, 35–36
  goals for 21st century,
    111–112
  gravity portion, 26–27
  history, 107–108, 110–115
  indoor pollution, 180
  interagency cooperation,
    116–117
  judicial power, 89, 90
  limitations on, 101–102

National Environmental
  Justice Advisory Counsel
  (NEJAC), 43
National Environmental
  Performance Partnership
  System (NEPPS), 111
Office for Criminal
  Investigations, 17
Office of Enforcement and
  Compliance Assurance,
  17, 148
Office of Environmental
  Equity, 42
Office of Policy, Economics,
  and Innovation
  (OPEI), 111
Office of Reinvention, 111
oversight power, 103
penalties for noncompliance,
  99, 113, 252
Policy on Civil Penalties,
  26–27
proposed cabinet-level
  agency, 147–148
reforms, 111–112
regional offices, 118
source of law, 14
strategic plan of 1997, 116
strategic plan of 2000-2005,
  111–112
structure, 115–116
Environmental racism and
  justice, 41–43
Environmental Results
  Programs, 113
Environmental Working
  Group, 226
EPA rating definitions, 156
EPAct of 1992, 344–345
Equal protection clause, 41
Error, prejudicial, 77
Escherichia coli (E. coli),
  219
*Essay on the Principle of
  Population,*, 424
Estuaries, 396, 397, 398, 404,
  407–408
Estuaries and Clean Water
  Act of 2000, 407
Estuary Restoration Act of
  2000, 407–408
Ethics, 131
*Ethyl Corporation v. United
  States EPA*, 263
Ethylene dibromide
  (EDB), 275
European Chemicals
  Agency, 283
European Community
  (EC), 440

European Union (EU),
  439–440
  green taxes, 136
Eutrophication, 223
Evidence, preponderance of, 16
Examination, 76
Executive branch, 3,
  creation of administrative
    agencies, 90
  limits on administrative
    agencies, 102–103
  as source of law, 11–13
Executive orders, 13, 42, 102,
  304, 343
Exposure assessment, 265
Extinction crisis, 416–418. *See
  also* Endangered species
Extractive Industries
  Review, 438
Exxon *Valdez*, 17, 364, 366

Factories. *See* Industrial
  plants
Fairchild, 328
Fecal coliforms, 219
Federal Actions to Address
  Environmental Justice
  and Minority Populations
  in Low-Income
  Populations, 42
Federal Aviation Agency, 107
Federal Energy
  Administration, 341
Federal Energy Office
  (FEO), 341
Federal Energy Regulatory
  Commission (FERC), 107,
  dams, 373
  NEPA lawsuits, 158
Federal Environmental
  Conflict Resolution
  (ECR) Roundtable, 83
Federal Environmental
  Pesticide Control Act of
  1947, 272
Federal Food, Drug, and
  Cosmetics Act (FFDCA),
  278
Federal Insecticide, Fungicide,
  and Rodenticide Act
  (FIFRA), 97, 271–278. *See
  also* Pesticides
  cancellation of registration,
    274–276
  change of use, 276
  enforcement, 277
  penalties for violations,
    277–278
  registration of pesticides,
    272–274

reregistration, 274
worker protection standard
    program, 276–277
Federal Land Policy and
    Management Act, 391
Federal Maritime Com-
    mission, 119
Federal Mediation and
    Conciliation Service
    (FMCS), 81
Federal Motor Vehicle Control
    Program, 200
Federal preemption, 30
Federal Register, 249–250
    agency rules, 14, 91, 92–93
    environmental documents, 93
    executive orders, 13
    website, 13, 93
Federal supremacy, 30
Federal Tort Claim Act, 102
Federal Trade Commission
    (FTC), 89
Federal Violence Against
    Women Act, 32
Federal Water Pollution Control
    Act (FWPCA), 230
    of 1948, 236
    of 1972, 237
Federal water Pollution
    Control Administration,
    236–237
Federal Water Quality
    Administration, 107
Federalism, 29–30
Felony, 16
Fifth Amendment, 36–43
    due process clause, 36–37
    grand jury, 63
    takings clause, 37–39
Finding of No Significant
    Impact (FONSI), 156, 160
Fiore, William, 17
*Fischer v. Johns-Manville
    Corporation*, 289–290
Fish and Wildlife Service, 67
    endangered species, 121,
        397, 416
    "overenforcement", 67
Five haloacetic acids
    (HAA5), 225
Flaschner Judicial Institute, 61
Flooding
    global warming, 183
    wetlands, 397
Fluoride, 252
FONSI, 156, 160
Food and Drug Administration
    (FDA), 100
Food Quality Protection Act
    (FQPA), 274, 278–280

For cause dismissal, 75
Ford, Gerald
    energy crisis, 342
    surface mining, 357
Ford Motor Company, 343
Forest and Rangelands
    Renewable Resource
    Planning Act of 1974,
    391–392
Forest Emergency Recovery
    and Research Act, 394
Forest Reserve Act of 1891, 390
Forest Service, 121
    northern spotted owl, 413
    rangelands, 388–389
    standing, 65
Forest Stewardship Council
    (FSC), 388
Forests, 387–388
    fire prevention, 393
    global warming, 182
    national, map of, 390
    ownership, 395
    part of global commons, 429
    Rio Summit, 462
Fortune Magazine, 5
Forum *non conveniens*, 59
Fossil fuels. *See* individual fuels
Foundation for Research on
    Economics and the
    Environment (FREE),
    61–62
Fourteenth Amendment, 36–43
    equal protection clause, 41
    just compensation, 37
Fourth Amendment, 35–36
"Fourth branch" of
    government, 46, 90
Frank Weeden Foundation, 458
Free market, pollution and,
    114, 260
Free rider problem, 130–131
Freedom of Information
    Act, 101
*Friends of the Earth (FOE) v.
    Laidlaw Environmental
    Services*, 68
Fuel additives. *See* Gasoline
Fuels. *See* Individual fuels;
    Renewable fuels
Futura Coatings, 270
F-wastes, 306

Gamma rays, 224
Gasoline
    cleaner, 202–203
    lead-free, 201
    prices, 202
    underground storage tank
        (UST) program, 327–330

General Accounting Office
    (GAO)
    National Energy Strategy
        (NES), 343
    New Source Review (NSR),
        198–200
    no-net-loss policy, 404–407
    nuclear plant safety, 370
General Agreement on Tariffs
    and Trade (GATT),
    462, 463
General Electric Co., 23–24
Generally achievable control
    technologies (GACT), 205
Genetically engineered (GE)
    crops, 271
Geneva Protocol, 443
Geophysical Research
    letters, 182
Geothermal energy, 377
Giardia lamblia, 220
Ginsburg, Ruth B.
    EPA oversight, 110
    ripeness, 69–70
    standing, 68
Gist, Reginald, 117
Global commons, 428–429,
    448–459
Global Environment Facility
    (GEF), 438–439
Global Environment Outlook
    Project (GEO), 425, 435
Global extinction crisis,
    416–418
Global Nuclear Energy
    Partnership Program
    (GNEP), 367
Global Resource Information
    Database (GRID), 435
Global warming. *See* Climate
    change
Goddard Institute for Space
    Studies, 179
Good neighborliness
    principle, 432
Gorbachev, Mikhail, 436
Gore, Al, 141
Gorsuch, Anne (Burford), 108
Gothenburg Protocol, 443
Government agencies. *See*
    Administrative agencies
Government in Sunshine
    Act, 101
Government Performance and
    Results Act (GPRA), 308
Grand juries, 63
Grand Old Party (GOP), 115
Grasslands, 390
Gravity portion, 26
Grazing, 388–389

Great Britain. *See* United Kingdom
Great Lakes, 408–409
Great Lakes Binational Toxics Strategy, 408
Great lakes Water Quality Agreements (GLWQA), 408
Great Republican Environmental P. R. Campaign, The, 143
Green Building Tax Credit program, 137
Green Cross International, 436
Green Power Partnership, 345
Green products, 141
Green taxes, 136–137
Greenhouse effect, 179
Greenpeace, 444
Groundwater
  protection, 230–254
  rights to, 230–235
Guinn, Kenny, 371
Gun-Free School Zone Act, 32

Habitat Conservation Plans (HCP), 412
Halons, 178
Hansen, Jim, 392
Hardin, Garrett, 129–130
Hayden, Charles, 357
Hazard identification, 264
Hazardous and Solid Waste Amendments of 1984 (HSWA)
  groundwater, 235–236
  hazardous waste disposal, 301
  inspection of facilities, 277, 320
  RCRA enforcement, 312–313
  small-quantity generators, 301, 308
  TSDFs, 310
  underground storage tank (UST) program, 327–330
USTs, 327, 328, 330
Hazardous material releases, 314–317. *See also* Underground storage tank (UST) program
  Brownfields, 325–327
  emergency response plans, 314–317
  federal response to contaminated sites, 317–327
  liability, 322–324, 325–326
  prioritizing sites, 320
  remedial response, 319–325
  removal action, 318–319

Hazardous Substances Response Trust Fund (Superfund). *See* Superfund Act (CERCLA)
Hazardous waste, 304–312. *See also* Superfund Act (CERCLA); Waste
  amount generated, 299
  commerce clause, 31–36
  cradle to grave tracking, 307–308
  electroplating, 241, 306
  EPA identification lists, 306
  facility standards, 310–311
  identification, 304–306
  international law, 443–445
  mixed with nonhazardous waste, 306
  permits, 308–310
  reactive, 305–306
  recycled, 304–305
  refundable deposits, 144
  solid waste exemptions, 306
  states with greatest generation, 300
  toxic waste, 305
  transboundary movement, 283, 444
Health, Education, and Welfare (HEW)
  1967 Air-Quality Act, 189–190
  Clean Air Act of 1963, 188–189
  Motor Vehicle Act of 1965, 189
Healthy Forests Restoration Act of 2003, 393
Heavy metals, 223
Helsinki Protocol, 443
Helsinki Rules, 433
Herbicides, 226, 271
Hewlett Packard, 327
Hing Mau, Inc., 278
Hodel, Donald, 362
Hodel v. Virginia Surface Mining and Reclamation Association, Inc., 31–32
Homestead acts, 389
Hormones, 226
Houlton Citizen's Coalition v. Town of Houlton, 35
House Republican Policy Committee's principles for reauthorization, 414
Hudson River, 23, 113
Huish Detergents, Inc. v. Warren County, KY, 35

Human-induced climate change (global warming), 451–452
Hydraulic head, 303
Hydrochlorofluorocarbons (HCFCs), 449
Hydrogen fuels, 377
Hydropower, 373–374
Hydrothermal energy, 377
Hypoxic zones, 398

IBM, 327
Illinois Central Railroad Co. v. Illinois, 45
"Incentives for Self-Policing: Discovery, Disclosure, Correction and Prevention of Violations". *See* Audit Policy
Incineration, 296–297
Indictment, 16
Indoor pollution, 186–187
Industrial plants
  New Source Review (NSR), pollutant discharge, 238–244
Industrial Technologies Program (ITP), 347
Inert ingredients, 280
Inhofe, James M., 104
In-house counsel, 60
Injunction, 134–135, 209
Inland wetlands. *See* Wetlands
Institute for Environmental Conflict Resolution, 82–83
Intel, 327
Interagency Testing Committee, 269
Intergovernmental Panel on Climate Change (IPCC), 179
International Convention for the Prevention of Pollution from Ships, 455
International Convention on Oil Pollution Preparedness, Response, and Cooperation, 456
International Convention on Standards of Training, Certification, and Watch Keeping for Seafarers, 456
International Court of Justice, 432, 433, 446–447
International Joint Commission (IJC), 408
International Law Association, 432
International Law Commission (ILC), 432
International law(s), 424–472

air pollution, 442–443
biodiversity, 427–428, 456–459, 461–462
choice of forums, 446–448
climate change, 451–452
conventional, 431–432
customary, 432–434
future, 460–466
global commons, 428–429, 448–459
hazardous waste, 443–445
institutions affecting, 434–441
key issues, 425
Kyoto protocol, 452–454
Madrid Protocol, 459–460
marine pollution, 454–456
nature of, 430–431
need for, 424–430
overpopulation, 424, 426–427
ozone layer, 448–451
persistent organic pollutants (POPs), 445–446
Ramsar Convention, 403
sources, 431–434
trade agreements, 462–466
transboundary pollution, 430
International Organization for Standardization (ISO), 145
International Register of Potentially Toxic Chemicals, 436
Internet lobbying, 5–6
Interpretive rule (of agency), 93
Interrogatories, 72–73
Interstate commerce. *See* Commerce clause
Interstate Commerce Commission (ICC), 89, 107
standing, 66
Ionizing radiation, 223–224
Iroquois Pipeline, 17
ISO 14000 standards, 145–146
Isotopes, 224

Jefferson, Thomas, 61
Johannesburg World Summit on Sustainable Development, 12
Johnson, Stephen, 114, 147
Judgement notwithstanding the verdict (judgment n.o.v.), 77
Judges, 60–62
administrative law judge (ALJ), 90, 96–97, 115
appellate, 61

environmental impact statement (EIS), 66, 155
federal courts, 62
state courts, 62
trial court, 61, 62
Judgment n.o.v. (judgment notwithstanding the verdict), 77
Judicial branch, 3, limitations on administrative agencies, 104–106
as source of case law, 9–11
Judicial review, 11
Jurisdiction, 55
concurrent, 58–59
federal, 58
over the person, 70–71
state, 58
subject matter, 57
Jury, 62–63
federal *vs.* state courts, 59
grand, 63
instructions, 76–77
mock, 75
petit, 62–63
selection, 74–75
shadow, 75
Just compensation, 37–38

Kantor, Mickey, 463, 465
Kelo v. *London*, 41
Kemeny Commission, 370
Kempthorne, Dirk, 358
Kempthorne bill, 415
K-wastes, 306
Kyoto Protocol, 183–184, 452–454
Kyoto Treaty, 12, 113, 147

Landfill Methane Outreach Program (LMOP), 145
Landfills
bioreactor, 303
closure process, 311
design, 302
hazardous waste, 304–312
methane gas, 376
regulations, 302–303
Landowners Equal Treatment Act, 415
Larsen B ice shelf, 181
Law(s). *See also* International law (s); specific legislation
administrative agencies as source, 14
case, 14
civil, 15–16
classifications, 14–16
common, 10
criminal, 15–16

criminal prosecutions, 16–29
executive branch as source, 11–13
executive orders as source, 13
legislative branch as source, 3–9
need for, 127–132
private, 14–15
process of making, 6–7, 9
public, 14–15
signing statements, 13
state, 30
statutory, 14
Lawsuits. *See* Litigation
Lawyers, 60
Leachate, 303, 309
Lead, 174
Lead Industries Association, Inc. v. EPA, 263
League of Conservation Voters, 148
lobbying, 5
Leavitt, Mike, 114, 147
Legionella disease, 218
Legislation. *See also* Law(s); specific legislation
enabling, 90
Legislative branch. *See also* Congress
limitations on administrative agencies, 101–106
as source of statutory law, 3–9
Liability
Brownfields, 325
hazardous materials releases, 314–317
international law, 432
market share, 288
oil spills, 365–366
strict product, 284–285
Lieberman, Joseph I., 104
Linowes Commission, 359
Litigation, 15, 52–79. *See also* Trial
alternatives, 79–84
appellate procedure, 77–79
posttrial, 77
pretrial, 70–74
steps, 63–79
threshold issues, 63–70
trial, 74–77
Lobbying, 3, 5, 7
Local unwanted land uses (LULUs), 230
Locke, John, 29
London Convention on the Prevention of Marine Pollution by Dumping of Wastes and Other Matter, 455

Long Island Lighting
  Company, 207
Long Range Transboundary
  Air Pollution (LRTAP),
  442–443
Long Term 2 Enhanced
  Surface Water Treatment
  Rule (LT2 rule), 251
Long-arm statute, 71
Lowrance, Sylvia, 148
*Lucas v. South Carolina
  Coastal Council*, 38
*Lujan v. Defenders of
  Wildlife*, 65

Madrid Protocol, 459–460
Majority opinion, 78
Malthus, Thomas Robert, 424
Man and the Biosphere
  (MAB) program, 458
Marbury v. Madison, 11
Marine Mammal Protection
  Act, 463
Marine pollution, 454–456
Marine Pollution (MARPOL)
  Convention, 455
Marine Protection, Research,
  and Sanctuaries Act of
  1972, 401–402
Market forces, 144–145
Market share liability, 288
Marketable emissions permits,
  134, 136
MARPOL Convention, 455
Massachusetts v. EPA, 185–186
Material safety data sheet
  (MSDS), 315
Maximum achievable control
  technology (MACT),
  204–205
Maximum Contaminant Level
  Goals (MCLGs), 249
Maximum Contaminant Levels
  (MCLs), 249
Maximum extent practicable
  (MEP), 242
McDonald's, 140
McGinty, Kathleen, 150, 151
McNeil Generating
  Station, 377
Mediation, 82–84
Mercedes-Benz, 463
Mercury, 205–207
Methane Outreach, 345
Methemoglobinemia, 223
Methyl bromide, 449, 450
Methyl parathion, 21, 227
Methyl tertiary butyl ether
  (MTBE), 202–203
Miccosukee Tribe, 392

*Michigan Citizens for Water
  Conservation v. Nestle
  Waters North America*, 235
Migratory Bird Rule, 32–33,
  399, 400
Miller bill, 415
Miller Report, 143
Million Solar Roofs
  Initiative, 375
Mine Safety and Health
  Administration, 121
Mineral content, 224
Mineral Leasing Act of 1920,
  359, 390
Mining, coal
  commerce clause, 33–35
  environmental problems,
  355–357
  regulation of, 357–360
  types, 354
  zinc emissions, 106
Mining Law of 1872, 389
Misdemeanor, 15
Mobile source standards,
  200–203
Mock jury, 75
Money damages, 62, 133
Montreal Protocol, 448
Montreal Protocol Multilateral
  Fund, 448
Montreal Protocol on
  Substances That Deplete
  the Ozone Layer, 12
Mootness, 69
Mosquitoes, 218
Motions
  directed verdict, 76
  dismissal, 75, 349
  judgment notwithstanding
  the verdict, 77
  judgment on pleadings, 64, 72
  posttrial, 77
  preliminary relief, 72
  pretrial, 72
  summary judgment, 73
Motor Vehicle Air-Pollution
  Control Act of 1965, 189
Motor Vehicle Control Act
  of 1960, 188
  of 1965, 189
Mountaintop removal, 355, 356
Muller, Paul, 261
Multilateral environmental
  agreements (MEAs), 465
Multiple-Use Sustained Yield
  Act of 1960, 390, 409
Multi-Sector General Permit
  (MSGP-2000), 243
Multi-Sector General Permit
  (MSGP-2006), 243

Municipal separate storm
  sewer system (MS4), 242
Municipal solid waste. *See also*
  Solid waste; Waste
  definition, 301
Municipal solid waste landfills
  (MSWLF). *See* Landfills

N. fowleri, 220
Nader, Ralph, 463–464
Naegleria fowleri, 220
Naphthalene, 278
National Academy of Public
  Administration, 110
National Academy of Sciences
  global warming, 179
  no-net-loss policy, 405
  oil seepage, 366
National Aeronautics and
  Space Administration
  (NASA), 178
National Air Pollution Control
  Administration, 107
National Ambient Air Quality
  Standards (NAAQSs),
  174, 191–197
  air-quality regions, 191
  automobile inspection/main-
  tenance programs, 197
  no significant deterioration
  (NSD), 197
  nonattainment, problem of,
  193–196
  permit programs, 196–197
  state implementation plans
  (SIPs), 192–193
National Audubon Society, 6
*National Audubon Society v.
  Superior Court (Mono
  Lake)*, 233
National Biological Survey, 142
National Commission on Air
  Quality, 176
National Drinking Water
  Advisory Council, 250
National Energy Act of
  1978, 354
National Energy Plan
  (NEP), 342
  George W. Bush, 367
  Jimmy Carter, 342
National Energy Policy
  (2001), 352
National Energy Policy Plans
  (DOE), 347
National Energy Strategy
  (NES), 343
National Environmental
  Justice Advisory Counsel
  (NEJAC), 43

National Environmental Performance Partnership System (NEPPS), 111
National Environmental Policy Act (NEPA), 44, 149–160
alternatives to EIS, 158–160
Council on Environmental Quality (CEQ), 149, 150–152
effectiveness, 160
environmental impact statement (EIS), 153
lawsuits, 158
leases for offshore drilling, 350
procedure under EIS requirement, 156–158
threshold considerations, 152–156
National Estuary Program, 404
National Forest Management Act of 1976, 391
National forests. *See* Forests
National Highway Traffic Safety Administration (NHTSA), 113, 203
National Institute for Occupational Safety and Health (NIOSH), 121. *See also* Occupational Safety and Health Administration (OSHA)
National Interim Primary Drinking Water Regulations, 249
National Law Journal
Clinton administration, 141–142
environmental racism, 41–43
National Marine Fisheries Service (NMFS), 410
National monuments, 143, 392
National Oceanic and Atmospheric Administration (NOAA), 402
coastal zones, 403–404
marine sanctuaries, 401–402
National Park Service, 121
National Parks and Public Lands Act, 392
National Pesticide Telecommunications Network, 280
National Pollution Discharge Elimination System (NPDES), 238
National Primary Drinking Water Regulations (NPDWRs), 251

National Priorities List (NPL), 320
National Research Council
Endangered Species Act, 409–416
risk assessment, 263–264
National Research Council of the National Academy of Sciences, 414
National Resources Conservation Service, 120
National Resources Defense Council v. Train, 174
National Response Center, 318, 319
National Security Council, 150
National Snow and Ice Data Center, 181
National Technology Initiative, 343
National Wilderness Preservation System, 390
National Wildlife Federation, 5
National Wildlife Refuge System, 121
Nat'l Parks Conservation Ass'n v. Manson, 68–69
Natural gas, 360–361
Natural Resource Defense Council, 5
Natural resources, 386–423
endangered species, 409–416
forests, 387–388
Global Extinction crisis, 416–418
Great Lakes, 408–409
public lands, 386, 389–395
rangelands, 388–389
wetlands, estuaries, and coastal areas, 395–398, 399–408
wild and scenic rivers, 409
Natural Resources Defense Council, 5, 199
Nature Conservancy, 458
"Navigable waters", 399
Negligence, 284–285
NEPA Task Force, 160
New Source Review (NSR), 113, 146
New York state
auto emissions standards, 185
green taxes, 136–137
New York Times, 143
New York v. EPA, 200
Ninth Amendment, 44
Nitrogen, 223
Nitrogen oxides, 170–171

control program, 200
international protocols, 443
Nixon, Richard M.
1973 energy crisis, 340–342
Clean Air Act, 191
water pollution act, 237
"No net loss" policy, 113, 404–407
No significant deterioration (NSD), 197
"No surprise" rule, 412, 415
Non conveniens, 59
Nongovernmental organizations (NGOs), 430
Non-*legionella* bacteria, 218
Non-point source pollution, 245, 403, 429
Nordic Convention, 447
North American Free Trade Agreement (NAFTA), 462, 463
North American Waterfowl Management Plan, 404
North Pole, 180
Northern spotted owl, 413
Northwest Forest Plan, 414
Northwest Ordinance of 1787, 45
Northwest Science and Environment Policy Center, 271
Northwestern Hawaiian Islands Marine National Monument, 401–402
Norton, Gale, 146, 147, 358
Not In My Backyard (NIMBY), 309
Notice, 71, 72
Notice-and-comment, 91
NRDC v. United States EPA, 263
Nuclear energy, 366–372
history of development, 367–368
nuclear waste, 368–369
oldest power plants, 369
problems, 368–369
regulation, 370–372
Nuclear Regulatory Commission (NRC), 301
Nuclear waste, 366, 368–369, 370–372
Nuclear Waste Policy Act of 1982, 370
Nuisance, 133
proving a case of, 76
Nutrients, 222–223
NYPDES Primary Industry Categories List, 239

Occupational Safety and
  Health Administration
  (OSHA), 121. *See also*
  National Institute for
  Occupational Safety and
  Health (NIOSH)
  cooperation with EPA, 116
  environmental responsibili-
  ties, 121
  health and safety standard,
  defined, 105
  judicial limitations on, 105
  rule making authority, 91
  source of law, 14
Ocean dumping, 455–456
Oceans, 429, 454
O'Connor, Sandra D.
  interstate waste disposal, 35
  standing, 66
Office of Air and Radiation,
  205
Office of Compliance and
  Enforcement, 17
Office of Energy Efficiency
  and Renewable
  Energy, 379
Office of Enforcement and
  Compliance Assurance,
  17, 18
Office of Environmental
  Equity, 42
Office of Environmental
  Policy, 150–151
Office of Management and
  Budget (OMB), 12
  George H. W. Bush
  administration, 141
  limits on administrative
  agencies, 102
Office of Personnel
  Management (OPM), 12
Office of Pesticide Programs
  (OPP), 272
Office of Pipeline Safety, 119
Office of Policy, Economics,
  and Innovation (OPEI),
  111, 113
Office of Pollution Prevention
  and Toxics (OPPT), 162
Office of Reinvention, 111
Office of Solid Waste, 304
Office of Strip Mining, 342
Office of Surface Mining
  Reclamation and
  Enforcement (OSM),
  357, 358
Office of Technology
  Assessment, 270
Office of Wastewater
  Management, 257

Office of Water, 404
Offshore drilling, 348
Offshore Oil Spill Pollution
  Protection Fund, 365
Ohio Citizen Action, 226
Ohio Valley Environmental
  Coalition, 358
Oil. *See* Petroleum
Oil and grease, 221, 238
Oil Pollution Act
  of 1924, 236
  of 1990, 237
  liability for oil spills, 365, 366
  penalties for violations, 19
Oil Spill Program, 365
Oil spills, 364–366
Old-growth forests, 387, 413
OMB Watch, 114
Omnibus National Parks and
  Public Lands Act, 392
OPEI (Office of Policy,
  Economics, and
  Innovation), 111, 113
Open dump, 301
Open pit mining, 356
Opinion (court), 78
Opinion, public. *See* Public
  opinion
Organic chemicals, 220–222,
  248, 266. *See also* Toxins
  international law, 281–283
  new, treatment of, 269–271
  old, treatment of, 268–269
  in water, 248
Organization for Economic
  Cooperation and
  Development
  (OECD), 445
Organization of Petroleum
  Exporting Countries
  (OPEC), 340
OSHA (Occupational Safety
  and Health
  Administration), 121
Oslo Protocol, 443
Our Common Future, 436
Outer Continental
  Shelf Leasing Act
  (OCSLA), 361
Outer continental shelf
  (OCS), 142
Overburden, 306, 356
Overdrafting, 236
Overpopulation, 424, 426–427
Owl, northern spotted, 413
Oxygenated fuel, 201
Ozone, 169, 171, 173
Ozone layer
  depletion, 177–178, 448–451
  international law, 446–448

Pacific Legal Foundation, 39–40
Pacific Northwest forests, 143
Pacific Northwest National
  Laboratory, 349
Pacific Yew, 413
*Paepke v. Building
  Commission*, 45–46
Palazzolo v. Rhode Island, 40
P-and U-wastes, 306
Paraquat, 284
Parkland, national, 392
Particulates, 173–174
Partnership for a New Generation
  of Vehicles, 345, 347
Pathogens, 218–220
PCBs (polychlorinated
  biphenyls), 23–24, 113
Peremptory challenge, 75
Performance-Based
  Environmental
  Leadership programs, 113
Permanent damages, 134
Permit programs, 196–197
Persistent organic pollutants
  (POPs), 445–446
Personal injury case, 15
Personal service, 71
Pesticide Environmental
  Stewardship Program
  (PESP), 145, 280
Pesticides, 116, 187. *See also*
  Federal Insecticide,
  Fungicide, and
  Rodenticide Act (FIFRA)
  common products, 276
  in foods, 271
  labeling, 272, 282
  lowered risks, 279
  registration, 272–276
  regulation, 277–278
  removed from market,
  267–268
  U.S. and world use of,
  compared, 281–283
Petit juries, 62–63
Petrocco (David) Farms, Inc., 277
Petroleum
  consumption, production,
  and importation, 341
  offshore development
  problems, 361–363
  oil spills, 364–366
  onshore development
  problems, 360–361
Pfiesteria piscicida, 220
PH
  measure of water quality,
  224–225
  of solid waste, 305
  of various substances, 176

Pharmaceuticals, 226, 387, 461
Phosphorus, 222
Plaintiff, 15, 62, 70, 74
Pleadings, 70, 72
Pocket veto, 9
Polar sea ice, 180, 181
Policy. *See* Environmental policy
Policy statement (of agency), 93, 268
Pollutant discharge, 238–244
Pollution. *See also* Water-quality problems
  air, 168, 179–186
  alternative ways to control, 132–134
  charges, 135–136
  as free market external-ity, 131
  indoor, 186
  ISO 14000 standards, 146
  marine, 454–456
  market forces, 144
  nonpoint source, 245
  prevention program, 162, 163
  transboundary, 441–442
  voluntary control programs, 145
Pollution Prevention Act of 1990, 160–162
Pollution Prosecution Act of 1990, 17
Polychlorinated biphenyls (PCBs), 113, 221
Polycyclic aromatic hydrocar-bons (PAHs), 221
Poole, Lee, 277
Population. *See* Overpopulation
Population Bomb, The, 139
Posttrial motions, 77
Potable water. *See* Drinking water
Potentially responsible parties (PRPs), 318
Power plants. *See also* Nuclear energy
  dependence on coal, 354–355
  deregulation, 352
  emissions, 355
  mercury emissions, 205, 355
  New Source Review (NSR), 198–200
Power Resources Office, 120
Powerplant and Industrial Fuel Use Act (PIFUA), 354
Precedent, 10–11, 78
Preemption, federal, 30, 33

Prejudicial error, 77
Pre-manufacturing notice (PMN), 269–271
Preponderance of evidence, 16
Preservationists, 386
President's Annual Report on Environmental Quality, 150
Pretrial conference, 74
Pretrial motions, 72
Price-Anderson Act of 1957, 367
Private laws, 14–15. *See also* Law(s)
Private nuisance, 134
Private property
  endangered species, 411
  framers of Constitution, 29
  proposed legislation, 415–416
  rights advocates, 39, 40
  takings clause, 37–43
Privilege, attorney-client, 60
Procedural due process, 36–37
Product liability, 285
Project Independence, 342
Project XL, 111, 112
Proper purpose, 37
Property and Environmental Research Center (PERC), 114
"Property Firsters", 39
Property Owners Protection Act, 415
Proprietary action, 33
Protocol on Liability and Compensation, 445
Protozoa, 220–221
Public awareness, 84
Public Health Security and Bioterrorism Preparedness and Response Act of 2002, 253
Public Health Service Act of 1912, 236
Public lands
  agencies responsible for, 389
  forests, 387–388
  rangelands, 388–389
  regulation, 389–395
Public Law 96-295 (nuclear reactors), 370
Public laws. *See also* Law(s)
Public nuisance, 134
Public opinion
  in 1990s, 144–145
  energy policy, 348
  environmental enforcement, 17–18
Public Rangelands Act of 1978, 392

Public trust doctrine, 44–47
Public water systems. *See* Drinking water
Publicly owned treatment works (POTWs), 240
Punitive damages, 288–289
Punte Arenas, Chile, 178
Putin, Vladimir, 454

Quayle, Dan, 103
Questions of fact, 74

Radiation, 223–224, 228–229
Radionuclides, 228–229
Radon, 228–229
  in air, 228
  number of deaths from, 228
  in water, 228–229
Radon Gas and Indoor Air-Quality Act, 186, 210
Ramsar Convention, 403
"Ramsar List", 403
Rangelands, 388–389
Rangelands Renewable Resource Planning Act of 1974, 392
Rapanos v. *United States*, 33, 400
REACH (Registration, Evaluation, and Authorization of Chemicals), 283
Reactive waste, 305–306
Read the Label FIRST!, 273
Reagan, Ronald
  coal-leasing, 359
  Department of the Interior, 359
  energy policy, 342–343
  standing, 66
  EPA, 108
  executive orders, 102
  limitations on administrative agencies, 101–106
  Montreal Protocol, 12
  offshore drilling, 362
  solar energy, 375
  surface mining, 358
Reasonable doubt, 16
Recess appointment, 114
Record of Decision (ROD), 321
Recycling, 296, 298, 305–306, 444
Redirect examination, 76
Reformulated Gasoline Program, 464
Regional Seas Programme, 435
Registration, Evaluation, and Authorization of Chemicals (REACH), 283

Reg-neg, 95
Regulation, 4, 129–132. *See also* Law(s)
Regulators. *See* Administrative agencies
Rehnquist, William H., 34, 54
Reilly, William K., 24, 42, 108, 141
Remedial design/remedial action (RD/RA) phase, 321
Remedial Investigation/ Feasibility Study (RI/FS), 320
Renewable fuels, 372–377
    biomass energy, 376–377
    consumption percentages, 372
    geothermal energy, 377
    hydrogen, 377
    hydropower, 373–374
    solar energy, 374–375
    wind energy, 375–376
Reply, 72
Report to Congress on the Endocrine Disrupter Screening Program (EPA), 280
Reporters (case law), 9
Republican Party, 143
Request (discovery), 73
Residual Risk Report to Congress, 205
Resource conservation, 301
Resource Conservation and Recovery Act (RCRA), 23. *See also* Waste management
    amendments of 1984, (*See* Hazardous and Solid Waste Amendments of 1984 (HSWA))
    criminal liability, 25
    enforcement, 22, 312–314
    environmental racism, 41
    penalties for violations, 20, 21, 22
Resource recovery, 296
Restatement (Second) of Torts, Section 402A, 284–285
Reuse, 296
Reynolds, Shirley, 67
Rice paddies, 182
Rio Declaration, 461
Rio Summit, 12, 282, 452, 460
Riparian water rights, 231–232
Ripeness, 69
Risk assessment, 263–264
Risk characterization, 265–268
Risk management plan (RMP), 205

River Oder case, 433
Rivers, 409
Rivers and Harbors Act of 1899, 236
Roadless Area Conservation Rule, 392
Rotterdam Convention on Prior Informed Consent (PIC), 282–283, 445
Royal Dutch/Shell, 135–136
Ruckelshaus, William, 108
Rule making (agency), 90–96
    exempted, 93–94
    formal, 92–93
    hybrid, 93
    informal, 91–92
    judicial review, 94
    problems, 95–96
    public participation, 91, 93, 94
    regulated negotiation, 95
Rules of civil procedure, 63
Runoff, 407

S. D. Myers, 466
Safe Drinking Water Act (SDWA), 230
    drinking water, 248–254
    environmental racism, 41–42
    groundwater, 246–248
Safe Harbors, 412
Safety-Kleen Corporation, 270
Sagebrush Rebellion, 39
Salvage Convention, 456
Sanitary landfill. *See* Landfills
Santa Barbara oil spill, 139, 237
Scalia, Antonin
    Clean Air Act, 192
    standing, 66, 67
Scenic rivers, 409
Schaeffer, Eric, 113, 147, 199
Schistosomiasis, 218, 220
Science Advisory Board (SAB), 108
Scientific Assessment of Ozone Depletion: 2002, 178
Scientific Assessment Reports, 178
SCRAP 1 (Students Challenging Regulatory Agency Procedures), 66
Search and seizure. *See* Fourth Amendment
"Section 5 notice", 269
Securities and Exchange Commission (SEC), 103
Security Council, 431, 434
September 11, 2001, 317, 340
Septic systems, 230, 248
Service (of summons), 70–71

Setting Priorities, Getting Results: A New Direction for EPA, 110
Sewage. *See* Wastewater treatment
Shadow jury, 75
Shell Oil, 349
Shrimps, 465
Sick building syndrome, 186
Sierra Club
    lobbying, 6
    standing, 65–66
Sierra Club v. Morton, 65, 66, 85
Signing statements, 13
Silent Spring, 139
Simon, Julian, 268, 426
Simpson Construction Company, 313
Sindell v. Abbott Laboratories, 288
Small Business Liability Relief and Brownfields Revitalization Act, 326
Small municipal separate storm sewer systems (MS4s), 242
Smog, 171, 173
Snake River dams, 373
Sofia Protocol, 443
Solar energy, 374–375
Sole Source Aquifer Protection Program, 247
Solid content, 224
Solid waste. *See also* Waste
    definition, 301
    hazardous, defined, 304–306
Solid Waste Agency of Northern Cook County v. United States Army Corps of Engineers, 400
Solvents, 178, 187, 222
Source reduction, 161, 296, 297
Source Water Assessment and Protection (SWAP) Program, 250
Source Water Assessment Program, 247
Sphaerotilus natans, 221
Standing, 63–69
    animals, 67
    environmental organizations, 65–69
    plaintiffs against "overenforcement, 67
    tort law, 132–133
Stare decisis, 10, 11
State implementation plans (SIPs), 192–193

Status and Trends of Wetlands in the Conterminous United States 1998 to 2004, 405
Statute(s), 3, 9. *See also* Law(s)
enabling legislation, 90
long-arm, 71
Statutory law, 3. *See also* Law(s)
Steel Co. v. Citizens for a Better Environment, 67–68
Stenographer (court reporter), 73
Stockholm Convention on Persistent Organic Pollutants, 445–446
Stockholm Declaration, 431
Storage tanks. *See* Underground storage tank (UST) program
Stormwater discharge, 242
Stormwater Pollution Prevention Plan (SWPPP), 244
Strategic Petroleum Reserves (SPR), 360
Strategies for a Clean Energy Future, 135
Strict product liability, 284–285
Strip mining, 355, 356–357. *See also* Mining, coal
Suarez, John, 148
Subject matter jurisdiction, 57–59
Subsidies, 134–135
Substantive due process, 37, 37
Sulfur dioxide, 169–170
international protocols, 442–443
trading program, 136
Summary judgment, 73
Summons, 70–71
Superfund Act (CERCLA), 314
Brownfields, 325–327
citizen awards, 99–100
criticisms, 324
emergency response plans, 314–317
environmental racism, 41
Hudson River, 23, 113
overview, 314
penalties for violations, 41
remedial response, 319–325
removal action, 318–319
Superfund Amendments and Reauthorization Act of 1986 (SARA), 314
Supremacy clause
state *vs.* federal laws, 30
treaties, 12

Supreme Court, U.S., 54. *See also* Court cases; specific cases
appeals to, 79
attitude in 1990s, 141–144
commerce clause, 32
current justices, 54
public trust doctrine, 45–47
takings clause, 37–43
Surface mining, 355, 356–357
Surface Mining Control and Reclamation act of 1977 (SMCRA), 357–359
Surface water
ambient water-quality control, 244–246
discharge controls, 238–244
penalties for violation, 246
protection, 246–253
terrorism threats, 253–254
Surface Water Treatment Rule, 251
Suspended solids, 224
"Swampbuster" bill, 403–404
Synthetic organic substances. *See* Organic chemicals

Tailpipe emissions. *See* Automobile emissions
Takings clause, 37–39
Tampa Electric Company, 199
Tanknology-NDE, International, Inc., 23, 328
Tanner et al. v. Armco Steel et al., 44
Taxes, green, 136–137
Terrorism threats, 253–254
Texas Environmental Task Force, 117
Texas Natural Resource Conservation Commission, 117
Texas Parks and Wildlife Department, 117
34/50 Project, 145
Thomas, Craig, 415
Thomas, Lee, 108
Three Gorges Dam, 374
Three Mile Island, 367
Threshold issues, 152–156
case or controversy, 69
ripeness, 69–70
standing, 63–69
Tort law, 132–134. *See also* Toxic torts
Total Coliform Rule (TCR), 251
Total Maximum daily loads (TMDLs), 245
Total organic carbon (TOC), 221

Toxic Release Inventory (TRI), 316
Toxic Substances Control Act (TSCA), 97, 268–271
Toxic substances, controlling, 261–294
dose-response assessment, 265
exposure assessment, 265
FFDCA, 278
FIFRA, 271–278
FQPA, 278–280
hazard identification, 264
identification, 261–262
new chemicals, 269–271
old chemicals, 268–269
Pesticide Environmental Stewardship Program (PESP), 280
progress, 280–281
risk assessment, 263–264
risk characterization, 265–268
scientific uncertainty, 262–263
TSCA, 268
Toxic substances, international regulation, 281–283
Toxic torts, 283–290. *See also* Tort law
enterprise liability, 287–288
establishing causation, 285–287
punitive damages, 288–290
theories of recovery, 283–285
Toxicity Characteristic Leaching Procedure (TCLP), 305
Toxics Release Inventory (TRI), 111
Toxins. *See also* Organic chemicals; individual substances
airborne, 175
controlling, 261–294
defining, 261–262
in discharge, 238–246
federal regulation, 268–280
Great Lakes, 408–409
identification, 264
international regulation, 281–283
laws regulating, 271–277
risk assessment, 263–264
scientific uncertainty, 262–263
tort cases, 283–290
trace organic, 221–222
Trace organics, toxic, 221–222

Trade, 462–466
Tragedy of the Commons, The,
    129–130
Trail Smelter arbitration, 432
Train, Russell, 108
Transboundary pollution, 430,
    441–442
Transcontinental Gas Pipe
    Line Corporation, 270
Transportation, energy policy,
    346–347
Treaties. *See also* International
    law(s)
    executive branch, 12–13
Treatment, storage, or disposal
    facility (TSDF), 307
    inspection, 307
    permits, 308–310
    standards, 310
    states with TSDFs without
        permits, 309
Trial, 74–77
    closing arguments, 77
    defendant's case, 76
    jury instructions, 76–77
    jury selection, 74–75
    opening statements, 75
    plaintiff's case, 76
    posttrial motions, 77
Trial courts, 55, 57
Trihalomethanes (THMs), 225
TSCA, 268
Turbidity, 224
Turtles, 465

Ultraviolet (UV) radiation, 177
UN Security council, 446–447
Underground Injection
    Control Program
    (UIC), 246
Underground storage tank
    (UST) program, 327–330
UNEP Draft Principles of
    Conduct, 447
*Unified National Strategy for
    Animal Feeding
    Operations,* 242
Uniform Hazardous Waste
    Manifest, 307
United Kingdom, 180, 439
    climate change mea-
        sures, 184
    green taxes, 136
United Nations, 426,
    434–437
    Educational, Scientific, and
        Cultural Organization
        (UNESCO), 458
    Environment Programme
        (UNEP), 178, 434–436

Food and Agriculture
    Organization
    (UN/FAO), 281
Organization for Economic
    Cooperation and
    Development
    (OECD), 445
Security Council, 431, 446
Sustainable Development
    Commission, 460
World Commission on
    Environment and
    Development (WCED),
    436–437
United Nations and the Food
    and Agriculture
    Organization (UN/FAO),
    281–282
United Nations Convention on
    Biological Diversity, 461
United Nations Environment
    Programme (UNEP), 178
United Nations Framework
    Convention on Climate
    Changes, 451–452, 454
United States Code, 9
*United States Code
    Annotated,* 9
*United States v. Alcan Aluminum
    Corporation,* 323
United States v. Burns, 323
*United States v. Carolawn
    Chemical Company,* 322
*United States v. Fleet Factors
    Corporation,* 323
*United States v. Hayes
    International
    Corporation,* 25
United States v. Lopez, 32
United States v. Mottolo, 323
United States v. Park, 25
*United States v. Students
    Challenging Regulatory
    Agency* Procedures
    (SCRAP 1), 66
Uruguay Round, 464
U.S. Advanced Battery
    Consortium, 343
U.S. Centers for Disease
    Control and Prevention
    (CDC), 220
U.S. Coast Guard, 364
*U.S. Congressional News and
    Administrative
    Reports,* 10
U.S. Department of
    Agriculture (USDA), 242
    CAFOs (concentrated ani-
        mal feeding operations),
        230, 242–243

Food Safety and Inspection
    Service (FSIS), 278
National Forests, 121
U.S. Fish and Wildlife
    Service, 121
U.S. Forest Service, 12. *See also*
    Forest Service
U.S. Geological Survey, 435
U.S. Geological System, 226
U.S. National Research
    Council, 269
U.S. Supreme Court. *See*
    Supreme Court, U.S.
USDA's Food Safety and
    Inspection Service
    (USDA/FSIS), 278
Utilitarians conservationists, 386

Venue, 59
Verdict, directed, 76
Veto, pocket, 9
Viruses, 219
Voir dire, 74–75
Volatile organic
    compounds, 200

Wall Street Journal
    environmental enforce-
        ment, 18
    Gore interview, 141
    source reduction, 161
Warrant, 36
Waste. *See also* Hazardous
    waste
    amount generated, 298, 299
    commerce clause, 33–35
    municipal solid waste,
        301–304
    problems, 297–301
Waste management, 295–314.
    See also Landfills;
    Resource Conservation
    and Recovery Act
    (RCRA); Underground
    storage tank (UST)
    program
    cradle to grave tracking,
        307–308
    EPA goals, 297
    hazardous waste, (*See* also
        Hazardous waste), 304–312
    municipal solid waste,
        301–304
    recovery amounts and
        rate, 298
    techniques, 295–314
Waste Wise, 145
Wastewater treatment, 238–244
Water Alliances for Volunteer
    Efficiency (WAVE), 145

Water hardness, 224
Water Quality Act of 1987
    (WQA), 236, 237
Water rights, 231
    appropriative, 231, 232–234
    groundwater, 231, 235–236
    riparian, 231–232
Water temperature, 225
Waterfowl, 403, 404
Water-quality control, 217–260
    ambient water quality,
        244–245
    drinking water protection,
        248–253
    groundwater protection,
        246–248
    properties of water, 224–225
    surface water protection,
        236–237
    terrorism threats, 253–254
    water pollutants, 217–225
    water rights, 231
Water-quality problems
    coastal contamination,
        229–230
    concentrated animal feeding
        operations (CAFOs), 230
    copper, 227–228
    lead, 227, 228
    measures of water quality,
        224–225
    pollutants, 217–225

radon and radionuclides,
    228–229
toxic organics, trace levels
    of, 225–227
Watt, James, 359
Waxman, Henry, 348
Weeden (Frank) Foundation,
    458
Welfare (public), 14, 192
Wells. *See* Groundwater
Wetlands, 395–409
    benefits, 397
    causes of loss and
        degradation, 407
    coastal, 396–397
    commerce clause
        restrictions, 399–401
    destruction, 397–398
    features, 395, 396
    inland, 395
    no-net-loss policy,
        404–407
    percentage lost, 398
    regulations, 399–408
    takings clause, 37–43
White House Council on
    Competitiveness, 103
Whitman, Christine Todd, 113,
    114, 147
Whitman v. *American
    Trucking*, 195
Whitney v. United States, 39

Wild and Scenic Rivers Act of
    1968, 409
Wild rivers, 409
Wilderness Act of 1964, 390–391
Wildfires, 393
Wind energy, 375–376
"Wise use" movement, 146
Worker Protection Standard
    (WPS), 276
Work-product doctrine, 60
World Bank, 437–438
World Commission on
    Dams, 373
World Commission on
    Environment and
    Development (WCED),
    150, 436–437
World Conservation Union
    (IUCN), 418
World Health Organization
    (WHO), 218
World Meteorological
    Organization (WMO), 178
World Trade Organization
    (WTO), 462
World Wildlife Foundation,
    108, 458
Worms, 219–220

Yellowstone National Park,
    68, 144
Yucca Mountain, 371